A GUIDE TO
Microsoft®
Proxy Server 2.0

David Johnson

J. Michael Stewart

Andy Ruth

COURSE
TECHNOLOGY

ONE MAIN STREET, CAMBRIDGE, MA 02142

an International Thomson Publishing company I(T)P®

Cambridge • Albany • Bonn • Boston • Cincinnati • London • Madrid • Melbourne • Mexico City
New York • Paris • San Francisco • Singapore • Tokyo • Toronto • Washington

A Guide to Microsoft® Proxy Server 2.0 is published by Course Technology.

Publisher:	Keith Weiskamp
Acquisitions Editor:	Shari Jo Hehr
Managing Editors:	Paula Kmetz, Kristen Duerr
Product Managers:	Ann Waggoner Aken, Jennifer Normandin
Production Editors:	Kim Eoff, Roxanne Alexander
Technical Editing:	Richard Ingram
Composition House:	GEX, Inc.
Text Designer:	GEX, Inc.
Cover Designer:	Wendy J. Reifeiss
Marketing Specialist:	Cynthia Caldwell
Marketing Manager:	Tracy Foley

© 1999 by Course Technology—I**T**P®

For more information contact:

Course Technology
One Main Street
Cambridge, MA 02142

ITP Europe
Berkshire House 168-173
High Holborn
London WCIV 7AA
England

Nelson ITP Australia
102 Dodds Street
South Melbourne, 3205
Victoria, Australia

ITP Nelson Canada
1120 Birchmount Road
Scarborough, Ontario
Canada M1K 5G4

International Thomson Editores
Seneca, 53
Colonia Polanco
11560 Mexico D.F. Mexico

ITP GmbH
Königswinterer Strasse 418
53227 Bonn
Germany

ITP Asia
60 Albert Street, #15-01
Albert Complex
Singapore 189969

ITP Japan
Hirakawacho Kyowa Building, 3F
2-2-1 Hirakawacho
Chiyoda-ku, Tokyo 102
Japan

Trademarks

Course Technology and the Open Book logo are registered trademarks and CourseKits is a trademark of Course Technology. Custom Edition is a registered trademark of International Thomson Publishing.

I**T**P®   The ITP logo is a registered trademark of International Thomson Publishing.

Some of the product names and company names used in this book have been used for identification purposes only and may be trademarks or registered trademarks of their respective manufacturers and sellers.

Disclaimer

Course Technology reserves the right to revise this publication and make changes from time to time in its content without notice.

ISBN 0-619-03538-2

Printed in Canada

2 3 4 5 6 7 8 9 WC 02 01 00

Brief Table of Contents

TABLE OF CONTENTS

PREFACE

Welcome to *A Guide to Microsoft Proxy Server 2.0!* This new book from Course Technology offers you real-world examples, interactive activities, and numerous hands-on projects that reinforce key concepts and help you prepare for the Microsoft Certification Exam #70-088, "Implementing and Supporting Microsoft Proxy Server 2.0." This book also features troubleshooting tips for solutions to common problems that you will encounter.

There are extensive career opportunities for well-prepared Internet administrators. This book is designed as your doorway into Internet and gateway administration through Microsoft Proxy Server. If you are new to Proxy Server or gateway administration, this is your ticket to an exciting future. If you have experience working with Proxy Server, you will find that the book adds depth and breadth to that experience. Also, the book provides the knowledge you need to prepare for the Microsoft Certification Exam #70-088, "Implementing and Supporting Microsoft Proxy Server 2.0." The exam is one of the available electives, and it is a crucial step in becoming a Microsoft Certified Systems Engineer (MCSE).

Because Proxy Server is closely tied to Windows NT Server, it fits into both large and small organizations. It provides the cornerstone on which to build an Internet Web site, or an intranet, while protecting the rest of your network from the outside world. The success of Windows NT Server is reflected in the huge number of software vendors and developers who develop in this environment or who have switched from other environments to Windows NT Server.

When you complete this book, you will be at the threshold of a Internet/intranet administration career that can be very fulfilling and challenging. This rapidly advancing field offers many opportunities for personal growth and for contributing to your business or organization. This book is intended to provide you with knowledge that you can apply right away and a sound basis for understanding the changes that you will encounter in the future. It also is intended to give you the hands-on skills you need to be a valued professional in your organization.

This book is filled with hands-on projects that cover every aspect of installing and managing Microsoft Proxy Server. The projects are designed to make what you learn *come alive* by actually performing the tasks. In addition to the hands-on projects, each chapter offers case projects that put you in the position of a consultant working in a variety of situations to fulfill the needs of clients. Also, every chapter includes a range of practice questions to help prepare you for the Microsoft certification exam. All of these features are offered to reinforce your learning, so you will feel confident in the knowledge you gain from each chapter.

Chapter 1, "Introduction to Microsoft Proxy Server 2.0," provides a brief history of proxy servers and firewalls, particularly the Microsoft Proxy Server product, as well as explaining its components, hardware, and software requirements. In Chapter 2, "Proxy Server 2.0 Architecture," you are given a detailed look at how the Proxy Server services work together to provide secure access to the Internet. Because of its importance in the Proxy Server environment, Chapter 3, "Understanding TCP/IP," reviews the TCP/IP protocol suite, its history, and its structure. In addition, it discusses IP addressing, subnet masks, and TCP and UDP ports, which are all very important for a successful Proxy Server implementation. Chapter 4, "Internet Information Server Overview," looks at IIS 3.0 and 4.0 and how Proxy Server utilizes their features to provide secure Internet access.

After reviewing the important building blocks of a Proxy Server, Chapter 5, "Planning Your Proxy Server Implementation," steps you through the planning process including needs assessment and capacity planning, choosing an Internet connection and ISP, and the physical requirements for your Proxy Server, based on the size of your network and the type of Internet services you are offering. Chapter 6, "Installing Microsoft Proxy Server 2.0," steps you through the installation process including configuring the Local Address Table and configuring your Proxy Server to support multiple protocols. Chapter 7, "Proxy Client Configuration," discusses the configuration process for many types of clients including Windows, Macintosh, and UNIX.

Chapter 8, "Proxy Server Security," discusses one of the most important aspects of any Proxy Server installation, security. It steps you through the security options available to you and the implementation of each of those options, including packet filtering and logging to track how your Proxy Server is used. In Chapter 9, "Managing and Tuning Proxy Server," you learn how to administer each of the Proxy services, as well as the Performance Monitor counters that can be used to measure your Proxy Server's performance. Chapter 10, "Internet Access Via Proxy Server," discusses in greater detail the process of connecting your Proxy Server to your ISP and configuring its caching options. In Chapter 11, "Managing Multiple Proxy Servers," you learn about Proxy Server arrays and chains, as well as the different methods for balancing the load amongst multiple Proxy Servers.

In Chapter 12, "Network Address Translation and DNS Issues," we begin to look at some of the issues that arise with Proxy Server installations. Chapter 12 provides a detailed discussion of DNS and WINS and things to watch out for when these systems are used with your Proxy Server. Chapter 13, "Complex Deployment and Configuration Issues," continues the discussion of Proxy Server issues focusing on reverse hosting and reverse proxying, as well as coexistence with Microsoft Exchange Server 5.5. Chapter 14, "Troubleshooting Proxy Server," discusses the various troubleshooting tasks and tools used in a Proxy Server environment, including the Registry Editor, Performance Monitor, and Event Viewer. Finally, there are three appendixes in this book. Appendix A provides a detailed discussion of the Microsoft Exam Preparation Guide for the Proxy Server 2.0 exam (#70-088). It addresses each of the points in the Exam Preparation Guide and serves as a refresher before you take the exam. Appendix B lists the well-known and registered TCP and UDP ports for use in configuring your Proxy Server. Lastly, Appendix C discusses the pre-defined WinSock Proxy protocols and how they are used to communicate with the Internet.

FEATURES

To aid you in fully understanding Proxy Server 2.0, there are many features in this book designed to improve its value.

- **Chapter Objectives** Each chapter in this book begins with a detailed list of the concepts to be mastered within that chapter. This list provides you with a quick reference to the contents of that chapter, as well as a useful study aid.

- **Illustrations and Tables** Numerous illustrations aid you in the visualization of common setups, theories, and architectures. In addition, many tables provide details and comparisons of both practical and theoretical information.

- **Chapter Summaries** Each chapter's text is followed by a summary of the concepts it has introduced. These summaries provide a helpful way to recap and revisit the ideas covered in each chapter.

- **Review Questions** End-of-chapter assessment begins with a set of review questions that reinforce the ideas introduced in each chapter. These questions not only ensure that you have mastered the concepts, but are written to help prepare you for the Microsoft certification examination.

- **Hands-on Projects** Although it is important to understand the theory behind the technology, nothing can improve upon real world experience. With the exception of those chapters that are purely theoretical, each chapter provides a series of exercises aimed at providing you with hands-on implementation experience.

- **Case Projects** Finally, each chapter closes with a section that proposes a certain real-world situation. You are asked to evaluate the situation and decide upon the course of action needed to remedy the problems described. This valuable tool helps the student sharpen decision-making and troubleshooting skills — important aspects of set-up and administration.

TEXT AND GRAPHIC CONVENTIONS USED IN THIS BOOK

Where appropriate, additional information and activities have been added to this book to help the reader better understand what is being discussed in the chapter. Icons throughout the text alert individuals to additional materials. The icons used in this textbook are described below.

 Note icons present additional helpful material related to the subject.

 Tip icons highlight suggestions on ways to attack problems you may encounter in a real-world situation. As experienced network administrators, the authors have practical experience with how networks work in real business situations.

 Caution icons appear in the margin next to concepts or steps that often cause difficulty. Each caution anticipates a potential mistake and provides methods for avoiding the same problem in the future.

 **Hands-on project** icons precede each hands-on activity in this book.

 Case project icons are located at the end of each chapter. They mark a more involved, scenario-based project. In this extensive case example, you are asked to independently implement what you have learned.

Where Should You Start?

This book is intended to be read in sequence, from beginning to end. Each chapter builds upon those that precede it, to provide a solid understanding of Proxy Server 2.0. After completing the chapters, you may find it useful to go back through the book, and use the review questions and projects to prepare for the Microsoft certification exam for Proxy Server (#70-088). Readers are also encouraged to investigate the many pointers to online and printed sources of additional information that are cited throughout this book.

INSTRUCTOR'S MATERIALS

The following supplemental materials are available when this book is used in a classroom setting. All of the supplements available with this book are provided to the instructor on a single CD-ROM.

Electronic Instructor's Manual. The Instructor's Manual that accompanies this textbook includes:

- Additional instructional material to assist in class preparation, including suggestions for lecture topics, suggested lab activities, tips on setting up a lab for the hands-on assignments, and alternative lab setup ideas in situations where lab resources are limited.

- Solutions to all end-of-chapter materials, including the Project and Case assignments.

Course Test Manager 1.1. Accompanying this book is a powerful assessment tool known as the Course Test Manager. This cutting-edge Windows-based testing software helps instructors design and administer tests and pre-tests. In addition to being able to generate tests that can be printed and administered, this full-featured program also has an online testing component that allows students to take tests at the computer and have their exams automatically graded.

PowerPoint presentations. This book comes with Microsoft PowerPoint slides for each chapter. These are included as a teaching aid for classroom presentation, to make available to students on the network for chapter review, or to be printed for classroom distribution. Instructors, please feel at liberty to add your own slides for additional topics you introduce to the class.

TRANSCENDER CERTIFICATION TEST PREP SOFTWARE

Bound into the back of this book is a CD-ROM containing Transcender Corporation's Implementing and Supporting Microsoft Proxy Server 2.0 certification exam preparation software with one full exam that simulates the Microsoft Certification Exam (#70-088).

ACKNOWLEDGMENTS

David Johnson: I'd like to thank the staff at Coriolis for their continued support and great work. Thanks especially to Ann Waggoner Aken, Kim Eoff, Robert Clarfield, Cynthia Caldwell, and Tony Stock for seeing this book through to completion. This may have taken a little longer than we originally planned, but it was well worth the wait! Thanks also to the staff at LANWrights. Ed, as always, thanks for the opportunity. Mary and Dawn, thanks for all your hard work in putting this book together. And of course, my co-author Michael, thanks for filling in where needed on short notice. Finally, Barry Shilmover, thank you for all your hard work and dedication to this project. Without you, this would have been a much more strenuous task.

Andy Ruth: Thanks to the staff at Coriolis for believing in this project and LanWrights for allowing me to take part. Thanks to Dad and Mom for making sure I had the tools necessary to complete the task. You did good.

James Michael Stewart: Thanks to my boss, Ed Tittel, for including me in this book series. Thanks to all my co-workers, whose efforts in the trenches have enabled this series to grow to fruition. To my parents, Dave and Sue, thanks for love and understanding. To Mark, even considering the miles, there is never a closer friend. To HERbert, your trust and affection are precious gifts. And finally, as always, to Elvis—with my ear to the radio, my heart toward Graceland, and my hand on meatloaf, I eagerly await your immanent return.

PREPARING FOR MICROSOFT CERTIFICATION

Microsoft offers a program called the Microsoft Certified Professional (MCP) program. Becoming a Microsoft Certified Professional can open many doors for you. Whether you want to be a network engineer, product specialist, or software developer, obtaining the appropriate Microsoft Certified Professional credentials can provide a formal record of your skills to potential employers. Certification can be equally effective in helping you secure a raise or promotion.

The Microsoft Certified Professional program is made up of many courses in several different tracks. Combinations of individual courses can lead to certification in a specific track. Most tracks require a combination of required and elective courses. One of the most common tracks for beginners is the Microsoft Certified Product Specialist (MCPS). By obtaining this status, your credentials tell a potential employer that you are an expert in a specialized computing area such as personal computer operating systems on a specific product, like Microsoft Windows 95.

How Can Transcender's Test Prep Software Help?

To become a Microsoft Certified Professional, you must pass rigorous certification exams that provide a valid and reliable measure of technical proficiency and expertise. The CD-ROM contained in this book, Transcender Corporation's Limited Version certification exam preparation software, can be used in conjunction with the book to help you assess your progress in the event you choose to pursue Microsoft professional certification. The Transcender CD-ROM presents a series of questions that were expertly prepared to test your readiness for the official Microsoft certification examination on Implementing and Supporting Microsoft Proxy Server (Exam #70-088). These questions were taken from a larger series of practice tests produced by the Transcender Corporation — practice tests that simulate the interface and format of the actual certification exams. Transcender's complete product also offers explanations for all questions. The rationale for each correct answer is carefully explained, and specific page references are given for Microsoft product documentation and Microsoft Press reference books. These page references enable you to study from additional sources.

Practice test questions from Transcender Corporation are acknowledged as the best available. In fact, with their full product, Transcender offers a money-back guarantee if you do not pass the exam. If you have trouble passing the practice examination included on the enclosed CD-ROM, you should consider purchasing the full product with additional practice tests and personalized feedback. Details and pricing information are available at the back of this book. A sample of the full Transcender product is on the enclosed CD-ROM, including remedial explanations.

The Transcender product is a great tool to help you prepare to become certified. If you experience technical problems with this product, please e-mail Transcender at *course@transcender.com* or call (615) 726-8779.

Want to Know More about Microsoft Certification?

There are many additional benefits to achieving Microsoft Certified Professional status. These benefits apply to you as well as to your potential employer. As a Microsoft Certified Professional (MCP), you will be recognized as an expert on Microsoft products, have access to ongoing technical information from Microsoft, and receive special invitations to Microsoft conferences and events. You can access a comprehensive, interactive tool that provides full details about the Microsoft Certified Professional program online at *www.microsoft.com/mcp/mktg/cert.htm*. For more information on texts at Course Technology that will help prepare you for certification exams, visit our site at *www.course.com*.

When you become a Microsoft Certified Product Specialist, Microsoft sends you a Welcome Kit that contains:

- An 8-½" × 11" Microsoft Certified Product Specialist wall certificate. Also, within a few weeks after you have passed any exam, Microsoft sends you a Microsoft Certified Professional transcript that shows which exams you have passed.

- A Microsoft Certified Professional program membership card.

- A Microsoft Certified Professional lapel pin.

- A license to use the Microsoft Certified Professional logo. You are licensed to use the logo in your advertisements, promotions, proposals, and other materials, including business cards, letterheads, advertising circulars, brochures, yellow page advertisements, mailings, banners, resumes, and invitations.

- A Microsoft Certified Professional logo sheet. Before using the camera-ready logo, you must agree to the terms of the licensing agreement.

- A Microsoft TechNet CD-ROM.

- A 50% discount toward a one-year membership in the Microsoft TechNet Technical Information Network, which provides valuable information via monthly CD-ROMs.

- Dedicated forums on CompuServe (GO MECFORUM) and The Microsoft Network, which enable Microsoft Certified Professionals to communicate directly with Microsoft and one another.

- A one-year subscription to Microsoft Certified Professional Magazine, a career and professional development magazine created especially for Microsoft Certified Professionals.

- A Certification Update subscription. Certification Update is a bimonthly newsletter from the Microsoft Certified Professional program that keeps you informed of changes and advances in the program and exams.

- Invitations to Microsoft conferences, technical training sessions, and special events.

- Eligibility to join the Network Professional Association, a worldwide association of computer professionals. Microsoft Certified Product Specialists are invited to join as associate members.

A Microsoft Certified Systems Engineer receives all the benefits mentioned above as well as the following additional benefits:

- Microsoft Certified Systems Engineer logos and other materials to help you identify yourself as a Microsoft Certified Systems Engineer to colleagues or clients.

- Ten free incidents with the Microsoft Support Network and a 25% discount on purchases of additional 10-packs of Priority Development and Desktop Support incidents.

- A one-year subscription to the Microsoft TechNet Technical Information Network.

- A one-year subscription to the Microsoft Beta Evaluation program. This benefit provides you with up to 12 free monthly beta software CDs for many new Microsoft software products. This enables you to become familiar with new versions of Microsoft products before they are generally available. This benefit also includes access to a private CompuServe forum where you can exchange information with other program members and find information from Microsoft on current beta issues and product information.

Certify Me!

So you are ready to become a Microsoft Certified Professional. The examinations are administered through Sylvan Prometric (formerly Drake Prometric) and are offered at more than 700 authorized testing centers around the world. Microsoft evaluates certification status based on current exam records. Your current exam record is the set of exams you have passed. To maintain Microsoft Certified Professional status, you must remain current on all the requirements for your certification.

Registering for an exam is easy. To register, contact Sylvan Prometric, 2601 West 88th Street, Bloomington, MN, 55431, at (800) 755-EXAM (3926). Dial (612) 896-7000 or (612) 820-5707 if you cannot place a call to an 800 number from your location. You must call to schedule the exam at least one day before you want to take the exam. Taking the exam automatically enrolls you in the Microsoft Certified Professional program; you do not need to submit an application to Microsoft Corporation.

When you call Sylvan Prometric, have the following information ready:

- Your name, organization (if any), mailing address, and phone number.

- A unique ID number (e.g., your Social Security number).

- The number of the exam you wish to take (#70-88 for the Implementing and Supporting Microsoft Proxy Server 2.0 exam).

- A payment method (e.g., credit card number). If you pay by check, payment is due before the examination can be scheduled. The fee to take each exam is currently $100.

READ THIS BEFORE YOU BEGIN

To complete the projects and assignments in the book, you will need access to a file server and a workstation. The server should be equipped with Microsoft Windows NT Server 4. A few projects require Internet access for information searches. These projects are not mandatory; however, the projects will give you experience using this resource as a prospective server administrator.

System Requirements. The recommended software and hardware configurations are as follows:

Workstation Clients

- Windows 95 or Windows NT Workstation
- Pentium with 16 MB of RAM minimum
- VGA monitor
- Mouse or pointing device
- Network interface card cabled to the file server
- Hard disk with at least 110 MB free
- CD-ROM drive
- Internet access and a browser (recommended but not required for selected research assignments)

File Server

- Listed in Microsoft's Hardware Compatibility List
- 32-bit computer with an 80486 33 MHz or faster processor
- VGA or better resolution monitor
- Mouse or pointing device
- High density 3.5-inch floppy disk drive
- CD-ROM drive
- 32 MB or more memory
- One or more hard disks with at least 125 MB of disk storage free
- Network interface card for network communications
- Tape system (recommended but not required)
- Modem (recommended but not required)
- Printer (to practice setting up a network printer)

System Requirements for Test Prep Software:

- 8 MB RAM (16 MB recommended)
- VGA/256 Color display or better
- 8X CD-ROM Drive
- Windows NT 4.0 or Windows 95

System Requirements for Transcender Corporation's Test Prep Software

- 8 MB RAM (16 MB recommended)
- VGA/256 Color display or better
- CD-ROM drive
- Microsoft Windows 3.1, Windows for Workgroups 3.11, Windows NT 3.51, Windows NT 4.0, or Windows 95/98, or Windows 2000 Professional

Upgrade to the full version of ProxyCert 2.0a

The full version includes Transcender's new test engine and gives you:

- · Three full-length exams, including a Computer Adaptive Testing option
- · Detailed Score History - Breaks down your score so you can pinpoint weak areas
- · Expanded Printing Options - You can now print by section, string or keyword
- · Random Exam Option - Randomize test items from all three tests to create additional exams
- · Detailed answer explanations, including documented references for every question
- · Money Back if You Don't Pass Guarantee*
  - *see our Web Site for guarantee details*

To upgrade to the full version:

1. Install ProxyCert 2.0a Limited version on the computer system with which you will use the full version.
2. When the program starts, choose "Order Full Version."
3. To upgrade immediately, enable your Internet connection, and go to http://www.transcender.com/upgrade/limited/proxycert2.
4. Follow the instructions posted at the above listed URL.
5. If you do not wish to purchase your upgrade on-line, mail us the completed coupon below (no reproductions or photocopies please). Enclose a check or money order, payable to Transcender Corporation, for $129, plus $6 shipping ($25 outside U.S.).

Terms and Conditions:

Maximum one upgrade per person. Pre-payment by check, money order or credit card is required. For your protection, do not send currency through the mail.

Send to: Upgrade Program
Transcender Corporation
242 Louise Avenue
Nashville, TN 37203

Please send me the ProxyCert 2.0a Upgrade. Enclosed is my check or credit card number, payable to Transcender Corporation for $129 plus $6 ($25 outside the U.S.). TN residents add $10.64 for sales tax.

Name_____   School_____

Address_____   Credit Card: VISA MC AMEX DISC

City_____ State_____   CC#_____

Zip_____ Country_____   Expiration Date_____

Phone_____   Name on Card_____

E-Mail_____   Signature_____

CRS042799

INTRODUCTION TO MICROSOFT PROXY SERVER 2.0

In this chapter, we'll introduce you to Microsoft's Proxy Server 2.0. In doing so, we'll take a brief look at where proxy servers came from, what Proxy Server 2.0 offers, and why you would want to use a proxy server on your network.

AFTER READING THIS CHAPTER AND COMPLETING THE EXERCISES, YOU WILL BE ABLE TO:

- Understand the basic history of proxy servers, from firewalls to content caching
- Understand the need for and use of a proxy server
- Identify the key benefits of a proxy server
- Understand the main components of Proxy Server 2.0
- Identify the hardware and software requirements of Proxy Server 2.0

STATE OF THE NETWORK ENVIRONMENT

The use of the Internet in today's business, nonprofit, and private worlds is growing at a substantial rate. The benefits of connecting an organization's network to the worldwide communication medium of the Internet are so glaringly obvious that to fail to establish such a connection spells stagnation for many "unplugged" networks. Communication, customer interaction, 24-hour technical support, increased productivity, expanded research capabilities, and geographically unlimited collaboration are some of the positive results of an Internet-accessible network.

However, Internet access is not exactly a brightly lit path. Networks of any size must seriously contend with increased security problems when connected to the Internet. Unauthorized access, private data distribution, and system integrity failure are all serious threats to your network's well-being and to your organization as a whole. But there are still further risks you must consider when you connect to the Internet: loss of work due to nonproductive Internet use, the difficulties of managing vast new resources, and handling the cost of the connection.

FIREWALLS

The first stage in combating the drawbacks of Internet access was to address the issue with a new type of software and/or hardware product called a firewall. A *firewall* is designed to restrict unauthorized or unlawful entry into an organization's network from some external point, such as the Internet. Most worthwhile firewalls deploy a multilayer scheme to restrict access, typically at the packet level or the Network and Application layers of the OSI (Open System Interconnection) model. Some routers are also labeled as firewalls, even though they are only capable of restricting traffic based on packet filtering.

Firewalls are often deployed to restrict traffic for security reasons, but they can and do offer several other benefits, including an alert or alarm capability to inform administrators of attempted unauthorized access, the existence of repeat access attempts, or the identification of corrupt communication pathways. Such notification is often an invaluable tool for preventing future system breaches or pressing legal charges against would-be or repeat attackers. In addition to alerts, firewalls can establish and maintain secure network links over wide area network (WAN) or Internet connections to form virtual private networks (VPNs). A *virtual private network* is a network consisting of computers that use public network links (i.e., the Internet) to maintain secure, low-cost, and reliable communication. The most common use for a VPN is to connect remote branches to a central business headquarters. This is a reliable and cost-effective method for connecting distant computers to improve organizational communication and transactions.

In the last few years, Internet firewalls have received a lot of attention. Many product vendors have expended significant effort to develop, improve, and expand their firewall products to keep up with user demand, potential and kinetic risk, and network technology. The growth process for firewalls has been swift, moving from solutions developed internally—which often failed, were expensive to develop, and a beast to maintain—to standardized solutions available commercially. As firewalls become more commonplace in the network environment, they are being deployed in more specialized applications, offer a broader range of value-added services, and grant users and administrators seamless interaction with existing communication systems.

CACHING CONTENT

The ability of a firewall or another software product to cache content is a new paradigm in the world of computers. It has only been in the last year or two that this development has been given serious consideration to address the problem of overtaxing the bandwidth of a network communication link. A *content caching* server provides improved network performance, greater reliability, and reduced cost by storing frequently accessed remote data locally. Caching servers have taken on the name of application proxies, or *proxy servers*, because they act as moderators or go-betweens for clients and remote hosts. The early deployments of caching or proxy servers still required a separate firewall because the functions were still considered distinct operations.

Content caching improves network performance by reducing network traffic. Network traffic is reduced when requested content is read from local storage instead of being requested from its original remote host. The less frequently a remote resource is accessed, the less traffic occurs on the outbound link. This improves the performance from a user's perspective because requested data is displayed promptly. The benefit of reduced network traffic can often be translated into network cost savings because communication pipeline increases are not necessary as often, less data transfer often means less cost, and faster performance reduces time lost waiting for resources.

It should not be too much of a stretch in reason to see how a product that stores a duplicate copy of a remote resource locally can also be used to restrict access to remote resources. There are several ways to prevent resources from being accessed: exclusions based on IP addresses, domains, or Uniform Resource Locators (URLs); application or information service exclusions; and user or group exclusions. When a caching or proxy server is used to prevent resource access, it is called *site filtering,* or *user access control.* This feature gives administrators some ability to focus general Internet usage toward more productive resource locations.

Internet Service Providers (ISPs) are using content caching servers to improve performance for customers. By caching sites that are accessed frequently, they can distribute content faster and reduce the load on their typically overburdened backbone links. This improves response time for everyone, including other users on other ISPs accessing the same resource—the less simultaneous competition for access to a resource, the faster the host machine can respond to a request. As an ISP's user base expands, content caching will play a critical role in its ability to offer information services that are responsive while keeping backbone connection charges down. As push technology becomes more commonplace in distributing personal and corporate content, caching systems will adapt to distributing content pushed from external resources to multiple internal (i.e., behind the caching server) clients.

PROXY SERVERS

The next step in the evolution of network communication products is the proxy server. A proxy server takes the capabilities of a firewall and combines them with the functions of a content caching server. The resultant hybrid is a tool that can cache oft-used content, protect a network from unauthorized access or use (whether originating from inside or outside of the network), and hide the identity of internal clients by requesting resources on their behalf. Another way of stating this is that a proxy server acts as a secure Internet gateway for network clients.

A properly installed and operational proxy server is completely transparent to both the user and the resource host. The only time a user will interact directly with the proxy server is when a restricted resource is requested; then the proxy server will issue a restriction warning instead of returning the desired item.

A proxy server is deployed on a multihomed server. A *multihomed server* is a computer that has two or more network interfaces and is connected to different networks. A proxy server will often have one connection to the Internet and one or more connections to an organization's internal network (see Figure 1.1). With such a configuration, the private network can be restricted by preventing IP routing across the proxy server. Thus, only the most secure server, the one hosting the proxy server, is accessible from the Internet.

OVERVIEW OF PROXY SERVER 2.0

In Microsoft's valiant efforts to stay up-to-date with the rapid forward movement of Internet technologies, it has produced Proxy Server 2.0. Proxy Server 2.0 is the latest incarnation of the proxy product originally released in November 1996. Although it was not the first proxy server for the Microsoft

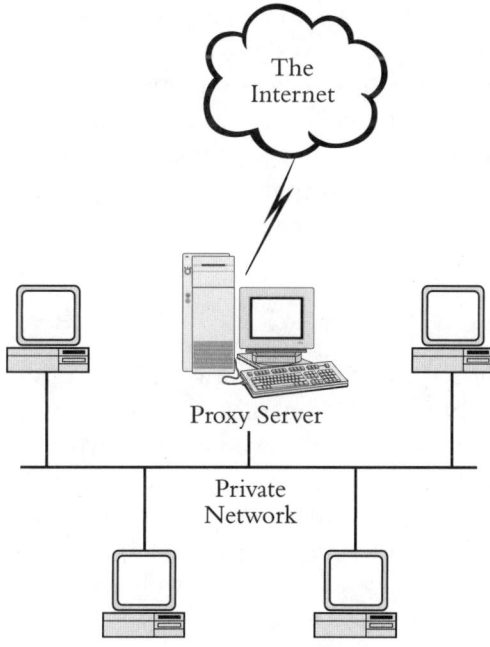

Figure 1.1   A proxy server mediating between a private network and the
Internet.

Windows platform, it quickly gained on its competitors, such as Netscape's
Proxy Server.

The original 1.0 version of Microsoft Proxy Server offered content caching, site
restriction, and some application restrictions and circuit-layer restrictions, but it
did not offer all of the security benefits of a true firewall. Plus, many large
organizations found it necessary to deploy groups of proxy servers to handle the
traffic load and still provide adequate performance. Proxy Server 2.0 was released
just under a year after its predecessor. It was designed to pick up where the first
version left off by including true firewall capabilities and improved scalability
features.

According to Microsoft, Proxy Server 2.0 includes "high performance Web
caching and firewall security in one affordable, integrated product." Proxy
Server 2.0 fulfills this legacy by being the first caching server to offer true
firewall capabilities and the first firewall to support high-performance caching of
content.

From the perspectives of simultaneous users, amount of content, performance, and cost, Proxy Server 2.0 is capable of supporting networks of any size. Thus, both small and large organizations can reap the benefits of Proxy Server. In fact, when Proxy Server's performance is compared to that of other or more traditional methods, the average improvement is 50 percent. In other words, deploying Proxy Server on your network to replace current Internet connection technologies can improve the overall performance of your system rather than hinder it.

FLEXIBLE SECURITY

Proxy Server acts as a firewall-security-enhanced gateway between a local area network (LAN) and the Internet. Through dynamic packet filtering, Proxy Server maintains a protected environment in which unwanted traffic is filtered. With the addition of Application-layer security and circuit-layer security, Proxy Server offers as much protection as any standalone firewall product on the market. Alerting and logging capabilities further expand the security benefits of this product, providing administrators with warnings and a paper trail to track down possible perimeter breaches.

Proxy Server 2.0 can be combined with the Microsoft Routing and Remote Access Service Update for Windows NT Server to provide complete VPN services. This includes secure WAN connections, inexpensive communication costs, and reliable network links. Proxy Server can help you exploit the Internet as your own vehicle for network communications.

Additional security features include virus scanning, JavaScript and ActiveX filtering, and site-restriction enhancements. In addition, more security features can be integrated with or installed into Proxy Server 2.0 from third-party manufacturers. Proxy's extensibility and standards compliance make it an excellent platform for other vendors and internal programmers to modify and enhance.

SOLID PERFORMANCE

Proxy Server 2.0 introduces new scalability and performance features to enhance the speed and depth of content caching. Array-based caching and hierarchical or chain-based caching enable multiple installations of Proxy Server to act together interactively instead of separately. Caching can be tuned to the particular needs or resource-access habits of your users. Thus, distributed caching that focuses on high-turnover material or oft-accessed resources is a vast improvement over time-based caching. Microsoft developed a new protocol standard to manage and control this new distributed caching technique: the *Cache Array Routing Protocol (CARP)*.

With an overall network bandwidth usage reduction of 50 percent, Proxy Server's caching abilities reduce user wait time, eliminate network congestion, and improve administration control over resources. The key abilities of caching that provide such a performance improvement are the automated intelligent filtering and storage of data. This includes proactive caching, where frequently accessed sites are updated locally on a regular basis based on usage history.

EASY ADMINISTRATION

Microsoft has been focusing on maintaining tight integration amongst its products, especially in the realm of server software. Fortunately, Proxy Server 2.0 is a shining example of Microsoft's success at obtaining this goal. Proxy Server 2.0 is integrated tightly into Windows NT Server 4.0. The most obvious and significant benefit of this is the similarity and homogeneity of the interfaces and administrative tools. With the exception of the Proxy Server configuration tool itself, most tasks are managed or viewed through existing NT Server utilities—including Performance Monitor, User Manager For Domains, Event Viewer, and IIS (Internet Information Server) Manager. In addition to the standard executable dialog box admin tools, Proxy Server 2.0 can be administered via the Web by using HTML-based administration or from a command prompt with command-line syntax and parameters.

Every function, feature, tool, and ability of Proxy Server is managed, accessed, controlled, or configured through an easy-to-use and understandable utility. This includes array administration, automation tuning, deployment, system configuration, and backup.

PROXY SERVER 2.0 FEATURES

Microsoft Proxy Server 2.0 is a rich and full-featured product, so much so that it has three distinct facets. It is a gateway service that enables multiple users to access the Internet over a single connection. It is a content caching system where resources that are accessed frequently are stored locally to improve performance. In addition, it includes a secure firewall system to restrict internal users from accessing some external resources and to prevent unauthorized access from points external to the network. With these features of Proxy Server, it is easy to see why it is such an important and revolutionary networking product.

PROXY SERVICES

To provide the widest range of support for standardized information services, Proxy Server uses three proxy subsystems: Web Proxy, WinSock Proxy, and SOCKS Proxy.

Web Proxy supports those protocols and communication mechanisms typically associated with Web documents, access, and interaction. This includes support for Hypertext Transfer Protocol (HTTP), File Transfer Protocol (FTP), Gopher, and Transmission Control Protocol/Internet Protocol (TCP/IP).

WinSock Proxy supports client applications designed around the Windows Sockets application programming interface (API). This includes utilities and services such as Telnet and RealAudio. Plus, this proxy subsystem is able to deliver content over TCP/IP or Internetwork Packet Exchange/Sequenced Packet Exchange (IPX/SPX). In other words, with WinSock Proxy, a LAN can operate with IPX/SPX and still be able to access WinSock Internet applications.

SOCKS Proxy is a cross-platform network service that creates a secured communications link between a client and a server. SOCKS Proxy supports SOCKS 4.3a and offers non-Windows or non-WinSock applications access to Internet services. SOCKS Proxy can be used for HTTP, FTP, Gopher, and Telnet, but it cannot be used with services that require the User Datagram Protocol (UDP), such as RealAudio, VDOLive, or Microsoft NetShow.

NEW FEATURES IN PROXY SERVER 2.0

Proxy Server 2.0 is able to boast such significant operational improvements due to the many new features and modifications added to the software since version 1.0. The new features of Proxy Server 2.0 include:

- Firewall security
  - Dynamic packet filtering
  - Reverse proxy
  - Reverse hosting
  - Server proxying
  - Realtime alerts and logging
  - VPN support
- Performance/cost savings
  - Array-based content caching
  - Hierarchical caching
  - Cache Array Routing Protocol (CARP) support
  - FTP caching
  - Performance improvement of 40 percent or better
  - HTTP 1.1 support
  - SOCKS support

- Management
  - HTML-based administration (available via Web download shortly after the Proxy Server 2.0 general release)
  - Command-line operation and scripting support
  - Array administration
  - Configuration backup and restore

These features are discussed in a bit more detail in the following sections, plus they are reviewed and referred to repeatedly throughout this book.

PRODUCT FEATURE DETAILS

Microsoft Proxy Server 2.0 offers a wide variety and depth of features, functions, and abilities. The following sections highlight many of these features. Most of the items discussed here in brief are examined more closely in subsequent chapters. Please use the table of contents and the index to locate related material elsewhere in this book.

EXTENSIBLE FIREWALL SECURITY

Proxy Server's extensible firewall security features include:

- **Packet-layer security with dynamic packet filtering** A dynamic and intelligent packet filtering process automatically determines which packets are allowed in or out. This type of packet reduction relieves the burden on the circuit- and application-layer proxy services, which in turn improves the performance of legitimate resource interaction. In addition to packet filtering, Proxy Server 2.0 also manages IP ports by only opening those ports needed and only when needed. This is handled automatically to reduce the number of open communication ports in both directions and results in a more secure environment.

- **Circuit-layer security** Both WinSock Proxy and SOCKS Proxy use an application-transparent circuit gateway to protect your network. Proxy Server 2.0 uses dynamic packet filtering at the circuit layer to improve security and simplify use. Circuit-layer security enables filtering or monitoring across numerous protocols simultaneously instead of the single protocol limitations of most application-layer proxies. This enables Proxy Server 2.0 to filter streaming audio and video, customized messaging protocols, and even Internet Relay Chat (IRC).

- **Application-layer security** The Application-layer security of Proxy Server 2.0 hides the internal IPX or IP address from external hosts, supports special capabilities such as virus scanning, is client neutral, and is able to interpret commands from PC clients within the application protocols of HTTP, SHTTP (Secure Hypertext Transfer Protocol), FTP, and Gopher.

- **Realtime security alerts** Proxy Server 2.0 keeps the administrator informed by issuing alerts when suspected network attacks are occurring. You can configure the system so alerts are issued by email or in the Event Log.

- **Reverse proxy** This special feature enables you to set up a World Wide Web publishing server within your network behind the Proxy Server and still be able to offer its contents to the Internet. Reverse proxy provides tighter security control over your Web site. The proxy server impersonates a Web server to the outside world, and only it communicates directly with the real internal Web server.

- **Reverse hosting** This feature is a companion to the reverse proxy feature in that it enables Proxy Server 2.0 to integrate several distinct Web servers that are hosted inside of your network into what looks like a single large Web site to all external viewers. This method of Web publishing maintains tight security, isolates the Web servers from the Internet, and offers you greater flexibility in design, layout, and navigation.

- **Server proxying** Server proxying is Proxy Server 2.0's ability to listen for or identify traffic bound for specific information service servers within the internal network and then forward those packets to the proper servers based on the request. This enables services such as Microsoft Exchange Server to operate as your primary Internet mail clearinghouse even if the computer on which the service is installed is located behind the proxy. This method of server proxying maintains a secure environment by offering administrators control over which packets are allowed access to the network.

- **Extensive logging support** Through its extensive logging capabilities, Proxy Server 2.0 can maintain a detailed paper trail. Activity on, through, and across the proxy perimeter can be recorded in standard log files or to ODBC (Open Database Connectivity) databases. The logging system also records all alert information and any firewall-related activities.

- **Virtual private networking (VPN) with Routing and Remote Access Service (RAS) Update** When used in combination with the Routing and Remote Access Service for Windows NT Server, Proxy Server 2.0 can establish secure WAN communication links with remote networks to create a VPN. Such a system is not only reliable and efficient, it is also extremely cost effective. The use of Proxy Server to establish a VPN also enables administrators to maintain resource access control from a single location.

- **Secure Sockets Layer (SSL) tunneling** Via the Web Proxy, Proxy Server supports SSL tunneling to maintain highly secure Web-based transactions. SSL is commonly used in electronic commerce or other state-dependent applications. SSL tunneling creates an encrypted communication path between the client and the remote server.

- **Full authentication/logging** The WinSock Proxy supports full encrypted authentication and maintains tight access control. In addition, all transactions are recorded to the logs.

- **Complementary third-party applications** Several third-party products are designed to integrate with Proxy Server 2.0 to add unique application-specific features or add alternative security measures. Such tools include virus scanners and JavaScript and ActiveX parsers/ blockers. All such products that integrate with Proxy Server do so via the Internet Server Application Programming Interface (ISAPI).

PERFORMANCE AND COST SAVINGS

The performance and cost-saving features of Proxy Server 2.0 include the following:

- **Array-based content caching** You can use a new array-based distributed caching method to configure several Proxy Server installations to operate as a single entity. This is called a proxy array. Array caching can be administered as a single, logical entity, and it can provide automated load balancing, add fault tolerance, and embody scalability.

- **Hierarchical content caching** When multiple LANs are connected, such as with multiple branch offices or within a large enterprise network, a hierarchical caching scheme can be implemented with multiple single proxies or arrays of proxies to distribute content based on location and use histories. Client requests are communicated upward through the proxy relation tree until the resource is located or finally retrieved from the Internet.

- **Cache Array Routing Protocol (CARP)** CARP is a new distributed caching protocol submitted by Microsoft to the IETF (Internet Engineering Task Force) as a new industry standard. CARP uses a queryless routing method to locate and retrieve data from distributed cache whether it is in an array-based or an hierarchical-based format. This method offers significant performance improvement over traditional location methods, especially on high-volume requests with multiple proxy servers.

- **Active intelligent caching** Proxy Server automatically monitors and examines the access patterns of users and the refresh rate of resources to establish a proactive preload of the sites that are used most commonly. This improves response time for users and reduces network load. This feature of Proxy Server is automatic and requires no additional administration.

- **FTP and HTTP cache support** Proxy Server 2.0 includes expanded support for HTTP 1.1 (instead of just HTTP 1.0 as in version 1.0) and FTP objects. This broadens the range of cacheable items, which ultimately results in improved performance for users. In addition to this expanded support, there is more control over Time-to-Live (TTL) settings for such objects to retain or release them with greater accuracy.

- **Hypertext Transfer Protocol (HTTP) version 1.1** Through the support of full HTTP 1.1, Proxy Server uses persistent connections (client-to-proxy and proxy-to-Internet) to improve resource access performance and response time. Note that full HTTP 1.1 support requires the final full release of Internet Information Server 4.0.

- **Improved cache and proxy performance** Proxy Server 2.0's performance shows a significant improvement over that of Proxy Server 1.0—over 40 percent. This improvement is gained through the advancements in cache methodologies and proxy techniques. This level of performance improvement is enjoyed even at a high level of security and access restrictions.

EASY, COMPREHENSIVE MANAGEMENT SUPPORT

Proxy Server 2.0 offers the following features for management support:

- **Windows NT Server integration** Proxy Server is a member of the BackOffice family, which is a group of server-level application packages that are integrated tightly into Windows NT Server. This integration provides Proxy Server with access to many services and tools already present in NT, resulting in simple management and better performance. Proxy Server uses the existing authenticated user base for security and access purposes, so user accounts do not need to be re-created for Proxy Server. A single user logon to NT gives the user access to all granted resources and access permissions made available via Proxy Server.

- **User access control** As part of the NT integration, access to all resources made available via Proxy Server can be controlled on a user and/or group basis just as with all other objects and resources within the NT resource space. Access is based on Internet protocol within each of the sub-proxies: Web, WinSock, and SOCKS.

- **Site filtering** Site filtering is a restriction mechanism within Proxy Server where access to Internet addresses can be controlled on a granting or denial basis based on IP address, IP range, or URL.

- **GUI-based administration** All of the confirmation, management, and administration tools for Proxy Server are constructed around the familiar Windows GUI interface. Thus, all of the controls, even those for managing proxy arrays and caching hierarchy, are easy to understand, read, and use.

- **HTML-based administration** As part of Microsoft's continued effort to integrate high-end server products with standard interaction methods (i.e., the Web), Proxy Server can be controlled through an HTML-based administration interface by using a Web browser from a local or remote computer. This adds flexibility to the product by not restricting management control to a single console. Note that the HTML-based administration tool is not shipped with the final release of Proxy Server 2.0; it must be downloaded from the Microsoft Proxy Web page.

- **Command-line administration** To further simplify administration by adding batch-file capabilities, Proxy Server includes command-line administration support. From a command prompt (a.k.a. MS-DOS prompt), you can manage and configure local and remote proxy servers.

- **Array administration** When you are working with a cache array, administration is simplified by allowing you to propagate configuration changes to all members of an array. Thus, you only need to make setting modifications once; the array system will handle the task of dispersing the configuration changes to all other members.

- **Configuration backup and restoration** All of the configurations and settings of Proxy Server can be stored in a configuration file (i.e., backed up) for the ease and convenience of rolling back to a previous state, simplifying new installations, and protecting your existing status.

- **Client auto-configuration** Proxy Server can configure many Web Proxy clients automatically through the use of predefined or customized JavaScripts. This enables you to maintain a single, central settings database for all clients throughout an enterprise. Each time you make a modification to the client settings, the clients will be automatically updated the next time they attempt to access a resource.

- **SNMP support** Proxy Server supports SNMP for active remote network monitoring for administrators who are using any standard SNMP (Simple Network Management Protocol) console, such as HP OpenView.

FLEXIBLE SUPPORT FOR NETWORKING AND APPLICATIONS

The following features add flexibility to the tasks of managing networking and applications:

- **IPX-to-IP gateway** This special gateway enables clients on an IPX network to access Internet information services served via Proxy Server 2.0. TCP/IP is no longer a requirement for a client or a network to gain access to Internet resources. The IPX-to-IP gateway currently supports Windows 95 and Windows NT Workstation 4.0 clients.

- **Auto-dial connection** Just as modem connections can be set to establish a link with an ISP each time Internet resources are needed, so too can the Proxy Server's ISP connection be set to connect when any client requests a resource not already stored in cache. Then, when the link is no longer in use, it is disconnected. This feature saves on connection fees and time-use charges. Auto-dial can also be used to create a secondary or backup link in the event of a primary link failure or overload.

- **SOCKS support** To provide wider and richer Internet proxy services for Macintosh, Unix, and other non-Windows clients, Proxy Server can act as a SOCKS server or as a SOCKS client to an upstream SOCKS server.

- **Unbeaten LAN and WAN connectivity options** Proxy Server is compatible with all network interface cards (NICs) or adapters that carry the Windows NT Compatible logo. If it is supported by Windows NT, it is supported by Proxy Server.

- **Great protocol support** Proxy Server is equipped with support for a wide range of common Internet protocols, plus its protocol base can be extended. Web Proxy supports the following protocols natively: HTTP, SHTTP, FTP, and Gopher. WinSock Proxy supports the following protocols natively: AlphaWorld, AOL, Archie, Echo, Enliven, IMAP4, IRC, Microsoft NetShow, MSN, NNTP, POP3, RealAudio, SMTP, Telnet, and VDOLive.

WHY USE A PROXY SERVER?

The most important reason to use a proxy server is to provide Internet access to a large number of internal clients without having several Internet connections. The features of firewall protection, content caching, and identification masking are all significant, but they are typically not the main issue when you are deploying a proxy server. For most organizations, offering Internet access to its users involves one of two possibilities:

- Install a modem on each client and install a phone line for each modem.
- Set up a small number of Internet-capable machines for the entire office to share.

Neither alternative offers a satisfactory solution, whereas Proxy Server offers a reliable, high-performance, cost-effective solution.

There are several disadvantages to adding a modem and phone line for each client, including:

- Expense of extra hardware for each client (modem, wall jack, etc.)
- Monthly expense of each phone line
- Inability to share a single line with multiple users
- Monthly expense of individual ISP accounts
- No managerial control over Internet use or retrieved content
- Security dangers from PCs with modems
- Poor resource-retrieval performance
- Possibly that one resource, if used by several people, must be downloaded individually

Sharing Internet-enabled PCs with several users introduces other drawbacks, such as:

- Extreme user inconvenience (moving from normal workstation to the Internet PC)
- Lack of availability (when others are using the Internet PC)
- All users restricted to the same service settings; no real or useful customization options
- Difficulty with individual tracking and use logging

But, the deployment of a proxy server on a network eliminates most of the disadvantages that plague traditional connection methods and offers many key advantages, namely:

- Sharing of a single Internet connection with multiple simultaneous users
- Single access-point or gateway management and monitoring
- Secure external resource access
- User- and group-based resource restriction

- Site-, service-, and content-based restrictions
- Use tracking and logging by user
- High performance due to caching
- Cost effective

It should be obvious that to use any method other than the deployment of a proxy server to provide Internet access to clients on a network will result in poor performance, complicated administration, and high cost.

WHY USE MICROSOFT PROXY SERVER 2.0?

Microsoft's Proxy Server 2.0 is a solid, reliable, high-performance product. It is unique in its field as both a secure firewall and a high-volume, scalable, distributed, caching proxy server. As a leader in the realm of NT, Proxy Server 2.0 is an obvious choice among the handful of competitors. In Table 1.1, the features of Microsoft's Proxy Server 2.0 are compared to those of Netscape's Proxy Server and Novell's Border Manager.

HARDWARE AND SOFTWARE REQUIREMENTS FOR PROXY SERVER 2.0

Microsoft Proxy Server 2.0 installs onto Windows NT Server 4.0. Thus, most of the hardware and software requirements are automatically met if they are already

Table 1.1 A proxy server competitive comparison.

Feature	Microsoft Proxy Server 2.0	Netscape Proxy Server 2.5	Novell Border Manager
Automatic active caching	Yes	Manual	Manual
Cache array load balance	Automatic	No	No
Firewall security	Yes	No	Yes
Static packet filtering	Yes	No	Yes
Dynamic packet filtering	Yes	No	No
Realtime alerts	Yes	No	No
Logging (text and ODBC)	Yes	No—text only	No—text only
Windows NT Server integration	Best	Minimal	No
GUI-based administration	Yes	No	Yes
Browser-based administration	Yes	Yes	No
Scriptable command administration	Yes	No	No
Auto dial	Yes	No	No
Built-in IPX-to-IP gateway	Yes	No	Yes

1

satisfied for NT Server. However, here is a detailed list of the requirements for Proxy Server 2.0.

SOFTWARE REQUIREMENTS

Proxy Server 2.0 requires that the following software is installed on the hosting server computer:

- Microsoft Windows NT Server 4.0
- Microsoft Internet Information Server 3.0 or greater
- Windows NT Server 4.0 Service Pack 3.0 or greater (included with Microsoft Proxy Server 2.0)

HARDWARE REQUIREMENTS

The hardware requirements for Proxy Server are basically the same as those for Windows NT Server 4.0; however, they should be modified to meet the expected workload.

The hardware requirements for up to 300 clients are:

- Intel 486 minimum/Pentium 133MHz recommended
- 24MB RAM minimum/32MB RAM recommended
- 10MB minimum/from 250MB to 2GB disk space recommended for caching

The requirements for 300 to 2,000 clients are:

- Intel Pentium 133MHz
- 64MB RAM minimum
- From 2GB to 4GB disk space for caching

The requirements for 2,001 or more clients are:

- Intel Pentium 166MHz or greater
- 64MB RAM minimum
- From 2GB to 4GB disk space for caching

CHAPTER SUMMARY

In this chapter, we discussed the origins of security as they relate to connecting a network to the Internet. Firewalls were the first major advancement in communication security. Soon firewalls were used for several purposes, including restricting internal access for external users, enabling controlled external access for internal users, and establishing WAN or VPN links over public communication networks. Eventually, a new type of server—the content caching server—was developed and deployed alongside and in conjunction with firewalls. Caching servers improved resource access by storing oft-retrieved remote files locally. ISPs adopted caching servers to improve performance for their customers.

Proxy servers are the result of the combination of firewalls and content caching systems. These multipurpose or multifunctional tools enabled network administrators to maintain a secure environment, to offer restricted Internet access, and to allow multiple users to reach out to the Internet on a single communication link.

Microsoft's Proxy Server 2.0 is a revolutionary product because it is the first caching server to offer true firewall capabilities and the first firewall to support high-performance caching of content. Proxy Server offers flexible security, solid performance, and easy administration. Version 2.0 of the software has many significant improvements over its predecessor, version 1.0. Some of the more significant advancements are scalability, distributed caching, and true firewall capabilities.

Proxy Server is made up of three sub-proxy systems: Web Proxy, WinSock Proxy, and SOCKS Proxy. The combination of these three components makes Proxy Server the most broadly applicable and supported proxy server on the market today.

KEY TERMS

- **Application layer**—The layer of the OSI model where network communications are interfaced with user applications.

- **application restriction**—A user access control where a specific protocol or application is restricted from use.

- **array-based content caching**—You can use a new array-based distributed caching method to configure several Proxy Server installations to operate as a single entity. Array caching can be administered as a single, logical entity, and it can provide automated load balancing, add fault tolerance, and embody scalability.

- **Cache Array Routing Protocol (CARP)**—As a new distributed caching protocol submitted by Microsoft to the IETF as a new industry standard, CARP uses a queryless routing method to locate and retrieve data from distributed cache whether it is in an array-based or hierarchical-based format. This method offers significant performance improvement over traditional location methods, especially on high-volume requests with multiple proxy servers.

- **circuit-layer restriction**—A user access control, where multiple protocols can be filtered or monitored simultaneously regardless of the application or data content.

- **content caching**—The function of a proxy server; frequently accessed data on a remote server is stored locally to speed client access and reduce network traffic.

- **File Transfer Protocol (FTP)**—The protocol used to transfer files to and from remote servers located across a TCP/IP-based network.

- **firewall**—A hardware and/or software product designed to restrict unauthorized or unlawful entry into an organization's network from some external point such as the Internet.

- **Gopher**—The protocol used to host the term-only information service of Gopher.

- **hierarchical caching**—When multiple LANs are connected, such as with multiple branch offices or within a large enterprise network, a hierarchical caching scheme can be implemented with multiple single proxies or arrays of proxies to distribute content based on location and use histories. Client requests are communicated upward through the proxy relation tree until the resource is located or finally retrieved from the Internet.

- **Hypertext Transfer Protocol (HTTP)**—The protocol used on the World Wide Web for the distribution of HTML documents over the Internet or an intranet.

- **Internet**—The collection of TCP/IP-based networks around the world. Information on nearly every subject is available in some form somewhere on the Internet. The Internet has become the communication medium of choice for both business and personal interaction.

- **Internet Service Provider (ISP)**—A company or organization that is in the business of selling access to the Internet and providing value-added network and communication services.

- **Internetwork Packet Exchange/Sequenced Packet Exchange (IPX/SPX- and NWLink-compatible transport)**—The protocol originally developed by Novell and commonly associated with NetWare. Many Microsoft products support IPX/SPX and compatible protocols (NWLink).

- **IPX-to-IP gateway**—A gateway that enables clients on an IPX network to access Internet information services via Proxy Server 2.0. No longer is TCP/IP a requirement for a client or a network to gain access to Internet resources. The IPX-to-IP gateway currently supports Windows 95 and Windows NT Workstation 4.0 clients.

- **local area network (LAN)**—A network that is confined to a single building or geographic area and consists of servers, workstations, peripheral devices, a network operating system, and a communications link.

- **Microsoft NetShow**—A streaming multimedia architecture and tool set developed by Microsoft.

- **multihomed server**—A computer that has two or more network interfaces and is connected to different networks.

- **network**—A collection of server and client computers that communicates over a wire-based media for the purpose of sharing resources.

- **Network layer**—The layer of the OSI model where addressing and routing are handled.

- **network traffic**—The actual digital communications that occur over the wire media of a network.

- **OSI (Open Systems Interconnection) model**—An international standard set by International Organization for Standardization (ISO) that defines a seven-layer model that specifies how networking protocols operate.

- **packet**—A single chunk of data that is transmitted across a network.

- **packet layer**—Another name for the network layer of the OSI model.

- **paper trail**—In relation to computers, a term that refers to the collection of electronic data in the form of logs, records, errors, or messages. A paper trail can be used to establish the sequence of events, process of occurrence, or evidence of failure.

- **proxy server**—A software product that acts as a moderator or go-between for a client and a remote host. Most proxy servers also offer content caching and firewall capabilities.

- **RealAudio**—A multimedia tool, protocol, and enhancement that streams audio (and video) over TCP/IP networks.

- **reverse hosting**—A feature of Proxy Server. Reverse hosting is a companion to the reverse proxy feature in that it enables several distinct Web servers hosted inside of your network to be integrated by Proxy Server into what looks like a single large Web site to all external viewers. This method of Web publishing maintains tight security, isolates the Web servers from the Internet, and offers you greater flexibility in design, layout, and navigation.

- **reverse proxy**—A feature of Proxy Server that enables you to set up within your network a World Wide Web publishing server behind the proxy server and still be able to offer its contents to the external world of the Internet. If you use reverse proxy, you have tighter security control over your Web site.

The proxy server impersonates a Web server to the outside world and only it communicates directly with the real internal Web server.

- **router**—A device or a software implementation that enables interoperability and communication across networks.

- **Routing and Remote Access Service Update**—A service update for Windows NT Server that adds routing capabilities to the RAS server and improves the features and performance of RAS (Remote Access Service).

- **Secure Sockets Layer (SSL) tunneling**—Proxy Server supports SSL tunneling via the Web Proxy to maintain highly secure Web-based transactions. SSL is commonly used in electronic commerce or other state-dependent applications. SSL tunneling creates an encrypted communication path between the client and the remote server.

- **security**—Protecting data by restricting access to only authorized users.

- **server proxying**—A feature of Proxy Server. Server proxying is the ability to listen for or identify traffic bound for specific information service servers within the internal network and then forward the packets to those servers. This enables services such as Microsoft Exchange Server to operate as your primary Internet mail clearinghouse even if the computer on which the service is installed is located behind the proxy. This method of server proxying maintains a secure environment by offering administrators control over which packets are allowed network access.

- **Simple Network Management Protocol (SNMP)**—A protocol used to monitor remote hosts over a TCP/IP network.

- **site filtering**—A security feature that prevents internal users from accessing specified sites by filtering responses from that site or preventing requests from being processed. Site filtering is a form of user access control.

- **site restriction**—Another term for site filtering; the specification of an IP address, domain name, or URL that is restricted.

- **SOCKS Proxy**—One of the components of Proxy Server. SOCKS Proxy is a cross-platform network service that creates a secured communications link between a client and a server. SOCKS Proxy supports SOCKS 4.3a and offers non-Windows or non-WinSock applications access to Internet services.

- **Telnet**—A TCP/IP utility that enables remote terminal emulation.

- **Transmission Control Protocol/Internet Protocol (TCP/IP)**—The most commonly used network protocol and the central protocol of the Internet.

- **Uniform Resource Locator (URL)**—The addressing scheme used to identify resources on the Internet. URLs are most commonly associated with Web resources and are used by Web browsers. A URL consists of a protocol type and a domain name as a minimum, plus it can identify a port, directory path, file name, and a defined named spot.

- **user access control**—A general term that refers to the security and control restrictions enforced by an administrator to specify or dictate the resources available to a user.

- **User Datagram Protocol (UDP)**—A connectionless TCP/IP protocol that provides extremely fast data transmission.

- **VDOLive**—A streaming audio and video protocol, and tool for TCP/IP networks.

- **virtual private network (VPN)**—A WAN that is provided by a common communications carrier. It works like a private network, but the backbone of the network is shared with all of the customers in a public network.

- **Web Proxy**—One of the components of Proxy Server. Web Proxy supports those protocols and communication mechanisms typically associated with Web documents, access, and interaction.

- **wide area network (WAN)**—A network that spans geographically distant segments. Often, the distance of two miles or more is used to define a WAN; however, Microsoft equates any RAS connection as establishing a WAN.

- **WinSock Proxy**—One of the components of Proxy Server. WinSock Proxy supports client applications designed around the Windows Sockets API. This includes utilities and services such as Telnet and RealAudio.

REVIEW QUESTIONS

1. Which of the following is typically not a benefit of connecting an organization's network to the Internet?
   a. improved communication
   b. customer interaction
   c. 24-hour technical support
   d. increased productivity
   e. expanded research capabilities
   f. unlimited, unrestricted, free high-bandwidth links
   g. geographically unlimited collaboration
2. What is the most serious drawback or consequence of connecting a network to the Internet?
   a. decline in employee productivity
   b. increased costs
   c. security
   d. the need for user training
   e. too much information

3. What was the first stage of or product used for securing networks connected to the Internet?

a. name and password authentication

b. proxy servers

c. content caching

d. firewalls

e. physical restrictions

4. On which levels or layers of the OSI model does a firewall typically operate? (Choose two answers.)

a. Transport

b. Application

c. Data Link

d. Physical

e. Network

5. What type of product was typically deployed alongside or in conjunction with a firewall to improve resource access performance and reduce network traffic?

a. content caching servers

b. routers

c. Web servers

d. Telnet hosts

e. multihomed servers

6. What is the primary function of a content caching server?

a. to allow several users to share a single Internet communication link

b. to store frequently accessed remote resources locally

c. to restrict external intrusion

d. to record user activity

e. to authenticate users and scan for viruses

7. Which of the following is not an example of proxy server user access control?

a. restricting access to a Web site based on URLs

b. preventing interaction with hosts of a specified domain name

c. disabling the transmission of a specific application's protocol

d. restricting a user from changing the contents of a locally stored file

e. preventing a client computer from using an Internet information service

8. ISPs have deployed proxy servers to improve performance for their users and reduce costs in relation to network traffic over backbone links. (True or False?)

9. A proxy server is a hybrid product that has the ability to perform what functions? (Choose all that apply.)

   a. protect a network from unauthorized access or use

   b. enable realtime video collaboration

   c. cache oft-used content

   d. create and publish HTML documents

   e. hide the identity of internal clients by requesting resources on their behalf

10. A properly installed and operational proxy server is completely apparent to both the user and the resource host. (True or False?)

11. A proxy server is usually installed on what type of computer?

    a. a standalone server

    b. a multihomed server

    c. a low-end client computer

    d. a server with a single NIC

    e. a client with an ISDN connection to an ISP

12. What features or improvements are found in Proxy Server 2.0 that were not present in its version 1.0 predecessor? (Choose all that apply.)

    a. true firewall capabilities

    b. HTTP 1.0 support

    c. distributed caching scalability

    d. circuit-layer security

    e. reverse hosting

13. What features typically only found in firewall products does Proxy Server 2.0 offer? (Choose all that apply.)

    a. circuit-layer security

    b. alerting

    c. application-layer security

    d. logging

    e. dynamic packet filtering

14. Proxy Server enables the construction of secure VPNs when it is combined with what Windows NT Server 4.0 update?

    a. BackOffice SDK (Software Development Kit)

    b. Service Pack 2

    c. Wolfpack

    d. Routing and Remote Access Service

    e. Internet Information Server 4.0

15. What is Microsoft's new caching protocol that has been submitted to the IETF for standardization?

 a. Hypertext Transfer Protocol (HTTP)

 b. CARP (Cache Array Routing Protocol)

 c. SNMP (Simple Network Management Protocol)

 d. Transmission Control Protocol/Internet Protocol (TCP/IP)

 e. Internetwork Packet Exchange/Sequenced Packet Exchange (IPX/SPX)

16. Proxy Server offers a performance improvement over traditional Internet connection methods by what percentage?

 a. up to 10 percent

 b. 20 to 30 percent

 c. 40 to 50 percent

 d. 70 to 80 percent

 e. over 90 percent

17. What are the three main components or sub-proxies of Proxy Server 2.0? (Choose three answers.)

 a. Web

 b. FTP

 c. SOCKS

 d. WinSock

 e. CARP

18. SOCKS Proxy enables support for what platform types?

 a. Unix

 b. Macintosh

 c. Intel/PC

 d. OS/2

 e. All of the above

19. The ability to host a single Web server inside your network and have the proxy server mediate between the Web server and the Internet is called:

 a. reverse hosting

 b. multiprotocol routing

 c. reverse proxy

 d. server proxying

 e. array caching

20. The ability to host multiple internal Web servers but to have Proxy Server integrate them into a fictitious single server for external users is called:
    a. reverse hosting
    b. multiprotocol routing
    c. reverse proxy
    d. server proxying
    e. array caching

21. What is the ability of Proxy Server to forward information-service-specific packets from external sources to internal servers called?
    a. reverse hosting
    b. multiprotocol routing
    c. reverse proxy
    d. server proxying
    e. array caching

22. What is the ability to configure multiple proxy servers to act as a single entity called?
    a. reverse hosting
    b. multiprotocol routing
    c. reverse proxy
    d. server proxying
    e. array caching

23. Proxy Server 2.0 is able to cache FTP objects. (True or False?)

24. What level of HTTP support does Proxy Server 2.0 feature?
    a. 1.0
    b. 1.1
    c. 3.2
    d. 2.0
    e. 4.0

25. Out of the box, Proxy Server can be configured and administered via a Web interface. (True or False?)

CASE PROJECTS

1. You administer a 10,000-user enterprise network. You have recently added a DS-3 digital link to a high-speed Internet backbone.

Required result: All users are able to connect to the Internet over the single DS-3 line.

Optional desired results: All users share a common cache set. The GENERAL users group is restricted from using RealAudio.

Proposed solution: Install multiple Proxy Servers. Link the servers together so they perform array caching. All clients have connectivity to and are configured to use a Proxy Server. Which results does the proposed solution produce?

   a. The proposed solution produces the required result and both of the optional desired results.

   b. The proposed solution produces the required result and only one of the optional desired results.

   c. The proposed solution produces the required result but neither of the optional desired results.

   d. The proposed solution does not produce the required result.

2. You administer a 10,000-user enterprise network. You have recently added a DS-3 digital link to a high-speed Internet backbone.

Required result: All users are able to connect to the Internet over the single DS-3 line.

Optional desired results: All users share a common cache set. The GENERAL users group is restricted from using RealAudio.

Proposed solution: Install multiple Proxy Servers. Link the servers so they perform array caching. All clients have connectivity to and are configured to use a Proxy Server. Configure a user access control in the WinSock Proxy that denies access to RealAudio for the GENERAL group. Which results does the proposed solution produce? Why?

   a. The proposed solution produces the required result and both of the optional desired results.

   b. The proposed solution produces the required result and only one of the optional desired results.

   c. The proposed solution produces the required result but neither of the optional desired results.

   d. The proposed solution does not produce the required result.

3. You attach your organization's network to the Internet using an ISDN line.

Required result: Prevent external access to your internal resources.

Optional desired results: Cache oft-used resources. Enable multiple users to access the Internet over the single ISDN line.

Proposed solution: Install a firewall. Which results does the proposed solution produce? Why?

a. The proposed solution produces the required result and both of the optional desired results.

b. The proposed solution produces the required result and only one of the optional desired results.

c. The proposed solution produces the required result but neither of the optional desired results.

d. The proposed solution does not produce the required result.

4. You administer a network that has recently been attached to the Internet. You install Microsoft Exchange Server to handle internal and Internet email.

Required result: Provide security for the internal network.

Optional desired results: Improve resource access performance. Maintain a usage history.

Proposed solution: Install Proxy Server 2.0. Enable server proxying for email packets. Restrict all other external access to the internal network. Configure all clients to use proxy services for Internet access. Turn on the logging capabilities of Proxy Server. Which results does the proposed solution produce? Why?

a. The proposed solution produces the required result and both of the optional desired results.

b. The proposed solution produces the required result and only one of the optional desired results.

c. The proposed solution produces the required result but neither of the optional desired results.

d. The proposed solution does not produce the required result.

5. There are four divisions to your organization. The divisions are evident on the internal network because each department has its own private Web server.

Required result: Establish a secure Internet connection to the current network.

Optional desired results: Combine the resources on the multiple Web servers into a single entity viewed by external users. Improve access performance.

Proposed solution: Create a new network of five server computers. Set up four with duplicates of the original Web servers. Configure the fifth as a proxy server with reverse hosting. Connect only the new five-server network to the Internet. Which results does the proposed solution produce? Why?

a. The proposed solution produces the required result and both of the optional desired results.

b. The proposed solution produces the required result and only one of the optional desired results.

c. The proposed solution produces the required result but neither of the optional desired results.

d. The proposed solution does not produce the required result.

MICROSOFT PROXY SERVER 2.0
ARCHITECTURE

Microsoft has positioned itself as the provider for all things Internet, both client side and server side. Proxy Server is an integral part of that plan in that it provides a secure method of connecting corporate computers to the Internet. In this chapter, we take a brief look at the Windows NT architecture and how Proxy Server 2.0 fits into that architecture. We also explore each of the Proxy services and their structure.

**AFTER READING THIS CHAPTER AND COMPLETING THE
EXERCISES, YOU WILL BE ABLE TO:**

- Understand where Microsoft Proxy Server fits in a Windows NT network
- Understand the components and functions of each service offered by Proxy Server

THE WINDOWS NT ARCHITECTURE

Before delving into the structure of Microsoft Proxy Server, it is important to understand the Windows NT architecture. As you may have learned in preparing for the Windows NT Server or Server in the Enterprise test, the Windows NT architecture is a layered model, similar to the OSI model for networking.

Fundamentally, the Windows NT operating system is made up of three main components: environment subsystems, executive services, and user applications.

The *environment subsystems* (Win16, VDM, POSIX, OS/2, and Win32) offer runtime support for a variety of applications under the authority of a single operating system. Just like the applications they support, Windows NT environment subsystems run in *user mode*, which means that they must access all system resources through the operating system's *kernel mode*.

The Windows NT *Executive Services* (I/O Manager, Object Manager, Security Reference Monitor, Local Procedure Call Facility, Virtual Memory Manager, and Process Manager) and the underlying Windows NT Kernel, define the kernel mode of the operating system and its runtime environment. Kernel mode components are permitted to access system objects and resources directly, and provide the many services and access controls that allow multiple users and applications to coexist and effectively interoperate.

User applications provide the functionality and capabilities that make Windows NT the most popular network operating system in use today. All such applications run within the context of one of the environment subsystems that operate in user mode. Figure 2.1 illustrates how each of these components interrelates.

Before addressing the components that apply specifically to the Proxy Server architecture and operation, a quick review of user mode, kernel mode, and the I/O Manager is in order.

 For more information on the environment subsystems and other components of the Windows NT architecture refer to Microsoft TechNet.

USER MODE VERSUS KERNEL MODE

To fully understand the Windows NT architecture and Proxy Server's place in that architecture, a clear distinction between Windows NT's kernel mode and user mode must be made. The main difference between the two modes lies in how memory is used by kernel-mode components and user-mode components.

User Mode

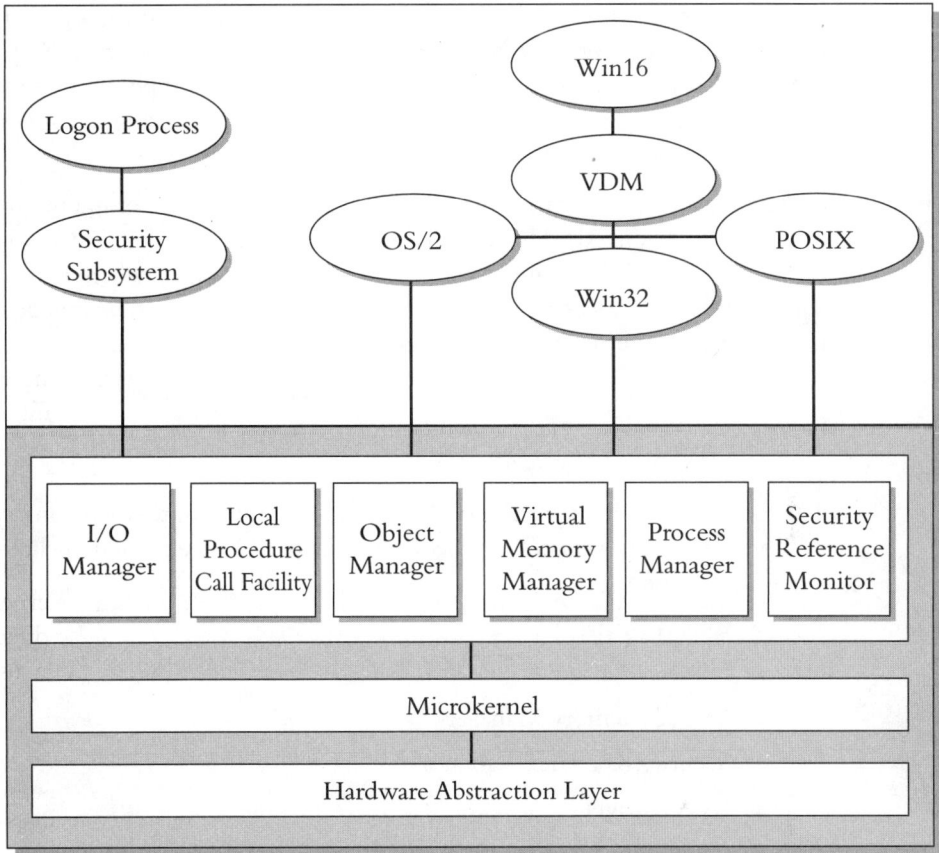

Kernel Mode

Figure 2.1   The many components that encompass the Windows NT architecture.

In user mode, each process operates as if the entire 4GB of virtual memory available to Windows NT is its exclusive property—with the understanding that the upper 2GB of addresses are always reserved for system use. This is true no matter what type of hardware Windows NT is running on.

This address space is entirely virtual, and must operate within the confines of whatever RAM is installed on a machine and within the amount of space reserved for the paging file. While the theoretical upper bound for Windows NT addresses may be 2GB (or 4GB, for system purposes), the true upper bound of the address space is always the sum of physical RAM size plus the amount of space in the paging file.

Although processes that operate in user mode may share memory areas with other processes to accomplish tasks such as passing messages or sharing information, they don't by default. This means that one user-mode process cannot crash another or corrupt its data. Because of this, applications appear to run independently, giving each one the illusion that it has exclusive possession of the operating system and the computer's hardware.

Processes running in user mode cannot access hardware or communicate with other processes directly. However, kernel mode processes are able to directly access all hardware and memory in the computer. Thus, when a particular application needs to access the hardware, it calls a user-mode function that ultimately calls a kernel-mode function.

The Windows NT Kernel consists of three parts: Windows NT Executive Services, the Windows NT Kernel itself (also known as the *microkernel*), and the *Hardware Abstraction Layer (HAL)*.

The Executive Services portion of the Kernel is the part of the operating system that provides basic services to the environment subsystems and includes the following components:

- Object Manager
- Process Manager
- Virtual Memory Manager
- Security Reference Monitor
- I/O Manager
- Graphical Device Interface (GDI) and Window Manager
- Device drivers

Although they share the same 4GB of virtual memory area, these components exist and operate independently of each other, so that modifying one service does not mean that the rest of the services must also be modified as a result. For the purposes of understanding how Proxy Server fits into the Windows NT architecture, only an examination of the I/O Manager is necessary. For more information on the other Executive Services of the Kernel, refer to Microsoft TechNet.

I/O Manager

The *I/O (input/output) Manager* provides a consistent interface for the majority of I/O operations on a Windows NT computer, including installed device drivers for the files systems, network adapters, and other peripherals such as CD-ROM drives, printers, or tape drives. The I/O Manager does not, however, manage screen-, keyboard-, or mouse-related I/O; these operations are handled by the GDI. The I/O Manager provides NT with the ability to interact with any installed device drivers without requiring the operating system itself to understand how such hardware works.

The I/O Manager's interaction with device drivers is layered so that one driver handles communication between the driver and the process making the request, while another driver manipulates the hardware. By using a layered system such as this, any of the Executive Services modules can be replaced or changed without affecting the operation of the system or how the applications must interact with device drivers.

MICROKERNEL

Beneath the collection of modules that comprise the Windows NT Executive Services in the Kernel, lies a special component sometimes called the microkernel (or more simply, the Kernel). The microkernel is the part of Windows NT that is responsible for scheduling threads and handling interrupts and exceptions as well as synchronizing activities among the various components of the Executive Services. If multiple processors reside in a computer, the microkernel also synchronizes processor activity and runs simultaneously on all processors. The microkernel is one of a small number of Windows NT components that always remains resident in memory, because it may be called on at any time to manage the rest of the system.

HARDWARE ABSTRACTION LAYER

The final piece of the puzzle and the foundation of the Windows NT Kernel is the Hardware Abstraction Layer (HAL). This component is written in a specific machine language so it can communicate with the computer's CPU as quickly as possible. The HAL is the main hardware-dependent portion of Windows NT, and its job is to make all CPUs look alike to the rest of the operating system. This layer enables Windows NT to work on computers with PowerPC, Alpha, and Intel CPUs.

NETWORKING ARCHITECTURE WITH WINDOWS NT

Now that you've learned a little about how the Windows NT Kernel and its services interact, a discussion of how the TCP/IP model works within the architecture is needed. The Microsoft networking structure operates in both kernel and user mode and is controlled by the I/O Manager.

As you may know, the OSI model is divided into seven layers (Application, Presentation, Session, Transport, Network, Datalink, and Physical), each of which performs a specific function in network communications. Similarly, the TCP/IP model is divided into four layers (Application, Transport, Internet, and

Network Interface) and the Windows NT Networking model is divided into six layers (Programming Interface, File System Drivers, Transport Driver Interface, Transport Protocols, Network Driver Interface Specification, and Network Adapters). Figure 2.2 shows how each of these networking models relates to each other.

All of the functions performed by each of these networking models take place through the control of the I/O Manager in the Windows NT Kernel. Each of the top layers provides the link to the user mode applications that use their services. The following sections describe the components of the Windows NT Networking model.

BOUNDARY LAYERS

Microsoft's architecture means that NT's networking services are delivered through a collection of components and their associated interfaces, called *boundary layers*. Often, a boundary represents nothing more than a group of settings that are used to define a desired network service. Other times, a boundary layer will consist of some application programming interface (API) designed to permit specific networking components to exchange information within Windows NT. The most important thing to remember in the Windows NT Networking model is that components deliver services and boundary layers permit components to exchange information and to communicate.

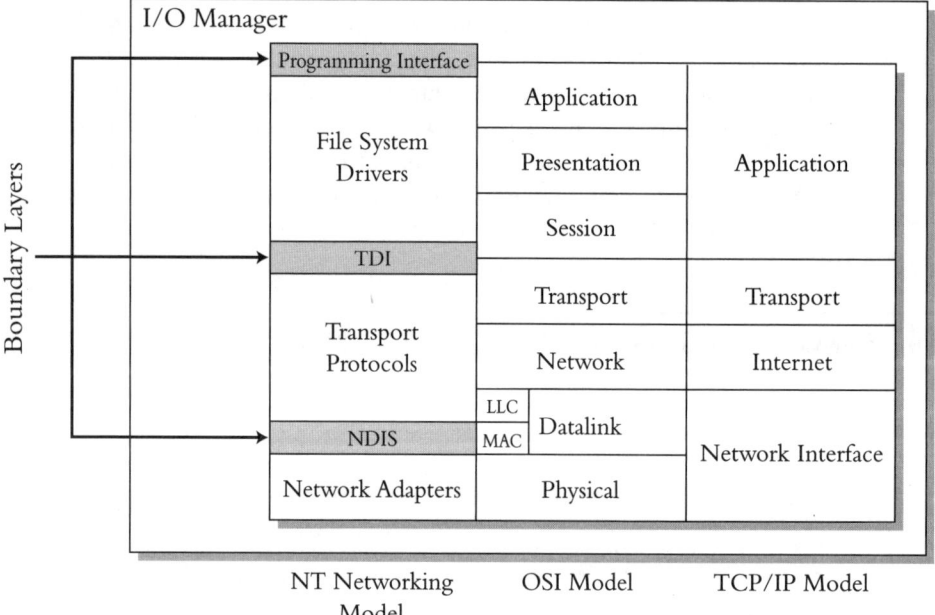

Figure 2.2   The many networking models at work in the Windows NT environment.

Boundary layers were designed to make it easy for programmers to create drivers for network adapters and to easily access other network components, such as file systems or protocols. Boundary layers separate components and provide access between the components they separate. By doing this, the generic Programming Interface permits user mode applications to communicate with one of NT's redirectors, the Server service, the Workstation service, or other high-layer network services.

The *Transport Driver Interface (TDI)* makes it possible for each of these services to interact with one or more available transport protocol drivers. This creates an open-ended networking environment, where services can be indifferent to the transports they will ultimately use, because the boundary layer handles the details of connecting a service to one or more transports.

Beneath the Transport Protocol Driver components, another boundary layer called the *Network Driver Interface Specification (NDIS)* resides. NDIS defines a specification for building network interface card drives that can support multiple interfaces in a single computer and one or more protocols for each such interface. NDIS 3.0 is the version supported in Windows NT 4.0 while NDIS 3.1 is supported in Windows 95 and Windows 98 as well. The NDIS 3.1 and NDIS 5.0 specifications are the only versions available that support the full-blown Microsoft plug and play specification.

PROGRAMMING INTERFACES

Programming interfaces are often referred to as application programming interfaces or APIs, but the terminology that Microsoft uses emphasizes that such interfaces can occur at almost any level in the operating system. These interfaces define the procedure calls or object references that permit applications or drivers to interact with system services such as the redirector.

 Some of the programming interfaces supported by Windows NT 4.0 include NetBIOS, WinSock, and NetDDE.

FILE SYSTEM DRIVERS COMPONENT

Due to the way Windows NT is designed, a computer accessing a file system across the network uses the same steps as a computer accessing a local file system. As shown earlier in Figure 2.2, these file system drivers operate at the OSI Application and Session layers. This means that user applications access local and remote file systems in the same way, making it easier to create the user application. In the Windows NT system, the redirector services distinguish between which file system is local and which file system is remote and take appropriate action to see that all requests for resources are satisfied. The Windows NT components that are considered file system drivers are: workstation services, named pipes, server services, and mailslots.

 Although these components are referred to as file system drivers, these components are also known as redirectors because they are able to redirect requests for remote resources to other systems on the network.

TRANSPORT DRIVER INTERFACE (TDI) BOUNDARY LAYER

The Transport Driver Interface (TDI) acts as a boundary layer to shield the redirectors from the details of network transport. To operate in a Windows NT environment, all transport protocols must conform to the TDI. Because of this requirement, Windows NT's services can function as if they were transport independent. The TDI boundary layer operates between the OSI Session and Transport layers.

TRANSPORT PROTOCOLS COMPONENT

Transport protocols deal with such functions as packet sequencing, data delivery, and integrity checks. In the Windows NT environment, the TDI permits multiple transport protocols to be active simultaneously. Consequently, connections made using any of the transport protocols that Windows NT supports—primarily NetBEUI, IPX/SPX, and TCP/IP—can coexist and interoperate effectively and reliably.

NETWORK DRIVER INTERFACE SPECIFICATION (NDIS) BOUNDARY LAYER

As you learned earlier in this chapter, the Network Driver Interface Specification (NDIS) provides the ability to install more than one network interface card in a single computer and for more than one protocol to operate on a single card. All Windows NT network drivers must conform to the NDIS 3.0 specification. NDIS defines a standard interface that structures the communication between compliant drivers and one or more of Windows NT's transport protocols. To extend the capabilities of any Windows NT machine, NDIS drivers permit multiple transport protocols to communicate using one or more network interface cards simultaneously. Among other things, this permits a properly configured NT machine to route packets from one network interface to another, or to communicate simultaneously across multiple networks.

The Windows NT network architecture relies heavily on NDIS. NDIS operates at the Media Access Control (MAC) address sublayer of the OSI Datalink layer. Any interface card that is NDIS-compatible can pass data to any Windows NT transport protocol.

MICROSOFT PROXY SERVER IN A WINDOWS NT NETWORK

As Microsoft has expanded its presence in the networking world, network administrators have looked to it for many different services, and it has risen to the challenge. As part of an Internet/intranet solution, Proxy Server works with Internet Information Server (IIS) to provide Web, FTP, Telnet, and Gopher services as well as basic TCP/IP access for users.

Historically, each user in a company who wanted to connect to the Internet had his or her own modem and user account at the local ISP. Although this system worked, it was slow and costly. With separate dial-up lines, modems, and accounts for each user, Internet connection costs skyrocketed.

The next-generation configuration, shown in Figure 2.3, pooled a company's modems at an NT Server acting as a modem server. Although this configuration centralized resources and simplified administration, it was still slow and not terribly secure.

With the introduction of Windows NT 4.0 and IIS, Microsoft was able to provide secure Internet services. IIS uses the Windows NT internal security system to ensure that only users with appropriate access are allowed to view and retrieve files. Microsoft Proxy Server, an extension of the IIS product, acts as a firewall between the Internet and your intranet.

As mentioned in Chapter 1, Proxy Server 2.0 requires Windows NT 4.0 with both Service Pack 3 and IIS 3.0 installed and configured. Because of this tight integration with the Windows NT platform Proxy Server is able to provide a secure connection to the Internet.

Like other networking services, Proxy Server operates through the I/O Manager and the Windows NT Networking model. Figure 2.4 shows how many of the Proxy Server components map to the TCP/IP and Windows NT Networking models.

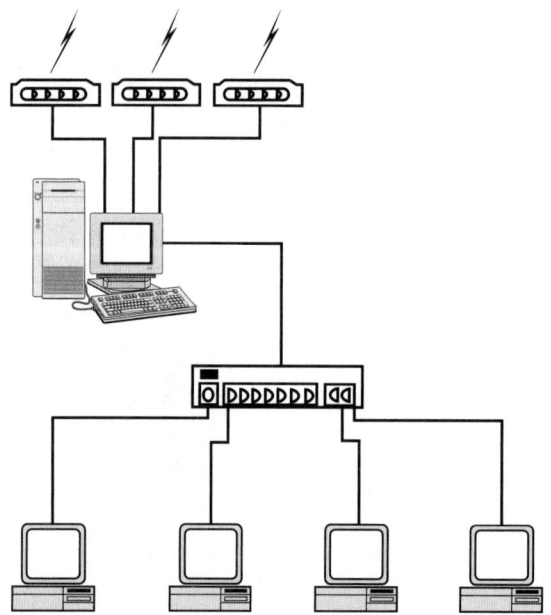

Figure 2.3   Modem pools allowed many users to share modem resources.

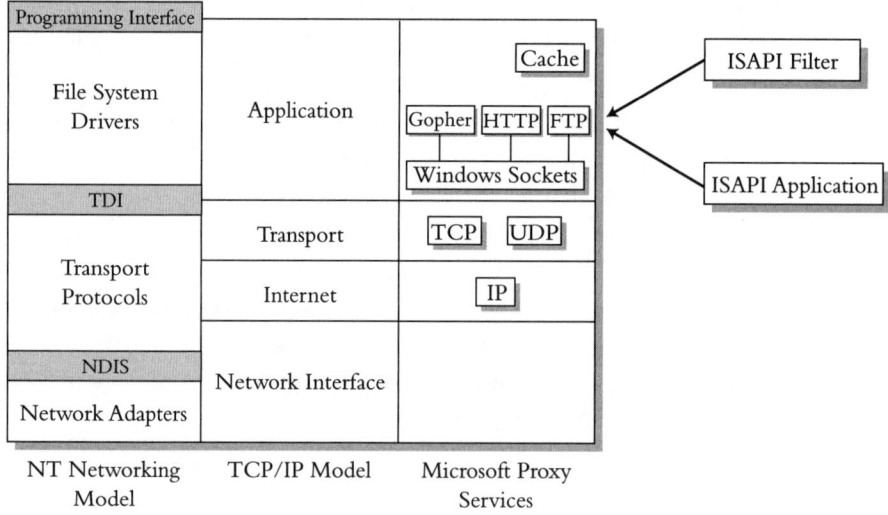

Figure 2.4   The Microsoft Proxy Server architecture.

OVERVIEW OF PROXY SERVER SERVICES

As you know, Microsoft Proxy Server includes three services that are used to provide proxy Internet access. By definition, proxy is the authority to act for another. This means that the proxy server takes on the role of both client and server for PCs communicating with the Internet. It acts as a client by forwarding requests from other clients on the network as if they were its own requests. In contrast, it acts as a server to internal clients by fulfilling their requests. The services offered by Proxy Server are:

- **Web Proxy** As its name implies, the Web Proxy service provides services for clients requesting Web documents. Web browsers that use this service must be *CERN* compliant, and most of today's browsers are, including Netscape Navigator and Microsoft Internet Explorer. Because the Web Proxy service supports this type of browser, computers of varying architectures—Windows, Apple, and Unix—can use the Web Proxy service.

- **WinSock Proxy** This service is used by Microsoft Windows applications (such as Internet Relay Chat, Microsoft NetShow, and RealAudio) that use Windows Sockets.

- **SOCKS Proxy** This service is used by other applications that use SOCKS version 4.3a. It is used to establish a secure channel between client and server across the Internet. *SOCKS* is used to provide Internet functions for applications such as Telnet, FTP, and Gopher.

The following sections provide a detailed discussion of each service, including its components and how it is used to access the Internet.

WEB PROXY SERVICE

As we have already stated, the Web Proxy service provides Internet access for CERN-compliant Web browsers. The Web Proxy service gives multiple computers the ability to use a single IP address (called secure IP address aggregation). It also provides extensive caching, data encryption using Secure Sockets Layer (SSL), client request logging, user-level security for each application protocol, and encrypted logon for browsers that support the Windows NT Challenge/Response authentication system.

The Web Proxy service acts as both a client, making requests to servers on the Internet, and as a server, fulfilling requests made by internal clients. By using the enhanced security of Windows NT and the functions of IIS, however, the Web Proxy service is much more than a relay between client and server. It is the Web Proxy service that requires IIS and utilizes its functionality to provide Web access.

CERN

CERN refers to the Conseil Européen pour la Recherche Nucléaire, or the European Laboratory for Particle Research, in Switzerland. What, you may ask, does this laboratory have to do with the Web and Web browsers? Most Internet applications, including the World Wide Web, are based on the Hypertext Transfer Protocol (HTTP). The first code libraries to use HTTP to support this type of client/server communication were developed at CERN. As CERN expanded its use of these libraries and added support for application-aware proxy, the Internet took notice and adopted the CERN-proxy protocol as the industry standard. As mentioned, the Microsoft Proxy Server Web Proxy service is fully compliant with this protocol.

Because the Web Proxy service is fully compliant with CERN proxy, it is able to service the requests of many different types of browsers. Not only will it successfully process Microsoft Internet Explorer requests from a Windows 95 machine, it will also handle requests from Netscape on Unix systems or CERN-compliant browsers running on Macintosh computers.

Most Web communication, whether it be WWW, FTP, or Gopher, uses HTTP as its transport. As with all protocols, HTTP has a specific set of commands that are used in client/server communication. The commands most often used are **Get** and **Post**. The **Get** command requests the document specified in the URL of the request. The **Post** command is used by the server to forward the information requested by the **Get**; the information is generally presented as an HTML page.

ISAPI Filter And ISAPI Application

The Web Proxy service is made up of two applications within the *Internet Server Application Programming Interface (ISAPI)*: the filter interface and the application interface. To understand how the Web Proxy service responds to requests from clients, it is important to understand each component and how it operates. Bear in mind that the Proxy Server ISAPI filter and application perform specific functions in the realm of Proxy services. Other ISAPI filters or applications can be created and called given certain circumstances.

The ISAPI filter provides an extension to the IIS Web server; the extension is used whenever the Web server receives an HTTP request. Because this filter is called every time a request is made to the server, it can be used to monitor or log requests, to modify a request if necessary, to provide for authentication, or to redirect a request to another server.

Once the Proxy Server ISAPI filter (which is located in W3PROXY.DLL) has been loaded, it examines each request made to the server to determine whether the request is a CERN-proxy request or a standard HTTP request. If in fact the request is a proxy request, the ISAPI filter adds instructions to route the response to the ISAPI application, which is also part of W3PROXY.DLL. If, however, the request is a standard HTTP request, meaning it does not contain protocol or domain name information, the filter makes no changes and passes the request to the IIS Web server for normal processing.

An ISAPI application performs a specific set of functions each time it receives a request. Different applications can be used to generate HTML dynamically or to provide an interface with a database. ISAPI applications are invoked only if the request calls the specific application. In the case of the Proxy Server ISAPI application, the Proxy Server ISAPI filter makes the call.

Each time a request is received from the ISAPI filter, the Proxy Server ISAPI application does the following:

- Validates the request by authenticating the client.
- Checks the domain filter to verify that the request is allowable.
- Checks the cache for the resource.
  - If the resource is found in cache, the ISAPI application verifies that the resource is current and sends the reply to the client.
  - If the resource is not in cache, the ISAPI application retrieves the resource from the Internet, sends it to the client, and updates the cache.

If the ISAPI application determines that the request is valid and it is not in the cache or that the cached copy needs to be updated, the application parses the URL to extract the protocol and the domain name for the resource. If it is an HTTP request, the application calls the necessary Windows Sockets API to process the request. At this point, the ISAPI application resolves the domain name from the DNS (Domain Name System) cache and connects to the remote site. Once a connection has been made, the application is able to send the request, receive the response, and forward the response to the client. At the same time, the Proxy Server ISAPI application saves a copy of the resource in the cache.

One other benefit of using the IIS Web server to support the ISAPI application is the Web server's use of HTTP *keep-alive* packets. Keep-alive packets allow TCP connections to remain intact after the server has responded to a request, which provides for greater performance if the client requests other resources from the same server within the time limit for connections. If this were not the case, each request to a site would go through the same steps of domain name resolution and TCP connection establishment.

Caching

Caching is the process of temporarily maintaining a local copy of a resource to speed up requests. When a copy of the requested resource is kept in cache, each time a local client makes a request for the resource, the request is fulfilled immediately rather than being passed to the Web server and through to the Internet. The Microsoft Proxy Server Web Proxy service uses two types of caching, passive and active, to achieve this increase in performance.

Passive caching is the basic mode of caching used by Proxy Server. As mentioned earlier, the Web Proxy service receives requests from internal clients and services those requests. To save time, the Web Proxy service will first check to see if the resource is in the cache; if it's not, the request is forwarded to the Web. The steps involved in caching are outlined in the flowchart in Figure 2.5.

In passive caching, an object is retrieved from the Internet and placed in cache and assigned a *Time-to-Live (TTL)*. For the duration of the TTL, all requests for the object are serviced from cache rather than being sent to the Web. After the

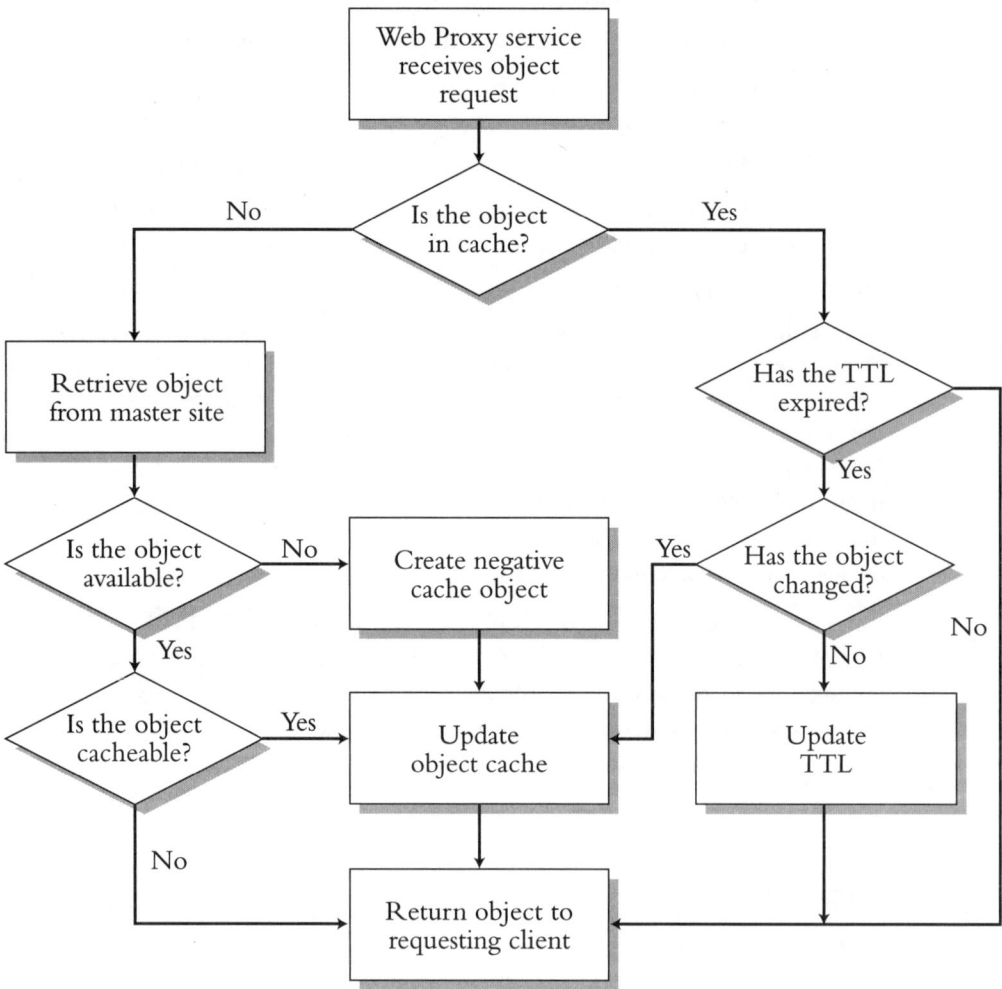

Figure 2.5   Caching is used by Proxy Server to speed Web access.

TTL has expired, the next request made for the object will be forwarded to the Web for service. Proxy Server will then store the object in cache again and assign it a new TTL as if it were a new object.

When a new request is made and the data is in the cache, Proxy Server determines whether or not the object is still usable based on TTL and whether the object has changed. If it is valid, it is sent directly to the client; if not, Proxy Server updates the object in cache and returns the object to the client.

In the event that the disk space set aside for the Proxy Serve cache is full, Proxy Server removes older objects from cache by using a formula that factors in the age, popularity, and size of the object.

Most Web browsers have a mechanism for bypassing the cache and retrieving an object directly from the Internet. With Internet Explorer, this is done by pressing F5; with Netscape Navigator, it is done by pressing the Reload button on the toolbar and the Shift key (Shift+Reload). By using these commands, you are instructing Proxy Server to retrieve the object without checking the cache.

Active caching works in conjunction with passive caching to optimize performance by increasing the likelihood that a frequently requested object will be serviced from cache. Active caching automatically generates requests for objects based on the popularity of the object, the TTL of the object, and the load the server is experiencing. Servers with higher loads will perform active caching less frequently than servers with lower loads.

WINSOCK PROXY SERVICE

The WinSock Proxy service provides many of the same features the Web Proxy service provides, including secure IP aggregation, Challenge/Response authentication, client request logging, and SSL tunneling encryption. In addition, it provides support for Windows Sockets version 1.1, filtering by a number of different variables, blocking external user access to the internal network, and compatibility with Microsoft Windows-based computers.

What exactly is WinSock? The Windows Sockets (WinSock) system is a mechanism for interprocess communication, whether the communication is between processes on the same computer or processes running on different computers across a LAN or WAN. This system defines a standard set of APIs that are used to communicate with one or more applications. The APIs support a client initiating a connection, a server accepting a connection, a client and server sending and receiving data over the connection, and the client or server terminating the connection when it is no longer needed.

The Windows Sockets APIs support a number of different protocol stacks. Windows Sockets is actually a port of Berkeley Sockets (Unix), with extensions for the Microsoft TCP/IP implementations of Win16 and Win32. In addition, Windows Sockets includes support for other transport protocols, such as NetBEUI and IPX/SPX. It is through this mechanism that Proxy Server can support an IPX/SPX-only network and still provide Internet connectivity. It is important to note, however, that although WinSock supports NetBEUI, the WinSock Proxy service, and by extension Proxy Server, does not. In addition, the WinSock Proxy service supports Windows Sockets version 1.1, but not version 2.0.

Windows Sockets supports two types of communication based on the transport protocols of the TCP/IP suite: TCP and UDP. Point-to-point connection-oriented communications, referred to as *stream-oriented communications* by Microsoft, are handled by the TCP protocol, whereas point-to-point or multipoint connectionless communications, called *datagram-oriented communications*, are handled by the UDP protocol. Both protocols will be covered in greater detail in Chapter 3. Most protocols used on the Internet, including HTTP, Gopher, and FTP, use connection-oriented, client/server communication. The client initiates a connection to the server to process a request. The server sits patiently waiting for clients to initiate connections, accepts those connections, and fulfills their requests.

Windows Sockets operates over communication channels called *sockets*. A socket is actually made up of two pieces of information, an address and a port. Ports are discussed more fully in Chapter 3, but for now, it is important to understand that a socket is created by combining an IP address and a TCP or UDP port. For example, the socket information for a connection between two computers using FTP contains the local IP address and port pair and the remote IP address and port pair, as shown in Figure 2.6.

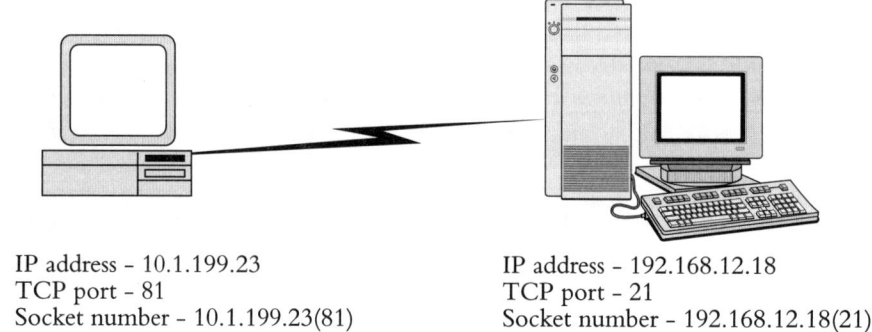

IP address – 10.1.199.23
TCP port – 81
Socket number – 10.1.199.23(81)

IP address – 192.168.12.18
TCP port – 21
Socket number – 192.168.12.18(21)

Figure 2.6   Sockets are created by combining the IP address and the port number being used.

WinSock Proxy Client

The WinSock Proxy service allows Windows Sockets applications to function as if they were directly connected to the Internet rather than through a gateway. This is an important distinction between Web Proxy and WinSock Proxy. CERN-compliant Web browsers are configured to use the proxy server and are aware of its existence. WinSock applications, on the other hand, still operate as though nothing were in between them and the Internet.

Each WinSock Proxy client computer is loaded with the DLL that corresponds to the version of Windows TCP/IP it is running, either WINSOCK.DLL (for Win16) or WSOCK32.DLL (for Win32). The Web Proxy client DLLs replace the DLLs that are installed when TCP/IP is loaded on the system. The old DLLs are retained, however, under a different name.

When a Windows Sockets application makes a request to the Internet, the WinSock Proxy client DLL intercepts the call and establishes a communication path between the internal application and the Internet application through Proxy Server. When a call is made that requires the old DLLs, the WinSock Proxy client DLL is given the name of the corresponding (renamed) DLL and forwards the request through it; that is, the Windows Sockets application links to the WinSock Proxy client DLL and the WinSock Proxy client DLL links to the renamed Windows Sockets DLL. In its role as interceptor, the WinSock Proxy client DLL can perform one of three things:

- Completely process the client's request itself
- Pass the request on to the renamed Windows Sockets DLL
- Pass control information to the WinSock Proxy service running on the Proxy Server computer

Unlike the Web Proxy service, the WinSock Proxy service operates as a standalone application on a Windows NT 4.0 Server. In addition to providing the transparent services just described, it also acts as a gateway for IPX/SPX networks that require Internet access.

WinSock Control Channel

To manage the connection between the client and the server, WinSock Proxy uses a *control channel* that allows Windows Sockets messages to be handled remotely. This control channel, which uses the connectionless UDP protocol, is established when the WinSock Proxy client DLL is loaded. Because UDP is connectionless, it is faster than other protocols that could be used, such as TCP. But also because it is connectionless, it is less reliable than other protocols; the WinSock Proxy client uses acknowledgment messages to add reliability.

The control channel is used for four main functions. The first is to provide routing information between the WinSock Proxy server and the WinSock Proxy client. When the client establishes a control channel, the server provides a list of local IP addresses in the form of a LAT (Local Address Table). The control channel is also used to make TCP connections from the WinSock Proxy client to the WinSock Proxy server. This channel is only used to establish a virtual connection between the client and the remote application. Once data begins to be sent, the control channel is not used. Maintaining UDP connections between WinSock clients and WinSock servers also falls within the control channel's realm of responsibility. This channel is used to establish connections between the WinSock Proxy client and WinSock Proxy server each time a new remote peer sends data. Once the session is established, it is no longer used. Finally, the control channel handles the redirection of Windows Sockets database requests, such as DNS resolution, by passing the request and response via the control channel.

 The control channel for Proxy Server 2.0 uses UDP port 1745 on the WinSock Proxy client and WinSock Proxy server computers.

SOCKS PROXY SERVICE

The SOCKS Proxy service supports SOCKS version 4.3a and most SOCKS 4.0 client applications. By nature, the SOCKS protocol functions as a proxy. It enables hosts on one side of a SOCKS server to gain full access to hosts on the other side of the server without requiring direct IP accessibility. This is done through two operations: **connect** and **bind**.

A SOCKS client sends a connect request to the SOCKS server when a connection to an application server, other than the other side of the SOCK server, is required. The connect request is made up of the following information: the SOCKS version number, the SOCKS command code, the destination IP address, the destination TCP port number, the user ID, and a null field. When the server receives the request packet, it processes it and sends a response packet to the client; the response packet contains the status of the request: granted, rejected, or failed.

If the request is granted, the client is immediately able to begin sending and receiving data through the SOCKS server. If the request is rejected or failed, the reply code contained in the response packet may give some indication as to the possible cause. In the event the request is rejected or failed, the SOCKS server immediately closes the connection.

The SOCKS **bind** operation is used to provide access control based on the TCP header information, such as the source and destination IP addresses and port numbers.

For more information on the SOCKS protocol and its various implementations, visit the *Internet Engineering Task Force (IETF)* Web site for the Authenticated Firewall Traversal (aft) working group at **http://www.ietf.org/html.charters/ aft-charter.html**. The SOCKS protocol is part of its responsibility. In addition, NEC is very involved with the SOCKS protocol, and information is available at its Web site at **http://www.socks.nec.com/**.

CHAPTER SUMMARY

The modularity of the Windows NT architecture allows for easy integration with any number of services, including Proxy Server. Microsoft's Proxy Server fits seamlessly into almost any network, its only requirements being at least one NT Server running IIS. Its support for clients running on different platforms makes it a good choice to provide secure Internet access for a network of any size.

The Web Proxy service supports any CERN-proxy-compliant browser, which includes most of today's browsers. This means that Web access can be granted to clients running on Unix, Macintosh, or Microsoft Windows. The Web Proxy service utilizes the security of Windows NT and the Web services of IIS to provide proxy access to the World Wide Web. In its role as proxy, it acts as both a client and a server, making requests and servicing the requests of internal clients. To do this, the Web Proxy service uses an ISAPI filter and application that intercept requests for Web objects and acts on them. To help speed the servicing of Web requests, the Web Proxy service uses two forms of caching: active and passive. Passive caching is performed by default and tries to ensure that requested documents do not have to be transmitted across the Internet multiple times. When an object is requested, it is placed in cache. Because most Web sites use the same object (such as a button or a background) multiple times, the chances that the object will be used again are high. Active caching tries to anticipate the needs of the clients by requesting popular documents on its own, before a client makes a request. By doing so, access speed is increased even more.

The WinSock Proxy service provides Internet connectivity for Windows Sockets applications. By intercepting a request on the client side, the WinSock Proxy service can determine whether Internet access is needed and forward the request to the WinSock Proxy service application running on the Windows NT Server. Unlike applications that use the Web Proxy service, client applications that use WinSock Proxy do not know they are using a proxy. The workings of the service are transparent to the applications. The WinSock Proxy service is unique in that it is not only able to provide Internet access for TCP/IP clients, it is also able to provide them for clients running only IPX/SPX. Through its use of a control channel, the WinSock Proxy service is able to utilize the faster UDP protocol to decrease connection time and DNS resolution time.

Finally, the SOCKS Proxy service provides Internet access for any computer running SOCKS version 4.3a. The SOCKS protocol is, by nature, a proxy protocol and an accepted IETF protocol. It is designed to be used through firewalls and proxy servers. SOCKS clients use **connect** and **bind** commands to connect to Internet sites and to retrieve information. When the client sends a connect request, the server sends a response that either accepts or rejects the connection. In the event that the connection is rejected or fails, the server's response packet can indicate why the connection was not granted.

Key Terms

- **boundary layer**—A portion of the Windows NT Networking model that allows programmers to easily create drivers to perform a specific networking function.

- **cache**—On a server, the area used to store objects requested from the Web so that subsequent requests can be processed locally, decreasing response time.

- **CERN**—Conseil Européen pour la Recherche Nucléaire, or the European Laboratory for Particle Research, which developed much of the HTTP protocol and an HTTP proxy system.

- **control channel**—Secondary channel used by the WinSock Proxy service to provide routing and connection information and management.

- **datagram-oriented communication**—Connectionless communication method used by UDP and the WinSock Proxy service.

- **environment subsystem**—Portions of the Windows NT architecture that operate in user mode that are responsible for managing applications for the operating system.

- **executive services**—Portions of the kernel mode that are responsible for specific operating system functions such as security and I/O.

- **Hardware Abstraction Layer (HAL)**—The portion of the executive services that is hardware-specific and provides a standard interface to the rest of the operating system.

- **Internet Engineering Task Force (IETF)**—Governing body of the Internet; made up of a number of working groups, including the Authenticated Firewall Traversal group, which lists among its responsibilities the SOCKS protocol definition.

2

- **Internet Server Application Programming Interface (ISAPI)**—A Windows Sockets programming interface that is used to provide services for the WinSock Proxy service in the form of the ISAPI filter and ISAPI application.

- **I/O Manager**—The executive service that is responsible for input and output, including all network functions.

- **keep-alive**—A type of packet that is used by TCP to maintain a connection between client and server.

- **kernel mode**—The area of the Windows NT architecture that is responsible for hardware access and operating system functions.

- **microkernel**—The portion of the executive services responsible for synchronizing services and interaction between the various managers and the Hardware Abstraction Layer.

- **Network Driver Interface Specification (NDIS)**—A specification to which Windows NT network drivers must conform that allows for multiple interface cards in a single computer and multiple protocols on each interface card.

- **socket**—A unique identification number created by combining a computer's IP address and the TCP or UDP port number being used.

- **SOCKS**—A protocol used to establish a secure proxy data channel between a client and server.

- **stream-oriented communication**—A connection-oriented communication method used by TCP that ensures data delivery.

- **Time-to-Live (TTL)**—The length of time an object may reside in cache.

- **Transport Driver Interface (TDI)**—A specification to which Windows NT protocols must be written to provide access to higher layer services.

- **user mode**—The area of the Windows NT architecture in which all applications operate.

REVIEW QUESTIONS

1. The two commands most often used in HTTP communication are
   _____ and _____ .

2. Windows Sockets is a system for supporting interprocess communication between application processes running on different machines across a LAN. (True or False?)

3. Stream-oriented communication is used by which of the following protocols?

   a. UDP

   b. TCP

   c. HTTP

   d. FTP

4. The _____ DLL contains the ISAPI filter and application used by the Web Proxy service.

5. Most protocols used on the Internet use connection-oriented, client/server communication. (True or False?)

6. Which of the following Internet standards groups includes a working group whose responsibilities include the SOCKS protocol?

   a. IIOC

   b. IETF

   c. IANA

   d. CERN

7. _____ caching takes into account the popularity of an object and server load.

8. Which of the following pairings correctly describes the Proxy service and the other Windows NT service it utilizes?

   a. Web Proxy and IIS

   b. WinSock Proxy and IIS

   c. Web Proxy and SMS

   d. SOCKS Proxy and User Manager

9. The SOCKS Proxy service provides access for IPX/SPX clients. (True or False?)

10. When an object is received from the Internet and placed in cache, it is assigned a _____ .

11. A SOCKS server rejection message will give no indication of the reason for the rejection. (True or False?)

12. What role did CERN play in the development of the Internet?

    a. devised the numbering system used for IP addressing

    b. provided cross-platform compatibility for TCP/IP

    c. implemented the first TCP ports

    d. developed an HTTP proxy system

13. The Web Proxy service runs on Windows NT 4.0 and requires _____ .

14. WinSock Proxy client computers, such as one running Windows 95, include all necessary drivers to utilize the WinSock Proxy service. (True or False?)

15. Which of the following ISAPI functions ensures that multiple requests to a single server do not each go through the full connection process?

    a. request redirection

    b. caching

    c. keep-alives

    d. TTLs

16. Active caching is more effective at decreasing response time than passive caching. (True or False?)

17. Which type of authentication is supported by Web Proxy service?

    a. Challenge/Response

    b. request/response

    c. standard IP authentication

    d. advanced IP authentication

18. The _____ Proxy service does not support Unix systems.

19. Microsoft Proxy Server 2.0 requires Service Pack _____ .

20. Datagram-oriented communication is used by the UDP transport protocol. (True or False?)

21. Which of the following is used by the WinSock Proxy service to manage connections?

    a. connection channel

    b. management channel

    c. access channel

    d. control channel

22. Telnet access is provided by the _____ Proxy service.

23. Servers with higher load levels perform active caching more often than servers with lower load levels. (True or False?)

24. Which of the following is not an option the WinSock Proxy client DLL can choose to fulfill a client request?

    a. send the request to the renamed Windows Sockets DLL

    b. completely process the request itself

    c. process a portion of the request and forward the remainder to the Proxy Server

    d. send the request to the WinSock Proxy service running on the Proxy Server

25. A socket number is generated using the IP address and subnet mask for a host. (True or False?)

26. Which of the following is a standard to which all network interface card drivers must conform to operate in a Windows NT network?
    a. NDIS
    b. TDI
    c. API
    d. OSI

27. The _____ is hardware-specific and is responsible for communicating directly with the CPU.

28. Applications that run in user mode are able to directly access all hardware on the computer. (True or False?)

29. NDIS operates at the _____ sublayer of the OSI model.

30. Which of the following are examples of boundary layers?
    a. programming interface
    b. transport protocols
    c. file system drivers
    d. transport driver interface

CASE PROJECTS

1. The Securities firm you work for has decided to implement realtime tickers on the desktop. There are 100 workstations installed; they all use Windows NT Workstation 4.0 and are linked using 100Mbps Ethernet.

   Required result: Ensure that the data that reaches the clients is accurate and up-to-date.

   Optional desired results: Internet access speed should be high. Software expenditures should be kept to a minimum.

   Proposed solution: Install Windows NT Server running Proxy Server and IIS. Configure the clients to use Internet Explorer through the Proxy Server. Limit the cache size and reduce the TTL for objects retrieved from the Internet. Install a high-speed link, such as a T1, to connect to the Internet. Which of the following does the proposed solution provide?

   a. The proposed solution provides the required result and both optional results.
   b. The proposed solution provides the required result and one optional result.
   c. The proposed solution provides only the required result.
   d. The proposed solution does not provide the required result.

2. Your network consists of 35 clients using a combination of Windows 95, Window NT Workstation, and Unix. The Windows 95 and Windows NT clients communicate with each other using IPX/SPX. There is no communication between the PC clients and the Unix clients.

   Required result: All clients must have Internet access.

   Optional desired results: Continue to use IPX/SPX for PC clients. Minimize client configuration.

   Proposed solution: Install Proxy Server 2.0 and configure the WinSock Proxy service to provide access for the clients. To save on processing power, disable the Web Proxy and SOCKS Proxy services. Which of the following does the proposed solution provide?

   a. The proposed solution provides the required result and both optional results.

   b. The proposed solution provides the required result and one optional result.

   c. The proposed solution provides only the required result.

   d. The proposed solution does not provide the required result.

3. Your network consists of 35 clients using a combination of Windows 95, Window NT Workstation, and Unix. The Windows 95 and Windows NT clients communicate with each other using IPX/SPX. There is no communication between the PC clients and the Unix clients.

   Required result: All clients must have Internet access.

   Optional desired results: Continue to use IPX/SPX for PC clients. Minimize client configuration.

   Proposed solution: Install Proxy Server 2.0 and configure the WinSock Proxy and SOCKS Proxy services to provide access for the clients. Which of the following does the proposed solution provide?

   a. The proposed solution provides the required result and both optional results.

   b. The proposed solution provides the required result and one optional result.

   c. The proposed solution provides only the required result.

   d. The proposed solution does not provide the required result.

UNDERSTANDING TCP/IP

Because TCP/IP is the protocol of the Internet, it is very important to understand how TCP/IP operates, how it is addressed, and how it is used to communicate over the Internet. Microsoft has an entire test dedicated to TCP/IP and its implementation; therefore, TCP/IP plays a significant role in the Proxy Server environment.

AFTER READING THIS CHAPTER AND COMPLETING THE EXERCISES, YOU WILL BE ABLE TO:

- Understand IP addressing, classes, and subnet masks
- Comprehend the role of gateways in a TCP/IP network
- Configure TCP ports
- Explore DHCP and WINS and how they are used for address management
- Understand the Domain Name System

TCP/IP OVERVIEW

The Transmission Control Protocol/Internet Protocol (TCP/IP) is the protocol suite used on the Internet, and therefore, it is used extensively with Microsoft Proxy Server. To fully understand how TCP/IP relates to Proxy Server, it is important to discuss its history, addressing scheme, and structure.

TCP/IP is a suite of protocols developed by the Department of Defense's (DOD's) *Advanced Research Projects Agency (ARPA)*. ARPA envisioned a network where researchers in different parts of the country (at the DOD, corporations, and universities) could share information with one another easily and quickly. At that point in time, everyone was using massive computers to assist in research, and one of the goals of this group was to provide a way to interconnect their networks. The other task was to provide interoperability between those networks.

From the need for interconnectivity came the *Internet Protocol (IP)*. The IP protocol was designed to provide a transport mechanism between the networks through a packet-switched environment. This, however, was the easy part.

Once it was proven that data could be transported from one site to another, the question of interoperability—application-to-application communication—was addressed. A number of issues regarding interoperability had to be addressed before the system would work. Disparate hardware, operating systems, file types, and terminal types were used at all sites. It was determined that to provide true interoperability between the systems, a series of hardware-independent application protocols had to be developed. Protocols were developed for file transfer and management, email, terminal emulation, printing, and network management.

In September 1969, four sites were connected to create the *Advanced Research Projects Agency Network (ARPANet)*. This network quickly grew to connect all major colleges and universities, and eventually allowed connections from corporations not involved in research. Because the ARPANet was originally funded by the DOD, it was deemed public domain; this was the beginning of today's Internet.

TCP/IP's vast acceptance has been driven by its use in the Unix environment and its ability to interconnect divergent technologies. It is by far the most widely used suite of protocols today, and it is expected to continue to be number one for the foreseeable future. The TCP/IP suite has grown from just a few protocols in 1969 to over 100 individual protocols today. These protocols do everything; they manage files, provide calendar and scheduling functions, transport World Wide Web pages, and configure a computer's IP settings automatically.

TCP/IP STRUCTURE

The TCP/IP suite is named for its two primary protocols—the Transmission Control Protocol (TCP) and the Internet Protocol (IP). Its protocols are divided into three categories according to their function:

- **Application protocols** Provide a specific function and interface for the user. For example, FTP is used for file transfer and manipulation, SMTP provides email transfer, and Telnet is a terminal emulation protocol.

- **Network protocols** Move packets around the network. Network protocols are responsible for addressing and routing the packets. IP is the most prevalent network protocol.

- **Transport protocols** Ensure delivery between computers on the network. They are responsible for providing a low layer connection for the applications through mechanisms such as flow control. TCP and UDP are examples of transport protocols.

It is important to know how these protocols interrelate and how they are used in a Proxy Server environment. The following list describes some of the most-used TCP/IP protocols:

- **Address Resolution Protocol (ARP)** ARP is a Network-layer protocol that provides association from logical (IP) addresses to physical (MAC) addresses. As you know, the network interface card (NIC) in a computer looks for packets with its physical address. IP has no knowledge of this address, so it uses ARP to discover the Media Access Control (MAC) address for a particular IP address. ARP does this by sending a broadcast requesting the MAC address.

- **File Transfer Protocol (FTP)** FTP is an upper-layer protocol encompassing the Session, Presentation, and Application layers. It is used for file transfer, file manipulation, and directory manipulation.

- **Hypertext Transfer Protocol (HTTP)** HTTP is perhaps the most widely used protocol today. This upper-layer protocol is used to deliver World Wide Web documents that have been written in HTML and other markup languages.

- **Internet Control Message Protocol (ICMP)** ICMP is another Network-layer protocol that is used to send control messages. The PING utility uses ICMP to request a response from a remote host. ICMP provides information such as whether the response was received and how long it took to make the trip.

- **Internet Protocol (IP)** IP is a Network-layer protocol that provides source and destination addressing and routing.

- **Routing Information Protocol (RIP)** As its name indicates, RIP is used to distribute routing information throughout a network. It is a Network-layer protocol that uses distance-vector routing algorithms to identify the best path through an internetwork.

- **Simple Mail Transport Protocol (SMTP)** Another upper-layer protocol, SMTP is used by messaging programs such as email.

- **Simple Network Management Protocol (SNMP)** As its name implies, SNMP is used to manage network devices. It can be used to configure devices, such as bridges, repeaters, and gateways. SNMP also uses MIBs and SNMP managers to monitor network events.

- **Telnet** Telnet (surprisingly, not an acronym) is an upper-layer protocol that is used for remote terminal emulation. It allows users to act as if they were directly connected to the computer. It is most often used as a configuration interface for networking devices, such as routers, and as a terminal program for mainframe and microcomputer systems.

- **Transmission Control Protocol (TCP)** TCP is a connection-oriented transport-layer protocol that accepts messages of any length from the upper layers and provides transportation to another computer. TCP is responsible for packet fragmentation and reassembly, and for sequencing.

- **User Datagram Protocol (UDP)** UDP is the counterpart to TCP. It provides connectionless Transport-layer functions for the TCP/IP suite.

TCP AND TCP PORTS

As mentioned earlier, the Transmission Control Protocol is the primary transport protocol of the TCP/IP suite. It is a connection-oriented protocol that provides reliable service across a network, including the Internet. TCP also increases its reliability by using acknowledgments, flow control, and checksum information.

For TCP to know which application is sending and receiving data, it uses *ports*. A port is used to name the ends of logical connections that carry on long-term conversations. Most TCP/IP protocols have been assigned their own port from 0 to 1023. These are called *well-known ports* and are assigned by the *Internet Assigned Numbers Authority (IANA)*. Other TCP/IP applications, such as proprietary programs, use ports above 1023. Table 3.1 contains a partial list of the well-known ports used in TCP/IP.

Table 3.1   The IANA has assigned well-known port numbers to most TCP/IP
protocols and functions.

Port Number	Keyword	Description
20	ftp-data	Port used to transfer data using FTP
21	ftp	Control port used by FTP
23	telnet	Port used by Telnet
25	smtp	Port used by SMTP (email)
80	www	Port used by HTTP (World Wide Web)
137	netbios-ns	Port used by the NetBIOS Name Service
161	snmp	Port used by SNMP
532	netnews	Readnews port

Because every packet that uses TCP includes port information, filters can be set
up to permit or deny a particular type of application communication on the
network. Microsoft Proxy Server takes full advantage of this option, and it is very
important to know the most often used ports. A complete list of the well-known
ports is available at **http://www.isi.edu/innotes/iana/assignments/port-
numbers.**

IP ADDRESSING

As mentioned earlier, IP is responsible for addressing and routing packets
through the network. To understand how this works, let's take a look at how all
packets are addressed.

Before a packet is placed on a network, it is given both a physical source address
and destination address. These addresses tell the computers on the network
where a packet came from and where it's going. The physical address for a
computer is its *Media Access Control (MAC) address.* In most cases, the MAC
address is burned into the NIC's ROM when the card is created.

As the packet traverses the wire, each computer looks at the destination address
to determine whether the packet's destination is that computer. If so, it reads the
packet, including the source information, and acts on the data in the packet.

Just knowing the physical address of a computer works fine in a small
environment where there are no networking devices such as routers or gateways.
Could you imagine, though, if your computer had to know the physical address
of every computer on the Internet in order to communicate? What if every
router that makes up the Internet had to have this information? In addition, how
many people know the MAC address of their computer—or even their server?
Not many.

IP uses a logical address that is assigned to each computer. Each IP address is 32 bits long and is represented as 4 bytes, also called octets, in decimal format. Hearken back to your binary-to-decimal conversion days. Each bit can be either on (1) or off (0). The decimal value of the number is calculated from right to left, and each consecutive bit is worth twice the previous bit. The first bit on the right is worth either 0 or 1, the second bit from the right is worth either 0 or 2, the third bit is worth either 0 or 4, and so on through 8, 16, 32, 64, and 128. If there are 8 bits together, the decimal representation can be from 0 (00000000) to 255 (11111111, or 1+2+4+8+16+32+64+128), which gives us 256 combinations of numbers. Table 3.2 shows a few other decimal representations of a byte.

To delineate between each byte in an IP address, these addresses are written in what is called *dotted-decimal format*. Each byte is separated by a period, or dot, so an IP address looks something like this: 205.199.10.1. Remember, though, that this is just a representation of the 32 bits that make up the address.

 Although IP addresses can range from 0 to 255, certain addresses are reserved for special use. Both 0 and 255 are reserved for broadcasts and should only be used in host IDs in special situations. In addition, any address beginning with 127 is treated as a *loopback address*. If a program such as PING uses this address, the traffic does not hit the network.

IP addresses are assigned and maintained by the *InterNIC (Internet Network Information Center)*. It is the InterNIC's responsibility to ensure that computers connected to the Internet have unique addresses. However, with the growth of TCP/IP and the Internet, unique addresses are in short supply. InterNIC has taken a number of steps to ease this problem, some of which will be discussed later. One of the biggest steps they have taken has been to assign particular addresses as *private addresses*, meaning they cannot be used to connect to the Internet. For companies that have closed and secure environments, these

Table 3.2   Decimal representations of a byte.

Bit Pattern	Decimal Equivalent	The Math Involved
10000000	128	0+0+0+0+0+0+0+128
01001100	76	0+0+4+8+0+0+64+0
01011100	92	0+0+4+8+16+0+64+0
11000000	192	0+0+0+0+0+0+64+128
01111111	127	1+2+4+8+16+32+67+0
11111010	250	0+2+0+8+16+32+64+128
00001010	10	0+2+0+8+0+0+0+0
01100011	99	0+2+4+0+0+0+64+128
10101001	169	1+0+4+0+16+0+0+128

addresses are ideal. Three groups of addresses have been assigned as private addresses according to class, which will be discussed in the next section. The private addresses are:

- Addresses beginning with 10 (one Class A address)
- Addresses beginning with 172.16 through 172.31 (16 Class B addresses)
- Addresses beginning with 192.168.0 through 192.168.255 (256 Class C addresses)

Private addresses cannot be sent over the Internet. If an Internet router receives a packet with either a source or destination address that is private, it will drop the packet.

ADDRESS CLASSES/CIDR

By definition, an internetwork is a group of interconnected networks that operate autonomously. In an internetwork, each network is assigned an address, and it is the responsibility of networking devices such as routers to move packets through the internetwork.

In a network using IPX/SPX, the network address is assigned by the administrator and is a hexadecimal representation of the bits in the address field. IPX then uses the MAC address of the NIC to ensure that the packet reaches its destination. An IPX packet includes separate fields for the network and host address. In contrast, IP uses a single address for both network and host.

The IP *address class* system was developed to delineate which bits of the IP address represent the network ID and which bits represent the host ID for a particular computer. The class of an IP address is defined by the value of the first octet of the address. The IP address class system is broken down this way:

- **Class A** The first octet is assigned by InterNIC, which leaves the last three octets to be assigned by the administrator. Class A addresses begin with ID numbers from 1 to 126. These addresses were designed with very large corporations in mind. A single Class A address provides for 16,387,064 (254×254×254) hosts. That's a lot of computers!

- **Class B** The first two octets are assigned by InterNIC and begin with IDs between 128 and 191. This leaves the last two octets for host IDs and provides 64,516 hosts per network.

- **Class C** The first three octets are assigned by InterNIC and begin with IDs between 192 and 223. A Class C address can have up to 254 hosts.

When internetworks use the class system, the network ID/host ID delineation is along octet lines, i.e., each decimal represents a line of demarcation between a network ID and host ID. Even if a corporation has been assigned a Class B address, if it has no need for more than 254 hosts on a network, or for many networks, it can use a Class C delineation.

SUBNET MASKS

The delineation between network ID and host ID is made by using a *subnet mask*. This section of the IP packet specifies which bits of the IP address denote the network ID and which bits denote the host ID. As mentioned, in networks using the class system, this distinction is made along class boundaries. Subnet masks are also written in dotted-decimal format. Let's look at how a computer uses a subnet mask to decide which part of an address is the network ID and which part is the host ID. It is important to understand subnet masking because this is where many IP problems start.

Remember that IP addresses are 32 bits long. Subnet masks are also 32 bits long and are used by the computer to determine whether the packet's destination is on the local subnet or a remote subnet; the computer makes this determination by making the delineation between network ID and host ID. Bits in a subnet mask are set to 1 starting at the far left. Each bit that is turned on denotes the network ID of the IP address, either source or destination. For example, an IP address using a Class A subnet mask has the first eight bits set to 1. This means that the first octet denotes the network, whereas the remaining three octets are the host ID. Here are a few examples of how this works:

IP Address:	100.202.230.99			
Subnet Mask:	255.255.255.0 (Class C)			
Binary Address:	01100100	11001010	11100110	01100011
Binary Mask:	11111111	11111111	11111111	00000000
Binary Network ID:	01100100	11001010	11100110	
Binary Host ID:				01100011
Decimal Network ID:	100.202.230			
Decimal Host ID:	99			

IP Address:	87.104.10.19			
Subnet Mask:	255.0.0.0 (Class A)			
Binary Address:	01010111	01000100	00001010	00010011
Binary Mask:	11111111	00000000	00000000	00000000
Binary Network ID:	01010111			

3

Binary Host ID:		01000100	00001010	01100011
Decimal Network ID:	87			
Decimal Host ID:	104.10.19			
IP Address:	87.104.10.19			
Subnet Mask:	255.255.0.0 (Class B)			
Binary Address:	01010111	01000100	00001010	00010011
Binary Mask:	11111111	11111111	00000000	00000000
Binary Network ID:	01010111	01000100		
Binary Host ID:			00001010	01100011
Decimal Network ID:	87.104			
Decimal Host ID:	10.19			

As you can see, even if a Class A address is used, it can have a different subnet mask to provide more networks with fewer hosts per network. If you think about it from a routing perspective, it makes sense. If, for example, a very large corporation had an internetwork covering the entire U.S. and parts of Europe, it would probably get a Class B address from InterNIC. If this company used its Class B address with only Class B subnet masks, it would have one very large network. From an IP perspective, every host would be on the same subnet and no routing would take place. All packets would be sent to all sites, leading to IP chaos. However, the company could use the Class B address with a Class C mask and have 254 individual subnets with 254 hosts per subnet. This type of configuration is much more manageable and gives the routers something to do. Just imagine what would happen if a Class A address used a Class A mask—16 million hosts across the globe with no routing. For this reason, you will most often find Class C masks being used.

However, because of the growth of the Internet and TCP/IP, there are not enough IP addresses to go around even with the class system in use. How many companies do you know that have less than 100 computers to connect to the Internet? If each company were given a Class C address—in the beginning they were—the addresses would quickly disappear. As mentioned earlier, this is one reason the private IP addresses were reserved for companies that do not connect to the Internet. But, something else had to be done to make the most of the available addresses until the next generation of TCP/IP is introduced.

To work around this problem, *Classless Inter-Domain Routing (CIDR)* was introduced. CIDR (pronounced "cider") removes the class boundaries for subnet masks and introduces a new system for determining the network and host ID of an address. Rather than using the dotted-decimal notation, CIDR specifies the exact number of bits representing the network ID. This specification is written after the IP address as a number following a slash: 202.248.130.128 /26. In this case, the network ID occupies the first 26 bits of the 32-bit address. The following two examples show how CIDR works:

IP Address:	152.98.212.156			
Subnet Mask:	/26 (CIDR)			
Binary Address:	10011000	01100010	11010100	10011100
Binary Mask:	11111111	11111111	11111111	11000000
Binary Network ID:	10011000	01100010	11010100	10
Binary Host ID:				011100
Decimal Network ID:	152.98.212.128			
Decimal Host ID:	28			

IP Address:	129.8.242.156			
Subnet Mask:	/21 (CIDR)			
Binary Address:	10000001	00001000	11110010	10011100
Binary Mask:	11111111	11111111	11111000	00000000
Binary Network ID:	10000001	00001000	11111	
Binary Host ID:			010	10011100
Decimal Network ID:	129.8.240			
Decimal Host ID:	2.156			

By using this method, ISPs and the InterNIC can provide a company with an address or range of addresses to fit its needs more specifically. This also means that an ISP can get one Class B address from InterNIC and provide addresses for a larger number of companies.

As mentioned, the subnet mask helps the computer determine whether the destination is on the local network or a remote network. When the packet is addressed, the computer looks at the network ID and determines whether it matches its own network ID. If so, it sends the packet down the wire, knowing it will reach its destination. If not, it sends the packet to a gateway.

GATEWAYS

A *gateway* is a device on the network—often a router or server acting as a router—that knows what path a packet should take to get from the local subnet to a remote subnet. Because a computer only knows about its own subnet, the gateway is the next hop for packets going to other subnets. It is important to know which computer is the gateway for a particular network. An incorrectly configured gateway setting is often the cause of many network problems. The most likely problem is that a computer can communicate with computers on its own subnet but not with computers on other subnets.

3

ADDRESS MANAGEMENT

As you can imagine, managing IP addresses, especially in large organizations, is a detailed and sometimes tedious task. Because each device on the network must be configured manually, there is room for error and many problems occur. For this reason, it is often best to automatically configure clients that will be using TCP/IP. It is important to remember that this type of configuration only works best for clients. Often, it would be counterproductive to automatically configure servers because each client would then need to be reconfigured with the server's new address.

DHCP OVERVIEW

The *Dynamic Host Configuration Protocol (DHCP)* was developed from Bootstrap Protocol (BOOTP), which provided IP addresses for diskless computers. DHCP is more dynamic, however, and provides for more extensive configuration. DHCP can not only be used to configure the IP address and subnet mask for a computer, it can also be used to configure its default gateway, DNS server addresses, and WINS server addresses. DHCP can also be used to configure more exotic IP settings, such as ARP cache time-out, NBT node type, and X Windows system font. The DHCP process is fairly intricate, and it is important to understand completely how DHCP assigns addresses for troubleshooting a network in which both a DHCP server and a Proxy Server are used.

When a client has been configured to use DHCP boots, it sends a special IP broadcast packet requesting an address. The DHCP server receives this request and offers an address to the client. If the offer is accepted, a DHCP lease is created, which allows the computer to use the address for a certain amount of time. Once half that time has expired, the client sends a new request to use the address it's using. Often, the request is granted and the timer is reset. However, if the server is unavailable or there is some reason the request cannot be fulfilled, the client's time keeps ticking away.

When 87.5 percent of the time has been used, the client will again try to lease the same address. If the server is still unavailable or the client receives a negative acknowledgment, the client will initiate the DHCP lease process from the beginning by sending a general broadcast request.

Why use DHCP? It makes it easy to configure a large number of clients. In addition, clients can be easily moved from one subnet to another without manual reconfiguration. One caveat in regard to moving DHCP clients: Always verify that no part of the client's IP configuration has been configured manually. For example, if a DHCP client has been configured to get its IP address and subnet mask (but not its default gateway) from the DHCP server and the client is moved, the client's gateway setting will have to be reconfigured.

WINS OVERVIEW

If you recall, Microsoft networking is based on the NetBIOS system, which requires a unique name be assigned to each computer on the network and then uses this name to address all communications. Although NetBIOS was originally designed to be used with NetBEUI, it can use TCP/IP or IPX as its transport. Because these protocols do not include name fields, a system must be used to assign names to addresses. The NetBIOS name is also known as the computer name in the Network Properties Identification tab. The *Windows Internet Name Service (WINS)* provides this function.

In a network that is not using WINS, name-to-address resolution is performed by using broadcasts, which can quickly bog down a network. In a WINS environment, a computer such as a Windows NT Server that is running the WINS service keeps track of all computers on the network, their computer names, and their IP addresses. All name queries are then sent to the WINS server first, eliminating broadcasts.

As a computer is powered on, it registers its name and address with the WINS server. When it does this, there is no discovery process, which further limits broadcasts, and the computer is sure to have a unique name assigned to it. The WINS server does not allow duplicate name registrations.

DNS OVERVIEW

The *Domain Name System (DNS)* is a key part of the TCP/IP suite and the Proxy Server environment. Although it will be covered in greater detail in Chapter 12, it is important to take a quick look at DNS and its use.

Although IP addresses are easier to remember than MAC addresses, they are still difficult for most people. The Domain Name System provides a hierarchical name-to-address association. It allows users to assign plain-language names to computers and associates those names to the computers' IP addresses. For example, the computer **www.lanw.com** may have an address of 192.168.10.100.

At the top of this hierarchical system are a set of domains under which all names are grouped. Those who are familiar with the Internet will recognize the first domains: .com, .org, .net, .edu, .gov, and .mil. These top-level domains were established for groups of computers in the United States and correspond to commercial, nonprofit organizations, Internet Service Providers, education centers (colleges and universities), government, and military sites. Other domains have been added to encompass organizations outside the United States.

DNS servers provide lookup services upon request. When a computer requests a name from a DNS server, it responds with the corresponding IP address. For DNS servers connected to the Internet, the list is exceptionally long and, in actuality, distributed among many servers. However, DNS can also be used on an intranet to provide lookup. A DNS server is included with Windows NT Server 4.0 and can be configured with local machine names to provide this type of service. The DNS server and WINS server can be used together to provide lookup services for both regular TCP/IP and NetBIOS over TCP transmissions. However, unlike WINS, which updates its database dynamically, a DNS server's database must be configured manually.

Although DNS provides centralized management of names and their associated addresses, the same functions are provided by HOSTS files on the computers. However, management of these files, especially in large networks, can quickly become an arduous task.

TCP/IP CLIENT CONFIGURATION

Client configuration for TCP/IP is usually very easy if you have the appropriate information. The station's IP address and subnet mask are required. In addition, the default gateway, DNS server address, and WINS server address may be supplied. As mentioned earlier, all of this information can be provided automatically by using DHCP. Figure 3.1 shows the TCP/IP properties section of the Network applet for a Windows NT Workstation 4.0 computer. Configuration is similar for Windows 95 and Windows NT Server 4.0 computers. This process is covered in detail in Hands-on Project 3.1.

CHAPTER SUMMARY

As you can see, TCP/IP plays an important role in networking, particularly in regard to the Internet and, consequently, Microsoft Proxy Server. To adequately support a Proxy Server implementation—and pass the Microsoft certification exam—you must understand the TCP/IP protocols and structure, TCP ports, IP addressing and subnet masks, TCP ports, DHCP, WINS, and DNS.

The TCP/IP protocol suite is by far the most dynamic and intricate suite of protocols in use today. Its wide acceptance hinges on its cross-platform compatibility and its use on today's Internet. The wide variety of protocols, each of which performs a specific function, ensures that the TCP/IP suite, or some variation thereof, will remain in use in the foreseeable future.

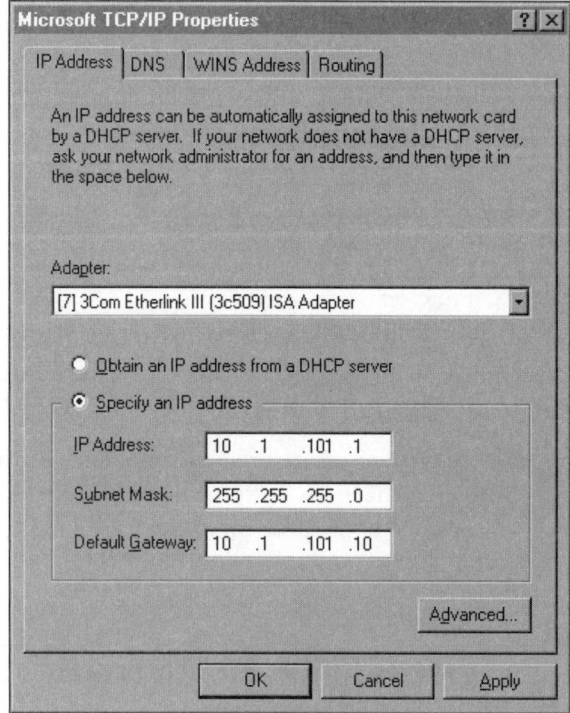

Figure 3.1   The TCP/IP Properties screen.

It is important to understand how each of the major protocols, especially those most often used on the Internet, interact with each other and with TCP. The TCP ports are an integral part of the security scheme that is available with Proxy Server, and you must be able to identify the correct port for a particular protocol.

IP addressing and subnet masks are the heart of the TCP/IP suite. The addressing scheme you use ensures that all computers attached to the Internet have unique addresses and are able to communicate effectively. Subnet masking and the problems associated with subnet masks are often the cause of network communication problems. To effectively troubleshoot a TCP/IP installation, you must have detailed knowledge of subnet masks and both the class system and CIDR, including how they function and how they are used to determine a packet's destination.

In the more advanced TCP/IP installations, additional servers, such as DHCP, WINS, and DNS, make troubleshooting more difficult. The key to effectively managing a TCP/IP network is fully comprehending these servers' functions.

Key Terms

- **address class**—Used to delineate the network ID and host ID portions of an IP address. The address classes make this distinction along byte boundaries.

- **Address Resolution Protocol (ARP)**—The protocol that determines the physical (MAC) address for a particular IP address.

- **Advanced Research Projects Agency (ARPA)**—The Department of Defense agency that initiated the project that created TCP/IP and the Internet.

- **Advanced Research Projects Agency Network (ARPANet)**—The predecessor to today's Internet; ARPANet linked colleges and universities to allow them to share research information over a packet-switched network.

- **application protocol**—An upper-layer protocol that provides an interface to the user and performs a specific function.

- **Classless Inter-Domain Routing (CIDR)**—The newest method for making the distinction between network ID and host ID. It counts the exact number of bits (from the left) that define the network ID.

- **Domain Name System (DNS)**—The worldwide system for plain-language assignment of names to IP addresses. It is hierarchically organized into six top-level domains.

- **dotted-decimal format**—The notation used to represent IP addresses. Rather than a string of 32 1s or 0s, the address is broken into bytes and represented decimally.

- **Dynamic Host Configuration Protocol (DHCP)**—A protocol based on BOOTP and used to automatically configure a client's IP settings, such as address, subnet mask, and default gateway.

- **File Transfer Protocol (FTP)**—An application protocol that is used to transfer files as well as manipulate files and directories.

- **gateway**—The next hop for a packet destined for a remote subnet.

- **Hypertext Transfer Protocol (HTTP)**—The protocol used on the Internet to transfer World Wide Web documents.

- **Internet Assigned Numbers Authority (IANA)**—The governing body of the Internet responsible for the DNS that ensures that each organization has a unique domain name.

- **Internet Control Message Protocol (ICMP)**—The protocol used by programs such as PING to return messages regarding the status of the transmission.

- **Internet Protocol (IP)**—The primary network protocol of the TCP/IP suite that is responsible for addressing and routing packets.

- **InterNIC (Internet Network Information Center)**—The governing body of the Internet responsible for, amongst other things, assigning IP addresses.

- **IP address**—The unique logical address assigned to a host on an IP network.

- **loopback address**— The IP address that is reserved for loopback testing (127.xxx.xxx.xxx).

- **Media Access Control (MAC) address**—The physical address of a network interface card. The MAC address is used at the Data Link layer to address packets.

- **network protocol**—Lower-level protocol responsible for addressing and routing packets.

- **port**—A designation used by TCP to determine which upper-layer protocol is communicating. Ports can be used to filter traffic on a network.

- **private address**—IP addresses set aside by InterNIC for use on networks not connected to the Internet.

- **Routing Information Protocol (RIP)**—A protocol used by TCP/IP to distribute information among routers.

- **Simple Mail Transport Protocol (SMTP)**—The primary protocol used today for email transfer across the Internet.

- **Simple Network Management Protocol (SNMP)**—A TCP/IP protocol that is used to monitor and configure networking devices such as routers.

- **subnet mask**—The method used by IP to determine which bits in an IP address denote the network ID and which bits denote the host ID. Bits that are masked represent the network ID.

- **Telnet**—An application protocol that provides remote terminal emulation in an IP network.

- **Transmission Control Protocol (TCP)**—The primary transport protocol of the TCP/IP suite. TCP is a connection-oriented protocol that ensures reliable delivery for upper-layer protocols.

- **transport protocol**—A protocol that ensures that packets are delivered between communicating computers.

- **User Datagram Protocol (UDP)**—The counterpart to TCP, UDP is a connectionless transport protocol that provides faster but less reliable service.

- **well-known ports**—Port numbers less than 1023 that are assigned to specific functions in a TCP/IP network.

- **Windows Internet Name Service (WINS)**—The service that keeps track of NetBIOS names and IP addresses for computers in a Windows network.

REVIEW QUESTIONS

3

1. Which of the following is the correct decimal representation of the number 119?

   a. 11101110

   b. 01110111

   c. 01111001

   d. 10110111

2. CIDR allows for more networks with fewer hosts per network. (True or False?)

3. At what percentage of the original lease does a DHCP-enabled client first request to use the same address?

4. Which subnet mask is most often used in large corporations that have a Class A or Class B address?

5. Which of the following is not a valid IP address?

   a. 199.230.256.100

   b. 112.2.1.122

   c. 99.89.99.199

   d. 186.113.200.202

6. The ARPANet originally connected four sites in the U.S. in 1969. (True or False?)

7. Which of the following protocols provides email transmission across the Internet?

   a. SNMP

   b. SMTP

   c. ICMP

   d. Telnet

8. What type of protocol provides addressing and routing functions?

9. WINS is responsible for associating names to IP addresses for the Internet. (True or False?)

10. Which protocol is responsible for discovering the MAC address associated with a particular IP address?

11. Which of the following network numbers accurately indicates the series assigned by InterNIC?

    a. 192.191.0.0

    b. 13.15.0.0

    c. 19.156.0.0

    d. 128.199.0.0

12. Which ports are considered well-known ports?

13. One of the primary tasks of ARPA was to provide interoperability between its research sites. (True or False?)

14. Which of the following addresses would be allowed across the Internet?

    a. 10.1.158.1

    b. 192.168.240.199

    c. 172.18.99.100

    d. 192.156.188.200

15. WINS provides a hierarchical name-to-address resolution database. (True or False?)

16. Which of the following is the CIDR representation of a Class C subnet mask?

    a. /24

    b. /26

    c. /8

    d. /16

17. The IP address that has been reserved for loopback testing begins with

    _____ .

18. Which of the following is used by a computer to determine the host ID portion of an IP address?

    a. gateway

    b. subnet mask

    c. DNS server

    d. host address

19. Which port is used as the control port for FTP?

20. Which of the following governing bodies of the Internet is responsible for assigning IP addresses?

    a. IEEE

    b. IETF

    c. InterNIC

    d. IANA

21. Using the class system for subnet masks, host IDs can be either 0 or 255. (True or False?)

22. If a computer is able to communicate with local computers but not with remote computers, what is the most likely problem?

    a. The DNS server setting is invalid or missing.

    b. The subnet mask setting is invalid or missing.

    c. The gateway setting is invalid or missing.

    d. The DHCP server setting is invalid or missing.

23. In what format are IP addresses written to allow for easier comprehension by humans?

24. Which of the following protocols accurately provides connectionless transport service for the TCP/IP suite?

    a. ICMP

    b. FTP

    c. TCP

    d. UDP

25. The Internet grew from a project funded by the Department of the Army. (True or False?)

HANDS-ON PROJECTS

The key to using TCP/IP in a network is a proper installation. To do this, we will step through the installation of TCP/IP on a Windows NT Workstation 4.0 computer. As mentioned in the text, the steps will be similar, if not exactly the same, for Windows 95 and Windows NT Server 4.0 computers. To perform the installation, it is necessary to have the Windows NT Workstation CD and to have either a modem or network interface card installed in the machine. The MS Loopback Adapter may also be installed, which will allow the user to load Protocols without requiring a physical modem or adapter card. To install it, right-click Network Neighborhood, select Properties, select Adapter, click Add and choose MS Loopback Adapter. Once the protocol suite and its supporting software is installed, we will use some of the programs to test our installation.

PROJECT 3.1

To install the TCP/IP protocol suite:

1. Select Settings | Control Panel from the Start menu.

2. Double-click on the Network icon. The Network applet appears (see Figure 3.2).

3. Select the Protocols tab in the Network applet. Click on the Add button. A window with a list of all protocols available in Windows NT appears.

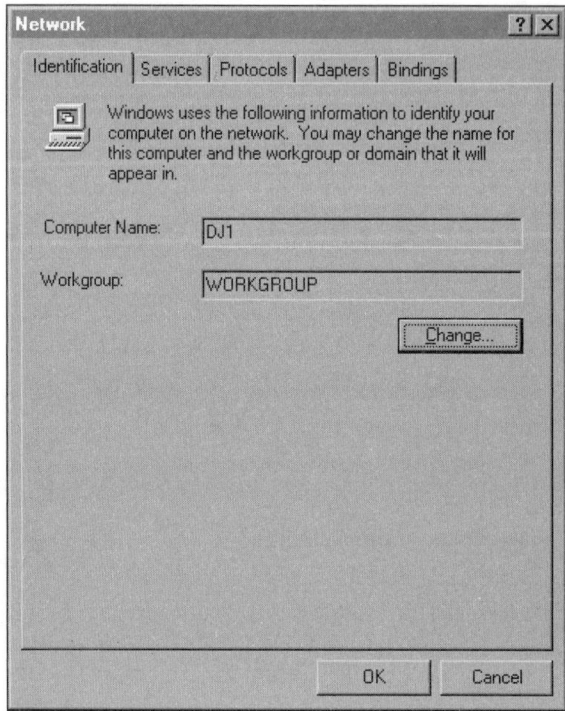

Figure 3.2   The Network applet in Windows NT Workstation.

4. Select TCP/IP Protocol from the list and click on OK.

5. As the protocol starts to install, you will be prompted with "If there is a DHCP server on your network, TCP/IP can be configured to dynamically provide an IP address. If you are not sure, ask your system administrator. Do you wish to use DHCP?"

   Select No because we will be supplying the IP address and subnet mask information.

6. You will then be prompted to supply the path to the Windows NT files. In most cases, this will be the CD-ROM. Enter the path for the files and click on Continue.

7. After the drivers and applications are installed on the computer, you will again be presented with the Network applet Protocols tab. Click on Close to continue the installation.

8. You will be presented with the TCP/IP Properties window, shown in Figure 3.3.

3

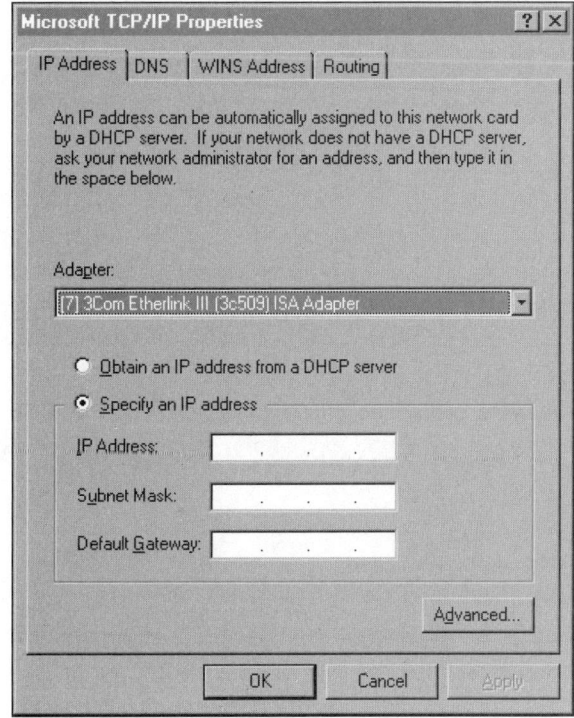

Figure 3.3   The TCP/IP Properties window will be displayed automatically.

9. Enter the IP address and subnet mask for your system. If you are working in a standalone environment, select any address. If you are working in a classroom environment, obtain your address and subnet mask from your instructor. For the purposes of this demonstration, we will be using 192.168.101.101 with a subnet mask of 255.255.255.0. In addition, you may enter a default gateway if you are operating in a internetwork.

10. Select the DNS tab, which is where all DNS information is entered if you are using DNS or connected to the Internet. Note that the NetBIOS computer name is automatically entered in the Host Name field. To add a DNS server to the search list, click on the Add button below the DNS Service Search Order window. Once your DNS information, if any, has been entered, click on OK.

11. After the system finishes its configuration, you will be asked to reboot the computer. Ensure that all other programs are closed and click on Yes.

12. Once the computer has finished rebooting, you are ready to move on to Project 3.2.

PROJECT 3.2

To verify that TCP/IP was installed correctly:

1. Open a Command Prompt window by selecting it from Start | Programs.

2. First, we will test the loopback address. If this test fails, TCP/IP did not load. From the Command Prompt, enter "PING 127.1.1.1". You should receive a response similar to that pictured in Figure 3.4.

3. Next, use the PING program again to test by PINGing the address you just assigned to the card.

4. Finally, if you are in a networked environment, PING another computer on your network. Another student's computer or the server would be best.

CASE PROJECTS

1. Your network has grown beyond the usefulness of NetBEUI and you are considering moving to TCP/IP. Your 65 computers do not need access to the Internet and, for security reasons, probably never will.

   Required result: Develop an addressing scheme for TCP/IP.

   Optional desired results: The system should support multiple subnets. The system should be easy to implement and support future expansion.

   Proposed solution: Utilize the private IP address 192.168.15.0 using a Class C subnet mask. Which results does the proposed solution provide?

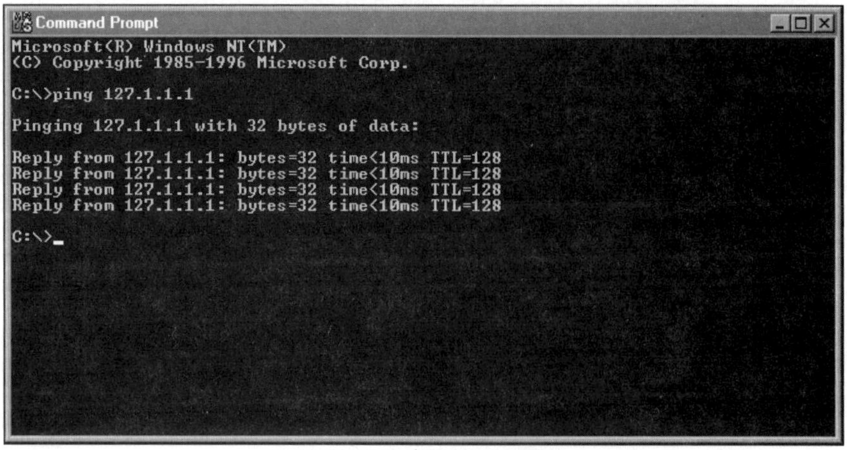

```
Command Prompt                                                    _ □ ×
Microsoft(R) Windows NT(TM)
(C) Copyright 1985-1996 Microsoft Corp.

C:\>ping 127.1.1.1

Pinging 127.1.1.1 with 32 bytes of data:

Reply from 127.1.1.1: bytes=32 time<10ms TTL=128
Reply from 127.1.1.1: bytes=32 time<10ms TTL=128
Reply from 127.1.1.1: bytes=32 time<10ms TTL=128
Reply from 127.1.1.1: bytes=32 time<10ms TTL=128

C:\>_
```

Figure 3.4   The loopback address response.

a. The proposed solution provides the required result and both optional desired results.

b. The proposed solution provides the required result and one optional desired result.

c. The proposed solution provides only the required result.

d. The proposed solution does not provide the required result.

2. You have been tasked with configuring 300 clients to use TCP/IP on your extensive internetwork.

Required result: Ensure that all computers on the network have unique addresses.

Optional desired results: Ensure that all computers are configured quickly. Ensure that all computers will have access to the Internet.

Proposed solution: Configure a DHCP server to provide client IP addresses. Use a range of addresses supplied by your ISP to provide Internet connectivity. Which results does the proposed solution provide?

a. The proposed solution provides the required result and both optional desired results.

b. The proposed solution provides the required result and one optional desired result.

c. The proposed solution provides only the required result.

d. The proposed solution does not provide the required result.

3. Sharon's computer has been moved from SubnetA to SubnetB. Your new network technician has configured her computer, and yet it is not able to connect to computers on the network.

Required result: Ensure that Sharon is able to communicate on the network.

Optional desired results: The solution should be easy to replicate if a similar situation arises. The solution should provide the new technician with feedback on where the configuration was wrong.

Proposed solution: Delete TCP/IP and re-install. Which results does the proposed solution provide?

a. The proposed solution provides the required result and both optional desired results.

b. The proposed solution provides the required result and one optional desired result.

c. The proposed solution provides only the required result.

d. The proposed solution does not provide the required result.

INTERNET INFORMATION SERVER OVERVIEW

Microsoft Proxy Server 2.0 has several software requirements, including Windows NT Server 4.0, Service Pack 3, and Internet Information Server 3.0 (or greater). Because of Proxy Server's reliance upon IIS, we'll explore that application throughout this chapter. In addition, we'll look into all of the Proxy Server requirements, with a significant focus on IIS 3.0+.

AFTER READING THIS CHAPTER AND COMPLETING THE EXERCISES, YOU WILL BE ABLE TO:

- Understand the requirements for Internet Information Server (IIS)
- Understand the functions and features of IIS

REQUIREMENT: WINDOWS NT SERVER 4.0

Proxy Server 2.0 was designed specifically to be deployed on Windows NT Server 4.0. It simply will not install onto NT Workstation, Windows 95, or earlier versions of Windows NT Server. Proxy Server is a true client/server application that relies upon the robustness of the hardware and the network operating system (NOS) comprising its host system.

For more information about Windows NT Server 4.0, please visit the Microsoft Web site's NT Server pages at **www.microsoft.com/ntserver/**.

REQUIREMENT: SERVICE PACK 3

Proxy Server 2.0 also requires that Service Pack 3 (standard international 40-bit or domestic 128-bit version) be properly installed onto NT Server. Several new drivers, kernel improvements, and software patches are required for Proxy Server to function properly. Proxy Server will not install if SP3 has not been applied.

For more information about Service Packs, please visit the Microsoft Web site's NT Server pages at **www.microsoft.com/ntserver/**. Click Downloads on the left-hand column to go to the downloads of the NT Server Web site. To download the Service Pack, click on the Windows NT 4.0 Service Pack 3 link, either on the far right-hand side of the window, or under the Service Packs and Updates heading on the Web page.

REQUIREMENT: IIS 3.0+

Proxy Server 2.0 requires Internet Information Server (IIS) 3.0 or greater. Even when Web and FTP service hosting is not required, Proxy Server requires several IIS components and the administration interface. Proxy Server will not install if IIS is not already present on the host server.

IIS 3.0 is no longer the latest release of the Microsoft IIS package. Internet Information Server 4.0 was released in mid-1998. In the next two sections, we'll look at both versions of IIS. However, our mention of IIS 3.0 is cursory. If you are using IIS 3.0, you already know most of this information anyway. If you are not already using IIS, there is no reason not to move right into IIS 4.0. IIS 4.0 offers a plethora of new features and improvements over its 3.0 predecessor.

INTERNET INFORMATION SERVER 3.0

Internet Information Server 3.0 was released in late 1996. This version expanded and improved the capabilities of IIS 2.0, which shipped as a component on the Windows NT Server 4.0 distribution CD-ROM. IIS 3.0 is a fast, easy-to-manage information service application that performs well on Windows NT Server 4.0. Creating rich interactive content and server-based applications is no longer a daunting task; it can now be attained by every Webmaster. IIS takes full advantage of Windows NT Server by relying on it to manage security, monitor performance, and support network communication. Furthermore, because of the tight integration of Windows NT Server and IIS, many other Microsoft products, from production to database tools, can be incorporated in Web applications. This greatly expands the capabilities and reach of IIS beyond simple static Web documents.

Five key IIS components or elements are sometimes referred to as the IIS toolkit: Active Server Pages, Index Server, NetShow, FrontPage Server Extensions, and Crystal Reports.

ACTIVE SERVER PAGES

Active Server Pages (ASP) is a Web programming technique and standard in which standard HTML documents are combined with programming or scripting languages to create dynamic content-directed Web documents. IIS 3.0 was the first Microsoft server product to include ASP support. With IIS 3.0 and ASP, you can easily create Web sites that include complex client/server applications without the hassles of incompatible systems or system-level programming.

Active Server Pages is a Web-development architecture and environment that is not dependent on IIS 3.0, but it works very well with it. ASP enables the smooth integration of HTML, scripts, and ActiveX components into an open, platform-independent, compilation-free Web application. In fact, ASP is typically faster than Common Gateway Interface (CGI) scripts or server-side programs. In addition, it can use server-side CGIs without significant loss of performance. As part of IIS 3.0, ASP runs as another thread within the IIS process space defined by the hosting virtual machine. The multithreaded architecture of IIS and ASP integration allows multiple Web sessions to occur simultaneously. Fortunately, ASP does not require alternative operating systems or development tools; instead, it uses the existing tools. This enables the current investment of capital, experience, and knowledge to be directly applied to this new technology without significant cost in dollars or effort.

Because ASP incorporates ActiveX scripting, you can use almost any scripting language. Thus, your current scripting investments can be leveraged against the new Web paradigm. ASP via IIS supports VBScript (Visual Basic Script) and Microsoft JScript natively. Many database interfaces are compatible with ActiveX scripting, including Oracle, Sybase, and Informix DBMSs (Database Management Systems). Using ASP, you can develop Web applications that can interact with virtually any application or system type present on a network. This means that even legacy and nonstandard computer systems and applications can continue their productive life even as your organization moves toward transforming your network into an intranet or extranet.

The use of legacy and nonstandard systems and applications via ASP does not require any special plug-ins or setups on the client's browser. All of the interaction with nonstandard or non–Web-enabled components is handled on the server side; the client browser simply receives a standard HTML document produced by the ASP scripts and the data pulled from its linked systems. Thus, ASP via IIS 3.0 is 100 percent compatible with every Web browser.

Active Server Pages is not a separate component of IIS 3.0. Rather, it is a fundamental core improvement over IIS 2.0. The process of installing ASP over/into IIS 2.0 effectively upgrades your system to IIS 3.0.

MICROSOFT INDEX SERVER

Index Server is a powerful content search engine designed to integrate with Internet Information Server. It is a full-text indexing tool that performs keyword queries across resources that are stored locally or resources accessed over a network (including the Internet). With support for plain text, HTML, and all of the document format types from Microsoft Office applications, Index Server is able to offer seamless search and retrieval access to your Web and standard productivity documents. Index Server also supports seven languages (English, French, German, Dutch, Spanish, Italian, and Swedish).

Index Server is an automatic system. Once you have defined the directories to be indexed, it updates its index files automatically each time a change is made. Every document is condensed into an exhaustive word index. This word index is what Index Server uses to perform keyword queries. It acts as a database, which speeds the search and response time in comparison to performing a resource-based search.

Index Server is the only Web search engine specifically designed to operate on Windows NT Server 4.0 and with Internet Information Server. This gives Index Server some significant advantages:

- Automated index updating due to tight integration with the NT file systems

- Complete security on a file-level basis maintained by NT Server and supported by Index Server to protect private data and to grant authorized access

- Ability to access any resource file located on any file system connected to and compatible with NT Server, including NetWare and Unix server file volumes

- High performance by relying on NT Server to maintain the operation environment and by demanding little system overhead, even during peak traffic times

4

MICROSOFT NETSHOW

Internet Information Server 3.0 is equipped with a broadly applicable multimedia distribution application—Microsoft NetShow. NetShow brings audio and video capabilities (including streaming, multicasting, and illustrated audio) to IIS-hosted Web sites. Several media types or formats are available on demand with both live and prerecorded distribution capabilities. NetShow does not rely on or prescribe to any one specific multimedia authoring environment; rather, it is capable of distributing media files authored from a wide variety of popular development tools.

NetShow is equipped with versatile administration tools that equip system operators with control over bandwidth use, performance management, and system monitoring. Broad support for third-party media types is maintained through NetShow's open architecture. NetShow includes full support for the Windows ACM/VCM codec (Audio/Video Compression Modules encoder/decoder) standard, so that even the most innovative multimedia can be made available on your network or Web site. In addition, NetShow uses Forward Error Correction (FEC) to compensate for poor network performance and to recover media streams automatically when transmission problems occur.

MICROSOFT FRONTPAGE SERVER EXTENSIONS

Microsoft FrontPage Server Extensions simplify using Microsoft FrontPage to build and manage IIS-hosted Web sites. These extensions can significantly reduce the amount of work involved in setting up an intranet or Internet Web site. This is the only Web-production suite that's fully integrated with IIS.

FrontPage server components and ISAPI (Internet Server Application Programming Interface) extensions are installed on any IIS server automatically. FrontPage Server Extensions are available for any viable NT 4.0 hardware platform, such as Intel, Alpha, and PowerPC. FrontPage supports NTLM authentication, also known as Windows NT Challenge/Response authentication, which requires only a single logon for Windows NT, Internet Information Server, and FrontPage, as well as secure administration through the Secure Sockets Layer (SSL). When Index Server is also installed, FrontPage automatically integrates its WebBot Search components with Index Server's utilities.

CRYSTAL REPORTS

Crystal Reports, Seagate Software's visual reporting tool, works with IIS to produce reports about what's happening on your Web server. You can also export Crystal Reports data to database applications. The following features make this application easy to use and learn:

- Crystal Reports wizards and templates
- A context-sensitive, step-by-step, on-screen tutorial
- The simple DataViews interface from Data Dictionary Builder
- One-step custom sort and calculations
- All those useful Windows NT functions, such as drag and drop, right-click-enabled menus, automatic styles, and undo

Crystal Report's output relies heavily on good graphics handling, such as drawing functions, and support for BMP, GIF, TIF, PCX, and TGA graphics formats, BLOB (Paradox and xBASE) bitmaps, integrated graphing styles, and OLE 2.0. Other useful and versatile features include:

- Powerful record selection
- Easy-to-use formula editing
- Drilldown and Search Dialogs
- Cross-tab reports
- Raw data storage for analysis
- Double-pass reporting
- Ability to link various databases into a single report
- Extensible Formula Language with user-defined dynamic link library (DLL) functions

Crystal Reports is compatible with Microsoft Access and Microsoft SQL Server.

IIS 3.0 INSTALLATION AND CONFIGURATION

The initial installation of IIS is as simple as it is with other Microsoft products. A setup wizard guides you through each required step. Most of the default settings that the wizard offers will suffice for normal implementations. Nevertheless, we have included a quick review of the setup process and the decisions you'll need to make along the way. Note that the installation process for IIS 3.0 is a two-step activity. First, you'll want to install IIS 2.0 from the Windows NT Server 4.0 distribution CD-ROM. Then you'll apply the Active Server Pages IIS 3.0 patch.

INSTALLING IIS 2.0

The installation procedure for IIS 2.0 from the original Windows NT Server (NTS) distribution CD-ROM assumes you did not install IIS as part of the original installation of NTS. If you recall, the installation wizard asked if you wanted to install IIS immediately after you specified whether the server was wired to a network. If you selected to skip the IIS installation when you installed NTS, you must complete the following steps. If you selected to install IIS as part of the NTS installation, you can skip this procedure and move on to installing IIS 3.0.

To install IIS 2.0, follow these steps:

1. Launch the INETSTP.EXE setup file located in the \I386\INETSRV directory of the distribution CD-ROM.

2. When prompted, select all but the Gopher service for installation.

3. When prompted, change the publishing directories to a data drive.

4. Select all listed ODBC drivers.

5. Reboot your system when the installation is complete.

INSTALLING IIS 3.0 AND THE ACTIVE SERVER PAGES PATCH

Because IIS 3.0 is no longer the current release of Internet Information Server, you may have difficulty locating and downloading the appropriate upgrade/ patch files. As of mid-1998, the IIS 3.0 files were still available for download. To locate the download area, follow these steps:

1. Go to the Microsoft IIS Web area at **www.microsoft.com/iis/**.

2. Select Download from the displayed menu on the left.

3. A page listing all of the currently available downloads is displayed.

4. Scroll down to the Archive section and select Internet Information Server 3.0.

5. Click on the Register & Download icon for your system type (Alpha, I386, or PPC).

6. Fill out the registration form and click on Submit User Info. You are presented with a feature selection page.

7. Check the features or components you want, plus the desired language type.

8. Click on the Next button at the bottom of this page for a list of download sites.

9. Select a site. A final page appears listing each of the download links that point to the files you need for the features and components you selected.

10. Click on each download link in turn and download the files.

After you have downloaded the required files, the installation process is as follows:

1. Execute ASP.EXE.

2. Allow the system to stop current IIS services.

3. Verify paths as defined during IIS 2.0 installation.

4. Instruct setup to restart IIS services when the patch is complete.

No reboot is necessary, but we recommend it anyway.

INSTALLATION CAVEATS

Part of the IIS installation process establishes a special user account and directory structure for the program's exclusive use. To truly understand the IIS environment, you must understand what the setup process did and why these settings are important:

- IIS creates a user account for anonymous access. This account is named IUSR_*<servername>* (where *<servername>* is the NetBIOS name for the server hosting IIS). This account has similar privileges to the Guest account, but it has no rights to log on locally.

- IIS also creates a default directory off the root of the boot partition (where the NT system files reside) called INETPUB, with subdirectories named FTPPUB, WWWPUB, and GOPHERPUB for FTP, Web, and Gopher services, respectively. If a service is not installed, its corresponding directory is not created. The IUSR account is granted read and execute access to these directories by default.

If you need more information about IIS 3.0 features, installation, configuration, use, or troubleshooting, we highly recommend the documentation found on TechNet. *TechNet* is Microsoft's best monthly publication. This $300-per-year CD-ROM subscription is well worth the cost. A monthly multi-CD-ROM contains all of the documentation for every major MS product, the Resource Kits, plus hundreds of white papers, FAQs, troubleshooting documents, book excerpts, articles, and other written materials. It also includes utilities, patches, fixes, upgrades, drivers, and demonstration software.

Microsoft Certified Systems Engineers (MCSEs) get a free one-year subscription. Periodically, Microsoft offers a special promotion where a single issue of TechNet can be obtained by participating in a review, questionnaire, or contest or by simply visiting a Web site. Such promotions are often advertised on Microsoft's IT home pages, located at **www.microsoft.com/ithome/**.

For more information on IIS 4.0, see *Internet Information Server 4.0 Exam Prep*, published by Certification Insider Press. Information on IIS 4.0 is included here for ease of reference and to provide you with a broader coverage of the background topics associated with Microsoft Proxy Server 2.0.

WHAT IS INTERNET INFORMATION SERVER?

Internet Information Server 4.0 (usually called IIS or IIS 4.0) is the latest release of the standards-based Web and FTP server from Microsoft. IIS is designed to operate on NT Server 4.0. It is an Internet-standards-compliant HTTP server that also includes FTP and several other valuable Web- and FTP-related services. IIS 4.0 gives you more publishing capabilities than most other Web servers. For instance, with IIS 4.0 you can perform the following tasks:

- Publish information on a Web or FTP site quickly and easily
- Develop and operate Web-based applications
- Manage and administer your Web site remotely across the Internet

In other words, IIS 4.0 permits you to fully design, create, deploy, and manage Web sites of any size, from individual personal pages to fully interactive high-traffic corporate Web sites. IIS not only makes the process of transforming business information into Web applications possible, it greatly simplifies the effort involved. Together, NT Server and IIS 4.0 make up a reliable, comprehensive, and adaptive Web server solution. Because IIS 4.0 is available as a free add-on to Windows NT Server 4.0, it also offers an outstanding value for organizations or individuals who want to turn to the Internet to disseminate information.

IIS 4.0 offers HTTP 1.1 support with full backward-compatibility with HTTP 1.0 for older browsers. HTTP 1.1 offers significant improvements in performance (it's 50 to 100 percent faster than HTTP 1.0), resulting in a more responsive Web experience for your users. To be more specific, the performance improvements conveyed in HTTP 1.1 and IIS 4.0 result from the following items:

- **Pipelining** HTTP 1.0 servers process only one resource request per client at a time. In other words, clients were forced to wait for each pending request to be processed before the next request could be sent. HTTP 1.1 uses *pipelining* to allow clients to send multiple requests simultaneously, without waiting for the server to respond to one request before sending another. Consequently, pipelining improves response time and Web display performance.

- **Persistent connections** Originally, HTTP was designed as a *stateless protocol*. In English, this means that no two packets transferred between a server and client had any kind of built-in relationship and that each packet transfer was treated as a separate request for service. Thus, for each item in a typical Web document—HTML, GIFs, Java applets, and so on—a separate connection between the client and server had to be established. So, if eight items made up a document, eight connections would be created between client and server, and only one item would be transported per connection. The overhead involved in establishing, maintaining, and tearing down such connections is high when compared to the amount of data sent across them. To reduce this overhead, IIS 4.0 uses *persistent connections* to send multiple objects across a single connection. This can be a tremendous boon to performance because the amount of overhead involved in a data transfer actually decreases as the amount of data to be transported increases when persistent connections are used.

- **Chunked transfers** IIS also supports ASP, which can interact with programs or user input to create Web pages on the fly as users demand their delivery. ASP files vary in size because of their dynamic behavior. HTTP 1.0 can experience difficulties when delivering data if the size of the information to be transported is unknown at the beginning of the transfer. HTTP 1.1 is able to transmit such variable-sized documents more efficiently through the use of a technique known as *chunking*. Chunking is a process whereby a transmission of arbitrary length is decomposed into multiple elements (called chunks) of varying sizes, each with its own header and size indicator. Because chunks can be composed and transmitted on the fly as a dynamic page "builds itself," this method greatly increases efficiency when information is delivered from ASP documents.

- **Proxy support** HTTP 1.1 includes caching information that's built right into the protocol itself. This data includes time of creation, expiration dates, and other measures of "data freshness" that provide servers and proxies with the information necessary to manage cached resources effectively. Furthermore, HTTP 1.1 can provide these details in the form of automatically generated metadata so that Web pages can be cached effectively without requiring any changes to the underlying content.

Other benefits of IIS 4.0 reach beyond performance. Its new wizards can help you create Web sites, while its versatile administration tools make it much easier to manage and maintain such sites. With these new capabilities, IIS 4.0 has become a premier Web server for Windows NT. Here are some of the other noteworthy highlights you'll find in IIS 4.0:

- Integrated setup
- Flexible management
- Complete content control
- Configuration backup and restoration
- Hosting of multiple Web sites on a single Web server
- Allocating network bandwidth
- Familiar Windows NT Server administration tools

Each of these topics will be explained in the sections that follow, starting with integrated setup.

INTEGRATED SETUP

IIS 4.0 is no longer distributed as an individual, separate product. It is now an integral part of the Windows NT 4.0 Option Pack. This product distribution contains IIS 4.0 (and all its many subcomponents), Windows NT Service Pack 3, Internet Explorer 4.01, Transaction Server 2.0, Message Queue Server Standard Edition, Site Server Express, and Connection Services for Microsoft RAS. Although not too many of the other products touch directly on IIS 4.0, it is necessary to install Service Pack 3 before installing IIS 4.0; likewise, users and administrators will obtain the best results from using IIS 4.0 if they also install Internet Explorer 4.01.

The integrated setup wizard for the Option Pack lets you install IIS and other components easily and simultaneously. The wizard asks you which components to install, requests a few additional parameters, and then completes the installation. The Option Pack simplifies the process of configuring an entire Web publication system so that Web applications can be developed and deployed with great ease and speed.

You can download the Windows NT 4.0 Option Pack from **www.microsoft. com/ntserver/basics/whatsnew.asp**. (Warning: The full version of the

Option Pack for Windows NT Server is 87MB!) The Option Pack installation is quite similar to the installation for Internet Explorer 4.01, where only those components selected are actually downloaded. Should additional components need to be installed later, only the additional files that are necessary will be retrieved. The Option Pack is also included on the distribution media for Microsoft's Windows NT Server 4.0 Enterprise Edition, or it may be purchased separately at a local reseller for under $100.

When you install IIS 4.0 on multiple servers at the same time, you can build an unattended installation script to install Windows NT Server 4.0, Service Pack 3, Internet Explorer 4.01, and any or all components of the Option Pack across the network on any number of designated target machines.

FLEXIBLE MANAGEMENT

IIS includes a useful collection of management and administration tools that can give administrators complete control and insight into the operation of their Web servers and related components. In addition, by using IIS Administration Objects (IISAOs), administrators can create customized interfaces to meet their particular needs or work flows. This provides extremely useful functionality if you manage multiple servers or work in a widely distributed network environment.

Windows-Based Administration

With the release of version 4.0, the most obvious change to IIS is its introduction of the Microsoft Management Console (MMC), shown in Figure 4.1. The MMC is a Windows-based tool that provides total management of all services and applications within a single framework. The MMC is also Active Desktop capable and will eventually be used to manage and control aspects of entire Windows NT systems. In fact, Windows NT 5.0's control mechanisms center around snap-ins for MMC, making this tool the nerve center for Windows NT's future generations.

MMC offers administrators control over every aspect of their Internet sites through a unified, standardized interface. Every component of IIS and the Option Pack can be managed by using an MMC snap-in; these components currently include the Web Server, FTP Server, Simple Mail Transfer Protocol (SMTP) services, Network News Transfer Protocol (NNTP) services, Transaction Server, and Index Server. And because MMC is inherently Web based, it also provides remote management capabilities alongside customized console controls. We expect third parties to create snap-ins to MMC, so it will truly become the general management console for the Windows NT environment in future releases.

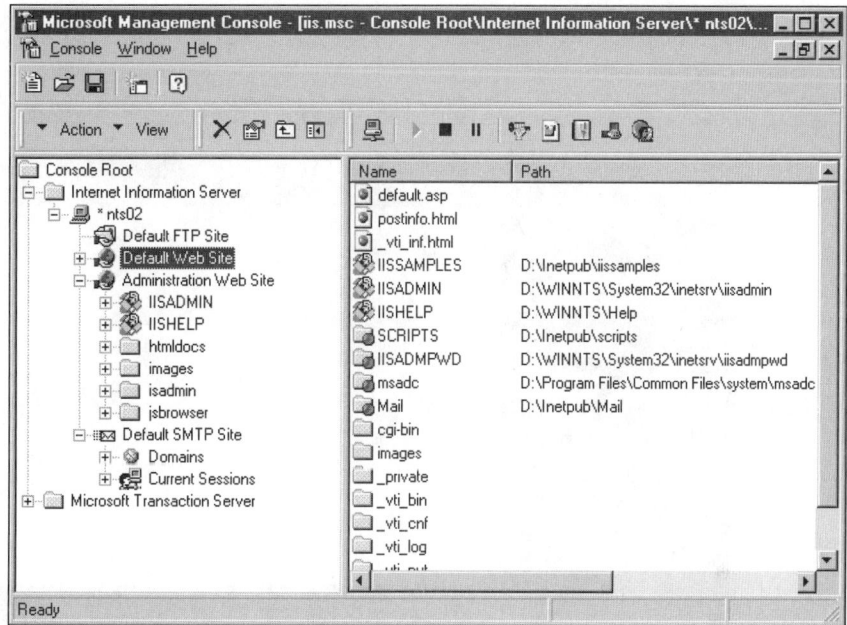

Figure 4.1   The Microsoft Management Console (MMC).

Web-Based Administration

IIS 4.0 also incorporates a new and improved Web-based interface (see Figure 4.2) for administrative tasks, called HTML Administration (HTMLA). This interface uses Active Server Pages (ASP) and JavaScript and maximizes your ability to manage an Internet site from any workstation equipped with a Web browser. This gives single-site administrators the freedom to travel; plus, it allows Internet Service Providers (ISPs) or other multisite Web hosting services to grant individual customers administrative control over their own particular Web sites.

IIS Administration Objects

In IIS 4.0, new IIS Administration Objects (IISAOs) can be used to control an entire server programmatically through automated objects. IISAOs enable command-line administration of Web servers through scripts or command prompts, permit the definition of customized interfaces for all kinds of administrative purposes, and support the automation of common Web administration tasks, such as HTTP log analysis, file clean-up, and directory management.

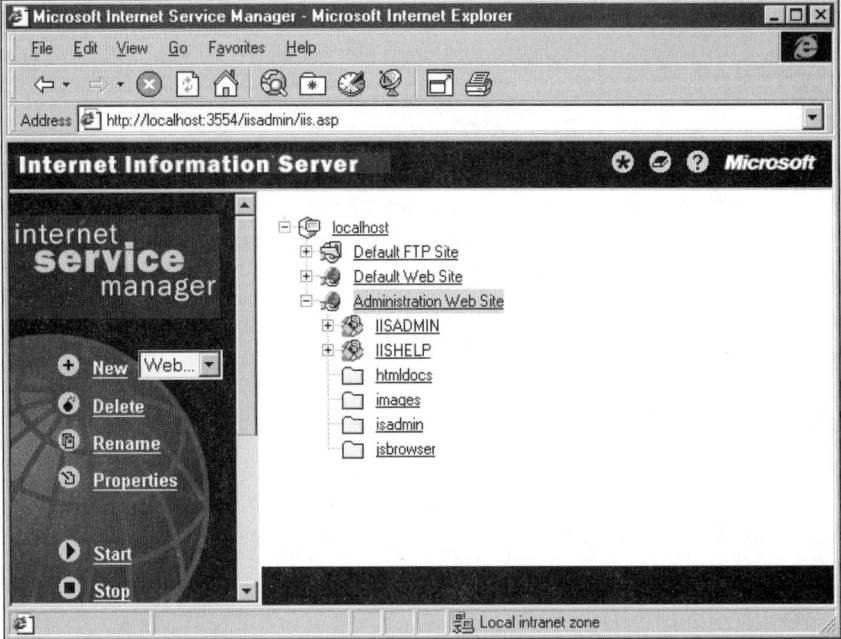

Figure 4.2   The IIS's HTML Administration (HTMLA) interface, as seen through Internet Explorer 4.01.

COMPLETE CONTENT CONTROL

With improved, more fine-tuned control of Web sites and the flexibility of IIS Administration Object properties, IIS offers more ways to control and obtain information about an entire Web server or an individually hosted Web site than most other Web servers do. By defining properties on a Web server properly (for any individual Web site, virtual directory, or even individual files), you gain more control over your Web documents and publications.

With IIS 4.0, you can reduce log file sizes by choosing to log hits on HTML documents rather than using the default method, which is to log hits on every object within a Web document (GIFs, WAVs, Java applets, and so on). This approach provides more accurate information on site visits rather than tracking access to individual elements.

IIS 4.0 also lets you assign Secure Sockets Layer (SSL) 3.0 security to individual directories rather than to an entire Web site. You can reduce redundant tasks by selecting upline settings to apply to downline objects (that is, a Web site's settings can apply to all the virtual directories under its purview, or a Web server's settings can apply to all hosted Web sites on that machine, and so forth). Fine-tuning content control can also improve performance by reducing the number of logging tasks that the server must complete for each requested document or object.

BACKING UP AND RESTORING IIS CONFIGURATION DATA

It's easy to back up and restore IIS 4.0 configuration data. In fact, IIS configuration settings can be imported from or exported to individual files on a per-server basis, but the same technique applies to individual sites, individual directories, and even individual files. This enables administrators to maintain accurate configuration backups, supports easy system rollback and restoration of previous configurations, and permits configuration data to be transferred directly from one server to another in the form of configuration data files.

HOSTING MULTIPLE WEB SITES

With previous versions of IIS, each Web site that was hosted on a single implementation of IIS had to have its own unique IP address. However, through the use of HTTP 1.1 host headers, IIS 4.0 permits hosting of multiple Web sites on a single IP address. This reduces administrative difficulties, permits many more sites to be hosted on a single IIS 4.0 installation, and reduces the costs associated with IP address registration and leasing. However, it's also important to note that HTTP 1.1 is not supported fully by all Web browsers. Therefore, deployment of this feature should be limited to intranet environments, or suitably formatted failover error messages should be incorporated until the majority of browsers used on the Internet support HTTP 1.1 host headers.

 Hosting multiple Web sites is not a problem for Netscape Navigator or Microsoft Internet Explorer versions 3.0 and higher.

ALLOCATING NETWORK BANDWIDTH

Any installation of IIS that supports multiple Web sites can offer guaranteed bandwidth to each individual site by using a technique called *bandwidth throttling*. Thus, high-priority sites or sites with higher traffic rates can be allocated a larger portion of a server's available bandwidth to ensure timely content delivery to clients. Bandwidth throttling can improve performance for low-end sites that are restricted to a smaller portion of the server's available bandwidth as well. That's because bandwidth throttling also guarantees pipeline size on a per-site basis and helps prevent connection terminations or interference owing to widely fluctuating bandwidth or network delays.

FAMILIAR WINDOWS NT SERVER ADMINISTRATION TOOLS

Because IIS 4.0 is so tightly integrated with Windows NT Server 4.0, little additional knowledge is required to administer it. Most of the management and administration tools used by NT Server can also be used to manage and control various aspects of IIS. User accounts, including an anonymous account, must be managed through the Administrative Tools utility called User Manager For Domains. Likewise, NT's built-in Performance Monitor and Network Monitor can also be used to locate bottlenecks, to track system performance, and to isolate network communication problems related to IIS, just as they can be used for the same purposes for other server-based applications.

By registering its own unique objects and counters, IIS adds numerous Web services and operations that are specific to Performance Monitor. Inspection and graphing of these objects can provide valuable insight into how IIS is behaving and what impact it can have on an NT Server. Within the application itself, IIS also traps security and application events that it sends to the Windows NT Event Viewer for inclusion in the log files. This makes it possible to audit IIS-related objects and events and offer additional sources of information about IIS usage, access, and attempted security violations that may sometimes occur when crackers try to break into a Web server.

IIS COMPONENTS

As mentioned previously, IIS 4.0 is distributed as part of the Windows NT Option Pack. The Option Pack contains seven distinct software components, or applications, that can be installed as an integrated system to support a broad range of Internet publishing, communications, and management capabilities. As Microsoft continues to integrate these products, the division between one product or service and another is becoming somewhat blurry.

In addition to the individually named components in the Option Pack (IIS 4.0, Service Pack 3, Internet Explorer 4.01, Transaction Server 2.0, Message Queue Server Standard Edition, Site Server Express, and Connection Services for Microsoft RAS), the Option Pack also includes numerous other unnamed components. They are installed along with IIS's Web and FTP services and include Index Server 2.0, Certificate Server 1.0, several data access (database) and development (software development kits, or SDK) components, SMTP service, NNTP service, the Microsoft Management Console (MMC), and the Microsoft Distributed interNet Applications (DNA) architecture. Strictly speaking, these are not IIS components, but at the same time, IIS could not function correctly or be as flexible if they were not present.

In the following sections, all of the IIS and Option Pack components are discussed briefly. These items are covered in more depth in subsequent chapters of this book.

INDEX SERVER 2.0

IIS 4.0 includes an updated and improved version of the Index Server software. Index Server provides site content indexing and searching services to IIS-based Web sites. It includes a set of default and customizable interface query forms that offer users a wide range of content search options. Index Server 2.0 includes support for ASP, processes SQL queries, provides a number of new content filters, and can now search content across multiple languages. Index Server 2.0 also offers improved performance, adds the ability to fine-tune the scope and range of searches, and delivers enhanced cache-management capabilities. This version is also subject to using a Web browser for MMC administration. All of these features make Index Server 2.0 a powerful and comprehensive content search engine. Given its inclusion with IIS 4.0 at no extra charge, Index Server has become the search engine of choice for IIS-based Web servers.

4

CERTIFICATE SERVER 1.0

Digital certificates have two primary purposes: to certify the identity and authenticity of a Web site and to authenticate user identities. Web site identity verification must be performed through contact with a certificate authority of some kind. But until the release of IIS 4.0 and Certificate Server 1.0, organizations were unable to use built-in IIS technology for client/server authentication. Certificate Server gives individual Web servers the ability to issue, revoke, and renew X.509 digital certificates for client use.

Once issued, digital user certificates can be used to prove a client's identity, to maintain status information about clients, and to circumvent manual user authentication processes. Certificate Server can also be used in a more conventional way through its support of the Secure Sockets Layer (SSL) and Private Communications Technology (PCT) protocols for authenticated, secure communications.

SITE SERVER EXPRESS 2.0

An express version of the full-blown Microsoft Site Server product (available separately) is included as part of the IIS 4.0 Option Pack. Site Server Express delivers a variety of analysis tools to keep tabs on Web sites, but it also incorporates several publishing utilities to facilitate content development. The Usage Import And Report Writer translates cryptic IIS log files into easy-to-read documents that contain information about hits, users who visit the site, length of stay, visitation patterns, and more. The Content Analysis module creates a graphical representation of a Web site and can also check for broken links. The Web Publishing Wizard makes it easy for content developers to create and post new documents to any IIS-based Web site.

MICROSOFT TRANSACTION SERVER 2.0

The integration of Microsoft Transaction Server (MTS) into IIS 4.0 brings new robustness, fault tolerance, and programmable extensibility to IIS and Web applications. Basically, a transaction server creates a software environment in which any kind of transaction—an information transfer, a financial transaction, a database update, or any other kind of activity that involves important or sensitive data—is guaranteed to either complete successfully or leave the data completely unchanged. Thus, incomplete or failed transactions can never leave an underlying database, be they financial records or other information, in an uncertain state or introduce an incomplete set of changes.

MTS allows IIS to play host to distributed transaction applications. MTS simplifies Web application development for multiuser environments by handling most of the basic low-level system interaction. Through MTS, any Web application can be launched as a separate process that can persist beyond a single client request, and its operation and system resources will not interfere with IIS or any other active Web applications. Also, the use of MTS guarantees that the data used in distributed applications will not be left in an uncertain or incomplete state, even when network or communications problems cause transactions to fail when they're not completed.

MICROSOFT MESSAGE QUEUE SERVER 1.0

As Web applications for distributed deployment become more commonplace, the reliability for these applications to communicate with one another or between their own distributed components becomes increasingly important. The Microsoft Message Queue (MSMQ) Server enables applications to communicate by using a message queue, even when remote systems may be offline or otherwise unavailable.

Basically, a message queue provides a holding tank for information that must be exchanged between application components (or individual applications) that the producing application or component can write to at any time, and the consuming application can check anytime to see if it has any messages waiting. Because this permits applications or components to exchange data without requiring realtime communications, it makes it much easier for such software elements to exchange data and instructions. From an IIS perspective, the range of flexibility and fault tolerance supported for distributed Web applications that use MSMQ is greatly extended by its integration of these components or capabilities:

- **Microsoft Transaction Server** Guarantees that all messages are properly delivered.

- **ActiveX support** Makes it easy to plug in external programs and software widgets to create and process messages.
- **Asynchronous communications** Makes it possible for components to communicate without being active at the same time or without establishing communications in realtime.

INTERNET CONNECTION SERVICES FOR MICROSOFT RAS 1.0

Internet Connection Services (ICS) is an extension and upgrade to Windows NT Server's Remote Access Service (RAS). ICS adds several enhancements to RAS, including customizable client dialers, centrally administered network phone books, Remote Authentication Dial In User Service (RADIUS) authentication support, and improved administration and management tools.

ICS is designed primarily for situations where large numbers of dial-up users, such as ISPs, access one or more servers to establish network communications. Because of its convenient user setup and installation capabilities, and its improved management facilities, ICS reduces operations and connectivity costs, improves and simplifies end-user support, and enables new Internet business solutions. Most of the improvements found in ICS also appear in the Routing And Remote Access Service (RRAS) update for NT Server, which appeared initially as part of the NT Server Service Pack 2.

SMTP SERVICE

IIS now includes a Simple Mail Transfer Protocol (SMTP) client service. This service allows Web applications to send and receive email messages. In addition, it permits Web server events to trigger email notifications to designated administrators. The SMTP service gives each Web server an email message box in which error messages, user feedback, or undelivered messages can be deposited for manual processing. This capability makes it easier for users to communicate with Web-site operators and provides for asynchronous information delivery to Web administrators.

NNTP SERVICE

With support for the Network News Transfer Protocol (NNTP), IIS 4.0 can host one or more independent online discussion groups. Such discussion groups permit individual users to post questions and return later to read replies. They also permit any visitors to follow the sequence of questions and answers, called message threads, that are posted to the group. This NNTP service makes an excellent tool for information exchange, online technical support, or any other kind of dialog that involves multiple users and that works with message threading. Most newsgroups focus around some particular topic or area of interest and involve numerous ongoing message threads on subtopics that relate in some way to the newsgroup's focus.

IIS-based discussion groups can be accessed through a Web interface to NNTP or through any NNTP-compliant newsreader. However, the version of NNTP included with the Windows NT Server Option Pack is designed to handle only private discussion forums; this implementation does not support Usenet newsfeeds, nor can it handle message replication from global Usenet NNTP news services. To add complete Usenet news services to an Internet site, you must purchase and implement Microsoft Exchange Server 5.5 or some other third-party NNTP news server for Windows NT; these alternatives include complete NNTP support (including newsfeeds and message replication).

DATA ACCESS AND SDK COMPONENTS

Because IIS supports several standard data access models and components, IIS-based Web applications enjoy broad communication capabilities with databases and other information delivery applications. IIS includes ActiveX Data Objects (ADO), Remote Data Service (RDS), and Open Database Connectivity (ODBC) drivers. Because ordinary Web documents are usually static and offer only limited access to background server functionality, these tools offer powerful means for Web content developers to enhance the interactivity of their Web documents and to drive those documents from external data repositories of all kinds.

In addition, the IIS 4.0 Software Development Kit (SDK) contains detailed documentation that describes how to build custom methods and interfaces for existing components; the custom methods and interfaces can expand and enhance Web applications that use ASP, custom IIS configurations, unique model and object types, logging adaptations, and server extensions. The Microsoft Script Debugger can be used to easily debug ASP and several types of programming scripts—including scripts written with Visual Basic Scripting Edition (VBScript), JScript (Microsoft's JavaScript), or Java—to help simplify Web application development.

MICROSOFT MANAGEMENT CONSOLE

As described earlier, the Microsoft Management Console (MMC) represents a new and powerful management, administration, and control interface for Windows NT. MMC appears within the NT 4.0 environment when IIS 4.0 is installed, but it will be a standard component in NT 5.0. MMC replaces numerous other interfaces and utilities, including elements that appear under the Start | Programs | Administrative Tools menu.

The MMC can manage and control all aspects of a networked Windows NT environment—including those services added by IIS—through the use of programmatic controls called *snap-ins*. Every significant component of IIS has an associated snap-in that delivers administrative control over that component and its related objects. MMC can be accessed through a Web interface or controlled by using command-line instructions through the new Windows Scripting Host (WSH), a language-independent scripting host for 32-bit Windows platforms (including Windows 95 and Windows 98, as well as Windows NT).

WINDOWS DNA ARCHITECTURE

In its continued effort to develop better support for distributed applications, Microsoft has created an environment called *Distributed interNet Applications (DNA)*. DNA is a Windows-based architectural framework that enables the deployment of scalable, multitiered distributed application components on any type of network. DNA combines Internet access, communications link establishment and management, client/server computing, TCP/IP communications, transactions, and more into a coherent programming structure. Basically, DNA is a system that enables all IIS components and related services, Windows NT Server, and its clients to interact reliably, efficiently, and at peak performance levels.

SERVICE PACK 3

Service Packs represent Microsoft's post-release method for correcting bugs and other errors found in its software products. Any Service Pack usually includes a collection of code replacements, patches, error corrections, new applications, version upgrades, or service-specific configuration settings that correct, replace, or hide deficiencies in an original product.

Service Packs can be downloaded from the Microsoft Web site or FTP site and are regularly included on Microsoft's monthly TechNet CD-ROMs; however, Service Pack 3 (SP3) for Windows NT 4.0 is also included with the Option Pack. This is not merely a convenience; SP3 must be installed on Windows NT Server if you wish to install IIS 4.0 and related components. For that reason, be sure to install SP3 before attempting to install IIS or any other applications from the Option Pack.

Service Pack installation is not always reliable, nor does it always leave a system fully operational. That's why we strongly recommend that you perform a full backup of a Windows NT computer before attempting to install a Service Pack. Nine times out of 10, a Service Pack installation will succeed, but we've found ourselves with an unsuccessful installation more often than we would like (Service Pack 2 for Windows NT 4.0 is almost infamous in this regard, in fact).

4

Based on our experience, the best approach to installing IIS 4.0 is as follows:

1. Install Windows NT Server 4.0 on a blank computer.

2. Install any additional services or drivers from the original CD-ROM.

3. Apply Service Pack 3.

4. Install IE 4.0.

5. Install IIS and any related components from the Option Pack.

If you install any items from the original CD-ROM or install OEM- or vendor-supplied drivers, services, or applications, you should always reapply the Service Pack. But keep in mind that each time you apply the Service Pack, you are once again in danger of losing your system. Service Packs replace numerous important system components, including DLLs and VXDs; thus, it is not uncommon for some applications or the system as a whole to fail immediately after a Service Pack is applied.

 For more information on Service Packs, please visit the Windows NT Server Web area and follow the appropriate menu selections to the Service Pack area. The steps required to download Service Pack 3 are outlined in the earlier section "Requirement: Service Pack 3" and are similar to the steps required to download IIS 3.0.

If you find the Web site interface for obtaining Service Packs difficult and complex, you are in good company. It sometimes seems that Microsoft doesn't want you to know about problems with its software products and goes out of its way to make it difficult to access fixes. Alternatively, you can jump straight to the FTP area where Service Packs are stored by using the following URL in a Web browser or by using server name and directory location inside an FTP client. Here's the URL (which when dissected means an FTP server named **ftp.microsoft.com**, in the BUSSYS/WINNT/… subdirectory under an anonymous login in an FTP client):

ftp://ftp.microsoft.com/bussys/winnt/winnt-public/fixes/usa/nt40/

INTERNET EXPLORER 4.01

Internet Explorer 4.01 for Windows NT 4.0 is included with the Option Pack. IE 4.01 is required for use with certain aspects of IIS 4.0 (particularly MMC) and for several of its related components. Be sure to install IE 4.01 immediately after installing SP3 and before installing IIS or any of the other applications from the Option Pack.

As of this writing, Internet Explorer 4.01 is the latest Web browser from Microsoft. This revolutionary tool grants users a wider range of access to Internet- and intranet-based content than previous implementations did. IE4 supports reliable, secure communications across the public Internet through SSL, certificates, authenticode technology, and security zones. IE4 supports Cascading Style Sheets, Dynamic HTML, Java, ActiveX, and the XML-based Channel Definition Format (CDF) for push content. With features that include comprehensive history lists, powerful search facilities, folder-based control of favorite site URLs, and AutoComplete (which completes known URLs as soon as a sufficiently unique string has been entered), navigating and using IE4 is simple, fast, and elegant.

As an IIS administrator, however, you'll also use IE4 to interact with the online documentation and to perform local site tests. Nevertheless, IE4 is the best browser for your internal and Internet users to employ when interacting with your IIS-4.0-based Web sites. In fact, the remote HTML administration tools that enable site operators to manage their Web document collections across the Internet work best when they are used with IE4. You will probably find yourself using the Option Pack CD-ROM to install IE4 on all your network clients.

For more details about IE4, please visit the Microsoft Internet Explorer Web area at **www.microsoft.com/ie/**.

IIS FEATURES

The features list for IIS 4.0 is huge. Microsoft spent considerable time and effort to improve IIS 3.0. The fruits of its labors show in the broad range of features, functions, support, and capabilities that were added to IIS 4.0. In the following sections, many of these features will be highlighted; they are also covered in more depth and detail in subsequent chapters in this book.

INTERNET STANDARD SERVICES

As mentioned earlier, IIS 4.0 is fully compliant with the HTTP 1.1 standard. This includes support for persistent connections, pipelining, chunking, host headers, and more. Some of the most important client/server communication features added to HTTP 1.1 include HTTP **PUT** and HTTP **DELETE** for easier Web publishing. HTTP **PUT** uses HTTP to transfer files to a Web server, and HTTP **DELETE** deletes files from a Web server. Support for HTTP 1.1 does not exclude browsers that conform only to HTTP 1.0 from interacting with IIS 4.0. IIS 4.0 maintains backward compatibility; if an older browser accesses the server, the software simply responds by using an HTTP level that is supported by that browser.

As part of IIS's ability to host multiple Web sites off of a single IP address, it includes backward-compatible support for older browsers that do not provide native support for host headers. *Host headers* are delivery and communication mechanisms used by IIS to distribute data for multiple Web sites by using transferred session information. Where host headers are not supported, IIS uses a less-sophisticated method to "multiplex" Web sites. Basically, when host headers are in use, the responsibility for tracking the location of a particular browser within a Web site returns to the server instead of remaining with the client.

 With the addition of native support for NNTP and SMTP, Web authors, administrators, and visitors can stay more informed, and avenues of communication are broadened.

IMPROVED SETUP AND ADMINISTRATION

IIS 4.0 is easier to set up than ever before, especially the version that's distributed as part of the Windows NT Server Option Pack. With that offering, it's also no longer necessary to install each IIS component separately; the Option Pack permits all (or some) of them to be installed together. This kind of setup integration permits installations of IIS that are not only more powerful, but also more likely to be properly configured right from the start. In addition, any options not initially selected can be added easily without complicated reconfiguration or reinstallation.

The upgrade path from IIS 2.0, IIS 3.0, or even IIS 4.0 beta 3 is relatively painless. Microsoft has taken great pains to ensure that when you install the final release over an existing installation, as much configuration and setup information as possible is maintained. This provides easy upward migration without requiring the entire Web server to be reconfigured.

If you're not installing from an Option Pack, IIS's setup utility pulls its distribution files from Microsoft's Internet site. One significant benefit of this installation method is that only those distribution files needed for the components you selected will be downloaded. Also, when other components are added to an existing installation, only those distribution files you need to add the new components will be downloaded. This permits fast, efficient Internet installation of this product and its ancillary components.

Much like the batch or unattended installation facilities for Windows NT, IIS installation can also be automated. An answer file guides the setup process, thereby eliminating any need for human intervention. Automated installations simplify the IIS deployment process on enterprise intranets or on mirrored or distributed Web hosts.

A new paradigm for systems management—namely the MMC—is introduced to Windows NT through IIS 4.0. MMC, which is a standard feature in the forthcoming Windows NT 5.0 release, revolutionizes IIS administration and management tasks (and will soon have an impact on every other aspect of

Windows NT configuration and management, as even a cursory inspection of Beta 2 for this product will quickly demonstrate).

A related feature of MMC is the modular nature of each management utility. Most of its components can be launched from the Windows NT command line. This gives administrators a wider range of control over their systems. Because command-line administration can be applied from any command line— provided a network target is identified—this facility permits scheduled execution of batch files to perform routine IIS management tasks, either locally or across the network.

4

IIS also permits individual site operators to be identified and specific areas of management access assigned to each one. This facility allows specific Web site operators to obtain access to a broad range of administration controls for their particular sites without granting carte blanche to an entire Web server. This more granular set of access controls greatly simplifies the distribution of management responsibilities for multisite IIS installations. Site administrators may be granted total control over their sites, but they will be unable to make security or configuration changes to other such sites, nor will they be permitted to manage or change the Web server itself.

IIS even supports configuration replication. This allows multiple IIS installations to behave as if they were a single logical server. All configuration settings that apply to a master IIS server will be replicated automatically to all other "slaved" IIS installations. This technique provides an affordable way to increase the handling capacity for any heavily visited Web site simply by creating additional copies on other machines across which user visits can be distributed to spread out the processing load.

A wider range of flexibility is available through the Web-site-specific application of special ISAPI (Internet Server Application Programming Interface) filters (an alternative to the CGI invocation methods used on other Web servers). The advantage that ISAPI has over CGI is that a CGI invocation requires a system to launch or access a separate process in which to run the underlying code, whereas ISAPI is designed to run within the same process space occupied by IIS. This produces better performance because ISAPI does not incur the kind of system overhead that process spawning used for CGI imposes. It also provides better resource utilization because ISAPI code can share resources and memory with IIS rather than requiring more expensive parameter-passing techniques to move data from the server to a CGI program and back again.

For IIS installations that host multiple Web sites and maintain separate instances of ISAPI filters, administrators have the ability to fine-tune each site individually. This provides great flexibility for supporting interactive pages or other kinds of Web documents that must accept and react to input from users.

With version 4.0, IIS's logging capabilities are expanded to support standard W3C extended logging formats and techniques. These industry-standard logging formats permit administrators to customize Web logs and to take advantage of a broad range of third-party products that have been developed to analyze and interpret the contents of such logs. Even better, IIS 4.0 log files can be configured to record only those information fields that are considered to be important or relevant to a site and to exclude all others. This produces smaller logs, delivers more focused data, and helps support faster server performance. As with previous versions of IIS, the 4.0 logging system also supports COM-designed custom logging capabilities.

WEB APPLICATIONS

With the tight integration of several applications from the Option Pack, IIS's ability to support distributed Web applications is greatly improved. Transactional ASP files enrich commerce and business communications by improving script management. ASP files can execute specific transactions within the context of the Microsoft Transaction Server. Therefore, if a script fails, the transaction is aborted and no data will be left in an uncertain state. This provides a more secure, reliable, and faster communication link between business partners and between vendors and their customers.

IIS 4.0 is also more immune to failed processes than previous versions. With IIS 4.0, it's possible to launch each application or subprocess in a separate Windows NT virtual machine. This approach isolates each Web site and application from the core IIS system. Then, should any Web site or application fail or stall, the rest of the system will not be affected and will continue to run unabated. Then, when a failed application is requested, IIS can restart that process by creating a new virtual machine in which the application will run. This provides IIS with a crash-protection system and enables automatic recovery from process failures. By launching each process separately, individual components can even be loaded and unloaded from memory as needed without restarting the entire IIS environment.

With IIS 4.0, script programmers can reap the benefits of the built-in Microsoft Script Debugger. This tool provides realtime interactive feedback when you are designing and troubleshooting Active Server Pages. This is a great deal easier than creating such pages with regular file outputs to produce trace values for subsequent analysis, which was the only debugging technique available to ASP programmers in earlier IIS implementations.

Using the clustering services of Windows NT Server Enterprise Edition, IIS can perform server failover. For example, if two sites are hosted on two separate IIS installations and one of the servers fails, the other server can automatically take over and host both sites if the proper kind of equipment and software is in place.

The Microsoft virtual machine, which provides Java support, has been updated to improve performance, provide more robust applications, and support server-side component execution.

IMPROVED SECURITY AND AUTHENTICATION

With the addition of the Certificate Server to IIS, organizations are now able to establish their own X.509 digital certificate authorities. This improves client or customer recognition and provides improved certificate and identity authentication services. Likewise, improved SSL protocol support grants IIS greater control over secure communications. *Server Gated Crypto (SGC)* is an extension to SSL that grants IIS the ability to use 128-bit encryption.

Some firewall filtering capabilities, such as refusing service based on a client's domain, are also built into IIS 4.0. This feature can be used to block unwanted access or to simply restrict access to a limited number of users.

CONTENT CONTROL AND ADMINISTRATION

IIS 4.0 incorporates several improvements in the area of managing and controlling Web site content. Index Server 2.0 adds a vastly greater range of indexing and searching capabilities than Index Server 1.0 supplies. A powerful search engine in its own right, Index Server permits HTML documents, text-only files, Microsoft Office documents, Adobe PDF files, and numerous other file formats to be searched online. When used in conjunction with ASP, ActiveX, and SQL, Index Server is much more than a typical search engine.

Given the widespread concerns about approved or age-controlled content, IIS also supports the assignment of content ratings on a per-document or per-site basis. Currently, IIS uses PICS (an XML-derived notation that stands for Platform for Internet Content Selection) rating labels to define a Web resource's content. This permits monitoring software to forbid access to inappropriate content based on the values of such rating labels.

Because of the need for immediate, accurate, and up-to-date information, it can sometimes be critical to know how old or how fresh a document is. Through assignment of content expiration dates, IIS can inform you and your users whenever a document's content has aged beyond a preset threshold date. One primary purpose of this feature is to tell proxy and caching systems when to refresh resources pulled from a Web server; another is to remind content developers that it's time to revisit and possibly replace what might be outdated content. Given IIS's support for event-based email, using such expiration dates to trigger messages to document owners is a natural extension of the system's capabilities.

IIS can add redundant information, standard information, or control data to documents as a header or footer. This reduces author responsibilities and ensures consistency across all documents on an entire Web site.

In the IIS environment, client-focused error messages can be customized to provide more specific information or to route users to new locations for more information should they seek it. Errors can forward users to other documents, return informational documents, or even launch applications. This certainly beats inflicting the three-digit HTTP error codes on hapless users, and it provides an opportunity to solicit their feedback about errors when they are sent to a forwarding page. These kinds of error-handling techniques can help to put a more human touch on your Web site.

As a scaled-back version of Site Server, Site Server Express can be used to replicate the content tree of an entire server to another server. This one-to-one replication feature simplifies distributed Web hosting, site management, site backup, and new site rollouts. Finally, a new system for defining directory and file aliases or redirection improves your abilities to send or forward users from one Web document or URL to another Web document or location.

IMPROVED DOCUMENTATION

One of the most often overlooked features in IIS is its documentation. All the IIS documentation can be accessed through a Web browser, even when IIS is not functioning (see Figure 4.3). This Web-based documentation is similar to the standard Help system found in Windows. The IIS documentation can be perused on a content or title basis, by keyword, or by using a full-text search engine. With support for numerous multimedia enhancements, step-by-step tours, and interactive tutorials, the documentation for IIS 4.0 is a marked improvement over that for previous versions of this software.

IIS AND WINDOWS

IIS 4.0 is designed for deployment on Windows NT Server 4.0 or Windows NT Server 4.0 Enterprise Edition. Theoretically, IIS 4.0 can support an unlimited number of simultaneous Internet/intranet Web users (but please read license restrictions within the IIS documentation to decide which restrictions apply to your particular installation). Despite IIS's open-ended capabilities, network and Internet communications media and hardware can limit access to Web sites, especially for those that handle large numbers of users or high volumes of traffic.

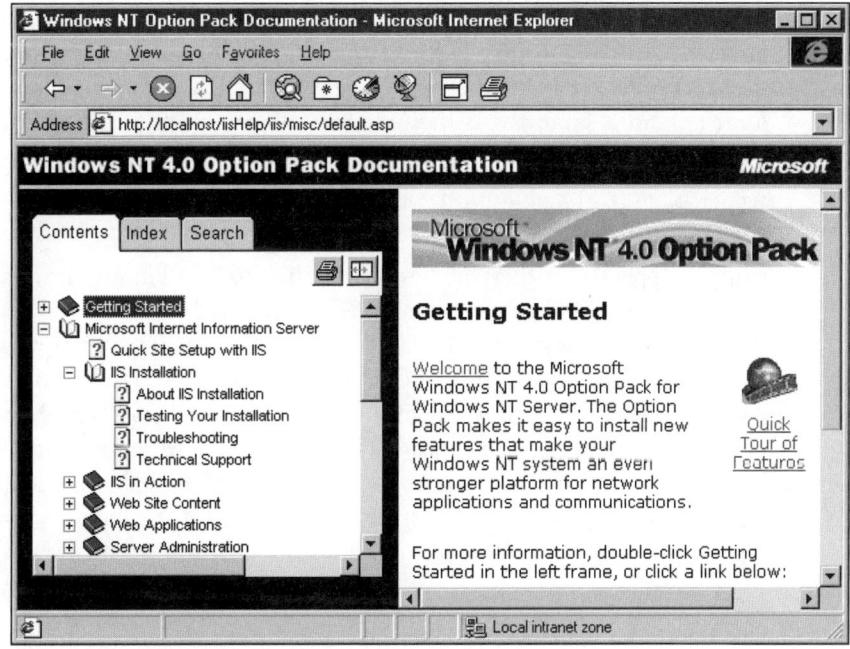

Figure 4.3   The Option Pack Documentation, as seen through
Internet Explorer 4.01.

To Windows NT 4.0 Workstation, Windows 98, or Windows 95 users, Microsoft offers Personal Web Server (PWS) 4.0, which includes most of the improvements found in IIS 4.0. However, PWS does not include Site Server Express, Index Server, or Certificate Server. Also, PWS is not designed to support high-volume data transfers or large numbers of users; rather, PWS is limited by its license agreement to support only 10 simultaneous connections. Its primary purpose is simply to provide content sharing within an intranet workgroup or among a small group of friends or co-workers across the Internet.

IIS On Your Intranet

Today's networks are adapting quickly to users' needs for the same wide range of information services, applications, and protocols that existed previously only on the Internet. The move to Internet-originated services within private networks has spawned the development of intranets and extranets. An *intranet* is a network that uses TCP/IP and one or more information services within a private, restricted environment to change or improve communications; the term is meant to indicate that it creates an Internet-like environment within the confines of a particular organization. On the other hand, an *extranet* represents a subsection of a private network built specifically for two or more organizations to share (usually, all must be served by the same communications provider, who provides a backbone that links all the parties). Extranets often provide high-speed Internet access to their participants, but such access is usually controlled from behind a protective structure (firewall, proxy, etc.) that sits between the extranet and the Internet.

Web-based documents and information make up the most common information service deployed on intranets and extranets. With an ever-expanding range of applications, the Web has proven itself to be a kind of universal interface to almost every kind of computer and for most kinds of services. Although some areas are still being explored and perfected, it is clear that most network operating systems and user applications are heading squarely to the Web. You've probably already noticed a growing trend for products to claim Web, HTTP, or HTML compliance or support. That's because the near ubiquity of Web browsers actually makes it easier for developers to build products that support this variety of interfaces and formats—a clear case of making a virtue out of a necessity.

Using IIS on your intranet gives you a head start if you're following this trend. If you transform your current internal methods for communications, scheduling, document tracking, collaboration, and project management into one or more multifaceted Web-based applications, you can realize some startling benefits. These include improved productivity, simplified training, reduced costs, increased quality and quantity of information, improved auditing and tracking, simplified workflow, and more.

IIS 4.0 and the other components of the Option Pack were designed to aid you in developing and deploying Web-based applications. You'll be hard-pressed to find another set of products that is as well integrated, that offers as broad a range of functionality and capability, that provides such high performance, that complies with so many standards, and that is supported by as many third-party vendors as IIS.

CHAPTER SUMMARY

Proxy Server 2.0 has three central software or environmental requirements: Windows NT Server 4.0, Service Pack 3, and Internet Information Server 3.0 (or greater). IIS 2.0 shipped with Windows NT Server 4.0; it was actually included on the distribution CD-ROM. IIS 3.0 was released within a few months after NTS's August 1996 release date. The current version, IIS 4.0, was released in late 1997.

IIS 3.0 expanded and improved the capabilities off IIS 2.0. IIS 3.0 is a fast, easy-to-manage information services application that performs well on its native NOS platform of Windows NT Server 4.0. IIS takes full advantage of Windows

NT Server by relying on it to manage security, to monitor performance, and to support network communication. There are five key components or elements of IIS that are sometimes referred to as the IIS toolkit: Active Server Pages, Index Server, NetShow, FrontPage Server Extensions, and Crystal Reports.

Internet Information Server 4.0 (referred to as IIS or IIS 4.0) is the latest full-release version of the standards-based Web and FTP application server from Microsoft. It's designed to operate on the Windows NT Server 4.0 network operating system. IIS is an Internet-standards-compliant HTTP server that offers FTP and several other valuable Web/FTP-related services. IIS 4.0 grants you the ability to design, create, deploy, and manage Web sites of any size.

IIS 4.0 offers HTTP 1.1 support with full backward compatibility with HTTP 1.0 for older browsers. HTTP 1.1 offers significant improvements in performance (as much as 50 to 100 percent in some circumstances), which results in a more responsive Web experience for your users. The performance improvements of HTTP 1.1 and IIS 4.0 are a result of pipelining, persistent connections, chunked transfers, and proxy support.

Microsoft no longer distributes IIS 4.0 as an individual, separate product. IIS 4.0 is now an integral part of the Windows NT 4.0 Option Pack. This collection of products contains IIS 4.0 (and its subcomponents), Service Pack 3, Internet Explorer 4.01, Transaction Server 2.0, Message Queue Server Standard Edition, Site Server Express, and Connection Services for Microsoft RAS.

IIS offers a useful collection of management and administration tools to give you complete control and insight into the operation of your Web server and its related components. In addition, by using the IIS Administration Objects (IISAOs), you can create customized interfaces to meet your particular needs or workflows. Local management is performed through a new IIS snap-in for the Microsoft Management Console (MMC). Remote management is performed through the HTML administration interface—an ASP- and JavaScript-based Web tool.

With the improved fine-grained control and flexibility inherent in its object properties, IIS offers more specific control and information about an entire Web server or any individual Web site on a multihomed server. By defining properties properly on a Web server, a Web site, a virtual directory, or even individual files, you can exercise more control over your Web site and its constituent parts. Secure Sockets Layer (SSL) 3.0 security can be assigned to individual directories rather than to an entire Web site. Fine-tuned content controls can also improve performance by reducing the number of metering or logging tasks spawned by the server for each client request for some document or object.

Previous versions of IIS required that each Web site hosted on an IIS server have its own unique IP address. IIS 4.0, with the use of HTTP 1.1 host headers, enables multiple Web sites to be hosted on the same IP address. A single IP address for multiple Web sites reduces administration, allows more sites to be hosted from a single installation, and reduces the costs associated with IP registration, address management, and leasing.

Any multihomed installation of IIS can offer guaranteed bandwidth to each site via bandwidth throttling. Therefore, higher-priority sites or sites with greater popularity can be allocated a larger portion of available bandwidth to ensure rapid response to their clients.

Because IIS 4.0 is tightly integrated with Windows NT Server, little additional knowledge is required to administer this application. Most of the management and administration tools used by NT Server may also be used to manage and control various aspects of IIS. User accounts, including the anonymous accounts, can be managed through User Manager For Domains. Performance Monitor and Network Monitor can be used to locate bottlenecks, to track system performance, and to isolate network communication problems.

IIS 4.0 includes an updated and improved Index Server 2.0. Index Server brings site content indexing and searching to IIS-hosted Web sites. A set of default or customized interface query forms offers users a wide range of search options. With support for ASP, use of SQL queries, new content filter types, multiple language support, improved performance, fine-tuned scope/range control, updated cache management, and new MMC administration, Index Server 2.0 is a full-featured content search engine.

Certificate Server gives individual Web servers the ability to issue, revoke, and renew X.509 digital certificates for clients. Such certificates are used to ensure a client's identity, to maintain status information about clients and certificates, and to circumvent manual user authentication. Certificate Server also supports SSL and Private Communications Technology (PCT) protocols for authenticated, secure communications.

An express version of the Microsoft Site Server is included with the IIS 4.0 Option Pack. This application gives you a wide variety of analysis tools to keep tabs on your Web sites and several publishing utilities for creating and publishing content. The Site Server Express Usage Import And Report Writer translates cryptic IIS log files into easy-to-read documents that contain information such as hits, user information, length of stay, and more. The Content Analysis module creates a visual representation of a Web site and can check for broken links. The program's Web Publishing Wizard makes it easy for content developers to post new documents to an IIS-based Web site.

The integration of Microsoft Transaction Server (MTS) into IIS 4.0 has brought new robustness, fault tolerance, and programmable extensibility to IIS and Web applications. MTS allows distributed transaction applications to be developed for

IIS. It simplifies Web application development for multiuser environments by providing much of the basic low-level system interaction structure. Through MTS, each Web application can be launched as a separate process that can persist beyond a single client request, and its operation and system resources will not interfere with IIS or any other active Web application.

As distributed Web applications become more commonplace, communications between applications, or among distributed components of a single application, become increasingly important. The Microsoft Message Queue (MSMQ) Server enables applications to communicate through a message queue even when remote systems are offline. Because MSMQ integrates with MTS, the range of flexibility and the fault tolerance of distributed Web applications are greatly enhanced.

4

Internet Connection Services (ICS) is an extension and upgrade for Windows NT Server's Remote Access Service (RAS). ICS adds several enhancements to RAS, including customizable client dialers, centrally controlled network phone books, new RADIUS authentication support, and improved administration and management tools. ICS was designed to help reduce ISP and connectivity costs, to improve and simplify end-user operation, and to enable new Internet business solutions.

IIS now includes an SMTP client service that allows Web applications to send and receive email messages. In addition, Web server events can trigger email notification to administrators. The SMTP service gives the Web server an email message box in which error messages, user feedback, or undelivered messages can be deposited for manual administrator processing.

With added NNTP support, IIS can host discussion groups. These discussion groups can be accessed using a standard Web browser with appropriate plug-ins or through any NNTP-compliant newsreader. The version of NNTP that ships with IIS is designed to host private discussion forums and does not support news feeds or message replication from global Usenet NNTP news services.

Because IIS supports numerous standard data access models and components, Web applications obtain broad communication capabilities with databases or other information delivery systems. IIS includes ActiveX Data Objects (ADO), Remote Data Service (RDS), and Open Database Connectivity (ODBC) drivers. In addition, the IIS 4.0 Software Development Kit (SDK) contains detailed documentation about developing custom methods and interfaces for existing components; the custom methods and interfaces can enhance Web applications that use ASP, custom IIS configurations, unique model and object types, logging adaptations, and server extensions.

The Microsoft Script Debugger can be used to easily debug ASP and several types of programming scripts—such as Visual Basic Scripting Edition (VBScript), JScript (Microsoft's JavaScript), and Java—to simplify Web application development.

The Microsoft Management Console (MMC) is a new management, administration, and control interface for Windows NT. Every significant component of IIS has an associated snap-in that provides administrative control over that component and its related objects. MMC can be accessed through a Web interface or controlled via command-line instructions by the new Windows Scripting Host (WSH), a language-independent scripting host for 32-bit Windows platforms.

In its continued effort to develop true distributed applications, Microsoft has created a framework called Distributed interNet Applications (DNA). DNA is Windows based and enables the deployment of scalable, multitiered, distributed applications over any kind of network. Basically, DNA is a system that defines an underlying programming structure that enables all the components and related services within IIS, Windows NT Server, and network clients to interact reliably and efficiently.

Service Packs are Microsoft's method for correcting bugs and errors found in its software products once they've gone to market. A Service Pack is a collection of replacement code, patches, error corrections, new applications, version upgrades, or service-specific configuration settings that correct, replace, or hide the deficiencies of some original product. Service Packs are typically downloaded from the Microsoft Web site or FTP area, but SP3 for Windows NT 4.0 is part of the Option Pack. This is not just a convenience; SP3 is required to run IIS 4.0 and related components. Be sure to install SP3 before attempting to install IIS or any other application from the Option Pack.

Internet Explorer 4.01 for Windows NT 4.0 is included in the Option Pack. IE 4.01 is a requirement for IIS 4.0 and several of its related components. Be sure to install IE 4.01 immediately after installing SP3 and before installing IIS or any of the other applications from the Option Pack.

All of IIS 4.0's documentation can be accessed through a browser, even when the IIS server is not functioning. The Web-based documentation is similar to the standard Help system found in Windows. The documentation can be perused by content, title, or keyword or through a full-text search. This documentation includes multimedia enhancements, step-by-step tours, and interactive tutorials, making the IIS 4.0 documentation a marked improvement over previous versions.

IIS 4.0 is designed for deployment on Windows NT Server 4.0 or Windows NT Server 4.0 Enterprise Edition. IIS 4.0 supports an unlimited number of simultaneous Internet or intranet Web users. Users of Windows NT 4.0 Workstation, Windows 98, or Windows 95 can install Personal Web Server (PWS) 4.0, which reflects most of the improvements found in IIS 4.0. However, PWS does not include most of IIS's ancillary components, nor can it handle large numbers of users or high traffic volumes.

KEY TERMS

- **Active Server Pages (ASP)**—A Web-document technology that combines standard HTML with a programming or scripting language. This combination results in customized Web documents based on client browser, user feedback, server-side settings, or even database-stored values.

- **ActiveX Data Objects (ADO)**—Language-independent, vendor-neutral interfaces for accessing or retrieving data. They enable a single interface or control to be employed by users for interacting with multiple data sources, including databases, indexed file systems, and messaging systems.

- **applet**—The designation for a Java-based application that runs within the context of an HTML document as opposed to a full-blown Java application that runs by itself outside any Web context.

- **asynchronous communications**—An exchange of messages in which the sender can transmit a message at any time and the receiver can accept that transmission when it is convenient to do so (email, for example).

- **AutoComplete**—An Internet Explorer feature that compares user input in the IE Address box to its existing history and favorites lists and completes strings that it can recognize from this internal store of URLs.

- **bandwidth throttling**—A feature of IIS where the amount of bandwidth for all sites and/or individual sites is limited or restricted to improve overall performance or to prevent one site from hijacking all available bandwidth over the Internet/intranet link.

- **Certificate Server**—An application used to issue, verify, and revoke X.509 digital certificates for the purposes of client and server authentication and identification.

- **Channel Definition Format (CDF)**—An XML-based markup language used to package text and binary data for Web-based delivery, primarily for so-called "push" (where the server initiates the data transfer) and "pull" (where the client initiates the transfer) data transfers. Microsoft uses CDF for its Active Update technology and for various forms of push delivery.

- **chunked transfers**—An HTTP 1.1 communications feature for efficient transmission of ASP documents. A single transmission of unknown length is broken into multiple pieces of known length, which improves overall

4

performance and delivery time for an ASP page and for other documents of unknown length.

- **Common Gateway Interface (CGI)**—A standard specification associated with HTTP that defines how Web browsers can communicate with and request services from Web servers; also names a format and syntax for passing data from browsers to servers through HTML-based forms or document-based queries in HTML.

- **counter**—When used in the context of the Windows NT Performance Monitor, an attribute of a registered object for which Performance Monitor can collect or monitor data or events. Counter data provides the basic data for Performance Monitor reports.

- **Distributed interNet Applications (DNA)**—A new programming architecture developed by Microsoft and used to design scalable, multitiered, distributed computing solutions over any type of network.

- **Event Viewer**—An NT administration tool used to view NT System, Security, and Application logs where details of system-level operation errors, audit events, and application operation events are recorded.

- **event-based email**—Email messages that are issued by a program in response to the occurrence of certain events; IIS 4.0 supports this type of messaging in response to errors or other recognizable server events.

- **File Transfer Protocol (FTP)**—The protocol used to transfer files to and from remote servers located across a TCP/IP-based network.

- **firewall**—A special-purpose Internet access server that sits between the public side of an Internet connection and the private network to which it is attached; it filters inbound traffic to deflect unauthorized access and outbound traffic to limit users to appropriate sites and to deny access to inappropriate sites.

- **FTP server**—A network application that fulfills requests from FTP clients for files.

- **host headers**—A delivery and communication mechanism used by Internet Information Server (IIS) to distribute multiple sites by using transferred session information that allows multiple Web sites to be hosted over a single IP address.

- **HTML Administration (HTMLA)**—The Web-based administration tool that enables remote management of IIS from any Web client.

- **HTML Document**—A text file that contains properly formatted HTML markup and textual content—among possible other items such as scripting language, graphics, and multimedia files—that a Web browser interprets to create a formatted display of the content (also referred to as a Web document).

- **HTTP 1.1**—The latest standard version of the HTTP protocol used to support communications between a Web server and a Web client. HTTP 1.1 includes pipelining, persistent connections, chunked transfers, and improved proxy support, which ultimately result in a 50 to 100 percent performance improvement.

- **Hypertext Markup Language (HTML)**—The programming or typesetting type of language used to create Web documents.

- **Hypertext Transfer Protocol (HTTP)**—The high-level, TCP/IP-based transport protocol used to move requests for documents and user input from a Web browser to a Web server; it is also used to move Web server replies to user requests (usually HTML documents and ancillary document elements) to a user.

- **IIS Administration Objects (IISAOs)**—Automated objects used to control an entire server programmatically. IISAOs enable command-line administration via scripts or command prompts, customized interfaces, and automation of common tasks.

- **Index Server**—An IIS add-on application that brings site-content indexing and searching to Web sites. With support for ASP, use of SQL queries, new content filter types, multiple language support, improved performance, fine-tuned scope/range control, updated cache management, and new MMC administration, Index Server 2.0 is a full-featured content search engine.

- **Internet Connection Services (ICS)**—An extension module to Windows NT Server RAS that adds customizable client dialers, centrally controlled phone books, new RADIUS authentication support, and improved administration and management tools.

- **Internet Explorer**—The Microsoft Web browser. IE4 offers reliable secure communications over the public Internet through the use of SSL, certificates, authenticode, and security zones. IE4 supports Cascading Style Sheets, Dynamic HTML, Java, ActiveX, and the Channel Definition Format (CDF) for push content. With features such as history, search, favorites, and AutoComplete, navigating and using IE4 is simple, fast, and elegant.

- **Internet Information Server (IIS)**—The Web and FTP network server application developed by Microsoft for the Windows NT platform. Its latest release, IIS 4.0, includes several new features and enhancements that simplify the process of developing and deploying Web applications and Web sites.

- **Internet Server Application Programming Interface (ISAPI)**—A Web-server-specific API defined by Microsoft and Process Software Corporation and designed to permit Internet browsers to access remote server applications and services more efficiently than the standard Common Gateway Interface (CGI).

4

- **Internet Service Provider (ISP)**—A commercial operation that's in the business of reselling bandwidth for connections to the Internet; ISPs usually offer all kinds of consulting, programming, and networking management services in addition to Internet access.

- **JavaScript (JScript in Microsoft terminology)**—A standard text-based scripting language that may be included within HTML documents to support interactivity, to invoke external programs, or to perform basic tasks on behalf of the document in which it appears.

- **Message Queue Server (MSMQ)**—An application that manages the communications between multiple applications or components within a single computer or across networks.

- **message replication**—An important aspect of a full-blown NNTP service, message replication represents the mechanism whereby new messages from newsgroups are propagated (and old messages are deleted) across the Internet from their points of origin to all other NNTP servers that carry the newsgroup's contents.

- **Microsoft Management Console (MMC)**—A Windows-based tool that provides total management of all services and applications within a single utility. The MMC is also Active-Desktop capable and will eventually be used to access management and control aspects of the entire Windows NT system. In fact, Windows NT 5.0's control mechanisms center around snap-ins for MMC.

- **Microsoft Script Debugger**—An IIS tool that offers programmers a simplified method of debugging and troubleshooting ASP applications. This tool supports several common scripting languages, including Visual Basic Scripting Edition (VBScript), JScript (Microsoft's JavaScript), and Java.

- **Network Monitor**—The NT administration tool that captures packets of network traffic sent to or from a single server. Captured packets can be filtered and their contents examined. Network Monitor is not a full-fledged network sniffer; however, the SMS (Systems Management Server) version of Network Monitor is a fully functional network sniffer.

- **Network News Transfer Protocol (NNTP)**—The TCP/IP protocol that defines a network news transport service. NNTP is the Internet standard for exchanging Usenet messages, but it may also be used for transport of threaded messages for private newsgroups (as is the case for the NNTP Services included with IIS 4.0).

- **network operating system (NOS)**—A software product that controls the basic system-level functions of a computer's devices (hard drive, video, keyboard, etc.) and also has the ability to participate in a network as either a server or workstation. A NOS typically grants the computer the ability to access resources from other computers and to offer its own resources out to the network.

- **newsfeed**— A source of NNTP newsgroup messages and traffic usually associated with Usenet or a private news replication service.

- **NNTP Services**—The IIS add-on that allows discussion groups to be hosted within a single server. This is not a full-featured NNTP server; it cannot interact with Usenet newsfeeds.

- **object**—When used in the context of Performance Monitor, an object refers to a named entity within the NT operating system (or some entity from an external application that registers with Performance Monitor) for which data can be acquired and monitored at the OS level.

- **Open Database Connectivity (ODBC)**—A Microsoft database-programming interface that uses standardized programming language components to enable Windows-based applications to access databases over a network.

- **Option Pack**—The Windows NT 4.0 Option Pack is a product release for Windows NT Server and NT Workstation. The Option Pack contains IIS 4.0 (and its PWS 4.0 equivalent), plus several other components, including Service Pack 3, Internet Explorer 4.01, Transaction Server 2.0, Message Queue Server Standard Edition, Site Server Express, and Connection Services for Microsoft RAS.

- **patch**—A special type of code fix, often associated with Service Packs, where binary code for an operating system or application is edited in place, permitting changes to be applied to the code without replacing entire files.

- **Performance Monitor**—The Windows NT administration tool that is used to monitor the performance of the network, the computer, applications, and even subsystems.

- **persistent connections**—A communications method used by HTTP 1.1 where a single communication link between a client and server is used to transfer multiple objects associated with a single resource request. This reduces the communications overhead of establishing, maintaining, and tearing down these connections (which is high in comparison to the amount of data sent over them) and results in faster performance.

- **Personal Web Server (PWS)**—A "light" version of IIS that ships with Windows NT Workstation, Windows 98, and Windows 95. PWS was designed for small-scale data and document sharing and supports a maximum of 10 simultaneous connections at any time.

4

- **pipelining**—A communications method used by HTTP 1.1 where clients do not need to wait for a confirmation or completion of each request before sending another, which improves response time and reduces the time required to display the requested resource.

- **Private Communications Technology (PCT)**—A security protocol for Web-based commerce and financial transactions. PCT supplies authentication and encryption capabilities designed to work with credit card processing on the Web. Sometimes defined as Personal Communications Technology.

- **proxy**—A product or tool used for several purposes, including isolating a private network's client identifiers (IP Address, NetBIOS name) from the Internet, caching commonly accessed sites on a local server, allowing multiple users to employ a single Internet connection, and enabling an entire network to access the Internet without requiring IP addresses to be reissued or reconfigured. IIS's support for HTTP 1.1 includes extended support for proxy servers, meaning IIS documents are able to inform proxy servers of the expiration date of each resource to force refreshing.

- **proxy support**—Technology for including freshness information in documents or data records; designed to inform proxy servers about when and how cached data must be refreshed or reloaded.

- **Remote Access Service (RAS)**—A series of facilities built into Windows NT (single connection at a time for Windows NT Workstation, unlimited connections for Windows NT Server) that provides dial-in access to NT, and in turn to the network to which that machine is attached. RAS also provides dial-out access for machines with network access to a RAS Server (Windows NT Server only).

- **Remote Data Service (RDS)**—A feature of IIS that enables client-side data caching in Web applications to reduce server traffic and overhead.

- **Routing And Remote Access Service (RRAS)**—An update to Windows NT RAS (originally appeared in Windows NT SP2) that adds software-based routing services to basic RAS and provides important patches and fixes to the original RAS release.

- **Secure Sockets Layer (SSL)**—A Transport-layer technology for data encryption and authentication between a Web browser and a Web server. Originally developed by Netscape, SSL has become a de facto industry standard to negotiate point-to-point security between a client and server. SSL sends data over a numbered IP socket, which is a secure channel defined at the TCP/IP connection layer.

- **server failover**—The process whereby one server in a clustered or linked Windows NT Server group can take over for another member of the group should that member fail.

- **Server Gated Crypto (SGC)**—An extension to the SSL specification that gives IIS the ability to use 128-bit authentication technology (it is therefore unavailable outside the U.S. because of export restrictions on such encryption/authentication technology).

- **Service Pack (SP)**—A patch/fix released by Microsoft to correct bugs and errors found in the released versions of software. Service Packs are identified by number; as of this writing, three Service Packs for Windows NT have been released: SP1, SP2, and SP3. Interim updates and releases from Microsoft that occur between Service Packs are called hot fixes.

- **Simple Mail Transfer Protocol (SMTP)**—The TCP/IP protocol that governs email transmission and reception on the Internet. SMTP supports text-oriented email between devices that support the Message Handling Service (MHS).

- **Site Server Express**—An application used to analyze a Web site's usage, content, and layout. It also offers features that simplify the publishing of new documents to existing Web sites.

- **SMTP Services**—The IIS add-on that brings some email services to Web applications. Allows an IIS host to send and receive email. This is not a full-featured email server; it does not have POP support, nor does it have the ability to create multiple inboxes for email.

- **Software Development Kit (SDK)**—A programming reference, syntax guide, and development software to aid developers, vendors, and individual programmers in creating extensions, add-ons, or alterations to Microsoft software products.

- **stateless protocol**—A network protocol that doesn't maintain information about prior communications or data transfers between clients and servers; therefore, each transfer must negotiate a new connection and proceed without reference to prior or pending transfer requests and replies. HTTP is a stateless protocol.

- **TechNet**—A monthly Microsoft CD-ROM-based publication that costs approximately $299 a year and includes Resource Kits, Service Packs, Option Packs, the Microsoft Knowledge Base, evaluation copies of applications, and all kinds of other useful information about Microsoft products and technologies. Also available at **www.microsoft.com/technet**.

- **Transaction Server (MTS)**—An application and programming structure that brings transaction monitoring, fault tolerance, and distributed architecture to Web applications.

4

- **Transmission Control Protocol/Internet Protocol (TCP/IP)**—The standard protocol suite atop which the Internet and intranets operate. TCP/IP is named after the reliable connection-oriented TCP transport protocol and the underlying connectionless IP network protocol.

- **Uniform Resource Locator (URL)**—The primary naming scheme used to identify Web locations and resources. URLs define the protocols to be used, the domain name of the server where a resource resides, the port address to be used for communication, and the directory path to access a named Web document or some other resource.

- **User Manager For Domains**—An NT administration tool used to manage user accounts and group memberships within a network.

- **VBScript**—Abbreviation for Visual Basic Scripting Edition, which is a version of Microsoft's Visual Basic programming environment designed for use within a variety of applications (including Web documents) to add basic programming and interactive capabilities.

- **virtual machine**—A concept that applies to Windows NT (and numerous other operating systems) wherein applications behave as if they have exclusive access to a computer because the operating system gives them a private address space and allows them to behave as if no other programs are active on a machine. Windows NT automatically launches all 32-bit applications, each within its own virtual machine; IIS 4.0 makes it possible to run individual IIS components and add-ons within their own virtual machines as well.

- **Web object**—Any component or subcomponent of a Web document that is required to complete, build, or produce the final formatted outcome desired by the document's creator. A Web object can be an HTML file, an ASP document, a Java applet, a graphic, a multimedia file, or a database interface component.

- **Web server**—A network application that fulfills requests from Web clients (Web browsers) for Web documents from a Web site.

- **Web site**—A collection of Web documents that focus on a single purpose or content topic and are linked together to form a cohesive whole. A Web server can host multiple Web sites, a Web site can comprise several Web documents, and a Web document can comprise several Web objects or components.

- **Windows NT Server 4.0**—The latest version of the network operating system developed by Microsoft. This software product boasts several key features, including security, fault tolerance, high performance, central administration, scalability, and auditing.

- **Windows NT Server 4.0 Enterprise Edition**—A scaled-up release of Windows NT Server 4.0 designed specifically for enterprise network deployment. It boasts several key improvements, including server clustering, 4GB memory tuning, eight CPU SMP support, and Microsoft Message Queue Server.

- **X.509**—That part of the international ITU-T X.500 Security Recommendation that deals with Authentication Frameworks for Directories. X.509 also includes a specification for a digital certificate that binds some recognizable entity's distinguished name (such as a username, a server name, and so forth) through the use of a digital signature, which contains the name of the certificate issuer (also known as a certificate authority) as well.

4

REVIEW QUESTIONS

1. IIS 4.0 supports HTTP 1.1. Which feature of HTTP 1.1 enables a single IP address to host multiple Web sites?

    a. chunked transfers

    b. pipelining

    c. persistent connections

    d. host headers

2. IIS 4.0 supports HTTP 1.1. This means that Web browsers that do not support this HTTP standard (that only support HTTP 1.0) will be unable to access any resources hosted by IIS 4.0. (True or False?)

3. What is the HTTP 1.1 communications feature that allows a client to send multiple requests to a Web server without waiting for a confirmation or response?

    a. pipelining

    b. persistent connections

    c. chunked transfers

    d. proxy support

4. The Windows NT 4.0 Option Pack includes several add-ons or additional applications that can be installed along with IIS 4.0. Which of the following items appear in the Option Pack?

    a. Transaction Server 2.0

    b. Site Server Express

    c. Message Queue Server Standard Edition

    d. Routing And Remote Access Service Update

5. What are the means by which the Option Pack can be obtained?

   a. Download it from Microsoft Web site.

   b. Obtain it from the Option subdirectory on the original Windows NT Server 4.0 distribution CD-ROM.

   c. Order the CD-ROM from a local reseller.

   d. Purchase the Windows NT Server 4.0 Enterprise Edition.

6. Which items, components, or applications must be present on the server before you install IIS 4.0?

   a. Service Pack 3 for Windows NT 4.0

   b. NetBEUI

   c. Internet Explorer 4.01

   d. Windows NT 4.0 Workstation

7. Which tool or utility permits IIS 4.0 site operators to remotely manage their Web sites?

   a. IIS MMC snap-in

   b. Server Manager

   c. HTMLA

   d. Script Debugger

8. What type of IIS 4.0 objects can be used to control an entire server programmatically?

   a. Web objects

   b. IIS Administration Objects (IISAOs)

   c. file system objects

   d. SMTP objects

9. What administration component of Windows NT 5.0 is already available to users of Windows NT 4.0 when they install IIS 4.0?

   a. Microsoft Management Console

   b. Microsoft Transaction Server

   c. Microsoft Message Queue Server

   d. Microsoft Administration System

10. The logging capabilities of IIS 4.0 are such that you can reduce the size of the log file by instructing the system to record Web document hits instead of hits to each Web object. (True or False?)

11. IIS 4.0 settings and configuration can be saved to a file. If an undesired change is made to the IIS configuration, this file can be used to roll back to the previous configuration. (True or False?)

4

12. Which of the following items can be defined on a directory basis (as opposed to a whole Web-site basis) within IIS 4.0?

    a. Read and Execute permissions

    b. bandwidth throttling

    c. HTTP keep-alives

    d. SSL security

13. Which Windows NT Server utilities can be used to monitor and troubleshoot IIS activities?

    a. User Manager For Domains

    b. Performance Monitor

    c. Network Monitor

    d. Event Viewer

14. IIS 4.0 is an upgraded and improved version of the previous release, IIS 3.0. Which new features of IIS 4.0 are not found in IIS 3.0?

    a. SMTP

    b. Web

    c. NNTP

    d. Gopher

15. Which IIS tool or application can be used to provide site visitors with access to a search engine so they can locate relevant or interesting content quickly?

    a. Transaction Server

    b. Certificate Server

    c. Index Server

    d. Message Queue Server

16. Regarding the services and applications supported by IIS 4.0, which of the following statements are true?

    a. HTML, Text, Microsoft Office, and Adobe PDF documents can be searched.

    b. Client identities can be tracked and verified.

    c. A single Web server can be duplicated to three or more other servers simultaneously.

    d. Applications can communicate even if network connections are broken.

17. Which of the following capabilities are added to IIS 4.0 when Certificate Server is installed?

    a. Issue X.509 digital certificates.

    b. Allow remote applications or components to communicate.

    c. Use certificates to maintain client data.

    d. Enable Web applications to send email messages.

18. Which add-on application from the Option Pack can be used to analyze the traffic on your Web site?

a. Transaction Server

b. Message Queue Server

c. Index Server

d. Site Server Express

19. When you install IIS 4.0 over an existing installation of IIS 3.0, you will be forced to reconfigure all settings and redefine all virtual directories. (True or False?)

20. Which component from the Option Pack adds RADIUS authentication support to Windows NT?

a. Message Queue Server

b. Internet Connection Services

c. Transaction Server

d. NNTP Service

21. Active Server Pages can be made error free through the use of which IIS 4.0 utility?

a. Java Virtual Machine

b. Microsoft Script Debugger

c. W3C logging

d. ODBC drivers

22. With the NTTP Service installed, IIS 4.0 can host an entire Usenet newsgroup newsfeed. (True or False?)

23. Which of the following database components are supported by IIS 4.0?

a. ActiveX Data Objects (ADO)

b. Remote Data Service (RDS)

c. Open Database Connectivity (ODBC)

d. Routing And Remote Access Service (RRAS)

24. The documentation for IIS 4.0 and all components available on the Option Pack can be accessed through a Web browser. What special capabilities does this method offer users?

a. listing by keyword

b. listing by topic

c. interactive tutorials

d. full-text searching

25. IIS is designed as a robust Internet Web and FTP server; therefore, it cannot be used within a private network or intranet. (True or False?)

26. HTTP **PUT** uses HTTP to transfer files to Web clients. (True or False?)

27. HTTP **DELETE** uses HTTP to delete files from a Web server. (True or False?)

28. Internet Explorer 4.0 must be installed to support IIS 4.0 installation and configuration. (True or False?)

29. Which of the following represents a source for Windows NT Service Pack 3.
    a. the Microsoft Web site
    b. the Microsoft FTP site
    c. the TechNet CD-ROM
    d. the Windows NT 4.0 Option Pack

30. Which of the following statements best defines bandwidth throttling?
    a. a method to restrict bandwidth for IIS Web sites on a per-site basis
    b. the phenomenon that occurs when the Internet slows down because of heavy loading
    c. an intranet-specific method for controlling access to IIS-based Web sites
    d. a way of providing guaranteed bandwidth for individual Web sites on multihomed IIS servers

HANDS-ON PROJECTS

In the projects that follow, you will visit the Microsoft IIS Web site, traverse the Windows NT Option Pack CD-ROM, and review some of the other Web servers on the market today, all to familiarize you with IIS. To complete these projects, you will need access to the Internet and the Windows NT Option Pack.

PROJECT 4.1

In this project, you will explore the Microsoft Internet Information Server Web area. To complete this project, you must have Internet access and a Web browser. Preferably, your computer should be running Windows NT Server 4.0 and Internet Explorer 4.01.

To explore the IIS Web site, follow these steps:

1. Boot your Windows NT Server computer.
2. Open your Web browser by double-clicking on the Internet Explorer icon. This automatically connects you to the Internet and the IE window opens.
3. Select Open from the IE File menu. The Open dialog box appears.

4. Type "www.microsoft.com/iis/" in the Open dialog box Open field and click on OK. The IIS Web area eventually loads and displays in your browser.

5. Click on the Product Guide item on the menu on the left side of the document. A submenu of additional items appears.

6. Click on the What's New item below Product Guide. The What's New document appears.

7. One by one, select and read each of the documents below the Product Guide top-level menu item.

8. Select the next top-level menu item. One by one, select and read each of the documents below each of the top-level menu items.

9. Select the Home Page top-level menu item. This returns you to the original document loaded in Step 4.

10. Click on the Windows NT 4.0 Option Pack hyperlink on the right side of the document. The Windows NT 4.0 Option Pack Web page loads.

11. Review each of the top-level menu items and their subitems on this document.

12. Exit Internet Explorer.

PROJECT 4.2

In this project, you will explore the Windows NT 4.0 Option Pack CD-ROM. To complete this project, you must have a computer running Windows NT Server 4.0 and Internet Explorer 4.01. In addition, you'll need the Windows NT 4.0 Option Pack CD-ROM.

To explore the Option Pack CD-ROM, follow these steps:

1. Boot your Windows NT Server computer.

2. Place the Windows NT 4.0 Option Pack CD-ROM in the CD-ROM drive. Internet Explorer automatically launches and displays the Welcome screen from the Option Pack CD-ROM.

3. Click on the Learn About hyperlink on the left-hand side of the document. This displays a document listing the contents and brief descriptions of the Option Pack. Read this document.

4. Click on Release Notes on the left-hand side of the document. This displays the release notes for the Option Pack. Read this document.

5. Click on Install on the left-hand side of the document. This displays the list of items required to install IIS and the Option Pack components.

6. Click on the Real License Information hyperlink. This displays the License for the Option Pack. Read this document.

7. Click on Internet Explorer's back arrow to return to the Install document. No other actions can be taken from this document since selecting any of the other links will launch the installation of Option Pack components. Installation of IIS and Option Pack components is discussed in later chapters.

8. Close Internet Explorer. Eject the Windows NT 4.0 Option Pack CD-ROM from your CD-ROM drive.

PROJECT 4.3

In this project, you will continue to explore the Windows NT 4.0 Option Pack CD-ROM. To complete this project, you need to have a computer running Windows NT Server 4.0 and Internet Explorer 4.01. In addition, you will need to have the Windows NT 4.0 Option Pack CD-ROM.

To explore the Option Pack CD-ROM, follow these steps:

1. Boot your Windows NT Server computer.

2. Place the Windows NT 4.0 Option Pack CD-ROM in your CD-ROM drive.

3. After Internet Explorer loads automatically, close it.

4. Select Start|Programs|Windows NT Explorer.

5. Select the CD-ROM drive letter in the left pane of Windows NT Explorer. The CD-ROM's root contents are displayed in the right pane.

6. Notice the multiple folders that appear on this CD-ROM. The AUTORUN.INF file automatically launches Internet Explorer with the <CD-ROM drive letter>:\SETUPCD\WINNT.SRV\INSTALL.HTM file when the disc is inserted in to the CD-ROM drive.

7. Double-click on the WINNTSP3 folder in the right pane. The folder opens and displays its contents in the right pane.

8. Double-click on the SPREAD.TXT file. A text editor opens and displays this text file. Read this document and then close the text editor.

9. Close Windows NT Explorer. Eject the Windows NT 4.0 Option Pack from the CD-ROM drive.

PROJECT 4.4

In this project, you will explore the WebServer Compare Web site. To complete this project, you'll need Internet access and a Web browser. Preferably, your computer should be using Windows NT Server 4.0 and Internet Explorer 4.01.

To explore the WebServer Compare Web site, follow these steps:

1. Boot your Windows NT Server computer.
2. Open your Web browser by double-clicking on the Internet Explorer desktop icon. This automatically connects you to the Internet and the IE window opens.
3. Select Open from IE's File menu. The Open dialog box appears.
4. Type "webcompare.internet.com" in the Open dialog box Open field and click on OK. The WebServer Compare Web area eventually loads and displays in your browser.
5. Select Microsoft Internet Information Server from the long list of servers under the Quick Compare heading on the left side of the document. A review of the major features of this product is displayed. Read or scan this document.
6. Select Netscape FastTrack Server from the long list of servers under the Quick Compare heading on the left side of the document. A review of the major features of this product is displayed. Read or scan this document and compare the features to those of IIS.
7. Select WebSite Pro from the long list of servers under the Quick Compare heading on the left side of the document. A review of the major features of this product is displayed. Read or scan this document and compare the features to those of IIS.
8. Select Purveyor WebServer from the long list of servers under the Quick Compare heading on the left side of the document. A review of the major features of this product is displayed. Read or scan this document and compare the features to those of IIS.
9. If you wish, review any of the other listed Web servers.
10. Close Internet Explorer.

 **C**ASE **P**ROJECTS

1. Your supervisor has assigned you the task of selecting a Web server to be deployed throughout your enterprise network to support internal private Web sites. Write a three-to-four-paragraph report explaining the benefits of using IIS 4.0 in this situation.

2. IIS supports HTTP 1.1 and boasts a significant performance improvement because of its support for those Web browsers that also support HTTP 1.1. Write a three-to-four-paragraph report explaining how HTTP 1.1 can offer performance improvements and include the four significant features of HTTP 1.1 discussed in this chapter.

3. The Windows NT 4.0 Option Pack includes IIS and several other components. These components are designed to work together as a tightly integrated Web-applications platform. Write a paragraph about each of the major components found in the Option Pack.

4. IIS 4.0 offers a wide range of management and administration tools and capabilities. Write a four-to-five-paragraph report discussing at least four methods, tools, or processes that can be used to manage and/or administer IIS 4.0.

5. IIS 4.0 boasts a more secure and controlled environment for Web applications. Write a three-to-four-paragraph report briefly discussing at least five methods, processes, or applications that can be used to enhance or control the security and reliability of IIS-hosted Web sites.

PLANNING YOUR PROXY SERVER IMPLEMENTATION

The first step in deploying Microsoft Proxy Server 2.0 is to determine exactly what you need. Making this determination is a multipart process. You need to be aware of your current network capabilities, know the extent of Internet access you wish to enable, and determine whether Proxy Server will provide you with the features and control required for your specific situation. In this chapter, we'll discuss how to avoid deployment failures by assessing your needs for Proxy Server 2.0.

AFTER READING THIS CHAPTER AND COMPLETING THE EXERCISES, YOU WILL BE ABLE TO:

- Plan your Proxy Server deployment
- Determine your current and required network capacity
- Assess your Internet access needs
- Understand why the Internet is such a useful resource
- Understand the services and capabilities offered by Proxy Server
- Design a network and Proxy Server layout
- Locate and select a worthwhile ISP
- Determine your bandwidth needs
- Plan out the hardware needs of the Proxy Server host

AVOIDING DEPLOYMENT FAILURE

The one factor that most often determines whether an installation is successful is planning. Planning involves several phases, including understanding your current capabilities, determining your current needs, extrapolating your future needs, and finding a viable solution. Failing to seriously ponder each phase can result in poor performance, inadequate capacity, or service denial (in other words, a deployment failure).

When you are planning future network capacity, it is important to determine what services, users, or data will be present on the network. Take the time to complete a thorough needs assessment. A bit of formal analysis now will ease the process of upgrading and configuring the system later. Don't succumb to the "easy way out." Planning is a long and arduous task that is overlooked far too often. We cannot stress just how important ample planning is in regard to Proxy Server installation.

NETWORK CAPACITY

The *capacity* of a network is its ability to support the amount of data transmitted over it. A network that can support the activity of your organization today may not be able to support the increased activity level when Internet access is offered via Proxy Server. You need to carefully consider the performance ramifications of adding new information services to an already overtaxed network.

Proxy Server's ability to cache oft-accessed resources only saves on performance over the Internet communication link (labeled "ISP Link" in Figure 5.1); it does not decrease the amount of data ultimately transferred to the client (labeled "private network" in Figure 5.1). Even if 100 percent of requested data is stored in the proxy server's cache, it will still traverse your network to the client computer. This means an increase in network traffic on your private network.

You should use Performance Monitor and Network Monitor to obtain or define a baseline profile of the performance levels of your current network. This involves sampling various aspects of your network over several days. Then examine these readings to decipher what is normal and abnormal about how your network performs. This includes pinpointing what areas of your network experience the most load and which users or applications are causing the most traffic.

Compare the actual traffic and performance levels on your network with the known capacity of the hardware that makes up your network. For example, if you are using 10Mbps NICs and hubs on your network, and the average

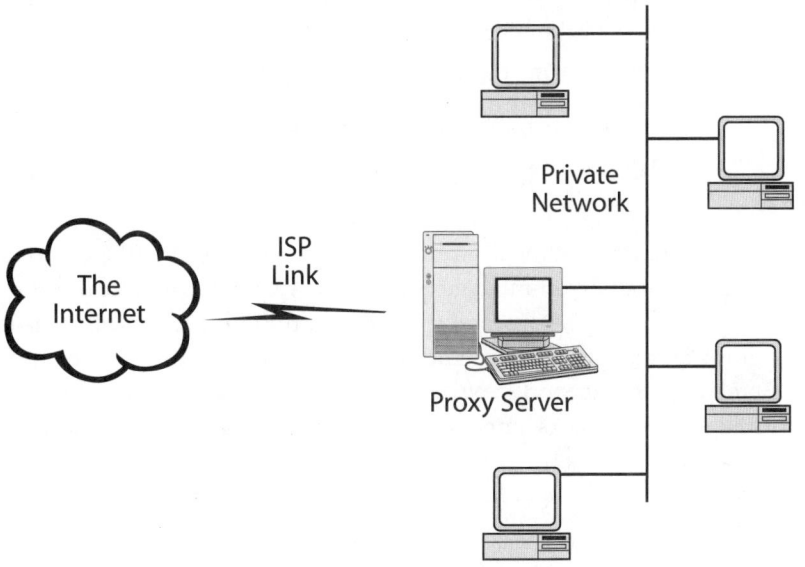

5

Figure 5.1   A typical configuration among Proxy Server, the Internet, and a LAN.

network load is around 7 or 8Mbps, then you have little room for additional traffic. A network operating consistently at 70 percent of available capacity would experience a severe performance degradation if Internet information services were added to the existing system.

Even if your network has little or no room for additional traffic, it does not rule out the ability to add information services moderated by Proxy Server. It does demand one of two courses of action, however: Either decrease or restrict current internal activities or upgrade the capacity of the system to accommodate the additional traffic.

Adding one or more Internet information services to your current network services or capabilities will increase network traffic levels significantly. More often than not, this requires that the capacity of your network be expanded. Ultimately, the amount or level of hardware needed by your network is in direct relation to the level of information transferred or stored on that network.

When you are considering a capacity expansion, you should also consider these additional points:

- How many new information services will you allow or enable over Proxy Server?

- Will access to these information services be restricted by user, group, time, or data size?

- Will additional storage capacity on clients and servers be required?

- Will the user community grow significantly in the next year?

- At what point of community or user growth will additional capacity be required?

Obviously, some of the answers to these questions cannot be determined exactly. But the process you must go through to even estimate a reasonable or ballpark answer should give you useful insights into the intricacies and relationships of a growing network. The insights you gain will enable you to avoid performance problems. All networks experience a high rate of growth, thus, many forecast values are difficult or impossible to predict. But good estimates are always worth the effort. Failing to plan ahead and include significant room for growth—typically 40 percent additional capacity or more—will quickly result in network overload.

ASSESSING THE NEED

Assessing your needs consists of making a list of the services and features required on your network to improve or expand its current capabilities. This list can include information services, security restrictions, and content sources. To help you focus on this process, we have included many of the questions you should ask yourself:

- What are the top three reasons you need to add Internet access to your network?

- How will your products and/or services be improved with Internet access?

- If you don't add Internet access, will your organization remain as a leader in your field? If so, for how long?

- What are your current needs? Will they really be met by simply adding Internet access?

- Has your organization been too quick to adopt previous business technologies only to have them fail to produce promised results?

- What network or communications technologies have been deployed within your organization most recently?

- If you could do things over, would you deploy these same technologies again? If so, would you deploy them in the same way and in the same time frame?

- What benefits and drawbacks did you reap from the deployment?

5

- Is Internet access just today's latest business fad, or does it really offer solid tangible benefits?
- What is the opinion of your competition regarding Internet access on their private network?
- Will your organization be able to enjoy the specific benefits of Internet access? Do the benefits fit your business model or product field?
- Have other companies in your field added Internet access to their networks? If so, what results have they obtained?
- What is the return on investment (ROI) for adding Internet access to your current network?
- How will your products' and/or services' profit margins be affected by Internet access?
- What effect, if any, will Internet access have on your business, and will customers or consumers be able to recognize or care about it?
- Is the addition of Internet access to your current network approved by the governing body of your organization?
- Does this governing body understand the technology and the ramifications it can have?
- Who is ultimately responsible for the deployment of Internet access on your network?
- Are improvements to the network properly funded? Are they included in the budget?
- If budgeted funds are insufficient, what part of deployment can be sacrificed?
- If extra funds remain after deployment is complete, what will be done with the surplus?
- What exactly are you expecting to occur once Internet access is added to your system?
- Once basic Internet access is deployed, will the network have the capability of supporting expanded services and functions?
- What Internet information services will be supported, allowed, or deployed?
- What capabilities and services are you expecting to deploy or derive from Internet access?
- What capabilities and services will you prevent or deny in relation to Internet access?

- If full open access is not granted, what restrictions will be in place and who will determine them?

- Why are these restrictions necessary?

- Are decisions about restrictions open to discussion?

- What is more important, service reliability or speed of access?

- What compromises are you willing to make to sustain reliability over speed (or vice versa)?

- What content filters will be put into place? Who is responsible for implementation and maintenance of these filters?

- Will filtering result in improved productivity?

- What is the opinion of users about content restrictions?

- What penalties will be enforced against users who violate (or attempt to violate) access restrictions?

- What is the purpose of the restrictions, rules, and regulations on access or services?

- Do access restrictions improve your organization's products and services?

- Have you documented the logic used to construct or describe your security or restriction system?

- What does "user satisfaction" really mean to you and your organization?

- Knowing that Internet access is typically 1/10 to 1/100 slower than local network access, what level of performance do you require or expect for each user accessing Internet resources? (That is, do you want 56Kbps per simultaneous user, or is 28Kbps or even 10Kbps sufficient?)

- To improve your network's performance, what services or capabilities are you willing to sacrifice?

- If your Internet access links go down, what projects, tasks, or abilities will be affected?

- What level of data transfer (i.e., use of bandwidth or network load) do you expect to occur on your network after Internet access is enabled?

- If this level doubles, can your network continue to provide adequate performance?

- What are the traffic patterns over a typical workday or workweek?

- What are your current and expected peak load times?

- What contingencies are in place to handle high network loads?

- What level of sustained network activity will prompt you to upgrade the system?

- What will it cost to improve the internal network's bandwidth?

- Are your current network media (NIC, hubs, repeaters, cables, etc.) upgradeable, expandable, or replaceable?

- Do you need a dedicated or on-demand Internet connection?

- Will the majority of information flow out from your network or in from the Internet?

- What restrictions on "outsiders" do you plan to implement?

- Will traveling or home-based users be allowed to connect via remote access or VPN?

- How important is it to restrict or control access to your internal information?

- What does your organization consider a security breach?

From this lengthy list of questions, you should be able to derive a clear perspective on your present situation and what you can afford, what you want, or what you need in terms of Internet access. Gaining this knowledge is an important step in the process of deploying any new technology, including Proxy Server 2.0.

WHY CONNECT TO THE INTERNET?

The Internet is the worldwide communications network that supports the largest conglomeration of knowledge and information in history. The Internet connects people from around the world to information of all kinds and to each other. Many businesses have discovered the benefits the Internet offers in the areas of productivity, communication, service, and quality. Although the Internet is not without its failings and nonprofessional material, connecting to it is a useful and worthwhile task.

There are several solid business reasons to make Internet access a staple on an organization's network. In the following sections, we'll highlight some.

IMPROVED CUSTOMER ACCESS

The Internet gives customers a 24-hour interface point with your organization. No matter what the service or product, a Web or FTP site can give remote employees and customers the added value, support, or information they need—exactly when and how they want it. You can provide email access, online help, troubleshooting, and product updates without burdening or increasing your present staff. Or you can host a newsgroup or forum where customers can get help in a timely manner.

However, improved access for customers also opens the door to access from undesirable sources. Proxy Server offers several features to improve the border security of your network, including limited access for public consumption, controlled or restricted access to authorized users, and denial of service for identified points of hostility.

REMOTE ACCESS

Depending on the nature of your organization, you may be able to offer virtual private network (VPN) links to customers, branch offices, or vendors. VPN links will provide you with reliable, secure network-to-network communication without the expense of leased long-distance links. Also, through a single Internet connection, multiple end users or LANs can connect back to your LAN, which eliminates the expense of maintaining multiple modems and access lines.

CONTENT CONTROL

By attaching your network to the Internet, you'll have several new opportunities to share or profit from existing warehousing of data. Depending on your organization, you can filter some of your nonconfidential data for public viewing. You can also provide additional levels of data access to authorized users, vendors, or customers. Republishing and repackaging existing data is a sure way to improve the productivity and profitability of every man-hour and project.

ONLINE MARKETING AND ADVERTISING

Once you are online, your ability to cheaply and easily disseminate marketing propaganda and advertisements is expanded. However, before your eyes glaze over with the thought of blanketing the world with a daily advertorial, remember that the Internet is a consumer-regulated market. There are both acceptable and unacceptable forms of capitalism. Requested mailings, Web sites, banners, focused newsgroups, and specialized chat sessions are palatable. Global email and unsolicited or off-topic postings (a.k.a., *spamming*) are vigorously opposed and often affronted.

RESEARCH

The Internet is a vast, ever expanding collection of information. By mining the data that exists on the Internet, many organizations have discovered methods for improving their products and services or for creating new products and services. For example, you can review and parse existing data banks or perform focused surveys and questionnaires; these methods can provide you with a wealth of information that is unobtainable by any other means.

COMMUNICATION

Without exception or pause, the Internet has become the most important communication medium since the spoken word. There is no faster, cheaper, more reliable, or more direct method of communication, nor is there one that is more user- and environmentally friendly. Short of transferring a physical object from point A to point B, the Internet is the best way to communicate.

PROXIED INTERNET INFORMATION SERVICES

5

Proxy Server 2.0 has many capabilities, including conglomerated access, content caching, and firewall security. But most users will only care about the information services they can access through Proxy Server. Fortunately, Proxy Server 2.0 offers a wide range of capabilities that support most of the currently available communication protocol technologies in use on the Internet today. Through one or more of the proxy subsystems—Web, WinSock, and SOCKS—nearly every data service can be accessed by users located behind Proxy Server.

The most common Internet information services are email, Web, and FTP. But they are not the only services with which users will want to interact. Others include streaming multimedia, Internet Relay Chat (IRC), and Network News Transfer Protocol (NNTP) Usenet newsgroups. In fact, many information service protocols are already built into Proxy Server; plus, you can expand coverage to other protocols via the WinSock or SOCKS proxy services.

Web Proxy supports those protocols and communication mechanisms typically associated with Web documents, access, and interaction. This includes support for Hypertext Transfer Protocol (HTTP), Secure HTTP (HTTPS), File Transfer Protocol (FTP), Gopher, and Transmission Control Protocol/Internet Protocol (TCP/IP).

WinSock Proxy supports client applications designed around the Windows Sockets API. This includes utilities and services such as Telnet and RealAudio. This proxy subsystem is also able to deliver content over TCP/IP or Internetwork Packet Exchange/Sequenced Packet Exchange (IPX/SPX). In other words, with WinSock Proxy, a LAN can operate with IPX/SPX and still be able to access WinSock Internet applications. Other protocols supported by WinSock Proxy include AlphaWorld, AOL, Archie, Echo, Enliven, IMAP4, IRC, Microsoft NetShow, MSN, NNTP, POP3, SMTP, and VDOLive.

SOCKS Proxy is a cross-platform network service that creates a secured communications link between a client and a server. SOCKS Proxy supports SOCKS 4.3a and offers non-Windows or non-WinSock applications access to Internet services. SOCKS Proxy can be used for HTTP, FTP, Gopher, and

Telnet, but it cannot be used with services that require the User Datagram Protocol (UDP), such as RealAudio, VDOLive, or Microsoft NetShow.

PROXY SERVER 2.0 CAPABILITIES

At this point, you should have a good idea of what you need Proxy Server to accomplish for you. But you need to be sure that Proxy Server offers the features and abilities to support your needs. Proxy Server is a multifaceted product that should be examined from several different viewpoints. These viewpoints are highlighted in the remainder of this section.

Proxy Server 2.0 enables several users to use a single Internet connection simultaneously. This means that instead of a dial-up connection for every computer on the network, a single high-speed connection can sustain the Internet needs of multiple users. But just because two or more users can access the Internet over the same link, you shouldn't assume that you can get away with only installing a standard connection between a phone line and a modem. For Proxy Server to adequately support two or more users, you need a communication pipeline with enough bandwidth. This may mean an Integrated Services Digital Network (ISDN) line, a fractional T1, or even a full T1. Connection size selection is discussed later in this chapter.

Proxy Server 2.0 can also be configured to use two or more Internet connections to support the network's Internet access needs. This is typically set up by installing Proxy Server on multiple computers, each with a single communication link. The servers are tied together in a caching scheme. This is a scalability feature that allows Proxy Server to support two or more users by simply distributing the load across multiple servers and Internet connections.

Proxy Server 2.0 has true firewall capabilities to prevent external users from accessing data stored on your internal network. Control of external access is handled in several ways. One is by simply preventing IP forwarding from occurring over the Proxy Server host. Another is to properly set all permissions on resources and to require Windows NT challenge/response user authentication. Yet another is to enable inbound packet filtering so you can define what packet types are allowed into the network.

Proxy Server 2.0 can also be used to control, restrict, or prevent internal users from gaining access to external resources. This is typically called outbound access. Outbound access can be controlled in several ways: group/user permission by Internet service; resource restriction by IP address, subnet, or domain; and protocol denial by port address.

Proxy Server 2.0 can improve resource access time through its caching capabilities. *Caching* is the process of saving a copy of an accessed remote resource locally. The next time the same or another user requests that resource, it will be pulled from the local cache instead of being pulled from the Internet again. Caching greatly improves the performance and response time of Internet services, especially for larger resources or very frequently accessed resources.

Proxy Server 2.0 can impersonate a Web server, which gives you the ability to set up a Web server inside of your network but offer the site's contents to the Internet. This feature is called *reverse proxy*. It effectively proxies your internal data to external users in the same way it proxies external resources for internal users. This configuration offers you a secure Web publishing environment.

Proxy Server 2.0 has a further expansion on the reverse proxy service: *reverse hosting*. This is another form of Web publishing to the external Internet from internal Web servers. However, this feature combines or integrates the contents of multiple distinct internal Web servers into a single entity that is viewed by external users. Thus, Internet users see a single Web site instead of multiple individual servers. Once again, this type of Web publishing offers significant security and greater control over site design and layout.

Proxy Server 2.0 is able to examine inbound traffic to determine whether to allow it to pass; plus, it can intercept predefined packet types to forward them to a specific server inside the network. This is known as *server proxying*. This feature is most often used with email services when an email server, such as Microsoft Exchange Server, is located behind Proxy Server on the internal network. Server proxying offers security without sacrificing flexibility and specialized information services capabilities.

Proxy Server 2.0 helps you keep track of what actually occurs on, around, through, and near your network. The extensive logging capabilities act as an ever vigilant sentry to keep you informed of suspicious activity. Events can trigger alerts to notify you of a serious breach.

In conjunction with Routing and Remote Access Service for Windows NT Server, Proxy Server 2.0 can expand your communication and networking capabilities by adding secure VPN support. This allows remote users to establish reliable and secure network links from their remote client over the Internet to the central LAN. This greatly reduces communication costs and gives administrators central control over LAN access.

As you can see, Proxy Server 2.0 is a multifunctional product that offers many features and functions heretofore unknown in the Windows NT Server environment. Proxy Server's communication, networking, and resource access solutions are sure to meet and exceed your system's needs and your personal expectations.

PHYSICAL SERVER LAYOUT

The layout, design, and construction of your network, especially when you are connecting to the Internet via Proxy Server 2.0, is crucial to successful deployment. The configuration possibilities of a network attached to the Internet and moderated by Proxy Server 2.0 are quite varied. Depending on your needs and your particular system's initial configuration, you can deploy Proxy Server to maximize your network's strengths and to supplement its weaknesses.

The basic layout configuration is a LAN (labeled "private network" in Figure 5.1) or a workstation connected behind Proxy Server, which is in turn connected to the Internet over a single link. For most small to midsized networks, this basic layout will suffice to provide adequate proxied Internet access.

Another possible configuration is that of a proxy cache array. A proxy cache array provides load balancing, fault tolerance, and scalability. A set of Proxy Servers configured in an array act as a single unit and are administered as a single unit. An array provides a type of distributed caching where downstream Proxy Servers offload cache hits to other members of the array. This configuration is depicted in Figure 5.2.

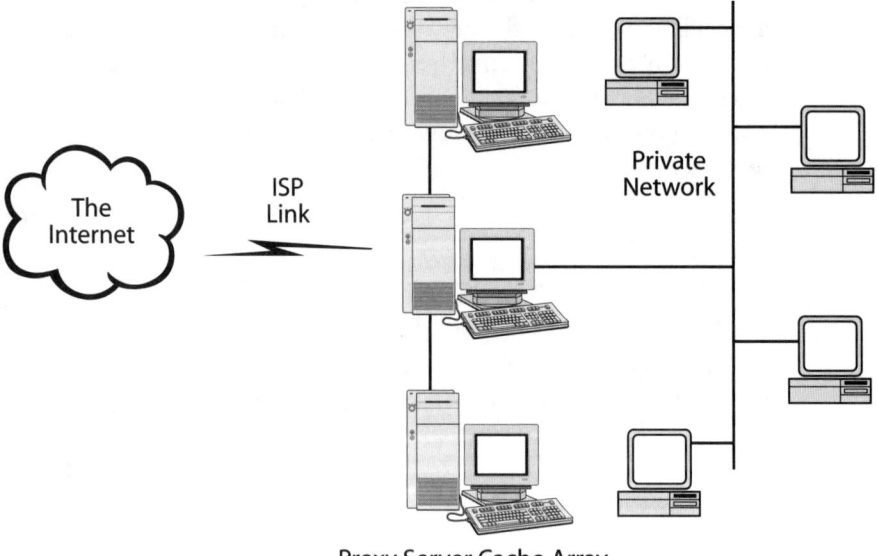

Proxy Server Cache Array

Figure 5.2   A typical configuration among Proxy Server, a LAN, and the Internet: cache array.

This configuration does not require that all of the Proxy Servers be located on the same side of the Internet connection. For example, one or two arrayed Proxy Servers can be located at the ISP with other Proxy Servers situated on the LAN. This type of layout is often used by ISPs or large organizations to improve performance and provide fault tolerance.

Another improvement or layout variation for a cache array is to add extra Internet links. This provides greater bandwidth and improves fault tolerance. The additional ISP links can be used just as often as the primary link, or they can be reserved for use only when the primary link is overtaxed, nonfunctional, or unavailable. This configuration is depicted in Figure 5.3.

The next configuration is a caching chain, or hierarchical caching. Chaining Proxy Servers is slightly different than connecting them in a array. In a chain, each Proxy Server remains an individual unit and is individually administered. When a client requests a resource, the first Proxy Server in the chain is accessed. If it cannot provide the resource, it repeats the request to the next Proxy Server. This continues through the chain until the final Proxy Server requests the resource from the Internet. This configuration is depicted in Figure 5.4.

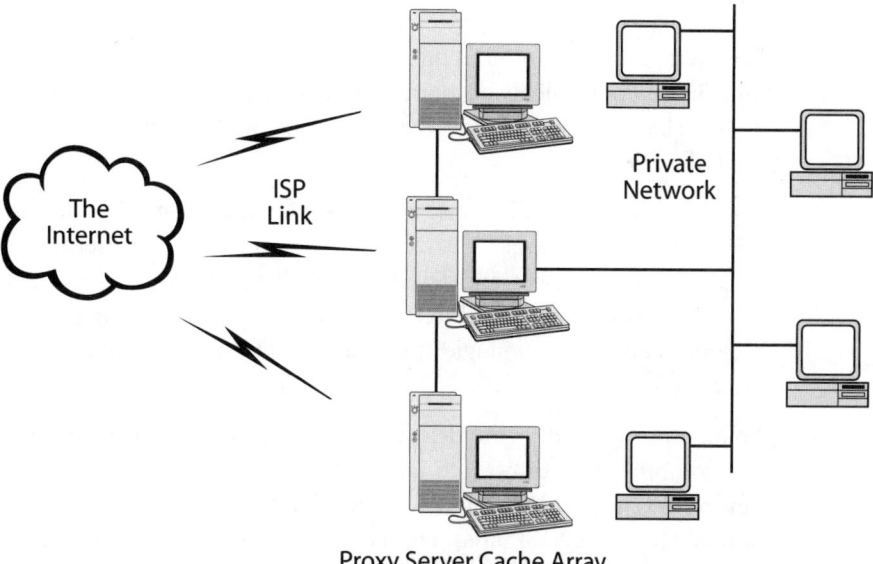

Proxy Server Cache Array

Figure 5.3   A typical configuration between Proxy Server, a LAN, and the Internet: cache array with redundant or backup ISP links.

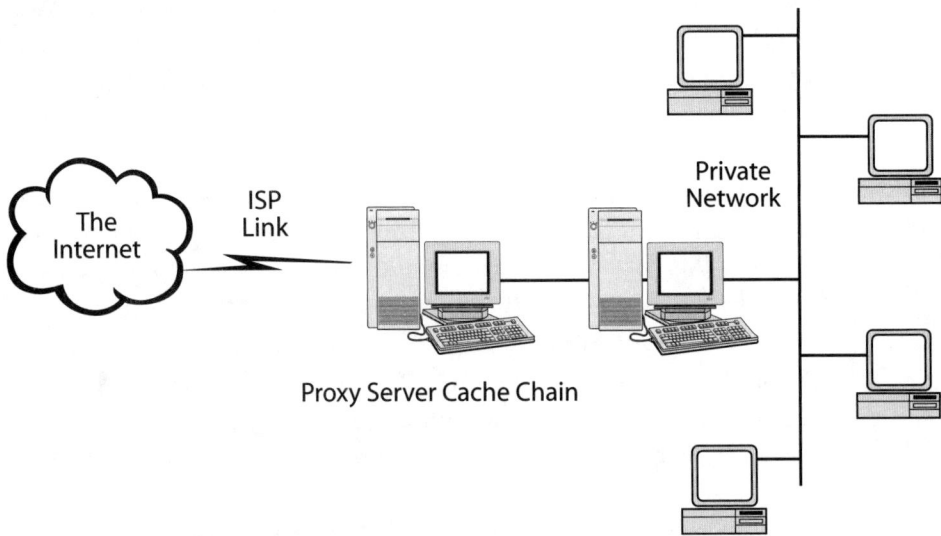

Figure 5.4   A typical configuration among Proxy Server, a LAN, and the Internet: cache chain.

At first glance, chaining may seem to be a poor-performance layout. In practice, however, spreading out caching responsibilities ultimately improves the response time. In addition, clients do not necessarily need to be pointed at the first proxy in the chain. Depending on the network layout, clients can point to proxies located further up the chain.

Cache chaining is not limited to a linear configuration. Forking is possible, in which there are multiple "first-level" proxies. These "first-level" or "down-level" proxies point to fewer and fewer "upper-level" proxies. The upper-most-level proxy is connected to the Internet. Typically, a forked chain is used to connect multiple networks to a single ISP access point. This configuration is depicted in Figure 5.5.

You are not limited to the depicted layouts we've described in this chapter. You can combine features of each layout to construct your own. For example, it is possible to connect multiple LANs via chained proxies to a cache array that has multiple redundant ISP links. This configuration is depicted in Figure 5.6.

Ultimately, let your current network layout and resource needs guide your Proxy Server deployment layout. You should consult other chapters in this book that discuss chaining, arrays, caching, and configuration to determine which options provide you with the most beneficial features.

5

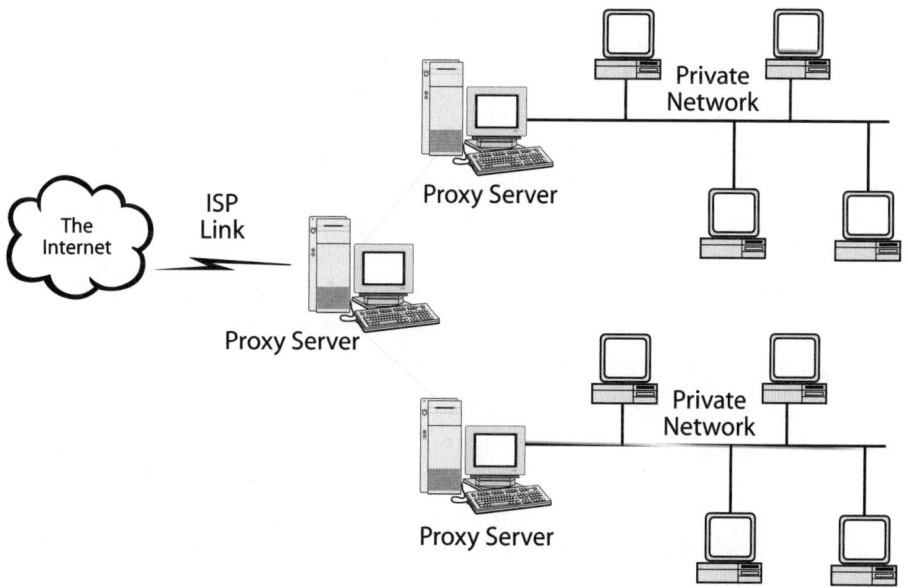

Figure 5.5 A typical configuration among Proxy Server, a LAN, and the Internet: forked cache chain with multiple LANs.

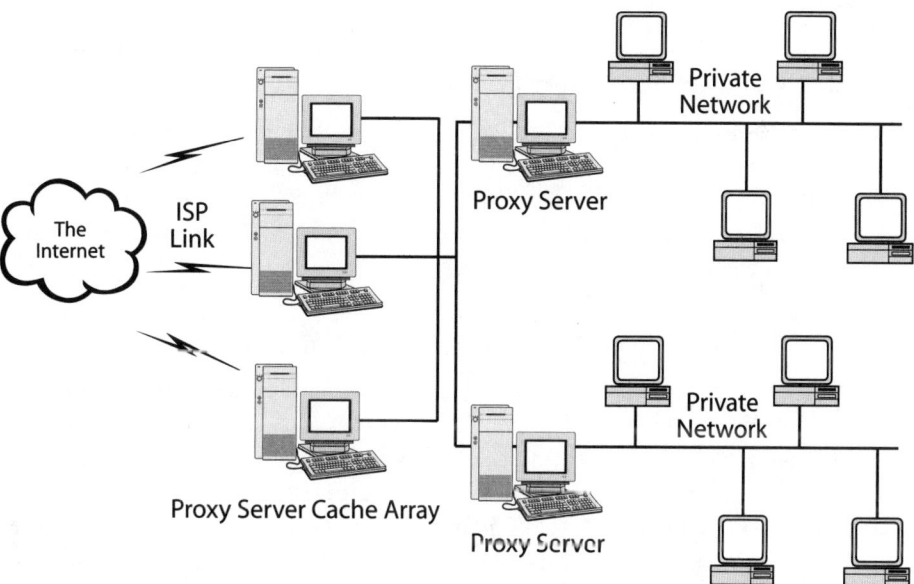

Figure 5.6 A typical configuration among Proxy Server, a LAN, and the Internet: multiple LAN caching chain linked to a cache array with multiple ISP links.

You should take note that all of these Proxy Server configurations have a few key layout features in common. First, the LAN (or workstation) has no other Internet access points other than those provided by Proxy Server. If another unrestricted Internet access pathway exists, Proxy Server will not be able to control Internet access, improve performance, or act as a firewall. Second, Proxy Server is always deployed on a computer that has no other significant purpose than to provide proxy services. If other services are active on the proxy host, security may be compromised and Proxy Server may not be able to perform its moderation functions properly. If you keep these two items in mind when you design your network/proxy layout, you should be able to avoid most layout-related problems.

There is another configuration option that you should be aware of (it is discussed in Chapter 10): using proxy on a network that is not connected to the Internet. In such a configuration, Proxy Server is used to isolate a portion of the network from the rest of the organization. This is a bit extreme and useless for small networks, but enterprise networks can extract many benefits from such a setup. You can view a large private network as a small version of the Internet and the isolated portion as a small LAN to be protected. Thus, internal proxy servers help control access to sensitive or mission-critical data, improve system performance, reduce network traffic, and give each department control over inbound and outbound resource access.

FINDING THE RIGHT ISP

Connecting your network to the Internet involves working with an *Internet Service Provider (ISP)*. An ISP is a service company that sells network access to the Internet; it purchases bandwidth in bulk and in turn resells it in smaller packages. You should evaluate an ISP in the same manner you would evaluate any other supplier or vendor.

HISTORY OF ISPs

The Internet was developed by more than random chance. Careful planning, lots of money, intense research, and over 20 years were required to establish the worldwide communication network known as the Internet. The Internet started as a research project for the U.S. Department of Defense (DOD) in the early 1970s. With the development of the TCP/IP protocol suite, large packet-switching internetworks, namely ARPANET (Advanced Research Projects Agency Network) and NSFNet (National Science Foundation Network) were created. These networks linked government agencies and university-level educational facilities to improve research and development projects. The expense for the initial network that grew into the Internet was funded by the U.S.

government. As the size of the network grew, its user base expanded from government to educational institutions to individuals.

The success of the internetwork was soon noticed by the business community. The fast, efficient communication ability of the young Internet offered business a cheaper method of communication. The Internet grew by leaps and bounds as for-profit businesses began to pour funds into the backbone and structure of the Internet. Some companies started selling access to the growing internetwork; they were the first forerunners of today's ISPs.

The Internet is not just a single large network. It is a conglomeration of thousands of networks. Some of them provide links or bridges or communication paths between other networks. The networks that support a significant portion of cross-network traffic are known as *backbones*. Backbones must be high-bandwidth, high-performance networks. The companies that own and maintain these networks sell access to their backbone to other networking companies. Eventually, an ISP sells you or your organization access to their network. Sometimes an ISP's network is directly connected to a backbone; other times the ISP is connected to a network that is connected to a backbone.

Types Of ISPs

There are three major groupings of ISPs:

- Online global/national corporations
- Small local businesses
- Hobbyists/amateurs

Online global/national corporations are those ISPs that have points of presence across the country or even around the world. Typically, you will not deal directly with ISPs of this level because they are most often in the business of wholesaling access to local business ISPs instead of end users. However, if your organization is of significant size, this type of ISP may be the only one that can adequately supply your connection needs. Service from corporate ISPs is often high, with little or no room for negotiation. And although technical support may be available 24 hours a day, 7 days a week, your specific issue or problem may not be as important to them as it is to you.

The small local business ISPs have one or only a few points of presence. Local ISPs are often more responsive to customer needs and can be flexible on service costs. The scope and value of services provided by a local ISP vary greatly, but with a little time and effort (as described later), you should be able to find a provider to meet your needs.

A hobbyist or an amateur access provider is often a small or upstart business. Most ISPs of this nature offer little in the way of value-added services, have limited bandwidth choices, and have unreliable service. We do not recommend using an amateur ISP for business Internet access.

LOCATING AN ISP

Finding the right ISP for your organization will involve some work on your part. Mainly, it requires you to seek out possible ISPs, interview them, and make an informed decision. You should be looking for a quality provider that is currently supporting professional or business customers. There are several ways to initially locate or discover ISPs, but just because an ISP is easy to find doesn't mean its service is acceptable. We suggest making a list of four or five ISPs and evaluating them in light of specific criteria we'll discuss later in this chapter.

Here are a few methods for finding an adequate ISP:

- **Word of mouth** Ask friends or colleagues for references to ISPs with which they have had experience. Because an ISP is typically an important relationship, most customers will not hesitate to let you know what they think about the service they are paying for.

- **Newspaper and magazine advertisements** ISPs commonly use print advertisements to gain attention. Check the business and technology sections of your local newspaper to see who wants your business in your area.

- **Business, competition** Ask other business owners or even your competitors who they use for Internet service.

- **Vendors** Ask your hardware and software vendor/supplier/retailer for recommendations. It is not uncommon for technical salespeople to be aware of related products and services available locally.

- **Yellow pages** The phone book is now a great place to look for ISPs. Check out the entries under Internet, Computers, Computer Services, Network, Access Providers, or Online Access.

- **Radio and television** Many well-to-do ISPs are spending the money to advertise on radio and television. But just because they can afford the expense, they shouldn't necessarily be your only choice. It does, however, mean they are making a profit, which is a good sign.

- **Search engines** All of the Web-based search engines can provide you with an extensive list of ISP possibilities. Just search for "Internet Providers", "Internet Service Providers", and "Internet Access Providers".

- **www.thelist.com** This Web site is a comprehensive database of ISPs. It is a well-organized collection of ISP information that is worth looking into.

- **Dlist** Dlist is another online resource worth looking into. Dlist, or "Definitive listing of ISPs," is an email distribution of ISP information. To get the Dlist, just send an email to **mj@ora.com.** In the body of the email message, type "request dlist". Within minutes, you'll receive an automated response that contains the list.

Once you've made a short list of ISP possibilities, run the list through the following gambit of tests.

ISP TORTURE CHAMBER

It is not impossible to switch from one provider to another, but it is fairly difficult and confusing. Take the time to ensure that everything you'll need in the foreseeable future is provided by the ISP you select. You should use the criteria discussed in the following sections to examine every potential ISP.

Technical Support

Your ISP should be able to provide you with technical support, advice, and consultation. Find out what technical support assets are available from an ISP; this includes any technical certification or education, length of experience, and troubleshooting success history. Find out the size of the technical support staff and the hours of availability. Ultimately, you'll need to make a judgment call—if you have an emergency, will your ISP be able to offer a helping hand?

You need to know if technical support is provided as part of normal service or if it is provided on a paid basis only. Most often there is a sliding scale of basic technical support.

Here are a few more items to ponder when you are making your ISP selection:

- What is covered by the ISP's technical support?
- In what area does the ISP claim they have no responsibility to aid you with a problem?
- Does technical support stop on their end of the communications link or on your network's communications device? Does it cover your clients?

Geographic Location

Because you will be using the link between you and your ISP a great deal, it is unwise to select an ISP located a great distance from your network. Connecting to an ISP in a different area code, city, or state will cost more in line charges. Most likely, you will not be using a telephone-line dial-up connection, but other dedicated digital subscriber lines have distance costs just the same. If you have a choice, closer is always better than farther away.

Internet Information Services

Usually, if you have a connection to the Internet through an ISP, you are able to access every information service type available anywhere in the world. But some ISPs have taken the liberty of restricting or blocking some of these services for various reasons. Illegal activity, too much bandwidth waste, not enough storage capacity, or nonprofessional content are all reasons you may not be able to access everything that exists on the Internet. More often than not, the restrictions imposed by an ISP will correspond to your own organization's desired access limitations, but you should still inquire about them.

Communication

Unlike most vendors from whom you purchase a product or service, you will develop a close relationship with your ISP. They are the one link in the configuration of Internet communication that can bring everything to a halt when it fails, and it's not under your control. Timely communication between an ISP and users is an important consideration. Look into the ISP's availability by phone, email, and the Web. If you fail to get a human on the phone or don't get a response to your email within 24 hours, you should look elsewhere for Internet service. An ISP that communicates with its customers is an ISP that values customer satisfaction.

Remote Connectivity

If members of your organization travel frequently, you may want to inquire about out-of-town access methods. Some ISPs have contracts with other ISPs across the country to provide their users with consistent access while they are on the road. If you plan to implement VPN services, discuss your technologies with the ISP to guarantee that its routers, gateways, and servers can handle the load and will allow the specialized connections to take place.

Payment Methods

At first glance, paying for Internet service may seem simple, but complications can surface. Ask the ISP how it expects to be paid and how invoicing or billing is handled. You should also ask about prepaid discounts for purchasing months, quarters, or years of access in advance.

Some ISPs have strict policies about missed or late payments. Make sure you understand the fine print on such infractions. Even if you are one day late, an ISP can terminate your service.

If your access needs are complicated, elaborate, or extensive, discuss ways to reduce the charges. Obviously, an ISP is in business to make money, but it also wants satisfied customers. Some payment schemes can be massaged to fit your budget or access needs. Besides, it never hurts to ask.

In general, the more speed and the longer contract you buy, the better terms you will get. Often, you'll be offered good terms up front, and you can usually negotiate down a bit. Consider negotiating more than just price. There are other useful services an ISP may be willing to provide based on your monthly commitment.

Downtime

Even the largest ISPs that span the globe have one problem in common with small local ISPs—humans run the computers and problems do occur. No service is 100 percent guaranteed. What is important is how an ISP deals with system failures and downtime. Ask the ISP about downtime history and what efforts were made to restore service. Ask if refunds or discounts are available for serious lapses in connection time.

Business Background

Never hook up your organization's network to an ISP that is less than two or three years old. Success comes with maturity, and experience has no substitute when dealing with the Internet. The longer an ISP has been in business, the more information you can find about it. Inquire with the Better Business Bureau, request customer references, ask to speak with customers who stopped working with the ISP, and look for any business report or study about it. Ask to see a business plan, financial statement, and any documents about the goals or future of the business.

Compatibility

Even the best of ISPs will be worthless to you if their hardware and software are incompatible with yours. Generally, because the communication link will be a TCP/IP connection, there is very little chance that a communication problem will exist. But if your ISP runs Unix and you are running NT, it will not be able to offer you much in the way of useful technical support if something on your end goes awry.

You can improve the compatibility of your ISP by using the same brand or manufacturer of communication device on your end of the link. When possible and practical, duplicate the computer setups and networking hardware employed by the ISP—any equipment you have in common with the ISP is another area where you can take advantage of its expertise.

Backbone Providers

An Internet backbone provides the highest quality and speed of Internet access possible. You should contract with an ISP that is as close to one or more backbones as possible. The further away from a backbone your connection is, the more inconsistent your bandwidth and response time will be.

ISP Peak Time

ISPs have hundreds or thousands of customers. You need to know when the ISP experiences its highest level of network traffic. This will be a combination of the Internet's own peak times and the ISP's customer-use patterns. You can't completely avoid peak time, but you can use this information to schedule your automated service and caching systems. Most ISPs maintain bandwidth and throughput statistics for their own use; it shouldn't take much effort to distribute this information to you.

Bandwidth Options

Your network needs will grow, and you will eventually require larger connection pipelines to your ISP. Make sure your ISP already has the next level of bandwidth available. Also make sure it has an ongoing plan for expansion: adding new levels of services as they become available and keeping them reasonably cost effective. Don't get stuck with an ISP that can only offer you modem and ISDN access.

Fine Print

Always get everything regarding your account with the ISP in writing and signed by you and the ISP. This is the only way to get what you ask (and pay) for. If it is not in writing when you sign the contract and hand over the first payment, you have no basis to demand it. Special services, unique configurations, technical support depth, and any added services must be spelled out. Every time either you or the ISP needs to alter or change the inventory of services, this document needs to be re-created or at least properly amended.

CONNECTION COSTS

Connecting your network to the Internet is going to cost you more than just the monthly fee charged by an ISP. You must take several other aspects into consideration. Cost is not always measured in dollars—opportunities, resource availability, and productivity are just as much "legal tender" in the business world.

Attaching your network to the Internet will involve considerable changes to its current configuration. This reconfiguration of your network will cost you in time, learning new technologies, purchasing new equipment, and troubleshooting the changes. If everything goes well, you can enjoy the new services; if not, you'll have to deal with the expense of lost productivity.

Spending less money on hardware, software, or ISP service may initially seem like a money saver. But if you spend more time troubleshooting problems and replacing components, you'll end up spending more than if you had purchased quality. More often than not, it is the hidden costs behind inexpensive purchases that cause the greatest loss of profit and productivity.

SELECTING A PIPELINE

Pipeline is a slang term referring to the communications link between your network and an ISP; it is the link that gives you access to the Internet. The term "pipeline" is appropriate because the ability for a connection to support significant amounts of data protection is dependent upon the size and cost of the link. Choosing the most appropriate link for your network is a bit of a guessing contest. Until you actually get everything deployed, you won't know for sure just exactly how much traffic will occur over the link and how popular Internet access will be.

Let's ignore for the moment that you will be using Proxy Server 2.0 to reduce traffic over the Internet link. We will assume each person will always pull resources directly from the Internet. This effectively defines a worst-case scenario when every user requests a resource that is not in cache. Using the following formula you can estimate the size of a connection (a.k.a. the pipeline size) required to offer multiple simultaneous users a reasonable level of Internet performance:

Number of users × Bandwidth required per user × 1.4 = Pipeline size

The number of users in this equation should be the actual user count (i.e., users who will be given access to resources over the Internet link). The bandwidth required per user equals how much data per second is minimally required for each user. This value is based on the information services supported on your network. If users only have email, a bandwidth of .5 to 1Kbps each is sufficient. But if FTP, Web, and streaming multimedia are supported, 5 to 10Kbps each may be enough. The 1.4 is a multiplying factor to add in 40 percent growth space.

For a network that has 100 Internet users who need 5Kbps each, this formula claims that a 700Kbps link would be sufficient. That would be five or six ISDN lines or a fractional T1. You may think this is too much bandwidth for such a small network because Proxy Server will be in use and rarely will all 100 users be accessing Internet resources simultaneously. Discuss your needs and plans with the ISP before making a decision to deploy less than this formula recommends. When it comes to networking, especially when connecting to the Internet, you can never have too much bandwidth. No matter what size pipeline you install, your Internet use will grow to consume every last bit of available bandwidth. Look ahead, take precautions, discuss options in-depth with your ISP, and don't spend more than you can afford.

Most ISPs will offer several options in communication link sizes and cost. Here is a list of some of the more common options:

- **Plain Old Telephone Service (POTS)** An analog communications link with a maximum bandwidth of 56Kbps.

- **Integrated Services Digital Network (ISDN)** A digital communications link with a maximum bandwidth of 128Kbps per dual-channel line.

- **56Kbps leased line** A digital communications link with a bandwidth of 56Kbps.

- **T1 and fractional T1** A digital communications link with a bandwidth of 1.544Mbps for a full T1 or in 56 or 256Kbps fractional T1 chunks.

- **Others** Several other digital communication link technologies may be available in your area with a wide variety of bandwidths. They include cable modems, Asynchronous Transfer Mode (ATM), Frame Relay, Switched Multimegabit Data Service (SMDS), Digital Subscriber Line (DSL), and Synchronous Optical Network (SONET).

Most of these options are available in either dedicated or nondedicated form. With dedicated service, you are assigned exclusive access to a specific communications port. Dedicated service guarantees your connection, but it has a price. With nondedicated service, you must compete with other users to gain access to a pool of communications ports. Nondedicated service does not guarantee access at any time and is therefore much less expensive. We recommend dedicated service for a network connection. Nondedicated service can impose complications for a network and thus should only be considered if dedicated service is cost prohibitive.

POTS

Plain Old Telephone Service (POTS) connections are the most common connection type, but they offer limited bandwidth, typically 28 to 56Kbps. POTS connections use standard telephone lines and modems to establish communication. POTS lines should not be used as the primary connection method for networks. These types of lines should be reserved for remote connections or emergency backup links.

ISDN

Integrated Services Digital Network (ISDN) is a relatively new digital communications link that can be used for network traffic, faxes, or standard voice phone conversations between other ISDN or POTS endpoints. ISDN is available in two forms—BRI and PRI. Basic Rate Interface (BRI) is made up of two 64Kbps (B) channels for data and a 16Kbps (D) channel for call management—known as 2B+D. When both B channels are in use, 128Kbps is obtained. Primary Rate Interface (PRI) is made up of 24 B channels and one D channel—24B+D. When all 24 B channels are in use, PRI has a bandwidth of 1.544Mbps (equivalent to a T1).

ISDN requires a special adapter to interface a computer with the communications network. These devices are called ISDN modems, or interfaces (they only share the namesake with POTS modems). They act just like a NIC, whereas POTS modems actually transform the digital computer signal into analog tones.

ISDN lines offer sufficient bandwidth for small-to-moderate networks. They should be considered an entry level option. ISDN can also serve as an adequate backup link if higher bandwidth options are chosen for primary links.

56Kbps Leased Lines

A 56Kbps (56K) leased line is a dedicated, high-speed communications circuit. A 56K link is a direct link between two points that bypasses the phone company central office. A 56K line can only be used to communicate directly with the network located at the other end. A Data Service Unit/Channel Service Unit (DSU/CSU) is required at each end of the link. A DSU/CSU is the device that connects a computer to the 56K communication line.

However, 56K lines are being phased out of some areas in favor of ISDN or fractional T1s. If 56K is still available, it may be a cost-effective option, but only if you don't plan to switch ISPs.

T1 And Fractional T1

A T1 is a digital communications link that supports a bandwidth of 1.544Mbps. Like 56K lines, T1s are point-to-point direct communication lines, and they require a DSU/CSU at each end. The T1 line is actually made up of 24 wires, each of which operates at 64Kbps. It is possible to lease only part of a T1 (between 1 and 23 lines); this is called a fractional T1.

T1 lines are fairly expensive, but you do get what you pay for. T1 and larger fractional T1s are cost prohibitive to all but larger organizations. But if you really need that much bandwidth, you can find a way to finance it.

Other Connection Types

The previously mentioned communication link types are the most common and the ones most likely to be available in your area. However, several new technologies have recently hit the market or are in their final stages of testing. Keep an eye out for these (discussed in the following sections) and other high-speed, low-cost technologies that may offer greater benefits than existing solutions.

T3

A T3 line offers the equivalent bandwidth of 28 T1 lines, or 44.736Mbps. Most backbone networks use T3s as their primary minimum connection speed. The T3 line is cost prohibitive for all but the largest organizations. Fees for installation, equipment, and setup can be over $13,500, with a monthly cost of over $47,000.

Cable Modems

Cable modems are a new technology that enables high-speed downlinking of resources, but has limited capabilities for uplinking. This means you can retrieve data quickly, often at T1 speeds, but uploading is limited to 600Kbps or less. Cable modems are able to deliver this level of data by using the existing cable television distribution network. Cable modems are intended more for home or Small Office/Home Office (SOHO) use and may not be a viable solution for commercial networks. The cable modem itself costs between $150 and $1,000, with a monthly cost that is just under ISDN prices.

ATM

Asynchronous Transfer Mode (ATM) is a high-bandwidth technology that offers speeds from 155Mbps to as much as 2.4Gbps. ATM is a cell-switching technology and is a leading member of the Cell Relay Service (CRS) family of solutions. ATM is currently used for CD-quality audio transmission, realtime video, video conferencing, and high-quality voice transmission by several international and national telephone companies. Attaching a network over ATM is fairly cost prohibitive.

Frame Relay

Frame Relay is a transport method used over many packet-switching networks, including ISDN, T1, ATM, X.25, and SONET networks. It is not a connection pipeline on its own. However, its value lies in the ability to offer variable bandwidth on-demand. By establishing a temporary point-to-point connection with a specified bandwidth, Frame Relay is able to guarantee timely delivery, and customers can be billed on a sliding time and bandwidth scale. Frame Relay has a maximum bandwidth of 1.544Mbps.

SMDS

Switched Multimegabit Data Service (SMDS) is another transport method. It is similar to Frame Relay, but it can offer even greater speeds, up to 44.736Mbps (T3). SMDS is an extremely expensive technology.

DSL

Digital Subscriber Line (DSL) is another new development; it can transmit 6Mbps of data over standard telephone wires. But like cable modems, it has a greater downstream load than upstream (640Kbps or less). DSL is slowly being deployed and supported by the telephone company in limited areas across the U.S. A DSL modem costs under $1,500, and the service will run between $200 and $1,200 a month, depending on the maximum speed you desire.

SONET

Synchronous Optical Network (SONET) is a new fiber-optic network technology that offers gigabit transmission rates. However, it is currently used in limited areas to link telephone switching areas. SONET can be used as the transmission medium for ATM or SMDS.

5

DOES SIZE MATTER?

The size of your network does matter. Well, actually, only the amount of data that is transferred matters. The physical size and the number of computers on your network are related to the amount of traffic, but the relation is ancillary. You should also take note that no two networks are the same. They vary in an infinite number of possibilities. So our recommendations and the recommendations of Microsoft may not be the absolute best fit for your specific situation. Take the time to examine every aspect of your network before accepting the recommendations of experts who have no direct experience with your system.

With that in mind, we will still review some common or basic configurations for networks of various workloads (which coincidentally correspond to geographic size and number of computers).

 In all of the following computer configurations, it is assumed that you are using components that are compatible with Windows NT Server and that NT Server is already installed.

LOW-VOLUME NETWORKS

A low-volume network is typically a network in a small or home office with 10 or fewer computers. Low-volume networks can obtain adequate Internet access by using a single Proxy Server connected to a single ISDN line.

Microsoft recommends the following minimum requirements for the computer hosting Proxy Server:

- Intel Pentium 133 or faster
- 2GB of storage space for caching
- 32MB of RAM or more

MODERATE-VOLUME NETWORKS

A moderate-volume network is typically a network in a midsized company with under 1,000 computers. Moderate-volume networks can obtain adequate Internet access by using two or more Proxy Servers arranged in an array or chain connected to multiple ISDN lines or a fractional T1.

Microsoft recommends the following minimum requirements for the computer hosting Proxy Server:

- Intel Pentium 166 or faster
- 2 to 4GB of storage space for caching
- 64MB of RAM or more

HIGH-VOLUME NETWORKS

A high-volume network is typically a network in an enterprise corporation with thousands of computers. High-volume networks can obtain adequate Internet access by using multiple Proxy Servers in a combined array and chain combination connected to a T1 line or greater.

Microsoft recommends the following minimum requirements for the computer hosting Proxy Server:

- Intel Pentium 200, Pentium Pro 166 or faster
- 8 to 16GB of storage space for caching
- 128 to 256MB of RAM or more

CHAPTER SUMMARY

In this chapter, we discussed the importance of planning your Internet access deployment. This includes examining your existing network to understand what capabilities you currently have. With this foundation of information, you can effectively plan out the requirements for adding new capabilities and features.

Examining network capacity involves establishing a baseline of current performance and then reexamining the same network after each significant system change. This is the only way to obtain specific details on the ability of your network to support the new traffic load sufficiently.

In helping you to examine and assess your network and Internet needs, we asked many questions related to information services, proposed restrictions, growth expectations, security factors, and more. Take the time to answer these questions to get a better idea of your exact requirements.

We discussed the Internet and its usefulness. The benefits of adding Internet access to your network includes improved customer access and communication, remote access capabilities, content and resource control, online marketing and advertisement, research, and general communication.

When it is used to connect a network to the Internet, Proxy Server offers you control of the data flow, but you can still allow most (if not all) common information services to be accessed by your internal users. Proxy Server is able to support a wide range of services by using three types of proxy systems—Web, WinSock, and SOCKS.

5

In addition to supporting most information services, Proxy Server offers many other features. Proxy Server 2.0 enables several users to use a single Internet connection simultaneously, it can be configured to use two or more Internet connections to support the network's Internet access needs, and it has true firewall capabilities to prevent external users from accessing data stored on your internal network. Proxy Server 2.0 can also be used to control, restrict, or prevent internal users from gaining access to external resources. Proxy Server 2.0 can improve resource access time through its caching capabilities, and it can impersonate a Web Server, which gives you the ability to set up a Web server inside of your network but offer the site's contents to the Internet.

Proxy Server 2.0 has a further expansion on the reverse proxy service: reverse hosting. This is another form of Web publishing to the external Internet from internal Web servers. Proxy Server 2.0 is able to examine inbound traffic to determine whether to allow it to pass or not. It can also intercept predefined packet types to forward them to a specific server inside the network. Proxy Server 2.0 aids you in keeping track of what actually occurs on, around, through, and near your network. In addition, a combination of Proxy Server and Routing and Remote Access Service for Windows NT Server can expand your communication and networking capabilities by adding secure VPN support.

Once you have concluded that Proxy Server can meet your needs, you'll need to design a network layout to include Proxy Server. There are several possibilities: a single Proxy Server with a single Internet connection, a Proxy Server cache array with one or more Internet connections, a Proxy Server caching chain, and further combinations.

Locating an ISP can be a lengthy process, but because it is the most important link between you and the Internet, it is worth the effort. After locating candidates, you should examine ISPs in light of several criteria, including technical support, location, services offered, communication, remote access, payment options, downtime management, background, compatibility, backbone providers, peak time, and bandwidth options. And no matter who you contract with, always get everything in writing.

The costs of connecting to the Internet are more than just the monthly fees charged to you by the ISP and telephone company. Remember that in a business environment, opportunities, resource availability, and productivity are just as important as money in terms of cost.

Once you select an ISP, you also need to determine your bandwidth needs. Several options are available to you, from ISDN to T1. Take the time to discuss your needs with your ISP before making a definite decision.

The size of your network in terms of the amount of transmitted data should help you determine the needs of the computer hosting Proxy Server as well as the number of Proxy Servers required. Low-traffic networks can often perform adequately with a single moderate computer hosting Proxy Server. High-traffic networks will require several high-performance computers hosting Proxy Server.

Key Terms

- **56Kbps (56K) leased line**—A digital communications link with a bandwidth of 56Kbps.

- **ARPANet (Advanced Research Projects Agency Network)**—The first internetwork that used the TCP/IP protocol.

- **backbone**—A high-bandwidth, high-performance network link. Most ISP's networks are directly connected to a backbone; other times the ISP is connected to someone else's network, which is connected to a backbone.

- **cache array**—A Proxy Server 2.0 configuration where two or more Proxy Servers are configured as a single entity.

- **caching chain**—A Proxy Server 2.0 configuration where two or more Proxy Servers are configured so the downline Proxy Servers are dependent on the upline Proxy Servers.

- **Data Service Unit/Channel Service Unit (DSU/CSU)**—The device that connects a computer to a 56K communication line.

- **dedicated service**—Exclusive access to a specific communications port. Dedicated service guarantees you a connection, but it has a price.

- **Integrated Services Digital Network (ISDN)**—A digital communications link with a maximum bandwidth of 128Kbps per dual-channel line.

- **Internet Relay Chat (IRC)**—An Internet information service in which numerous users anywhere in the world can communicate in realtime through a text interface.

- **Internet Service Provider (ISP)**—A service company that sells network access to the Internet; most ISPs purchase bandwidth in bulk and in turn resell it in smaller packages.

- **internetwork**—A network of networks; the term used to describe the early deployment of the system that became the Internet.

- **National Science Foundation Network (NSFNet)**—A network designed for use by educational and research facilities created soon after ARPANET.

- **network capacity**—The amount of data transmission a network is able to handle.

- **Network Monitor**—A Windows NT Server utility that can inspect network packets, traffic, and protocols.

- **Network News Transport Protocol (NNTP)**—The protocol that supports Usenet newsgroups.

- **newsgroup**—A messaging system on an intranet or the Internet where you can read and post information in a form called articles.

- **nondedicated service**—A type of service in which you must compete with other users to gain access to a pool of communications ports. Nondedicated service does not guarantee access at any given time and is therefore much less expensive.

- **Performance Monitor**—A Windows NT utility used to monitor the activity of the system, including memory, CPU, services, applications, communication ports, networking, and more.

- **pipeline**—A term that refers to the communications link between your network and an ISP. The ability for a connection to support significant amounts of data protection is dependent on the size and cost of that link.

- **Plain Old Telephone Service (POTS)**—An analog communications link with a maximum bandwidth of 56Kbps.

- **reverse hosting**—Web publishing to the external Internet from internal Web servers; reverse hosting combines or integrates the contents of multiple distinct internal Web servers into a single entity that is viewed by external users. Thus, Internet users see a single Web site instead of multiple individual servers.

- **server proxying**—The ability of a server to examine inbound traffic in order to intercept predefined packet types and forward them to a specific server inside the network. Server proxying offers security without sacrificing the flexibility and capabilities of specialized information services.

5

- **spamming**—The distribution of unsolicited and unwelcome messages via email or newsgroups, often with the purpose of selling some product or service.

- **T1 and fractional T1**—A digital communications link with a bandwidth of 1.544Mbps (for a full T1) or in 56 or 256Kbps fractional T1 chunks.

- **Usenet**—The term used to refer to the collection of 20,000+ NNTP-based newsgroups supported on the Internet.

REVIEW QUESTIONS

1. How will the traffic level of your internal network change if you deploy Proxy Server 2.0 to provide caching for your existing Internet access?

   a. no significant change

   b. a significant reduction in traffic

   c. a significant increase in traffic

2. Obtaining a baseline of current network activity before deploying Proxy Server 2.0 and adding Internet access is an important step of planning. (True or False?)

3. At what current performance level should you seriously consider upgrading your network capacity before adding Internet access with Proxy Server 2.0?

   a. 15%

   b. 45%

   c. 50%

   d. 70%

   e. 100%

4. When you are deciding how much to improve your network capacity, which of the following are important items to consider?

   a. How many new information services will you allow or enable over Proxy Server?

   b. Will the user community grow significantly in the next year?

   c. Will access to these information services be restricted by user, group, time, or data size?

   d. What bandwidth requirement does each new Internet service require, demand, or use?

5. What is a good padding value for giving your network room to grow when you expand its current capabilities?

   a. 5%

   b. 15%

   c. 40%

   d. 70%

   e. 100%

6. The benefit of improved customer access enables you to do what?

   a. give customers 24-hour access to information on your products and services

   b. distribute patches and fixes via FTP

   c. control the computer of anyone who connects to the Internet

   d. offer menu-driven technical support

   e. communicate with customers via email

7. What is the ability for network users to gain access to the internal LAN while they are traveling known as?

   a. content control

   b. research

   c. marketing

   d. remote access

   e. fault tolerance

8. Proxy Server is able to offer such a wide variety of protocol support due to what three components?

   a. Web Proxy

   b. Protocol Proxy

   c. WinSock Proxy

   d. SOCKS Proxy

   e. Port Proxy

9. Hypertext Transfer Protocol (HTTP), Secure HTTP (HTTPS), File Transfer Protocol (FTP), Gopher, and Transmission Control Protocol/Internet Protocol (TCP/IP) are the only protocols supported by which Proxy Server 2.0 component?

   a. Web Proxy

   b. WinSock Proxy

   c. SOCKS Proxy

5

10. Which Proxy Server 2.0 component supports Internet service for non-Windows and non-WinSock applications but cannot support proxy services that require UDP?

    a. Web Proxy

    b. WinSock Proxy

    c. SOCKS Proxy

11. Which Proxy Server 2.0 component supports AlphaWorld, AOL, Archie, Echo, Enliven, IMAP4, IRC, Microsoft NetShow, MSN, NNTP, POP3, SMTP, and VDOLive multimedia/specialty protocols, plus both TCP/IP and IPX/SPX?

    a. Web Proxy

    b. WinSock Proxy

    c. SOCKS Proxy

12. Proxy Server 2.0 allows several users to use a single Internet connection simultaneously. (True or False?)

13. Proxy Server 2.0 can manage or control access to external resources in several ways. Which of the following describe possible methods?

    a. disabling of IP forwarding

    b. group/user permission by Internet service

    c. use of Windows NT Challenge/Response

    d. resource restriction by IP address, subnet, or domain

    e. protocol denial by port address

14. Which of the following are caching methods, technologies, or configurations used by Proxy Server 2.0?

    a. chaining

    b. fractal

    c. array

    d. hierarchical

    e. inverse delegation

15. Proxy Server 2.0 is only able to cache and proxy external resources to internal users; it cannot be used to proxy or cache internal resources for external users. (True or False?)

16. The ability of Proxy Server 2.0 to listen for packets of a specific type, such as email, and forward them directly to a specified internal server is known as what?

    a. reverse hosting

    b. IP forwarding

    c. reverse proxying

    d. chain caching

    e. server proxying

17. What Windows NT Server add-on component is required in order to use Proxy Server 2.0 in a VPN configuration?

   a. Workstation Service

   b. File and Print Services for Microsoft Networks

   c. Routing and Remote Access Service

   d. Replication

   e. IIS 4.0

18. If you need to connect multiple LANs to the Internet through a single communications link, which of the following configurations should you use?

   a. array cache

   b. forked caching chain

   c. stepped array

   d. linear linked line

19. The Proxy Server 2.0 features of cache arrays, cache chains, and multiple ISP links can be combined together. (True or False?)

20. Proxy Server 2.0 can be deployed on a network that has no connection to the Internet to provide control divisions. (True or False?)

21. In any Proxy Server configuration, what two layout features are very important?

   a. that you only use 1 Proxy Server per 100 users

   b. that there are no other access points to the Internet that are not controlled by a Proxy Server

   c. that caching only be enabled for administrative-level users

   d. that the computer hosting Proxy Server is an Alpha AXP system

   e. that the computer hosting Proxy Server does not support any other network service

22. Which of the following are important criteria for choosing an ISP?

   a. technical support

   b. location

   c. Internet services

   d. downtime management

   e. business background

   f. compatibility

   g. backbone providers

   h. peak time

   i. bandwidth options

23. For small or low-traffic networks, which bandwidth option is the most cost effective and efficient?

   a. POTS

   b. ISDN

   c. T1

   d. SMDS

24. A full T1 offers what level of bandwidth?

   a. 128Kbps

   b. 600Kbps

   c. 1.544Mbps

   d. 44.736Mbps

25. The Microsoft recommendations of Intel Pentium 200, Pentium Pro 166, or faster, 8 to 16GB of storage space for caching, and 128 to 256MB of RAM or more are associated with a network with what level of volume?

   a. low

   b. moderate

   c. high

CASE PROJECTS

1. Your network has 1,000 users who need to use the Internet.

Required result: Provide each user with adequate bandwidth, even if all 1,000 users are active at one time.

Optional desired results: Minimize the load on any given server. Reduce the traffic load over the ISP link as much as possible.

Proposed solution: Contract with an ISP for an ISDN line. Install Routing and Remote Access Service. Which results does this solution deliver?

   a. The proposed solution produces the required result and both of the optional desired results.

   b. The proposed solution produces the required result but only one of the optional desired results.

   c. The proposed solution produces the required result but neither of the optional desired results.

   d. The proposed solution does not produce the required result.

2. Your network has 1,000 users who need to use the Internet.

Required result: Provide each user with adequate bandwidth, even if all 1,000 users are active at one time.

Optional desired results: Minimize the load on any given server. Reduce the traffic load over the ISP link as much as possible.

Proposed solution: Contract with an ISP for an ISDN line. Install Proxy Server 2.0. Enable caching. Which results does this solution deliver?

a. The proposed solution produces the required result and both of the optional desired results.

b. The proposed solution produces the required result but only one of the optional desired results.

c. The proposed solution produces the required result but neither of the optional desired results.

d. The proposed solution does not produce the required result.

3. Your network has 1,000 users who need to use the Internet.

Required result: Provide each user with adequate bandwidth, even if all 1,000 users are active at one time.

Optional desired results: Minimize the load on any given server. Reduce the traffic load over the ISP link as much as possible.

Proposed solution: Contract with an ISP for a T1 line. Install Proxy Server 2.0. Enable caching. Which results does this solution deliver?

a. The proposed solution produces the required result and both of the optional desired results.

b. The proposed solution produces the required result but only one of the optional desired results.

c. The proposed solution produces the required result but neither of the optional desired results.

d. The proposed solution does not produce the required result.

4. Your network has 1,000 users who need to use the Internet.

Required result: Provide each user with adequate bandwidth, even if all 1,000 users are active at one time.

Optional desired results: Minimize the load on any given server. Reduce the traffic load over the ISP link as much as possible.

Proposed solution: Contract with an ISP for a T1 line. Install Proxy Server 2.0 on 6 machines. Configure a 6-system cache array. Which results does this solution deliver?

a. The proposed solution produces the required result and both of the optional desired results.

b. The proposed solution produces the required result but only one of the optional desired results.

c. The proposed solution produces the required result but neither of the optional desired results.

d. The proposed solution does not produce the required result.

5. You have three networks that need Internet access.

Required result: Connect all three LANs over a single T1 communications link.

Optional desired results: Maintain a LAN-specific cache for each LAN. All LAN caches should offload unfulfilled caching hits to a master cache.

Proposed solution: Contract with an ISP for a single T1 link. Install Proxy Server 2.0 on four machines, one on each LAN and one as the T1 host. Configure the proxies in a three-forked caching chain. Which results does this solution deliver?

a. The proposed solution produces the required result and both of the optional desired results.

b. The proposed solution produces the required result but only one of the optional desired results.

c. The proposed solution produces the required result but neither of the optional desired results.

d. The proposed solution does not produce the required result.

INSTALLING MICROSOFT PROXY SERVER 2.0

In this chapter, you will learn to install Microsoft Proxy Server 2.0, to install only the Microsoft Proxy Server 2.0 documentation, to configure the Local Address Table (LAT) for the highest level of security, and to configure multiple-protocol support. Proper configuration of the connection to the Internet and of the client will be covered in detail in this chapter, as well as installation and configuration of multiple communication protocols. Finally, the authentication process will be reviewed, and configuration options associated with that process will be covered.

AFTER READING THIS CHAPTER AND COMPLETING THE EXERCISES, YOU WILL BE ABLE TO:

- Understand some of the security issues involved in connecting to the Internet
- Install Microsoft Proxy Server 2.0
- Configure and establish a connection with an ISP
- Configure the Local Address Table (LAT)
- Configure Microsoft Proxy Server 2.0 for multiple protocols
- Configure Microsoft Proxy Server 2.0 for various levels of user authentication

SECURITY CONCERNS

When you connect your network to the Internet, you give unwanted users a potential opening to break into your network. Microsoft Proxy Server 2.0 provides a secure, cost-effective path for connecting your users to the Internet. It gives you a single point of connection that allows you to monitor and control what sites your users can access.

IP forwarding can be disabled, which hides your internal IP addresses, and packet filtering can be enabled, which blocks certain types of packets—such as Network News Transfer Protocol (NNTP) packets, for instance. Proxy Server also provides a secured path for Internet users to access your Web server through a process called reverse proxy, which was discussed in Chapter 5.

PROXY SERVER LICENSING

Licensing for Microsoft Proxy Server 2.0 falls under the standard Microsoft licensing agreement. For Proxy Server, as with IIS and Site Server, no client access licenses are required. However, as you know, Proxy Server requires Windows NT Server 4.0 and IIS 3.0 or higher. Valid licenses of each of these servers must be present for the Proxy Server installation to comply with the licensing agreement. The Proxy Server license can be transferred between two systems as long as it is completely removed from the original system. Like all Microsoft products under this agreement, it cannot be rented or leased. It can, however, be sold with the understanding that no copies will be kept in any form. The Proxy Server software cannot be decompiled or reverse-engineered. Finally, Microsoft requires that all benchmark and testing results be submitted to Microsoft before they are released to any third party.

INSTALLING MICROSOFT PROXY SERVER 2.0

Refer to Chapter 1 for the hardware requirements for installing Microsoft Proxy Server 2.0. Make sure your hardware is suitable for the number of clients you'll support. Before you install Microsoft Proxy Server 2.0, you'll need to make sure things are ready for installation:

- Make sure you have at least 100MB of free disk space on the server disk drive. The disk must be formatted with the New Technology File System (NTFS) to support the cache system.

- You'll need administrative privileges. The account you use to log in must be a member of the Administrators group.

- The network interface card (NIC) for the internal network must be installed and configured correctly with the protocol that is used on that network. The protocol can be either TCP/IP or NWLink.

- Make sure the interface used to connect to the Internet (NIC, modem, or ISDN adapter) is configured with the TCP/IP protocol. Note that when you configure the TCP/IP protocol, you will be prompted to provide an IP address and subnet mask. If you are using an Internet Service Provider (ISP) to gain access to the Internet, this information should be obtained from your ISP.

- The computer must be running NT Server 4.0 as a domain controller or member server and Service Pack 3 must be applied.

- Internet Information Server 3.0 (or newer) must be installed.

The installation of Microsoft Proxy Server 2.0 is covered in detail in Hands-on Project 6.1. The following list includes the three installation options that can be selected, the amount of space you'll need, and a brief description of what functionality each component provides:

- **Install Microsoft Proxy Server (9541K)** This option (shown in Figure 6.1) installs and configures Microsoft Proxy Server 2.0. Four separate components can be selected: Install Server, Install NT Intel/ W95 Client Share, Install NT Alpha Client Share, and Install Win 3.x Client Share.

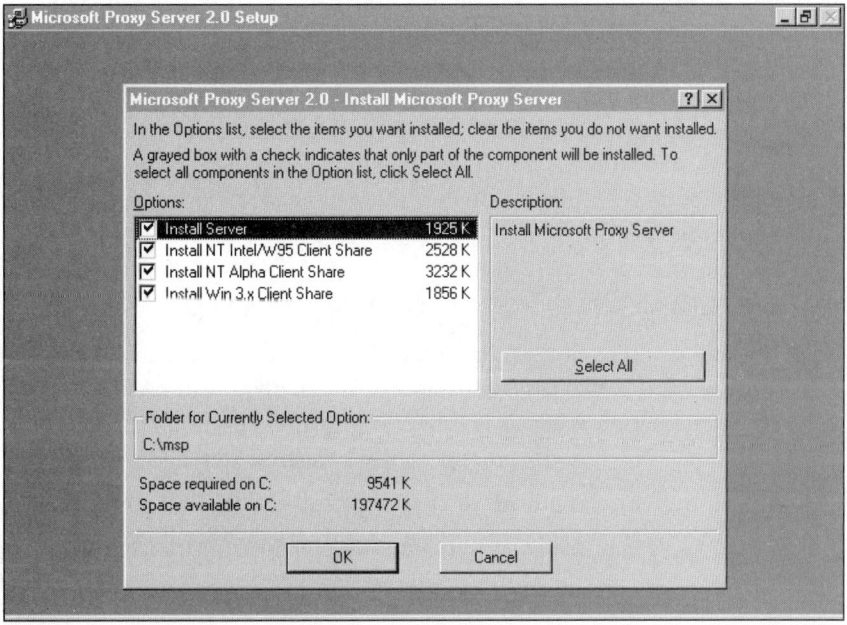

Figure 6.1   Client software installation.

- **Install Administration Tool (1505K)** This option installs the administrative tools during the installation of Microsoft Proxy Server 2.0.

- **Install Documentation (3328K)** This option installs only the documentation for Proxy Server 2.0. The option is available at the beginning of the setup process.

After selecting components to install, click the Continue button. If either of the following situations occur, an error message will appear:

- If enough disk space isn't available to install the selected options, an error message will appear indicating that you need to free some disk space before continuing.

- If the Service Advertising Protocol (SAP) agent is not installed, an error message will appear prompting you to install the SAP agent and the installation process will end. The SAP agent is used by servers to advertise their services and addresses on a network.

Setup stops the WWW service and the Microsoft Proxy Server Cache Drives dialog box appears (see Figure 6.2). By default, caching is enabled, and the local drives are listed in the Drive list box.

If a server services 24 Web Proxy service clients, it is recommended that you allocate 112MB or more to cache. This represents 100MB of initial cache storage and 0.5MB for each additional client. The amount of caching space you'll need to support a given number of clients varies depending on the configuration and load on the system; typically, increasing the amount of disk space allocated to cache benefits the cache.

After configuring the cache options, you must identify all internal addresses for your network and exclude all external addresses. This is done in the Construct Local Address Table dialog box (see Figure 6.3). The steps required to construct a table of the IP addresses of your internal network are covered in detail in Hands-on Project 6.1.

INSTALLING THE DOCUMENTATION ONLY

The documentation can be installed without installing any other components of Microsoft Proxy Server 2.0. This does not require the computer on which the documentation is being installed to be running Microsoft Windows NT Server. To install only the documentation, follow these steps:

1. Run setup from the root directory of the Proxy Server CD.

2. When the Microsoft Proxy Server Installation Options dialog box appears, clear all options except the Install Documentation checkbox.

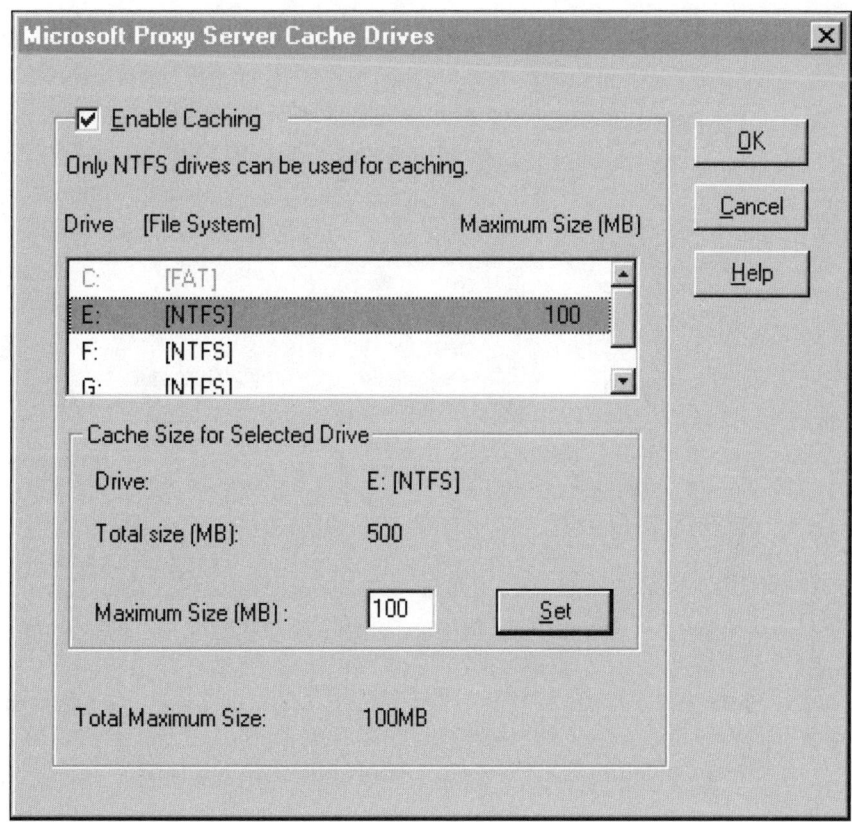

Figure 6.2   Setting disk and space options for caching.

3. After setup is complete, navigate to the documentation by choosing Start | Programs | Microsoft Proxy Server | Microsoft Proxy Server Documentation.

The Install Documentation option makes it possible for you to study and review the online documentation even if you don't have a computer that meets the requirements for running Microsoft Proxy Server 2.0.

CONFIGURING PROXY SERVER AUTO DIAL

Proxy Server can be configured to automatically dial out to an ISP to establish an Internet connection. Proxy Server *Auto Dial* uses Microsoft Windows NT Server *Remote Access Service (RAS)* and *Dial-Up Networking* to establish the connection.

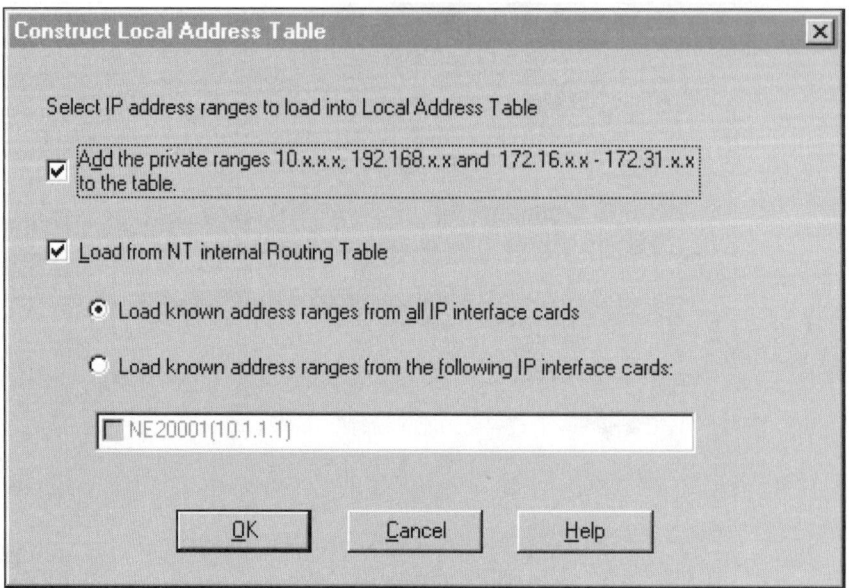

Figure 6.3   Constructing the Local Address Table.

Proxy Server Auto Dial is activated when an event occurs that requires connection to the Internet. The following events will activate Auto Dial and are configurable through the Auto Dial Configuration tool:

- When the Web Proxy service requests an object that cannot be located in cache
- When the WinSock Proxy service has any client request
- When the SOCKS Proxy service has any client request

Proxy Server Auto Dial allows you to reduce connection time to the Internet by establishing a connection only when it is needed. The Auto Dial feature can also be used as a fault-tolerance measure by acting as a backup connection if a continuous Internet connection fails. For example, if a T1 link goes down, Auto Dial can establish a backup connection using ISDN or regular phone lines.

To configure Proxy Server Auto Dial, Windows RAS must first be installed and Dial-Up Networking must be configured. To install RAS and to configure Dial-Up Networking, follow these steps:

1. Install RAS (through Network Properties).
2. Configure the Phonebook entry.
3. Configure RAS services.

To configure the Auto Dial feature, do the following:

1. Configure Auto Dial credentials.

2. Configure Auto Dial hours of operation.

3. Restart the Proxy Server service.

RAS is used to configure the modem in a Windows NT computer and can be installed as part of the Windows NT Server installation process or after the network operating system is installed through the Network Properties applet in the Control Panel. When you install RAS, you'll need the following information:

- Modem manufacturer and model

- Type of communication port used for the RAS connection

- TCP/IP configuration information

- Modem settings, such as baud rate, stop bits, and start bits

SECURITY SETTINGS

It is suggested that RAS be configured only for dialing out to increase security. It is also suggested that the RAS server be installed on a computer other than the one hosting Proxy Server if possible.

Dial-Up Networking is used to provide the connection information to RAS for establishing a connection with a remote computer. A connection is established by creating a Phonebook entry in the Dial-Up Networking applet, which is in My Computer. The following list includes the information you will need:

- A name for the Phonebook entry

- The phone number or numbers used to establish a connection

- The dial-up server type

- Script information (if a script is used)

- Security level (plain text, NT challenge/response)

- X.25 information

After you install RAS and create a Phonebook entry, RAS must be configured to use the Proxy Server Auto Dial:

1. Stop and disable the Remote Access Auto Dial Manager service. This is done through the Services applet in the Control Panel. To disable the service, select the Remote Access Auto Dial Manager service, click the Startup button, and select Disable. To stop the service, click Stop.

2. Set the Remote Access Connection Manager service for automatic startup. Select the Remote Access Connection Manager service, click the Startup button, and select Automatic.

After you configure RAS and Dial-Up Networking, you will need to configure the Proxy Server Auto Dial credentials for dialing out, enabling dial-up for Proxy Server services, and limiting the times the dial-out connection functionality is available. This is done through the Auto Dial Configuration tool. To configure the Auto Dial function (Figure 6.4), follow these steps:

1. Choose Start|Programs|Microsoft Proxy Server and double-click Auto Dial Configuration.

2. In the Configuration tab, select the events that will start the Auto Dial feature. Select the times that the Auto Dial feature will be enabled.

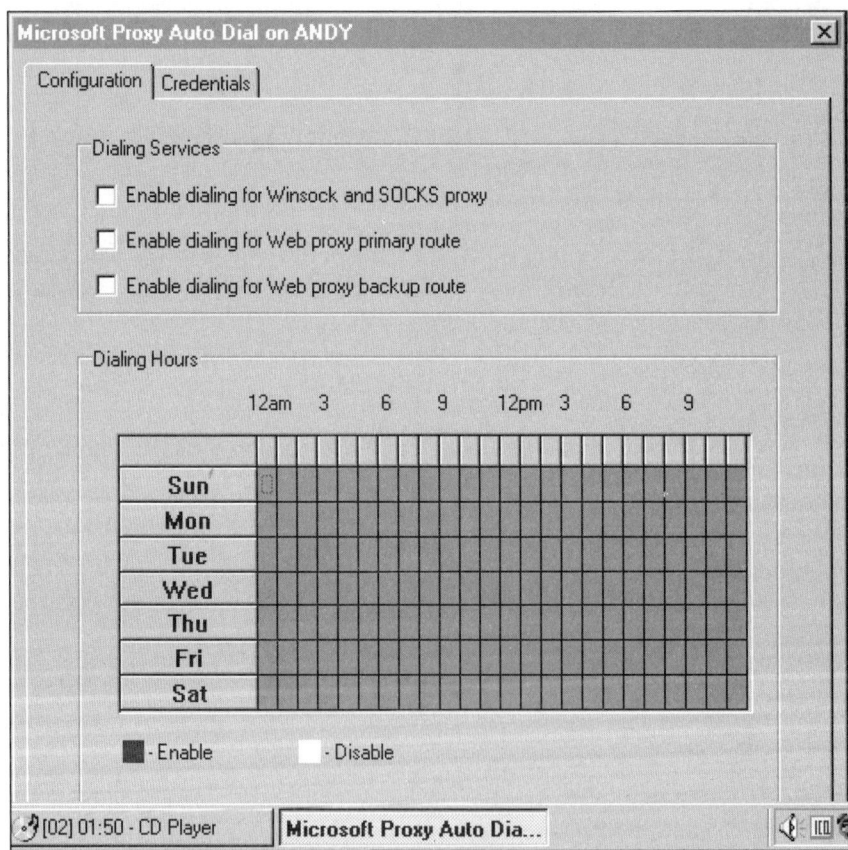

Figure 6.4   Configuring Auto Dial.

3. In the Credentials tab, configure the RAS Phonebook entry, username, and password that will be used to launch and authenticate the connection.

Before the Proxy Server Auto Dial feature can be used to establish a connection to an ISP, the World Wide Web, Web Proxy, WinSock Proxy, and SOCKS Proxy services must be stopped and restarted if one of two conditions exist:

- When Proxy Server Auto Dial is used the first time, the services must be initialized to use Auto Dial.

- When the Proxy Server Auto Dial settings are changed, the services must be stopped and restarted before the changes will take effect.

We will cover the configuration of the Microsoft Proxy Server 2.0 environment, clients, and security in the chapters that follow. The changes that are made to the system by installing Microsoft Proxy Server 2.0 are as follows:

- The Web Proxy service is installed on the server and is added to the Internet Service Manager, which is installed with Internet Information Server (IIS).

- The WinSock Proxy service is installed on the server and is added to the Internet Service Manager.

- The SOCKS Proxy service is installed on the server and is added to the Internet Service Manager.

- The HTML online documentation is installed and copied to the %SYSTEM_ROOT%\HELP\PROXY directory.

- A cache is created on an NTFS partition.

- The *Local Address Table (LAT)* is created.

- Proxy Server Performance Monitor counters are installed.

- The client installation and configuration software is copied to the MSP\CLIENTS folder and shared as MSPCLNT.

ROUTING AND REMOTE ACCESS SERVICE (RRAS)

Routing and Remote Access Service (RRAS) is a new product that extends the abilities of Windows NT Server to support, among other things, enhanced RAS and the Point-to-Point Tunneling Protocol (PPTP). PPTP is a fairly new protocol that provides secure, encrypted RAS connections over the Internet by creating virtual private networks (VPNs.) It is possible for Proxy Server and

RRAS to be installed and operating on the same physical machine, but some configuration caveats should be kept in mind:

- For a PPTP session to be established across the Internet through a Proxy Server, both the PPTP Receive and PPTP Call filters must be enabled on the Proxy Server.

- The RRAS hotfix must be applied after RRAS has been installed on the server.

It is important to remember these configuration considerations in the event that a PPTP connection from the Internet is unsuccessful.

ADDING OR REMOVING PROXY COMPONENTS

After Proxy Server is installed, components can be added or removed, bad or missing files can be replaced, or the entire Proxy Server product can be removed. The process to perform these three tasks is similar to the process used with Microsoft Office to perform the same tasks.

To add or remove selected Proxy Server components:

1. Run Setup from the root directory of the Proxy Server CD. The Setup dialog box appears.

2. Click on Add/Remove and add or remove the desired components.

To restore bad or missing files:

1. Run Setup from the root directory of the Proxy Server CD. The Setup dialog box appears.

2. Click on Reinstall and follow the online instructions. The files that are missing or corrupted are replaced.

To remove Proxy Server:

1. Run Setup from the root directory of the Proxy Server CD. The Setup dialog box appears.

2. Click on Remove All. A message appears asking you to confirm the removal of Microsoft Proxy Server 2.0.

3. Click Yes. Proxy Server is removed from the server.

LOCAL ADDRESS TABLE (LAT)

The Local Address Table (LAT) is a database that contains a series of IP address pairs that define your internal network address space. Each pair of addresses can define one IP address or an entire range of addresses. Figure 6.5 is an example of a LAT with the default entries included.

The LAT is configured during the Proxy Server installation process, which is covered in detail in Hands-On Project 6.1. After it is installed, you can configure the LAT with the Web Proxy Service tool, which is located in the Internet Service Manager. Microsoft Proxy Server uses the lists of IP addresses found in the NT Server routing table to generate the LAT during installation. It is extremely important that all entries in the LAT be from your internal network and that the LAT contains no entries from an external network.

When the client Setup program is run, the information contained in the LAT is downloaded to the client and stored in the \MSPCLNT directory in a file named MSPLAT.TXT. The server updates the file on the client regularly to keep the file current.

After client setup, each time a WinSock application on a client attempts to establish connection to an IP address, the LAT file is checked to determine if the IP address is local to the internal network or on an external network. If the address is local, a direct connection is established. If the connection is remote, the connection is made through the WinSock Proxy service.

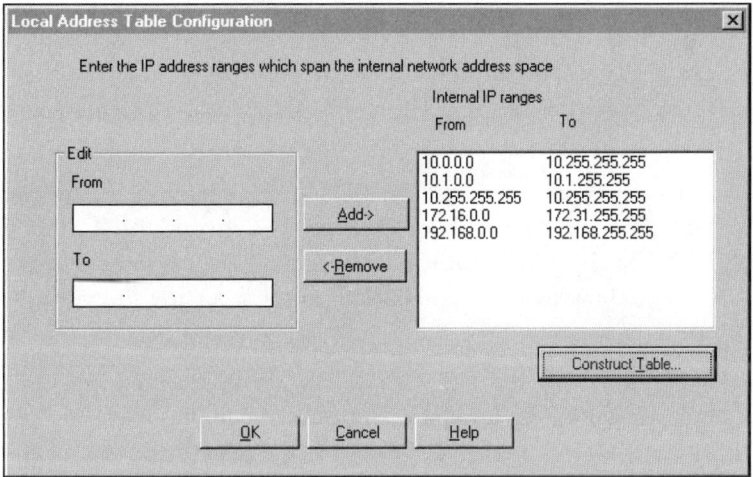

Figure 6.5 Example of a Local Address Table (LAT).

In certain cases, a client may need additional entries in the LAT for connection to internal IP addresses. Because MSPLAT.TXT is copied over by the server on a regular basis, the client should create a custom file named LOCALLAT.TXT and place it in the \MSPCLNT directory. The client will then use both files to determine whether the destination is local or remote.

 To customize the LAT for individual clients, create a file named LOCALLAT.TXT and place it in the \MSPCLNT directory instead of modifying the information in the MSPLAT.TXT file downloaded by Proxy Server.

MULTIPLE-PROTOCOL CONFIGURATION

Microsoft Proxy Server acts as a firewall or gateway by forwarding the packets on the internal network that have external destinations and receiving packets from external sources to forward to the internal client.

The client can run NWLink (Microsoft's version of IPX/SPX, which is used with Windows NT), or TCP/IP, or both. If the internal client uses NWLink to send the packet, Proxy Server will convert the packet to TCP/IP for delivery to the external address.

If a TCP/IP packet is received for an internal client running only NWLink, Proxy Server will convert the TCP/IP packet to NWLink for delivery to the internal client.

If both the TCP/IP and IPX/SPX protocols are in use by the client, the client can be forced to use the IPX/SPX protocol to communicate with Microsoft Proxy Server, as shown in Figure 6.6. This screen is reached by opening the MSP Client applet in the Control Panel on the client computer.

On a network running IPX/SPX only, Proxy Server might have only the IPX/SPX protocol configured on the internal network's NIC. Some clients may have both the IPX/SPX and TCP/IP protocols configured on their computers because they installed the TCP/IP protocol for use in connecting to an ISP via the RAS support.

Simply disabling the TCP/IP protocol while on the local area network (LAN) will not work. The WinSock Proxy client computer will still detect the presence of the TCP/IP protocol, assume it is operational, and attempt to create IP sockets.

It is preferable to configure the internal Microsoft Proxy Server client to use only the IPX/SPX protocol rather than both the IPX/SPX protocol and the TCP/IP protocol. An internal address has no chance of being compromised when you use the IPX/SPX protocol only.

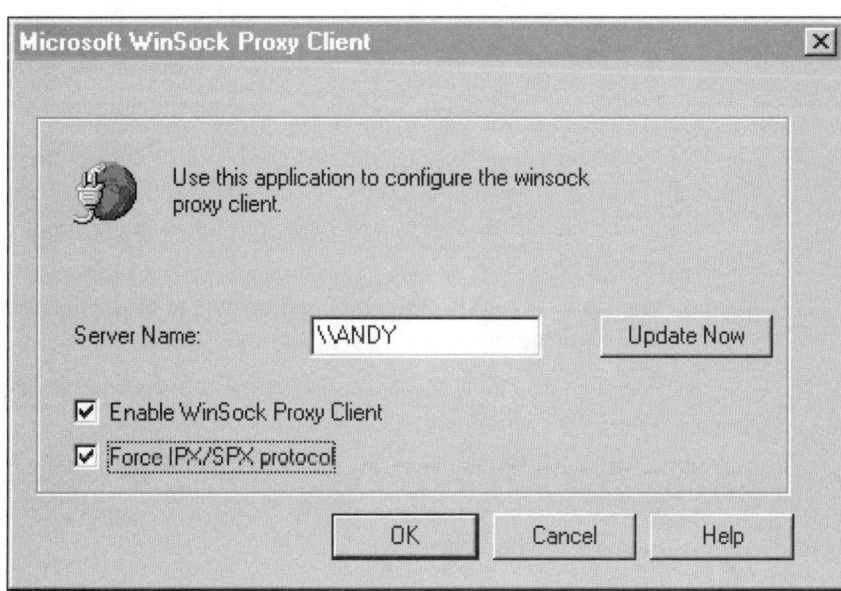

Figure 6.6   Forcing the client to use IPX/SPX.

6

CLIENT CONFIGURATION

Proxy Server Setup creates the MSP\CLIENTS folder and shares it as MSPCLNT. The share permissions are set to Read for the group Everyone. Under the MSPCLNT share, additional folders that contain client-specific files are created. The share point is created automatically during installation.

The clients that will be supported and will consequently have folders under the MSPCLNT share are configured during the Microsoft Proxy Server 2.0 installation. There are two ways the client can connect to and be configured to use the Proxy Server: connecting with a Web browser and attaching to the Proxy Server share.

To configure the client by connecting with a Web browser:

1. Start the Web browser on the client computer.

2. Connect to the Proxy Server at **http://*proxy_server_computer_name*/ MSProxy/**.

3. A Web-based WinSock Proxy client installation screen appears. Click the Click Here link to begin installation.

To configure the client by attaching to the Proxy Server share:

1. Choose Start|Run.

2. In the Run dialog box, type "*proxy_server_computer_name*\Mspclnt" and click OK. This connects you to the share on the proxy server.

3. Double-click on Setup. The client installation begins.

The WinSock Proxy client can be removed from the system by selecting Uninstall from the Microsoft Proxy Client group that was created during installation. The client installation will make the following changes to the client computer:

- The LAT file (MSPLAT.TXT) will be copied to the client. Proxy Server updates this file on a regular basis.

- Windows-based clients (Windows 3.x, Windows 95, Windows NT) will have a WSP client icon added to the Control Panel.

- A Microsoft Proxy Client Program group will be created.

- WINSOCK.DLL is renamed WINSOCK.DLX and replaced with Remote WinSock from WinSock Proxy client.

- MSPCLNT.INI is copied to the client.

Once the WinSock Proxy client is installed, the client can only gain access to the external network (Internet) through the Proxy Server. If direct access is needed, the client can temporarily disable the WinSock Proxy client.

To disable the WinSock Proxy client:

1. In the Control Panel, open the WSP Client applet.

2. Clear the Enable WinSock Proxy Client checkbox and reboot the system.

To reenable the WinSock Proxy client:

1. In the Control Panel, open the WSP Client applet.

2. Select the Enable WinSock Proxy Client checkbox and reboot the system.

CHAPTER SUMMARY

In this chapter, you learned the requirements for installing Microsoft Proxy Server 2.0. The computer on which the installation will take place has to be running Microsoft Windows NT Server with Service Pack 3 applied, and Internet Information Server 3.0 (or higher) must be installed.

During the installation process, selections can be made to install Microsoft Proxy Server 2.0 or to install the documentation only. After installation is complete, Proxy Server Auto Dial can be configured from the Auto Dial Configuration tool, which is installed under the Microsoft Proxy Server tools along with the Internet Service Manager tool.

To configure Auto Dial, first RAS must be configured, and a Phonebook entry for connecting to the ISP of choice must be made. Proxy Server's Auto Dial feature uses this information to establish the connection. The services that instigate the Auto Dial feature are configurable and include WinSock, SOCKS, Web Proxy primary route, and Web Proxy backup route. You can also configure the Auto Dial service to work only during certain times of the day.

You learned that the Local Address Table (LAT) can be automatically configured during the installation process and that entries can be made for all internal network cards. The LAT should only contain IP addresses that reside on the internal network. This can include IP addresses for local computers and routers.

Client configuration is accomplished by connecting to Proxy Server with a Web browser or by connecting to a share on Proxy Server. To connect to Proxy Server using a Web browser, the client selects **http://*Proxy_Server*/MSProxy/**. To connect to the Share point created when Microsoft Proxy Server is installed, the client connects to *PROXY_SERVER*\MSPCLNT and runs setup.

After the client installation is complete, the MSP Client applet is added to the Control Panel on the client. This applet allows the client to enable and disable the WinSock Proxy client and force the WinSock Proxy client to use IPX/SPX for communications with Proxy Server.

KEY TERMS

- **Auto Dial**—The service that connects to the Internet automatically when an event that requires connection to the Internet occurs.
- **Dial-Up Networking**—A Windows NT utility that controls the dial-out capabilities of RAS.
- **Local Address Table (LAT)**—The table of all internal IP address pairs on the internal network where Microsoft Proxy Server is installed. This list is used to control access between clients on the internal network and remote IP addresses on external IP networks (or the Internet). The LAT is registered and stored in a text-based file (MSPLAT.TXT) within the installed directory for Microsoft Proxy Server (C:\MSP\CLIENTS). This file is distributed to clients during setup and updated periodically by Microsoft Proxy Server.
- **Remote Access Service (RAS)**—The Windows NT service that provides network communication for remote clients.

REVIEW QUESTIONS

1. You are planning to install Microsoft Proxy Server version 2.0 on your Windows NT Workstation. Which of the following would you need to do? (Choose all that apply.)

   a. Ensure that Microsoft TCP/IP is installed on the system.

   b. Configure NWLink.

   c. Add Internet Information Server to your system if it is not already installed.

   d. Upgrade to Windows NT Server version 4.0.

   e. Install Microsoft Service Pack 3 or later.

   f. Install NetBEUI.

   g. Install Internet Explorer version 4.0 or later.

2. What types of partitions can Microsoft Proxy Server 2.0 utilize for caching? (Choose all that apply.)

   a. File Allocation Table

   b. Virtual File Allocation Table

   c. New Technology File System

   d. High Performance File System

   e. Network File System

   f. DR-DOS

3. What is the minimum amount of memory that Microsoft recommends for a Microsoft Proxy Server 2.0 installation on an Intel 486DX2/66?

   a. 8MB

   b. 16MB

   c. 24MB

   d. 32MB

   e. 64MB

4. How many network adapters are required for a Microsoft Proxy Server 2.0 computer that will access the Internet via an ISDN modem connection and provide proxy services to 50 internal clients?

   a. 0

   b. 1

   c. 2

   d. 3

   e. 4

   f. 5

5. What is the minimum amount of memory Microsoft recommends for a Microsoft Proxy Server 2.0 installation on a Digital Equipment Corporation Alpha AXP Server?

   a. 8MB

   b. 16MB

   c. 24MB

   d. 32MB

   e. 64MB

6. If you plan to install Microsoft Proxy Server 2.0 to provide services for 400 Web Proxy client computers, how much disk space would you have to allocate for caching?

   a. 100MB

   b. 200MB

   c. 300MB

   d. 400MB

   e. 500MB

7. Your proxy server is expected to support 20 internal clients connecting to the Internet. The computer on which you plan to install MS Proxy Server has Windows NT Server 4.0 and Internet Information Server 3.0 installed. The single network adapter in this computer provides intranet site hosting for your LAN. You have not yet connected your LAN to the Internet, but you plan to connect via a router. What is the minimum additional hardware you would need to add to the computer that is to host Proxy Server?

   a. one digital modem

   b. two modems

   c. three network adapters

   d. one network adapter

   e. one CSU/DSU

8. You have an Intel Pentium system with 64MB of RAM running Windows NT Server version 4.0 and Internet Information Server 3.0. You would like to install Microsoft Proxy Server version 2.0 on this system. You will have to manually stop the WWW publishing service to install Proxy Server on this system. (True or False?)

9. You are planning to install Microsoft Proxy Server with your newly purchased MS Proxy Server CD from Microsoft. The computer you plan to use as the proxy server is running Windows NT Server 4.0, TCP/IP, Windows NT Service Pack 3, and IIS 3.0. The computer has a Pentium 100MHz processor, 512K pipeline burst cache, and 64MB of RAM with a

4GB disk drive and 100MB of free space. A 10BaseT network adapter connects the computer to your LAN and an ISDN modem using Microsoft Dial-Up Networking connects it to the Internet. You want to host 200 Web Proxy clients on your LAN. Which of the following Microsoft installation recommended requirements has not been met?

a. memory

b. software requirements

c. Web Proxy cache

d. processor

e. network connection

f. Internet connection

g. connection to client computers

10. Microsoft Proxy Server 2.0 should install properly on a Digital ALPHA AXP with 16MB of RAM and 500MB of free disk space if you are only planning to support 200 Web Proxy clients. (True or False?)

11. Which addresses does Microsoft Proxy Server Setup require that you add to the Local Address Table? (Choose all that apply.)

a. IP address of your ISP

b. IP address of your Internet Information Server

c. IP addresses on your internal network

d. IP addresses of the network card that connects to your ISP

e. IP addresses of the network cards in your system that are attached to the LAN

12. Which of the following methods can a WinSock Proxy client use to connect to Microsoft Proxy Server? (Choose all that apply.)

a. computer name

b. IPX network number

c. IP address

d. NetBIOS Scope Identifier

e. DFS share name

13. If you want local servers to use Proxy Server when connecting to some, but not all, Internet sites, which of the following choices do you have? (Choose all that apply.)

a. Click on Use Proxy Server For Local Servers in the Advanced Client Configuration dialog box.

b. Configure the IP addresses of the sites to which you do not want clients to connect without using Proxy Server.

    c. Configure the IP addresses of the sites to which you would like Proxy Server to allow clients to connect without having to go through Proxy Server.

    d. Configure the domain names of the sites to which you do not want clients to connect without using Proxy Server.

    e. Configure the domain names of the sites to which you would like Proxy Server to allow clients to connect without having to go through Proxy Server.

14. Which of the following is/are not true of the default Microsoft Proxy Server 2.0 installation? (Choose all responses that are not true.)

    a. Packet filtering is disabled.

    b. 100MB is set up as the default Web Proxy cache.

    c. C:\MSPROXY is the default Web proxy installation directory.

    d. C:\%SYSTEMROOT%\MSPROXY is the default installation directory.

    e. 100MB plus 0.5MB for each client is set up as the default Web Proxy cache.

15. Which of the following is the best definition for the LAT?

    a. The LAT, or Local Address Table, defines the IP addresses that belong to the internal network.

    b. The LAT, or Local Address Table, defines the IP addresses that belong to the internal network adapters on MS Proxy Server.

    c. The LAT, or Local Address Table, defines the IP addresses that belong to the external network.

    d. The LAT, or Local Access Table, defines the IP addresses that belong to the internal network.

    e. The LAT, or Local Access Time, defines the MS Proxy Server availability hours.

16. Which file contains the LAT for a client computer that is regularly updated by the MS Proxy Server?

    a. LAT.INI

    b. LAT.TXT

    c. MSPLAT.TXT

    d. MSPCLIENT.TXT

    e. MSPCLIENT.INI

17. Assume you have installed Microsoft Proxy Server version 2.0 on an Alpha AXP with computer name APPROX and IP address 192.168.1.1. The installation proceeded normally and all of the default options were configured. You haven't created any additional shared folders since installation. How can you begin installation of the client computers? (Choose all that apply.)

    a. Connect the client browsers to **http://192.168.1.1/MSProxy/**.

    b. Connect the client computers to \\192.168.1.1\CLIENTS and run the client setup program.

    c. Connect the client computers to \\192.168.1.1\MSPCLNT and run the client setup program.

    d. Connect the client computers to \\APPROX\CLIENTS and run the client setup program.

    e. Connect the client browser to **http://192.168.1.1/Clients/**.

18. Microsoft Proxy Server 2.0 can be installed on which of the following systems?

    a. DEC Alpha AXP

    b. Intel P200

    c. Intel 486DX

    d. Intel 386DX

    e. All of the above

19. Microsoft Proxy Server 2.0 requires at least a ___ MB _____ partition in order to install.

    a. 10, FAT

    b. 100, FAT

    c. 10, NTFS

    d. 100, NTFS

    e. 50, HPFS

20. What is the default port configured for Web browsers in the Client Installation/Configuration section of MS Proxy Server 2.0 Setup?

    a. 70

    b. 80

    c. 90

    d. 100

    e. 120

21. What is the default size of the Microsoft Proxy Server cache during installation?

   a. 10 times the number of clients

   b. 0.5 times the number of clients

   c. 40% of the corpus

   d. 100MB

   e. 200MB

22. When you are installing Microsoft Proxy Server version 2.0, which of the following are installation choices? (Choose all that apply.)

   a. Install ODBC 3.0 drivers.

   b. Install IE 4.0 Integration Components.

   c. Install Microsoft Proxy Server.

   d. Install Administration Tool.

   e. Install Documentation.

23. When you use Microsoft Proxy Server 2.0 to connect to an external network, you should not configure a default gateway on a network adapter that is used to connect your Proxy Server computer to your internal network. (True or False?)

24. What is the default installation folder for Microsoft Proxy Server as displayed in the Microsoft Proxy Server Setup dialog box?

   a. C:\MSP

   b. C:\MSPROXY

   c. %SYSTEMROOT%\SYSTEM32\DRIVERS\ETC

   d. %SYSTEMROOT%\SYSTEM32\PROXY

   e. %SYSTEMROOT%\SYSTEM32\MSPROXY

HANDS-ON PROJECTS

In this project, you will install Microsoft Proxy Server 2.0 and accept the default settings. Make sure the computer you are using meets the minimum hardware and software requirements. Also, make sure you have installed the SAP agent service, which can be verified from the Network Properties|Services tab.

 ## PROJECT 6.1

1. To install Microsoft Proxy Server 2.0, insert the Proxy Server CD. AUTORUN.INF will start the installation wizard (see Figure 6.7) if that feature is enabled on your system. If not, run SETUP.BAT from the MSPROXY directory.

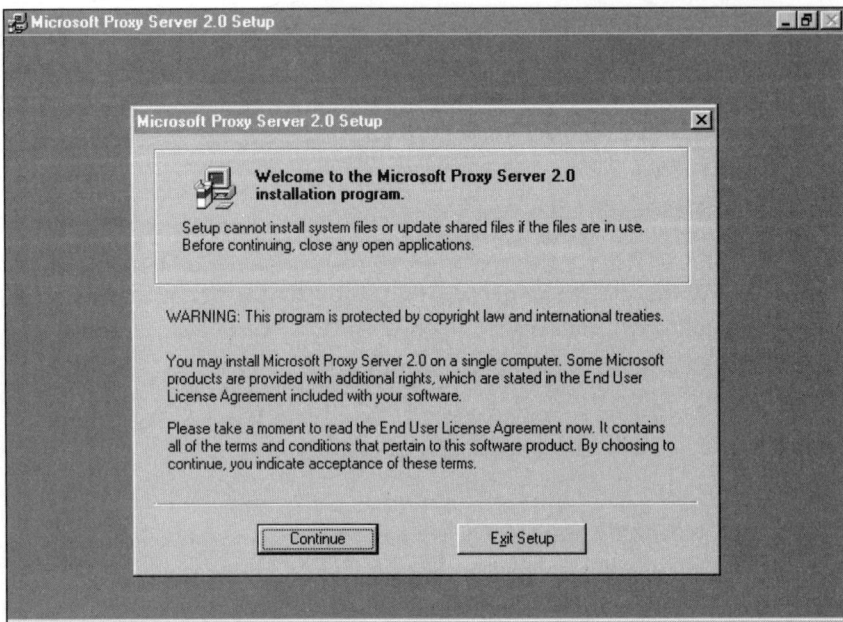

Figure 6.7   The Proxy Server Setup Wizard start screen.

2. Click on Continue. The Microsoft Proxy Server Setup dialog box appears
   and prompts you for the CD key.

3. Enter the 10-digit key found on the sticker on the back of the CD-ROM
   case. Click on OK. The Product Identification dialog box appears.

4. Click on OK. The system will search for installed components, and the
   Microsoft Proxy Server Setup dialog box opens and displays the default
   destination folder in which Proxy Server will be installed.

5. If desired, change the folder in which Proxy Server will be installed by
   clicking on the Change Folder button and providing the new destination
   path. After modifying the path, click on the large button next to Installation
   Options.

6. The Microsoft Proxy Server 2.0 Installation Options dialog box appears (see
   Figure 6.8). By default, all components are selected. Accept the default
   settings by clicking on Continue. This will install Microsoft Proxy Server 2.0,
   the Administrative Tool, and the online documentation. If not enough disk
   space is available to install the selected options, an error message will appear
   indicating that you need to free some disk space before continuing. If the
   SAP agent is not installed, an error message will appear prompting you to
   install the SAP agent and the installation process will end.

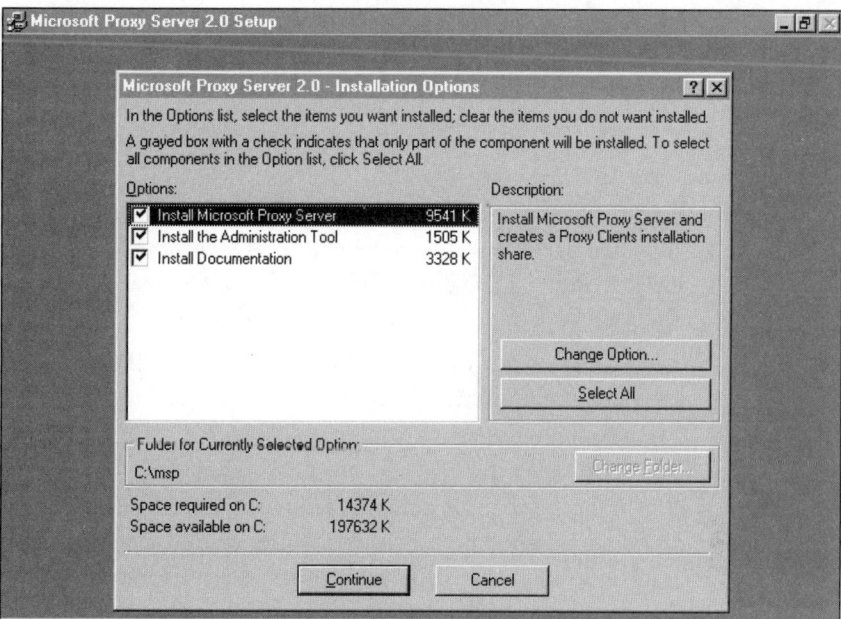

Figure 6.8   The Microsoft Proxy Server Installation Options dialog box.

7. Setup will stop the WWW service and the Microsoft Proxy Server Cache Drives dialog box appears. By default, caching is enabled, and the local drives are listed in the Drive list box.

8. To assign a partition to store cache data, select the drive from the list, enter the amount of space to use for caching in the Maximum Size (MB) box, and click on the Set button. Repeat as necessary to assign additional drives to store cached information. Note that only partitions that are formatted with NTFS are accessible for assigning cache storage.

   The minimum requirement for disk caching storage is 100MB plus an additional 0.5MB for each Web Proxy service client. Also note only local disk drives can be used for caching. Configure the cache options and click on OK.

9. The Local Address Table Configuration dialog box appears. To construct a table of the IP addresses of your internal network, click on the Construct Table button. The Construct Local Address Table dialog box appears. The default selections for constructing the Local Address Table (LAT) are to include the private IP address ranges and to load from the NT internal routing table the known address ranges for all IP interface cards.

10. To include the IP address ranges that are defined as private address ranges, select Add Private Ranges. This option includes the address ranges that are defined for intranet use in the current Request for Comments (RFC). If these addresses are used, they will not be routed across the Internet. They are

reserved for private, intranet use and one is defined for each address class. The reserved address ranges are as follows:

- Class A reserved range: 10.X.X.X
- Class B reserved range: 172.16.X.X to 172.31.X.X
- Class C reserved range: 192.168.X.X

11. To select the network interface cards on the server whose IP addresses will be included in the Local Access Table (LAT), select the Load from NT Internal Routing Table option. Two choices are available under this option:

- Load known address ranges from all IP interface cards.
- Load known address ranges from the following IP interface cards. This box lists the configured network interface cards. Select the card you wish to include.

12. Click on OK after making selections. The entries for the options selected appear in the Internal IP ranges portion of the Local Address Table Configuration dialog box (Figure 6.9). You should receive a setup warning message indicating that you should verify the addresses added to the LAT to ensure that they are all correct.

The entries included in the Local Address Table should only contain the private IP address ranges and IP addresses for your internal network. At this point, you can add additional IP addresses to the LAT.

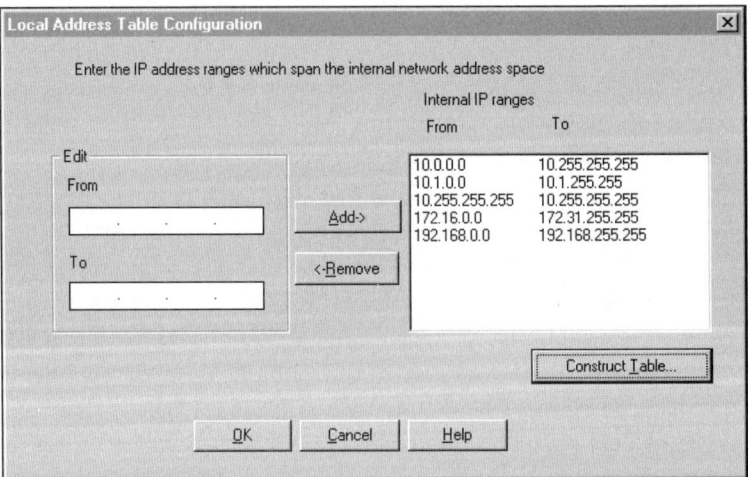

Figure 6.9 The Local Address Table Configuration dialog box.

13. To add a single entry, enter the IP address in the From and To box under Edit and click on Add. To add a ranges of addresses, enter the starting address in the From box under Edit and the ending address for the range in the To box, then click on Add.

14. Click on OK to accept the default settings. You will receive a setup warning message indicating that you should verify the addresses added to the LAT to ensure all of the addresses are correct. Then you will return to the Local Address Table Configuration dialog box.

15. Click on OK. The Client Installation/Configuration dialog box appears (see Figure 6.10).

16. Use the choices under WinSock Proxy Client to specify how the client setup program will configure WinSock Proxy clients that install from this server. In this selection, you provide either the computer name or the IP address of the proxy server. The default selection is the computer name.

6

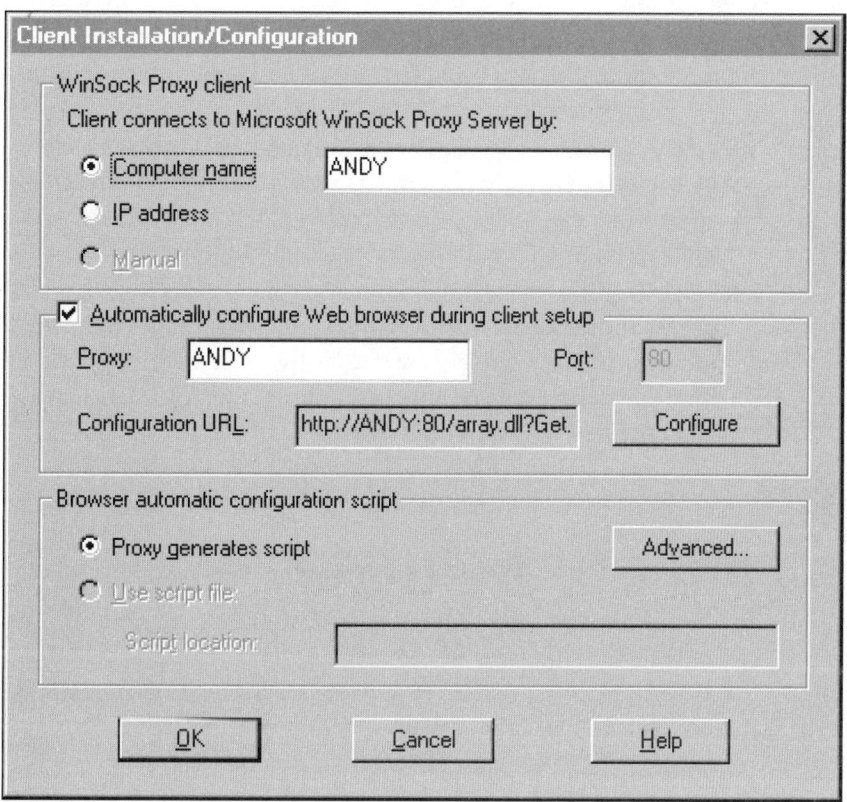

Figure 6.10   The Client Installation/Configuration dialog box.

17. If you select the Automatically Configure The Web Browser During Client Setup checkbox, client setup will modify the client Web browser network setting to send client requests to the proxy server rather than the external network or the Internet. A configuration area will allow you to use a custom URL script to configure the client rather than the default one supplied with Proxy Server.

18. If you click on the Advanced button under Browser Automatic Configuration Script, the Advanced Client Configuration dialog box appears. To return to the Client Installation/Configuration menu, click on the OK button to accept the configuration options selected and described below:

   ■ You can select whether Proxy Server will be used for local servers.

   ■ You can select which IP addresses will be excluded from Proxy Server.

   ■ You can select which domains to exclude from Proxy Server. The entries are typed in the box under the option and separated by semicolons. The domains mentioned in this area are Internet domains, not Microsoft NT network domains.

   ■ You can enable a backup route either to the Internet or to another Proxy Server.

19. Accept the default settings by clicking on OK. The Access Control dialog box appears. This box allows you to control the proxy clients' Internet access and enables the Access Control option. The Access Control setting can be modified through the Proxy Server Administration tool.

20. Click on OK to accept the settings for the Access Control box. Proxy Setup checks for disk space, completes the installation, and restarts the Internet services. After the services are started, the Microsoft Proxy Server 2.0 Setup box appears and displays a successful installation message. Click on OK to end the Proxy Server Setup Wizard.

 CASE PROJECTS

1. You administer a 200-client network. Your internal network uses IPX/SPX only for communications; however, some clients have TCP/IP installed for RAS to remote clients. You want to install Microsoft Proxy Server and have all client computers connect to the Internet through the Proxy Server.

   Required result: All client computers must use IPX/SPX to connect to Microsoft Proxy Server.

   Optional desired results: Client computers that are using TCP/IP for RAS can continue to do so. Client computers will use the WinSock Proxy client to connect to the Internet.

Proposed solution: Install Microsoft Proxy Server and configure it to use TCP/IP to connect to the Internet. Enable IPX/SPX on the Proxy Server as well. Install the WinSock Proxy client on all of the client computers. Remove TCP/IP from all client computers. Which results does the proposed solution produce?

    a. The proposed solution produces the required result and both of the optional desired results.

    b. The proposed solution produces the required result but only one of the optional desired results.

    c. The proposed solution produces the required result but neither of the optional desired results.

    d. The proposed solution does not produce the required result.

2. You administer a 200-client network. Your internal network uses IPX/SPX only for communications; however, some clients have TCP/IP installed for RAS to remote clients. You want to install Microsoft Proxy Server and have all client computers connect to the Internet through the Proxy Server.

Required result: All client computers must use IPX/SPX to connect to the Microsoft Proxy Server.

Optional desired results: Client computers that are using TCP/IP for RAS can continue to do so. Client computers will use the WinSock Proxy client to connect to the Internet.

Proposed solution: Install Microsoft Proxy Server and configure it to use TCP/IP to connect to the Internet. Enable IPX/SPX on the Proxy Server as well. Install the WinSock Proxy client on all of the client computers. Disable TCP/IP from the network adapter on each client computer. Which results does the proposed solution produce?

    a. The proposed solution produces the required result and both of the optional desired results.

    b. The proposed solution produces the required result but only one of the optional desired results.

    c. The proposed solution produces the required result but neither of the optional desired results.

    d. The proposed solution does not produce the required result.

3. You administer a 200-client network. Your internal network uses IPX/SPX only for communications; however, some clients have TCP/IP installed for RAS to remote clients. You want to install Microsoft Proxy Server and have all client computers connect to the Internet through the Proxy Server.

Required result: All client computers must use IPX/SPX to connect to Microsoft Proxy Server.

Optional desired results: Client computers that are using TCP/IP for RAS can continue to do so. Client computers will use the WinSock Proxy client to connect to the Internet.

Proposed solution: Install Microsoft Proxy Server and configure it to use TCP/IP to connect to the Internet. Enable IPX/SPX on the proxy server as well. Install the WinSock Proxy client on all of the client computers. Check the Force IPX/SPX Protocol option on the WinSock Proxy client computers. Which results does the proposed solution produce?

    a. The proposed solution produces the required result and both of the optional desired results.

    b. The proposed solution produces the required result but only one of the optional desired results.

    c. The proposed solution produces the required result but neither of the optional desired results.

    d. The proposed solution does not produce the required result.

4. You manage a network with 300 client computers that will use Microsoft Proxy Server to connect to the Internet. The Proxy Server, named NT_PROX, has been configured and the default installation and share options were chosen. You want to install the 300 client computers as WinSock Proxy clients. NT_PROX is running both NWLink and TCP/IP. All clients on the network are using the NWLink, but some also use TCP/IP.

Required result: All clients must be configured with the WinSock Proxy client.

Optional desired results: Clients must use NWLink to connect to MS Proxy Server. TCP/IP should remain enabled on the client computers that already have it.

Proposed solution: Connect the client computers to \\NT_PROX\PROXCLNT to install the WSP on the client computers. Check the Force IPX/SPX Protocol option on the client computers and be sure to enable the WinSock Proxy client software. Which results does the proposed solution produce?

    a. The proposed solution produces the required result and both of the optional desired results.

    b. The proposed solution produces the required result but only one of the optional desired results.

    c. The proposed solution produces the required result but neither of the optional desired results.

    d. The proposed solution does not produce the required result.

5. You are planning to install a proxy server on your network. You have chosen three different computers as candidates to become the Microsoft Proxy Server. The first candidate is a Windows NT server with a RISC R4000 processor, 24MB of RAM, and 100MB of free disk space on a FAT partition. The second candidate is a Windows NT Server with an Intel Pentium 120 processor, 32MB of RAM, and 500MB of free disk space on an NTFS partition. The third is a Windows NT Server with an Intel Pentium 133 processor, 16MB of RAM, and 400MB of hard disk space on an NTFS partition. All three computers are running Internet Information Server 2.0 and two network cards running TCP/IP. You plan to use a router connected to your ISP for Internet connectivity.

Required result: Install and configure Microsoft Proxy Server 2.0 on a computer that meets the minimum installation requirements.

Optional desired results: The MS Proxy Server computer should be able to support 300 WinSock Proxy clients. Clients should not be able to connect to the Internet except through the computer running MS Proxy.

Proposed solution: Add eight or more megabytes of RAM to the RISC R4000 computer and install Microsoft Proxy Server on that computer. Which results does the proposed solution produce?

a. The proposed solution produces the required result and both of the optional desired results.

b. The proposed solution produces the required result but only one of the optional desired results.

c. The proposed solution produces the required result but neither of the optional desired results.

d. The proposed solution does not produce the required result.

6. You are planning to install a proxy server on your network. You have chosen three different computers as candidates to become the Microsoft Proxy Server. The first candidate is a Windows NT Server with an Alpha processor, 24MB of RAM, and 100MB of free disk space on a FAT partition. The second candidate is a Windows NT Server with an Intel Pentium 120MHz processor, 32MB of RAM, and 500MB of free disk space on an NTFS partition. The third is a Windows NT Server with an Intel Pentium 133 processor, 16MB of RAM, and 400MB of hard disk space on an NTFS partition. All three computers are running Internet Information Server 2.0 and two network cards running TCP/IP. You plan to use a router connected to your ISP for Internet connectivity.

Required Result: Install and configure Microsoft Proxy Server 2.0 on a computer that meets the minimum installation requirements.

Optional desired results: The MS Proxy Server computer should be able to support 300 WinSock Proxy clients. Clients should not be able to connect to the Internet except through the computer running MS Proxy.

Proposed solution: Install Microsoft Proxy Server on the Pentium 133. Configure the WinSock Proxy cache for the NTFS partition and add 150MB to the cache. Connect Proxy Server's network card to the router that provides Internet services. Connect the other network card to the LAN.

Which results does the proposed solution produce?

   a. The proposed solution produces the required result and both of the optional desired results.

   b. The proposed solution produces the required result but only one of the optional desired results.

   c. The proposed solution produces the required result but neither of the optional desired results.

   d. The proposed solution does not produce the required result.

7. You are planning to install a proxy server on your network. You have chosen three different computers as candidates to become the Microsoft Proxy Server. The first candidate is a Windows NT Server with an Alpha processor, 24MB of RAM, and 100MB of free disk space on a FAT partition. The second candidate is a Windows NT Server with an Intel Pentium 120 processor, 32MB of RAM, and 500MB of free disk space on an NTFS partition. The third is a Windows NT Server with an Intel Pentium 133 processor, 16MB of RAM, and 400MB of hard disk space on an NTFS partition. All three computers are running Internet Information Server 2.0 and two network cards running TCP/IP. You plan to use a router connected to your ISP for Internet connectivity.

Required result: Install and configure Microsoft Proxy Server 2.0 on a computer that meets the minimum installation requirements.

Optional desired results: The MS Proxy Server computer should be able to support 300 WinSock Proxy clients. Clients should not be able to connect to the Internet except through the computer running MS Proxy.

Proposed solution: Install Microsoft Proxy Server on the Pentium 120. Configure the WinSock Proxy cache for the NTFS partition and add 150MB to the cache. Connect Proxy Server's network card to the router that provides Internet services. Connect the router's network card to the LAN. Configure the WSP clients to connect to the MS Proxy Server. Which results does the proposed solution produce?

   a. The proposed solution produces the required result and both of the optional desired results.

   b. The proposed solution produces the required result but only one of the optional desired results.

   c. The proposed solution produces the required result but neither of the optional desired results.

   d. The proposed solution does not produce the required result.

8. You attach your organization's network to the Internet using an ISDN line from your Windows NT Server (which is currently only using half of your ISDN connection). You want to configure Microsoft Proxy Server on your Windows NT Server, which meets or exceeds all installation requirements,

so WinSock Proxy clients can benefit from its caching capabilities. You also want to restrict clients from using specifically forbidden Internet sites.

Required result: Install Microsoft Proxy Server 2.0 on your Windows NT server.

Optional desired results: Ensure that your computer uses both lines of your ISDN connection. Keep clients from accessing **www.forbidden.com** and **123.167.3.45**.

Proposed solution: Install Microsoft Proxy Server on your Windows NT Server. Configure a cache of about 110MB on your NTFS partition. Which results does the proposed solution produce?

a. The proposed solution produces the required result and both of the optional desired results.

b. The proposed solution produces the required result but only one of the optional desired results.

c. The proposed solution produces the required result but neither of the optional desired results.

d. The proposed solution does not produce the required result.

9. You attach your organization's network to the Internet using an ISDN line from your Windows NT Server (which is currently only using half of your ISDN connection). You want to configure Microsoft Proxy Server on your Windows NT Server, which meets or exceeds all installation requirements, so WinSock Proxy clients can benefit from its caching capabilities. You also want to restrict clients from using specifically forbidden Internet sites.

Required result: Install Microsoft Proxy Server 2.0 on your Windows NT Server.

Optional desired results: Ensure that your computer uses both lines of your ISDN connection. Keep clients from accessing **www.forbidden.com** and **123.167.3.45**.

Proposed solution: Install Microsoft Proxy Server on your Windows NT Server. Configure a cache on your NTFS partition of about 300MB. Install enable multilink and ensure that two entries have been included for your ISDN phone numbers in the Phonebook. Also, ensure that multiple lines are configured for your Dial-Up Networking client. Which results does the proposed solution produce?

a. The proposed solution produces the required result and both of the optional desired results.

b. The proposed solution produces the required result but only one of the optional desired results.

c. The proposed solution produces the required result but neither of the optional desired results.

d. The proposed solution does not produce the required result.

CHAPTER SEVEN

PROXY CLIENT CONFIGURATION

One of the most attractive features of Microsoft Proxy Server 2.0 is its ability to support a wide variety of clients, including Windows, Unix, and Macintosh systems. In this chapter, you will learn how to configure the many types of clients supported by Microsoft Proxy Server 2.0.

AFTER READING THIS CHAPTER AND COMPLETING THE EXERCISES, YOU WILL BE ABLE TO:

- Determine which clients require which proxy services
- Configure Proxy Server clients
- Modify the client configuration files

MAKING THE CONNECTION

The first step in configuring a proxy client is ensuring that a connection between the client and the server exists. Because Microsoft Proxy Server 2.0 supports such a large variety of clients, this can be an extensive project, but one that will ultimately pay off in the long run.

As you learned in Chapter 2, Microsoft Proxy Server 2.0 not only supports TCP/IP (the Internet Protocol suite), it also has the ability to function as an IPX-to-IP gateway. This is important when you are considering the Proxy Server implementation for your network. One other major consideration is the non–Windows clients you have on your network and whether they are using SOCKS or CERN-compliant Web browsers.

Both considerations, however, hinge on the ability of the client to communicate with the server and to be granted access to its resources. One of the biggest problems that looms over administrators configuring Proxy Server clients is the lack of connectivity. It is important to verify that the client computer is able to locate the server, whether through the Network Neighborhood or by using the PING utility.

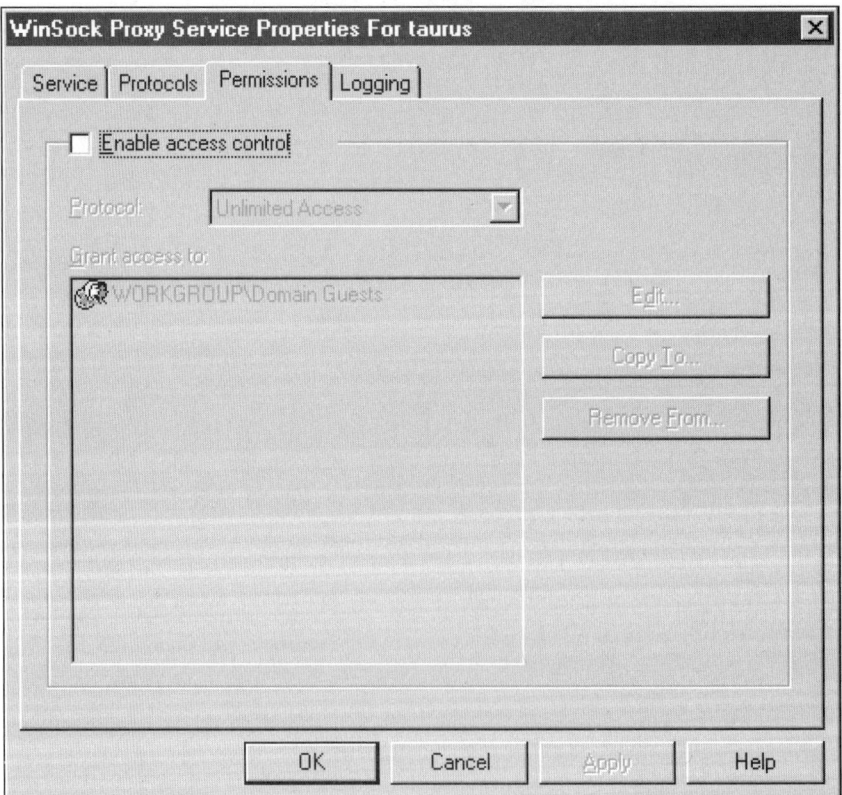

Figure 7.1 WinSock Proxy access control disabled.

Another consideration with regard to client configuration is how security is administered on the Proxy Server. Remember that, if the Proxy Server components are configured with access control disabled (as shown in Figure 7.1), clients are not required to log on to the server to use its services. However, if access control is enabled, the clients must have accounts on the Proxy Server and appropriate permissions to access the system.

Remember that each proxy service manages access control in a different way. The Web Proxy service provides access controls through only four settings: FTP Read, Gopher, Secure, and WWW (as shown in Figure 7.2).

 The WWW permission provides access to Web sites that use both HTTP and HTTPS, the SSL version of the HTTP protocol. The Secure permission provides access to sites that use other SSL protocols, such as Snews.

By using the Copy To and Remove From options in the Permissions tab of the Web Proxy Service Properties dialog box, you can grant a particular user or group access to a number of protocols. For example, to add the same group's

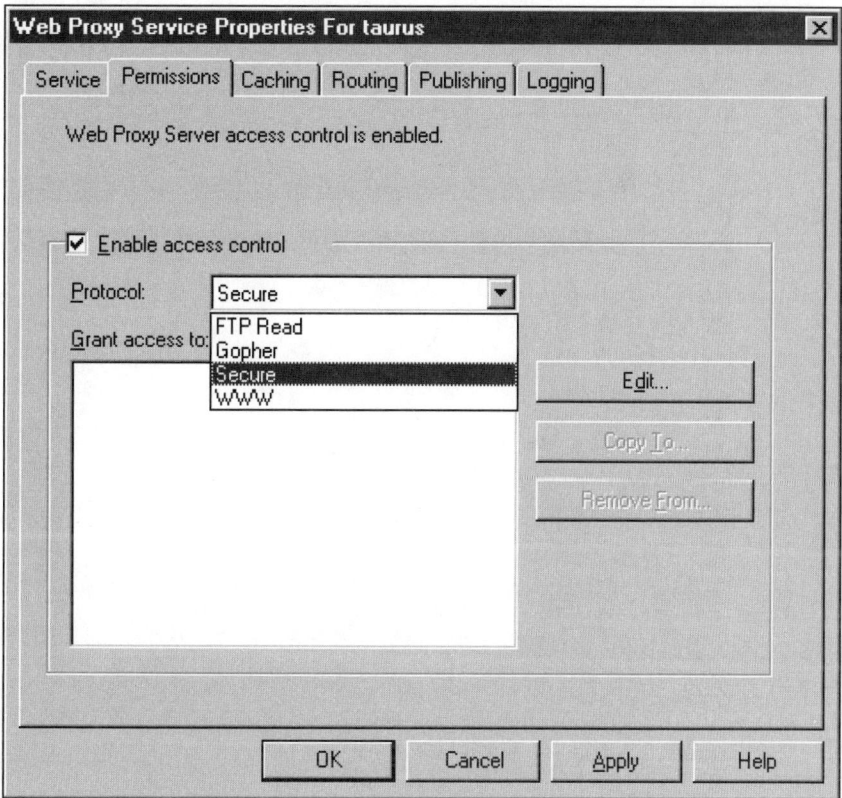

Figure 7.2   The access controls available to the Web Proxy service.

permissions to all protocols, you must first configure access for one protocol to a user or group. Next, select the group and click on Copy To on the Permissions tab. The Service Selection dialog box appears (see Figure 7.3). Ctrl+Click to select each protocol to which you want to copy the group's permissions and then click on OK.

The permissions available to WinSock Proxy clients are much more extensive and detailed. Each protocol allowed by the WinSock Proxy service is defined through the Protocols tab of the WinSock Proxy Service Properties dialog box, shown in Figure 7.4. Each protocol is discussed in detail in Appendix C.

The protocols defined in the Protocols tab are then used to assign permissions through the Permissions tab, the same way they are assigned for the Web Proxy service. One option that is available in the WinSock Proxy Service Permissions dialog box that is not available in the Web Proxy Service Permissions dialog box is the Unlimited Access option. This permission grants unlimited access to all protocols for members of the specified group. This configuration is often used to provide administrators unlimited access to the Internet while restricting access for the majority of the Proxy Server clients.

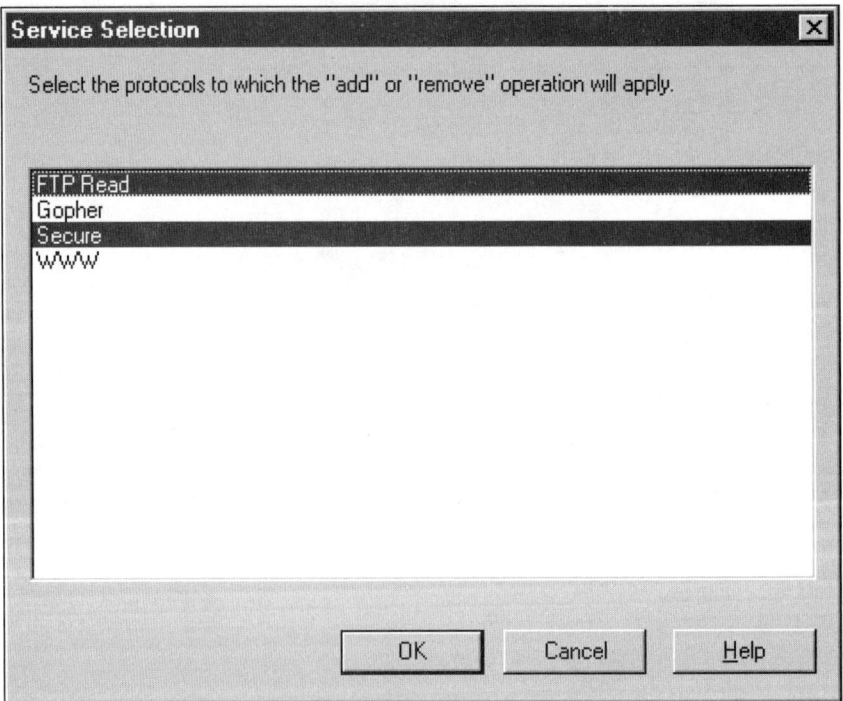

Figure 7.3   The Service Selection dialog box.

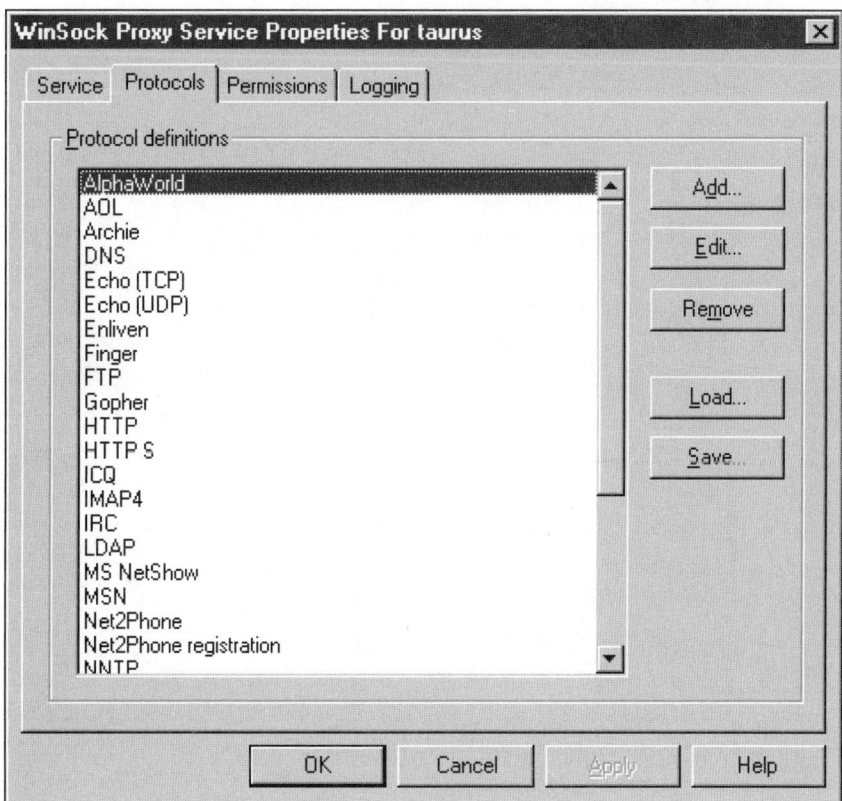

Figure 7.4   Many protocols are predefined for the WinSock Proxy service.

Permissions of the SOCKS Proxy service are handled differently than they are for the other services. The SOCKS Permission dialog box, shown in Figure 7.5, is used to configure specific access for SOCKS Proxy clients. Because the SOCKS Proxy service does not rely on Windows NT security, there is no configuration for user and group access. Access is instead granted or denied to all clients by domain or zone name or by IP address. The same configurations are available to limit access to specific destinations. You can also limit access to the SOCKS Proxy service by port; to do so, check the Port checkbox at the bottom of the window and specify the operator (equal, not equal, greater than, less than, greater than or equal, or less than or equal) and the port number.

CONFIGURING CLIENT COMPUTERS

Once you have verified that the client computers are able to communicate with the Proxy Server and that permissions, if they are being used, have been configured correctly, you are ready to configure the client computers to use the Proxy Server.

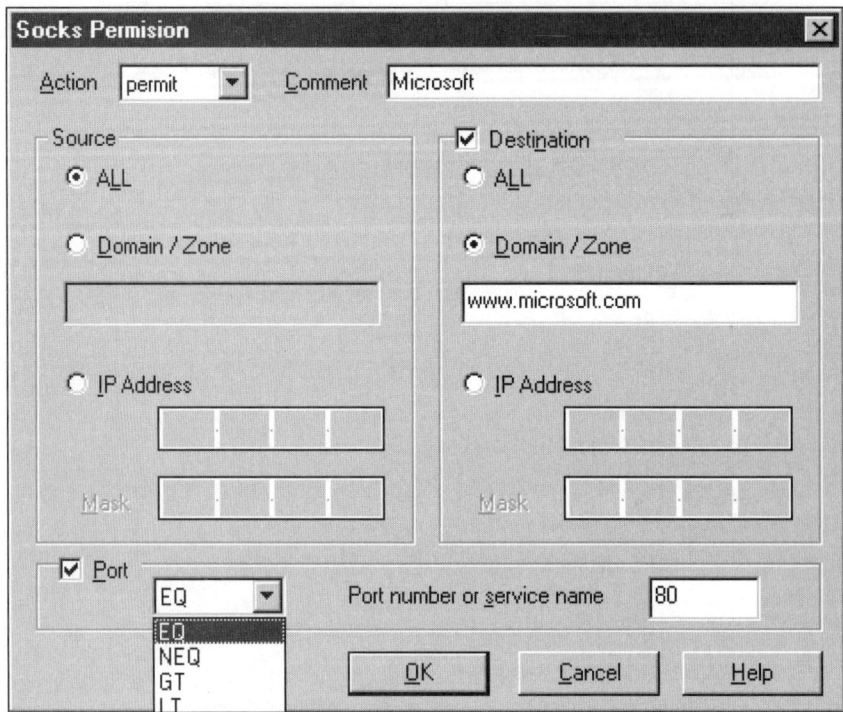

Figure 7.5   Defining SOCKS permissions.

CERN-COMPLIANT WEB PROXY CONFIGURATIONS

As you know, for a client computer to use the Web Proxy service, its browser must be CERN-Proxy compliant. This includes most of the Web browsers available today, including Microsoft Internet Explorer, Netscape Communicator (Navigator), and Opera. To change the settings for these clients, use the Web browser's configuration dialog box, which is usually accessed through the Settings or Options menus. The following sections discuss how to set these options for Microsoft Internet Explorer 4.0 and Netscape Communicator 4.0.

Microsoft Internet Explorer 4.0

The Proxy Server configuration for Microsoft Internet Explorer 4.0 is accessed by choosing Internet Options from the View menu. You can configure many aspects of Internet Explorer through the Internet Options dialog box, including the Proxy Server settings, which are configured through the Connection tab, as shown in Figure 7.6.

The Address setting can be the Proxy Server's IP address, its DNS name, or in the case of Windows clients, its NetBIOS computer name. The port settings must coincide with the settings used in the Permissions tab of the Web Proxy Service Properties dialog box; 80 is the general setting for WWW.

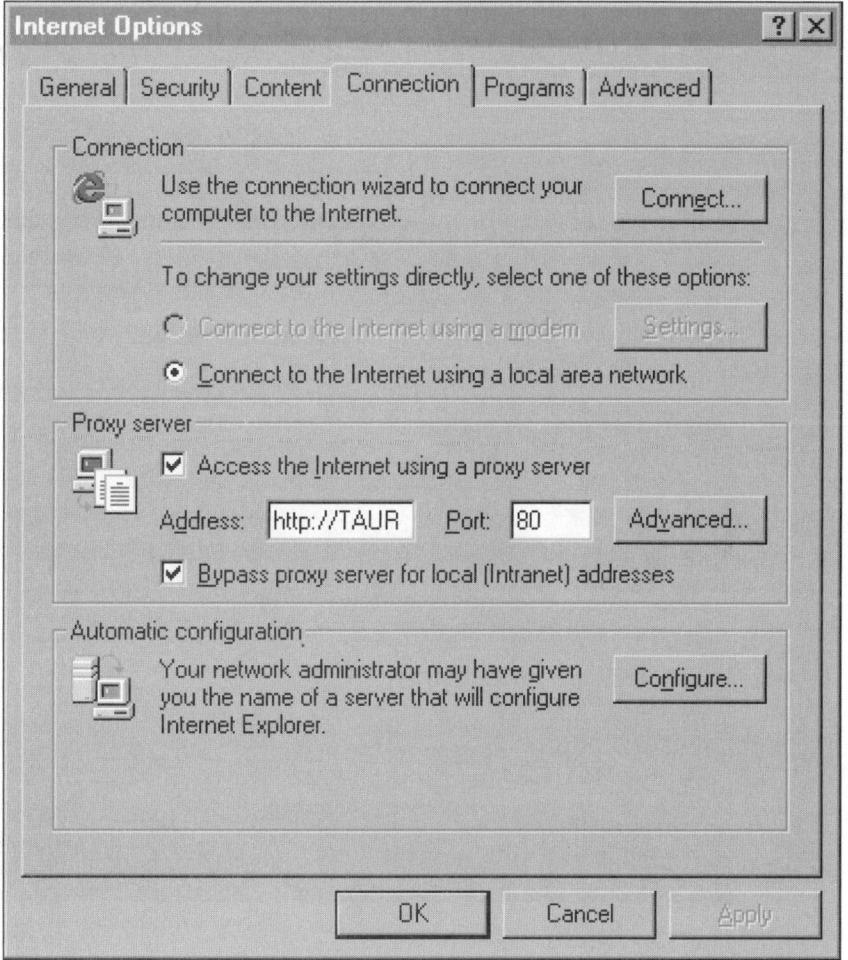

Figure 7.6 Proxy server settings for IE 4.0.

When you click on the Advanced button, the Proxy Settings dialog box appears (see Figure 7.7). Here you can configure a different Proxy Server and port for a number of basic Internet protocols, including HTTP, FTP, Secure, Gopher, and SOCKS. This configuration is useful when you have specific Proxy Servers performing specific functions, such as a server dedicated to FTP access.

 To operate on the Proxy Server computer correctly, a browser must be configured to use the IP address of the local NIC as its proxy address. You cannot use the server's computer name or DNS name because the address returned by the name resolution process may be the address of the interface connected to the Internet and will therefore be filtered by the Local Address Table (LAT).

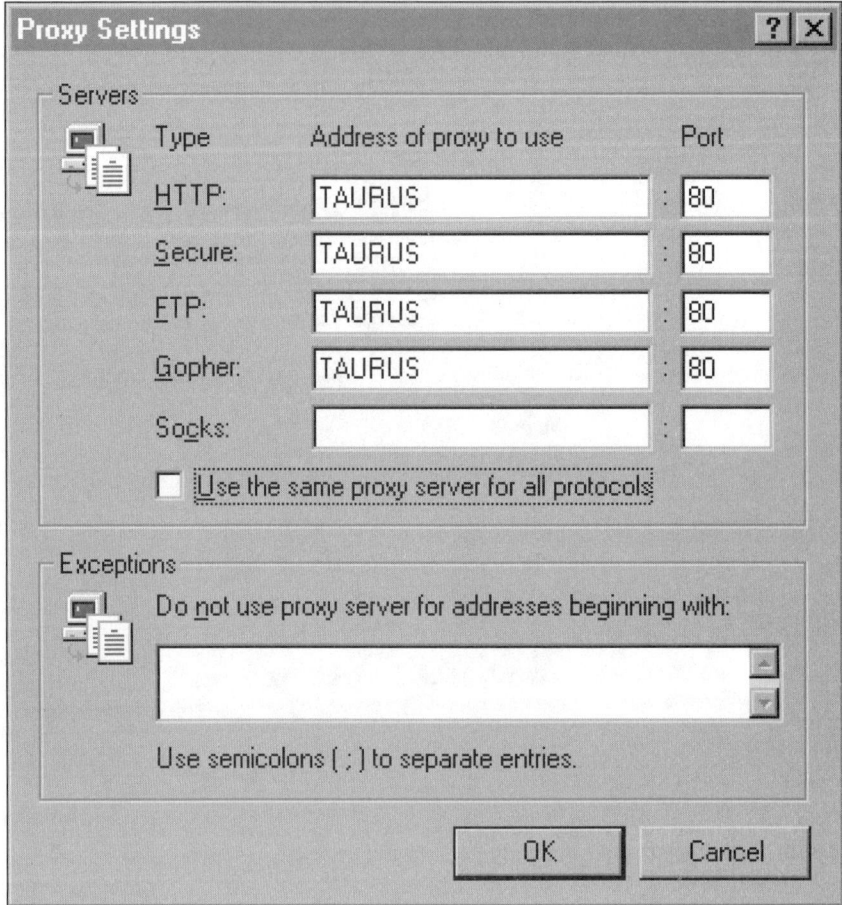

Figure 7.7   The advanced proxy settings allow users to configure multiple proxy servers.

Netscape Communicator 4.0

The Proxy Server configuration settings for Netscape Communicator 4.0 are accessed by choosing Preferences from the Edit menu. Select Advanced from the tree on the left and choose Proxies to invoke the dialog box shown in Figure 7.8. Notice that, unlike IE 4.0, there is no general proxy server configuration option.

To define the proxy server setting, you must select Manual Proxy Configuration and click on the View button. This brings up the Manual Proxy Configuration dialog box, shown in Figure 7.9. Again, notice that unlike IE, there is no option to use the same settings for all protocols. However, each option has the same settings by default. Also notice that Netscape provides settings for the Wide Area Information Service (WAIS) protocol, which is seldom used today.

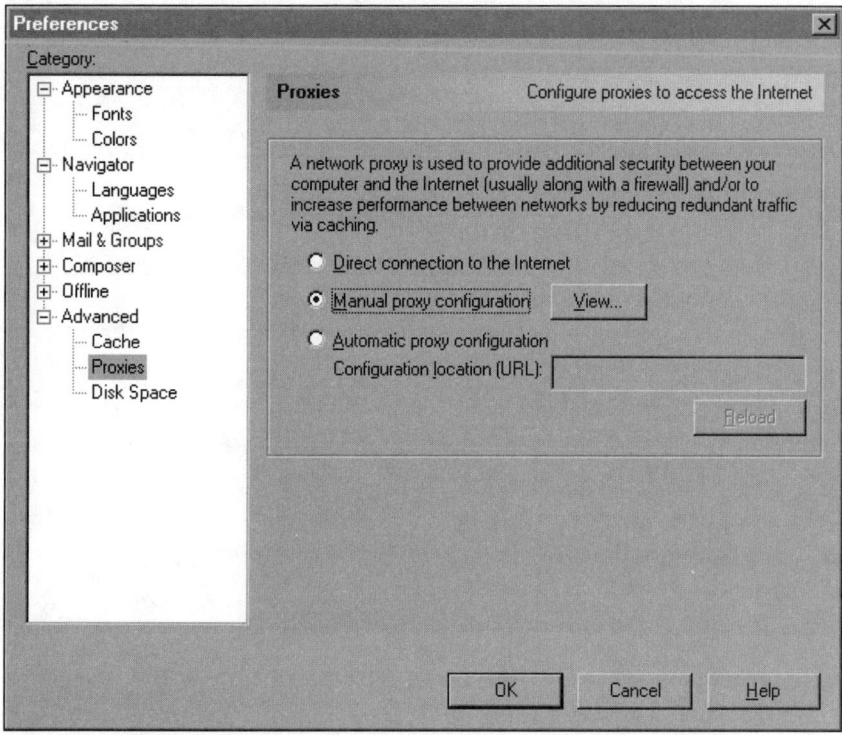

Figure 7.8   Proxy configuration options for Netscape Communicator.

The WAIS protocol is a legacy Internet system that is used to search cataloged resources. It is generally used today only in education to access older documents.

WINSOCK PROXY CLIENTS

As you've learned, the WinSock Proxy service operates differently than the Web Proxy service. One of the key differences is that WinSock Proxy (WSP) clients must be Windows computers and must be configured with client software. The client software intercepts Windows Sockets requests and directs them to the WinSock Proxy service. This means that any Windows Sockets program is able to use the WinSock Proxy service transparently. For example, although a Web browser may be configured to access the Proxy Server directly, other Windows Sockets programs, such as an email program like Eudora Lite or an FTP program like WS-FTP, may not have the configuration options available. These programs make standard requests to the Internet; the requests are intercepted by the WSP client software and redirected to the Proxy Server for access.

When Proxy Server is installed on a Windows NT Server, a share called MSPCLNT is automatically created and points to the C:\MSP\CLIENTS

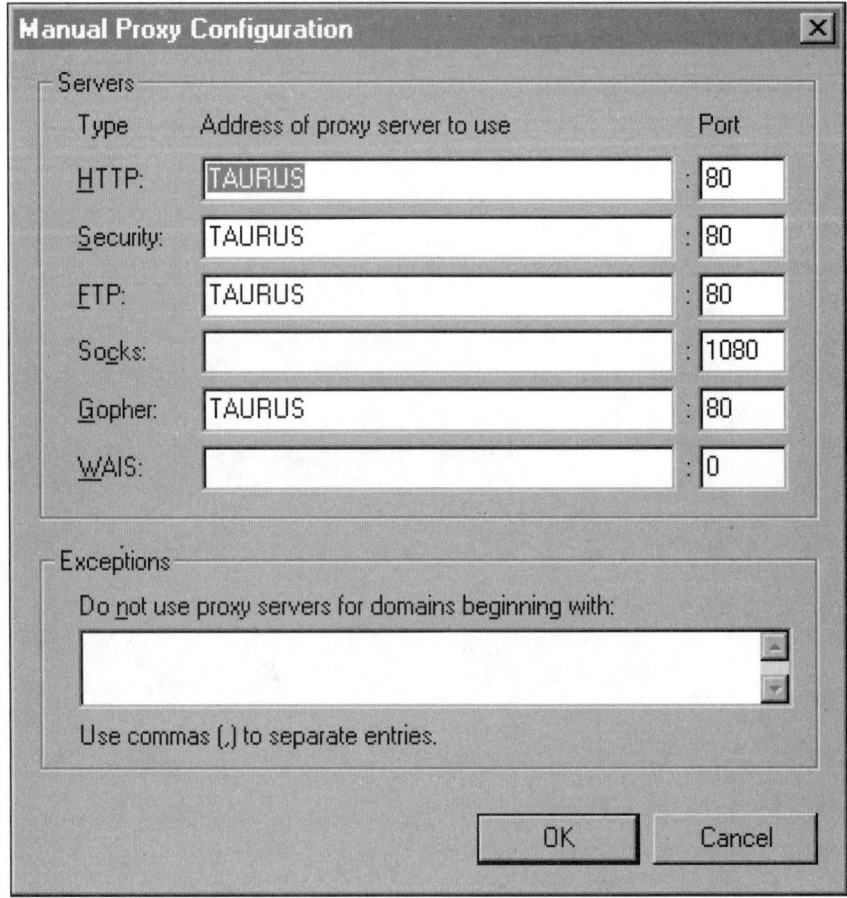

Figure 7.9   Proxy settings for Netscape Communicator are configured
through the Manual Proxy Configuration dialog box.

directory, assuming Proxy Server is installed on the C: drive. You can start the
WSP client installation program in one of the following ways:

- Connect to the Proxy Server, open the MSPCLNT share, and run
  SETUP.EXE. This starts the Microsoft Proxy Client Setup application,
  which is shown in Figure 7.10.

- From a Web browser, go to the **//servername/MSProxy** URL
  (*servername* is the name of your proxy server). This brings up the Web
  page shown in Figure 7.11. Click on the WinSock Proxy 2.0 Client link.
  Depending on the browser you are using, you will be prompted to
  either launch the Setup program (Microsoft Internet Explorer) or to
  save the SETUP.BAT file to launch later (Netscape Navigator). Whether
  you run the program immediately or save it to disk and run it later, you
  will start the Proxy Client Setup application (shown in Figure 7.10).

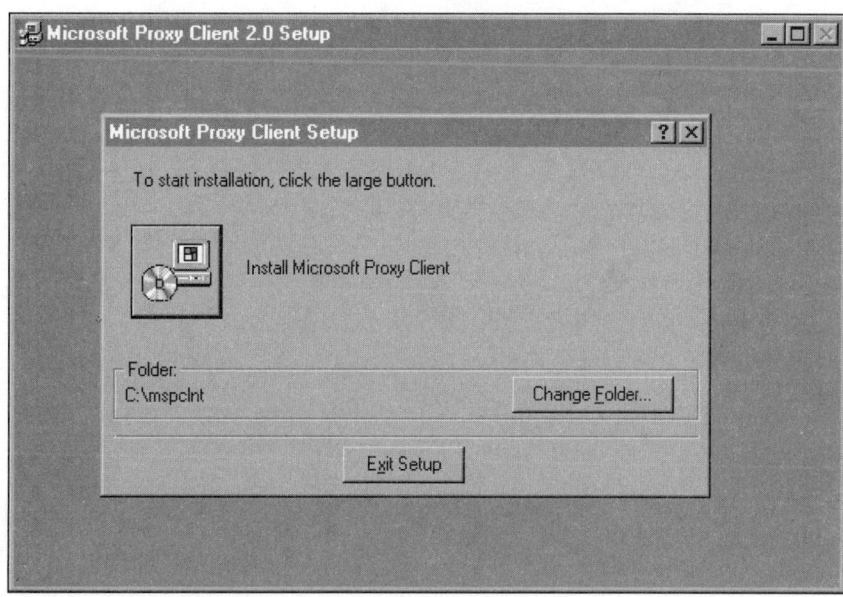

Figure 7.10   The Proxy Client Setup application.

From the Proxy Client Setup application, select the location for the WSP client software and click on Install Microsoft Proxy Client. It is often best to accept the default settings for the client software location. However, if you want to install

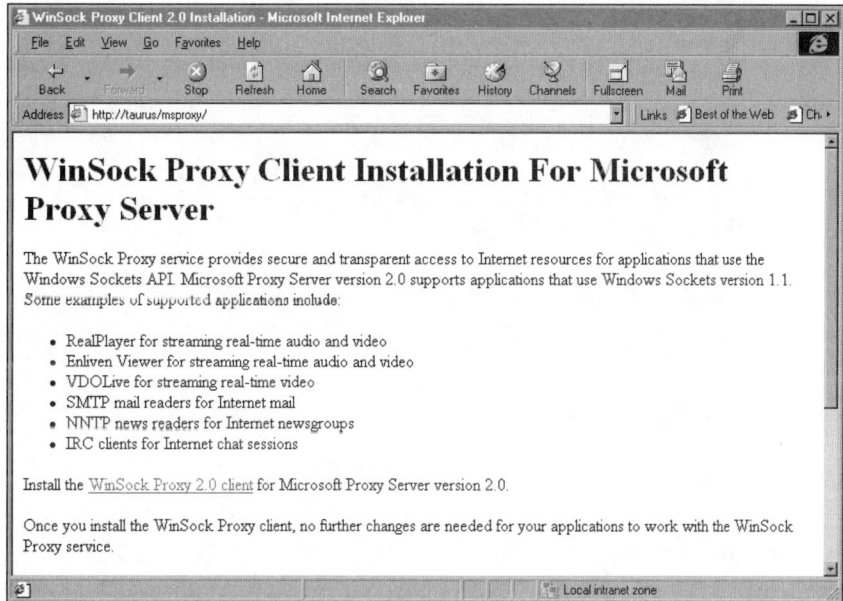

Figure 7.11   Launching the Proxy Client Setup application from a Web browser.

the software in a folder other than the default, click on Change Folder in the Proxy Client Setup application and select a new path. The program will install the software, copy the configuration files (MSPCLNT.INI, MSPLAT.TXT, etc.) from the proxy server, and prompt you to restart Windows. After restarting, the computer will be configured to use the WSP client software.

The few configuration options available from the client side for the WSP client software are configured through the WSP applet in the Control Panel (Start | Settings | Control Panel). As Figure 7.12 shows, the configuration options are limited to entering the Proxy Server name, updating the configuration, enabling the WSP client software, and forcing the use of the IPX/SPX protocol.

Click on Update Now to download the configuration files from the Proxy Server listed in the Server Name box. The Force IPX/SPX Protocol option is used with clients that are configured with both TCP/IP and IPX/SPX (NWLink), such as computers on IPX networks that have dial-up Internet connections. It forces the client computer to connect to the proxy server by using IPX/SPX rather than attempting to connect with TCP/IP.

 Each time the WSP client software is enabled or disabled, the computer must be restarted for the change to take effect.

Here are a few caveats to remember when you are dealing with the WSP client software:

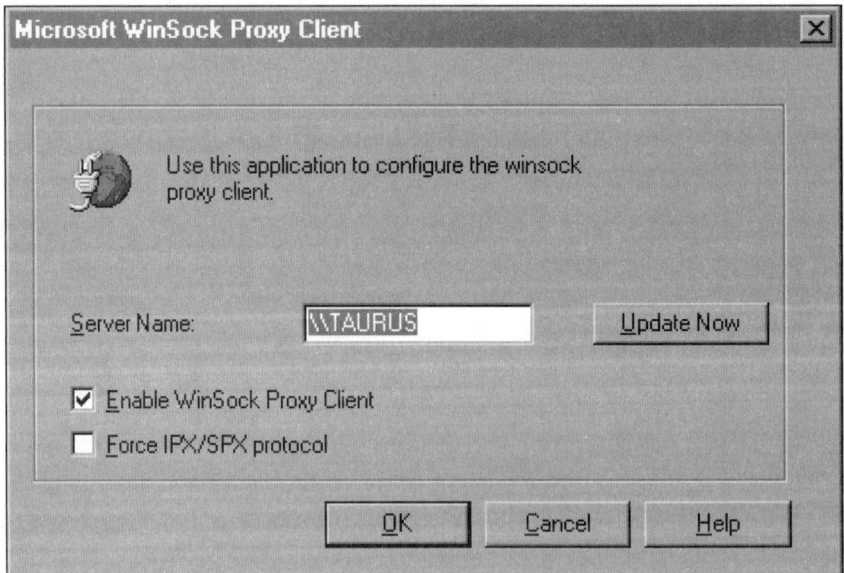

Figure 7.12 The WSP client configuration options.

- Although some Windows Sockets applications may provide settings to direct requests to the Proxy Server, do not utilize these settings. The WSP client software will intercept and redirect the requests independently.

- If the WSP client software is loaded on a workstation that is able to use 16-bit Windows Sockets applications, the user may be required to log on to the domain again through the Domain Credentials dialog box.

- In the event that a Windows NT client that has the WSP client software installed is upgraded, the WSP client software must be reinstalled. The upgrade process replaces WSOCK32.DLL, which is used by the WSP client software. Reinstallation may be required, for example, if a Windows NT Workstation 3.51 computer is upgraded to Windows NT Workstation 4.0.

- Microsoft Exchange Server cannot operate with the WSP client software installed. Exchange clients, such as Outlook or MS Mail, are able to effectively use the WSP client, but the Exchange Server software cannot function as a WSP client. For more information on using Microsoft Exchange Server with Microsoft Proxy Server, refer to the Exchange Server documentation.

Although the configuration options for the WinSock Proxy client software are limited on the client side, they are a bit more extensive on the server side. As mentioned earlier, when the WSP client software is installed, it also copies MSPLAT.TXT and MSPCLNT.INI to the local system for use by the WSP client software.

The greatest configuration benefit is seen when the WSP software is allowed to configure the client's Web browsers automatically. The basic settings in the Client Installation/Configuration dialog box, shown in Figure 7.13, define the contents of MSPCLNT.INI.

You can configure how the Proxy Server will be identified, whether to configure the client's browsers automatically and what settings will be used, and whether to configure the browsers to use Automatic Configuration.

The Proxy Server can be identified by either its computer name (which is its NetBIOS name defined through the Network applet) or its IP address, or it can be identified manually. If you choose the manual setting, the Server IP Address section of the MSPCLNT.INI file is not overwritten. This is useful when the administrator wants to manually configure the Server IP Address section, such as when there are multiple WinSock Proxy servers on a particular network.

When the Automatically Configure Web Browser During Client Setup option is checked, the Proxy Client Setup application will search for Web browsers, and

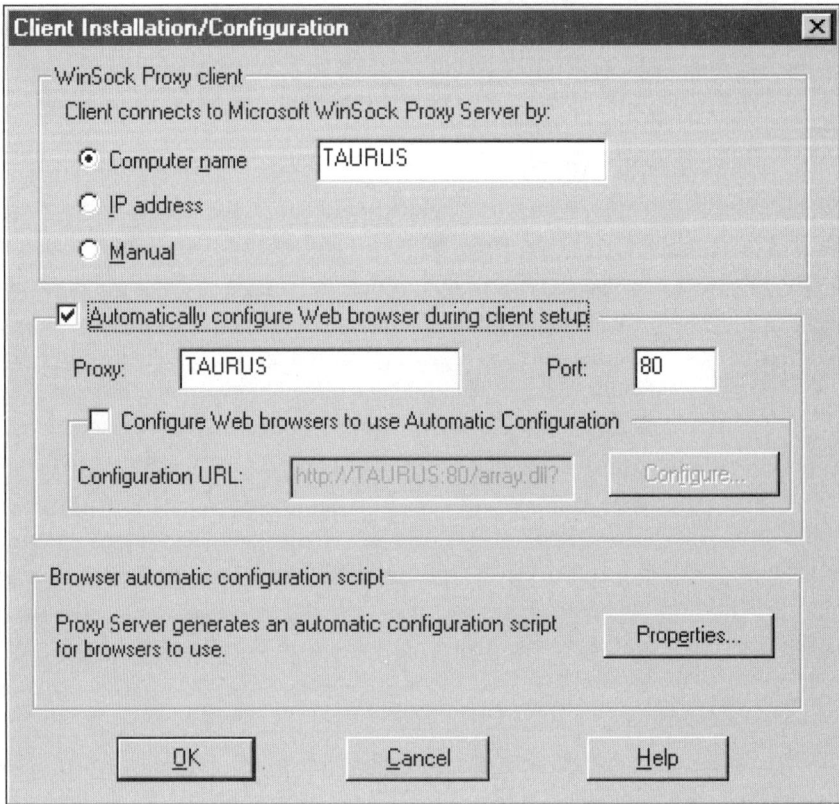

Figure 7.13   Web browsers can be configured automatically through the WinSock Proxy service.

the information shown in the Proxy and Port boxes will be copied into the browser's configuration. This ensures that all clients' browsers are correctly configured to use the Proxy Server.

Some browsers, such as IE and Navigator, can be configured automatically with scripts generated by the Proxy Server. This option is enabled by checking the Configure Web Browsers To Use Automatic Configuration option. The default URL is accessed when a client browser connects to the Proxy Server. A script that is able to configure the browser can be created manually and used by clicking on Configure and changing the Configuration URL setting.

Configure the script the browser uses when it accesses the default URL by clicking on the Properties button in the Browser Automatic Configuration Script area. The Advanced Client Configuration dialog box appears (see Figure 7.14), which you can use to set the parameters for the default configuration script.

The settings available through the Advanced Client Configuration dialog box are the same as the settings that can be set manually through the browser's

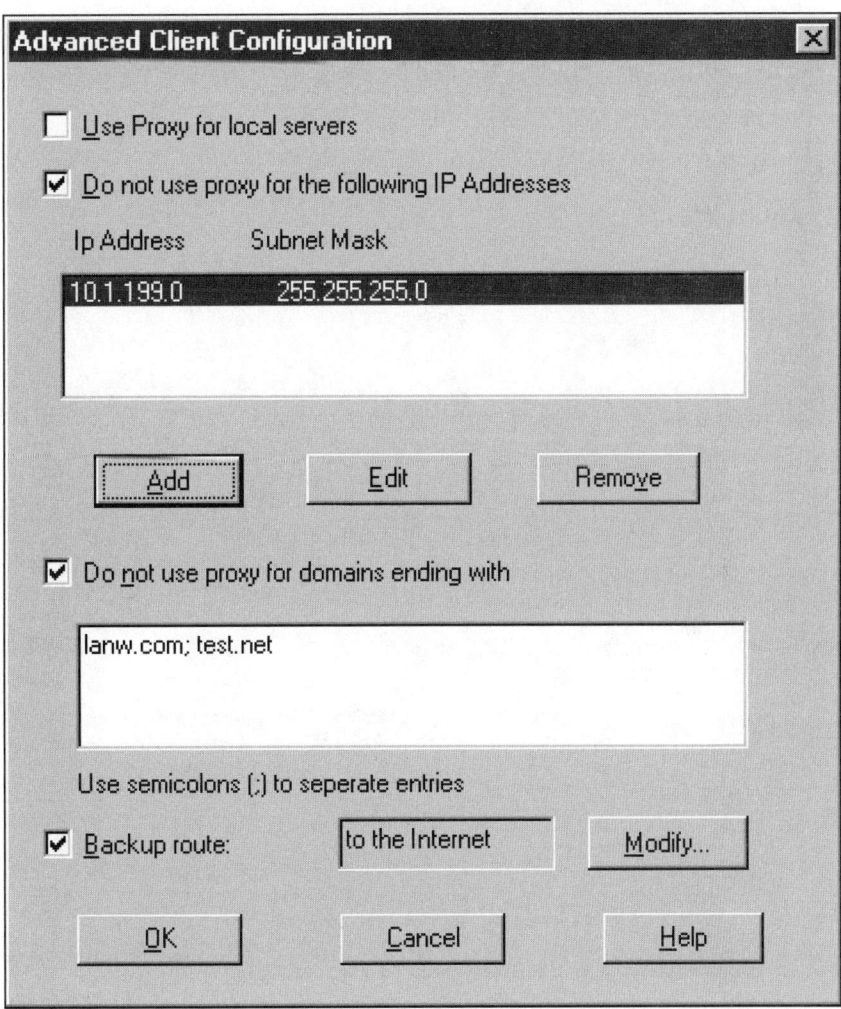

Figure 7.14   The Advanced Client Configuration dialog box is used to generate the default configuration script.

configuration applet. The settings defined by the script are invoked when the WSP client Web browser first accesses the Proxy Server. However, if a change has been made to the configuration, both Navigator and Internet Explorer provide options for updating the settings immediately. In Navigator, this is done by choosing Edit | Preferences | Advanced | Proxies. Click on Reload to access the script again and redefine the browser's settings. In IE, this task is performed in much the same way. Select View | Internet Options and click on the Connection tab (shown in Figure 7.15). Click on Configure in the Automatic Configuration area and then click on Refresh.

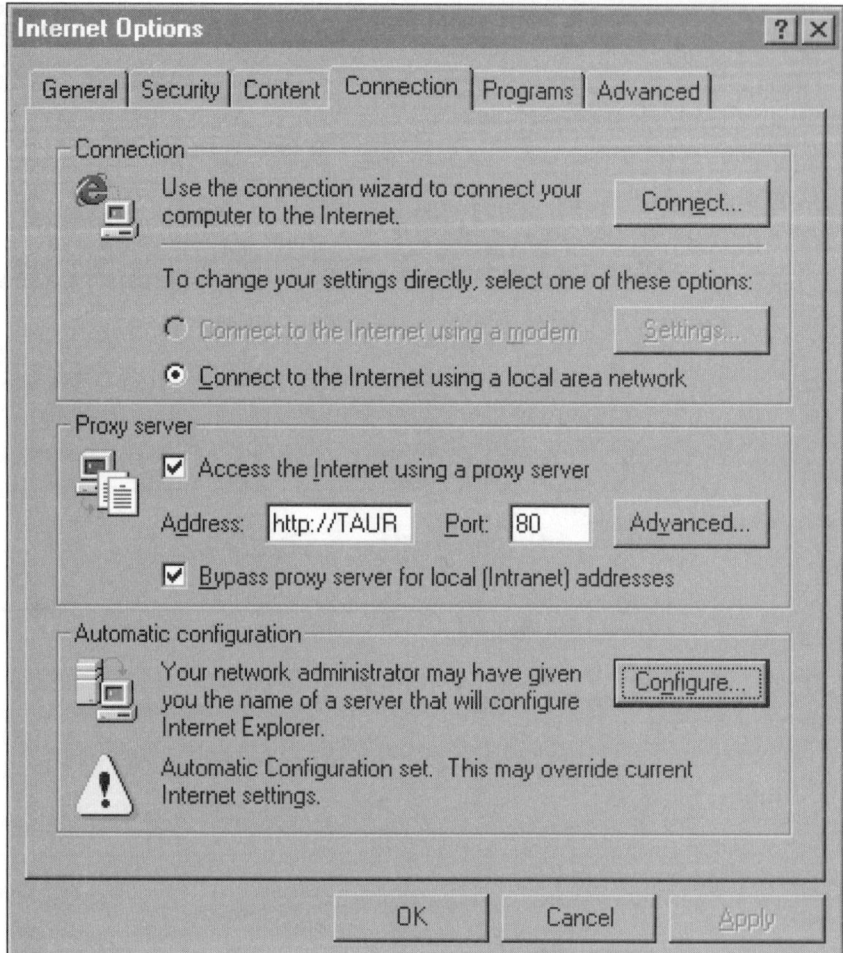

Figure 7.15   Internet Explorer can be forced to access the configuration script through the Internet Options dialog box.

CLIENT CONFIGURATION FILES

The MSPCLNT.INI file contains the settings for the WSP client software. This file is created during the Proxy Server setup and is copied to the clients as the WSP client software is installed. By default, MSPCLNT.INI is downloaded from the Proxy Server each time the client computer is started and is refreshed every six hours. The Path1 setting (which will be discussed in greater detail in the next section) in the Master Config section of the INI file defines the first location the WSP client software will look for a new MSPCLNT.INI file when the time comes for the file to be refreshed.

The server's copy of MSPCLNT.INI can be updated one of two ways: through the Client Configuration dialog box, which is accessed through the WinSock

Proxy Service Properties dialog box, or by using any standard text editor. As with all Windows INI files, MSPCLNT.INI is a regular text file that is divided into sections that define the configuration areas available. Each section in the MSPCLNT.INI file starts with a section header enclosed in brackets, such as [Servers IP Addresses]. The following is a sample MSPCLNT.INI file:

```
[Master Config]
Path1=\\TAURUS\mspclnt\
[Servers Ip Addresses]
Name=TAURUS
[Servers Ipx Addresses]
Addr1=00131313-000000000001
[Common]
WWW-Proxy=TAURUS
Set Browsers to use Proxy=1
Set Browsers to use Auto Config=1
WebProxyPort=80
Configuration Url=http://TAURUS:80/array.dll?Get.Routing.Script
Port=1745
Configuration Refresh Time (Hours)=6
Re-check Inaccessible Server Time (Minutes)=10
Refresh Give Up Time (Minutes)=15
Inaccessible Servers Give Up Time (Minutes)=2
LocalDomains=mynet.com
[raplayer]
RemoteBindUdpPorts=6970-7170
LocalBindTcpPorts=7070
[rvplayer]
RemoteBindUdpPorts=6970-7170
LocalBindTcpPorts=7070
[net2fone]
ServerBindTcpPorts=0
```

As mentioned earlier, the Master Config section specifies the UNC path to the shared directory on the Proxy Server containing the master copies of the

7

configuration files. If a Proxy Server array is used on the network, this section contains the paths to the MSPCLNT shares on all array members.

There are two settings available for the Servers IP Addresses section: Name= or Addr1=. This section contains the information used by the client to connect to the Proxy Server or servers. When the Name setting is used, it lists either the computer name or the DNS name of the Proxy Server. If a Proxy Server array is used, the computer name of each server is entered. However, in the case of a Proxy Server array with a single DNS entry, only one name will appear. When the Addr setting is used, the IP address of the server's local NIC appears. Multiple entries (Addr1, Addr2, Addr3) indicate either multiple network interface cards in one server or multiple servers.

The Servers IPX Addresses section defines the IPX addresses for the Proxy Server. On a network that includes Novell NetWare servers or IPX routers, which define the network number and IPX frame type used on the network, the settings are automatically configured with the internal network number of the Proxy Server and the Media Access Control (MAC) address of the server's interface card. However, on a network that does not include NetWare servers or IPX routers, the information that is entered includes the Proxy Server's internal network address, but the MAC address section is represented as 000000000001, as shown in the sample MSPCLNT.INI file.

There are a number of settings that fall into the Common section of the INI file:

- **WWW-Proxy** Defines the server that is used for Web access.

- **Set Browsers To Use Proxy, Set Browsers To Use Auto Config** Define the modifications the INI file will make to the client's browsers.

- **WebProxyPort** Defines the port on which the Web Proxy service listens for client requests.

- **Configuration URL** Lists the path to the automatic browser configuration script, which will be discussed in detail in "Using Scripts To Configure Browsers" later in this chapter.

- **Port** Defines the TCP port the Proxy Server uses for the control channel. In most configurations, this setting should not be changed.

- **LocalDomains** A list of suffixes for names that are resolved locally.

- **Configuration Refresh Time (Hours)** As you can imagine, the Configuration Refresh Time defines the number of hours the client waits before downloading updated configuration files from the Proxy Server.

- **Re-check Inaccessible Server Time** Defines the number of minutes the WinSock client will wait before redirecting a request that was made in an inaccessible server.

- **Refresh Give Up Time** Defines the number of minutes a client will wait before it attempts to update its configuration files if the initial attempt failed.

- **Inaccessible Servers Give Up Time** Defines the number of minutes the client will wait before redirecting a request if all servers are marked inaccessible.

In the sample INI file, notice that there are additional settings for special applications such as RealAudio, RealVideo, and Net Phone. These sections define the ports used for the applications and are added automatically depending on the configuration of the Proxy Server.

 It is important to remember that, although the MSPCLNT.INI file operates from the client computer, changes made to the version on the client will be overwritten when the refresh time has expired or when the computer is restarted.

MSPLAT.TXT is one of the configuration files that is copied to the client computer periodically. You learned in Chapter 6 that the LAT is a static file that defines the internal IP addresses on your network. There may be occasions when the MSPLAT.TXT file that is copied from the server does not contain some of the addresses that a particular client needs to access the internal network. When this happens, a specialized file can be created on the client computer that contains the information that is specific to that client. This file, called LOCALLAT.TXT, resides in the \MSPCLNT directory with the other configuration files, but it is not overwritten when the client is refreshed.

NWLINK CLIENTS

As you've learned, the WinSock Proxy service, in conjunction with the WSP client software, is able to support clients using NWLink (IPX/SPX) as their default transport protocol. For these clients, the WinSock Proxy service acts as an IPX/SPX-to-TCP/IP gateway.

There are few caveats to working with IPX-only clients. In fact, IPX-only clients and TCP/IP WSP clients operate identically. The first consideration is that NWLink clients must use the WinSock Proxy service and client software. Even with a CERN-compliant browser and access to the server, if the WSP client software is not loaded, the client will not be able to access the Internet because the WSP client software intercepts all Web requests and forwards them to the Proxy Server. If it didn't, the IPX/SPX protocol would disregard HTTP or FTP requests.

One other major consideration is that the WSP client software only supports specific IPX clients. For example, it does not support IPX-only Windows 3.1 or

Windows for Workgroups 3.11 clients. However, it does support Novell's Client 32 for Windows 95. For this reason, if you have legacy systems on your network, it is very important to know which proxy services support which client types.

MACINTOSH AND UNIX CLIENTS

Configuration options for Macintosh and Unix clients are limited to two areas: CERN-compliant browsers and SOCKS client applications. Any CERN-compliant browser can easily access the Web Proxy service when it is configured properly. SOCKS client applications must also be configured to use the Proxy Server to access the Internet.

As you may recall from Chapter 2, SOCKS is by definition a proxy environment. SOCKS applications are cognizant of the proxy server, as opposed to WSP client applications that operate as if they were connected directly to the Internet.

USING SCRIPTS TO CONFIGURE BROWSERS

As mentioned throughout this and other chapters, it is possible to configure a browser's proxy settings automatically by using scripts. Both Netscape Navigator 3.0 or higher and Internet Explorer 4.0 and higher use JavaScript to modify browser settings. The scripts are downloaded to the client computer when the browser is initialized and are run each time a browser requests a URL to determine the path the request will take. It should be noted that, although these scripts modify the operation of the browser, the changes they make are not visible in the configuration areas of the browsers.

Both Netscape and Microsoft have software available to administer their browsers and create scripts centrally. Netscape's Mission Control software is able to manage all browser settings from a central location. Likewise, Microsoft's Internet Explorer Administration Kit (IEAK) provides centralized administration of Internet Explorer 4.0 and higher.

Microsoft provides another configuration option that is not available for Netscape browsers. In addition to running script files to configure Internet Explorer, you can use Internet Communication Settings (.INS) files. Unlike JavaScript files, INS files modify the settings in the browser so they can be viewed. In addition, the options available for configuration reach far beyond just the Proxy Server settings.

INS files are actually INI files with a different extension. They are laid out the same way, with each section beginning with the section name in brackets. The following is a sample INS file:

```
[Branding]
Language Locale=en
Language ID=9
Window_Title_CN=DJ's Web Service
Window_Title=IE 4.0 from DJ's Web Service, Inc.
Toolbar Bitmap=D:\InetPub\wwwroot\tb.bmp
User Agent=
Platform=2
CabsURLPath=d:\inetpub\wwwroot
InsVersion=1998.04.10.00
Type=2
[URL]
AutoConfig=1
Help_Page=http://help.lanw.com
Quick_Link_1_Name=Internet Start
Quick_Link_1=http://home.microsoft.com
Quick_Link_2_Name=Cnet News
Quick_Link_2=http://www.news.com
Home_Page=http://www.lanw.com
Search_Page=http://www.yahoo.com
AutoConfigURL=http://taurus/test2.ins
AutoConfigJSURL=
AutoConfigTime=25
Quick_Link_3_Name=
Quick_Link_3=
Quick_Link_4_Name=
Quick_Link_4=
Quick_Link_5_Name=
Quick_Link_5=
[Internet_Mail]
Window_Title=Outlook Express from DJ's Web Service, Inc.
[Favorites]
CNN Games.url=http://cnn.com/games/crossword/default.htm
MTV.url=http://www.mtv.com/
```

7

```
[Proxy]
HTTP_Proxy_Server=taurus:80
FTP_Proxy_Server=taurus:80
Gopher_Proxy_Server=taurus:80
Secure_Proxy_Server=taurus:80
Socks_Proxy_Server=taurus:80
Use_Same_Proxy=1
Proxy_Enable=1
Proxy_Override=<local>
[Mail_Signature]
Signature_Text=Something wicked this way comes.
Use_Mail_For_News=1
Use_Signature=1
[Signature]
Signature_Text=Something wicked this way comes.
Use_Signature=1
```

As you can see, this configuration file provides a number of options, including Proxy Server settings, a standard email signature, favorites, and the bitmap used on the toolbar. Figure 7.16 shows an Internet Explorer window that has been configured by using the sample INS file.

 The INS file must be placed in a directory serviced by the IIS WWW Service and accurately addressed in the browser's configuration.

By using the configuration options available in the Internet Communication Settings file, you are able to strictly control a browser's appearance and settings. From a Proxy Server standpoint, it is helpful to have the ability to easily configure all browsers with the same settings. But beyond that, you can specify a home page, search pages, and other links that will ease your users' access to the Internet. Remember that, in most cases, such as home page or Proxy Server settings, changes that users make to their browser's configuration will be rewritten when the computer is restarted. For more information on the options available for Internet Communication Settings files, refer to the Internet Explorer Administration Kit documentation or Microsoft TechNet.

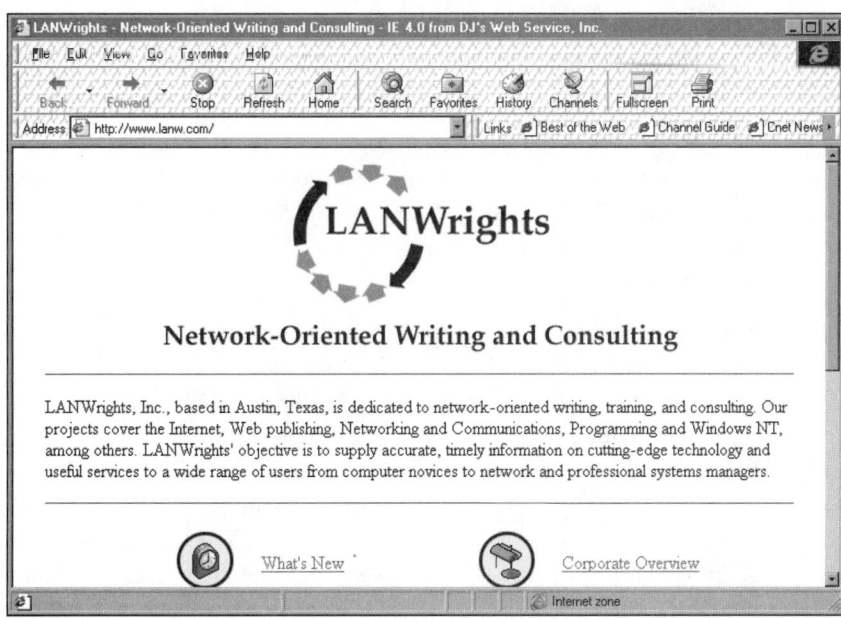

Figure 7.16   An instance of IE configured with the sample INS file.

CHAPTER SUMMARY

Microsoft Proxy Server 2.0 supports a wide range of clients, from Windows 3.1 PCs to Unix systems and from TCP/IP-enabled clients to those running only IPX/SPX. It is this diversity that gives Microsoft Proxy Server its edge.

The first, and perhaps most important, step in configuring a client computer to use Proxy Server is to ensure that the client can communicate with the server and that permissions have been assigned correctly. Once this has been established, the client is ready to utilize the services available.

The most basic client configuration method occurs with TCP/IP clients utilizing the Web Proxy service through CERN-compliant Web browsers. These browsers recognize the existence of a proxy server and can be easily configured to direct all requests through the server. It is because CERN-compliant browsers and TCP/IP are supported on all platforms that Microsoft Proxy Server supports all types of clients.

As you've learned, the WinSock Proxy service provides Internet connectivity for Windows clients and Windows Sockets applications. Clients must be configured to use the WinSock Proxy service by installing the WinSock Proxy (WSP) client software, which intercepts all Windows Sockets requests and redirects them to the WinSock Proxy service as necessary. Because of the way the client software operates, Windows Sockets applications (such as FTP or email applications) are not aware of the Proxy Server and act as if they are connected directly to the Internet. In addition, the WinSock Proxy service gives IPX-only clients the ability to connect to the Internet by acting as a gateway between IPX and TCP/IP.

The WSP client software uses configuration files that are copied from the server periodically. These files can be managed from the WinSock Proxy Service Client Configuration dialog box, or they can be edited manually. In addition, the WSP client software allows the client's Web browsers to be automatically configured to use the Proxy Server.

Finally, you can use JavaScript configuration files to configure both Navigator and Internet Explorer. These scripts are accessed each time the browser starts and determine the path a URL request will take. In addition, Microsoft gives you the option to configure the browsers through Internet Communication Settings files, which you can use to configure more than just the proxy server settings. They can be used to modify the look and feel of the browser, the favorites and quick links, and the home and search pages. This gives the administrator the ability to ensure that all browsers on the network use the same basic configuration.

KEY TERMS

- **CERN-compliant browser**—A Web browser that supports Proxy HTTP and is configured to use the Proxy Server.

- **Internet Communication Settings (INS) file**—Configuration files that can be used to configure Internet Explorer settings.

- **Internet Explorer Administration Kit (IEAK)**—A set of applications that can be used to centrally administer Microsoft Internet Explorer installations.

- **JavaScript**—A scripting language based on Java that is used for, among other things, automatic browser configuration.

- **LOCALLAT.TXT**—A client-specific version of the Local Address Table (LAT) that is not replaced each time the client is restarted.

- **Mission Control**—A set of applications that can be used to centrally administer Netscape Navigator installations.

- **MSPCLNT.INI**—The configuration file that defines the operation of the WinSock Proxy client software.

- **Wide Area Information Service (WAIS)**—A legacy Internet protocol, supported by Netscape, that was used to search cataloged documents. It is seldom used today.

- **WinSock Proxy (WSP) software**—An application loaded on the client computer that intercepts Windows Sockets requests and directs them to the Proxy Server. This software is required for IPX-only clients and Windows clients that are not using CERN-compliant software.

REVIEW QUESTIONS

1. Which of the following accurately describes client configuration supported by Microsoft Proxy Server 2.0?
   a. Macintosh system running TCP/IP and using the WSP client software
   b. Windows 3.1 system running IPX/SPX and using Internet Explorer
   c. Unix system running TCP/IP and using Internet Explorer
   d. Windows 95 system running TCP/IP and using the WSP client software

2. An IPX-only computer using a CERN-compliant browser does not require the WSP client software. (True or False?)

3. The _____ Proxy service provides the same configurations for both inbound and outbound access restrictions (All, Domain/Zone, and IP Address.)

4. MSPCLNT.INI settings can be managed, at least in part, by clicking on _____ in the WinSock Proxy Service Properties dialog box.

5. To use an INS file, it must be placed in a directory that is serviced by the IIS WWW Service, preferably WWWROOT. (True or False?)

6. In the WSP Client applet, click on _____ to immediately copy new configuration files from the proxy server.

7. Which of the following proxy server settings are available to Internet Explorer but not to Navigator?
   a. A general proxy server configuration.
   b. WAIS Proxy configuration
   c. Secure Proxy configuration
   d. Use the same settings for all protocols.

8. If access control is not enabled for a particular service, the client is not required to log on to the proxy server. (True or False?)

9. A client's _____ defines specific IP address settings and is not overwritten during a refresh.

10. Microsoft Exchange client computers are able to operate effectively as WinSock Proxy clients. (True or False?)

11. The default port for all proxy configurations is _____ .

7

12. The WSP client software can only be loaded on a client computer by connecting to *//servername/MSProxy* through a Web browser. (True or False?)

13. Which of the following services does not rely on the Windows security structure?

    a. WinSock Proxy service

    b. SOCKS Proxy service

    c. FTP service

    d. Web Proxy service

14. _____ is Microsoft's implementation of the IPX/SPX protocol.

15. Which of the following IPX implementations are supported by Proxy Server 2.0 and the WSP client software?

    a. Macintosh IPX/SPX

    b. Windows 3.11 IPX/SPX

    c. Windows 95 NWLink

    d. Novell Client 32

16. Often, the first step in diagnosing a client configuration problem is verifying that the client is able to communicate with the server. (True or False?)

17. The _____ section of an INS file can be used to configure a browser's home page and search page.

18. The WinSock Proxy service supports a wide variety of clients across multiple platforms. (True or False?)

19. Which of the following files are updated periodically by the WSP client software?

    a. MSPCLNT.INI

    b. LAT.TXT

    c. LOCALLAT.TXT

    d. PROXY.INI

20. By default, the WSP client software will download new copies of the configuration files every six hours. (True or False?)

21. _____ is by definition a proxy environment.

22. Which of the following accurately describes methods in which Netscape Navigator can be automatically configured?

    a. INS file

    b. Default script (ARRAY.DLL?GET.ROUTING.SCRIPT)

    c. JavaScript file

    d. INI file

23. The MSPCLNT.INI _____ setting defines the location from which the client will request updated configuration files.

24. When you are using the WSP client software, it is necessary to configure Proxy Server settings in all applications in which they are available. (True or False?)

25. Which of the following MSPCLNT.INI settings would be used to connect to a Proxy Server array that consists of SERV1, SERV2, and SERV3 and has a single DNS entry of SRVARRAY1?

   a. Name=SERV1

   b. Name1=SERV1, Name2=SERV2, Name3=SERV3

   c. Name=SRVARRAY1

   d. Name1=SRVARRAY1, Name2=SERV1, Name3=SERV2, Name4=SERV3

26. Which of the following settings in the Client Installation/Configuration dialog box prevents part of the MSPCLNT.INI file from being overwritten during a refresh?

   a. server identified by DNS name

   b. server identified manually

   c. server identified by IP address

   d. server identified by computer name

27. Both the Web Proxy and WinSock Proxy services provide access based on an extensive list of protocols. (True or False?)

HANDS-ON PROJECTS

In the Hands-on projects for this chapter, you will configure both Microsoft Internet Explorer 4.0 and Netscape Navigator 4.0 to use a Proxy Server and the Web Proxy service. You will load the WSP client software and look at its configuration. For each project, you will need IE 4.0, Navigator 4.0, another non-browser Internet application (such as WS-FTP), TCP/IP connectivity to the Proxy Server, the Proxy Server's IP address, and access to the Proxy Server console.

PROJECT 7.1

In this project, you will configure Internet Explorer 4.0 to use Proxy Server on your network:

   1. Before jumping right in and configuring the browser, you must verify the connectivity to the Proxy Server. Open a Command Prompt window by selecting Start | Programs | Command Prompt.

2. In the Command Prompt window, PING your Proxy Server by typing "ping *server_ip_address*", where *server_ip_address* is the IP address for your Proxy Server. If DNS is in use on your network, you can PING the server's DNS name instead. You should receive a response similar to Figure 7.17.

3. The success of the PING in Step 2 indicates that, on the most basic level, there is connectivity between the client and the Proxy Server. Next, go to the Proxy Server console and log on as Administrator to verify the permissions for the Web Proxy service.

4. Open the Internet Service Manager by selecting Start | Programs | Microsoft Proxy Server | Internet Service Manager. Notice that all six services are up and running.

5. Select the Web Proxy service and press Enter. This invokes the Web Proxy Service Properties dialog box.

6. Click on the Permissions tab.

7. Verify that the Enable Access Control option is not checked. Leave the Internet Service Manager up, but close the Web Proxy Service Properties dialog box by clicking on OK.

8. Now you're ready to configure the Web browser. Return to the client computer and log on as Administrator.

9. Open Internet Explorer by selecting Start | Programs | Internet Explorer | Internet Explorer.

10. From the View menu, select Internet Options.

11. Select the Connection tab.

12. Check the Access The Internet Using A Proxy Server checkbox. Enter the name of your Proxy Server in the Address box and 80 in the Port box. Your window should look similar to Figure 7.18.

```
Command Prompt                                               _ □ ×
Microsoft(R) Windows NT(TM)
(C) Copyright 1985-1996 Microsoft Corp.

E:\>ping 10.1.128.15

Pinging 10.1.128.15 with 32 bytes of data:

Reply from 10.1.128.15: bytes=32 time<10ms TTL=128
Reply from 10.1.128.15: bytes=32 time<10ms TTL=128
Reply from 10.1.128.15: bytes=32 time<10ms TTL=128
Reply from 10.1.128.15: bytes=32 time<10ms TTL=128

E:\>_
```

Figure 7.17   A successful PING.

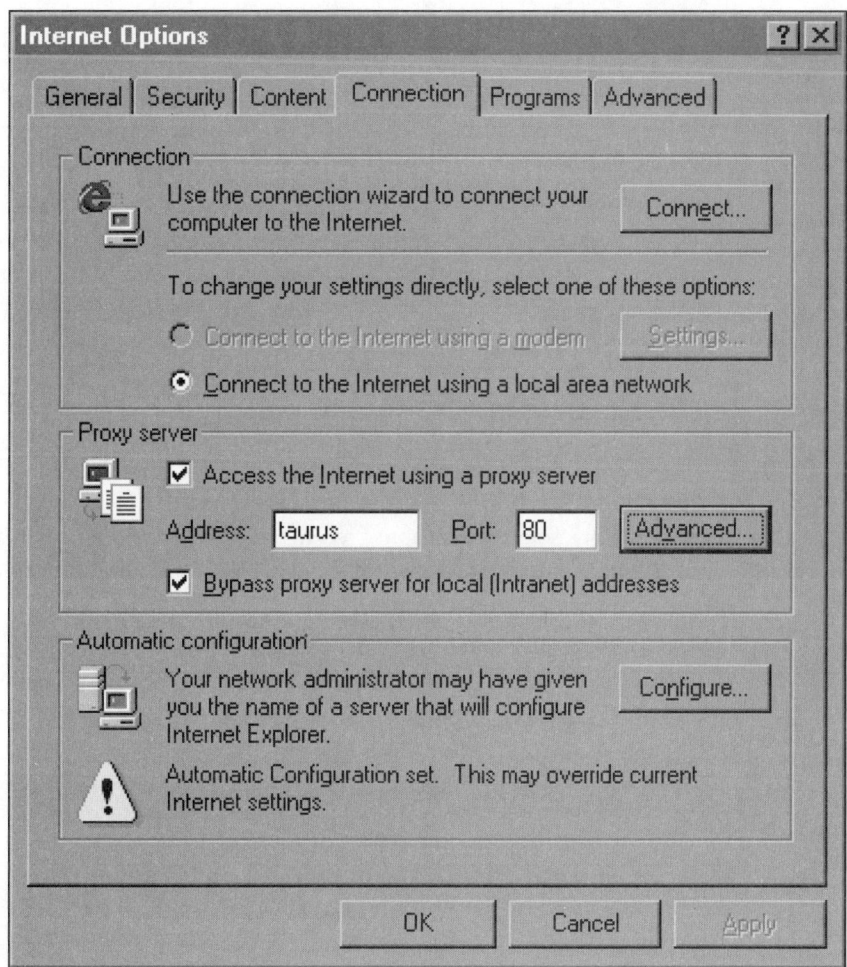

Figure 7.18   The Internet Options dialog box in Internet Explorer 4.0.

13. Click on OK to save the configuration, then close and reopen Internet Explorer.

14. Your browser should now be configured to access the Internet through the Proxy Server. Attach to several Web sites to test this configuration.

15. To demonstrate the effectiveness of access control configurations, close Internet Explorer and return to the Proxy Server console.

16. Reopen the Web Proxy Service Properties dialog box by selecting the service and pressing Enter.

17. Click on the Permissions tab.

18. Select Enable Access Control.

19. Select WWW from the Protocol list.

20. Click on Edit to invoke the WWW Permissions dialog box, which is used to define the list of users and groups that will be granted access to the Web through the Web Proxy service. The list should currently be empty.

21. Click on Add to bring up the Add Users And Groups dialog box. If you have been exposed to assigning permissions in Windows NT, this dialog box will look familiar.

22. Select the group Domain Guests and click on Add. The group is entered in the lower section of the window.

23. Ensure that Full Access is listed in the Type Of Access box and click on OK to return to the WWW Permissions dialog box, shown in Figure 7.19.

24. Click on OK twice to return to the Internet Service Manager. Leave the ISM open and return to the client machine.

25. If you are not still logged on as Administrator, do so.

26. Open Internet Explorer and attempt to connect to a Web site. Notice that, unlike before, you are prompted to enter a network password. If you recall, the Administrator user is not a member of the Domain Guests group and therefore has not been granted access to the Web Proxy service.

27. Click on Cancel. Notice that the message "Error: Access denied" is displayed in the browser. Leave Internet Explorer open on the client machine and return to the Proxy Server.

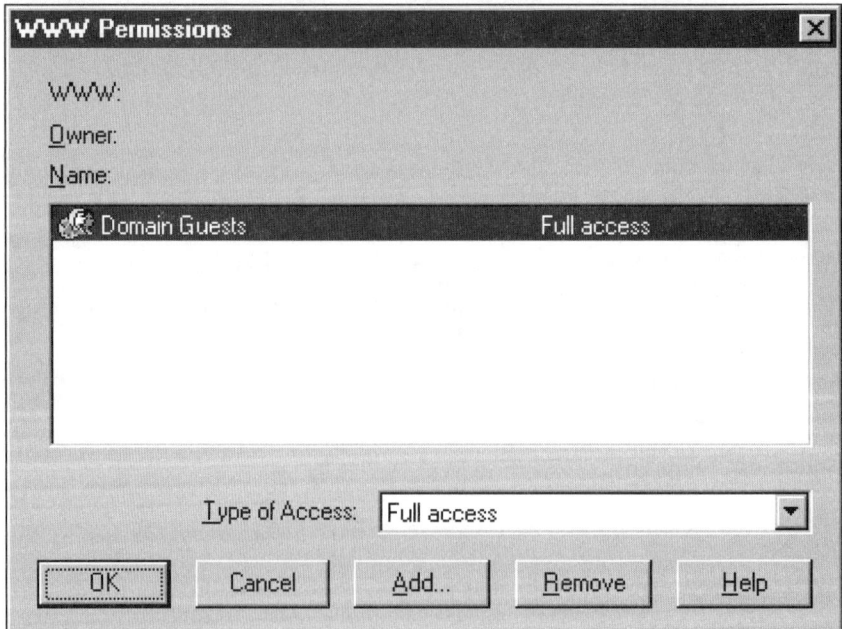

Figure 7.19   The Domain Guests group has been granted full access to the Web Proxy service.

28. Repeat Steps 16 and 17 to reach the Permissions tab of the Web Proxy Service Properties dialog box.

29. Deselect the Enable Access Control option and click on OK.

30. Return to the client and attempt to access the same Web site. Access should be granted to the site without incident.

31. Close Internet Explorer.

 **PROJECT 7.2**

In this project, you will step through similar steps to configure Netscape Navigator 4.0 on the client computer:

1. Open Netscape Navigator.

2. Select Preferences from the Edit menu.

3. In the Category box, click on the **+** next to Advanced and select Proxy.

4. Select the Manual Proxy Configuration option and then click on View.

5. Enter your Proxy Server name and port information into the appropriate boxes. Populate only the HTTP, Security, FTP, and Gopher options, as shown in Figure 7.20.

6. Click on OK twice to return to Navigator. To ensure that the configuration changes have taken effect, stop and restart Navigator.

7. Connect to a number of Web sites. Access should be granted without incident.

 **PROJECT 7.3**

In this project, you will install and configure the WSP client software:

1. Before beginning the WSP client configuration process, open your other, non-browser Internet application. Because the client computer is only configured to use the Web Proxy service, connecting to the Internet should fail. Remember this, because at the end of the project, the attempt to connect should succeed.

2. Open Windows NT Explorer by selecting Start | Programs | Windows NT Explorer.

3. Double-click on Network Neighborhood to view all computers on your network.

4. Double-click on the icon for your Proxy Server.

5. Double-click on MSPCLNT in the list of available shares.

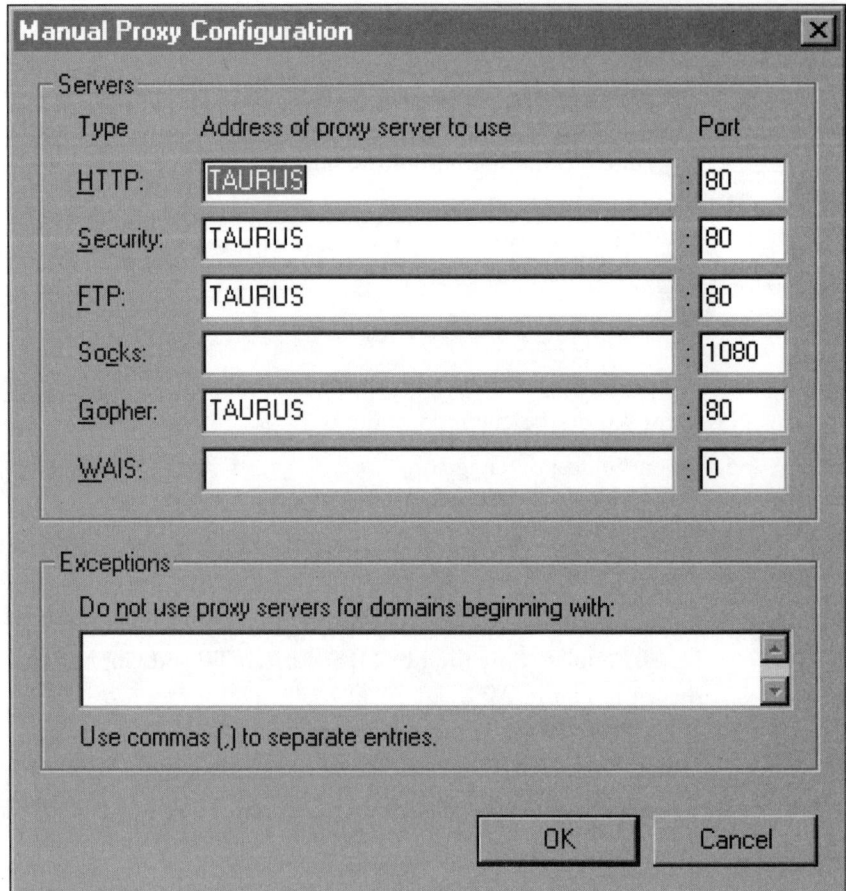

Figure 7.20   The proxy server options for Netscape Navigator.

6. Double-click on SETUP.EXE to launch the WSP client installation program.

7. After the program launches, click on Continue.

8. The options available in the WinSock Proxy Client Setup dialog box (shown in Figure 7.21) are limited to selecting the directory to which the client software should be installed and proceeding with the installation. Click on Install Microsoft Proxy Client to proceed with the installation.

9. The setup program now checks for necessary disk space and installs the software. When you receive the message that the software was installed successfully, click on OK.

10. Click on Restart Windows Now to complete the installation and restart the computer.

11. Once the computer has restarted, open the Control Panel by selecting Start | Settings | Control Panel.

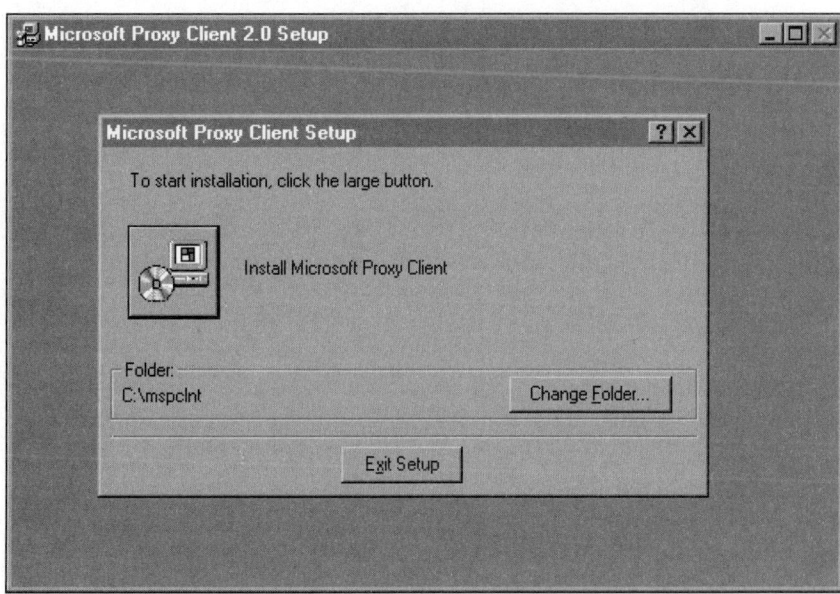

Figure 7.21   The WinSock Proxy Client Setup dialog box.

7

12. Double-click on the WSP client icon to open the configuration program.

13. Note that there are few configuration options for the WSP client. For more information on the options available, please refer to the WinSock Proxy Clients section of this chapter. Click on OK to close the WSP client configuration program.

14. To test the WSP client software, open your non-browser Internet application and attempt to connect to the Internet. The connection should be successful.

CASE PROJECTS

1. You have been given the task of providing Internet connectivity to your 300-node network, which is made up of a combination of Windows 3.11 and Windows 95 clients. You are currently running IPX/SPX and NWLink to provide access to your Windows NT and NetWare servers.

   Required result: Provide Internet connectivity to all clients on the network.

   Optional desired results: Continue to use NWLink as the primary network protocol. Keep administration requirements to a minimum.

   Proposed solution: Install a Microsoft Proxy Server computer to connect to the Internet. Enable NWLink on the internal network interface. Use the WinSock Proxy service and the WSP client software to provide connectivity for the IPX clients. Which results does the proposed solution provide?

a. The proposed solution provides the required result and both optional results.

b. The proposed solution provides the required result and one optional result.

c. The proposed solution provides only the required result.

d. The proposed solution does not provide the required result.

2. Your network consists of 35 Macintosh, 100 Windows 95, and 25 Windows NT Workstation clients, all connected to three Windows NT servers. The primary network protocol is TCP/IP.

Required result: Provide Internet access to all clients.

Optional desired results: Continue to use TCP/IP as the primary network protocol. Ensure that specific users' access to the Internet can be restricted.

Proposed solution: Install Microsoft Proxy Server 2.0 on one of the existing Windows NT Servers. Configure TCP/IP on the server's internal and external network interfaces. Install Microsoft Internet Explorer on all computers to provide access to the Internet. Which results does the proposed solution provide?

a. The proposed solution provides the required result and both optional results.

b. The proposed solution provides the required result and one optional result.

c. The proposed solution provides only the required result.

d. The proposed solution does not provide the required result.

3. Your network consists of 300 Windows 95 clients connected to Windows NT and NetWare servers. They are currently configured for both IPX/SPX to connect to the NetWare servers and TCP/IP to connect to a Unix system.

Required result: Provide all clients Internet access.

Optional desired results: To reduce overhead on the proxy server, enable only the required services. Provide access for FTP and email packages in addition to Web access.

Proposed solution: Install Microsoft Proxy Server 2.0. Configure TCP/IP on the server's internal network interface. To reduce overhead, only enable the WWW service. Which results does the proposed solution provide?

a. The proposed solution provides the required result and both optional results.

b. The proposed solution provides the required result and one optional result.

c. The proposed solution provides only the required result.

d. The proposed solution does not provide the required result.

4. Your network consists of 300 Windows 95 clients connected to Windows NT and NetWare servers. They are currently configured for both IPX/SPX to connect to the NetWare servers and TCP/IP to connect to a Unix system.

   Required result: Provide all clients with Internet access.

   Optional desired results: To reduce overhead on the proxy server, enable only the required services. Provide access for FTP and email packages in addition to Web access.

   Proposed solution: Install Microsoft Proxy Server 2.0. Configure NWLink on the server's internal network interface. Install the WSP client software on all clients and enable Force IPX/SPX. To reduce overhead, enable only the WinSock Proxy service. Which results does the proposed solution provide?

   a. The proposed solution provides the required result and both optional results.

   b. The proposed solution provides the required result and one optional result.

   c. The proposed solution provides only the required result.

   d. The proposed solution does not provide the required result.

7

PROXY SERVER SECURITY

Microsoft Proxy Server 2.0 offers a wide variety of security features to control unauthorized intrusion and restrict unproductive resource access. Both ends can be accomplished through several means. This chapter focuses on securing your installation of Proxy Server and configuring the services to control inbound and outbound access.

AFTER READING THIS CHAPTER AND COMPLETING THE EXERCISES, YOU WILL BE ABLE TO:

- Secure the environment for Proxy Server
- Use Proxy Server's security measures
- Set permissions for each proxy service
- Define protocols and ports for maximum control
- Use domain filters and packet filters
- Configure proxy alerts
- Initiate and manage Proxy logging

SECURING A PROXY INSTALLATION

Proxy Server's primary purpose is to give your network users access to the vast resources of the Internet. However, by opening the door to let internal users reach out, you also increase the possibility of unwanted external users getting in. To reduce the risk involved with opening a communication channel with the Internet via Proxy Server, you need to make several configuration changes to the Windows NT Server that is hosting Proxy Server.

The default settings in Windows NT Server 4.0 do not protect your network as you would expect. Instead, Microsoft has left it up to you to set up the security so you can configure it to meet your specific needs and network configuration. Although this is considerate, it leaves the uninformed systems operator with an insecure system. Fortunately, Proxy Server is not as susceptible to this failing as Windows NT Server. Once Proxy Server is installed, you must enable and grant access in and out of your network via the new proxied services; they are not available to users by default. Specifically, Proxy Server's default settings prevent Internet users from gaining internal access because IP forwarding is disabled on the host server and all inbound service ports are ignored. Only when you enable inbound service ports or reenable IP forwarding can external users gain internal access.

In the following sections, we'll look at several configurations and features that can be used to increase or decrease the security level on your Proxy host server and, by extension, your entire internal network. Take note that these items are discussed as if only a single Proxy Server is being used; if multiple instances of Proxy Server are present on the network, these changes will need to be made to each instance.

IP FORWARDING

IP forwarding is the Transmission Control Protocol/Internet Protocol (TCP/IP) configuration that enables the Windows NT computer to pass on IP packets to other segments of the network on multihomed computers. Remember that a multihomed computer is any machine with two or more network interfaces—a network interface can be a network interface card, a modem, or some other type of communications device that NT can use to pass network packets. The control for this feature is located on the Routing tab of the TCP/IP Properties dialog box (see Figure 8.1), which is accessed through the Protocols tab of the Network applet in the Control Panel.

IP forwarding is disabled (unchecked) by default when you install TCP/IP on a fresh installation of Windows NT. If it is enabled, Proxy Server will disable it as part of its installation process. If Remote Access Service (RAS) or Routing and

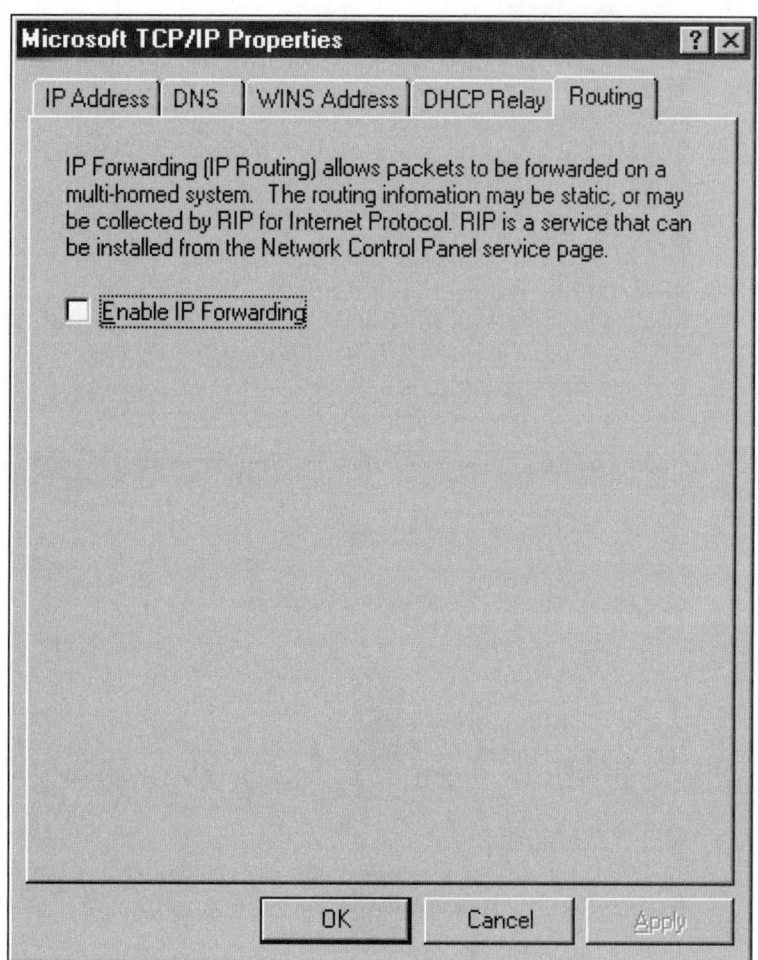

Figure 8.1   The Routing tab of TCP/IP Properties.

Remote Access Service (RRAS) is installed after Proxy Server, the RAS installation process will reenable IP forwarding. So make sure IP forwarding is set properly each time you install or modify the network communications of your host server.

The proper setting for IP forwarding is dependent on the function or requirements for the host server. If you want communications that are initiated externally to reach your network, IP forwarding should be enabled. If you do not want external communications to reach your network, disable IP forwarding. In either case, external communications can still reach the host server if the inbound port is open and the system is listening for communications.

PROXY ACCESS CONTROL

During the installation of Proxy Server, you were asked whether or not you wanted to enable access control for the Web Proxy and WinSock Proxy services. It is recommended that you enable access control. Otherwise, you will not be able to set password authentication schemes to restrict or control access over these services. A Web Proxy or WinSock Proxy service on which access control is not enabled is insecure. If you decide not to enable access control for these services during installation, you may open up insecure channels into your network. You'll need to open the Properties dialog box for these proxy services through the Microsoft Management Console and enable access control on the Permissions tab (see Figure 8.2).

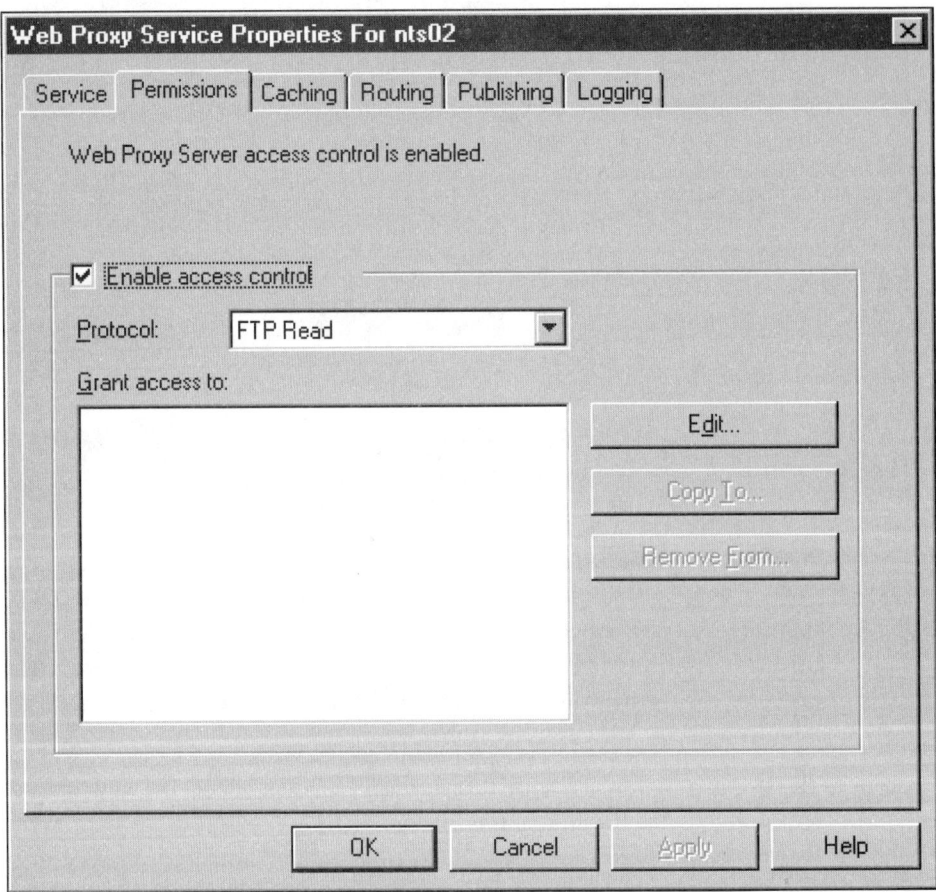

Figure 8.2   The Permissions tab of the Web Proxy's Properties dialog
box showing enabled access control.

LAT AND EXTERNAL IP ADDRESSES

The *Local Address Table (LAT)* lists the IP addresses that have valid access to the services offered by Proxy Server. LAT should contain only those local internal IP addresses that need access. You can always expand the LAT to include new or additional internal IP addresses, so it is wise to be too restrictive rather than too permissive. However, under no circumstances should you ever add an external IP address to the LAT. Doing so will give the external host access to your internal network; that is, it will create an insecure environment. Figure 8.3 shows the LAT Configuration dialog box.

STRICT PASSWORD POLICY

Access to services hosted by Proxy Server is gained by a username and password. In the NT networking system, this information is usually only entered once—at the time of domain logon. The access token assigned to the user at that time is used to determine valid access at all other security checkpoints. Proxy Server services are no different. However, if an external user provides Proxy Server with a valid name and password, that external user is granted the access permissions assigned to that user account. Thus, it is important (and hopefully, obvious) to construct, maintain, and enforce a strict password policy. Each user's password should be hard to guess (long, mixed case, punctuation, alphanumeric, changed every 30 days, etc.). By using the Windows NT Account Policy dialog box (shown in Figure 8.4), you can enforce strict passwords to improve the security of your network.

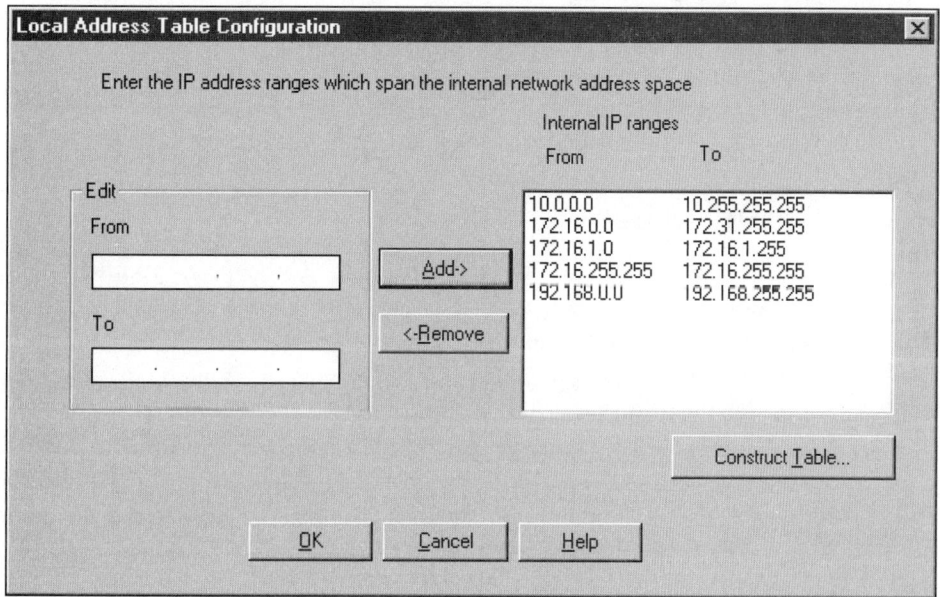

Figure 8.3 The LAT Configuration dialog box.

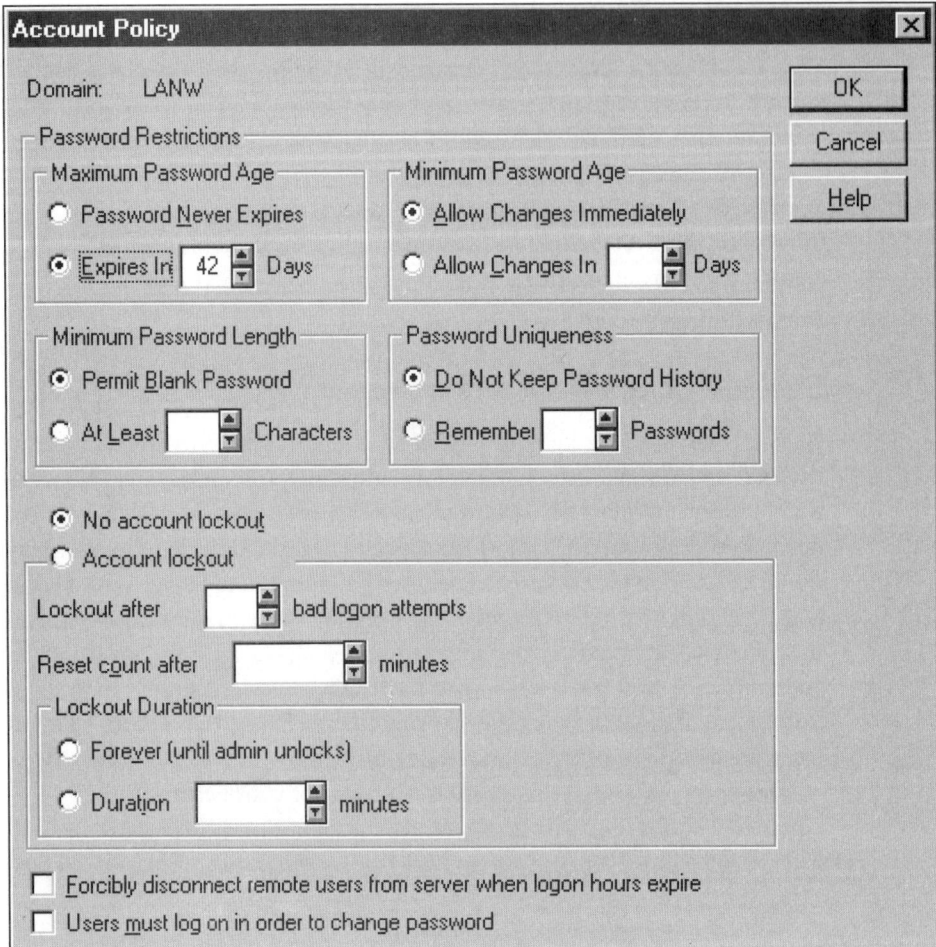

Figure 8.4 The Windows NT Account Policy dialog box.

GROUP AND USER RIGHTS

The more users there are with high levels of access, the more opportunities there are for unwanted users to gain access to a high-level user account. Restrict membership in administrative-level groups to only those users who actually need such privileged access. This includes assigning Full Control rights to resources. In addition, review the assignments of user rights to determine if a more restricted configuration can provide the access and features users need in order to perform their daily activities without opening additional security holes. Logging on to servers locally, rebooting systems, taking ownership of objects, managing security logs, logging on as a service, adding workstations to the domain, and acting as part of the operating system are all user rights that should be granted with extreme caution. User rights can be set in User Manager for Domains/Policies/User Rights.

SERVER SERVICE AND SHARES

Disable or remove binding of the Server service with Internet adapters or interfaces when access to these devices off of the host server is not absolutely necessary. If such service is needed, check all permissions on resource shares from the host to ensure that they are defined properly. On host servers connected to the Internet, all shares and directories should be set to Read Only. Any other services or protocols that are not required by the Internet interface should also be unbound. It is crucial not to run Server Message Blocks (SMBs) over the Internet because they are easily snooped for content and usernames. Also, you can prevent external users from gaining access to your internal NetBIOS-to-IP address-mapping name table by unbinding the WINS client.

NETWORK DRIVE MAPPINGS

All network drive mappings on the host server should be disabled. Do not map any network shares or resources located anywhere on the network to the host Proxy Server. Such mappings can give external users access to internal network resources in spite of other security restrictions, such as disabling IP forwarding. This is especially important if Web services are hosted from the same physical server as Proxy Server.

USE NTFS

Because it is the only file system supported by Windows NT that contains security features, all volumes on a Proxy Server host should be formatted with NTFS. This gives you the widest range of access control over the file and directory objects found on the server.

OTHER APPLICATIONS

Do not install any services or applications on the host server that are not absolutely necessary. The fewer items operating on the server, the less likely a configuration or administration error can be exploited by an external user. This includes not installing or disabling FTP and/or Gopher from Internet Information Server (IIS) if these services are not required or will not be used.

DNS AND GATEWAY

Remove Domain Name System (DNS) and gateway references from the TCP/IP configuration on the host server. This prevents external users from obtaining this information and exploiting it to bypass Proxy Server's security. If the Dynamic Host Configuration Protocol (DHCP) is in use, make sure DNS and gateway references are not distributed by the DHCP server.

DISABLE RPC PORTS

Windows NT TCP/IP services use ports 1024 through 1029 to transmit and listen for Remote Procedure Calls (RPCs). These RPC ports should be disabled on all Internet (or otherwise externally connected) servers to prevent users from issuing RPC commands on your network.

NT DOMAINS

When and where possible, Proxy Server should be installed on a Windows NT Server host that is a standalone domain member instead of a domain controller. This prevents a compromised host server from giving an external user access to your Security Accounts Manager (SAM) database.

If you are installing Proxy Server in a multidomain environment, you can install it on a Windows NT Server host that is its own Primary Domain Controller (PDC) and its only member. Then, by establishing a one-way trust relationship to one of the existing domains, Proxy Server will be the trusting domain and the user-hosting internal domain will be the trusted domain. If the Proxy Server host or domain is compromised, no domains will trust the Proxy domain, so the rest of the network is not compromised. If multiple Proxy Servers are needed, they can be installed on Backup Domain Controller (BDC) or member servers of the Proxy domain.

PASSWORD AUTHENTICATION

The Proxy Server Web Proxy service uses the same password authentication schemes the IIS Web service uses—namely, anonymous logon, basic authentication, and Windows NT Challenge/Response authentication. WinSock Proxy service uses Windows NT Challenge/Response authentication only to secure WinSock applications. Because non-Microsoft browsers and utilities may not fully support the Challenge/Response etiquette, may reject the client configuration JScript, or may incorrectly interpret SSL use, you may have to use basic authentication to allow them to operate properly.

If anonymous access is enabled, all anonymous users assume the identity of the IUSR_*servername* account. Any resources to which this account has access (either directly or via group memberships) are accessible by all anonymous users.

USE PERMISSIONS

Access to the protocols supported by the Web Proxy and WinSock Proxy services are controlled through use or user permissions. Each protocol is configured individually (and separately for each proxy service) to enable or restrict users and groups from gaining access. Permissions are established through the Permissions tab in the WinSock Proxy Properties dialog box (see Figure 8.5) and should be granted to groups rather than individual user accounts. Therefore, it is a good idea to plan out the permission structure and create multiple groups to provide the most control over granting protocol access.

 The permission settings for HTTP and HTTPS (SSL) are the same. Thus, granting access to HTTP also grants access to HTTPS, and denying access to HTTP also denies access to HTTPS. The Secure protocol assignment is reserved for special secure port protocols other than 443, such as Snews.

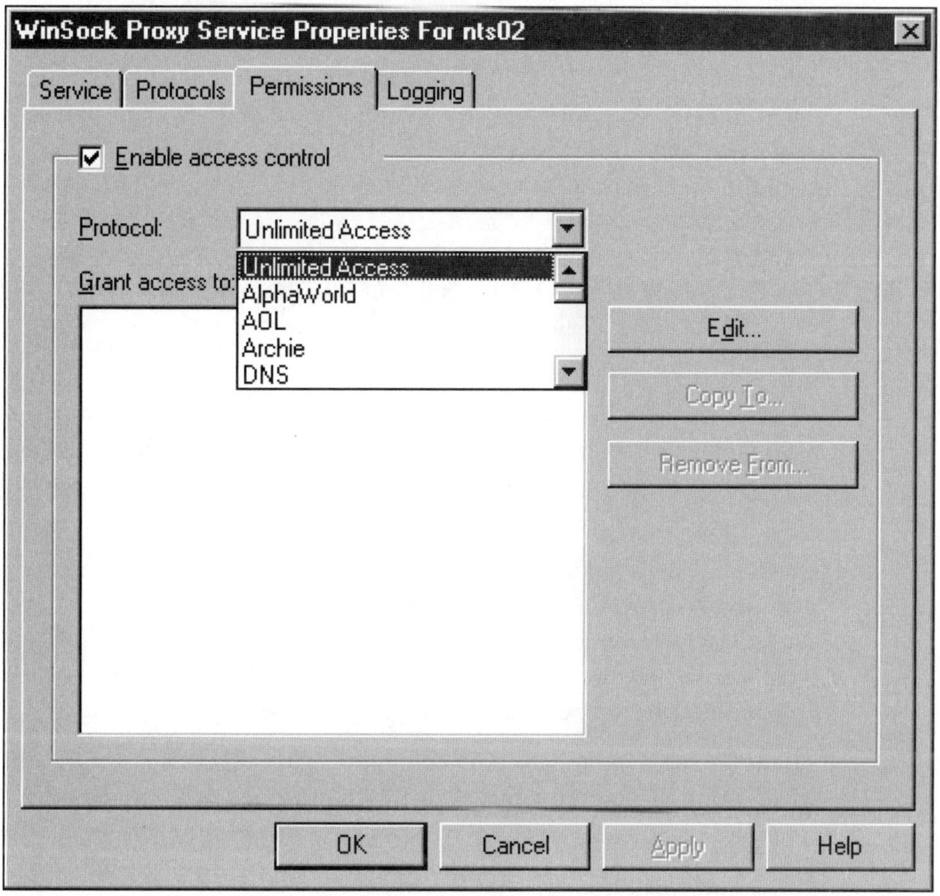

Figure 8.5   The WinSock Proxy Properties dialog box Permissions tab.

To set permissions on a protocol, launch the Internet Service Manager (ISM) by choosing Start|Programs|Windows NT 4.0 Option Pack|Microsoft Internet Information Server|Internet Service Manager. You should notice that the ISM for IIS 4.0 is significantly different from the ISM of IIS 3.0; it is now called the Microsoft Management Console instead of ISM. Select either the Web Proxy or WinSock Proxy service. Select Properties from the Action menu, select the Permissions tab, and select the Enable Access Control checkbox. To grant or deny access to a protocol, select it from the list of protocols and click on Edit. This brings up the Permissions dialog box, where users and groups can be selected and granted or denied access. To speed up the process, you can select the permissions for one user or group and copy them from one protocol to another. When Enable Access Control is checked, only those users specifically granted access can use the protocols hosted by that proxy service; all other users are not validated.

The Unlimited Access selection in the list of protocols is a special device that grants full access to every protocol and all inbound/outbound ports on the host server. This setting grants users full control over all protocols and all ports via the WinSock Proxy service, including those that are not specifically defined. Do not grant this access type to general users.

PROTOCOL AND PORT SECURITY

A protocol's definition determines which Windows Sockets applications can use that protocol to access the Internet. Each protocol definition also specifies which communication ports can be used for inbound and outbound traffic. By modifying a protocol's definition (through the WinSock Properties dialog box—see Figure 8.6), you can gain increased security control of your hosted services.

Socketed connections are established for Windows-Sockets-based applications by combining their application port(s) with IP addresses; this enables these applications to function properly over network connections. WinSock Proxy can also be used to redirect inbound ports by redirecting a Listen( ) call. This feature enables server proxying, where specific packets, such as email, sent to a defined port are captured and redirected to a specific internal server.

By modifying a protocol's port definitions, you effectively alter the ports to which users and groups assigned to that protocol have access. In other words, once you grant a user access permission to a protocol on the Permissions tab, you grant them access to the inbound and outbound port definitions for that protocol as defined on the Protocols tab (these tabs appear on the Properties dialog box of the WinSock Proxy in the Microsoft Management Console).

By default, inbound access to administrative types of protocols are disabled—this includes Telnet and FTP. If you choose to enable inbound use of these protocols via Proxy Server, you must implement additional security, such as:

- Establishing a strict accounts policy to enforce tough passwords
- Enabling WinSock Proxy access control
- Allowing protocol/port access only to users who require it
- Avoiding the use of the Unlimited Access option to grant blanket access
- Making sure remote users are not granted unneeded access
- Establishing separate user accounts for remote users instead of using their normal domain account

To establish protocols for the same application, but with different port assignments and user/group access, you can define new protocols, as shown in Figure 8.7. The Protocol Definition dialog box is accessed by selecting a protocol from the list of Protocol definitions and clicking the Edit button on the Protocols tab of WinSock Proxy Service Properties dialog box (see Figure 8.6). For example, if you need to grant most users outbound access to FTP, but one

8

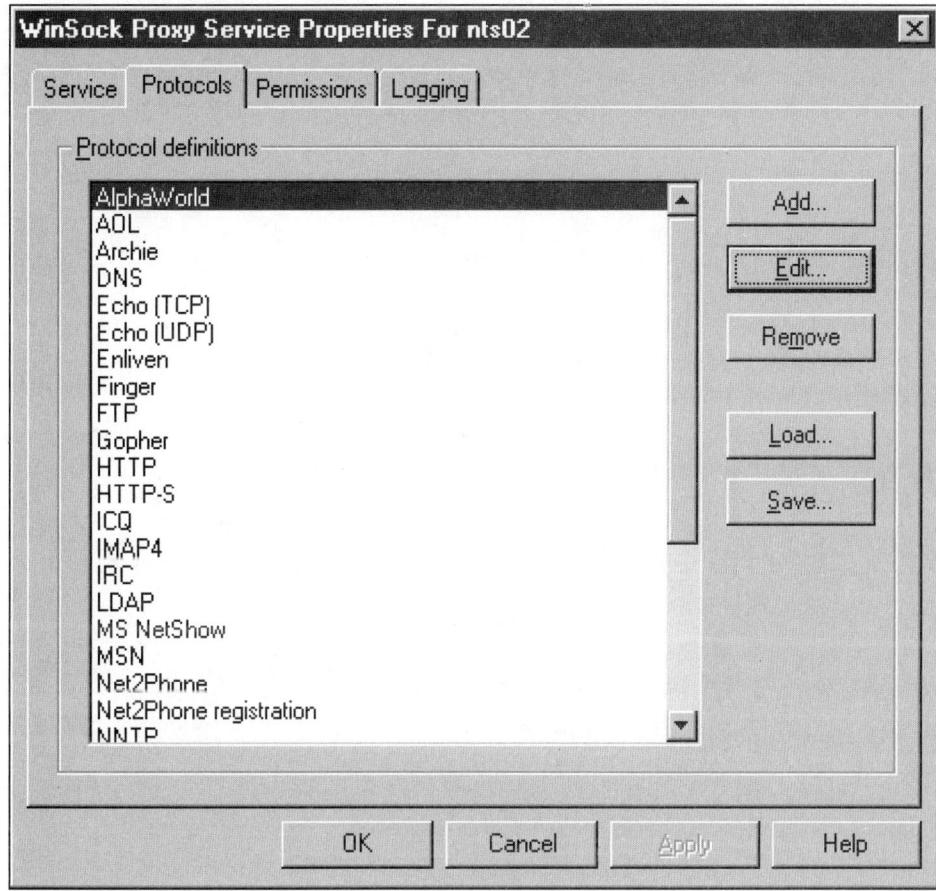

Figure 8.6 The Protocols tab of the WinSock Proxy Properties dialog box.

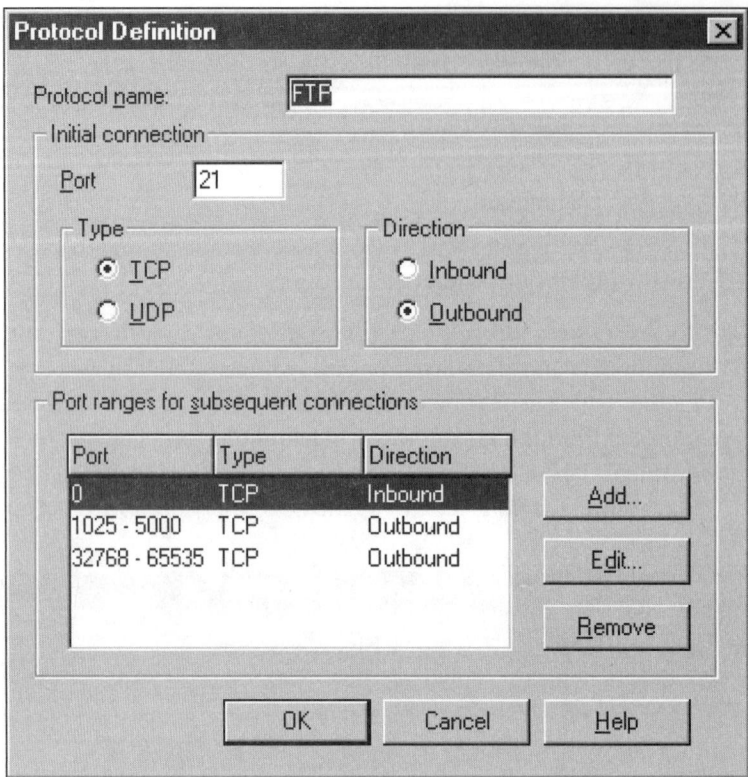

Figure 8.7 The Protocol Definition dialog box.

user needs inbound access, you can define the existing FTP protocol for outbound access, grant it to all users, create another protocol named FTP (inbound), and assign it to the one user who needs it. By default, all newly created protocols do not have any granted permissions; users and groups must be granted specific access on the Permissions tab to use new protocols.

When you are creating new protocols on the Protocols tab of the WinSock Proxy Properties dialog box, you will need to supply or define:

- Protocol name
- Initial connection port number
- TCP or UDP type
- Inbound or outbound communication
- Any subsequent connection Port Range Definitions of port, type, and direction

The Port Range Definitions are port ranges for subsequent connections made after the initial request is sent to the initial connection port. A port range setting of 0 is known as Port_Any—this allows the server to select any available port from 1024 to 5000. To remove protocol definitions, select the definition and click on the Remove button.

SOCKS SECURITY

SOCKS Proxy redirects API calls in much the same way WinSock Proxy does. However, SOCKS does not use true Windows NT Challenge/Response; instead, it uses IP addresses and the Identification (Identd) protocol to authenticate SOCKS Proxy clients. This variation in authentication methods occurs because SOCKS Proxy supports SOCKS version 4.3a standards. You can set SOCKS permissions through the Permissions tab in the SOCKS Proxy Properties dialog box, as shown in Figure 8.8.

To minimize conflict and security breaches, any client application operating through the SOCKS Proxy should be disabled through the WinSock Proxy. Also,

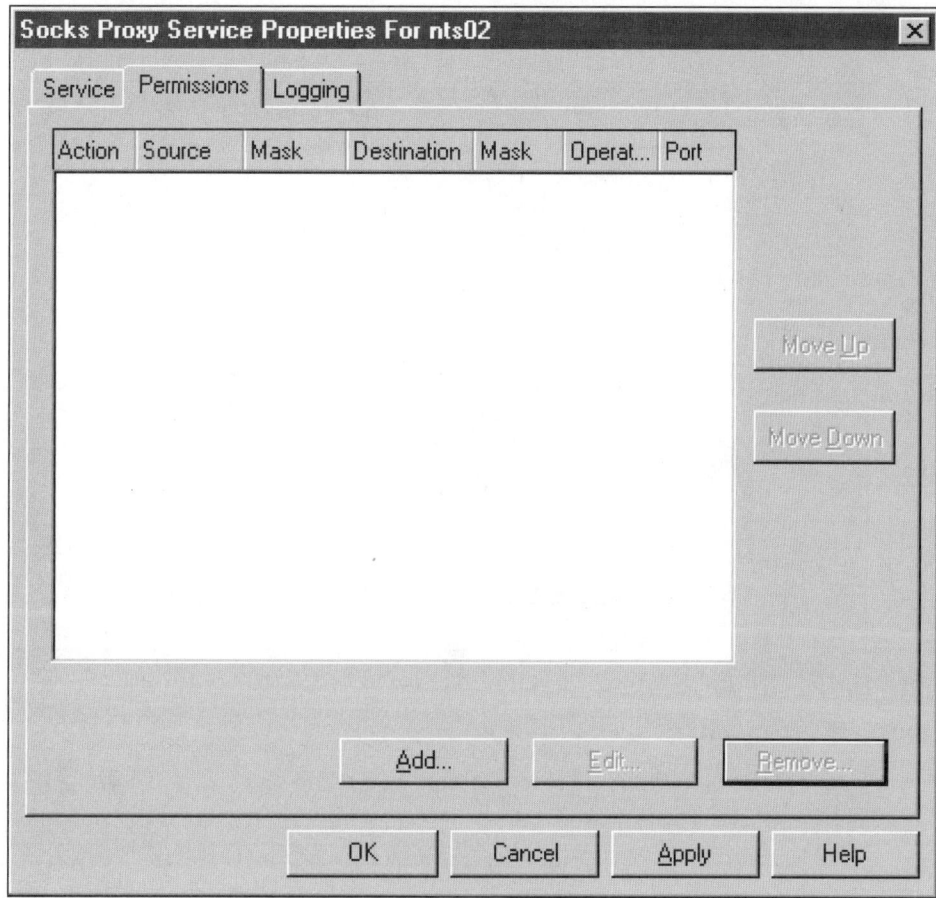

Figure 8.8   The Permissions tab of the SOCKS Proxy Properties dialog box.

the SOCKS Proxy is dependent on the Web Proxy service. If Web Proxy is not running or fails, SOCKS Proxy will not be available. Furthermore, SOCKS Proxy does not support any client applications that use the UDP protocol (RealAudio, VDOLive, Microsoft NetShow), nor is the IPX/SPX protocol supported.

Fortunately, all SOCKS client requests are denied by default. To enable SOCKS client request access, you must define SOCKS permission rules (see Figure 8.9). A rule consists of a defined source and destination address (a domain for a group or an IP and subnet mask for an individual computer), a defined port range, and whether or not access is granted or denied. SOCKS Proxy determines if a specific client has authorized access to a requested resource as follows:

- The resource requested is inspected for a specific denial defined for the requesting client.

- The resource requested is inspected for a specific allowance defined for the requesting client.

- If neither are defined, then access is denied to the requesting client.

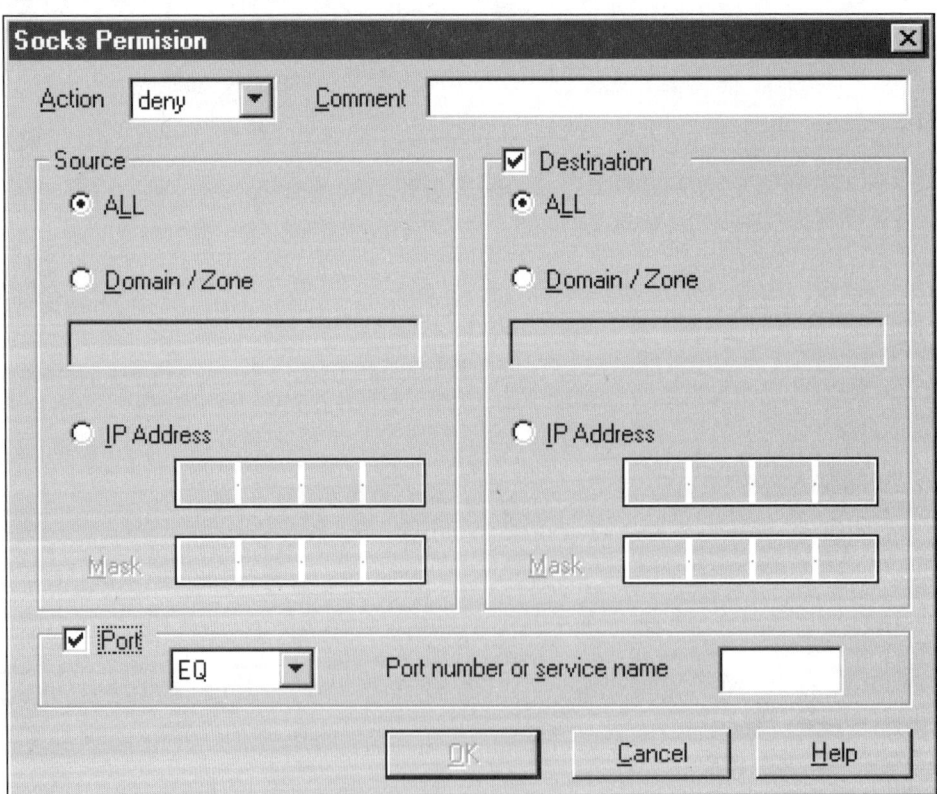

Figure 8.9   The SOCKS Permission dialog box.

To add or deny access to SOCKS, you need to define or edit a permissions rule from the Permissions tab of the SOCKS Permissions dialog box. All of the required elements of the SOCKS Permissions dialog box are self-explanatory except for the port range. The port range setting offers you a pull-down list of options and a field to define a port number or service name. The options are:

- **EQ** Equal to
- **NEQ** Not equal to
- **GT** Greater than
- **LT** Less than
- **GE** Greater than or equal to
- **LE** Less than or equal to

You can define multiple rules to accommodate the specific port structure you need. Rules that appear on the Permissions tab are processed in order from top to bottom. You can use the Move Up and Move Down buttons to manage the processing order. Subsequent rules do not alter the permission states of ports, services, or addresses defined by processed rules located higher on the list. In other words, once a service rule is denied or granted, another rule cannot reverse the setting. To remove/delete a rule, select it and click on the Remove button.

IDENTD SIMULATION SERVICE

SOCKS Proxy service uses Identd as part of its authentication method. Identd assigns a temporary unique identifier to each user. Proxy Server 2.0 ships with an Identd Simulation service, which can be installed to grant Microsoft Proxy client access to services that require Identd identification. The MS Identd Simulation service creates a random false username for each client and supplies it to the requesting servers to give Microsoft SOCKS Proxy clients access where they would be denied otherwise.

The IDENTD.EXE file located on the Proxy Server distribution CD is used to install the service. The manual installation procedure is as follows:

1. Create a directory named IDENTD on the host Proxy Server.
2. Copy the IDENTD.EXE file from the Proxy Server CD to this directory.
3. At a Command Prompt, change directories into the IDENTD directory.
4. Type "identd –install" and press Enter.
5. Type "net start identd" and press Enter.
6. Create a bidirectional packet filter for the Identd service, using TCP on port 113.

To remove the Identd service, follow these steps:

1. At a Command Prompt, change directories into the IDENTD directory.
2. Type "net stop identd" and press Enter.
3. Type "identd –uninstall" and press Enter.
4. Remove the packet filter for the Identd service.

DOMAIN FILTERS

A *domain filter* is a Proxy Server security tool used to limit access to external Internet resources by internal clients. To enable domain filtering, use the Domain Filters tab of the Security dialog box (see Figure 8.10). To access the Security dialog box, click on the Security button under Shared services on the Service tab of the Web, WinSock, or SOCKS Proxy Server's Properties dialog box in the Microsoft Management Console.

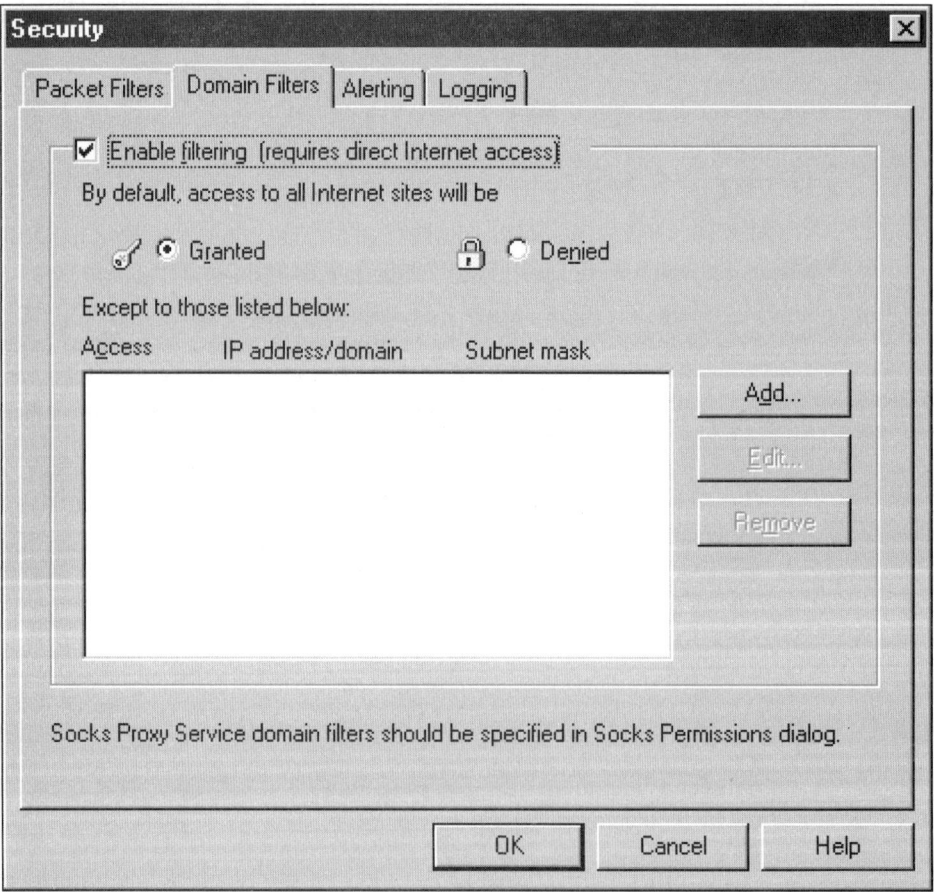

Figure 8.10   The Domain Filters tab of the Security dialog box.

Domain filters work by either blocking access to all sites except those specified or granting access to all sites except those specified (see Figure 8.11). Once the selection is made, you can use the Add button to add IP addresses and domains to the exceptions list on the Domain Filters tab. Exceptions can consist of a single computer's IP address, a group of computers' IP address and subnet mask, or an entire domain.

If multiple Proxy Servers are being used in a chained or cascading configuration, the Proxy Server that is farthest upstream must have direct Internet access for domain filtering to function. This is due to the inability of downstream Proxy Servers to perform name resolution.

With domain filtering enabled, each request from an internal client is checked. If the request is destined to a permitted site, it is processed. If the request is destined to a restricted site, it is refused and an error message is returned to the client.

To effectively block Internet resource site access from WinSock clients, you must define both an IP address (single or range) and a domain name for the site. Likewise, to grant access under blanked denial, both the IP address and domain name must be excluded for WinSock clients.

When domain filtering is used, it applies to all traffic encountered over the network interface. Because packets will be inspected before they are passed on to services, applications, or the internal network, domain filters apply equally to Web, WinSock, and SOCKS Proxy services.

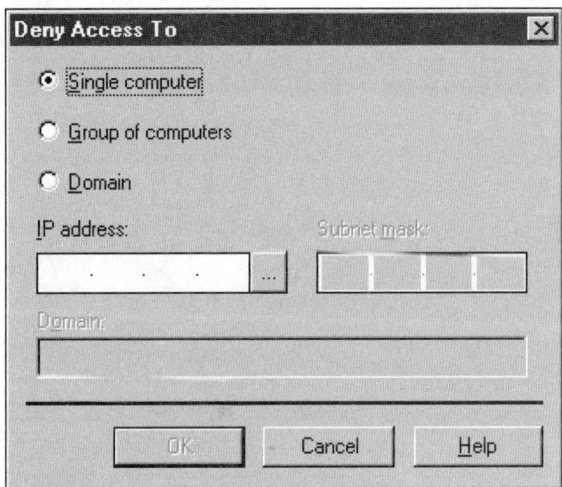

Figure 8.11   The Deny Access To dialog box.

PACKET FILTERS

A packet filter is another Proxy Server security tool; it filters traffic based on the protocol/application of individual packets. To enable packet filtering, use the Packet Filters tab of the Security dialog box (see Figure 8.12). To access the Security dialog box, click on the Security button under Shared services on the Service tab of Web, WinSock, or SOCKS Proxy Server's Properties dialog box in the Microsoft Management Console. Packet filtering is a firewall-level security feature that gives you precise control over inbound and outbound communication flow to and from the Proxy Server host.

A packet filter is used to block specific packets from crossing Proxy Server's boundary while allowing others to pass through. Proxy Server supports both inbound and outbound packet filtering to give you the widest range of firewall-level security control over network traffic.

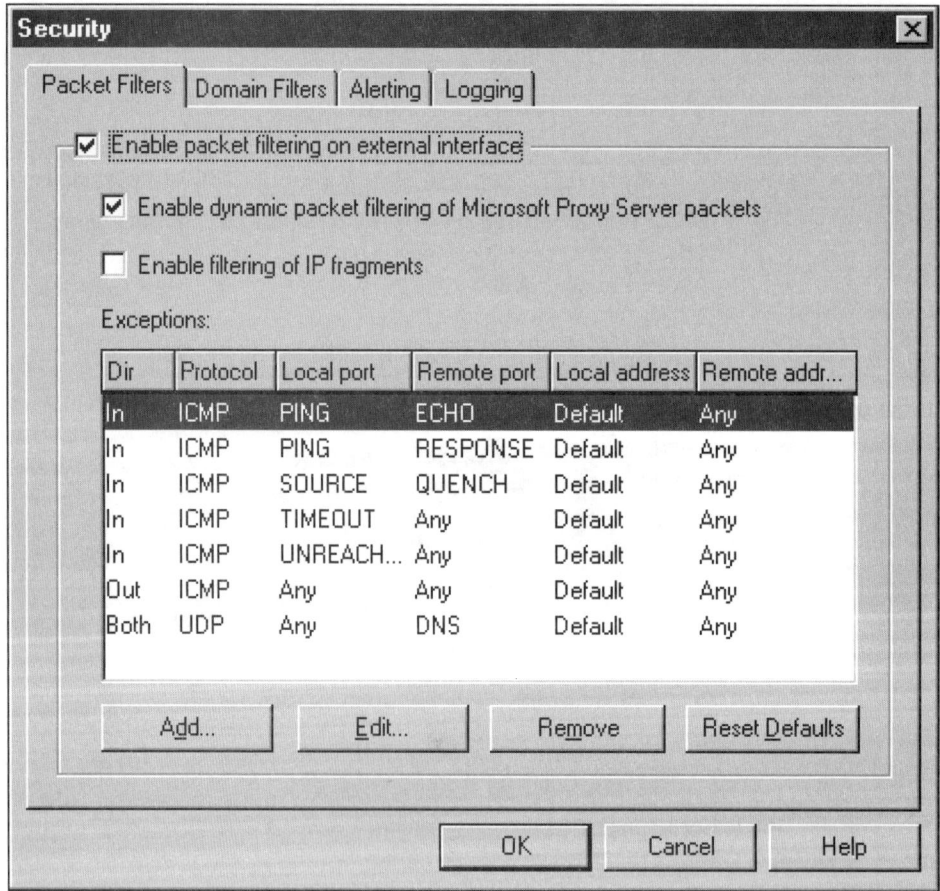

Figure 8.12 The Packet Filters tab of the Security dialog box.

Packet filtering is disabled by default. Before packet filtering can be enabled, a network interface (an ISP link to the Internet) must be installed and made active on the host server. If you are using a nondedicated Internet connection, you'll need to configure Auto Dial before you enable packet filtering. The button to reach the Auto Dial configuration dialog box is located below the Security button on the Service tab of Web, WinSock, or SOCKS Proxy Server's Properties dialog box in the Microsoft Management Console. Packet filters only apply to external network interfaces; they are not used on the internal network adapter where NT's own security measures (password authentication and user permissions) are in effect.

When packet filtering is enabled, every packet encountered by the host server is intercepted and inspected before it is passed on to the services or applications active on the host or into the internal network. This includes Web, WinSock, and SOCKS Proxy Server services. Thus, Proxy Server automates the task of verifying access restrictions before passing IP packets to a network's circuit and Application-layer services.

Dynamic packet filtering enables Proxy Server to open and close valid excepted ports to send and receive packets. When communication is initiated, a port is opened. When communication is complete, Proxy Server closes the port. This reduces the number of open and exposed ports (both inbound and outbound), plus it limits the amount of time a port is open to the Internet. Once packet filtering is enabled, all packets are denied access except those listed as exceptions. In addition, filtering can occur on datagrams and packet fragments if you select that option on the Packet Filters tab. This setting will prevent address spoof, SYN, and FRAG attacks from reaching your network.

If dynamic packet filtering is disabled, static packet filtering is enabled. This means that all ports defined in the exception list will remain open at all times. Generally, static filtering is only used with applications that require Internet access and are hosted on the same Windows NT Server as Proxy Server (such as Exchange Server or Routing and Remote Access Service).

A packet filter exception is created by clicking on the Add button. To define the exception, you'll need to provide parameters such as data flow, the transport protocol used, the remote (source) IP address of the host, the remote (source) service port used, and the local (destination) service port, as shown in Figure 8.13.

Several exception filters are predefined. Be sure to review these existing filters to determine if they are adequate for your needs; then make any changes, deletions, or additions as necessary. Remember that a packet filter defines packet types that will be allowed into your network. All other packets are denied access. If you do not have a packet filter defined for a specific port, you have effectively blocked all usage of that port. Several services require multiple filter definitions to allow proper communications, especially those services/protocols that have an initialization or

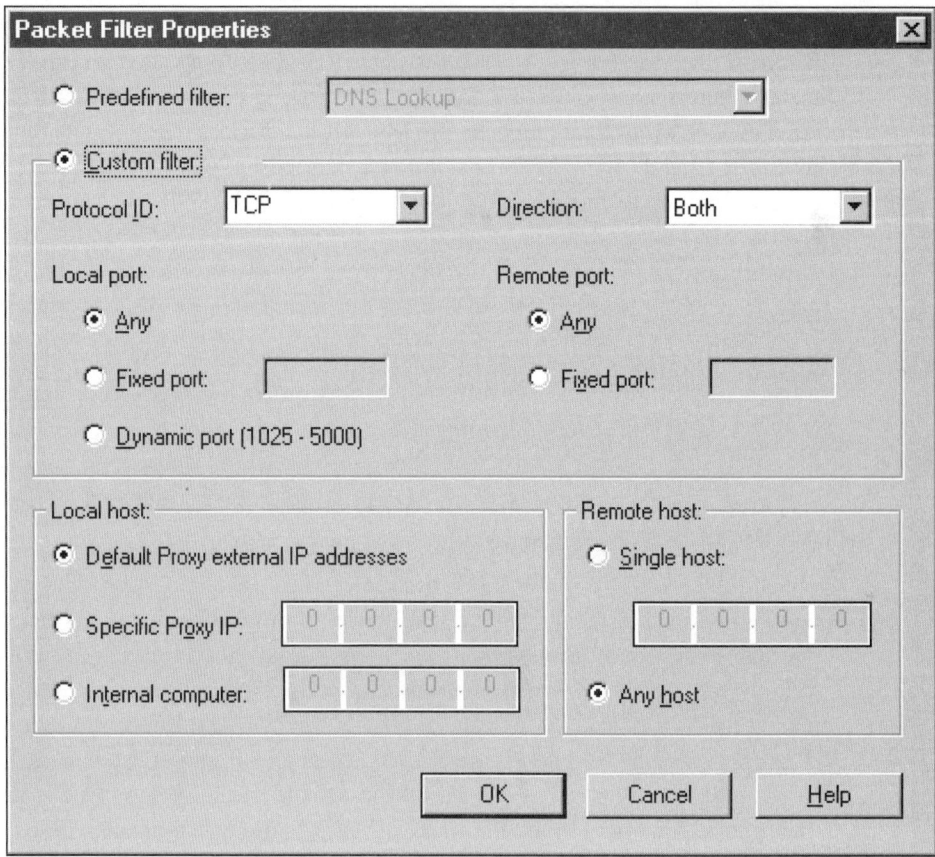

Figure 8.13   The Packet Filter Properties dialog box.

call port and a subsequent communications port, or those services/protocols that support simultaneous bidirectional communication on two different ports.

 When packet filtering is enabled, it applies to all traffic encountered over the network interface. Because packets are inspected before they are passed on to services, applications, or the internal network, this also means that packet filters apply equally to Web, WinSock, and SOCKS Proxy services.

PROXY ALERTS

Proxy Server can be configured to issue alerts when specified events occur. Proxy Server's ability to issue realtime alerts enables administrators to be aware of critical or potentially damaging situations as they occur. Proxy Server can monitor and issue alerts for several suspicious network events, including frequent rejected packets, attempted protocol violations, and storage volumes reaching capacity.

Alerts are configured on the Alerting tab of the Security dialog box (see Figure 8.14). To access the Security dialog box, click on the Security button under Shared services on the Service tab of Web, WinSock, or SOCKS Proxy Server's Properties dialog box in the Microsoft Management Console.

Alerts are automatically recorded in the packet filtering log and the Proxy Server service logs. You can also include alert messages in the System log, which is viewed through the Event Viewer, and you can send an SMTP email message to an administrator.

A rejected packet alert is issued when a specified number of events occurs per second. Rejected packets are packets that are sent to an illegal, unknown, or denied port, are frame/packet anomalous, or are dropped because of too much network traffic. A high rate of rejected packets might indicate an active attack on your network.

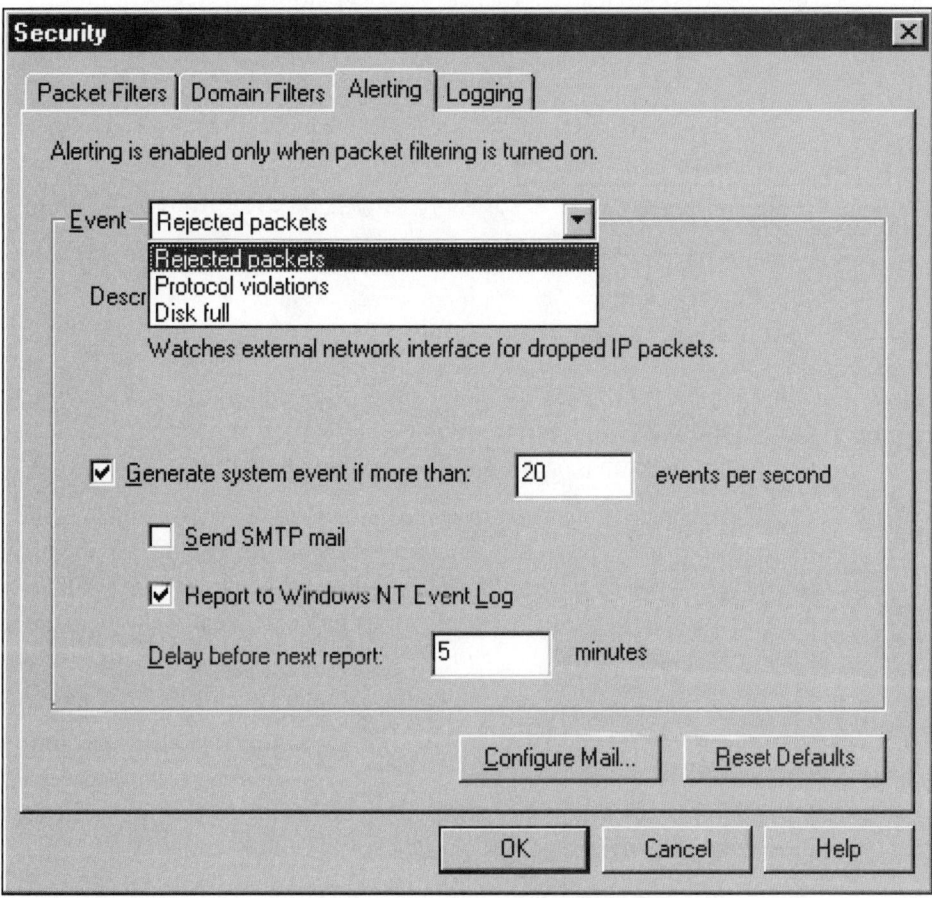

8

Figure 8.14   The Altering tab of the Security dialog box.

A protocol violation event is used when filtered packets or frames that violate the standard structure for protocol packets are found. Packet violations are also common indicators of network attacks.

A disk full alert is issued when the storage volume hosting any of the service logs or the packet log becomes full. When this alert is issued, you need to free up space on the volume or alter the destinations of the log files.

 For rejected packets and protocol violation alerts to be issued, packet filtering must be enabled.

To configure alerts, follow these steps:

1. Select the Alerting tab from the Security dialog box.
2. Select the event type for which you want to configure the alert response (rejected packets, protocol violations, or disk full).
3. Check the Generate System Event If More Than checkbox and define an integer value in the Events Per Second field.
4. If desired, select the Send SMTP Mail option to send alerts via SMTP email.
5. If desired, select the Report To Windows NT Event Log option.
6. Set the time to delay before issuing another alert of this event type.
7. Repeat Steps 2 through 6 for each event type.
8. Click on OK to save the changes.

You can also click on the Configure Mail button on the Alerting tab to configure the SMTP options, or you can click on the Reset Default button to return all alert settings back to post-installation defaults.

The Configuration Mail button reveals a configuration box where SMTP email message alert parameters are defined (see Figure 8.15). The parameters include the domain name of the SMTP server, the port (the default for SMTP is 25), the email address of the person to notify, and a name to list as the message originator. Once these parameters are defined, click on the Test button to send a sample message using the provided parameters.

When you use email alerts, it is highly recommended that you use only an internal SMTP email server and not an external public SMTP server. This will provide you with the highest level of security and prevent external users from intercepting the alert messages.

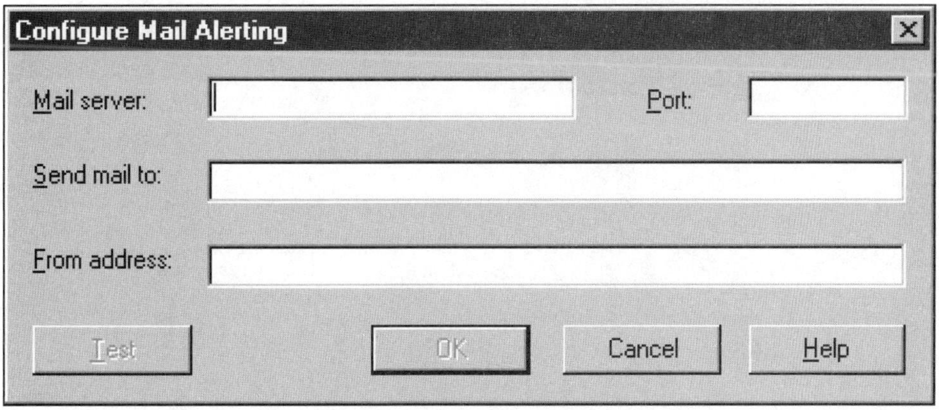

Figure 8.15   The Configure Mail Alerting dialog box.

WINDOWS NT SYSTEM LOG AND ALERT EVENTS

If the Report To Windows NT Event Log option is selected on the Alerting tab of the Security dialog box (see Figure 8.14), each occurrence of an alert is recorded in the System log. You can use the Event Viewer to review the event. Each event recorded in the System log will be tagged with a source name to indicate what type of event was recorded. Table 8.1 lists the source names and what they mean. Figure 8.16 shows a sample System log alert event as seen in the Event Viewer.

PROXY LOGGING

Proxy Server has multiple logs to record the various activities of the proxy system. For example, a Web Proxy log is configured through the Web Proxy Logging tab shown in Figure 8.17. Each proxy service—Web, WinSock, and SOCKS—has its own log; there is also a security filtering log that records events related to packet traffic. The security filter log only records rejected or dropped packet events.

Table 8.1   The source names listed in the System log for alert events.

Source Name	Description
MSProxyAdmin	Proxy Server administrative events
PacketFilterLog	Packet filter alert events (filtered frames)
SocksProxy	SOCKS Proxy service events
SocksProxyLog	SOCKS Proxy logging events
WebProxyCache	Web Proxy caching events
WebProxyLog	Web Proxy logging events
WebProxyServer	Web Proxy service events
WinSockProxy	WinSock Proxy service events
WinSockProxyLog	WinSock Proxy logging events

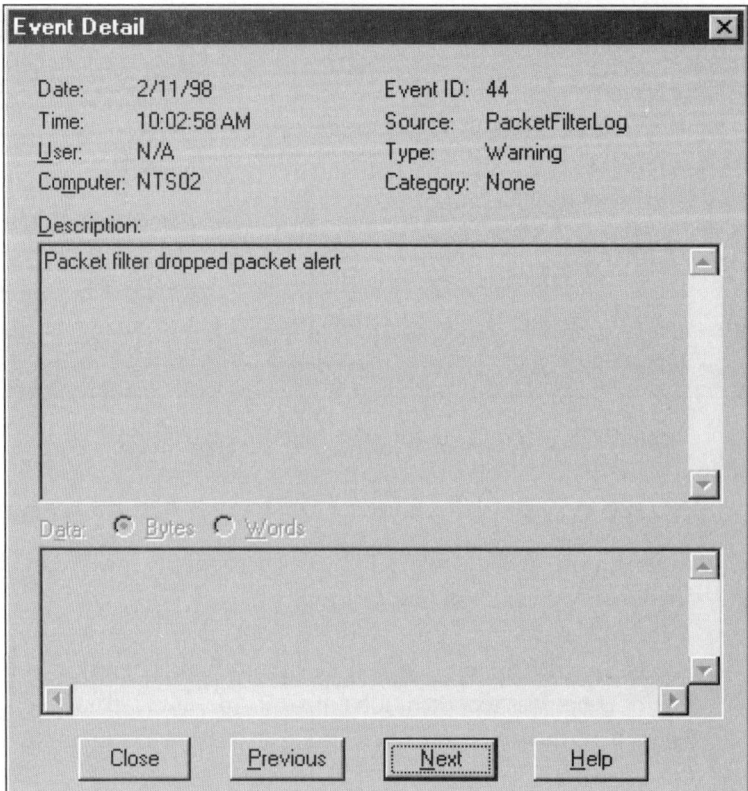

Figure 8.16   A sample System log alert event as seen in the Event Viewer.

Logs are stored in a text file format or in an ODBC-compliant database table format. The database table format is compatible with many database tools, including Microsoft Access and Microsoft SQL Server. Logs can be stored on remote or network drives, but for best performance and security, it is recommended that you store logs on volumes local to the host server. By default, logging is recorded in a text file when it is initially enabled.

The configuration tabs for all four of the logs are the same. Logging is enabled by selecting the Enable Logging Using checkbox at the top of the Logging tab.

Logging format can be set to regular or verbose. Regular logging records a limited number of data fields, whereas verbose logging records all available information. Table 8.2 lists the data items that are recorded for each of these log format types.

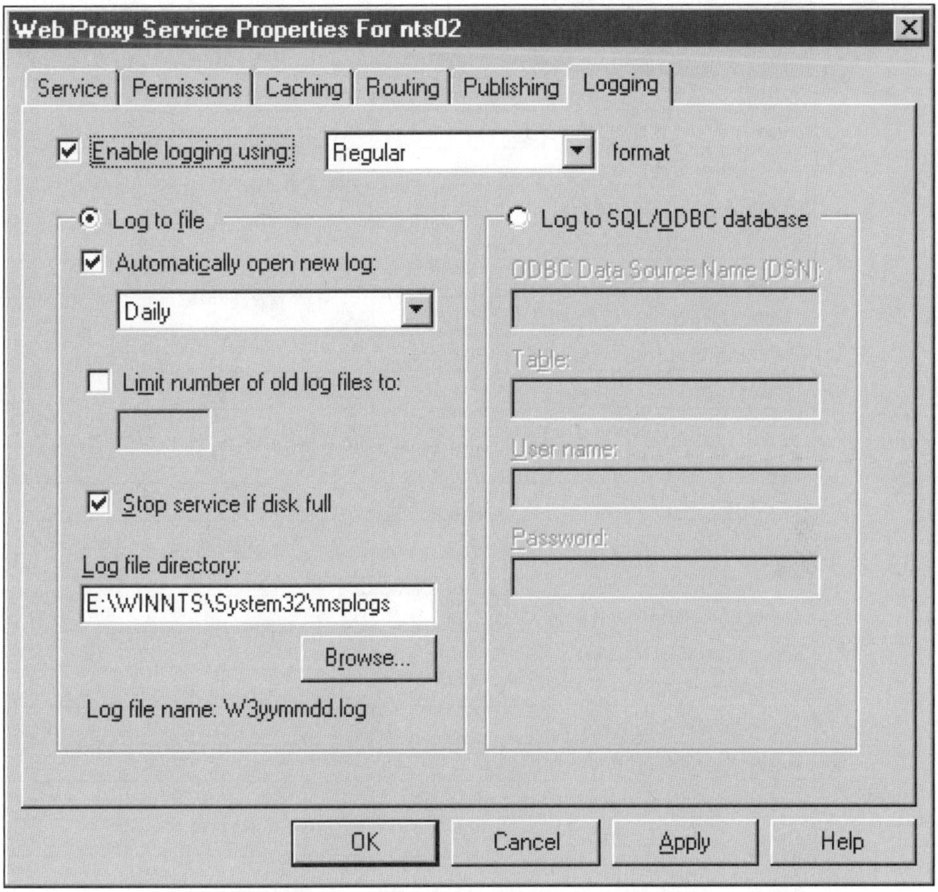

![Web Proxy Service Properties For nts02 dialog box showing the Logging tab. Tabs across the top: Service, Permissions, Caching, Routing, Publishing, Logging. "Enable logging using" is checked with "Regular" format selected. "Log to file" radio button is selected with "Automatically open new log" checked set to "Daily". "Limit number of old log files to:" is unchecked. "Stop service if disk full" is checked. Log file directory: E:\WINNTS\System32\msplogs. Browse button. Log file name: W3yymmdd.log. The "Log to SQL/ODBC database" section is grayed out with fields for ODBC Data Source Name (DSN), Table, User name, Password. Buttons at bottom: OK, Cancel, Apply, Help.]

Figure 8.17   The Web Proxy Logging tab (WinSock Proxy, SOCKS Proxy, and Security are similar).

Log entries may contain extended characters outside of the normal ASCII characters supported by text editors and database applications. Make sure the text editor you use to read a text log file is capable of reading and displaying OEM characters (for example, Notepad) and that the Data Source Name (DSN) is set to use OEM-to-ANSI conversion for database reading.

LOGGING TO A TEXT FILE

Logging to a text file is selected by default. The configurations options for text file logging are displayed in the left-hand side of the Logging tab. The options are as follows:

- Automatically open a new log on a daily, weekly, or monthly basis.
- Retain only a specified number of old logs.

Table 8.2   The data items recorded in regular or verbose log formats.

Field Name	Regular Logging	Verbose Logging
Authentication Status (ClientAuthenticate)		X
Bytes Received (BytesRecvd)		X
Bytes Sent (BytesSent)		X
Client Agent (ClientAgent)		X
Client Computer Name (ClientIP)	X	X
Client Platform (ClientPlatform)		X
Client User Name (ClientUserName)	X	X
Destination Address (DestHostIP)		X
Destination Name (DestHost)	X	X
Destination Port (DestHostPort)	X	X
Log Date (LogTime)	X	X
Log Time (LogTime)	X	X
Object MIME (MimeType)		X
Object Name (Uri)	X	X
Object Source (ObjectSource)	X	X
Operation (Operation)		X
Processing Time (ProcessingTime)		X
Protocol Name (Protocol)	X	X
Proxy Name (ServerName)		X
Referring Server Name (ReferredServer)		X
Result Code (ResultCode)	X	X
Service Name (Service)	X	X
Transport (Transport)		X

- Stop this service when the disk where log events are recorded becomes full.

- Define the directory into which log files are placed. The default is C:\WINNT\SYSTEM32\MSPLOGS\.

Log files have automatic names of:

- C:\WINNT\SYSTEM32\MSPLOGS*W3<DATE>*.LOG for the Web Proxy service

- C:\WINNT\SYSTEM32\MSPLOGS\WS*<DATE>*.LOG for the WinSock Proxy service

- C:\WINNT\SYSTEM32\MSPLOGS\SP*<DATE>*.LOG for the SOCKS Proxy service

- C:\WINNT\SYSTEM32\MSPLOGS\PF<*DATE*>.LOG for packet filter events

The <*DATE*> portion of the file name is replaced with *yymmdd* for daily logs, W*yymmw* for weekly logs, and M*yymm* for monthly logs—*yy* is the two-digit year (00 to 99), *mm* is the two-digit month(01 to 12), *w* is the one-digit week within a month (1 to 4), and *dd* is the two-digit day of the month (01 to 31).

The data items recorded in a text file are comma delimited. This means that each field is separated by a single comma. Make sure that any parsing tools used to convert the log files support comma-separated values (CSVs).

LOGGING TO A SQL/ODBC DATABASE

Logging to a SQL/ODBC database file is not selected by default. It must be enabled by selecting the correct radio button on the Logging tab (see Figure 8.18). Open Database Connectivity (ODBC) is a standard application programming interface (API) used to construct platform- or application-independent databases. Database logging requires significantly more system resources than text logging, so on heavily trafficked networks, ODBC logging may degrade performance.

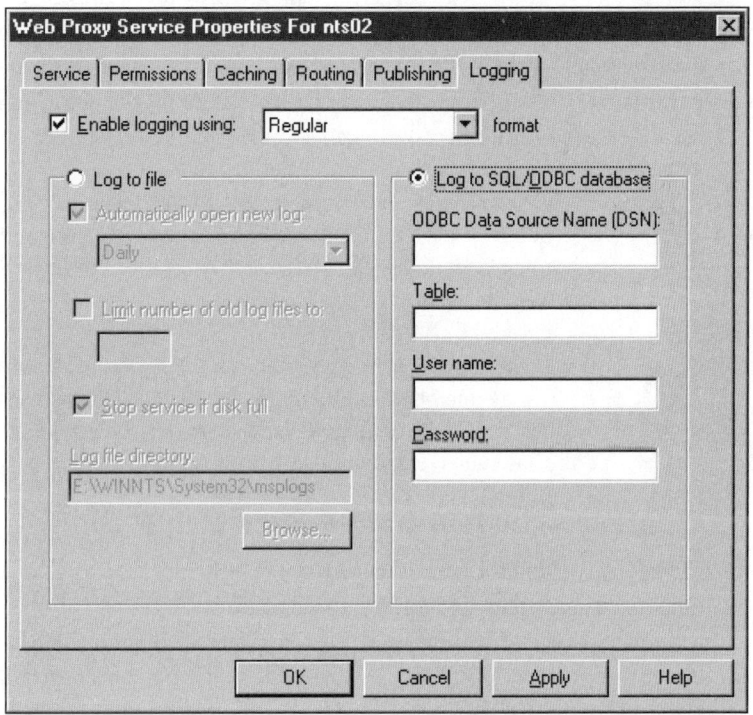

Figure 8.18   Log To SQL/ODBC Database selected on the Logging tab.

ODBC logging requires several more steps than text logging. These steps include:

1. Install the database application.
2. Install the ODBC driver for the database.
3. Create a system Data Source Name (system DSN) for the database.
4. Create a table in your database application with the necessary fields.
5. Configure the log for the database.

Installing The Database

The database you will use to analyze the logged data does not need to be installed on the Proxy Server host; it can be installed on any server on the network. Refer to the database product's documentation for installation requirements and instructions.

Installing The ODBC Driver

An ODBC driver (version 2.5 or later) is required to use the database logging options of Proxy Server. This ensures that the driver supports Data Source Names (DSNs) so Windows NT services can actually use ODBC. ODBC drivers are included on the Windows NT Server distribution CD or by the vendor of the database application. ODBC drivers are typically installed through the Internet Information Server Setup program. By re-executing the setup utility and selecting Add/Remove Components, you can add ODBC Drivers and Administration.

 Proxy Server does not support the ODBC driver for Microsoft Access 2.0. The 32-bit ODBC drivers shipped with Microsoft Office 95 Professional Edition and Microsoft Access for Windows 95 (and later versions) should be used instead.

 If multiple Proxy Server computers are configured as an array, and each array member is to log to an ODBC database, database logging should be configured for each array member after the array has been created.

Creating A System Data Source Name

ODBC uses a logical name known as the system DSN to refer to the driver and other parameters that are required to access data. Once the ODBC driver is installed, a unique system DSN must be defined for database logging. Whatever DSN is used, it must match the DSN defined by ODBC. DSNs are created from the Control Panel with the ODBC Data Source Administrator applet. Click on Add on the System DSN tab to select a driver to define a new DSN. Depending on the driver and database, several specific parameters and configuration details will be requested. Refer to your database's documentation for more details on creating new DSNs.

Creating A Database Table

Create a database table file using the data types and field names that are appropriate for your database application. Sample SQL database table template files are included with Proxy Server. They are placed in C:\WINNT\HELP\PROXY\MISC on the host computer during setup. MSP.SQL can be used for creating a database table for Web Proxy, WinSock Proxy, or SOCKS Proxy services. PF.SQL can be used for creating a database for packet filtering. These files can be used with either Microsoft SQL Server or Microsoft Access. For more information about database table template files, refer to your database application's documentation.

Configuring The Log

The final step in configuring SQL/ODBC database logging is to actually configure a proxy service to log on the appropriate Logging tab. This step can only be taken after the previous four steps have been completed successfully (see "Logging To A SQL/ODBC Database" earlier in this chapter). The configuration options are located on the right-hand side of the Logging tab. The available parameters to define are:

- The ODBC Data Source Name (DSN) that was created in Step 3.

- The name of the table file created in Step 4.

- A valid username and password for the database.

SERVICE LOG FIELDS

Each of the Proxy Server services—Web Proxy, WinSock Proxy, and SOCKS Proxy—record four types of data in the log files (when logging is enabled). These data types are:

- Server information

- Client information

- Connection information

- Object information

Server Information Fields

Server information fields contain information that is related to or extracted from the server. The fields include:

- **Log Date** The date of the logged event.

- **Log Time** The time of the logged event.

- **Proxy Name** The NetBIOS name of the host computer.

- **Referring Server Name** The NetBIOS name of the downstream computer that routed the request (only used in chained configurations).

- **Service Name** The name of the logged service (CERNProxy for Web Proxy, WSProxy for WinSock Proxy, and SOCKS for SOCKS Proxy).

Client Information Fields

Client information fields contain information that is related to or extracted from the client. The log from Web Proxy contains more client information than the log from WinSock Proxy contains. Web Proxy clients communicate more information about themselves over HTTP than WinSock applications do. The client log fields are:

- **Authentication Status** Indicates if an authentic client connection is being used.

- **Client Agent** Defines header information from a client browser from Web Proxy or the name of the client application from WinSock Proxy.

- **Client Computer Name** The name of the client computer or the Proxy Name when active caching is transpiring.

- **Client Platform** Used only by WinSock to indicate the client operating system (the codes are listed in Table 8.3).

- **Client User Name** Name of the user account currently logged on to the client computer.

Table 8.3   The codes used to define client operating systems.

Field Entry	Client Operating System
0:3.1	Windows 3.1
0:3.11	Windows for Workgroups
0:3.95	Windows 95 (16-bit)
1:3.11	Win32s
2:4.0	Windows 95 (32-bit)
3:3.1	Windows NT 3.1
3:3.5	Windows NT 3.5
3:3.51	Windows NT 3.51
3:4.0	Windows NT 4.0

Connection Information Fields

Connection information fields contain information that is related to or extracted from the client-to-server or server-to-server connections. They include:

- **Bytes Received** Used by Web Proxy to indicate the number of bytes received from the client. A hyphen, a zero, or a negative number means this information is not known.

- **Bytes Sent** Used by Web Proxy to indicate the number of bytes sent to the client. A hyphen, a zero, or a negative number means this information is not known. Used by WinSock to indicate the number of bytes sent when a connection terminates.

- **Destination Address** The IP address for the remote computer providing the requested resource.

- **Destination Name** The domain name for the remote computer providing the requested resource.

- **Destination Port** The reserved port number for the remote computer providing the requested resource.

- **Operation** Used by Web Proxy to indicate the HTTP method used—**GET**, **PUT**, **POST**, or **HEAD**. Used by Windows Proxy to indicate the current socket API call—Connect( ), Accept( ), SendTo( ), RecvFrom( ), GetHostByName( ), or Listen( ).

- **Processing Time** Indicates the time (in milliseconds) used by Proxy Server to process a connection.

- **Protocol Name** Used by Web Proxy to specify the protocol used (HTTP, FTP, or Gopher). Used by WinSock to specify the well-known destination port number for the socketed application.

- **Transport** Web Proxy always defined this as TCP/IP. WinSock Proxy can be TCP/IP, UDP, or IPX/SPX.

Object Information Fields

Object information fields contain information that is related to or extracted from the resource object. They include:

- **Object MIME** Used by Web Proxy to indicate the Multipurpose Internet Mail Extensions (MIME) type for the current object. Table 8.4 lists some supported MIME types.

- **Object Name** Used by Web Proxy to indicate the contents of a URL request.

- **Object Source** Used by Web Proxy to indicate the source of the object. This field can have the values listed in Table 8.5.

Table 8.4   Some supported MIME types.

MIME Type	Description
Application/x-msdownload	Application (executable)
Image/gif	GIF image file
Image/jpeg	JPEG image file
Multipart/x-zip	PKZIP archive file
Text/plain	Plain text file

- **Result Code**   Used by Web Proxy to indicate error and status codes. Windows (Win32) error codes have values less than 100, HTTP status codes have values from 100 to1000, and WinSock error codes have values from 10000 to 11004. Some of the supported values are defined in Table 8.6.

 Most connections have two log entries, one for connection establishment (result code of either 0 or 13301 and a byte count of 0) and a second for connection termination (result code of either 20000 or 20001 and the byte count).

PACKET FILTER LOG FIELDS

The Proxy Server packet filtering service records five types of data in its log file (when logging is enabled). These data types are:

- General information
- Remote information

Table 8.5   Object Source values and their descriptions.

Source Value	Description
0	No source information is available.
Cache	Source is the cache. Object returned from cache.
Inet	Source is the Internet. Object added to cache.
Member	Object returned from another array member cache.
NotModified	Source is the cache. Client performed an "If-Modified-Since" request and object had not been modified.
NVCache	Source is the cache. Object could not be verified to source.
Upstream	Object returned from an upstream proxy cache.
Vcache	Source is the cache. Object was verified to source and had not been modified.
VFInet	Source is the Internet. Cached object was verified to source and had been modified.

Table 8.6 Some of the supported error/status codes and their descriptions.

Value	Description
0	Successful connection
200	OK, Successful connection
201	Created
202	Accepted
204	No content
301	Moved permanently
302	Moved temporarily
304	Not modified
400	Bad request
401	Unauthorized
403	Forbidden
404	Not found
500	Internal server error
501	Not implemented
502	Bad gateway
503	Service unavailable
10060	Connection timed out
10061	Connection refused by destination
10065	Host unreachable
11001	Host not found
13301	Connection rejected by Proxy Server (due to filtering or protocol permissions)
20000	Normal connection termination
20001	Abortive connection termination

- Local information
- Filter information
- Packet information

Like the service logs, packet filtering logs can be either regular or verbose. Table 8.7 indicates which fields are included in each log format.

General Information Fields

General information fields contain information that is related to or extracted from general information:

- **PFLogTime** Time and date of packet reception.

Table 8.7   The field types included in the packet filtering regular and verbose log formats.

Field Name	Regular Logging	Verbose Logging
DestinationAddress	X	X
DestinationPort	X	X
FilterRule	X	X
Interface	X	X
IPHeader		X
Payload		X
PFLogTime	X	X
Protocol	X	X
SourceAddress	X	X
SourcePort	X	X
TcpFlags		X

Remote Information Fields

Remote information fields contain information that is related to or extracted from the remote computer:

- **Protocol**   Indicates the transport level protocol used by the connection (TCP, UDP, ICMP, etc.).

- **SourceAddress**   Indicates the IP address of the remote source computer.

- **SourcePort**   Indicates the service port number (if appropriate to the protocol) on the remote source computer.

Local Information Fields

Local information fields contain information that is related to or extracted from the local computer:

- **DestinationAddress**   Indicates the IP address of the local destination computer.

- **DestinationPort**   Indicates the service port number (if appropriate to the protocol) on the local destination computer.

Filter Information Fields

Filter information fields contain information that is related to or extracted from packet filters:

- **FilterRule**   Has a value of either 1 for accepted packet or 0 for dropped packet; only dropped packets are recorded in the filter log.

- **Interface (reserved for future use)** Indicates the interface in which the packet was received, but Proxy Server currently only supports a single interface per instance.

Packet Information Fields

Packet information fields contain information that is related to or extracted from packets:

- **IPHeader** Contains the entire IP header (in HEX format) of the packet that caused the alert event.

- **Payload** A partial listing (in HEX format) of the data packet that caused the alert event.

- **TcpFlags** Indicates the TCP flag value from the culprit packet's IP header (FIN, SYN, RST, PSH, ACK, or URG).

8

CHAPTER SUMMARY

In this chapter, we discussed the wide variety of security features Microsoft Proxy Server 2.0 offers to control unauthorized intrusion and restrict unproductive resource access. Both of these ends can be accomplished through several means. This chapter focused on securing your installation of Proxy Server and configuring the services to control inbound and outbound access.

Proxy Server's primary purpose is to give your network users access to the vast resources of the Internet. However, by opening the door to let internal users reach out, you also increase the possibility of unwanted external users getting in. To reduce the risk involved with opening a communication channel with the Internet via Proxy Server, you need to make several configuration changes to the Windows NT Server hosting Proxy, all of which were discussed in detail throughout this chapter.

Access to the protocols supported by the Web Proxy and WinSock Proxy services are controlled through use or user permissions. Each protocol is configured individually (and separately for each proxy service) to enable or restrict users and groups from gaining access. Permissions should be granted on a groups basis rather than individual user accounts. Therefore, it is a good idea to plan out the permission structure ahead of time and create multiple groups to provide the most control over granting protocol access.

The definition of a protocol determines which Windows Sockets applications can use it to access the Internet. Each protocol definition also specifies which communication ports can be used for inbound and outbound traffic. By modifying a protocol's definition, you can increase the security of your hosted services.

SOCKS Proxy redirects API calls in much the same way WinSock Proxy does. However, SOCKS does not use true Windows NT Challenge/Response; instead, it uses IP addresses and the Identification (Identd) protocol to authenticate SOCKS Proxy clients. This variation in authentication methods occurs because SOCKS Proxy supports SOCKS version 4.3a standards.

SOCKS Proxy service uses Identd as part of its authentication method. Identd assigns a temporary unique identifier to each user. Proxy Server 2.0 ships with an Identd Simulation service, which can be installed to grant Microsoft Proxy client access to services that require Identd identification. The MS Identd Simulation service creates a random false username for each client and supplies it to the requesting servers to give Microsoft SOCKS Proxy clients access where they would be denied otherwise.

A domain filter is a Proxy Server security tool that limits access to external Internet resources by internal clients. To enable domain filtering, use the Domain Filters tab of the Security dialog box. The Security dialog box is accessed by clicking on the Security button under Shared services on the Service tab of Web, WinSock, or SOCKS Proxy Service's Properties dialog box in the Microsoft Management Console.

A packet filter is another Proxy Server security tool; it limits access to external Internet resources by internal clients. To enable packet filtering, use the Packet Filters tab of the Security dialog box. Packet filtering is a firewall-level security feature that gives you precise control over inbound and outbound communication flow from the Proxy Server host.

Proxy Server can be configured to issue alerts when specified events occur. Proxy Server's ability to issue realtime alerts will keep administrators fully abreast of critical or potentially damaging situations. Proxy Server can monitor and issue alerts for several suspicious network events, including frequent rejected packets, attempted protocol violations, and storage volumes reaching capacity.

Proxy Server has multiple logs to record the various activities of the proxy system. Each proxy service—Web, WinSock, and SOCKS—has its own log, plus there is a security filtering log that records events related to packet traffic. The security filter log only records rejected or dropped packet events.

Logs are stored in a text file format or in an ODBC-compliant database table format. The database table format is compatible with many database tools, including Microsoft Access and Microsoft SQL Server. Logs can be stored on remote or network drives, but for best performance and security, it is recommended that you store logs on volumes local to the host server. By default, logging is recorded in a text file when it is initially enabled.

KEY TERMS

- **access control**—A feature of Proxy Server that enables user- and group-level control of service access by protocol and by extension port.

- **account policy**—A Windows NT security setting that defines restrictions on user passwords and failed logons.

- **binding**—Connecting a service or protocol to a network interface so that the service or protocol can use or be transported over that interface.

- **domain filter**—A Proxy Server security tool used to limit access to external Internet resources by internal clients by restricting domains, subnets, or individual computers.

- **Identd**—A simulated service of SOCKS Proxy that creates a random false username for each client and supplies it to the requesting servers in order to give Microsoft SOCKS Proxy clients access where they would be denied otherwise.

- **IP forwarding**—A feature of Windows NT's TCP/IP protocol that can forward IP packets across multihomed computers.

- **Local Address Table (LAT)**—A list of IP addresses that can have valid access to the services offered by Proxy Server.

- **packet filter**—A Proxy Server security tool that filters traffic based on the protocol/application of individual packets.

- **password authentication**—An NT security feature where users are verified on one of three different security levels: anonymous logon, basic authentication, or Windows NT Challenge/Response authentication.

- **RPC ports**—The TCP/IP service ports (1024 thorough 1029) used to Transmit Remote Procedure Calls (RPCs); they should be disabled on external interfaces.

- **Unlimited Access**—A WinSock Proxy setting that grants unlimited and unrestricted protocol access to a user/group.

- **user rights**—Security privileges within the Windows NT network environment that gives users/groups specific abilities, such as rebooting systems, taking ownership, or logging on as a service.

8

Review Questions

1. IP forwarding is disabled (unchecked) in which of the following circumstances? (Choose all that apply.)

   a. after TCP/IP is installed

   b. after RAS or RRAS is installed

   c. after Proxy Server 2.0 is installed

   d. after Windows NT is installed

2. What should your LAT file contain?

   a. all internal IP addresses

   b. IP addresses of remote servers

   c. the IP addresses of ISP-hosted DNS servers

   d. IP addresses of frequently accessed Internet FTP servers

3. Even with access control enabled for all of Proxy Server's services, what other security features or measures are required to protect the internal network? (Choose all that apply.)

   a. restrictive granting of user rights

   b. carefully planned group memberships

   c. strict accounts policy

   d. proper service binding

4. Proxy Server's host server should have all administrative shares from other servers mapped to local drive letters. (True or False?)

5. What two items of TCP/IP configuration should be removed from the Proxy Server's host computer's configuration? (Choose all that apply.)

   a. subnet mask

   b. DNS server

   c. IP address

   d. gateway

6. Proxy Server can be installed into its own domain in a multidomain network. This type of installation scenario will not compromise the integrity of the network if the Proxy domain is compromised. (True or False?)

7. What methods of user authentication are supported by the Web Proxy service? (Choose all that apply.)

   a. voice ID

   b. anonymous logon

   c. basic authentication

   d. Windows NT Challenge/Response authentication

8. Which user account is used by all anonymous users of the Web Proxy service?

   a. Guest

   b. Everyone

   c. IUSR_servername

   d. null

9. Granting or denying use permissions for the HTTP Web Proxy service protocol also affects which other protocol?

   a. FTP

   b. Gopher

   c. Telnet

   d. HTTPS

10. Use permissions of Web Proxy and WinSock Proxy are granted on a protocol-by-protocol basis to users/groups. (True or False?)

11. How can you grant unlimited and unrestricted access to all protocols and ports via WinSock?

   a. grant a user or group access to each protocol/port individually

   b. assign Unlimited Access to a user or group

   c. add a user to the WinSock Administrators group

   d. it is not possible

12. How are users granted access to specific ports under the WinSock Proxy?

   a. by selecting the port number and access direction on the Permissions tab

   b. by associated port ranges and user/groups on the Ports tab

   c. by creating separate protocols with unique port definitions and assigning access to these custom protocols

   d. it is not possible to assign port access

13. What is a socketed connection?

   a. a collection of known ports for a specific application

   b. a session's SOCKS Proxy communications link

   c. a dedicated semi-permanent pathway established across Proxy Server

   d. a WinSock connection created by combining the application ports with IP addresses

8

14. Which protocols under WinSock Proxy are by default disabled for inbound access? (Choose all that apply.)
    a. IMCP
    b. Telnet
    c. FTP
    d. DNS

15. Which security authentication scheme is used by SOCKS Proxy?
    a. Identd
    b. anonymous logon
    c. basic authentication
    d. Windows NT Challenge/Response authentication

16. Which service is dependent on the operation of Web Proxy to function?
    a. WinSock Proxy
    b. SOCKS Proxy
    c. packet filtering
    d. alert logging

17. Which types of applications are not supported by SOCKS Proxy?
    a. HTTP
    b. TCP
    c. UDP
    d. SMTP

18. By default, all access across SOCKS Proxy is denied. (True or False?)

19. Domain filters are defined using what data? (Choose all that apply.)
    a. single computer's IP address
    b. NetBIOS server name
    c. a group of computers' IP address and subnet mask
    d. entire domain

20. Which service requires that both the IP address and the domain name of a remote Internet site be granted or denied in order to properly control access?
    a. Web Proxy
    b. WinSock Proxy
    c. SOCKS Proxy

21. When packet filtering is enabled, each packet encountered by the host server is intercepted and inspected before it is passed on to the services or applications active on the host or into the internal network. (True or False?)

22. What is required to enable packet filtering?
    a. pause all IIS services through the Services applet
    b. install the packet filtering service through the Network applet
    c. an external network interface
    d. logging to ODBC
23. Which events can trigger Proxy alerts? (Choose all that apply.)
    a. attempted protocol violations
    b. storage volumes reaching capacity
    c. frequent rejected packets
    d. invalid name/password combination
24. What type of logging is enabled by default?
    a. log to text file
    b. log to SQL/ODBC database
    c. log to Event Viewer System log
    d. do not log
25. What is required to enable SQL/ODBC logging? (Choose all that apply.)
    a. an ODBC driver
    b. a database table
    c. system DSN
    d. an installed database application

HANDS-ON PROJECTS

In this section, we take you step-by-step through some common management tasks to help improve the security of your Proxy Server implementation.

 **PROJECT 8.1**

In this project, you will manage Web Proxy access permissions. To complete this project, you need to have a computer configured with Windows NT Server 4.0 and Proxy Server 2.0.

1. Launch Microsoft Management Console (Start | Programs | Microsoft Proxy Server | Microsoft Management Console).
2. Expand the Console Root, expand IIS, and expand the computer name.
3. Locate and select Web Proxy.
4. Select Action | Properties.

5. Select the Permissions tab.

6. Select Enable Access Control.

7. Select WWW from the pull-down Protocol list.

8. Click on the Edit button.

9. Click on the Add button.

10. Locate and select the Everyone group from the Add Users And Groups dialog box.

11. Click on Add, then click on OK to close the Add Users And Groups dialog box.

12. Click on OK again to close the WWW Permissions dialog box. Notice the listing of the Everyone group in the Grant Access To field on the Permissions tab.

13. Select the Everyone group listed in the Grant Access To field on the Permissions tab.

14. Click on Remove From.

15. Select WWW from the Service Selection dialog box.

16. Click on OK. Notice that the group was removed.

17. Click on OK to close the Web Proxy Properties dialog box.

PROJECT 8.2

In this exercise, you will create a domain filter (this exercise assumes an external interface has already been configured):

1. Locate and select Web Proxy.

2. Select Action | Properties.

3. Click on the Security button on the Services tab of the Web Proxy Properties dialog box.

4. Select the Domain Filters tab.

5. Select Enable Filtering.

6. Click on the Add button.

7. Type "172.16.1.1" as the IP address for a single computer and click on OK. Notice the Denied Access listing for this domain filter.

8. Select the 172.16.1.1 filter and click on Remove.

9. Deselect Enable Filtering. Do not close the dialog box; it will be used in the next exercise.

 **PROJECT 8.3**

In this exercise, you will create a packet filter:

1. Select the Packet Filters tab of the Security dialog box.
2. Select Enable Packet Filtering On External Interface.
3. Click on Add.
4. Select Predefined Filter.
5. Select SMTP from the pull-down list.
6. Click on OK. Notice the new packet filter listed in the Exceptions field.
7. Select the SMTP packet filter you just added and click on Remove. Do not close the dialog box; it will be used in the next exercise.

8

 **PROJECT 8.4**

Next you will configure alerting:

1. Select the Alerting tab of the Security dialog box.
2. Select Protocol Violations from the Event pull-down list.
3. Change the events per second to 3.
4. Deselect Report To Windows NT Event Log. Do not close the dialog box; it will be used in the next exercise.

 **PROJECT 8.5**

In this exercise, you will configure packet filtering:

1. Select the Logging tab of the Security dialog box.
2. Select Verbose from the Format pull-down list.
3. Select Weekly from the Automatically Open New Log pull-down list.
4. Select Limit Number Of Old Logs Files and enter a value of 5 in the field.
5. Click on OK to save the logging and alerting configuration changes.
6. Click on OK to close the Web Proxy Properties dialog box.
7. Exit MMC.

CASE PROJECTS

1. You suspect that a disgruntled customer has attempted to shut down your network by using TCP/IP packet flooding. What can you do to determine if this is true and to discover as much information as possible about the source of such attacks?

2. You've discovered that several employees are spending hours each day visiting unproductive Web sites when they have important deadlines approaching. After reviewing the log for Web Proxy, you discover that most of the activity is occurring on **www.toomuchfunforyou.com**. What can you do to improve the productivity of your employees?

3. You've installed a Telnet server on your internal network. You want to give a small group of users access to the Telnet server while they are traveling, but you do not wish to grant blanket access to all users on your network. What can you do?

4. The existing Windows-NT-based network is made up of several domains. Proxy Server is needed to control access over the Internet connection for the entire network. What is the best way to add Proxy Server to this system?

5. To support Unix clients on your network, you are using the SOCKS Proxy service. Several users have complained that since Proxy Server was deployed, they have been unable to gain access to IRC servers on the Internet. You verify that they have proper access and that the IRC protocol is enabled for both inbound and outbound communication. What else could be wrong and how can you fix it?

MANAGING AND TUNING PROXY SERVER 2.0

In this chapter, you will learn to perform the administrative tasks necessary to keep Microsoft Proxy Server 2.0 operating at its highest possible performance level. You will become acquainted with the tools Microsoft Proxy Server 2.0 provides to maintain Web Proxy, WinSock Proxy, and SOCKS Proxy. You will also become familiar with the Performance Monitor counters that are used to monitor Proxy Server 2.0, and you will be introduced to the tool that opens a Performance Monitor chart specifically configured for monitoring Proxy Server components. At the end of the chapter, the hands-on projects will take you step-by-step through many of the administrative tasks that are described throughout this chapter.

AFTER READING THIS CHAPTER AND COMPLETING THE EXERCISES, YOU WILL BE ABLE TO:

- Perform Web Proxy administrative tasks
- Perform WinSock Proxy administrative tasks
- Perform SOCKS Proxy administrative tasks
- Monitor Proxy Server performance

INTERNET SERVICE MANAGER

Internet Service Manager (shown in Figure 9.1) is used to access and administer Microsoft Internet Information Server and Microsoft Proxy Server 2.0. When the Proxy Server is installed, the Web Proxy, WinSock Proxy, and SOCKS Proxy icons are added to the Internet Service Manager tool.

Internet Service Manager can be accessed through either the Microsoft Internet Server group or the Microsoft Proxy Server group. To open the Internet Service Manager tool, select Start | Programs | Microsoft Proxy Server and click on Internet Service Manager.

The Internet Proxy Service Manager appears with a list of all installed Internet services. The Tools menu allows access to the Key Manager. Options that will allow connection or identification of other servers on the network that are providing Internet services are on the Properties menu (see Figure 9.2). A brief explanation of these options follows:

- **Connect To Server** Allows you to connect to a remote server, which provides a way to administer Internet Information Server and Proxy Server computers across the network.

- **Find All Servers** Finds and lists all Internet Information Server computers on the network by polling IPX/SPX routers and WINS servers and sending broadcast-based messages. Any computers found will be listed in the Internet Service Manager. Note that you must have administrative rights on the remote server to perform remote administration.

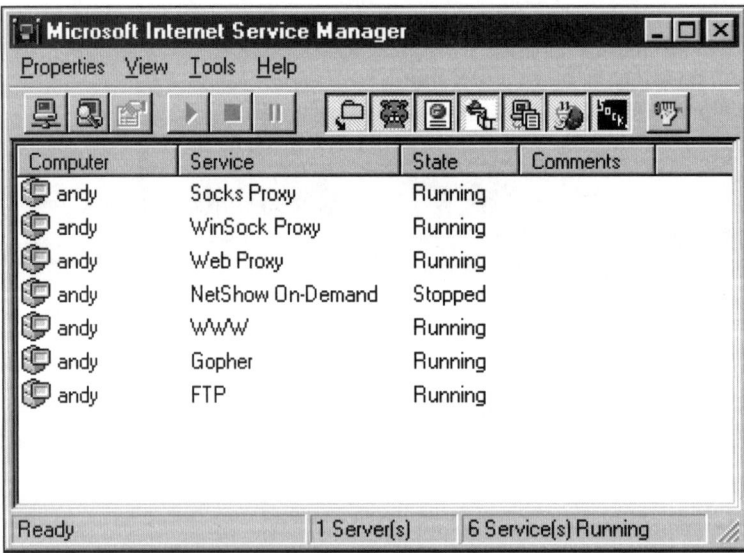

Figure 9.1   Internet Service Manager.

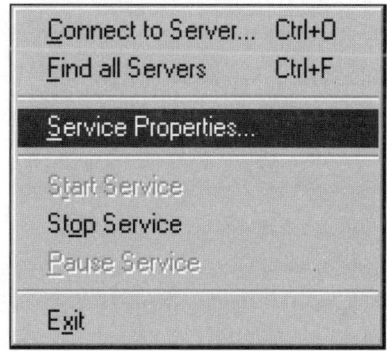

Figure 9.2   The Internet Service Manager Properties menu.

There are several viewing options available for the Internet Service Manager. There are three grouped areas, a refresh selection, and selection for displaying the toolbar and the status bar. The three grouped areas are as follows:

- In the Services area, each service is listed and can be selected for display. The All option places checkmarks next to all services.

- In the Sort area, there are options to sort by server, service, comment, or state of operation.

- In the View area, the display can be configured for Server view, Services view, or Report view.

WEB PROXY MANAGEMENT

The Web Proxy service provides a pathway to the Internet for CERN-compliant applications and supports requests from any CERN-compliant browsers, such as Microsoft Internet Explorer or Netscape Navigator.

The tool used to administer the Web Proxy service is the Internet Service Manager. When Microsoft Proxy Server 2.0 is installed, an icon is added to Internet Service Manager for Web Proxy service support. To Access this tool (shown in Figure 9.3), follow these steps:

1. Select Start | Programs | Microsoft Proxy Server and click on Internet Service Manager.

2. Select Web Proxy from the display window.

3. Select Service Properties from the Properties menu. The Web Proxy Service Properties dialog box appears.

There are six tabs that are used to configure the Web Proxy service properties. The following sections include a brief description of the information that can be configured on each tab.

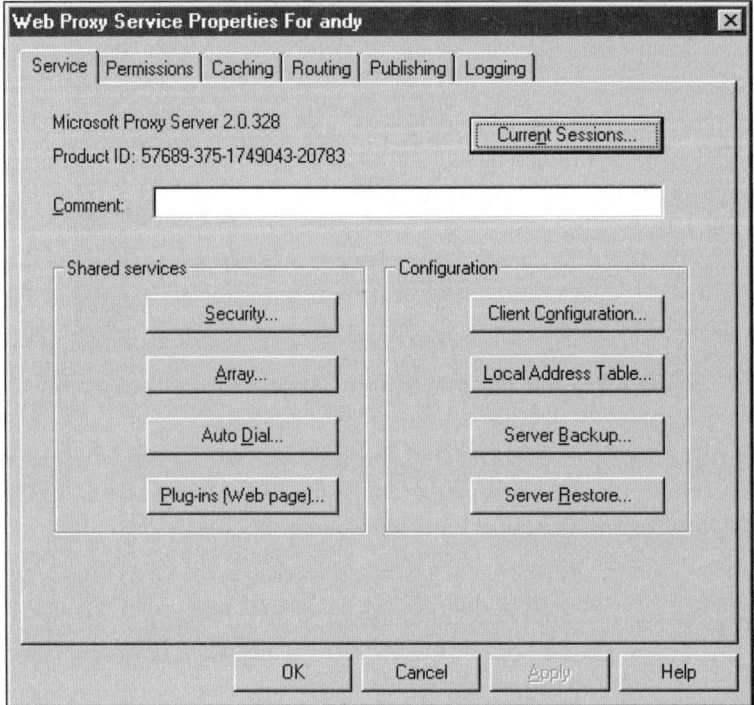

Figure 9.3 The Web Proxy Service Properties dialog box with the Service tab selected.

SERVICE PROPERTIES

When the Service tab is selected (see Figure 9.3), the Proxy revision and ID information is displayed. The Current Sessions button lists all connected users for the three proxy services. It also displays the time the client connected and the length of time the client maintained the connection. Below the Current Sessions button is a comment line where you can add a comment about the server or one of the services. The central area of the dialog box is divided into two parts: Shared Services and Configuration.

The Shared Services area has four buttons: Security, Array, Auto Dial, and Plug-ins. You can use the Shared Services area to configure and support the Web Proxy, WinSock Proxy, and SOCKS Proxy services. A brief description of each button follows:

- **Security** Configures the filters, of which there are two types: domain filters and packet filters. The Domain Filters tab is used to grant or deny access to specified Internet Web sites. The Packet Filters tab is used to filter IP packets on inbound and outbound communications, which allows specified protocols to be blocked or enabled. The Alerting tab is used with packet filtering to log suspicious network events, including dropped packets, SYN or FRAG attacks, and packets sent to an unused service port. The Alerts tab is used to configure the Proxy Server computer to generate a system event, to add the event to the event log, or to send SMTP mail to a specified address. A delay can be set so subsequent events will not be logged for a configurable amount of time. An SMTP message can also be sent if the hard disk is full. The Logging tab is used to configure the logging options for the WinSock Proxy, Web Proxy, and SOCKS Proxy services.

- **Array** Creates an array, which is a group of Proxy Server computers that are linked and use peer-to-peer communication. Arrays provide increased caching performance for the Web Proxy service and increased fault tolerance and load balancing for all the services. If synchronization is enabled, common configuration maintenance can be performed for all of the Proxy Server computers in an array.

- **Auto Dial** Sets up on-demand dialing of a RAS Phonebook entry by Microsoft Proxy Server. On-demand dialing is used when one of the Proxy Server services must establish a dial-up connection to the Internet rather than keep a constant connection to an Internet Service Provider (ISP). The Credentials tab specifies which RAS Phonebook entry is used to establish the connection. For the WinSock Proxy and SOCKS Proxy services, on-demand dialing is used for all client requests. For the Web Proxy service, on-demand dialing is used only when a client request cannot be located and processed by using objects from the Web Proxy cache. You can choose which services you want the Auto Dial feature enabled for by using the checkboxes on the Configuration tab. The choices are:

  - Enable dialing for WinSock and SOCKS Proxy

  - Enable dialing for Web Proxy primary route

  - Enable dialing for Web Proxy backup route

- **Plug-ins** Used by Microsoft Proxy Server 2.0 to support the installation of third-party software (plug-ins). When you click on the Plug-ins button, your Web browser opens and loads the Web page **http://www.microsoft.com/proxy/common/plugins.htm**. A list of plug-ins that can be installed appears, each of which can be downloaded.

The Configuration area has four configuration buttons, which are also shared for all three services:

- **Client Configuration** Opens a dialog box that is used to set the configuration options for client setup. During setup, Proxy Server Setup

9

installs a client setup program on the Proxy Server computer; client computers can connect to it and run client setup. You can configure client setup during the installation of Proxy Server or from the Web Proxy or WinSock Proxy Service Properties dialog box.

- **Local Address Table** Opens a dialog box that is used to view and modify the Local Address Table for the Proxy Server. The Local Address Table (LAT) is used to determine whether an IP address is local or remote by identifying all internal IP network addresses and excluding all external IP addresses. This information is maintained in a LAT, which is used by WinSock Proxy, Web Proxy, and SOCKS Proxy clients.

- **Server Backup** Specifies the directory to which the backup file is saved. The default is C:\MSP; it can be modified by typing the new path in the dialog box or by clicking on the Browse button.

- **Server Restore** Completes a partial or complete restoration of an earlier configuration of Proxy Server; click on the Server Restore button on the WinSock Proxy, Web Proxy, or SOCKS Proxy Service Properties dialog box. After choosing the restoration method to be used, enter the name of the configuration file in the Filename box or click on Browse to display the Browse For Folder dialog box, and choose the configuration file.

PERMISSIONS

You can use the Permissions tab (shown in Figure 9.4) to give a user or group permission to use Internet protocols on your Proxy Server. The permissions are configured and granted for each protocol that is installed. For instance, a user might have permission to use the FTP protocol but not the WWW protocol.

The following protocols can be configured from the Permissions tab:

- FTP Read
- WWW
- Secure
- Gopher

The proper way to provide permissions for the Web, File Transfer Protocol (FTP), and Gopher services is to create a group for each service in User Manager For Domains and to assign the users to groups following the *AGLP (Account, Global, Local, Permission)* method. Then for each protocol, you only need to

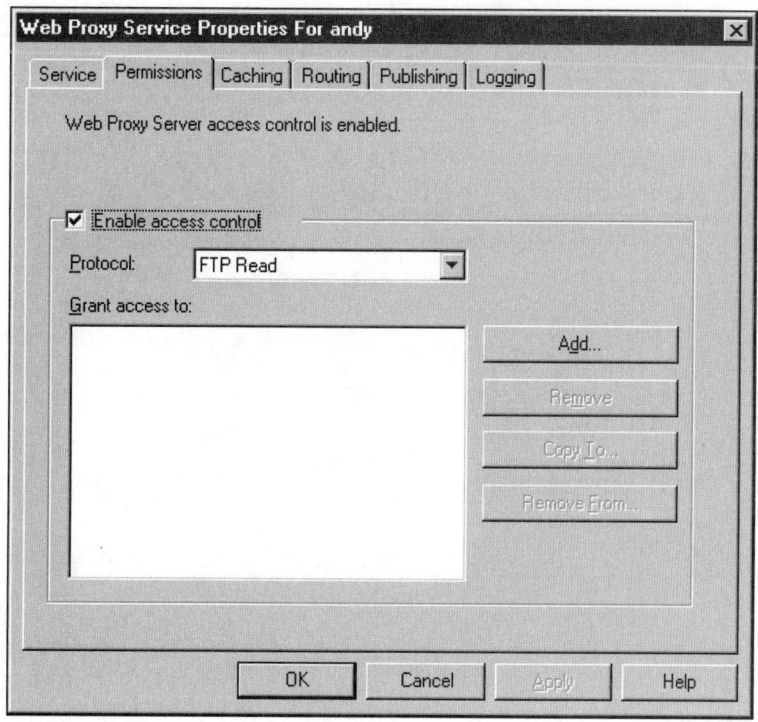

Figure 9.4   The Permissions tab of the Web Proxy Service Properties dialog box.

apply the permissions once for the group rather than by the individual. The AGLP method is as follows:

1. Add user accounts to global groups.

2. Add global groups to local groups.

3. Add local groups to the Access Control List (ACL) for a resource, such as the FTP service.

4. Assign permissions to the local group; provide the rights that will be the most restrictive and still allow the group to perform the given task.

CACHING

The Caching tab (shown in Figure 9.5) is used to enable or disable the caching feature and to configure caching operations. There are two forms of caching that can be used: active caching and passive caching. The cache area is actually hard disk space that is set aside for storing components of Internet sites that have been visited by the client. When the same site is accessed again, it will take less time to load because its information is stored locally.

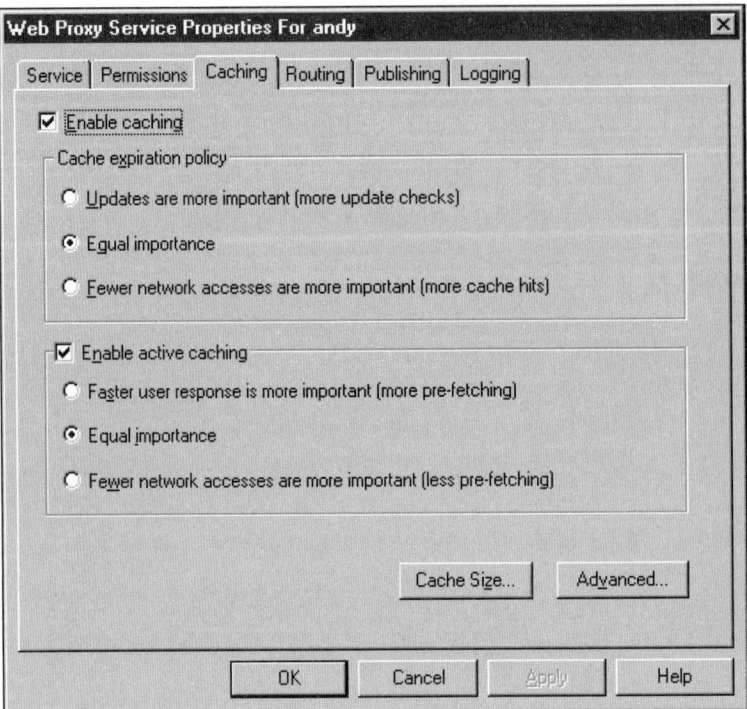

Figure 9.5 The Caching tab of the Web Proxy Service Properties dialog box.

The cache can operate in either Active or Passive mode:

- **Active mode** Enables the Web Proxy service to search the Internet for fresh copies of Web pages that are stored in cache. The update frequency for Proxy Server is configurable, so cache updates can be more important or less important than client requests. With active caching, the client is provided with the Web page much quicker because the copy in cache is always being kept up to date.

- **Passive caching** Proxy Server verifies that the Web page in cache is current.

By enabling the caching feature in Proxy Server, you can increase the Proxy Server's performance dramatically by decreasing the amount of time it takes for a client to retrieve an object from the Internet and reducing Internet traffic from your Proxy Server to the Internet.

The cache configuration option is very robust and allows particular Web sites to always be cached or never be cached. It also gives you the ability to set how much of the entry's Time-To-Live (TTL) expires before the entry is updated.

The two main areas under the Caching tab are Cache Expiration Policy and Enable Active Caching:

- **Cache Expiration Policy** Sets the freshness of the objects in cache. Freshness is a measurement of how long an object that is stored in local cache is used before remote retrieval is attempted. There are three settings:

  - Updates Are More Important (More Update Checks)

  - Equal Importance

  - Fewer Network Accesses Are More Important (More Cache Hits)

- **Enable Active Caching** Enables active caching (allowing the server to make network requests to update an object stored in cache) and configures how often and when active caching will take place. One of three selections can be made:

  - Faster User Response Is More Important (More Pre-fetching)

  - Equal Importance

  - Fewer Network Accesses Are More Important (Less Pre-fetching)

The Cache Size button allows you to adjust the size and location of the cache. Remember, the cache can only be placed on NTFS partitions. The size of the cache space that should be allocated depends on the amount of clients the Proxy Server is expected to support.

The Advanced button allows you to:

- Specify a maximum size allowed for cached objects.

- Return expired objects from the cache when the requested Internet site is unavailable and the cache does not contain an expired copy of the requested object.

- Filter the cache, listing specific URLs, sites, or directories that either should always be cached (subject to other caching rules) or can never be cached.

- Set the TTL parameters for HTTP and FTP cached objects.

 The cache file must be created on an NTFS partition. The Enable Caching checkbox is used to enable the caching feature of Proxy Server. Many people install Proxy Server just for the caching feature.

ROUTING

The Routing tab (shown in Figure 9.6) is used to configure the routing options, which direct client requests for Internet objects. Requests can be configured for routing through the array, to an upstream Proxy Server, or by directly connecting to the Internet.

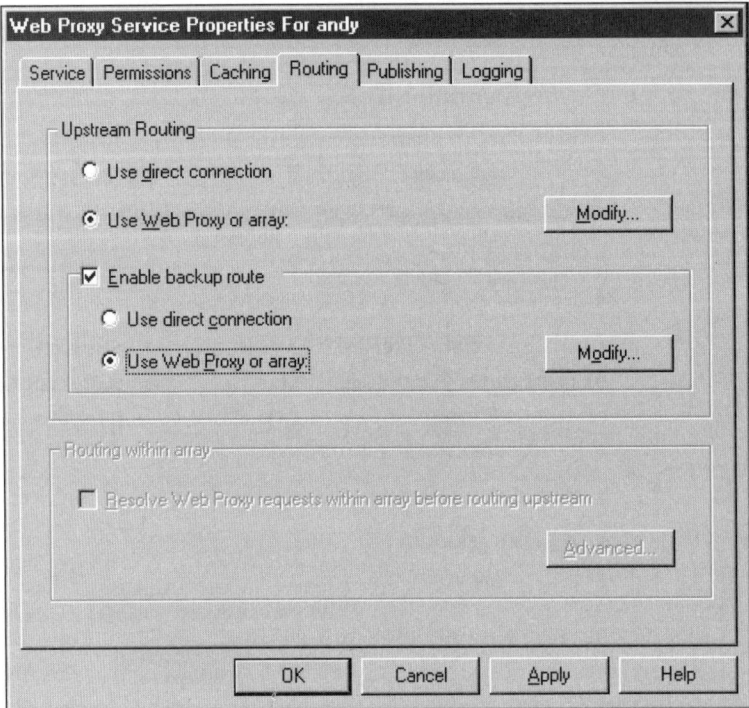

Figure 9.6 The Routing tab of the Web Proxy Service Properties dialog box.

There are two main areas on the Routing tab:

- **Upstream Routing** Allows you to configure the name of the upstream Proxy Server computer and port number, to automatically poll upstream Proxy Server computers for array information, and to set credentials for communication with upstream Proxy Server computers and arrays. This configuration option is made available by selecting Use Web Proxy Or Array, and if it is selected, allows the configuration of a backup route. The dialog box to configure primary and backup Proxy Server computer routes is identical.

- **Routing Within Array** If configured, routes Web Proxy clients through the array before sending the client request to an upstream Proxy Server or to the Internet. This option is available if the Proxy Server is a member of an array.

Routing and setting up arrays are covered in detail in Chapter 11.

PUBLISHING

The Publishing tab (shown in Figure 9.7) is used to configure reverse proxy and reverse hosting. This enables Proxy Server to respond to external requests by performing the following tasks:

- Rejecting external requests.
- Sending the requests to the local Web server or routing the request to another Web server. Downstream servers can be configured to publish Web pages through the Proxy Server.

Proxy Server allows computers sitting downstream from the Proxy Server to publish to the Internet. Proxy Server supports reverse proxy and reverse hosting. These two features enhance security by allowing any computer on the internal network to publish to the Internet. All incoming and outgoing requests are filtered through Proxy Server. In addition, Proxy Server can also cache incoming requests from the Internet, providing safe, easy access.

With reverse proxy, the incoming HTTP port of the Proxy Server "listens" for requests from the Internet and sends the requests downstream to the internal Web server. In reverse hosting, Proxy Server can maintain a list of several servers that have permission to publish to the Internet. Proxy Server will "listen" and respond to Internet requests on behalf of the internal Web server.

9

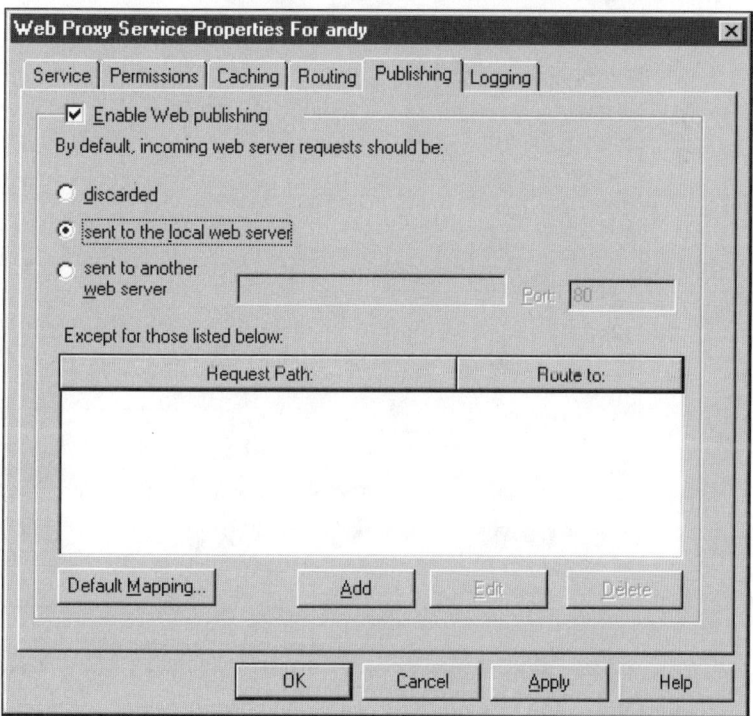

Figure 9.7   The Publishing tab of the Web Proxy Service Properties dialog box.

LOGGING

The Logging tab (shown in Figure 9.8) is used to set logging options for the Web Proxy, WinSock Proxy, and SOCKS Proxy services. Logging provides an audit trail and is key to securing a Proxy Server. Proxy Server can be configured to log information to a text file or to an ODBC database file. Note that logging to SQL/ODBC database files will place a greater strain on resources than logging to a text file will. The default file name used for the Web Proxy service is W3*YYMMDD*.LOG, and it is stored in the *SYSTEM_ROOT*\\SYSTEM32 directory.

The logging feature can log the following information:

- Server information
- Client information
- Connection information
- Object information

Use the Logging tab to set the logging options for the WinSock Proxy, Web Proxy, and SOCKS Proxy services. You can configure logging for packet filtering by clicking on the Security button and then clicking on the Logging tab of the Security dialog box.

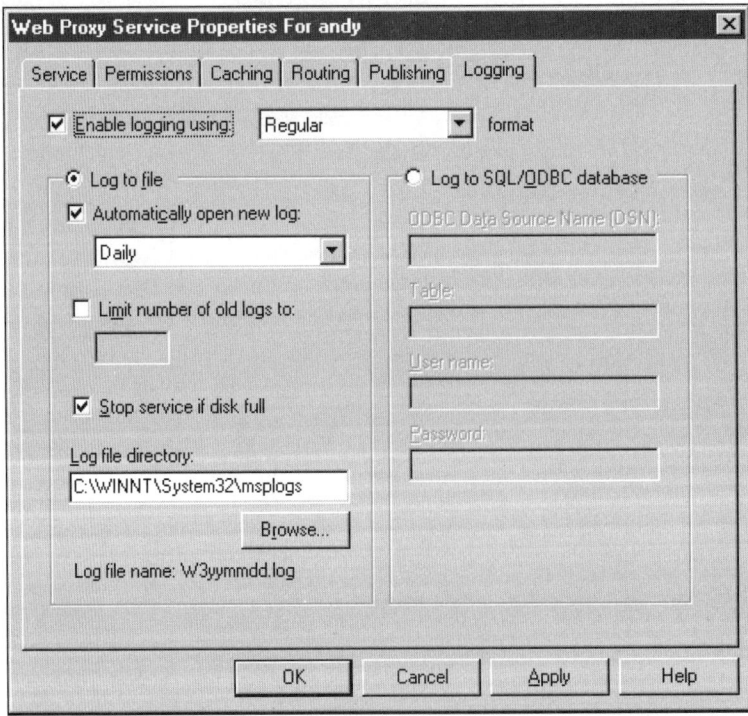

Figure 9.8   The Logging tab of the Web Proxy Service Properties dialog box.

Custom HTML error message pages that are returned to a Web Proxy client under specified error conditions can be configured. When Microsoft Proxy Server 2.0 is installed, the \ERRORHTMLS directory is created and contains a default file named DEFAULT.HTM, which should not be deleted. Additional HTML files can be created by using DEFAULT.HTM as a template and saving the files in an *ERRORCODE*.HTM file. These files are then returned and displayed in the client browser under the applicable error conditions. Any error conditions that do not have a corresponding custom HTML file will return and display the generic default HTM file.

The Web Proxy service uses the same password authentication methods for client requests as those allowed by the WWW service of Internet Information Server (IIS); they are actually set in the WWW service. The authentication methods used for client-to-server communication can include anonymous logon and basic authentication. It is important to remember that running the Web Proxy or WinSock Proxy service without access control enabled is not considered a secure operating condition. Without access control enabled, password authentication settings cannot be configured.

9

WinSock Proxy Management

The WinSock Proxy service is used by client Windows applications that use Windows Sockets to communicate on a network. This enables a Windows-Sockets-compatible application to perform as it would if it were directly connected to the Internet. The WinSock Proxy service provides support for applications such as IRC, RealAudio, and Microsoft NetShow.

The client Windows application makes Windows Sockets API calls to communicate with an application running on an Internet-based computer. The WinSock Proxy components redirect the necessary APIs to the Proxy Server computer, thus establishing a communication path from the internal application to the Internet application through the Proxy Server computer.

When a request is made by a WinSock client, the request to the Internet is done with the Proxy Server's external (Internet) IP address as the source address, which hides the internal IP address and allows use of unregistered or private addresses. All information about WinSock transactions can be logged using the same method that is available with the Web Proxy service.

The WinSock Proxy service is not detected when Find All Servers is used on remote server computers. To connect to the WinSock Proxy service on remote server computers, use Connect To Server and specify the server name for the connection. In addition, when the WinSock Proxy service is stopped, you can change configuration settings, but the changes do not take effect until you restart the service.

To reach the WinSock Proxy Service Properties dialog box (shown in Figure 9.9), follow these steps:

1. Select Start | Programs | Microsoft Proxy Server | Internet Service Manager. The Internet Service Manager appears.

2. Double-click on the WinSock Proxy icon. The WinSock Proxy Service Properties dialog box appears.

There are four tabs available for configuring the WinSock Proxy service: Service, Protocols, Permissions, and Logging. They allow you to control access by port number, protocol, and user or group. Each port can be enabled or disabled to allow communications by a specific list of users or user groups.

SERVICE

The information that can be configured under the Service tab is shared by the Web Proxy, WinSock Proxy, and SOCKS Proxy services and were detailed earlier in this chapter (see "Service Properties").

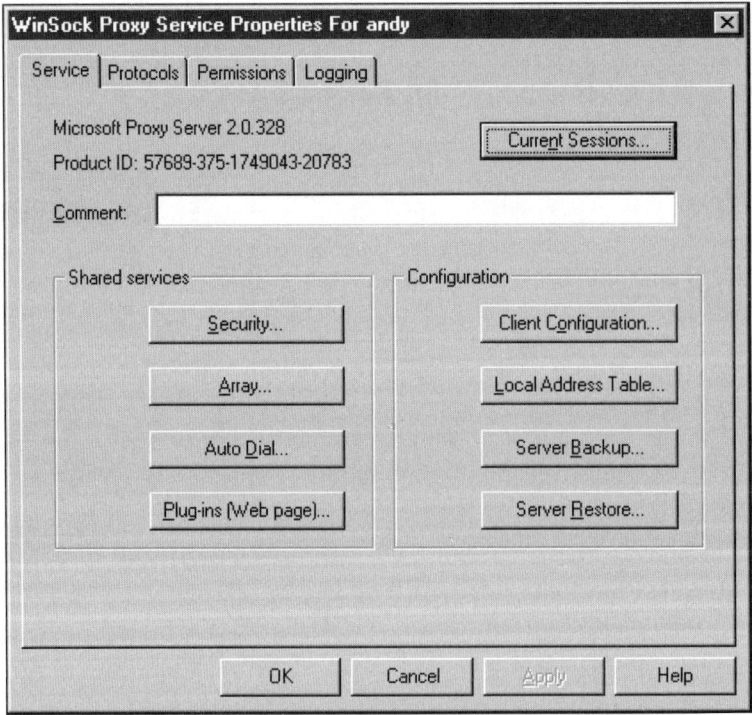

Figure 9.9   The WinSock Proxy Service Properties dialog box.

PROTOCOLS

The Protocols tab (shown in Figure 9.10) is used to determine which Windows Sockets applications will be allowed to access the Internet through the WinSock Proxy service. For each protocol configuration, use the Protocol Definition dialog box to determine which ports can be used for outbound and inbound connections.

To view a protocol's configuration, follow these steps:

1. Select the Protocols tab in the WinSock Proxy Service Properties dialog box.

2. Select the protocol to modify and click on the Edit button.

Protocols can be added, removed, and modified from this screen to allow each protocol to be used only for incoming or outgoing requests. The Unlimited Access selection in the protocol list allows access to all protocols and all ports of the Proxy Server. When it is assigned, this option allows a user to use any protocols or ports with the WinSock Proxy service, including those that are not defined. Users granted Unlimited Access are not affected by WinSock Proxy domain filtering.

9

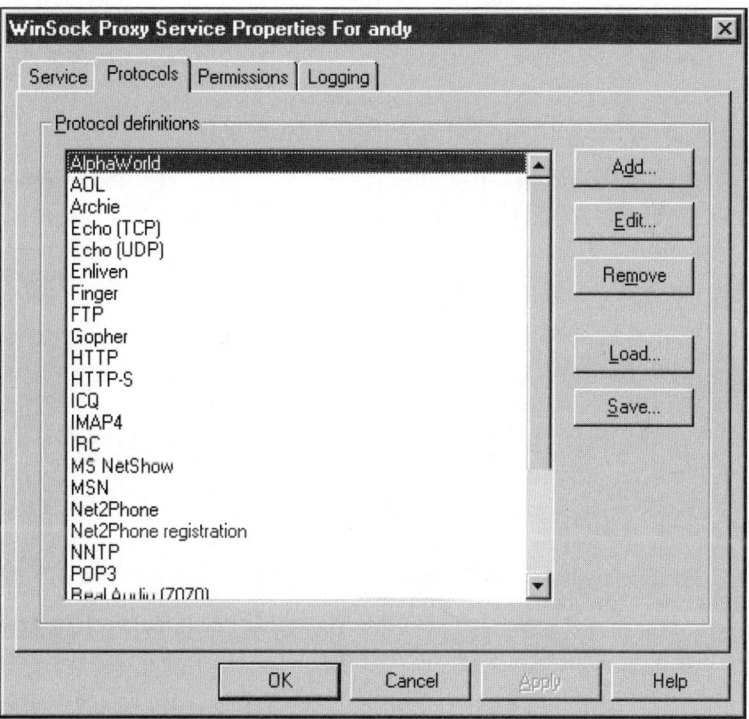

Figure 9.10   The Protocols tab of WinSock Proxy Service Properties dialog box.

The list of users allowed to initiate outbound connections on a port can be different than the list of users allowed to "listen" for inbound connections. Restrictions can also be made for access to remote Web sites by domain name, IP address, and subnet mask. Users can be granted access to all protocols except those listed or denied access to all Web sites except those listed. The settings are global and affect all users who access the Internet through the Proxy Server computer.

PERMISSIONS

The Permissions tab is used to designate which users or groups of users can use a particular protocol to access the Internet through the WinSock Proxy service. The setting can be done by protocol or by using the special Unlimited Access selection. It is suggested that the AGLP method of providing access permissions be used to configure each protocol.

LOGGING

The Logging tab configuration is the same as it is with the Web Proxy service. The location of the log file is common to all three services; only the file name changes. By default, the file name that is used for the WinSock Proxy service is WS*YYMMDD*.LOG.

SOCKS PROXY MANAGEMENT

The SOCKS Proxy service provides a secure channel between the client and server for applications that use SOCKS version 4.3a. It uses IP addresses and the Identification (Identd) protocol to identify and authenticate SOCKS Proxy clients.

The SOCKS Proxy service uses the TCP protocol to supply Proxy support for applications such as Telnet, FTP, and Gopher, but it does not provide support for RealAudio, streaming video, or NetShow. If logging is enabled, a new log can be created daily, weekly, or monthly and can be maintained in a text file or in an ODBC-compliant database (such as Microsoft SQL Server). There are three configuration tabs available in the SOCKS Proxy Service Properties dialog box: Service, Permissions, and Logging. To reach the SOCKS Proxy Service Properties dialog box, follow these steps:

1. Select Start | Programs | Microsoft Proxy Server | Internet Service Manager. The Internet Service Manager appears.

2. Double-click on the SOCKS Proxy icon. The SOCKS Proxy Service Properties dialog box appears.

SERVICE

The information that can be configured under the Service tab is shared by the Web Proxy, WinSock Proxy, and SOCKS Proxy services and were detailed earlier in this chapter (see "Service Properties").

PERMISSIONS

SOCKS clients establish a connection to the Proxy Server. After the proxy circuit is established, SOCKS relays application data between the client and the server. The Permissions tab (shown in Figure 9.11) on the SOCKS Proxy Service Properties dialog box displays an ordered list of entries.

A SOCKS permission is a rule entry in an ordered list. Each rule specifies a source, a destination address, and whether a request satisfying the rule entry is permitted or denied. The first rule entry in the list that matches the incoming client request is used to determine whether the request is permitted or denied. If a client request does not match any rule entry in the list, the request is denied. Each entry specifies a source, a destination, and whether a request satisfying the specification is to be permitted or denied. The first entry that satisfies a request is applied. The entries can be arranged by using the Move Up and Move Down buttons.

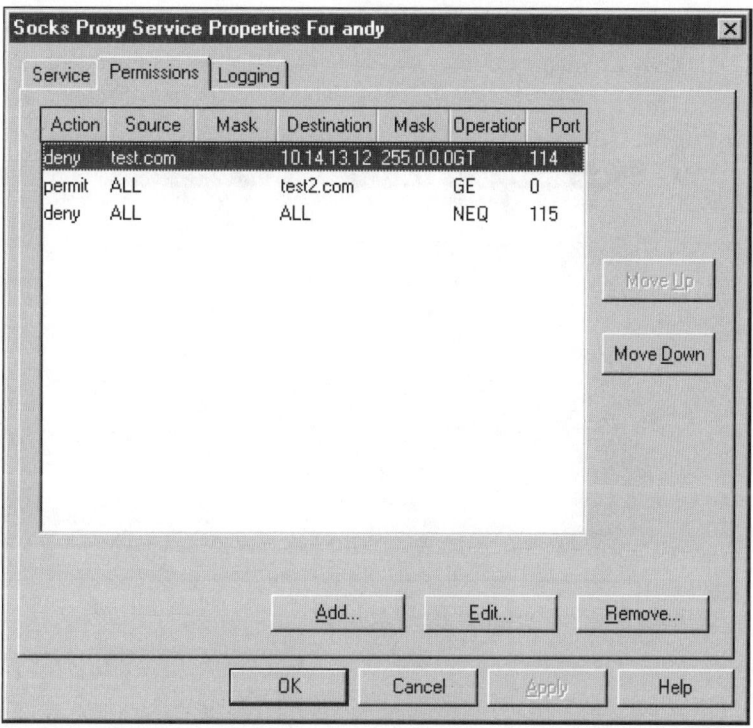

Figure 9.11   The Permissions tab of the SOCKS Proxy Service Properties dialog box.

LOGGING

The Logging tab configuration is the same as with the Web Proxy and WinSock Proxy services. The location of the log file is common to all three services; only the file name changes. By default, the file name that is used for the SOCKS Proxy service is SP*YYMMDD*.LOG.

PERFORMANCE MONITOR TOOL FOR PROXY SERVER

Performance Monitor (see Figure 9.12) is provided with Windows NT Server 4.0 to monitor NT Server activities. When Proxy Server is installed, additional software components are added to Performance Monitor so Proxy Server events can be monitored for optimization and troubleshooting purposes.

A menu option is added under the Proxy Server menu that will start Performance Monitor and display a chart of indicators that are specific to Proxy Server. Table 9.1 lists counters that are added when Proxy Server is installed or default filters included with Windows NT that may be useful in monitoring Proxy Server performance.

The Packet Filter counters are not available at the time of this writing, but they should be available with subsequent releases of Proxy Server 2.0. The available counters are shown in Table 9.1.

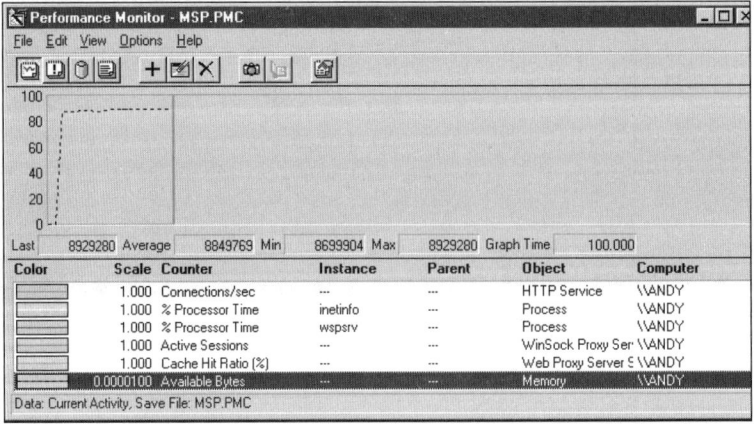

Figure 9.12   Performance Monitor.

Table 9.1   Performance Monitor counters.

Web Proxy Service Counters	Definition
Cache Hit Ratio (%)	The percentage of requests (out of the total number of requests to Web Proxy service) that have been served by using cached data.
Client Bytes Received/sec	The rate at which data bytes are received by Web Proxy Server from Web Proxy clients.
Client Bytes Sent/sec	The rate at which data bytes are sent by Web Proxy Server to the Web Proxy clients.
Client Bytes Total/sec	The sum of Client Bytes Sent/sec and Client Bytes Received/sec. This is the total rate of all bytes transferred between Web Proxy Server and Web Proxy clients.
Current Users	The number of users currently connected to Web Proxy Server.
DNS Cache Entries	The current number of DNS domain name entries cached by Web Proxy Server.
DNS Cache Flushes	The total number of times that the DNS domain name cache has been flushed or cleared by Web Proxy Server.
DNS Cache Hits	The total number of times a DNS domain name was found within the DNS cache.
DNS Cache Hits (%)	The percentage of DNS domain names (out of the total of all DNS entries that have been retrieved by Web Proxy Server) served by the Web Proxy Server cache.
DNS Retrievals	The total number of DNS domain names that have been retrieved by Web Proxy Server.
FTP Requests	The number of FTP requests that have been made to Web Proxy Server.
Gopher Requests	The number of Gopher requests that have been made to Web Proxy Server.
HTTP Requests	The number of HTTP requests that have been made to Web Proxy Server.
HTTPS Sessions	The total number of secure HTTP sessions serviced by the Secure Sockets Layer (SSL) tunnel.
Inet Bytes Received/sec	The rate at which data bytes are received by Web Proxy Server from remote servers on the Internet.
Inet Bytes Sent/sec	The rate at which data bytes are sent by Web Proxy Server to remote servers on the Internet.
Inet Bytes Total/sec	The sum of Inet Bytes Sent/sec and Inet Bytes Received/sec. This is the total rate for all bytes transferred between Web Proxy Server and servers on the Internet.
Maximum Users	The maximum number of users that have connected to Web Proxy Server simultaneously.
Sites Denied	The total number of Internet sites to which Web Proxy Server has denied access.

9

(continued)

Table 9.1 Performance Monitor counters *(continued)*.

Web Proxy Service Counters	Definition
Sites Granted	The total number of Internet sites to which Web Proxy Server has granted access.
SNEWS Sessions	The total number of SNEWS sessions serviced by the Secure Sockets Layer (SSL) tunnel.
SSL Client Bytes Received/sec	The rate at which Secure Sockets Layer (SSL) data bytes are received by Web Proxy Server from secured Web Proxy clients.
SSL Client Bytes Sent/sec	The rate at which Secure Sockets Layer (SSL) data bytes are sent by Proxy Server to secured Web Proxy clients.
SSL Client Bytes Total/sec	The sum of SSL Client Bytes Sent/sec and SSL Client Bytes Received/sec. This is the total rate for all bytes transferred between Web Proxy Server and secured Web Proxy clients.
SSL Sessions Scavenged	The number of Secure Sockets Layer (SSL) sessions closed because of idle time-out and excessive SSL demand.
Thread Pool Active Sessions	The number of sessions being actively serviced by thread pool threads.
Thread Pool Failures	The number of requests rejected because the thread pool was over-committed.
Thread Pool Size	The number of threads in the thread pool.
Total Cache Fetches	The total number of requests that have been served by using cached data from Web Proxy Server cache.
Total Failing Requests	The total number of Internet service requests that have not been processed by Web Proxy Server due to errors. Errors can be the result of Web Proxy Server failing to locate a requested server URL on the Internet or because of the client being denied access to the requested URL.
Total Internet Fetches	The total number of requests that have been served by using data retrieved from servers on the Internet.
Total Requests	The total number of Internet requests that have ever been made to Web Proxy Server.
Total SSL Sessions	The total number of Secure Sockets Layer (SSL) sessions serviced by the SSL tunnel.
Total Successful Requests	The total number of Internet requests that have been successfully processed by Web Proxy Server.
Total Users	The total number of users that have ever connected to Web Proxy Server.
Unknown SSL Sessions	The total number of unknown Secure Sockets Layer (SSL) sessions serviced by the SSL tunnel.

(continued)

Table 9.1   Performance Monitor counters *(continued)*.

Web Proxy Cache Counters	Description
Active Refresh Bytes Rate	The number of bytes of data per second retrieved from the Internet to proactively refresh popular URLs in the URL cache.
Active URL Refresh Rate	The number of popular URLs per second that are preemptively refreshed in the URL cache from remote URL sources on the Internet.
Bytes Committed Rate	The number of bytes of data per second committed to disk storage in the URL cache.
Bytes in Cache	The total number of bytes currently contained in the URL cache (stored on disk).
Bytes Retrieved Rate	The number of bytes of data per second retrieved from disk storage in the URL cache.
Max Bytes Cached	The maximum number of bytes that have been stored in the URL cache.
Max URLs Cached	The maximum number of URLs that have been stored in the URL cache.
Total Actively Refreshed URLs	The cumulative number of popular URLs in the URL cache that have been preemptively refreshed from the Internet.
Total Bytes Actively Refreshed	The cumulative number of bytes retrieved from the Internet to preemptively refresh popular URLs in the URL cache.
Total Bytes Cached	The cumulative number of bytes that have been stored in the URL cache.
Total Bytes Retrieved	The cumulative number of bytes that have been retrieved from the URL cache.
Total URLs Cached	The cumulative number of URLs that have been stored in the URL cache.
Total URLs Retrieved	The cumulative number of URLs that have been retrieved from the URL cache.
URL Commit Rate	The number of URLs per second committed to the URL cache.
URL Retrieve Rate	The number of URLs per second retrieved from the URL cache.
URLs in Cache	The current number of URLs in the URL cache.

9

(continued)

Table 9.1   Performance Monitor counters *(continued)*.

WinSock Proxy Service Counters	Description
Accepting TCP Connections	The number of connection objects that wait for TCP connection from the client after a successful remote connection.
Active Sessions	The number of active sessions.
Active TCP Connections	The number of active TCP connections.
Active UDP Connections	Total number of active UDP connections.
Available Worker Threads	The number of control channel worker threads that are available or waiting in the completion port queue.
Back-Connecting TCP Connections	Total number of connections that are waiting for an inbound connect( ) call to finish. These are connections from the WinSock Proxy service to a client after the WinSock Proxy service accepted a connection from the Internet on a listening socket.
Bytes Read/sec	Number of bytes per second read by the data pump.
Bytes Written/sec	Number of bytes per second written by the data pump.
Connecting TCP Connections	Total number of connections that are waiting for a remote connect( ) call to finish.
DNS Cache Entries	The current number of DNS domain name entries cached by the Web Proxy Server.
DNS Cache Flushes	The total number of times the DNS domain name cache has been flushed or cleared by the Web Proxy Server.
DNS Cache Hits	The total number of times a DNS domain name was found within the DNS cache.
DNS Cache Hits %	The percentage of DNS domain names (from the total of all DNS entries that have been retrieved by the Web Proxy Server) served from the Web Proxy Server cache.
DNS Retrievals	The number of DNS domain name entries that have been retrieved from the Web Proxy Server cache.
Failed DNS Resolutions	Number of calls to gethostname/gethostbyaddr that have failed.
Listening TCP Connections	Number of connection objects that wait for TCP connections from the Internet (after a successful listen).
Non-connected UDP Mappings	The number of mappings for UDP connections.
Pending DNS Resolutions	Number of calls to gethostname/gethostbyaddr that have not yet returned.

(continued)

Table 9.1 Performance Monitor counters *(continued)*.

WinSock Proxy Service Counters	Description
Successful DNS Resolutions	Number of calls to gethostname/gethostbyaddr that have returned successfully.
Worker Threads	The number of control channel worker threads and data pump worker threads that are alive.
SOCKS Proxy Service Counters	**Description**
SOCKS Client Bytes Received/sec	The rate at which data bytes are received by SOCKS Proxy Server from SOCKS Proxy clients.
SOCKS Client Bytes Sent/sec	The rate at which data bytes are sent by SOCKS Proxy Server to SOCKS Proxy clients.
SOCKS Clients Bytes Total/sec	The sum of SOCKS Client Bytes Received/sec and SOCKS Client Bytes Sent/sec. This is the total rate of all bytes transferred between SOCKS Proxy Server and SOCKS Proxy clients.
SOCKS Sessions	The total number of SOCKS sessions serviced by the SOCKS Proxy service.

9

If a network management tool is in use, Microsoft Proxy Server 2.0 comes with *Simple Network Management Protocol (SNMP) Management Information Base (MIB)* files, which are used to enable SNMP monitoring of the Web Proxy and WinSock Proxy services.

The MIB file for Web Proxy service monitoring is W3P.MIB. The MIB file for WinSock Proxy service monitoring is WSP.MIB. These files are not installed on the server by the Setup program. They are on the Proxy Server CD and can be copied from the \PERFCTRS directory. The correct MIB file for the server's processor architecture must be used.

The SNMP service uses object identifiers (OIDs) for MIB processing. The OID for W3P.MIB is 11. The OID for the WSP.MIB is 12.

MONITORING AND TUNING IN THE REAL WORLD

Now that you've explored the counters that are added to Performance Monitor, we can take a look at how to use Performance Monitor and other NT tools to identify problems with your Proxy Server configuration, client configurations, and your network in general.

Many of the counters previously listed in Table 9.1 can be used to identify specific occurrences on your network. Table 9.2 identifies some Performance Monitor objects and counters and the specific indications they provide.

Table 9.2 Performance Monitor counters and their indications.

Object	Counter	Indication
WinSock Proxy Server	Active Sessions	This counter, which displays the same information as the Current Sessions dialog box, can be used to identify the number of clients using the Proxy Server. Depending on the hardware that makes up the Proxy Server, the Active Sessions counter can provide an indication of when to add another Proxy Server to the network.
WinSock Proxy Server	Active TCP Connections and Active UDP Connections	Both of these counters are subsets of the Active Sessions counter and give greater insight into what type of sessions are in use on the Proxy Server.
Network Interface	Output Queue Length	This counter is a good indication of the amount of traffic on your network. It measures, in number of packets, the size of the output queue for a particular interface card. This number should never be greater than two. If this counter is larger than two for any NIC, the bottleneck is your network. In this case, the network should either be divided into two subnets or be upgraded to a faster transmission speed such as 100BaseT.
Network Interface	Bytes Total/sec	This counter displays the total number of bytes sent and received through a particular network interface per second. If this total is near the maximum throughput for your network, it is an indication of a bottleneck and the same steps should be taken as with the Output Queue Length.
Process	% Processor Time (wspsrv)	This counter is perhaps the best indication of whether a particular system is powerful enough to handle the services that are being requested. By using the Process object's % Processor Time counter, you are able to view the amount of time used by each service running on the system.
Processor	% Processor Time	This counter is the total % Processor Time being used by the computer. According to Microsoft, if this counter is consistently around 80%, the system is not powerful enough to handle the service requests and should be upgraded or the services divided onto multiple systems.
Memory	Page Faults/sec	As the number of page faults per second increases, the file server is having to swap more memory pages to the disk system. This problem can be easily corrected by adding more RAM to the server.

(continued)

Table 9.2   Performance Monitor counters and their indications *(continued)*.

Object	Counter	Indication
Web Proxy Server Service	Cache Hit Ratio (%)	As you've learned, caching increases the responsiveness of a Proxy Server to a client's request. If the Cache Hit Ratio (%) is high, it means that a large number of client requests are able to be serviced from cache. However, if this ratio is low, the majority of the requests are being directed to the Internet for service, which means slower performance and greater bandwidth usage. A low Cache Hit Ratio (%) indicates that the cache should be increased for the Proxy Server, or a caching array should be installed.
Web Proxy Server Service	Current Average Milliseconds/Request	This counter defines the average number of milliseconds it takes to service a client's request. As this number increases, it is an indication that the server is slowing down, either because there are too many requests, or too much network traffic.
Web Proxy Server Cache Object	Active Refresh Bytes Rate	This counter can be used to determine whether active caching is operating at its optimum performance level, which can then be used to determine whether to increase or decrease active caching.
LogicalDisk	Current Disk Queue Length	As with the Ouput Queue Length, this number should never be more than two. If so, it is an indication that the disk system is too slow for the I/O required to operate the Proxy Server. A faster disk is required. (Note: Enabling the PhysicalDisk and LogicalDisk counters increases the workload on the system and should be used only for short periods of time. To enable these counters, run Diskperf –y from a command prompt.)

In addition to the Performance Monitor counters described in the previous table, Performance Monitor alerts and logs can be used to notify an administrator when a particular threshold is met. These events can be logged to the Event Viewer for further analysis to aid in determining the optimum configuration for the Proxy Server.

NETWORK MONITOR

Among the tools included with Windows NT Server is Network Monitor. This network service must be added after the operating system is installed and can be used to monitor traffic between the server and other computers. Network Monitor captures packets sent to and from the host server and can analyze those packets to help you determine if there are problems on the network and, if so, where.

There are many features of Network Monitor that do not specifically apply to Proxy Server and are covered in other certification tests, such as NT Server, NT Server in the Enterprise, Networking Essentials, and TCP/IP. However, it is important to understand how Network Monitor works and how it can be used to watch traffic on your network and to the Internet.

 The version of Network Monitor that is included with Windows NT Server 4.0 is only able to track packets to and from the server. A more extensive version of Network Monitor is included as part of Microsoft's Systems Management Server (SMS). The SMS version is able to operate in "promiscuous" mode, which means that it is able to capture traffic destined for other computers on the network, rather than just for itself.

As mentioned, Network Monitor must be added to the network services. This is done by opening the Network applet, selecting the Services tab, clicking Add, and selecting Network Monitor Tools and Agent from the list of available services. Click OK to install the service, then click Close to close the Network applet. You will be prompted to restart the computer. Do so to complete the installation.

Once Network Monitor is installed, it can be used to capture data sent to and from the server. A capture is started after opening Network Monitor (Start|Programs|Administrative Tools (Common)|Network Monitor) by selecting Start from the Capture menu. This will capture all packets destined for or sent from the server running Network Monitor. To limit the data captured, a filter can be created. This will limit the traffic capture to that specified by the filter.

Once the capture is complete, the data can be analyzed by selecting Display Captured Data from the Capture menu. The dialog box that is invoked lists each packet that was captured. Double-clicking on any packet opens an analysis window that includes the packet's header information in the center of the screen, and the hexadecimal and binary representation of the data at the bottom of the screen.

The Network Monitor can be used to monitor traffic between the Proxy Server and the Internet, as well as easily identify communication problems between clients and Internet servers. For more detailed information on Network Monitor, refer to the Microsoft TechNet document "Network Traffic Analysis and Optimization (Windows NT 3.5x and 4.0 and Windows 95)."

CHAPTER SUMMARY

In this chapter, you learned to use the Internet Service Manager to configure and manage the Proxy Server components (Web Proxy service, WinSock Proxy service, and SOCKS Proxy service). The Internet Service Manager can be reached through the Internet Server menu or the Microsoft Proxy Server menu.

The Web Proxy service is used to provide a pathway to the Internet for CERN-compliant applications. It can be managed by opening the Internet Service Manager and double-clicking on the Web Proxy icon. This will open the Web Proxy Properties dialog box, which has six tabs for configuration of the service.

The Service tab is shared by all three services and displays ID- and revision-level information, current users, and the interface used to configure the Shared Services and Configuration information. The Shared Services area is used to set security, to configure the Array information, to configure the Auto Dial feature, and to install plug-ins. The Configuration area is used to configure clients, to modify the Local Address Table (LAT), and to configure the Proxy Server computer backup and restore information.

The Permissions tab in the Web Proxy Service Properties dialog box is used to configure access control for each of the four services: FTP Read, WWW, Gopher, and Secure. The Secure protocol supports Secure Sockets Layer connections.

The Caching tab is used to configure the system's active and passive caching, to set policy for what will be cached, and to designate how often the information in cache will be updated. How you configure caching will dramatically affect the performance of the Proxy Server. The cache area must be configured to use storage space on an NTFS partition, with a minimum space of 100MB.

The Routing tab is used to configure the route a client request will take to be fulfilled. The request can be configured to go directly to the Internet, to a proxy array, or in the event the information cannot be found in the primary proxy server for an individual client, through a series of proxy servers.

The Publishing tab is used to enable Web publishing. The terms used when an internal Web server is allowed to provide information for an Internet request are reverse proxy and reverse hosting.

The Logging tab is used to set logging options for the Web Proxy, WinSock Proxy, and SOCKS Proxy services; it provides an audit trail for Internet transactions. Information can be stored in a text file or in an ODBC database.

The WinSock Proxy service is used by client Windows applications that use Windows Sockets to communicate on the network. It provides support for applications such as IRC, RealAudio, and Microsoft NetShow. The WinSock Proxy icon is used to access the WinSock Proxy Service Properties dialog box. There are four tabs available for configuration: Service, Protocols, Permissions, and Logging.

The Service and Logging tabs are common to all three services. The Protocols tab is used to configure the protocols the WinSock Proxy service will recognize and whether each protocol is limited to inbound or outbound use. The protocols that can be configured include HTTP, RealAudio, Finger, POP3, and MS NetShow. The Permissions tab is used to determine which users and groups are allowed to use each of the defined protocols.

The SOCKS Proxy Service Properties dialog box is used to configure the SOCKS Proxy service, which provides a secure channel between a client and server for applications that support SOCKS version 4.3a. The SOCKS Proxy service uses the Identd protocol for identification and authentication of clients. The SOCKS Proxy Service Properties dialog box has three configuration tabs: Service, Permissions, and Logging.

The Service and Logging tabs are common to all three services. The Permissions tab is used to configure the client's permission to connect and perform various operations on a server. The entries that are defined can be ordered. The first entry that satisfies the client's entry is used to service that client.

When Microsoft Proxy Server 2.0 is installed, counters are added to Performance Monitor. The counters enable monitoring of the proxy services and can be used to tune their performance. A menu selection is available under the Proxy Server menu that will start Performance Monitor in Chart view and display information that is considered pertinent to the overall operation of the proxy services. SNMP MIBs can be found on the Proxy Server CD and can be installed and used by a network management tool.

KEY TERMS

- **AGLP (Account, Global, Local, Permission)**—Refers to the preferred method of assigning user permissions. User accounts are placed in global groups, which are added to local groups. Permissions are assigned to the local group.

- **cache**—Generally speaking, a temporary storage area that holds current information and is able to provide that information faster than other methods. In the case of the Web Proxy server, cache is local hard drive space on the Proxy Server computer that stores files received from a Web server. This provides the client with quicker access to Internet-based Web sites.

- **counter**—In Performance Monitor, a single collection point of information for a system resource. DNS Cache Hits under the Web Proxy Server Cache object is an example of a counter.

- **domain filter**—Used to grant or deny access to Internet domain sites; can include WWW, FTP, and Gopher sites.

- **instance**—In Performance Monitor, refers to multiple units of an object. For example, the PhysicalDisk object might have multiple instances if more than one hard disk is installed.

- **Local Address Table (LAT)**—Used to store all IP addresses that are internal to the network Microsoft Proxy Server 2.0 resides on.

- **Management Information Base (MIB)**—A set of manageable objects representing various types of information about a network device that an SNMP management tool can request.

- **object**—In Performance Monitor, an object is a system resource, such as the Web Proxy Cache object that groups counters together.

- **packet filter**—Used to reject packets of a certain type (for example, from a particular host or a particular protocol).

- **Simple Network Management Protocol (SNMP)**—A protocol used by network management tools to gather information from smart network devices. In SNMP, devices are logically grouped into a community. The device that provides the information to a management tool is known as an agent.

9

REVIEW QUESTIONS

1. You need to verify that all of the Proxy Server clients are able to use the RealAudio protocol. Select the screen that will provide this information.
   a. the Protocols tab in the Web Proxy Properties dialog box
   b. the Protocols tab in the WinSock Proxy Properties dialog box
   c. the Protocols tab under the SOCKS Proxy Properties dialog box
   d. the Protocols tab under Network Properties on each client's computer

2. You need to add a third-party plug-in to your Proxy Server. You understand the third-party plug-in can be found on the Microsoft Web site. You install the plug-in by:
   a. using the third-party plug-in installation program
   b. opening the WinSock Proxy Service Properties dialog box, selecting the Service tab, and clicking on Plug-ins
   c. opening the Network Properties dialog box, clicking on the Service tab, clicking on Add, selecting the plug-in from the list, and clicking on OK
   d. it can't be done; Microsoft Proxy Server 2.0 does not support third-party plug-ins

3. You have just installed a new hard disk for use as a cache storage area by the Proxy Server service. Which of the following would you need to do? (Choose the two best answers.)

   a. Format the partition as NTFS.

   b. Format the partition as FAT.

   c. Select the Caching tab in the WinSock Proxy Properties dialog box, click on the Cache Size button, and add the volume and space for the new drive.

   d. Select the Caching tab in the Web Proxy Properties dialog box, click on the Cache Size button, and add the volume and space for the new drive.

   e. Reinstall the Proxy Server software. During the installation, select the new drive as the cache area.

4. Users are complaining that access to the current sales information on an external server is extremely slow. What can you do to speed up access to that site?

   a. Disable caching.

   b. Enable active caching and add a cache filter for the URL of the sales site, forcing the site to be cached.

   c. Set the Cache Expiration Policy for Equal Importance.

   d. Enable active caching and add a cache filter for the URL of the sales site, forcing the site to not be cached.

5. Proxy Server can be configured for Auto Dial to establish a connection to an Internet Service Provider (ISP). (True or False?)

6. How do you configure Proxy Server so that the Internet Information Server (IIS) on your Proxy Server will be able to publish Web pages for use by your traveling sales force?

   a. Install IIS that is on the external network.

   b. Select Use Direct Connection under the Routing tab in the Web Proxy Service Properties dialog box.

   c. Select Enable Web Publishing under the Publishing tab in the Web Proxy Service Properties dialog box.

   d. Install IIS on the internal network.

7. Which of the following methods would you use to log information concerning the Web Proxy, WinSock Proxy, and SOCKS Proxy services into three different log files?

   a. Type the same file name in the Log file directory box on the Logging tab for each service.

   b. This cannot be done. By default, the Web Proxy, WinSock Proxy, and SOCKS Proxy services all log information to the same file.

    c. Enable logging. By default, the information will be placed in three separate files.

    d. Set the Web Proxy service to open a new file daily, the WinSock Proxy service to open a new file weekly, and the SOCKS Proxy service to open a new file monthly.

8. Which two of the following methods can you use to administer all of the Proxy Servers on your network from one location?

    a. Open Internet Service Manager and select Find All Servers from the Properties menu.

    b. Configure each of the Proxy Servers to be administered with the same TCP/IP address and subnet mask.

    c. Open Internet Service Manager, select Connect To Server from the Properties menu, and provide the name or IP address of the remote Proxy Server.

    d. Do nothing. All Proxy Servers will be listed automatically.

9. How can you view only the SOCKS Proxy service on all listed machines?

    a. Disable all services except the SOCKS Proxy service on all the Proxy Server computers.

    b. Enable all services except the SOCKS Proxy service on all Proxy Server computers.

    c. Select only SOCKS Proxy Service from the View menu in Internet Service Manager.

    d. Do nothing. This cannot be configured from Internet Service Manager.

10. You are preparing to contact Microsoft technical support for help with a WinSock problem, and you'll need to provide the revision level of the Proxy Server software. The disks are not nearby. What is the easiest way to obtain that information?

    a. Open Windows NT Diagnostics. The Proxy Server software revision level will be listed under the revision level of the NT Server product.

    b. Open Internet Service Manager. Double-click on the Web Proxy Service icon. The information will be displayed under the Service tab.

    c. Reinstall Microsoft Proxy Server 2.0. This information can only be obtained during the installation process.

    d. Open the Performance Monitor tool for Proxy Server. The information is displayed as a banner.

11. How can you make sure only the local Managers group is able to use the FTP Read protocol for the Web Proxy service?

    a. Open the Web Proxy Service Properties dialog box, select the Permissions tab, and enable access control, listing only the local Managers group under the FTP protocol.

9

    b. Click on the FTP Protocol button on the Security tab of Web Proxy Server Properties dialog box and type "Managers".

    c. Open the Network Properties dialog box, select the Protocols tab, select FTP, and add the local Managers group.

    d. Open User Manager For Domains, select the local Managers group, and add the FTP service to the group.

12. How do you configure caching to store Internet objects that are no larger than 500K?

    a. Select the Caching tab in the WinSock Proxy Service Properties dialog box, click on the Advanced button, select the Limit Size Of Cached Objects checkbox, and set the limit to 500K.

    b. Select the Caching tab in the Web Proxy Service Properties dialog box, click on the Advanced button, select the Limit Size Of Cached Objects checkbox, and set the limit to 500K.

    c. Select the Caching tab in the SOCKS Proxy Service Properties dialog box, click on the Advanced button, select the Limit Size Of Cached Objects checkbox, and set the limit to 500K.

    d. Select the Performance tab in the System Properties dialog box, click on the Change button under Virtual Memory, select the Limit Size Of Cached Objects checkbox, and set the limit to 500K.

13. How do you configure caching to provide the most current objects from the Internet?

    a. Select the Caching tab in the WinSock Proxy Service Properties dialog box and select the Enable Caching checkbox. Select the Updates Are More Important option.

    b. Select the Caching tab in the SOCKS Proxy Service Properties dialog box and select the Enable Caching checkbox. Select the Updates Are More Important option.

    c. Select the Caching tab in the Web Proxy Service Properties dialog box and select the Enable Caching checkbox. Select the Updates Are More Important option.

    d. Select the Routing tab in the Web Proxy Service Properties dialog box and select the Aggressive Caching checkbox.

14. The NetShow Protocol is configured from the WinSock Proxy Service Properties dialog box. (True or False?)

15. How do you configure the Web Proxy service to update objects that are stored in cache after one-half of the TTL has expired?

    a. Select the Caching tab in the Web Proxy Service Properties dialog box, select the Enable Active Caching checkbox, and select the Equal Importance setting.

b. Select the Caching tab in the Web Proxy Service Properties dialog box and click on the Advanced button. Under Object Time To Live, select TTL=__% and set the percentage box for 50%.

c. Select the Caching tab in the WinSock Proxy Service Properties dialog box and click on the Advanced button. Under Object Time To Live, select TTL=__% and set the percentage box for 50%.

d. Select the Caching tab in the SOCKS Proxy Service Properties dialog box and click on the Advanced button. Under Object Time To Live, select TTL=__% and set the percentage box for 50%.

16. How do you configure some free disk space so Proxy Server can use it for cache storage? (Select the best answer.)

a. Reinstall Microsoft Proxy Server 2.0. During the installation, configure the cache storage to include the free disk space.

b. Configure and format the free disk space with the FAT file system. Select the Caching tab in the Web Proxy Service Properties dialog box. Click on the Cache Size button, select the new partition, set the size of the cache, and accept the changes.

c. Configure and format the free disk space with the FAT file system. Select the Caching tab in the WinSock Proxy Service Properties dialog box. Click on the Cache Size button, select the new partition, set the size of the cache, and accept the changes.

d. Configure and format the free disk space with the NTFS file system. Select the Caching tab in the Web Proxy Service Properties dialog box. Click on the Cache Size button, select the new partition, set the size of the cache, and accept the changes.

e. Configure and format the free disk space with the NTFS file system. Select the Caching tab in the WinSock Proxy Service Properties dialog box. Click on the Cache Size button, select the new partition, set the size of the cache, and accept the changes.

17. How do you configure the Web Proxy, WinSock Proxy, and SOCKS Proxy services to log information into files and open new log files daily?

a. Open the Web Proxy Service Properties dialog box and select the Logging tab. Select the Enable Logging Using checkbox and the select Log To file. Select the Automatically Open New Log File checkbox and choose Daily from the drop-down list. Do the same from the WinSock Proxy Service and SOCKS Proxy Service Properties dialog boxes.

b. Open the Web Proxy Service Properties dialog box and select the Logging tab. Select the Enable Logging Using checkbox and then select Log To File. Select the Automatically Open New Log File and choose Daily from the drop-down list. This will automatically set the same options for the WinSock Proxy service and the SOCKS Proxy service.

9

   c. Open the WinSock Proxy Service Properties dialog box and select the Logging tab. Select the Enable Logging Using checkbox and then select Log To File. Select the Automatically Open New Log File checkbox and choose Daily from the drop-down list. This will automatically set the same options for the WinSock Proxy service and the SOCKS Proxy service.

   d. Open the SOCKS Proxy Service Properties dialog box and select the Logging tab. Select the Enable Logging Using checkbox and then select Log To File. Select the Automatically Open New Log File checkbox and choose Daily from the drop-down list. This will automatically set the same options for the WinSock Proxy service and the SOCKS Proxy service.

18. How do you enable clients to configure their Web browser software to use the Proxy Server?

   a. Have the client reinstall the Web browser software and select Use Proxy in the Advanced options.

   b. Do nothing at all. Client computers will automatically attempt to use the proxy server to connect to the Internet.

   c. From the Web Proxy Service Properties dialog box, click on the Client Configuration button and set the options so the client will automatically be configured during client setup.

   d. From the WinSock Proxy Service Properties dialog box, click on the Client Configuration button and set the options so the client will automatically be configured during setup.

19. Your boss uses a network management tool to monitor and service the network and has asked you to install the MIB files on the Proxy Server computer. How would you do this? (Select the best answer.)

   a. Copy W3P.MIB and WSP.MIB from the \PERFCTRS directory located on the Microsoft Proxy Server 2.0 CD. Tell your boss the object identifiers for the Web Proxy service and the WinSock Proxy service are 11 and 12, respectively.

   b. The MIB files are installed during the installation process. Tell your boss the object identifiers for the Web Proxy service and the WinSock Proxy service are 11 and 12, respectively.

   c. Select the Service tab in the Web Proxy Service Properties dialog box, click on the SNMP button, and configure for use with the management computer.

   d. Select the Service tab in the WinSock Proxy Service Properties dialog box, click on the SNMP button, and configure for use with the management computer.

20. You want to use Performance Monitor to view the Cache Hit ratio and see if changes need to be made to the cache settings. Select the easiest way to accomplish this task.

   a. Select Monitor Microsoft Proxy Server Performance from the Microsoft Proxy Server menu. Cache Hits is one of the counters monitored.

   b. Select the Caching tab in the Web Proxy Service Properties dialog box and click on the Monitor Hits button.

   c. Do nothing. This cannot be done.

   d. Open Network Monitor. Select the Cache Hits view.

21. How do you find the ratio between incoming and outgoing Internet traffic by your Proxy clients?

   a. Open Performance Monitor. Under the Web Proxy Server Service object, select the Inet Bytes Sent/sec counter and the Inet Bytes Received/sec counter and compare the two.

   b. Open Performance Monitor. Under the Web Proxy Server Service object, select the Sites Denied counter and the Sites Granted counter and compare the two.

   c. Select the Service tab in the Web Proxy Service Properties dialog box, click on the Counter button, and select the options you wish to view.

   d. Do nothing. This information cannot be monitored.

   e. Select the Logging tab in the SOCKS Proxy Service Properties dialog box and enable logging.

22. You are running out of disk space and want to be notified when the disk is full. Where is this option configured?

   a. Click on the Server Backup button on the Service tab of the Web Proxy Service Properties dialog box. Under the Alerting tab, configure the system to write an event in the event log and send a mail message.

   b. Click on the Current Sessions button on the Service tab of the Web Proxy Service Properties dialog box. Everyone connected will receive a message if the disk is full.

   c. Click on the Security button on the Logging tab of the Web Proxy Service Properties dialog box. Under the Alerting tab, configure the system to write an event in the event log and send a mail message.

   d. Click on the Security button on the Service tab of the Web Proxy Service Properties dialog box. Under the Alerting tab, configure the system to write an event in the event log and send a mail message.

23. You want to see how busy your Web Proxy Server is by finding out how many users are currently connected to the Web Proxy service. Select two ways this can be done.

9

    a. Click on the Current Sessions button on the Service tab of the Web Proxy Service Properties dialog box. A list of currently connected users will be displayed.

    b. Click on the Client Configuration button on the Service tab of the Web Proxy Service Properties dialog box. The currently connected users will be listed.

    c. Open Performance Monitor and select the Current Users counter under the Web Proxy Server Service object. This will display the currently connected users.

    d. Open Performance Monitor and select the Maximum Users counter under the Web Proxy Server Service object. This will display the currently connected users.

24. How do you find the total number of Internet requests that the Web Server has processed?

    a. Open Performance Monitor and select the DNS Retrievals counter under the Web Proxy Server Service object. This will display the total number of Internet requests that have been made.

    b. Open Performance Monitor and select the Total Requests counter under the Web Proxy Server Service object. This will display the total of Internet requests that have been made.

    c. Click on the Current Users button on the Service tab of the Web Proxy Service Properties dialog box. This will display the statistics for the Web Proxy service.

    d. Click on the Current Users button on the Service tab of the WinSock Proxy Service Properties dialog box. This will display the statistics for the Web Proxy service.

25. How can you find out how many URLs are cached?

    a. Click on the Cached URL Sites button on the Cache tab of the Web Proxy Service Properties dialog box. This will display the total number of URL sites currently in cache by name or IP address.

    b. Open Performance Monitor and select the URLs In Cache counter under the Web Proxy Server Service object. This will display the total number of URLs that are cached.

    c. Do nothing. This information cannot be gathered.

    d. Open Performance Monitor and select the URLs In Cache counter under the Web Proxy Server Cache object. This will display the total number of URLs that are currently stored in cache.

HANDS-ON PROJECTS

In this lab, you will use the Web Proxy Service Properties dialog box to configure the caching options and to configure the local Administrators group to be the only group allowed to use the Gopher protocol. Using the WinSock Proxy Service Properties dialog box, you will configure the local Users group to use the RealAudio protocol. With the SOCKS Proxy Service Properties dialog box, you will configure logging so a new log file is created weekly.

PROJECT 9.1

In this exercise, you will configure passive and active caching for the Web Proxy service. Then you will configure the Gopher protocol so that only the local Administrators group can use it. This will familiarize you with some of the settings that can be configured from the Web Proxy Service Properties dialog box.

To enable passive caching and set options, follow these steps:

1. Select Start | Programs | Microsoft Proxy Server and click on Internet Service Manager.
2. Select Web Proxy Service from the display window.
3. Select Service Properties from the Properties menu. The Web Proxy Service Properties dialog box appears.
4. Click on the Caching tab.
5. Select the Enable Caching checkbox. The option directly below the checkbox becomes active.
6. Select the Fewer Network Accesses option. This will provide the best user response and provide more cache hits.

To enable active caching and set options, follow these steps:

1. Select the Enable Active Caching checkbox on the Caching tab in the Web Proxy Service Properties dialog box. The active caching options become available.
2. Select the Faster User Response Is More Important option. This will enable the most aggressive active caching.
3. Click on the Cache Size button. This will open a window that displays all available drives and allow you to reconfigure the drives that are used for caching. Click on OK. You will return to the Caching tab.
4. Click on the Advanced button. A window that displays the advanced settings for the cache opens. Note the ability to limit the size of objects that will be cached and the configuration options for when cached objects will be refreshed. Click on OK. You will return to the Caching tab.
5. Click on OK to accept the passive and active caching options.

To configure the Gopher protocol permissions, follow these steps:

1. Select the Enable Access Control checkbox on the Permissions tab of the Web Proxy Service Properties dialog box. The Grant Access To dialog box appears.

2. Select Gopher in the Protocol area and click on the Add button. The Add Users And Groups dialog box appears.

3. Select the local Administrators group and click on the Add button.

4. Click on OK. You will return to the Permissions tab and the Administrators group will be listed. Click on OK.

 PROJECT 9.2

In this exercise, you will configure the RealAudio protocol for use by the local Users group. This will familiarize you with the protocols that are available from the WinSock Proxy Service Properties dialog box.

To configure the RealAudio protocol, follow these steps:

1. Select the Enable Access Control checkbox on the Permissions tab in the WinSock Proxy Service Properties dialog box. The Grant Access To dialog box appears.

2. Select RealAudio in the Protocol area and click on the Add button. The Add Users And Groups dialog box appears.

3. Select the local Users group and click on the Add button.

4. Click on OK. You will return to the Permissions tab, and the Users group will be listed. Click on OK.

5. Repeat Steps 2 through 4 for the second RealAudio Protocol entry.

 **PROJECT 9.3**

In this exercise, you will configure logging to create a new log file every week. This will familiarize you with the configurable options in the SOCKS Proxy Service Properties dialog box.

To configure a weekly log file, follow these steps:

1. Select the Enable Logging Using checkbox on the Logging tab in the SOCKS Proxy Service Properties dialog box.

2. Select the Log To File option.

3. Select Automatically Open New Log File.

4. Select the Weekly option for the log file. Click on OK. Note the file name and location that will be used by default.

In these labs, you configured the caching option in the Web Proxy Service Properties dialog box to support active and passive caching. You also configured the Gopher protocol for use by members of the local Administrators group only. For the WinSock Proxy service, you configured the RealAudio protocol for use by anyone that is a member of the local Users group. In the SOCKS Proxy Properties dialog box, you configured logging to log information and to open a new log file on a weekly basis.

To successfully pass the MCSE certification exam for Microsoft Proxy Server 2.0, as well as support a Microsoft Proxy Server 2.0 computer in the field, you must be aware of the protocols (and their configurations) that are supported by the Web Proxy, WinSock Proxy, and SOCKS Proxy services.

CASE PROJECTS

1. You administer a 200-client local area network. Your internal network uses only IPX/SPX for communications; however, some clients have TCP/IP installed for RAS to remote clients. You want to configure the cache to provide the quickest response to user requests.

   Required result: Internet objects must be stored locally.

   Optional desired results: Provide the best user response and maximize cache hits. Sites that are stored in cache must be updated every two hours.

   Proposed solution: Select the Enable Caching checkbox on the Caching tab of the Web Proxy Service Properties dialog box. Select the Fewer Network Accesses Are More Important option under Cache Expiration Policy. Which results does the proposed solution produce?

   a. The proposed solution produces the required result and both of the optional desired results.

   b. The proposed solution produces the required result but only one of the optional desired results.

   c. The proposed solution produces the required result but neither of the optional desired results.

   d. The proposed solution does not produce the required result.

2. You administer a 200-client local area network. Your internal network uses only IPX/SPX for communications; however, some clients have TCP/IP installed for RAS to remote clients. You want to configure the cache to provide the quickest response to user requests. You want to configure Microsoft Proxy Server on your Windows NT Server, which meets or exceeds all installation requirements, so WinSock Proxy clients can benefit from its caching capabilities.

Required result: Internet objects must be stored locally and updated every two hours.

Optional desired results: Provide the best user response and maximize cache hits. Internet objects that are larger than 5MB should not be cached.

Proposed solution: Select the Enable Caching checkbox on the Caching tab of the Web Proxy Service Properties dialog box. Select the Fewer Network Accesses Are More Important option under Cache Expiration Policy. Select the Enable Active Caching checkbox, then select the Faster User Response Is More Important option. Click on the Advanced button, select the Limit Size Of Cached Object To checkbox, and set the limit to 500K. Which results does the proposed solution produce?

  a. The proposed solution produces the required result and both of the optional desired results.

  b. The proposed solution produces the required result but only one of the optional desired results.

  c. The proposed solution produces the required result but neither of the optional desired results.

  d. The proposed solution does not produce the required result.

3. You administer a 200-client local area network. Your internal network uses only IPX/SPX for communications; however, some clients have TCP/IP installed for RAS to remote clients. You want to configure the cache to provide the quickest response to user requests. You want to configure Microsoft Proxy Server on your Windows NT Server, which meets or exceeds all installation requirements, so your Proxy Server computer can also provide access to Web pages on the local IIS Web server.

Required result: The internal IIS Web server must be able to publish Web pages that can be accessed from the Internet.

Optional desired results: Publish the Web pages on port 6450 rather than port 80. Publish all Web pages except **http://www.internal.phone.list.com**.

Proposed solution: Select the Enable Web Publishing checkbox on the Publishing tab of the Web Proxy Service Properties dialog box. Select the Discarded option. Click on the Add button under Except Those Listed Below. In the Mapping dialog box, enter the following URL in the To This URL field: "http://www.internal.phone.list.com" and accept the settings. Which results does the proposed solution produce?

  a. The proposed solution produces the required result and both of the optional desired results.

  b. The proposed solution produces the required result but only one of the optional desired results.

  c. The proposed solution produces the required result but neither of the optional desired results.

  d. The proposed solution does not produce the required result.

4. You attach your organization's network to the Internet using an ISDN line from your Windows NT Server (you are currently only using half of your ISDN connection). You want to configure Microsoft Proxy Server on your Windows NT Server, which meets or exceeds all installation requirements, so WinSock Proxy clients can benefit from its caching capabilities. You also want to restrict clients from using the Gopher protocol.

   Required result: Install Microsoft Proxy Server 2.0 on your Windows NT Server. Disable the Gopher protocol for all clients except members of the local Administrators group.

   Optional desired results: Ensure that your computer uses both lines of your ISDN connection. Limit HTTP protocol access to the local Users group.

   Proposed solution: Install Microsoft Proxy Server on your Windows NT Server. Configure a cache of about 300MB on your NTFS partition. Install and enable multilink and ensure that two entries have been included for your ISDN phone numbers in the Phonebook. Also, ensure that multiple lines are configured for your Dial-Up Networking client. Select the Enable Access Control checkbox on the Permissions tab of the Web Proxy Service Properties dialog box. Select Gopher from the list of available protocols and add the Administrators local group. Which results does the proposed solution produce?

  a. The proposed solution produces the required result and both of the optional desired results.

  b. The proposed solution produces the required result but only one of the optional desired results.

  c. The proposed solution produces the required result but neither of the optional desired results.

  d. The proposed solution does not produce the required result.

5. You administer a 200-client local area network. Your internal network uses only IPX/SPX for communications; however, some clients have TCP/IP installed for RAS to remote clients. You want to configure the cache to provide the quickest response to user requests. You want to configure Microsoft Proxy Server on your Windows NT Server, which meets or exceeds all installation requirements, so WinSock Proxy clients can benefit from its caching capabilities.

   Required result: Internet objects must be stored locally and updated every two hours.

   Optional desired results: Provide the best user response and maximize cache hits. Internet objects that are larger than 5MB should not be cached.

9

Proposed solution: Select the Enable Caching checkbox on the Caching tab of the Web Proxy Service Properties dialog box. Select the Fewer Network Accesses Are More Important option under Cache Expiration Policy. Select the Enable Active Caching checkbox, then select the Faster User Response Is More Important option. Click on the Advanced button, select the Limit Size Of Cached Object To checkbox, and set the limit to 500K. For the Object Time To Live options, select the Enable HTTP Caching checkbox and set the Maximum TTL to 120 minutes. Which results does the proposed solution produce?

a. The proposed solution produces the required result and both of the optional desired results.

b. The proposed solution produces the required result but only one of the optional desired results.

c. The proposed solution produces the required result but neither of the optional desired results.

d. The proposed solution does not produce the required result.

6. You administer a 200-client local area network. Your internal network uses only IPX/SPX for communications; however, some clients have TCP/IP installed for RAS to remote clients. You want to configure the cache to provide the quickest response to user requests. You want to configure Microsoft Proxy Server on your Windows NT Server, which meets or exceeds all installation requirements, so your Proxy Server computer can also provide access to Web pages on the local IIS Web server.

Required result: The internal IIS Web server must be able to publish Web pages that can be accessed from the Internet.

Optional desired results: Limit use of the Gopher protocol to the local Administrators group. Publish all Web pages except
http://www.internal.phone.list.com.

Proposed solution: Select the Enable Web Publishing checkbox on the Publishing tab of the Web Proxy Service Properties dialog box. Select the Sent To Local Web Server option. Click on the Add button under Except Those Listed Below. For the URL information, type "http://www.internal.phone.list.com" and accept the settings. Which results does the proposed solution produce?

a. The proposed solution produces the required result and both of the optional desired results.

b. The proposed solution produces the required result but only one of the optional desired results.

c. The proposed solution produces the required result but neither of the optional desired results.

d. The proposed solution does not produce the required result.

CHAPTER TEN

INTERNET ACCESS VIA PROXY SERVER

Connecting to the Internet is a major reason for installing Microsoft Proxy Server, and you need to be familiar with its configuration options. This chapter will give you a good understanding of how to configure the Local Address Table (LAT), the Auto Dial feature, and the cache, all of which are necessary for a successful implementation of Microsoft Proxy Server. It is important to understand all of Microsoft Proxy Server's configuration options before you implement it on your network; an incorrectly configured server can make your internal network vulnerable to attack via the Internet.

AFTER READING THIS CHAPTER AND COMPLETING THE EXERCISES, YOU WILL BE ABLE TO:

- Understand the structure of the Local Address Table and what information it should and should not contain
- Configure the Web Proxy cache
- Back up and restore the Proxy Server configuration

PROXY SERVER'S ROLE ON THE INTERNET

Microsoft Proxy Server provides an easy, secure, and cost-effective way to connect every desktop in an organization to the Internet. As Figure 10.1 shows, Proxy Server "listens" to your internal computers; when a client application makes a request to the Internet, Proxy Server translates the request and passes it to the Internet. When a computer on the Internet responds, Proxy Server passes that response back to the client application on the computer that made the initial request.

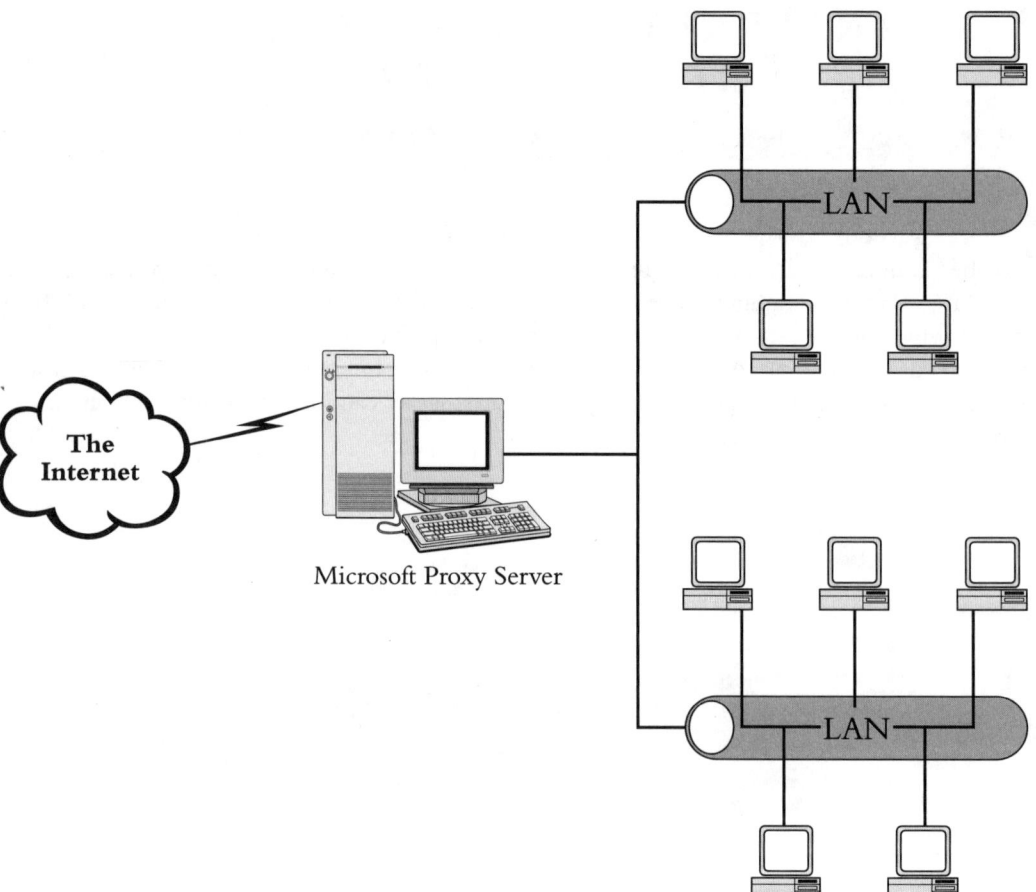

Figure 10.1   Proxy Server sits between a LAN and the Internet, "listening" for requests.

CONFIGURING AND MANAGING CLIENT INTERNET ACCESS

There are two ways to configure clients. You can modify the default settings specified during the Proxy Server setup or client setup, or you can modify the configuration parameters of existing clients by using Internet Service Manager (ISM) or Microsoft Management Console (MMC) with the Windows NT Option Pack. We'll cover several configuration and management tasks you can perform for the clients, including the following:

- Changing client configuration parameters
- Using client configuration scripts
- Editing the client configuration file
- Creating a client Local Address Table (LAT) file
- Configuring Web Proxy client applications
- Configuring WinSock Proxy client applications

 Do not configure the Proxy Server clients to use the Domain Name System (DNS) service for name resolution. The Proxy Server handles all local network name resolution.

10

MODIFYING CLIENT CONFIGURATION PARAMETERS

You can specify how WinSock Proxy client applications and Web browsers connect to the Proxy Server computer in the Client Installation/Configuration dialog box (see Figure 10.2). This information is configured during the Proxy Server installation.

The Client Installation/Configuration dialog box is divided into three sections:

- WinSock Proxy client
- Automatically configure Web browser during client setup
- Browser automatic configuration script

Use the WinSock Proxy client section to specify how WinSock clients connect to the Proxy Server. This connection can be made in one of three ways: by computer name, by IP address, or by manually entering the array name or the group of IP addresses for an array. If the Manual option is selected, you will have to edit the client configuration file, MSPCLNT.INI.

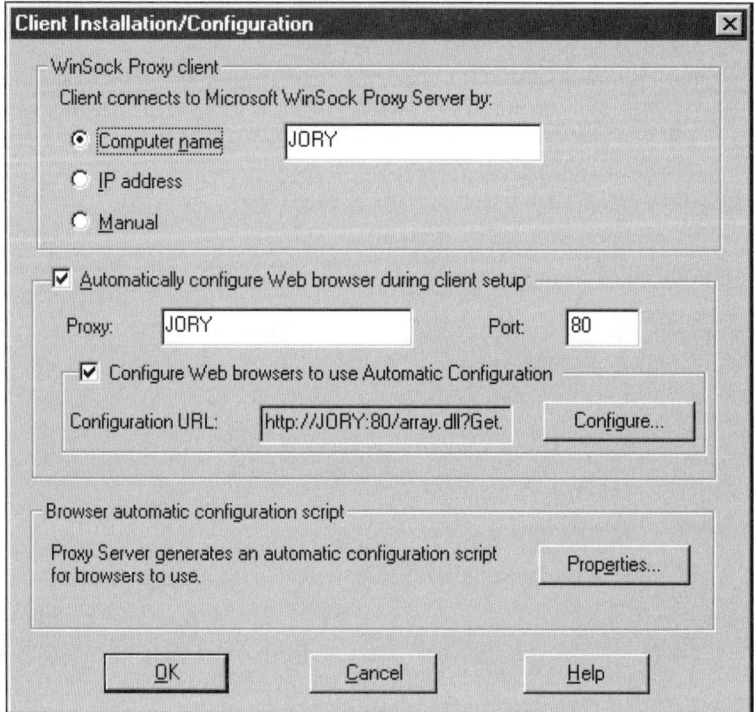

Figure 10.2   The Client Installation/Configuration dialog box.

You can specify that Web browsers use a configuration script (written in JavaScript) to determine how client requests are routed to the Proxy Server. You can route a client request to a Proxy Server or a Proxy Server array, or you can route it directly to the Internet. This eliminates the single point of failure by allowing you to transfer requests automatically from one Proxy Server to another.

You can configure a Web browser to run a client configuration script located at a specific URL. This script determines, in realtime, the client computer to which Proxy Server should connect. When you select the Automatically Configure Web Browser During Client Setup checkbox, the network configuration of the Web browser is modified to instruct the browser to direct all requests made to the Internet to a proxy server. Normally, the Web browser assumes that the client computer is directly connected to the Internet.

The default location for this script is **http://*servername*/array.dll?Get. Routing.Script**, where *servername* is the name of the Proxy Server. This is the script that is generated automatically, based on the configuration options set in the Advanced Client Configuration dialog box (shown in Figure 10.3), which you access by clicking on the Properties button.

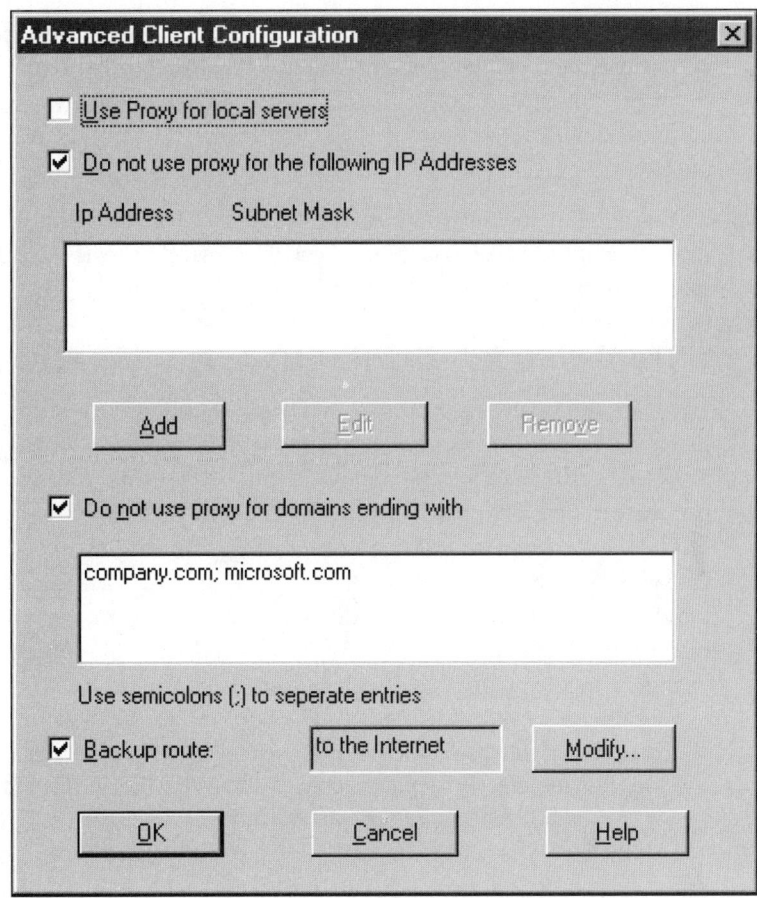

Figure 10.3   The Advanced Client Configuration dialog box.

The Advanced Client Configuration dialog box allows you to customize how the default script is generated. You can control the IP addresses and the domains that should not be routed through the Proxy Server as well as a backup route that should be used if the primary route is unavailable.

You can specify IP addresses that should not be routed through the proxy server by adding them to the list in the Advanced Client Configuration dialog box. The client computer will attempt to access the Internet directly for any IP address specified in this list. Because clients must be able to resolve each URL to an IP address, they should have access to a DNS server that can resolve Internet names. Click on the Add button and enter the IP address and the subnet mask to define which addresses for which the Proxy Server will not be used. You can also specify that all internal requests to internal servers pass through the proxy server by selecting the Use Proxy For Local Servers option. This allows you to improve browser performance by caching internal objects.

To specify domain names that should not be routed through Proxy Server, just enter the domain name to be excluded in the space provided on the dialog box. Separate multiple domain names with a semicolon (;). Again, the client computers will attempt to bypass the Proxy Server and access the Internet directly.

To configure a backup route to use when the primary route is unavailable, you can either specify that you want a direct connection to the Internet, or you can specify a route to another Proxy Server by selecting the appropriate checkboxes.

USING CLIENT CONFIGURATION SCRIPTS

You can optionally specify that a client configuration script located on the Proxy Server be downloaded each time a Web browser is opened. This improves browser performance and allows you to update browser configuration parameters. The downloaded script is executed each time the browser requests a URL, which helps to offload some of the routing work performed by the Proxy Server array. By using this type of script, you can easily update all browser settings for your clients without having to reconfigure each one manually. The client browser must be either Microsoft Internet Explorer 3.02 or higher or Netscape 2.0 or higher.

 If you use the JavaScript configuration script, you will see a benefit in routing performance only if the Web Proxy client browser points directly to a Proxy Server array.

EDITING THE CLIENT CONFIGURATION FILE

The client configuration information is stored in MSPCLNT.INI. A master copy of MSPCLNT.INI is generated during the Microsoft Proxy Server installation process and is stored in the C:\MSP\CLIENTS directory (where C is the drive letter where Proxy Server is installed). Every client configured to use the Proxy Server has a copy of this file in its MSPCLNT directory.

By default, the client configuration file is updated and copied to the client each time a client computer is restarted and every six hours thereafter. When the refresh is made, the client computer scans MSPCLNT.INI for the server share paths listed in the Master Config section. There has to be at least one path entry, which is tried first. The only time additional path entries are tried is when the preceding path did not supply updated files during a download.

You can modify the server's copy of the MSPCLNT.INI file in one of two ways:

- Reinstall the server and specify new information in the Client Installation/Configuration dialog box.

- Use a text editor to modify the MSPCLNT.INI file found in the C:\MSP\CLIENTS directory on the server.

You can modify the client's copy of the MSCPCLNT.INI file in one of two ways:

- Refresh the client's copy of the file by downloading the new version from the server.

- Use a text editor to modify the MSPCLNT.INI file.

 If you use a text editor to modify the MSPCLNT.INI file, you should also modify the server copy. If you do not, the client copy will be overwritten when it is refreshed by the server.

The following is an example of a MSPCLNT.INI file (Table 10.1 includes a description of each entry):

```
[Master Config]
Path1=\\JORY\mspclnt\
[Servers Ip Addresses]
Addr1=11.0.0.1
[Servers Ipx Addresses]
[Common]
WWW-Proxy=JORY
Set Browsers to use Proxy=1
Set Browsers to use Auto Config=1
WebProxyPort=80
Configuration Url=http://JORY:80/array.dll?Get.Routing.Script
Port=1745
Configuration Refresh Time (Hours)=6
Re-check Inaccessible Server Time (Minutes)=10
Refresh Give Up Time (Minutes)=15
Inaccessible Servers Give Up Time (Minutes)=2
Setup=Setup.exe
```

10

Table 10.1   The MSPCLNT.INI file entries.

Section	Entry	Description
[Master Config]	Path1	The UNC path to the shared directory on the Proxy Server that contains the master copy of the client configuration files. In an array, this is the path to the shared directories of all array members. This section is used for backward compatibility with Microsoft Proxy Server 1.0.
[Servers IP Addresses]	Name	The computer or DNS name for the Proxy Server computer used by the client. In an array, this is the DNS name for the array.
[Servers IP Addresses]	Addr1	The IP address of the Proxy Server used by the client. In an array, these are the IP addresses for each array member. Additional entries appear as Addr2, Addr3, etc. This entry does not appear if a computer or DNS name is used.
[Servers IPX Addresses]	Addr1	The IPX address of the Proxy Server used by the client. In an array, these are the IPX addresses for each array member. Additional entries appear as Addr2, Addr3, etc. This entry does not appear if a computer or DNS name is used.
[Common]	Port	The port that the Proxy Server uses for the Control Channel. Change it only if there is a port conflict with another service running on the Proxy Server.
[Common]	Configuration Refresh Time	The interval, in hours, that the client waits before requesting that the server download a new copy of the Local Address Table (LAT).
[Common]	Re-check Refresh Time	The interval, in minutes, that the WinSock client does not try to redirect a request by using an inaccessible server. The default value is 10 minutes.
[Common]	Refresh Give Up Time	The amount of time, in minutes, that the WinSock client attempts to refresh the configuration if the previous attempt failed. The default value is 15 minutes.

(continued)

Table 10.1 The MSPCLNT.INI file entries *(continued)*.

Section	Entry	Description
[Common]	Inaccessible Server Give Up Time	The interval, in minutes, that the WinSock client does not try to redirect a request if all servers are marked as inaccessible. The default value is 2 minutes.
[Common]	Set Browsers To Use Proxy	Set this value to 1 to have the client setup program configure the client's browser to use the Proxy Server. Set this value to 0 to prevent the client setup program from configuring the client to use the Proxy Server
[Common]	Configuration URL	The location of the configuration script that is used by the client computer to route to a particular Proxy Server in an array.
[Common]	LocalDomains	A list of domain names that are to be resolved locally. Separate different domains with a comma.
[Common]	WWW-Proxy	The Proxy Server the client setup program will configure the client browser to use if you set the Set Browsers To Use Proxy value to 1.
[Common]	WebProxyPort	The "listen-on" port used by the Web Proxy service.

10

CREATING A CLIENT LOCAL ADDRESS TABLE (LAT) FILE

When the client setup program is executed, it installs a file named MSPLAT.TXT into the MSPCLNT directory on the client computer. This file contains the Local Address Table (LAT). The LAT defines the IP addresses of the internal network. Like the client configuration file, the LAT configuration file is updated regularly from the Proxy Server. When a Windows Sockets application tries to connect to an IP address, the LAT is checked to determine whether the IP address is on the internal or external network. If the address is internal, the connection is made directly. If the address is external, the connection is made through the WinSock Proxy service on the Proxy Server.

Sometimes you must define different internal addresses so specific clients can gain access to certain internal servers. However, the server copy will overwrite any changes that you make to MSPLAT.TXT when the file is refreshed, so you can also create a custom LAT file for the client. Use a text editor to create this file, name it LOCALLAT.TXT, and place it in the client's MSPCLNT directory.

The client then uses both MSPLAT.TXT and LOCALLAT.TXT to determine which IP addresses are internal and which are external.

When you create the LOCALLAT.TXT file, enter the IP addresses as ranges or as a single IP address. For example:

```
192.168.12.0     192.168.12.255
192.168.12.50    192.168.12.50
```

CONFIGURING WEB PROXY CLIENT APPLICATIONS

A Web Proxy client is a client that uses a CERN application, such as a Web browser, and is configured to use the Web Proxy service. The client setup program configures the client's Web browsers. You can also configure the clients manually by changing the browsers' configuration parameters.

When you configure Web Proxy client applications, it is important to remember the following:

- Do not configure Web browser helper applications (for example, RealPlayer clients) as Web Proxy clients. These helper applications are used with the WinSock Proxy service and must not be configured to use the Proxy Server.

- Use an IP address rather than the domain or computer name to configure IPX Web Proxy clients. If the client computer is running only the IPX protocol, its Web browser will not be able to connect to the Web Proxy service if the Proxy Server is defined with a domain or computer name.

- With 16-bit applications, you may be required to enter additional information during the client logon procedure. A Domain Credentials dialog box may appear when an attempt is made to log on from the client computer if the computer is running Windows 95 or Windows for Workgroups.

CONFIGURING WINSOCK PROXY CLIENT APPLICATIONS

A WinSock Proxy client is a client that has Windows Sockets applications configured to use the WinSock Proxy service. The client setup program installs the WinSock client software. It is important to note that the client setup program does not configure the individual Windows Sockets applications; instead, it replaces the existing Windows Sockets DLL file that the applications use. The WinSock Proxy service supports Windows Sockets 1.1 applications. You will need to permit user access for specific protocols and service ports by configuring the WinSock service.

When you configure WinSock Proxy client applications:

- Do not set Windows Sockets applications to use the Proxy Server computer, even if the applications allow for this option.

- With 16-bit applications, you may be required to enter additional information during the client logon procedure. A Domain Credentials dialog box may appear when an attempt is made to log on from the client computer if the computer is running Windows 95 or Windows for Workgroups.

- Use an IP address instead of the computer name to configure IPX WinSock Proxy clients. If the client computer is running only the IPX protocol, its Web browser will not be able to connect to the WinSock Proxy service if the proxy server is defined with a computer name.

- If you upgrade your operating system on Windows NT clients, you will have to reinstall the WinSock Proxy client software. Once you upgrade the operating system, the WinSock Proxy client software is automatically disabled.

- If you are running a SOCKS client application through the SOCKS Proxy service, you should disable the WinSock Proxy client application.

10

CONFIGURING AND MANAGING SERVER INTERNET ACCESS

The following sections describe the Proxy Server parameters that you can set:

- Configuring Auto Dial
- Changing the Local Address Table
- Configuring the cache
- Backing up and restoring configuration

CONFIGURING AUTO DIAL

Auto Dial is an on demand dial-out feature of Microsoft Proxy Server. It works in conjunction with the Windows NT Remote Access Service (RAS) to schedule dial-out connection times to the Internet. Figure 10.4 shows the Auto Dial dialog box.

The Proxy Server will make an Internet connection in the following situations:

- **Web Proxy service** When the object being requested is not located in cache or when active caching is automatically refreshing cached objects.

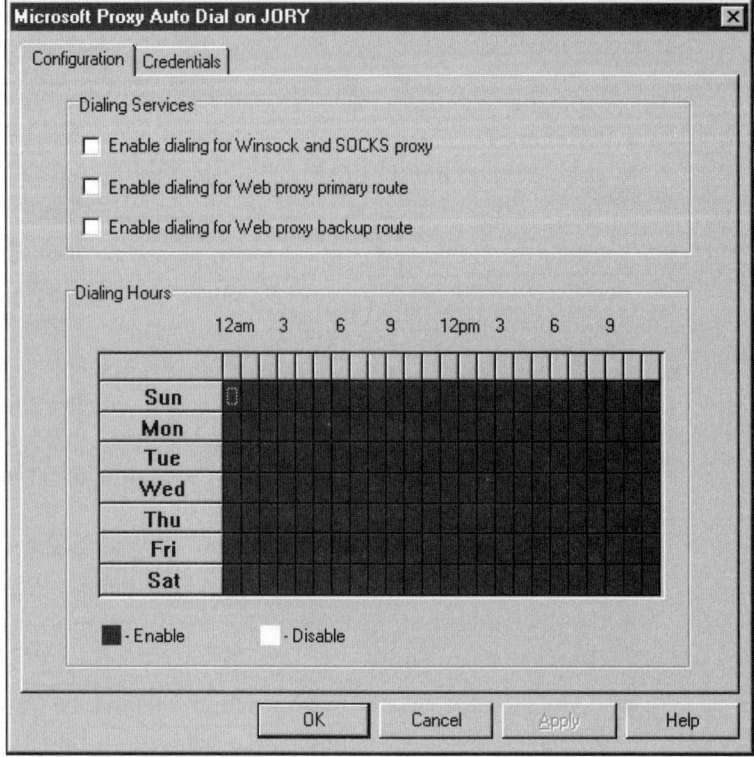

Figure 10.4   The Auto Dial dialog box.

- **WinSock Proxy service** All client requests are processed by using a dial-up connection.
- **SOCKS Proxy service** All client requests are processed by using a dial-up connection.

Auto Dial uses a RAS Phonebook entry to perform on-demand dial-out connections as a RAS client. To configure the dial-out connection, you must verify that a RAS client has already been installed and configured to operate with your modem or ISDN adapter.

You can schedule the Auto Dial feature by indicating the times the Proxy Server will use it in the Configuration tab of the Auto Dial dialog box. You will be required to enter the connection information (RAS Phonebook entry, username, password, and domain) in the Credentials tab of the Auto Dial dialog box.

  When Proxy Server is installed, packet filtering is disabled by default. You must configure Auto Dial before you can enable packet filtering.

To configure Auto Dial for dial-out to the Internet, perform the following tasks:

1. Verify that a RAS client has been installed.

2. Create a RAS Phonebook entry.

3. Configure Remote Access properties to use Auto Dial.

4. Unbind the WINS client from select network adapters.

5. Set your user credentials (if required by your ISP).

6. Set dialing services and dialing hours.

7. If necessary, stop and restart the proxy server services.

CHANGING THE LOCAL ADDRESS TABLE

As we mentioned earlier, the LAT is contained in MSPLAT.TXT and is created during the Proxy Server installation. The internal network information you provided during the install is used to create the LAT. Any external networks are excluded from the list. You can modify the existing LAT by adding or removing IP address pairs manually. Figure 10.5 shows the dialog box in which you can configure the LAT.

You can add a single IP address or a range of IP addresses. To add a single IP address to the LAT, enter the same address in the From field and the To field. To add a range of IP addresses to the LAT, enter the first address in the range in the From field and the last address in the range in the To field.

10

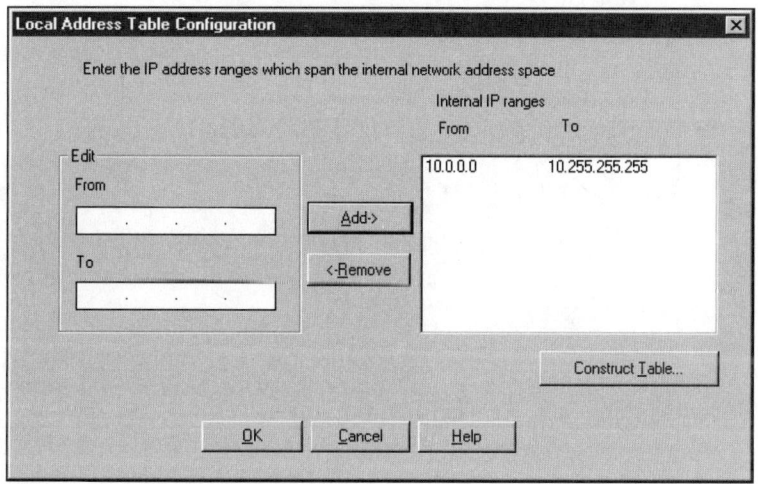

Figure 10.5   The Local Address Table Configuration dialog box.

CONFIGURING THE CACHE

Proxy Server's Web Proxy service uses caching to store copies of HTTP and FTP objects on the local machine. This improves performance from your users' standpoint and reduces bandwidth by accessing the cached objects from the local cache rather than from the Internet. The Web Proxy Service Properties Caching dialog box is shown in Figure 10.6.

 To use caching with Microsoft Proxy Server 2.0, you must install it on a computer that has at least one partition formatted as an NTFS volume. With Microsoft Proxy Server 1.0, you were able to place the cache on a FAT partition.

It is difficult to cache some Internet objects properly, such as objects that require authentication or are dynamically created. Proxy Server uses predefined criteria to determine whether or not an object can be cached.

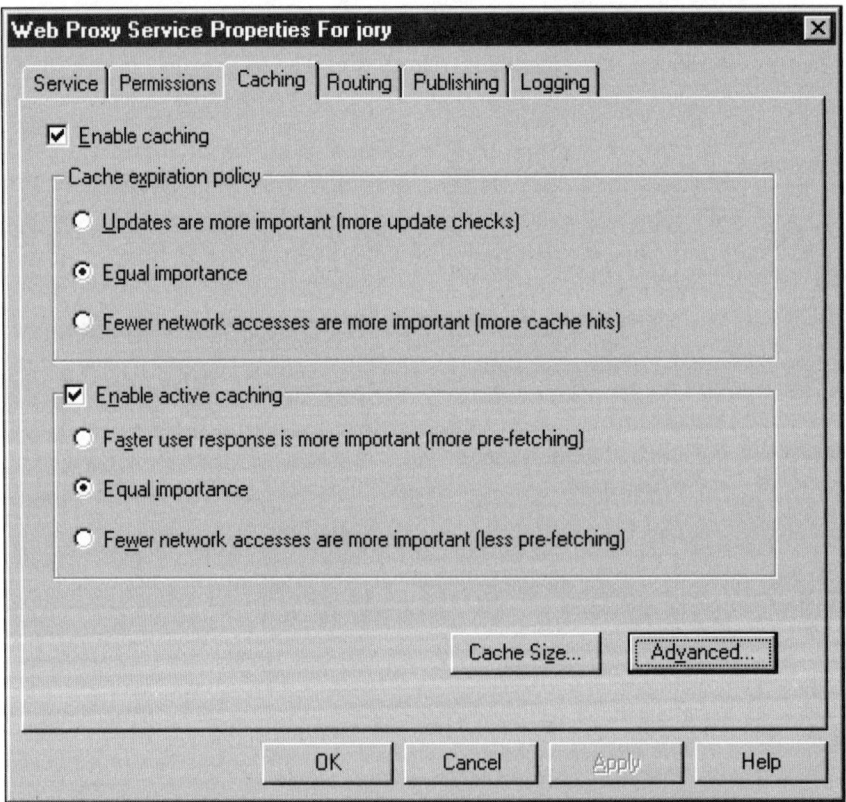

Figure 10.6   The Web Proxy Service Properties Caching dialog box.

Internet objects that require authentication or the Secure Sockets Layer (SSL) are not cached.

You have several configuration options when you configure a cache on Proxy Server:

- You can set passive caching parameters and a general expiration policy for object "freshness."
- You can set active caching parameters.
- You can change the cache drives and the total cache size.
- You can set advanced caching parameters, such as object Time-to-Live and object size.

BACKING UP AND RESTORING CONFIGURATION

All server configuration information can be backed up to a locally stored text file. By default, this information is stored in the C:\MSP\CONFIG directory. The file name is created by using the form.

`MSPyyyymmdd.mcp`

where *yyyy* is the year, *mm* is the month, and *dd* is the day.

You may do a partial or a full restore (or *roll-back*) to a previous configuration if you have backed up the server configuration to the file described in the preceding paragraph. A partial restore restores only the non-computer-specific configuration parameters, such as user permissions. A full restore restores all configuration parameters that belong to the server (including the ones for the partial restore).

 Be aware that when you are upgrading from Microsoft Proxy Server 1.0 to version 2.0, you should back up the Proxy Server 1.0 configuration, install Proxy Server 2.0, and restore the configuration files.

Several configuration parameters are not restored during a partial restore, including:

- The Web Proxy cache size and disk location
- The disk location for all service logs and the packet filter log
- The packet filter configuration
- The Auto Dial configuration
- The Server intra-array IP address
- The server alias used in the HTTP Via header for routing
- The Registry keys that cannot be configured through the ISM user interface

10

TUNING AND CONTROLLING INTERNET ACCESS PERFORMANCE

It can be difficult to fine-tune your Proxy Server performance; to do so, you need to take several criteria into consideration, including the number of users, the protocols used to access the Internet, and your available Internet bandwidth.

A nice feature of Microsoft Proxy Server 2.0 is the ability to set up a proxy array. With arrays, a group of Proxy Server computers can be configured and administered as a single entity with a large cache. Arrays also provide scalability and easier administration.

Table 10.2 shows Microsoft's recommended specifications for running Proxy Server. Be aware that these recommendations are based on the server running only Windows NT and Microsoft Proxy Server.

Use the following formula to select the amount of cache needed:

100MB + 0.5MB for each Web Proxy client.

For example, if you have 250 desktops that will use the Web Proxy service, you will require *at least* 225MB for cache.

INTERNET-SPECIFIC PROXY SERVER LOGGING

There are three service logs that record events generated by the Web Proxy, WinSock Proxy, and SOCKS Proxy services. There is also a separate packet log that records network packet events. You may have this information logged to a text file or to an ODBC-compliant database. It is possible to log to a remote drive; however, having the information logged to a local drive will improve performance.

Table 10.2   Microsoft Proxy Server minimum recommendations.

Scenario	Processor	Disk Space	RAM
Minimum	Intel 486 or faster	10MB	At least 24MB
Small office (300 desktops)	Pentium 133	250MB to 2GB	At least 32MB
Medium (300 to 2,000 desktops)	Pentium 166	2 to 4GB	At least 64MB
Large (2,000+ desktops)	1 Pentium 166 per 2,000	2 to 4GB/server	At least 64MB/server
ISP (1,000+ dial-up users)	1 Pentium 166 per 1,000	2 to 4GB/server	At least 64MB/server

By default, all information is logged to a text file, but you can configure each service separately to log to a text file or to a database. You can also select two logging modes: regular and verbose. The regular logging method has a smaller number of information fields that need to be logged. The verbose logging method logs all available information.

As a Microsoft BackOffice product, Proxy Server uses the Windows NT system event log to record events. You can use this information to monitor or troubleshoot a server problem. Table 10.3 lists the event source names that may appear in the NT system event log and a description of the types of events represented.

When the proxy information is logged to a text file (the default), the file locations for each log are:

- C:\WINNT\SYSTEM32\MSPLOGS\W3*FILENAME.LOG* for the Web Proxy service

- C:\WINNT\SYSTEM32\MSPLOGS\WS*FILENAME.LOG* for the WinSock Proxy service

- C:\WINNT\SYSTEM32\MSPLOGS\SP*FILENAME.LOG* for the SOCKS Proxy service

- C:\WINNT\SYSTEM32\MSPLOGS\PF*FILENAME.LOG* for packet filter events

The file name itself depends on how logging is configured. You can configure logging to create a new log each day, week, or month. For example, the log files for the SOCKS Proxy service would be:

- SP*YYMMDD*.LOG for daily logs

- SP*YYMMW*.LOG for weekly logs

- SP*YYMM*.LOG for monthly logs

Table 10.3   Microsoft Proxy Server source names.

Source Name	Description
MSProxyAdmin	Proxy Server administrative events
PacketFilterLog	Packet filter alert events
SocksProxy	SOCKS Proxy service events
SocksProxyLog	SOCKS Proxy logging events
WebProxyCache	Web Proxy caching events
WebProxyLog	Web Proxy logging events
WebProxyServer	Web Proxy service events
WinSockProxy	WinSock Proxy service events
WinSockProxyLog	WinSock Proxy logging events

10

The characters in italic represent the following:

- *YY* is a number from 00 to 99 that indicates the year.
- *MM* is a number from 01 to 12 that indicates the month.
- *W* is a number from 1 to 5 that indicates the week of the month.
- *DD* is a number from 01 to 31 that indicates the day of the month.

You can also log to any ODBC-compliant database (such as Microsoft SQL Server). Proxy Server has a SQL logging table tool, MKPLOG.EXE, that creates a Microsoft SQL Server table with the required field name, data type, and field length settings. MKPLOG.EXE must be executed from a Web browser on the computer on which the SQL server is located. This tool can be found in the IIS scripts directory (C:\INETPUB\SCRIPTS\TOOLS) on the computer running the proxy server. It is important to remember that this tool will create the database table only for Microsoft SQL Server. All other database tables must be created manually, and you cannot use this tool to create a packet filter log table.

TROUBLESHOOTING PROXY SERVER INTERNET CONNECTIONS

Proxy Server ships with a utility called mspdiag that is installed by default in the C:\MSP directory. You can use this utility to detect common configuration problems on the server, which can help you diagnose Internet connection problems. The tasks that mspdiag performs include:

- Verifying that Internet Information Server (IIS) 3.0 or later is installed
- Verifying that Windows NT Service Pack 3 or later is installed
- Verifying that valid IP addresses are assigned in the LAT
- Checking the status of the IIS WWW service
- Checking the status of the proxy services
- Checking to see if IP forwarding is disabled
- Checking to see if the default gateway is specified

Make sure that the LAT contains only internal network addresses. If there is an external network address in the LAT, both the clients and the Proxy Server will search for these addresses internally rather than on the Internet. Often you will notice slow connections from the client if the LAT is incorrectly configured.

CHAPTER SUMMARY

Connecting to the Internet is one of the main reasons for installing Microsoft Proxy Server on your network. It offers you security, increased performance, and fault tolerance. It is important to make sure that only your internal networks appear in the Local Address Table. If an external network is placed into the Local Address Table, you may be opening your internal networks to attacks via the Internet.

Another great feature of Microsoft Proxy Server is Auto Dial, which allows you to configure the times for the Proxy Server to dial your modem or to connect via your ISDN adapter to your Internet Service Provider for access to the Internet. There are several important steps that are necessary to make sure Proxy Server's Auto Dial feature is configured and operating properly: creating a RAS Phonebook entry, setting the dialing options and schedule, and setting any credentials required by your ISP.

Several tools are available for troubleshooting and monitoring Proxy Server. You can log Proxy Server messages to a text file or to an ODBC-compliant database. If you log to a database, you'll get more information out of your logs, but your proxy server may suffer a small performance hit because of the extra overhead required.

10

KEY TERMS

- **Auto Dial**—An on-demand dial-out feature of Proxy Server. Auto Dial works with the Windows NT Remote Access Service (RAS) and can be used to schedule dial-out connection times to the Internet through your Internet Service Provider (ISP).

- **cache**—A feature of Proxy Server that stores frequently accessed sites to be retrieved from the local hard drive rather than from the Internet.

- **client configuration script**—Allows for automatic configuration of Web Proxy clients to increase overall network performance when you are using arrays or chains. You can use predefined JavaScripts, or you can create your own scripts.

- **Local Address Table (LAT)**—Consists of a series of IP address pairs that define your internal network address space. Each address pair defines either a range of IP addresses or a single IP address.

- **roll-back**—The restoration of previous configuration values for a proxy server.

- **SOCKS Proxy service**—Provides SOCKS support. The SOCKS Proxy service supports any SOCKS client application that adheres to the SOCKS (version 4.3a or below) standard.

- **Web Proxy service**—Provides caching, cache routing (CARP), support for chains, and reverse proxying. The Web Proxy service supports any client that supports the HTTP protocol.

- **WinSock Proxy service**—Redirects Windows Sockets (WinSock) version 1.1 API calls, performs IPX-to-IP conversion, and provides server proxying. The WinSock Proxy service supports any client that supports WinSock 1.1 or above.

REVIEW QUESTIONS

1. You have several network interface cards in your Microsoft Proxy Server computer. There are two internal networks (192.168.12.0 and 192.168.13.0) and two external networks (204.35.4.0 and 207.54.34.0). Which networks would you place in the LAT?
   a. 192.168.12.0
   b. 192.168.13.0
   c. 204.35.4.0
   d. 207.54.34.0

2. Which of the following are required for Auto Dial to function?
   a. Configure your modem or ISDN adapter.
   b. Configure a RAS Phonebook entry.
   c. Configure a RAS Addressbook entry.
   d. Unbind the WINS client from the network adapter.

3. You have 550 client desktops that will access the Internet via the Proxy Server. You would like to configure the Proxy Server to cache common URLs. What is the minimum recommended cache size needed?
   a. Does not matter; cache will be dynamically allocated as needed.
   b. 200MB total
   c. 375MB total
   d. 5MB per URL accessed

4. Which configuration parameters are not restored during a partial restore?
   a. user permissions
   b. group permissions
   c. Web Proxy cache size
   d. Auto Dial configuration

5. One of your managers needs to access a private internal network (10.100.20.0). You do not want other users to have access to it through the LAT. What would you do?

    a. Create a LOCALLAT.TXT file on the manager's computer with the network range (10.100.20.0 to 10.100.20.255).

    b. Edit the manager's copy of MSPLAT.TXT and add the network range.

    c. Deny access to the network range by creating a LOCALLAT.TXT file on everyone's computer.

    d. Edit everyone's MSPLAT.TXT file and deny access to the network range.

6. You have 5,000 client desktops. How would you configure Microsoft Proxy Server?

    a. One server for all 5,000 clients.

    b. Two servers. Manually configure half the clients to each.

    c. Three servers. Manually assign an equal number of clients to each.

    d. Three servers in an array. Assign the clients to the array.

7. You upgraded your server from Microsoft Proxy Server 1.0 to Microsoft Proxy Server 2.0. Now caching does not work; why?

    a. Microsoft Proxy Server 1.0 is completely different from Microsoft Proxy Server 2.0; therefore, you cannot upgrade.

    b. The old caching directory was on a FAT partition; Microsoft Proxy Server 2.0 only supports logging to an NTFS partition.

    c. You are out of disk space. Add a drive.

    d. Add more memory.

8. You cannot configure a different LAT for each client. (True or False?)

9. If you modify the client's copy of the Proxy Server configuration file, the server copy will not be downloaded to the client when it is refreshed. (True or False?)

10. How is a configuration script generated?

    a. It can only be generated manually by the administrator.

    b. It is generated either manually or by using the parameters in the Advanced dialog box.

    c. It is configured upon installation and cannot be modified.

    d. It is configured by the users when they access the proxy server.

11. Where are the Web Proxy log files located?

    a. C:\WINNT\SYSTEM32\MSPLOGS\W3*FILENAME*.LOG

    b. C:\EXCHSRVR\MSPLOGS\W3*FILENAME*.LOG

    c. C:\WINNT\SYSTEM32\MSPLOGS\WP*FILENAME*.LOG

    d. C:\EXCHSRVR\SYSTEM32\MSPLOGS\WP*FILENAME*.LOG

10

12. There is an upgrade path from Microsoft Proxy Server version 1.0 to version 2.0. (True or False?)

13. Which of the following is not checked by the mspdiag diagnostic utility?

   a. whether Windows NT Service Pack 3 or later is installed

   b. whether both the TCP/IP and IPX protocols are installed

   c. whether IP forwarding is disabled

   d. whether Internet Information Server (IIS) 3.0 or later is installed

14. You will see a routing performance increase only when you connect to a proxy array. (True or False?)

15. Logging to an ODBC-compliant database will not affect Proxy Server performance compared to logging to a text file. (True or False?)

HANDS-ON PROJECTS

In the projects that follow, you will use the settings in the Client Installation/Configuration dialog box to modify basic client configuration parameters and to define the URL for a client configuration script. In the last project, you will modify the LAT for Proxy Server.

 ## PROJECT 10.1

To change the client configuration parameters for the WSP Client applet, follow these steps:

1. Select Computer name, IP address, or Manual in the WinSock Proxy client dialog box. Make sure that the server name is correct.

2. Select the Automatically Configure Web Browser During Client Setup checkbox and type the server name in the Proxy field.

3. Click on OK.

 ## PROJECT 10.2

To set the URL to use for the configuration script, follow these steps:

1. From the Client Installation/Configuration dialog box, select the Automatically Configure Web Browser During Client Setup checkbox and click on the Configure button.

2. To use the URL that Proxy Server generates by default, select Use Default Script Supplied By Server from the Configuration URL For Clients dialog box.

3. To use an alternate URL for a custom configuration script, select Use Custom URL and enter the path for the URL.

4. Click on OK to close the Client Installation/Configuration dialog box.

5. Click on OK to close the Properties dialog box.

PROJECT 10.3

To modify the LAT, follow these steps:

1. In Internet Service Manager (ISM), double-click on the computer name next to the Web Proxy, WinSock Proxy, or SOCKS Proxy service.

2. Click on Local Address Table in the Service Properties dialog box.

3. To add a range of IP addresses to the list, enter the first address in the range in the From field and the last address in the range in the To field and then click on Add. To add a single IP address to the list, type the same address in both the From and To fields and then click on Add.

4. Click on OK.

5. In Internet Service Manager, stop and restart the Web Proxy, WinSock Proxy, and SOCKS Proxy services.

10

CASE PROJECTS

1. You are required to set up Microsoft Proxy Server for Internet access to your network. Your Internet connection is a dial-up ISDN connection through your ISP.

   Required result: Connect your network to the Internet.

   Optional desired results: Configure the Proxy Server to connect only when there is a request made to the Internet (to save money on connection charges). Make sure there is fault tolerance in case the Proxy Server goes down for maintenance.

   Proposed solution: Install a Proxy Server in an array. Configure the Proxy Server with only your internal IP addresses in its Local Address Table. Configure Auto Dial to connect to the Internet only when needed. Which results does the proposed solution provide?

   a. The proposed solution provides the required result and both optional desired results.

   b. The proposed solution provides the required result and one optional desired result.

   c. The proposed solution provides only the required result.

   d. The proposed solution does not provide the required result.

2. You are required to set up Microsoft Proxy Server for Internet access to your network. Your Internet connection is a dial-up ISDN connection through your ISP.

   Required result: Connect your network to the Internet.

   Optional desired results: Configure the Proxy Server to connect only when there is a request made to the Internet (to save money on connection charges). Make sure there is fault tolerance in case the Proxy Server goes down for maintenance.

   Proposed solution: Install a proxy server in an array. Configure the Proxy Server with only your internal IP addresses in its Local Address Table. Which results does the proposed solution provide?

   a. The proposed solution provides the required result and both optional desired results.

   b. The proposed solution provides the required result and one optional desired result.

   c. The proposed solution provides only the required result.

   d. The proposed solution does not provide the required result.

3. You are required to set up Microsoft Proxy Server for Internet access to your network. Your Internet connection is a dial-up ISDN connection through your ISP.

   Required result: Connect your network to the Internet.

   Optional desired results: Configure the Proxy Server to connect only when there is a request made to the Internet (to save money on connection charges). Make sure there is fault tolerance in case the Proxy Server goes down for maintenance.

   Proposed solution: Configure the Proxy Server with only your internal IP addresses in its Local Address Table. Which results does the proposed solution provide?

   a. The proposed solution provides the required result and both optional desired results.

   b. The proposed solution provides the required result and one optional desired result.

   c. The proposed solution provides only the required result.

   d. The proposed solution does not provide the required result.

MANAGING MULTIPLE PROXY SERVERS

In this chapter, you will learn to configure multiple Microsoft Proxy Servers so the overall workload of proxy support will be distributed to provide client workload balancing and fault tolerance. These tasks are accomplished by configuring proxy arrays to distribute caching of Internet objects across all available members of the array. You will configure routes to the Internet so that if an array does not have a copy of a requested object, the object will be requested from an upstream Proxy Server.

You will also learn how to configure proxy arrays in a multiple-domain environment and deal with obstacles you may face when you work in an enterprise environment. This chapter's Hands-on Projects will take you step-by-step through the actual configuration of a proxy array environment.

AFTER READING THIS CHAPTER AND COMPLETING THE EXERCISES, YOU WILL BE ABLE TO:

- Configure and manage a multiple proxy environment
- Configure Proxy Servers into arrays
- Configure caching to span multiple Proxy Servers
- Balance client load across multiple Proxy Servers
- Configure Proxy Server routing
- Configure Proxy Server in a single- and multiple-domain environment

ARRAYS

"Array" is the term used to describe distributed proxying. In *distributed proxying* (shown in Figure 11.1), multiple Proxy Server computers are connected in a logical, peer-to-peer fashion to form an *array*. Each Proxy Server in the array is known as an *array member*. When you connect Proxy Servers in this fashion, the cache of each Proxy Server computer is combined to form one large, logical cache.

When one Proxy Server computer in an array is configured, all Proxy Server computers in the array are updated through a synchronization process, so virtual management of all Proxy Server computers is accomplished. Fault tolerance is provided because, when one Proxy Server computer goes down or is removed from the array, the other computers in the array are aware of the failure and "listen" for the return of the inoperative array member. Through a

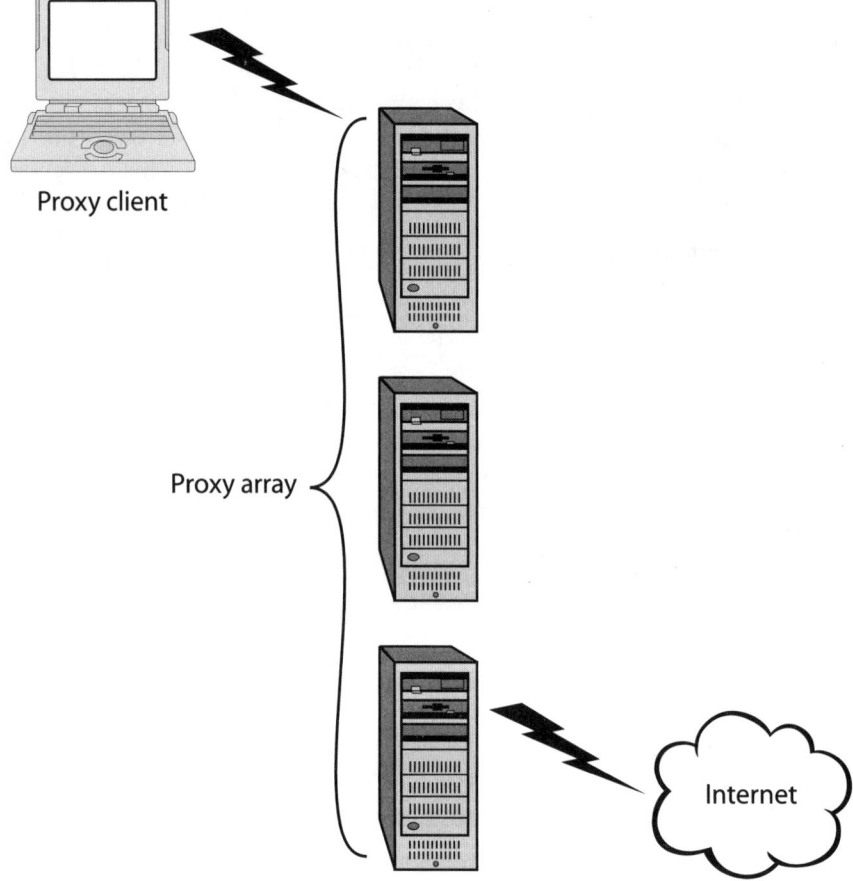

Proxy client

Proxy array

Internet

Figure 11.1   Distributed proxying.

synchronization process, every member of the proxy array is aware of the other members and their configuration. All members of a proxy array must be running Microsoft Proxy Server 2.0.

When a proxy array is configured, all members of the array pass configuration information to each other. By doing this, all array members have a current list of which array members are operational. The synchronization process can be configured for automatic synchronization. When automatic synchronization is enabled, the following parameters *are replicated* in the entire array. When replication occurs, the array member you are currently administering is always updated first.

- Domain filters
- Web Proxy service protocol access control information
- Web Proxy service caching options (including advanced caching options such as cache filters)
- Web Proxy service upstream routing options
- Web Proxy service publishing (reverse proxying) information
- WinSock Proxy service protocol definitions
- WinSock Proxy service access control information
- Socks Proxy service permissions
- Logging configuration for each service, including packet filter logging
- **Packet filter alerting** information
- Local Address Table (LAT) information
- Client configuration information

Information that is not shared through the synchronization process includes:

- Web Proxy service enable caching flag status
- Web Proxy service cache size and disk and directory location
- Logging directory information
- Packet filters, filter alerts, and logging information

To configure a new proxy array, follow these steps:

1. From Internet Service Manager, select the Web Proxy service for the computer you wish to configure. Next, select Service Properties from the Properties menu. The Web Proxy Server Service Properties dialog box opens.

2. Click on the Array button on the Service tab. The Array dialog box opens.

11

3. Click on the Join Array button to form an array with another Microsoft Proxy Server 2.0 computer. You're prompted to provide the name of the computer with which you wish to form an array.

4. After communications has been established with the other Microsoft Proxy Server 2.0 computer, you're prompted to provide the name of another computer. The two Microsoft Proxy Server 2.0 computers that formed the array are listed and the status for each machine is shown (see Figure 11.2).

5. Click on OK to accept the configuration. This returns you to the Web Proxy Service Properties dialog box. Click on Apply to implement the proxy array configuration.

6. Click on the Array button on the Service tab of the Web Proxy Service Properties dialog box. The Array dialog box opens. Note that the Synchronize Configuration Of Array Members option box is available. This option box is only available when there are no pending changes for the Join, Remove, or Leave buttons.

If an array already existed, you could have joined an existing array rather than creating a new one. By default, the array members are configured for automatic synchronization. The Array button is available and can be configured on the Web

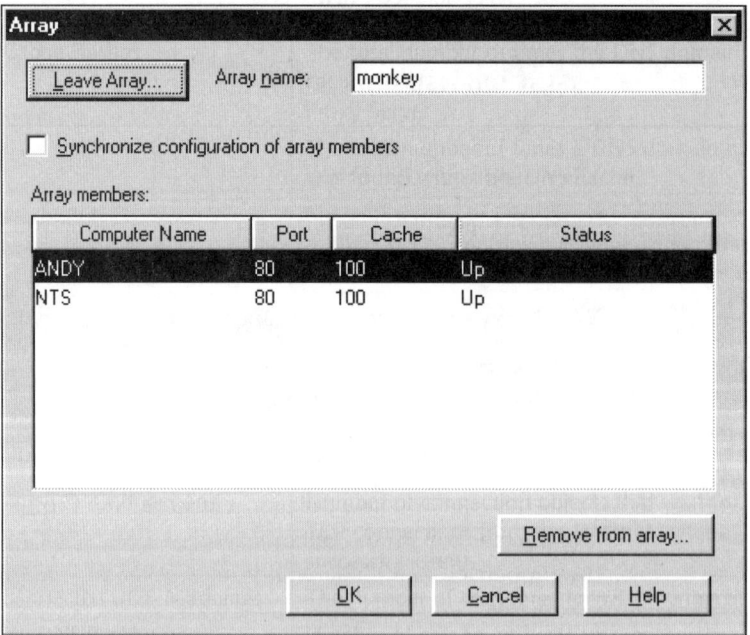

Figure 11.2   The Proxy Array dialog box.

Proxy Server, WinSock Proxy Server, and SOCKS Proxy Server Properties dialog boxes. To remove a Proxy Server from an existing array:

1. From Internet Service Manager, select the Web Proxy service for the computer you wish to configure. Select Service Properties from the Properties menu. The Web Proxy Server Service Properties dialog box opens.

2. Click the Array button on the Service tab. The Array dialog box opens.

3. Click on the Leave Array button on the Array dialog box. A warning box appears, asking if you are sure you wish to leave the array. If only two members are in the array, a message box will appear stating that both Proxy Servers will act as standalone proxy servers if this action is taken.

Updates from each array member will be sent to the other array members so that all members of the array are aware of each other's configuration and any configuration changes that may have occurred. If an array member is down, an error message stating an array member is down will be generated. This message can be viewed in the Event Viewer. The messages that can occur are:

- **132** The Web Proxy service detected that the array member *servername* is down.

- **133** The Web Proxy service detected that the array member *servername* is back up.

The synchronization process used by members of a proxy array works much the way the briefcase function on a portable computer works. If a document is located on a server, it can be copied to a client's briefcase. The client can work on the document away from the network. When the client is reconnected, the changes made to the copy of the document stored in the briefcase will be passed up to the network location. If someone else has made changes to the document, the client will receive a message back stating that the documents are out of synchronization. The client can replace the changes made on the other document or lose the changes made to his or her own document. If two Proxy Server array members are modified at or near the same time, a conflict can occur.

In a Proxy Server array, the replication process used to synchronize the information between array members takes place on the Proxy Server computer that is being altered. If someone else is modifying data at the same time you are, a conflict can occur. If the other Proxy Server changes have be applied and the synchronization process has started, but your changes have not been applied, a message will appear on your screen and you can do one of two things:

- **Refresh** If you select Refresh, all the changes you made will be discarded.

- **Overwrite** If you select Overwrite, your changes will stay in place and be replicated across the array.

11

If you have applied the changes to your Proxy Server and you receive changes from another Proxy Server, an Array Configuration Conflict message box appears. You have two choices:

- **Synchronize Now** If you select this option, you can select an array member to which all Proxy Servers in the array synchronize their cache.

- **Cancel** If you select this option, you are returned to Internet Service Manager and the warning message is effectively ignored.

The best policy to use when you are updating a Proxy Server is to attempt to avoid conflicts. This can be done by scheduling time intervals when changes can be made by each member of your administrative team. By doing this, changes will not be made to more than one array member at a time.

CACHING

Caching with multiple Proxy Servers allows several proxy server computers to be joined into an array, and the cache area available to each member of the array is compiled into one logical caching area. During the synchronization process detailed earlier, the content of each cache was not passed to other members of the array. A better method of determining the location of stored information has been devised.

The *Cache Array Routing Protocol (CARP)*, which is implemented in the Microsoft Proxy Server 2.0 product, is used to determine the location of locally stored URLs in the array member's cache, so queries need not be used to find out which Proxy Server is storing information. The CARP technique overcomes the limitations of the Internet Cache Protocol (ICP), which was introduced in 1995.

ICP was developed to allow proxy servers to query other proxy servers in an attempt to find locally stored Internet objects, but it does not scale well to large proxy server environments because each proxy member queries all other configured proxy servers before sending the request to the Internet. In a smaller networked environment, the excess traffic generated by the query process is acceptable, but in a large proxy server installation base, the traffic generated during the query process is not acceptable, and the delay before a request is released to the Internet is prohibitive.

CARP does not use a query process to locate locally cached information or determine where information will be stored. Instead, an algorithm is used to determine which array member will store the information. Every proxy server in the array is aware of the other array member's configuration information, and each uses the same algorithm to determine the location in which information will be stored. This allows for a *queryless* location of locally stored Internet objects through a *hashing* method.

Each member of an array keeps an "array membership list" with a Time-to-Live (TTL) assigned to it, which forces the list to be updated on a regular basis. Each member has a hash function computed for it; a hash function is computed for each URL that is stored as well. When the two are combined, the member with the highest number becomes the "owner" of the URL and stores it in cache. A simplified example of the hashing method follows:

Proxy 1 hash   25

Proxy 2 hash   14

Proxy 3 hash   17

URL hash   52

Proxy1 hash + URL hash = 77

Proxy 2 hash + URL hash = 66

Proxy 3 hash + URL hash = 69

The URL would be stored on Proxy Server 1. Each proxy member is using the same hash routine to determine the array member that will store each URL, so that no list of URLs needs to be passed between array members and no queries between array members need to be performed to determine where URLs are located. The hash values are actually 2^{32} wide, so information should be distributed evenly across all array members.

The hashing algorithm is part of the CARP definition so that all downstream servers that are CARP aware can determine where information will be stored. Clients that confirm to the industry-standard client Proxy Auto-Config (PAC) file can also hash to determine where information will be stored locally and which array member to solicit. Some of the advantages of CARP are:

- It uses algorithms on top of HTTP to distribute caching and to locate where URLs are and will be stored without having to maintain a list of stored URLs and their locations. Queries do not have to be performed to locate information, so efficiency is increased, network traffic is decreased, and scalability is achieved in multiple Proxy Server environments.

- Storage of Internet objects is more efficient because only one array member will store a URL locally rather than several Proxy Servers storing the same information, which can happen with ICP.

- It auto-tunes and recovers from the loss of an array member. Since the array member list is regularly updated by each member, each member

11

of an array knows of and removes downed members when they don't respond or are removed from an array. The hashing method determines where URLs will be stored.

- No new protocol is implemented. The CARP technique uses HTTP and is compatible with existing firewalls and other Proxy Servers.

- Clients can take part in CARP and can determine the location in which information will be stored locally. Since CARP can be implemented in the client PAC, each client can be configured to take advantage of CARP.

The status of each array member can easily be checked through any browser by typing "http://*membername*/array.dll?Get.Info.v1".

The information that is displayed will include the proxy array name, the member list Time-to-Live (TTL), and a copy of the list, which includes:

- The proxy array member's computer name.

- The IP address of the computer. If multiple IP addresses are defined, the address displayed will be the address used for proxy member communications.

- The TCP port number used for communications by array members. Note that, by default, the port that is used is the same port used by the HTTP protocol.

- The URL for ARRAY.DLL.

- The version of Proxy Server the member is running.

- How long the array member has been in its current operational state. This number is counted in seconds.

- The array member's current operational state. If a member server is not available, the operational state will be displayed as down.

- The load factor of the array member. This is a percentage based on the normal load, and by default, it is set to 100. This number is used in the hashing algorithm to help determine workload and where items will be cached.

- The cache size on the member server (in MB).

The information you receive will be similar to the following:

Proxy Array Information/1.0

ArrayEnabled: 1

ConfigID: 891315414

ArrayName: monkey

ListTTL: 3000

ANDY 10.1.1.1 80 http://ANDY:80/array.dll MSProxy/2.0 50161 Up 100 100

NTS 192.168.1.109 80 http://NTS:80/array.dll MSProxy/2.0 50161 Up 100 100

In this example, the monkey array is made up of two members which have two computers named Andy and NTS. The IP address of each is displayed along with vital statistics on how long each machine has been up and the cache size.

Array members can also be configured to route inside the array before they pass a request to an upstream router. This helps to increase overall efficiency by resolving more requests locally. To configure an array member to route requests within the array before forwarding the request to an upstream router:

1. From Internet Service Manager, select the computer name next to the Web Proxy Service icon for the computer to be configured.

2. Select Service Properties from the Properties menu. The Web Proxy Service Properties dialog box for the computer being modified opens.

3. Select the Routing tab. Select Resolve Web Proxy Requests Within Array Before Routing Upstream (under Routing Within Array). Click on the Apply button.

Requests that cannot be filled by the array member first contacted can now be resolved by other array members before the request is routed to an upstream Proxy Server. Requests will be resolved locally by an array member rather than routed to other Proxy Servers or to the Internet.

11

LOAD BALANCING MULTIPLE SERVERS

Load balancing is the act of making sure that clients are evenly dispersed across all available Proxy Servers in a proxy array, and there are several ways to do this. Web Proxy clients can be configured to route traffic across more than one gateway, but the WinSock service is configured to use only a specific gateway.

The best way to balance the workload for WinSock clients is to manually configure each client to go to specific Proxy Servers. If you have a particular group that uses the Internet frequently, try to identify and configure them so they use different Proxy Servers.

Web Proxy Server clients can be evenly distributed across all available Proxy Servers by using a Domain Name System (DNS) server and creating a CNAME resource record for each Proxy Server on your network. To do this, configure your DNS server by adding a CNAME resource record for each Proxy Server you want to distribute the client load across. Make sure each entry has the unique IP address for each Proxy Server but the same alias name. The DNS server will use a round robin method of providing name resolution to each client. This will evenly distribute the clients across all Proxy Servers.

When you use a DNS server to distribute clients evenly across all of the proxy servers, you don't take into account the physical location of each client. To distribute the workload in a network with multiple physical segments, or one that uses routers and WAN technology, it's more efficient to add multihomed entries in the WINS database for each proxy server.

In the Windows Internet Name Service (WINS) server, add a static multihomed entry for each proxy server computer that you want to distribute the workload across, using the same name for each entry. When a client requests the name of a Proxy Server, WINS will first attempt to provide the IP address of a Proxy Server that is local to the client. If the WINS server cannot provide an IP address for Proxy Server on the local subnet of the client, it will provide the address of a Proxy Server on the same network. Finally, the WINS server will provide the IP address of any Proxy Server. This configuration will provide the client with a local Proxy Server and better distribute the workload of each Proxy Server without generating excess network traffic.

Routes

Another way to share the cached information of multiple proxy servers is to route requests through them. This is known as *proxy chaining*, and in this configuration, not all proxy servers have to be running Microsoft Proxy Server 2.0.

In *hierarchical proxying* (Figure 11.3), individual proxy server computers or arrays are "chained" together. The communications path is hierarchical in structure rather than peer-to-peer as it is in distributed proxying. The Internet is the top of the communications path, and the client is the bottom. The Proxy Server computers or arrays in between are considered *upstream proxy servers* if they are above the other proxy server in the communications path. The lower proxy servers in the structure are known as *downstream proxy servers*. Hierarchical proxying is also referred to as *proxy chaining* or *cascaded proxying*. Hierarchical proxying provides load balancing and improved cache performance, but it doesn't offer fault tolerance. Microsoft Proxy Server 2.0 can be chained with Microsoft Proxy Server 1.0 computers as well as third-party proxy servers and firewalls.

Multiple proxy servers can be configured for either chaining or distributed proxying or a combination of both. With chaining, if a proxy server cannot fulfill a client request, it will pass the request to an upstream proxy server. If the upstream proxy server cannot fulfill the client's request, the request is passed to the Internet. Every proxy server computer in the chain is its own entity, and information about chained proxy servers is not passed between proxy servers.

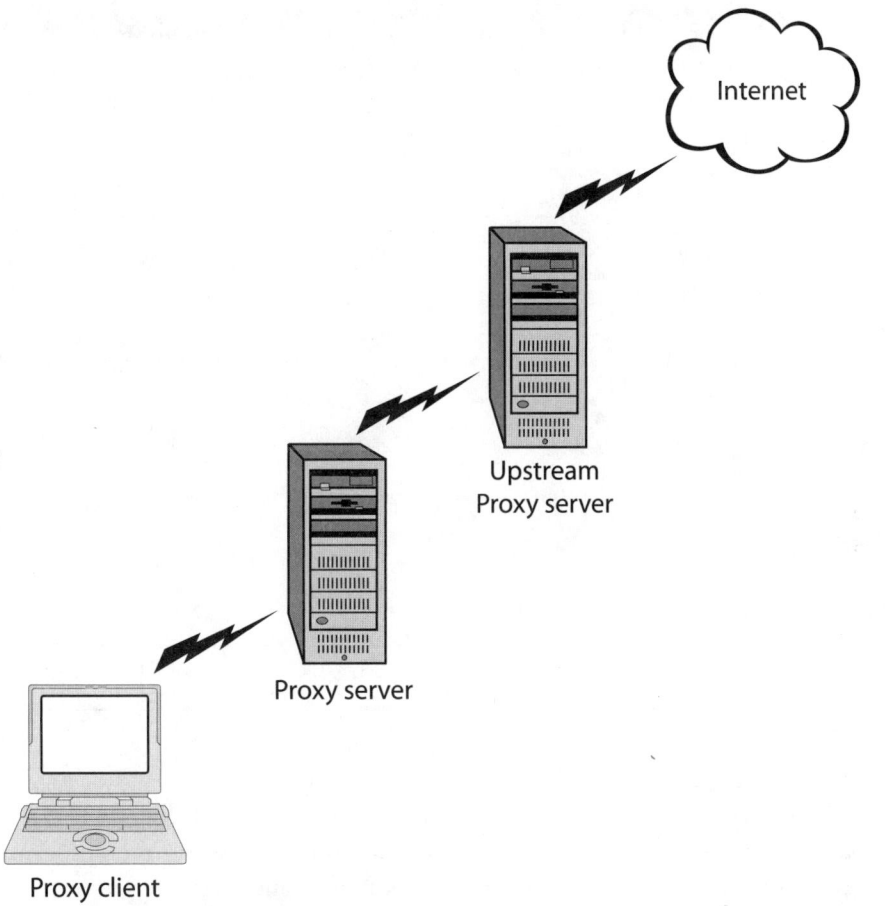

Figure 11.3   Hierarchical proxying.

With upstream routing, a primary upstream route can be configured; you can also configure a secondary or backup upstream route in the event the primary upstream router is unavailable. To configure an upstream router, follow these steps:

1. In Internet Service Manager (ISM), select the Web Proxy service for the computer for which you are configuring an upstream route. Select Service Properties from the Properties menu. The Web Proxy Service Properties dialog box appears.

2. Select the Routing tab. Select Use Web Proxy Or Array in the Upstream Routing area. The Modify button becomes active and you can configure an upstream proxy server or array. The Enable Backup Route option also becomes active, and you can configure an upstream backup route (see Figure 11.4).

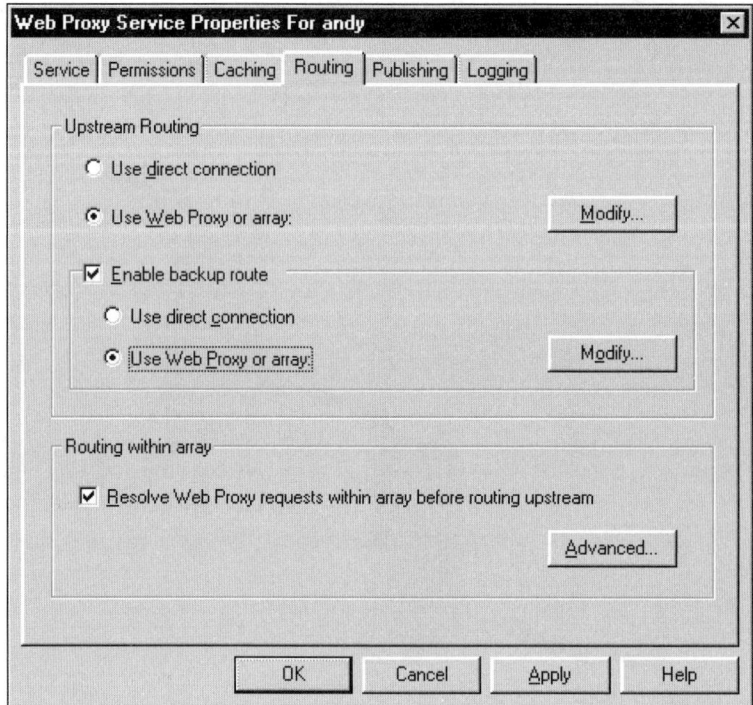

Figure 11.4 The Proxy Server Routing tab.

The Use Direct Connection option can be selected if you want the request routed directly to the Internet. While you are configuring the upstream Proxy Server, you can configure your Proxy Server to automatically gather proxy array information for the upstream array membership. You can also provide a valid username and password to be used for authentication by the upstream proxy server (if the proxy server is not a Microsoft Proxy Server, or if it is in a different domain).

In a proxy array, which is distributed proxying, the array acts as one logical entity and each array member shares information about its configuration with other array members. When a client makes a request, the request goes to the configured array member. If the array member doesn't have the requested object, a hash function is performed to determine the array member on which the object would be stored, and the request is forwarded to that array member. If that array member doesn't have the object, the request is passed to an upstream Proxy Server (if configured) and then forwarded to the Internet.

Some of the error messages that indicate problems with upstream routers are listed here (note these errors will appear in the system log and can be viewed with the Event Viewer):

- **130** The Web Proxy service detected that the upstream proxy *servername* is down.

- **131** The Web Proxy service detected that the upstream proxy *servername* is back up.

- **139** Proxy server *servername* requires proxy to proxy authentication. Proxy server *servername* is not configured to do so.

- **141** Proxy server detected a proxy chain loop. Please check the proxy server routing configuration on all chained proxies.

Most of the errors that are indicated are self-explanatory. If there is an array of Proxy Server computers, or if the Proxy Servers are chained, a user account and password that are valid on that Proxy Server must be used to provide access rights. If those rights have not been configured for a particular Proxy Server, an Error 139 will occur (the rights are configured by using the Advanced Routing options found under the Routing tab in the Web Proxy Server Properties dialog box). For Error 141, the Proxy Servers are configured as being upstream from each other, thus creating a loop.

SINGLE AND MULTIPLE WINDOWS NT DOMAINS

When the network that the proxy array supports is spread over a large geographical area, as is typically the case in a multiple-domain environment, the preferred method to discover a member of a proxy array is through the WINS service.

As noted previously, DNS uses a round robin method to provide the address of an array member to the client, whereas the WINS server service attempts to provide the IP address of the array member that is closest to the client.

The DNS method of distributing the client workload might provide the client with the IP address of an array member that is not located on the client's local subnet, which could have a negative impact on overall network performance.

In a single domain environment, the same user account can be used for authentication on all Microsoft Proxy Server 2.0 computers. If your Proxy Servers span multiple domains, a valid user account and password for each Proxy Server computer must be configured in order for the Proxy Server in an array or chain to operate properly. This is configured in the Advanced Options dialog box on the Routing tab of the Web Proxy Server Properties dialog box. To configure a user account to use for authentication, follow these steps:

1. From Internet Service Manager, double-click on the computer name next to the Web Proxy service icon for the computer you wish to configure. The Web Proxy Service Properties dialog box opens.

11

2. Select the Routing tab, which gives you access to the routing configuration information. The Upstream Routing Modify button allows you to add a user account and password for the Proxy Server you are configuring for access to an upstream Proxy Server. The Advanced button under Routing Within Array allows you to configure a user account and password to use when working within an array.

Two of the more common errors that will occur when user account authentication is not configured properly are 139 and 149, which were explained earlier.

CHAPTER SUMMARY

In this chapter, you learned the terminology Microsoft uses to describe multiple proxy server environments. You also learned how to configure Proxy Server arrays and routing. When you route requests for Internet objects through arrays or chained proxy servers, you are attempting to locate a locally cached Internet object rather than request it from an Internet-based computer. If the object cannot be found, the request will be forwarded to an Internet-based computer. This provides the proxy clients with the ability to quickly retrieve commonly requested URLs and helps to alleviate some of the traffic that is typically created when the Internet is accessed.

Two basic configurations that can be used within a multiple Proxy Server environment. The first is a peer-to-peer, or distributed, configuration known as an array. In this type of configuration, multiple Microsoft Proxy Server 2.0 computers can be logically connected to share each other's cache area by creating one logical cache out of all available storage. The algorithm that determines where data will actually be stored uses a method known as *hashing*, where data from the URL and each Proxy Server computer in the array is combined, and the computer with the highest combination is used to store the information. All proxy array members must be running Microsoft Proxy Server 2.0.

The second basic structure that can be used is a hierarchical structure known as chained proxy or proxy cascading. Proxy chaining is accomplished by configuring routes through various proxy servers in an attempt to locate locally stored data. The proxy servers that are receiving requests are known as upstream proxy servers, and the proxy server computers that are forwarding requests are known as downstream proxy servers. Any proxy server can be configured as an upstream proxy server, and it does not have to be running Microsoft Proxy Server 2.0. In a chained proxy environment, the proxy server computers need not communicate to pass configuration information.

The Cache Array Routing Protocol (CARP) was developed for and is used by Microsoft Proxy Server 2.0 computers to allow Proxy Servers in an array to communicate. CARP is not a protocol that has to be configured in routers and firewalls because it "rides" on top of the HTTP protocol. CARP also provides greater scalability in large install base Proxy Server environments because cached data isn't discovered by querying different Proxy Server computers; instead, it is located by performing a hash function. The hash function combines URL data with array member data to determine where information will be stored in the array.

In a multiple-domain environment, a valid user account and password must be used to establish communications between Proxy Servers in an array and between upstream and downstream Proxy Servers. Some best practices are as follows:

- Configure clients to use a proxy server array rather than a single Proxy Server. This provides the client with better proxy performance and fault tolerance.

- If possible, all of the Proxy Servers should be members of the same domain. This makes the authentication process much easier to configure and provides another layer of protection against unauthorized external detection of your internal network.

- Use WINS rather than DNS to distribute client workload. WINS will attempt to provide the client with the IP address of the closest Proxy Server, whereas DNS will use a round robin approach to distribute workload, with no regard to physical location of the client.

- If all Proxy Servers are running Microsoft Proxy Server 2.0, create a distributed proxying environment rather than a chained proxy environment by setting up a proxy array. This provides better overall support for the proxy client.

- If there are multiple administrators assigned to modify Proxy Server configuration in an array, assign times when each administrator can perform administrative tasks to avoid synchronization conflicts.

- If only one administrator is responsible for maintaining and configuring a Proxy Server array, modify only one Proxy Server array member at a time to avoid synchronization conflicts.

11

KEY TERMS

- **Cache Array Routing Protocol (CARP)**—A communication method that rides on top of the HTTP protocol to allow inter-Proxy-Server communications. This protocol was introduced with Microsoft Proxy Server 2.0 to allow efficient communications between Proxy Servers and to provide a method of queryless location of cached information in a multiple Proxy Server environment.

- **cascaded proxying**—In a multiple proxy server environment, a method of passing requests not found on one proxy server computer to an upstream proxy server computer. This is also known as hierarchical proxying or proxy chaining.

- **distributed proxying**—In a multiple Proxy Server environment, a method of logically connecting Proxy Server computers and associated cache so Internet objects are only stored one time and all members of the array will know where the object is stored. This provides the client with a higher percentage of "hits" when it is attempting to find objects stored locally and better utilizes the cache storage space. This configuration is also known as a proxy array. Members of an array must be running Microsoft Proxy Server 2.0.

- **Domain Name System (DNS) Server**—An industry-standard server that resolves host names to IP addresses.

- **hashing**—The method that determines where information will be stored in a proxy array. Proxy Server computer information is hashed and combined with hashed URL information. This is done for each array member. The member with the highest combined total stores the information.

- **hierarchical proxying**—In a multiple proxy server environment, a method of passing requests not found on one proxy server computer to an upstream proxy server computer. This is also known as chained proxying or cascaded proxying.

- **Internet Cache Protocol (ICP)**—A protocol developed in 1995 that allows Proxy Servers to "query" other Proxy Servers in an attempt to locate locally stored Internet objects.

- **Proxy Auto-Config (PAC) file**—An industry-standard file used to configure proxy clients. It allows clients rather than just proxy servers to take advantage of single-hop resolution.

- **proxy chaining**—In a multiple proxy server environment, a method of passing requests not found on one proxy server computer to an upstream proxy server computer. This is also known as chained proxying or cascaded proxying.

- **Windows Internet Name Service (WINS)**—A non-industry-standard service that resolves NetBIOS names to IP addresses. A Microsoft computer name is an example of a NetBIOS name, and WINS is the Microsoft NetBIOS name service that ships with the Microsoft Windows NT Server product.

REVIEW QUESTIONS

1. You need to create a proxy array between two Microsoft Proxy Server 2.0 computers. You would configure the array from which of the following?
   a. the Routing tab of the Web Proxy Service Properties dialog box
   b. the Caching tab of the Web Proxy Service Properties dialog box
   c. the Service tab of the SOCKS Proxy Service Properties dialog box
   d. the Protocols tab of the WinSock Proxy Server Properties dialog box

2. You are configuring an upstream Proxy Server on your Proxy Server computer and need to provide a valid user account and password for the proxy server. You would configure this from which of the following?
   a. the Service tab of the SOCKS Proxy Service Properties dialog box
   b. the Service tab of the WinSock Proxy Service Properties dialog box
   c. the Service tab of the Web Proxy Service Properties dialog box
   d. the Routing tab of the Web Proxy Service Properties dialog box

3. You are in the process of making changes to your Proxy Server, which is a member of a proxy array. While you are making the changes, but before you have saved them, you get an error message in a dialog box that will allow you to refresh or overwrite. What has happened?
   a. You have attempted to perform a configuration operation without having proper user permissions.
   b. Someone has made configuration changes to another Proxy Server array member and saved them while you were making changes to your array member.
   c. You have made configuration changes and saved them while someone else was making configuration changes.
   d. Some else is attempting to make configuration changes to the same array member at the same time you are.

4. CARP is the Cache Array Routing Protocol introduced with Microsoft Proxy Server 2.0. It provides greatly expanded scalability and efficiency by allowing queryless distributed caching. (True or False?)

11

5. Select the definition that best describes a proxy array.
   a. a multiple Proxy Server computer environment with a hierarchical structure
   b. a multiple Proxy Server computer environment with a distributed structure
   c. a single Proxy Server computer environment with a hierarchical structure
   d. a single Proxy Server computer environment with a distributed structure

6. Which answer is not true in a proxy array environment?
   a. A proxy array environment can integrate Microsoft Proxy Server 2.0 with other third-party proxy server products.
   b. Proxy arrays provide fault tolerance because Web Proxy clients can be configured to connect to a Proxy Server array rather than connect to a single Proxy Server computer.
   c. DNS can be configured to distribute proxy client workload.
   d. All array members can be configured to automatically update each other when configuration changes are made.

7. You have just configured a Proxy Server array member and saved the changes. A message appears on the screen asking if you would like to synchronize now or cancel. What has happened?
   a. You have attempted to perform a configuration operation without having proper user permissions.
   b. You have made configuration changes and saved them at the same time someone else has made configuration changes and saved them.
   c. Some else is attempting to make configuration changes to the same array member at the same time you are.
   d. Someone has made configuration changes to another Proxy Server array member and saved them while you were making changes to your array member.

8. Select all answers that do not apply to a chained proxy server environment.
   a. Provides better client response for Internet requests by filling more client requests locally.
   b. Has a hierarchical structure.
   c. Has a distributed structure.
   d. Updates upstream and downstream proxy server computers.
   e. Third-party proxy servers can act as upstream proxy servers.

9. In a Proxy Server array, not all information is replicated to each proxy member. Select the information that is not replicated to all proxy array members.

    a. a list of cached items

    b. Web Proxy cache size

    c. Web Proxy service protocol information

    d. Local Address Table (LAT) information

10. You have three Microsoft Proxy Server 2.0 computers that form a proxy array and one upstream Proxy Server to which requests are routed in the event an array member cannot fulfill a client request. All four Proxy Server computers are configured to provide 150MB of cache space. What is the proxy array's potential cache space?

    a. 450MB

    b. 600MB

    c. 150MB

    d. 300MB

11. Members of your support staff call and tell you that, while modifying an array member, they received a message stating they could refresh or overwrite changes, yet they had not applied any changes. What caused this?

    a. They were making changes to an array member and applied the changes, and someone else made changes to a different array member and applied the changes.

    b. They were making changes to an array member and applied the changes, and someone else made changes to a different array member and hadn't applied the changes.

    c. They were making changes to an array member but hadn't applied the changes, and someone else made changes to a different array member and did apply the changes.

    d. They were making changes to an array member but hadn't applied the changes, and someone else made changes to a different array member and hadn't applied the changes.

12. The hash function takes certain URL information that has been hashed and combines it with certain proxy array member computer information to determine at which upstream computer a site will be cached. (True or False?)

11

13. Which of the following statements are true about proxy arrays?

    a. Proxy Server arrays provide fault tolerance to clients.

    b. Proxy Server arrays will be slower than a single proxy server in providing clients with requested Internet information.

    c. Proxy Server arrays provide no fault tolerance to clients.

    d. Proxy Server arrays will be faster than a single Proxy Server in providing clients with requested Internet information.

14. You are at a client's computer troubleshooting a problem and want to get the status of the Proxy Server that should be servicing this client as well as the status of all the Proxy Servers in an array. What is the easiest way to do this?

    a. Call one of your other network support staff members and ask him or her to open Internet Service Manager and to check the status of each array member.

    b. In Control Panel, open the Proxy Server applet from the client machine and view the information.

    c. While in the client's Web browser, type "http://*membername*/array.dll?GetInfo.v1".

    d. Return to your machine, open Internet Service Manager, and view each Proxy Server computer in the array.

15. Which of the following has been implemented with Microsoft Proxy Server 2.0, runs on top of the HTTP protocol, and is an integral part of the proxy array environment's capability?

    a. RARP

    b. CARP

    c. HASH

    d. TCP

16. Which description best defines a proxy array?

    a. a distributed single Proxy Server environment with multiple clients that connect to a specific Proxy Server when accessing the Internet

    b. a hierarchical-structured multiple Proxy Server environment that provides better client response when accessing the Internet

    c. a hierarchical proxy client configuration that allows clients to connect to a Proxy Server through proxy clients

    d. a distributed, peer-to-peer-type multiple Proxy Server configuration that provides fault tolerance and better client response for the client when accessing the Internet

17. Using DNS to provide load balancing does take into account which of the following?

  a. the physical location of the client with respect to the Proxy Server

  b. the volume of Internet traffic the client generates

  c. the order in which the proxy servers show up when the DNS server provides resolution to the client

  d. how much cache is available on each Proxy Server in an array

18. Using WINS to provide load balancing does take into account which of the following?

  a. the physical location of the client with respect to the Proxy Server

  b. the volume of Internet traffic the client generates

  c. the order in which the Proxy Servers show up when the DNS server provides resolution to the client

  d. how much cache is available on each Proxy Server in an array

19. You are updating a Proxy Server array member and a Synchronization Conflict message appears giving you the choice to synchronize now or cancel. What does this indicate?

  a. You were making changes to an array member and applied the changes, and someone else made changes to a different array member and applied the changes.

  b. You were making changes to an array member but hadn't applied the changes, and someone else made changes to a different array member and did apply the changes.

  c. You were making changes to an array member and applied the changes, and someone else made changes to a different array member and hadn't applied the changes.

  d. You were making changes to an array member but hadn't applied the changes, and someone else made changes to a different array member and hadn't applied the changes.

20. You receive an error message that asks if you wish to refresh or overwrite while you are making changes to an array member. What will happen to your changes if you select Refresh?

  a. Your changes will be integrated with the changes made by the other array member.

  b. All changes you made will be discarded.

  c. Your changes will overwrite the changes made by the other array member.

  d. Your changes will be saved and implemented after the array is synchronized.

11

21. Select the answer that best describes the role of hashing in a Proxy Server array environment.

    a. Hashing is the method DNS uses to distribute clients evenly to all Proxy Server clients.

    b. Hash is the protocol used by array members to communicate.

    c. Hashing is performed on all available array members and on the URL the client requests. The array member with the highest hashed total is used to cache the Internet site locally.

    d. Hash is the protocol used by downstream clients to access upstream Proxy Servers.

22. You need to add a Proxy Server to an existing proxy array. You could accomplish this from which of the following?

    a. the Caching tab of the Web Proxy Service Properties dialog box

    b. the Service tab of the Web Proxy Service Properties dialog box

    c. the Service tab of the SOCKS Proxy Service Properties dialog box

    d. the Service tab of the WinSock Proxy Service Properties dialog box

23. Which of the following best describes a chained proxy environment?

    a. a hierarchical proxy client configuration that allows clients to connect to a proxy server through proxy clients

    b. a distributed, peer-to-peer-type multiple proxy server configuration that provides fault tolerance and better client response for the client when accessing the Internet

    c. a proxy server configured to respond to requests from the Internet and to forward them to an IIS server located on the internal network

    d. a hierarchical-structured multiple proxy server environment that provides better client response when accessing the Internet

24. Proxy chaining, cascade proxying, and hierarchical proxying all describe which of the following?

    a. a multiple proxy server computer environment configured as a proxy array

    b. a multiple proxy server computer environment configured for proxy routing

    c. a single proxy server computer environment configured as a proxy array

    d. a single proxy server computer environment configured for proxy routing

25. You want to distribute clients evenly across all array members on your local area network. You have decided to use the Microsoft DNS Server service to define all of your proxy array members and to provide IP address resolution to the array in a round robin fashion. How would you configure the DNS server?

   a. Make a PROXYA resource record and add the IP address of each array member to the record.

   b. Do nothing at all. Proxy Server will automatically add resource records to the DNS server for you when the Proxy Server registers with the WINS server.

   c. Make an A-type resource record for each array member and select the Enable Round Robin selection box under DNS Properties.

   d. Make CNAME resource records with one name and the IP addresses of each array member

HANDS-ON PROJECTS

In these projects, you will use Internet Service Manager to configure two Proxy Server computers to form an array. You will then use a Web browser to view array information. Finally, you will break the proxy array. You'll need two computers connected together on a network and running Microsoft Proxy Server 2.0 to complete these projects.

 **PROJECT 11.1**

To configure an array between two Proxy Server computers, follow these steps:

   1. From Internet Service Manager, double-click the Web Proxy service for the computer you wish to configure. The Web Proxy Service Properties dialog box opens.

   2. Click on the Array button on the Service tab. The Array dialog box appears.

   3. To form an array with another Microsoft Proxy Server 2.0 computer, click on the Join Array button. You'll be prompted to provide the name of the computer with which you wish to form an array. After communications has been established with the other Microsoft Proxy Server 2.0 computer, you are able to expand the array by providing the name of a third Microsoft Proxy Server 2.0 computer. The two Microsoft Proxy Server 2.0 computers that formed the array will be listed, and the status for each machine will be shown.

4. Click on OK to accept the configuration. This will return you to the Web Proxy Service Properties dialog box. Click on Apply to implement the proxy array configuration.

5. Click on the Array button on the Service tab of the Web Proxy Service Properties dialog box. The Array dialog box appears. Note that the Synchronize Configuration Of Array Members option box is available. This option box is only available when there are no pending changes for the Join, Remove, or Leave buttons.

 PROJECT 11.2

To view the array configuration information using a Web browser, follow these steps:

1. Open Microsoft Internet Explorer. Type "http://*servername*/array.dll?GetInfo.v1" in the address line and press Enter. Replace "servername" with the name of one of your two Proxy Servers. The configuration information and operation status of the array members appear.

2. Type "http://*servername*/array.dll?GetInfo.v1" in the address line and press Enter. Replace "servername" with the name of the second of your two Proxy Servers.

Compare the information in each window. Note any changes to the information.

 PROJECT 11.3

To remove a Proxy Server computer from an array, follow these steps:

1. From Internet Service Manager, select the Web Proxy service for the computer you wish to configure and select Service Properties from the Properties menu. The Web Proxy Service Properties dialog box appears.

2. Click on the Array button on the Service tab. The Array dialog box appears.

3. Click on the Leave Array button in the Array dialog box. A warning box appears asking if you are sure you wish to leave the array. If there are only two members in the array, a message box will appear stating that both Proxy Servers will act as standalone Proxy Servers if this action is taken.

4. Click on Yes to accept the change. The Web Proxy Service Properties dialog box appears. Click on OK to close the dialog box.

CASE PROJECTS

1. You administer a 2,000-client network. Your internal network uses TCP/IP for intranet communications. All of your clients use Proxy Servers to access the Internet. Each Proxy Server is a Pentium Pro 233 with 128MB of RAM and an 8GB hard disk. The hard disk has two 4GB partitions, both NTFS. The second partition is used strictly for Proxy Server cache storage. There is a Proxy Server on each physical network at your site. You use both WINS and DNS on your internal network to provide host and NetBIOS name resolution. You want to provide your clients with the quickest response to Internet requests and to use your cache space as efficiently as possible, but you don't want to increase internal network traffic.

   Required result: Clients must be configured to connect to the Proxy Server on their physical subnet if it's available.

   Optional desired results: Share proxy cache to provide optimum use of cache storage space. Provide the clients with fault tolerance in the event the Proxy Server on their physical segment is down.

   Proposed solution: Configure DNS with a CNAME resource record for each Proxy Server on your network. Use the same alias name for each record and the IP address of each Proxy Server. Which results does the proposed solution produce?

   a. The proposed solution produces the required result and both of the optional desired results.

   b. The proposed solution produces the required result but only one of the optional desired results.

   c. The proposed solution produces the required result but neither of the optional desired results.

   d. The proposed solution does not produce the required result.

2. You administer a 2,000-client network. Your internal network uses TCP/IP for intranet communications. All of your clients use Proxy Servers to access the Internet. Each Proxy Server is a Pentium Pro 233 with 128MB of RAM and an 8GB hard disk. The hard disk has two 4GB partitions, both NTFS. The second partition is used strictly for Proxy Server cache storage. There is a Proxy Server on each physical network at your site. You use both WINS and DNS on your internal network to provide host and NetBIOS name resolution. You want to provide your clients with the quickest response to Internet requests and to use your cache space as efficiently as possible, but you don't want to increase internal network traffic.

11

Required result: Clients must be configured to connect to the Proxy Server on their physical subnet if it's available.

Optional desired results: Share proxy cache to provide optimum use of cache storage space. Provide the clients with fault tolerance in the event the Proxy Server on their physical segment is down.

Proposed solution: Configure WINS with a multihomed entry for each Proxy Server on your network. Make sure each client is configured to use WINS for name resolution. Which results does the proposed solution produce?

   a. The proposed solution produces the required result and both of the optional desired results.

   b. The proposed solution produces the required result but only one of the optional desired results.

   c. The proposed solution produces the required result but neither of the optional desired results.

   d. The proposed solution does not produce the required result.

3. You administer a 2,000-client network. Your internal network uses TCP/IP for intranet communications. All of your clients use Proxy Servers to access the Internet. Each Proxy Server is a Pentium Pro 233 with 128MB of RAM and an 8GB hard disk. The hard disk has two 4GB partitions, both NTFS. The second partition is used strictly for Proxy Server cache storage. There is a Proxy Server on each physical network at your site. You use both WINS and DNS on your internal network to provide host and NetBIOS name resolution. You want to provide your clients with the quickest response to Internet requests and to use your cache space as efficiently as possible, but you don't want to increase internal network traffic.

Required result: Clients must be configured to connect to the Proxy Server on their physical subnet if it's available.

Optional desired results: Share proxy cache to provide optimum use of cache storage space. Provide the clients with fault tolerance in the event the Proxy Server on their physical segment is down.

Proposed solution: Configure DNS with a CNAME resource record for each Proxy Server on your network. Use the same alias name for each record and the IP address of each Proxy Server. Configure all of the Proxy Servers on the network to form a proxy array. Which results does the proposed solution produce?

   a. The proposed solution produces the required result and both of the optional desired results.

   b. The proposed solution produces the required result but only one of the optional desired results.

    c. The proposed solution produces the required result but neither of the optional desired results.

    d. The proposed solution does not produce the required result.

4. You administer a 2,000-client network. Your internal network uses TCP/IP for intranet communications. All of your clients use Proxy Servers to access the Internet. Each Proxy Server is a Pentium Pro 233 with 128MB of RAM and an 8GB hard disk. The hard disk has two 4GB partitions, both NTFS. The second partition is used strictly for Proxy Server cache storage. There is a Proxy Server on each physical network at your site. You use both WINS and DNS on your internal network to provide host and NetBIOS name resolution. You want to provide your clients with the quickest response to Internet requests and to use your cache space as efficiently as possible, but you don't want to increase internal network traffic.

   Required result: Clients must be configured to connect to the Proxy Server on their physical subnet if it's available.

   Optional desired results: Share proxy cache to provide optimum use of cache storage space. Provide the clients with fault tolerance in the event the Proxy Server on their physical segment is down.

   Proposed solution: Configure WINS with a multihomed entry for each Proxy Server on your network. Configure a proxy array using all Proxy Servers on your network. Configure the client to use WINS for name resolution. Which results does the proposed solution produce?

   a. The proposed solution produces the required result and both of the optional desired results.

   b. The proposed solution produces the required result but only one of the optional desired results.

   c. The proposed solution produces the required result but neither of the optional desired results.

   d. The proposed solution does not produce the required result.

5. You administer a 2,000-client network. Your internal network uses TCP/IP for intranet communications. All of your clients use Proxy Servers to access the Internet. Each Proxy Server is a Pentium Pro 233 with 128MB of RAM and an 8GB hard disk. The hard disk has two 4GB partitions, both NTFS. The second partition is used strictly for Proxy Server cache storage. There is a Proxy Server on each physical network at your site. You use both WINS and DNS on your internal network to provide host and NetBIOS name resolution. You want to provide your clients with the quickest response to Internet requests and to use your cache space as efficiently as possible, but you don't want to increase internal network traffic.

11

Required result: Make optimal use of available cache storage.

Optional desired results: Clients should be configured to connect to the Proxy Server on their physical subnet if it's available. Provide the clients with fault tolerance in the event the Proxy Server on their physical segment is down.

Proposed solution: Configure all Proxy Servers into a proxy array. Which results does the proposed solution produce?

   a. The proposed solution produces the required result and both of the optional desired results.

   b. The proposed solution produces the required result but only one of the optional desired results.

   c. The proposed solution produces the required result but neither of the optional desired results.

   d. The proposed solution does not produce the required result.

6. You administer a 2,000-client network. Your internal network uses TCP/IP for intranet communications. All of your clients use Proxy Servers to access the Internet. Each Proxy Server is a Pentium Pro 233 with 128MB of RAM and an 8GB hard disk. The hard disk has two 4GB partitions, both NTFS. The second partition is used strictly for Proxy Server cache storage. There is a Proxy Server on each physical network at your site. You use both WINS and DNS on your internal network to provide host and NetBIOS name resolution. You want to provide your clients with the quickest response to Internet requests and to use your cache space as efficiently as possible, but you don't want to increase internal network traffic.

Required result: Make optimal use of available cache storage.

Optional desired results: Clients should be configured to connect to the Proxy Server on their physical subnet if it's available. Provide the clients with fault tolerance in the event the Proxy Server on their physical segment is down.

Proposed solution: Configure each Proxy Server with an upstream proxy server. Which results does the proposed solution produce?

   a. The proposed solution produces the required result and both of the optional desired results.

   b. The proposed solution produces the required result but only one of the optional desired results.

   c. The proposed solution produces the required result but neither of the optional desired results.

   d. The proposed solution does not produce the required result.

7. You administer a 2,000-client network. Your internal network uses TCP/IP for intranet communications. All of your clients use Proxy Servers to access the Internet. Each Proxy Server is a Pentium Pro 233 with 128MB of RAM and an 8GB hard disk. The hard disk has two 4GB partitions, both

NTFS. The second partition is used strictly for Proxy Server cache storage. There is a Proxy Server on each physical network at your site. You use both WINS and DNS on your internal network to provide host and NetBIOS name resolution. You want to provide your clients with the quickest response to Internet requests and to use your cache space as efficiently as possible, but you don't want to increase internal network traffic.

Required result: Make optimal use of available cache storage.

Optional desired results: Clients should be configured to connect to the Proxy Server on their physical subnet if it's available. Provide the clients with fault tolerance in the event the Proxy Server on their physical segment is down.

Proposed solution: Configure all Proxy Servers into an array. For the client configuration, configure each client to use a proxy computer name rather than a specific address. Use WINS for name resolution and add a multihomed entry for each Proxy Server computer. Which results does the proposed solution produce?

a. The proposed solution produces the required result and both of the optional desired results.

b. The proposed solution produces the required result but only one of the optional desired results.

c. The proposed solution produces the required result but neither of the optional desired results.

d. The proposed solution does not produce the required result.

8. You administer a 2,000-client network. Your internal network uses TCP/IP for intranet communications. All of your clients use Proxy Servers to access the Internet. Each Proxy Server is a Pentium Pro 233 with 128MB of RAM and an 8GB hard disk. The hard disk has two 4GB partitions, both NTFS. The second partition is used strictly for Proxy Server cache storage. There is a Proxy Server on each physical network at your site. You use both WINS and DNS on your internal network to provide host and NetBIOS name resolution. You want to provide your clients with the quickest response to Internet requests and to use your cache space as efficiently as possible, but you don't want to increase internal network traffic.

Required result: Clients must be configured to connect to the Proxy Server on their physical subnet. If it's not available, the client should connect directly to the Internet.

Optional desired results: Share proxy cache to provide optimum use of cache storage space. Provide an upstream router for the proxy array.

Proposed solution: Configure all Proxy Servers into an array. For the client configuration, configure each client to use a proxy computer name rather than a specific address. Which results does the proposed solution produce?

a. The proposed solution produces the required result and both of the optional desired results.

b. The proposed solution produces the required result but only one of the optional desired results.

c. The proposed solution produces the required result but neither of the optional desired results.

d. The proposed solution does not produce the required result.

NETWORK ADDRESS TRANSLATION AND DNS ISSUES

The *Domain Name System (DNS)* and the *Windows Internet Name Service (WINS)* are used on networks to resolve names to addresses. Whereas WINS is used strictly in Windows environments, DNS is used to identify computers throughout the Internet. This chapter focuses on DNS and WINS and how they are used in a Proxy Server environment. We'll also discuss some Proxy-specific configuration considerations.

AFTER READING THIS CHAPTER AND COMPLETING THE EXERCISES, YOU WILL BE ABLE TO:

- Understand the Domain Name System, its role, and its structure

- Understand WINS and how it is used in a Microsoft network

- Understand Proxy Server load balancing and how it can be accomplished using DNS and WINS

THE DOMAIN NAME SYSTEM

As you know, all computers on the Internet are assigned IP addresses that they use to communicate with each other. As a conversation takes place between two computers, their IP addresses ensure that the data reaches the correct destination. But, as you also know, IP addresses can be confusing and difficult to remember. In the early days of the Advanced Research Projects Agency Network (ARPANet), it became necessary to develop a system to assign plain-language names to computers and to associate those names with IP addresses. The Domain Name System (DNS) was the eventual result, and it became the foundation of name resolution on the Internet. This system is a worldwide hierarchy administered by the Internet Network Information Center (InterNIC).

As you learned in Chapter 3, the Internet began as a Department of Defense project through the Advanced Research Projects Agency (ARPA) and was eventually named ARPANet. At that time, there were only a few dozen computers on the entire network and name resolution was handled by a file that was maintained on a single computer at the Stanford Research Institute (SRI). The file was called HOSTS.TXT, and it listed IP addresses in the left-hand column and computer names in the right-hand column. As the Internet grew, maintaining this single text file became an inefficient method for resolving computer names to IP addresses.

As a result of the network's growth, a distributed name resolution system called the Domain Name System was devised. DNS provides a method of name resolution that is similar to the HOSTS.TXT file, but it's more efficient. DNS does resolve computer names to IP addresses via manually configured files, but it uses a hierarchical database of names that is maintained across multiple computers. The hierarchical and distributed nature of DNS makes the system more efficient and easier to maintain than a single, massive text file.

The DNS history, concepts, and facilities are defined in Request for Comments (RFC) 1034, and RFC 1035 describes the implementation of DNS and the specification. These standards are accessed through the Standards section of the RFC editor at **www.isi.edu/rfc-editor/rfc.html**.

BIND

Berkeley Internet Name Domain (BIND) is a Domain Name System specification that was created at the University of California (UC), Berkeley. This implementation of DNS was originally written for Berkeley's 4.3 BSD Unix operating system and is currently the most popular implementation of DNS used today. BIND is, in fact, the basis for Microsoft's implementation of DNS, and consequently, Microsoft DNS supports BIND. However, it should be noted that BIND is not an official Internet specification and is not maintained as an RFC.

Windows NT supports the BIND specification through its BIND boot file, which is located in the %SYSTEM_ROOT%\SYSTEM32\DNS directory. The boot file is not required by Windows NT or DNS because DNS uses the settings in the Windows NT Registry. However, Windows NT will utilize the boot file to support BIND if instructed to do so through the Registry at HKEY_LOCAL_MACHINE\SYSTEM\CurrentControlSet\Services\DNS\Parameters. Microsoft recommends that this step only be taken when you are migrating from a BIND DNS system to the Microsoft DNS system.

One other caveat to using a BIND boot file: If you are migrating from a BIND system to Microsoft DNS, configure the DNS server to use the BIND boot file before you start the DNS Manager. Initializing the DNS Manager sets the DNS server to use the configuration settings in the Registry.

To use the boot file rather than the Registry settings, change the value in the EnableRegistryBoot key from 1 to 0. Then place the desired boot file in the %SYSTEM_ROOT%\SYSTEM32\DNS directory. Remember that, although this will initialize the DNS server from the BIND boot file, it should only be used to port an existing BIND boot file into the DNS configuration. To learn more about creating or maintaining a boot file, search on "The BIND boot file" in Microsoft TechNet.

THE DOMAIN NAME SPACE

The term *Domain Name Space* refers to the structure and data that create the distributed Domain Name System used on the Internet. This hierarchical system is made up of many levels, and many different computers are responsible for maintaining each piece of the hierarchy.

The top level of the hierarchy is called the root level; it contains (not surprisingly) the root name servers, which are maintained by the InterNIC. To provide complete name resolution, most DNS servers are configured with the IP addresses of these root servers. The next level contains the top-level domains, including com, net, org, edu, and several other name suffixes. The suffixes indicate country names or the types of domains that appear below them. For example, microsoft.com is a commercial organization, so it logically belongs under the com (commercial) group. The original seven domains (com, edu, gov, int, mil, net, and org) are often referred to as *generic domains*. Because the University of Texas is an educational institution, it is listed under the edu domain. There are domains that identify countries (such as uk for the United Kingdom or au for Australia). Many United States government agencies are starting to use the us domain to indicate the United States; however, this practice is not pervasive. Figure 12.1 shows a small sample of the Domain Name Space structure.

12

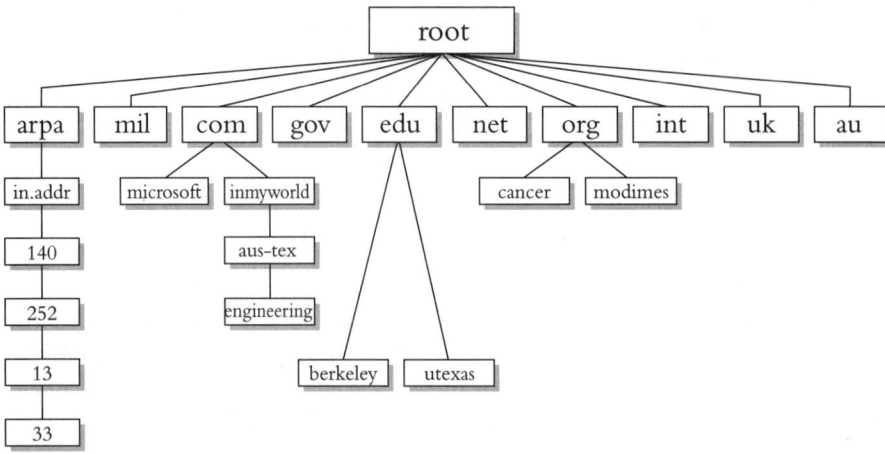

Figure 12.1   Part of the Domain Name Space structure.

Table 12.1 shows some of the domain suffixes in use today. Although it is a widely held belief that the original seven generic domains are for use only in the United States, there are many non-U.S. organizations that are part of the generic domains, and many U.S. organizations are part of the us domain.

Table 12.1   A portion of the top-level domains on the Internet.

Domain Suffix	Type
.com	Commercial organizations
.edu	Educational institutions
.gov	Government
.int	International organizations
.mil	Military operations
.net	Networking organizations
.org	Noncommercial organizations
.ae	United Arab Emirates
.us	United States
.uk	United Kingdom
.de	Germany
.au	Australia
.dz	Algeria
.bs	Bahamas
.cz	Czech Republic
.is	Iceland

In the Domain Name Space hierarchy, each computer is represented by a host name. The host name can be several layers deep in the hierarchical structure. For example, an FTP server at Microsoft could be (and in fact, is) named ftp.microsoft.com, or an email server in the engineering division in Austin, Texas, could be named pop3.engineering.aus-tx.inmyworld.com. No matter how long the name is, the host is an end point of the Domain Name Space hierarchical structure. This type of name is called a *Fully Qualified Domain Name (FQDN)* because it lists the full path through the hierarchy to the host.

Notice that an FQDN goes from the most-specific to the least-specific name. In the previous example FQDN, the "pop3" computer is in the engineering *subdomain* of the Austin, TX, subdomain under the inmyworld domain, and inmyworld is part of the commercial top-level domain. However, when you read the IP address for this computer, let's say 10.286.248.193, you actually read it from most general to most specific. For example, the address 10 belongs at the domain level and 193 identifies a specific computer on that network. This fact is important to remember when we discuss inverse name resolution (see "Inverse Queries" later in this chapter).

NAME RESOLUTION

As mentioned, the DNS name resolution process associates plain-language computer names to IP addresses so computers can use TCP/IP to communicate. Clients call a DNS server, and the DNS server attempts to provide complete name resolution services. As you'll learn in the following sections, if the DNS server cannot resolve an FQDN completely, it can collect additional information from other DNS servers to resolve the client's query.

In the DNS name resolution process, the client computer attempting to resolve a name is called the *resolver*. A server that provides name resolution services is known as a *name server*. The name server maintains a list of entries known as *resource records,* which map IP addresses to computer names.

 The term "resolver" actually refers to the software running on the client computer, rather than the computer itself. This software forwards name resolution requests to a name server.

NAME SERVER ROLES

There are actually four different roles that a name server can take, and any given name server may have multiple roles:

- A *primary name server* is responsible for a piece of the Domain Name Space hierarchy known as a zone. The information that creates the zone is maintained in a zone file that contains IP address-to-host name entries and other types of records, such as those identifying mail exchangers (email servers). The primary name server creates and maintains a given zone and is said to have authority for that zone. It also answers name resolution requests from resolvers.

- A *secondary name server* maintains a copy of the zone information it receives from the primary server or another secondary server. This allows a secondary server to provide redundancy for the zone's name list. A secondary name server reduces the load on the primary name server by answering name resolution requests from resolvers on the network. In addition, a secondary server provides fault tolerance for the zone by maintaining a copy of the zone list. For example, if the primary server experiences a critical hardware failure, the secondary server can continue resolving names because it has a copy of the list.

- A *master name server* is any name server that provides a zone list to a secondary name server. The process of copying a zone list is called a *zone transfer*. Because both primary name servers and secondary name servers can be configured to send zone transfers, either can be a master name server. Zone transfers are actually initiated by secondary name servers.

- A *caching-only name server* does just what its name implies—it caches name resolutions. The sole purpose of a caching-only name server is to increase the efficiency of name resolution. This type of name server does not keep a permanent zone list. A caching-only server resolves queries, often with the help of other name servers. However, once a caching-only name server resolves a query, it caches that name resolution; if another client asks for a name that has been resolved recently, the caching-only server can provide a name resolution immediately. Caching-only servers are useful when placed at the opposite ends of a slow wide area network (WAN) connection because they can answer resolver requests but do not require zone transfers.

NAME SERVER RESOLUTION

Name servers are not limited to their own databases and/or name caches when attempting to resolve name queries; they can also call on other name servers to assist in their resolution process. This enables the Domain Name Space hierarchy to work worldwide. For example, a name server in Australia can resolve the computer name of a host in North America by calling a name server (or several name servers, if necessary) in North America. In this hierarchical name resolution process, three types of queries are used: recursive, iterative, and inverse.

Recursive Queries

Recursive queries are most commonly issued by resolvers (clients). The resolver needs an absolute name resolution, which means that a complete IP address must be returned from the name server. For example, if a resolver wanted the IP address for the FTP server at the Microsoft site, it would send a recursive query to its name server asking, "What IP address corresponds to www.microsoft.com?" If the name server can't give the client a complete answer, then it must respond with a "bad IP address" message, which means the IP address is not available.

Iterative Queries

Iterative queries are most often used between name servers to obtain partial name resolutions. For example, a name server may not know the entire IP address for ftp.microsoft.com, but it might know the IP address for the name server that handles microsoft.com. In this way, the name resolution can occur in pieces. The original name server must do the legwork. It calls the name server for microsoft.com, which responds with the IP address for the FTP server. The client gets an absolute answer from the name server, but the resolution takes place in pieces.

Inverse Queries

Inverse queries are sent when a resolver requests a name that corresponds to a particular IP address. However, you must create a special domain for inverse queries (called in-addr.arpa). The in-addr.arpa domain maintains a reverse list of IP addresses to Internet names. One peculiar item about this domain (besides its name) is that IP addresses are listed in reverse order. As noted in the example earlier, the IP address 10.286.248.193 for pop3.engineering.aus–tx.inmyworld.com would be listed as 193.248.286.10 in the in-addr.arpa domain. Note that this matches the order of the FQDN—most specific on the left to least specific on the right.

12

NAME RESOLUTION STEPS

To fully understand the name resolution process used in DNS, consider the following example:

1. The client sends a recursive query to its name server; the recursive query requests the IP address for ftp.microsoft.com.

2. The name server looks in its DNS cache and database for the name and IP address. If it locates the information locally, it responds to the client's request immediately. If it does not find a matching entry, it queries the com top–level name server for the IP address of the microsoft.com name server.

3. The top–level name server provides the IP address of the lower-level name server for microsoft.com.

4. The client's name server is then able to contact the name server at microsoft.com directly and to request the name of ftp.microsoft.com.

5. When the client's name server receives the information from microsoft.com, it answers the resolver.

DNS CACHING AND TIME-TO-LIVE (TTL)

When a name server resolves a query, it places the name in a name cache so it can respond immediately rather than stepping through the entire resolution process if another request is made for the same name. Entries in the name cache are given a specific *Time-to-Live (TTL)*, which prevents a previously cached item from causing name resolution problems in the future. For example, you wouldn't want your name server to give you the old IP address for ftp.microsoft.com; you would want the most recent mapping. When a particular entry's TTL expires, it is removed from the cache.

Resolvers can also place entries in their own name caches. Resolver software is configured to adhere to the TTL's entries assigned by the name server. The resolver also removes the entry from its cache once the TTL has expired.

 If the IP addresses on your domain seldom change, you can configure a higher TTL to optimize your name resolution.

INSTALLING AND CONFIGURING DNS

In Windows NT, DNS is run as a network service. Just like other network services, DNS is installed through the Network applet's Services tab. To access the Network applet, follow these steps:

1. Right-click on Network Neighborhood and select Properties from the shortcut menu. The Network applet appears.

2. Select the Services tab and click on Add. The Select Network Service dialog box is invoked, from which you select Microsoft DNS Server, as shown in Figure 12.2. Click on OK to begin the installation.

3. You are prompted for the location of the Windows NT Server 4.0 setup files (usually the CD-ROM). Enter the appropriate location information and click on Continue.

4. Once the service has copied its files, click on Close to close the Network applet and complete the installation.

5. When prompted, click on Yes to reboot the computer.

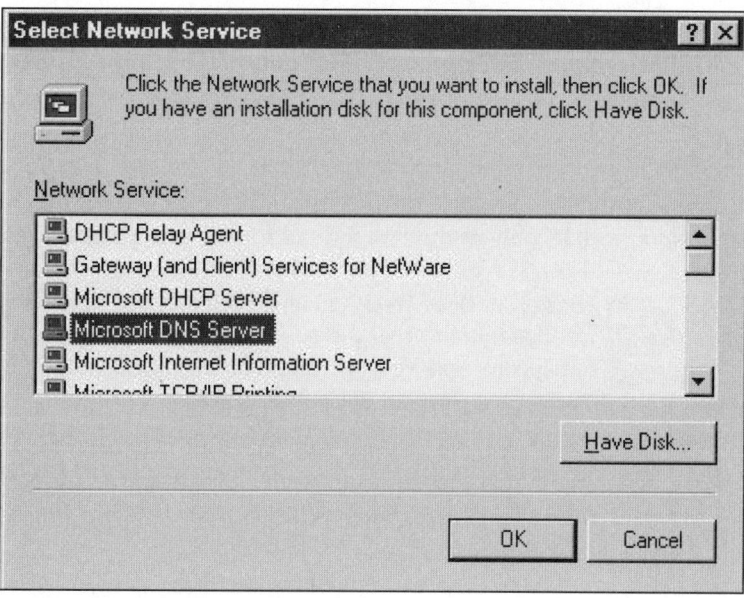

Figure 12.2   Installing Microsoft DNS Server.

CONFIGURING DOMAINS AND ZONES

Before you actually configure a name server, you should plan how your entire name structure is going to be internally configured. The scope of that assignment is far beyond this book and the Microsoft exam. More information on that subject is available in the Microsoft TechNet article "DNS And MS Windows NT 4.0."

Once you have determined which structure you are going to use for your piece of the Domain Name Space, you can begin to configure the servers, zones, and domains that will be under your control. The paragraphs that follow explain the creation process for these items.

You can configure your DNS server through the DNS Manager, which is added to the Administrative Tools (Common) group during the DNS server installation. When you open the DNS Manager, the domain structure is empty—essentially a clean slate. To add your DNS server to the domain, select New Server from the DNS menu. Enter the server name or IP address and click on OK. You can view the hierarchy that is configured below the server by double-clicking on the server object, which expands the tree. By default, new servers are configured as caching-only name servers, so only a cache object appears below a new name server.

Double-click on the cache object to expand its display information, which includes ARPA and NET settings. The right-hand pane of the DNS Manager displays a list of all root name servers that are preconfigured with your name server, as shown in Figure 12.3. This information comes from the CACHE.DNS file, which is located in the %SYSTEM_ROOT%\SYSTEM32\DNS directory. Double-click on the ARPA folder to expand it to include the IN-ADDR folder, which contains the information necessary for the inverse queries described previously. Double-click on the NET folder to display the ROOT-SERVERS folder, which contains the IP addresses for the root name servers on the Internet.

 Once your DNS server is running, you may see entries appear and disappear from the cache. These items represent the name resolutions that your server is making. When the TTL on the cached name expires, the entries disappear.

To configure your DNS server for use on your network, you must create a zone. To do so, right-click on the name server object and select New Zone from the shortcut menu. This invokes the Creating New Zone For Servername dialog box, shown in Figure 12.4.

The first step in creating a new zone is to specify whether you are creating a primary or secondary name server for the zone. For the initial creation of a zone, select Primary and click on Next. If at some point a secondary name server is added to the zone, you must enter the zone name and the name of a master name server. DNS imports the master name server's records automatically when a secondary zone is created.

The next step is to establish the zone information. Enter the domain name you are creating. For example, if your domain name is inmyworld.com, enter "inmyworld.com" in the Zone Name box and then press the tab key.

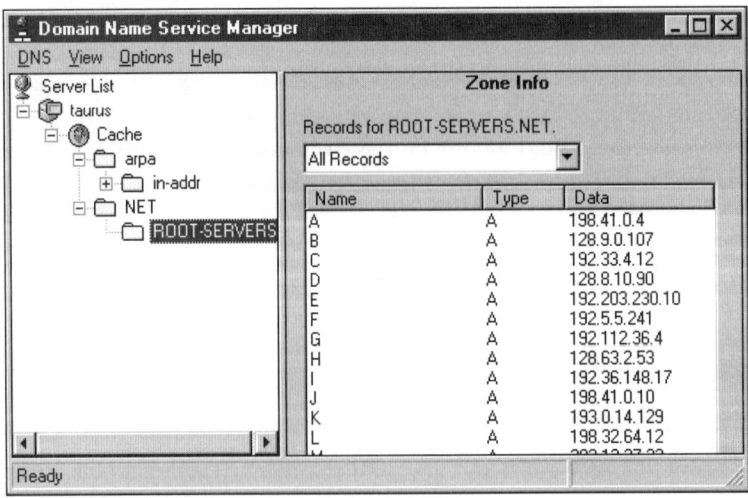

Figure 12.3 By default, the cache object includes a list of root name servers.

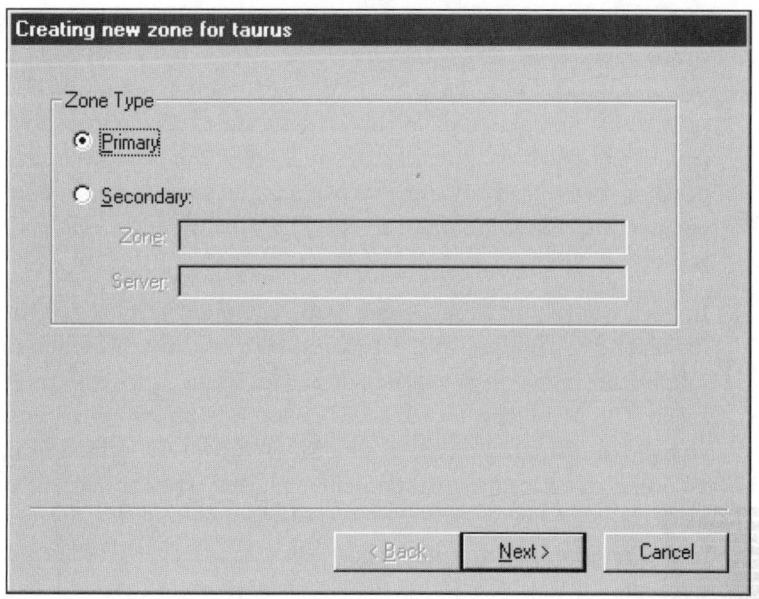

Figure 12.4   Creating a new DNS zone on server taurus.

The Zone File box is completed for you. By default, the file for your new domain is your domain name plus the extension .dns. This step creates an equivalent file in the %SYSTEM_ROOT%\SYSTEM32\DNS folder. For example, "inmyworld.com.dns" is entered into the Zone file box, which creates the file INMYWORLD.COM.DNS in the %SYSTEM_ROOT%\SYSTEM32\DNS folder. To complete the new zone creation, click on Next and then click on Finish. The new zone appears in the DNS manager, as shown in Figure 12.5.

12

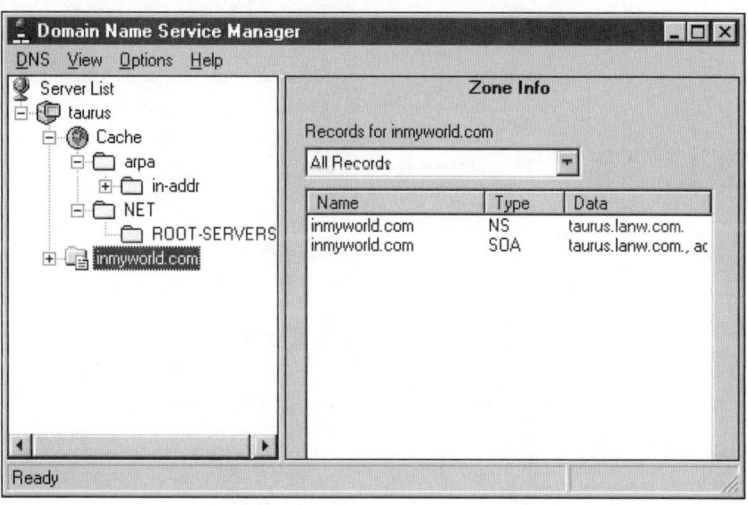

Figure 12.5   The new zone inmyworld.com has been created.

Once you have configured all of the zones required for this server, you can add subdomains. To do this, right-click on the zone and select New Domain from the shortcut menu. Enter the name of the new subdomain in the dialog box and click on OK. If multiple levels of subdomains are needed, repeat this process for each new object down the hierarchy. If you'll recall, the previous example of an FQDN, pop3.engineering.aus-tx.inmyworld.com, includes two subdomains: aus-tx and engineering. Figure 12.6 shows the DNS Manager's configuration for this DNS zone.

In each domain and subdomain, you may enter resource records that map host names to IP addresses. To create a resource record, right-click on the domain or subdomain in which it will be added and select New Record from the shortcut menu. The New Resource Record dialog box (shown in Figure 12.7) is invoked, and you are required to select the type of record (described in Table 12.2) as well as other information that depends on the type of record you selected. For example, an A record requires the host name and IP address, whereas an MX record requires the host name, mail exchange server DNS name, and Preference number.

INTEGRATING DNS WITH WINS

In addition to using other DNS name servers to resolve names, your DNS server can be configured to call a WINS server. The WINS server can help the DNS server with the host portion of the FQDN. For example, if your name server is

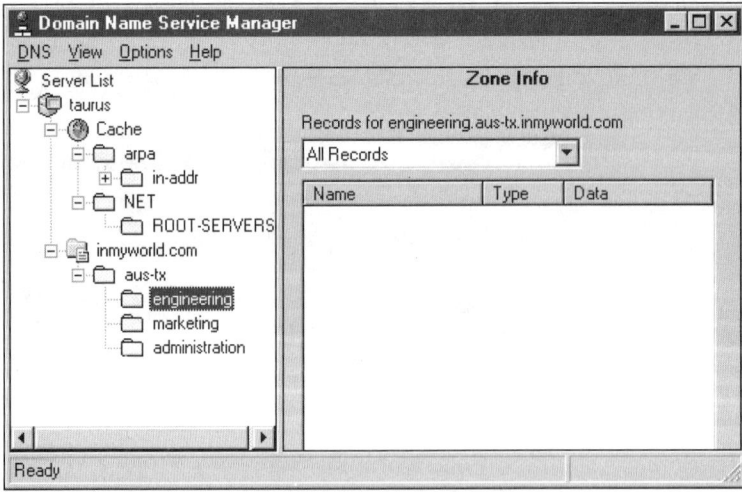

Figure 12.6   The domain structure for inmyworld.com.

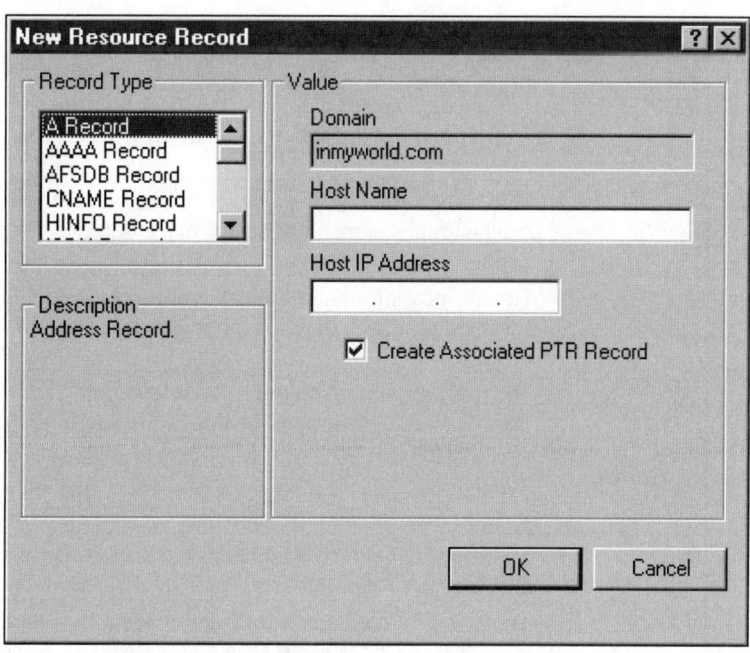

Figure 12.7 Resource records are added through the New Resource Record dialog box.

Table 12.2 DNS resource record descriptions.

Record Type	Description
A	The address record is used to map host names to IP addresses. Its counterpart, the PTR record, is used in the opposite way—to map an IP address to a host name in the in-addr.arpa domain. When you create an A record, you can create a PTR record automatically.
AFSDB	The AFSDB record specifies the location of either an Andrew File System (AFS) cell database server or a Distributed Computing Environment (DCE) cell's authenticated name server.
CNAME	The canonical name record creates an alias for specific hosts. The alias is used to hide the details of your network from the clients that connect to it. For example, ftp.inmyworld.com could be a CNAME record for the real name of the computer that runs the FTP service for InMyWorld, Inc. If the original FTP server fails and must be replaced, only the CNAME record needs to be changed in the DNS database.
HINFO	The host information record identifies a host's hardware type and operating system. RFC 1700 specifies the information that should be included in the CPU Type and Operating system fields.
ISDN	The ISDN record is a variation of the A record, but rather than map a host name to an IP address, it maps the host name to an ISDN address. This record type is used in conjunction with the RT (route through) record.

(continued)

Table 12.2   DNS resource record descriptions (*continued*).

Record Type	Description
MB	The mailbox record defines a DNS host with the specified mailbox. This is one of many experimental record types dealing with Internet mail.
MG	The mail group record is an experimental record type that specifies a mailbox that is a member of the mail group (mailing list) identified by the DNS domain name.
MINFO	The mailbox information record is an experimental record that specifies a mailbox that is responsible for the specified mailing list or mailbox.
MR	The mailbox rename record is an experimental record that specifies a mailbox that is the proper rename of the specified mailbox.
MX	The mail exchanger record specifies a mail exchange server for a DNS domain; the mail exchange server is a host that will either process or forward mail for the DNS domain.
NS	The name server record identifies the DNS name server(s) for the DNS domain. NS records appear in all DNS zones and reverse zones.
PTR	The pointer record maps an IP address to a host name in the in-addr.arpa DNS reverse zone and matches an A record.
RP	The responsible person record indicates who is responsible for the specified DNS domain or host.
RT	The route through record specifies an intermediate host that routes packets to a destination host. This record is used in conjunction with the ISDN and X25 resource records and is similar to the MX record type in its syntax and function.
SOA	The start of authority record indicates that this DNS name server is the best source of information for the data within this DNS domain. It is the first record in each of the DNS database files and is created automatically by the DNS Manager when you create a new zone.
TXT	The text record associates general information with an item in the DNS database. For example, a text record can be used to identify a host's location, such as "Third floor, Building B". The text string must be less than 256 characters long, but multiple TXT records can be associated with one host.
WKS	The well-known service record describes the services provided by a particular protocol on a particular interface (usually UDP or TCP).
X25	The X.25 record is a variation of the address record. Rather than mapping a host name to an IP address, the X.25 record maps the name to an X.121 address. Like ISDN, this record is used in conjunction with the RT record.

trying to resolve the name testing.engineering.aus-tx.inmyworld.com, a properly configured WINS server is able to assist in the resolution of the "testing" portion of the FQDN. WINS is discussed in greater detail later in this chapter.

To configure your DNS server to request resolution assistance from a WINS server, right-click on the icon for your domain and select Properties from the shortcut menu. Click on the WINS Lookup tab and check the Use WINS Resolution checkbox. Enter the IP addresses for the WINS servers that you would like your DNS server to contact when resolving host names, as shown in Figure 12.8.

When you enable WINS resolution, a WINS record is created in your domain. When you configure a zone to perform WINS lookup, be sure to configure all authoritative name servers for that zone with WINS lookup. Otherwise, name resolution on your domain may be inconsistent, which could be difficult to troubleshoot.

WINS AND REVERSE LOOKUP

Although WINS was not designed to provide reverse name resolution, DNS can be configured to call a WINS server for that purpose. To configure a WINS

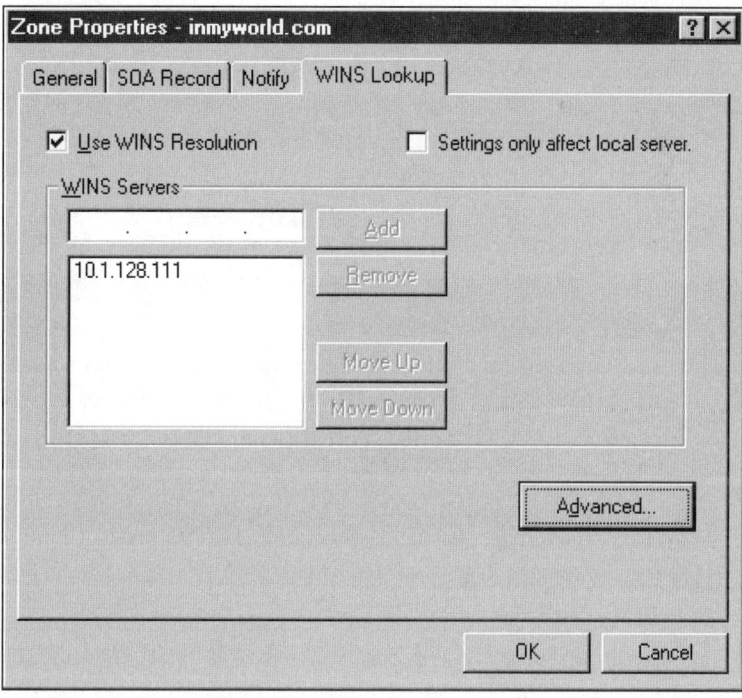

Figure 12.8   WINS resolution is enabled through the Zone Properties dialog box for a domain.

server, right-click on the in-addr.arpa domain for your site and select Properties. Click on the WINS Reverse Lookup tab and check the Use WINS Reverse Lookup checkbox. Enter the name of your DNS domain in the DNS Host Domain dialog box. The name you enter is appended to all WINS lookups for this domain before it is returned to the resolver.

DNS NOTIFY

The Microsoft DNS implementation includes DNS Notify, which allows master servers to inform secondary servers when changes have been made to the DNS database. The master name server prompts the secondary name servers to call for a zone transfer. To configure DNS Notify, right-click on your domain's icon and select Properties from the shortcut menu. Click on the Notify tab and enter the IP addresses of secondary servers in your zone. If you check Only Allow Access From Secondaries Included On Notify List, the name list will only be available to those name servers on the Notify list.

THE DNS ROUND ROBIN FEATURE

One area in which DNS affects the Proxy Server environment is through the use of the DNS *round robin* feature. This function is used to distribute the workload among multiple servers on a network. For example, Microsoft has multiple physical computers that create its FTP site. As a matter of fact, when you go to the Microsoft site, you don't know which physical server you are actually going to connect to. This is possible because DNS has the ability to resolve a host name to multiple IP addresses. If you enter the same host name a number of times, giving each a separate IP address, DNS will automatically rotate through each of the names in turn. For instance, if you associate www.inmyworld.com with three different IP addresses, DNS will answer queries for www.inmyworld.com with each address in the order it appears on the list.

This way, you can load-balance among multiple proxy servers. If your network operates with multiple gateways to the Internet, the DNS round robin feature will ensure that requests are forwarded to the proxy servers in an equitable manner.

CONFIGURING DNS CLIENTS (RESOLVER)

DNS client configuration is done through the properties of the TCP/IP protocol. On Windows NT computers, this is done through the Protocols tab of the Network applet. On Windows 95 computers, this function is found in the first screen of the Network applet. Once you have located the TCP/IP protocol, double-click on it to invoke the Properties dialog box. Select the DNS tab to configure the DNS settings for the computer. Figure 12.9 shows the DNS tab of the TCP/IP Properties dialog box on a Windows NT Workstation computer. For Windows 95 computers, the tab is called DNS Configuration and contains similar fields.

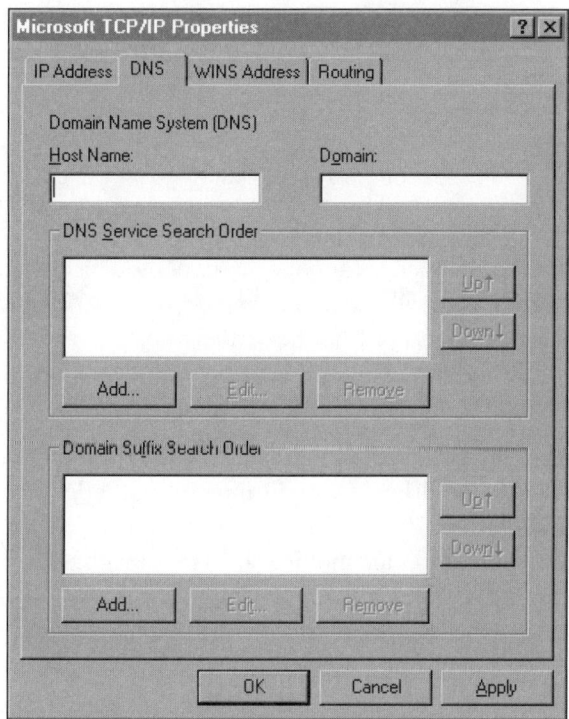

Figure 12.9   Configuring the DNS settings for a Windows NT Workstation computer.

By default, your computer's host name is identical to the computer name entered in the Identification tab of the Network applet. This name is appended to the domain name specified in the Domain box as the computer's FQDN. In the DNS Service Search Order section, you can enter the IP addresses for the name servers that will be contacted when you are attempting to resolve a computer name. Notice that you can also set the order in which these servers are accessed. Optionally, in the Domain Suffix Search Order section, you can enter the order in which you want the top-level domains to be searched. For example, you can enter "com", "edu", and "mil" in that order, which would indicate that the com domain is to be searched prior to the edu or the mil domains.

TROUBLESHOOTING DNS WITH NSLOOKUP

The DNS server system is not entirely automated, and for this reason, errors can occur. Aside from using the DNS Manager to view and correct entries, you can employ the *NSLOOKUP* utility to troubleshoot problems as they arise.

NSLOOKUP queries a name server to retrieve IP address information for a particular name. NSLOOKUP is a command-line utility that uses the following syntax:

```
nslookup [[-option ...] [computer-to-find]] | - [server]
```

NSLOOKUP operates in one of two modes: interactive and noninteractive. Most often, you will use noninteractive mode to look up a single record on the DNS server. Figure 12.10 shows the results of a noninteractive NSLOOKUP query. Notice that, as mentioned previously, a number of IP addresses can be configured for one host name.

To enter the NSLOOKUP's interactive mode, do not enter a computer to find on the command line. Once in interactive mode, you can issue multiple name queries. This mode is useful if you are not sure of the name you're looking for because you can enter multiple queries quickly. For more information on the Windows NT NSLOOKUP utility, check the WINNT.HLP file supplied with Windows NT 4.0 or refer to Microsoft TechNet.

WINS

Windows Internet Name Service (WINS) is the NetBIOS name server provided with the Windows NT 4.0 Server product. WINS differs from the name resolution techniques previously discussed in that it is a dynamic, or automatic, name resolution service. The WINS server is not configured manually; instead, it actually collects computer names and IP addresses from clients on the network. When a WINS client

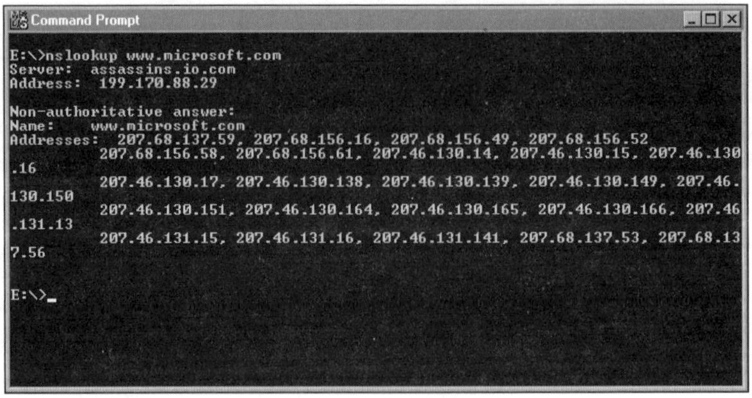

Figure 12.10 An NSLOOKUP noninteractive query.

wants to know the IP address of another computer on the network, it calls the WINS server to request the name resolution.

In Windows NT networks without WINS, NetBIOS names are resolved by using broadcasts. Whenever a computer wishes to communicate with another computer on the network, it sends a broadcast to the network and requests the computer's IP address. As you can imagine, in a large network, the amount of traffic generated by these broadcasts is rather large and can have a detrimental effect on performance. On a non-WINS network, the following NetBIOS name resolutions occur on a regular basis:

- When a computer is powered on, it announces itself by broadcasting its NetBIOS name. If there are no machines that already have that name, the computer claims the NetBIOS name and communicates on the network.

- If a computer is attempting to establish NetBIOS communications with another computer—for instance, by using a net send command to send a message to a destination machine—it uses the destination's NetBIOS name to broadcast a message requesting the IP address of that machine. When a response is received, communications are established and the message is sent.

- When a computer is shut down properly, it broadcasts a message releasing the NetBIOS name.

How Does WINS Work?

Perhaps the biggest benefit of using WINS is that it reduces the broadcast traffic on the network. The WINS process is simple to understand when it is broken down into three parts: name registration, name discovery, and name release. This is illustrated in the following list and in Figure 12.11:

- **NetBIOS name registration** When a WINS client initializes, it sends a directed message to a WINS server requesting registration of its name and IP address. The client is given the name for a fixed amount of time, or TTL, and the name is registered with the WINS server. When part of the TTL expires, the client attempts to renew the TTL for its NetBIOS name.

- **NetBIOS name discovery** When a WINS client attempts to establish communications with a destination computer, it sends a directed message to the WINS server requesting name resolution services. The WINS server replies with the IP address of the destination host.

- **Name release** When the client is shut down properly, the client sends a directed message to the WINS server releasing its NetBIOS name.

12

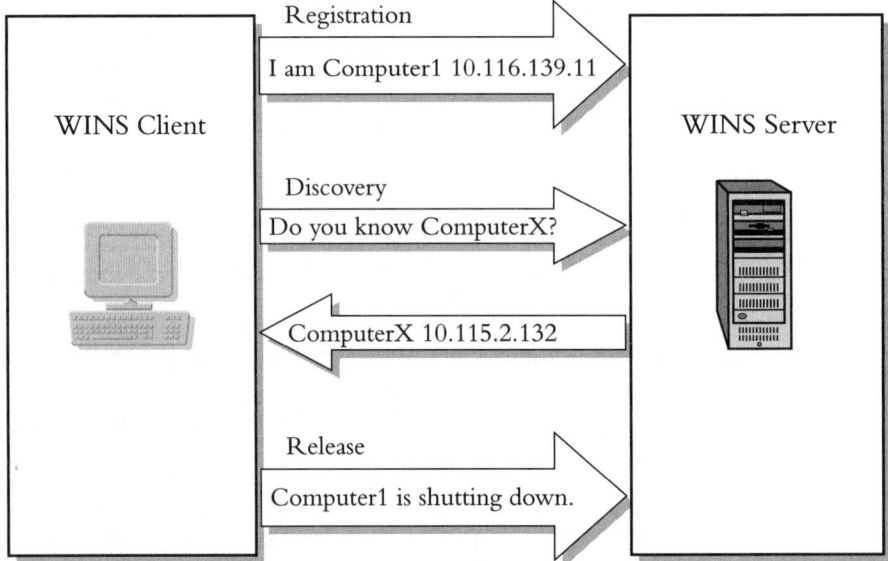

Figure 12.11   The WINS communication process.

The name is marked in the database of the WINS server, reflecting that the TTL for that record is zero. Once released, the name is available for use by another computer.

PLANNING AND IMPLEMENTING A WINS ENVIRONMENT

When you are planning to deploy WINS for your network, there are several things to consider:

- **Can all client computers use WINS?** Most systems that can communicate on a Microsoft network running Microsoft products can be configured to use WINS. If you have computers on your network that do not support WINS, you can configure static entries in the WINS server database for those clients. This enables the WINS clients to resolve the computer names of the non-WINS clients. However, the non-WINS clients cannot use the WINS database for name resolution unless they are on the same subnet as the WINS server. If the non-WINS clients are on a different subnet, you must provide an alternate name resolution method for the non-WINS clients, such as a HOSTS file, DNS name server, or a WINS Proxy Agent. WINS Proxy Agents are explained later in this chapter.

- **How many WINS servers are needed?** WINS servers can provide about 1,500 name registrations and 4,500 name resolutions per minute; a conservative estimate for a network is a WINS server and backup WINS server for every 10,000 clients. If one WINS server goes down, your clients may notice a slight degradation in performance, but the name resolution process will still proceed.

- **Will the network span a large distance and use WAN technologies?** If you use WAN technologies (such as T1 or ATM communications) to connect your network, you should consider putting a WINS server at the remote location. This enables NetBIOS name resolution services to be handled locally rather than across the WAN.

INSTALLING AND CONFIGURING A WINS SERVER

Only Windows NT Servers can be WINS servers. Installing the WINS service is similar to installing DNS or any other network service on Windows NT—by using the Network applet. To configure your Windows NT Server as a WINS server, perform the following steps:

1. Right-click on the Network Neighborhood icon and choose Properties from the shortcut menu. This invokes the Network dialog box.

2. Click on the Services tab and then click on the Add button.

3. Select Windows Internet Name Service from the list of services and click on OK.

4. Enter the path to the Windows NT Server source files, usually the CD, and click on OK.

5. Click on the Close button to complete the installation.

6. Click on Yes to reboot the computer when prompted.

After the system is restarted, a WINS Manager is added to the Administrative Tools (Common) area of the Start menu and WINS is ready for use. No further configuration is needed to make WINS operational, but further configuration should be considered to make the WINS deployment successful.

ADMINISTERING WINS

The WINS Manager is used to configure your WINS database. To open the WINS Manager, choose Start|Programs|Administrative Tools (Common)|WINS Manager.

When the WINS Manager first opens, you'll see your WINS server and related statistics. Like the many Windows NT utilities, the WINS Manager can also be used to remotely administer several servers. To add WINS servers to the WINS Manager, click on Server and select Add WINS Server. When prompted, enter the name or IP address of the WINS server you would like to add and click on OK. The WINS server appears in the list. To remove a WINS server from the list, select the server in the WINS Manager window, click on Server, and then click on Delete WINS Server. Confirm the deletion by clicking on OK.

WINS DATABASE

To look at the WINS database, select the Mappings menu, then select the Show Database option. The Show Database dialog box displays the current server and entries and gives you several view options for searching the database (see Figure 12.12). In the Mappings window, you can see which entries are active and which are static, as well as the expiration date for each entry. On the far right side of the Mappings window, you can see a column labeled Version ID. The Version ID number is used by replication partners to identify which changes to the database are the most recent. If you ever want to re-create the WINS database, click on the Delete Owner button to purge the entire database.

SCAVENGING

On the WINS Manager's Mappings menu, there is also an Initiate Scavenging option. *Scavenging* is a method of cleaning up entries in the WINS database. It checks the entries in the database against their owners. Entries that have expired or have no owner are removed from the database. Scavenging is an automatic function of

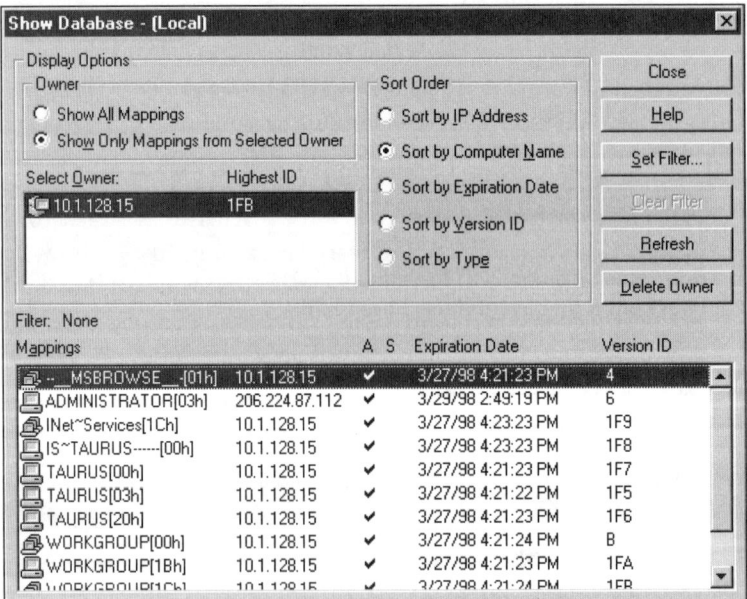

Figure 12.12 Viewing the WINS database.

WINS, but it can be started by selecting the Initiate Scavenging option. To configure the WINS server maintenance intervals, select Configuration from the Server menu. The WINS Server Configuration dialog box is displayed (see Figure 12.13).

The following list describes the options available for configuring the WINS server:

- **Renewal Interval** The maximum length of time the NetBIOS name is considered registered. In Windows NT 4, the default is 144 hours (6 days). After that, the client is expected to reregister its name with the WINS server; otherwise, the name is considered released.

- **Extinction Interval** Determines how long a released name is maintained in the database so that it does not have to be reentered if a WINS client attempts to reregister that name. By default, once an entry has been released for six days, it is considered extinct, which means that it will soon be removed from the WINS database. You can configure the extinction interval in hours, minutes, and seconds.

- **Extinction Timeout** Controls how long entries are extinct before being removed from the database. By default, an additional six days are given to extinct names before they are removed entirely from the database.

- **Verify Interval** Determines how long the WINS server allows entries from another WINS database (replication partner) to remain active in its database before those entries must be verified. The default setting is 576 hours (24 days).

The Pull Parameters and Push Parameters settings are used to configure intervals for WINS replication partners. They are discussed in the next section.

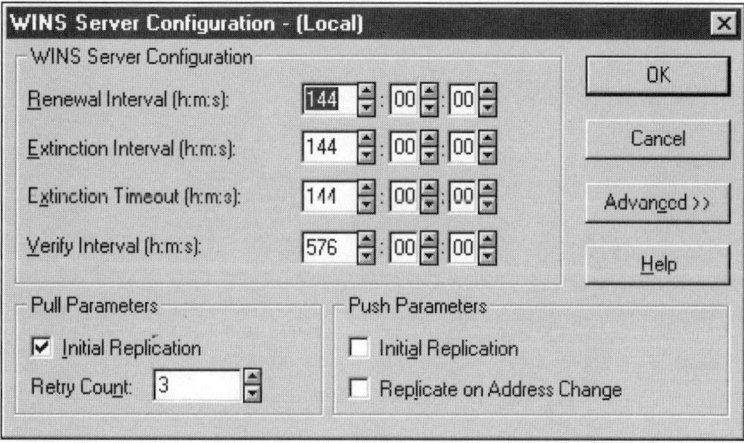

Figure 12.13   WINS maintenance interval configuration.

WINS REPLICATION PARTNERS

WINS servers are typically paired for redundancy; if one WINS server were to fail, the name resolution process would proceed, which would reduce the impact on users. WINS servers can be configured to update each other's name resolution database, which allows all WINS servers to have identical databases.

A WINS server that is configured as a push partner sends its database changes to its partner after a fixed number of changes have been made to the WINS database. A WINS server that is configured as a pull partner requests database changes from its partner at fixed intervals. A WINS server can be configured to synchronize its database with another WINS server as either a push partner, a pull partner, or both. These settings are configured through the Replication Partners option on the WINS Manager's Server menu. The Replication Partners dialog box is shown in Figure 12.14.

 Microsoft recommends that pull partners be configured on either side of a slow WAN link, which enables you to control when database changes are replicated over the link. Push partners are recommended for LAN connections only.

There are several configuration options in the Replication Partners dialog box, including the Push With Propagation option. If you enable this option, when

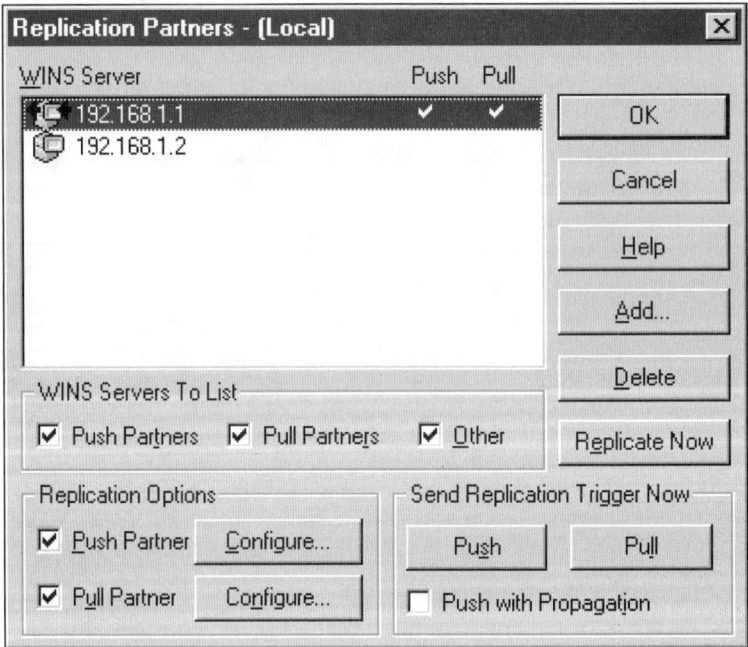

Figure 12.14 Configuring WINS replication partners.

your WINS server sends its database to its partner, the partner is prompted to push the changes to all of its partners.

Configuring WINS Clients

After the WINS servers are in place, you must configure the clients before you can use them. This is done at the client computer through the Network applet's TCP/IP Properties dialog box. Select the WINS Address tab, shown in Figure 12.15. Enter the IP address of the primary WINS server. If a secondary WINS server is available, enter its IP address in the appropriate box.

As mentioned earlier, DNS can use WINS to complete name resolution requests. WINS can also refer to a DNS server to complete NetBIOS name resolution requests. To enable this option, check the Enable DNS For Windows Resolution box. When a client's DNS information is configured, the host name is by default the same as the NetBIOS (computer) name. When a DNS record is created for the client, the same name is likely to appear in DNS and in WINS.

After completing the WINS configuration, click on OK to close the TCP/IP Properties dialog box and click on Close to close the Network applet. The

12

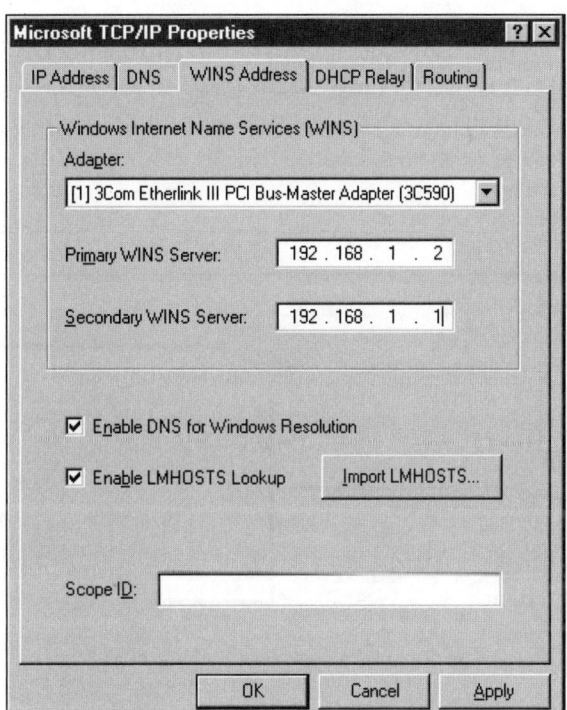

Figure 12.15   Configuring a client computer to use WINS.

system will complete its configuration and prompt you to restart the computer. Click on Yes to restart the computer with WINS enabled.

WINS Proxy Agents

Windows NT computers can be configured as WINS Proxy Agents, which allows the computer to forward the name resolution broadcasts of non-WINS clients to a WINS server. In effect, a WINS Proxy Agent allows non-WINS clients to use a WINS server for name resolution rather than relying on static files like LMHOSTS. Bridges and routers are not able to pass TCP/IP broadcasts, or any broadcasts, between network segments. On a single-segment network with both WINS and non-WINS clients, the WINS server receives a broadcast request for resolution and responds even though it is not a WINS request. However, on a multisegment network, when a non-WINS client is on one segment and the WINS server is on another, the broadcast never reaches the server. A WINS Proxy Agent acts as an intermediary to ensure that the non-WINS client's request is resolved. This process is outlined in the following steps and illustrated in Figure 12.16:

1. The non-WINS client broadcasts for name resolution on the local segment.

2. The WINS Proxy Agent picks up that name resolution broadcast.

3. The WINS Proxy Agent forwards the name resolution request directly to the WINS server.

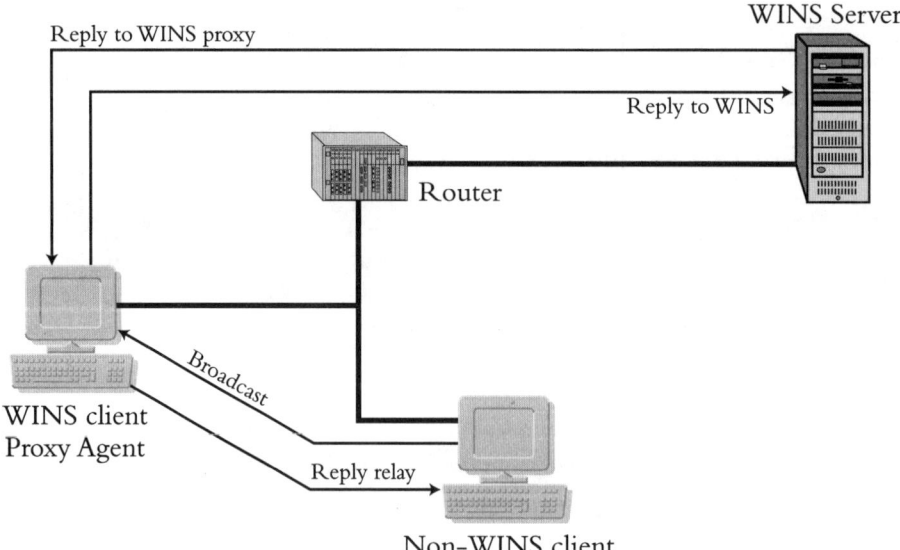

Figure 12.16   The WINS Proxy Agent process.

4. The WINS server responds to the WINS Proxy Agent with a name resolution.

5. The WINS Proxy Agent forwards the reply from the WINS server to the non–WINS client.

WINS Proxy Agents are required only on subnets that do not have a WINS server. If the routers on your network are configured to permit broadcasts (i.e., if UDP ports 137 and 138 are enabled), WINS Proxy Agents are not required. However, one of the primary reasons for installing bridges and routers is to limit the traffic on each network segment, including broadcast traffic. Enabling UDP ports 137 and 138 on your routers is not recommended because it increases network broadcast traffic, which creates the potential for broadcast storms.

Any computer running Microsoft Windows NT 4 that is configured as a WINS client can be configured as a WINS Proxy Agent. However, this option is not available in the WINS configuration area of the TCP/IP Properties dialog box; instead, it is a Registry setting. To configure a Windows NT computer to be a WINS Proxy Agent, change the Enable Proxy setting in the HKEY_Local_Machine\System\CurrentControlSet\Services\NetBT\Parameters to 1. After you make this change, close the Registry editor and restart the computer.

Microsoft recommends that you don't enable more than two WINS Proxy Agents per subnet. Enabling more than two WINS Proxy Agents could increase network traffic beyond acceptable limits because each WINS Proxy Agent will repeat all name resolution broadcasts that it receives.

12

Proxy Server DNS And WINS Issues

The majority of the issues that arise with Proxy Server and its interaction with WINS and DNS occur in the area of load balancing. By using DNS's round robin and multihomed WINS servers, you can ensure that the Internet access responsibilities are shared equally across multiple Proxy Server computers.

Load Balancing With DNS

As mentioned in "The DNS Round Robin Feature" section earlier in this chapter, DNS has the ability to evenly distribute requests among multiple servers. This feature ensures that the workload is balanced between all machines.

The first step in establishing this type of environment is creating multiple A resource records in the DNS database. The A records must have the same name but different IP addresses—one for each proxy server. DNS automatically responds to requests with each entry's IP address in the order it appears.

The second and final step in this configuration process is to ensure that all clients are pointing to the name used by DNS rather than a specific proxy server's name. Table 12.3 illustrates this point by showing you how Jim, a systems administrator at a medium-sized company, configured DNS for the proxy servers on his network.

The first step Jim must take is to configure his DNS server so it responds to requests for the Proxy Servers. To provide load balancing, Jim enters three A resource records on his DNS server with the configurations shown in Table 12.4.

Finally, Jim must configure each client to use InetServer as its proxy server.

LOAD BALANCING WITH WINS

Load balancing on a WINS-enabled network is handled much differently than it is on a DNS network. First, you must use the WINS Manager to make a static WINS mapping for the Proxy Servers. Select Static Mappings from the Mappings menu and click on Add Mappings to invoke the Add Static Mappings dialog box, shown in Figure 12.17.

The multihomed static mapping type is used to define computers with multiple network interface cards. However, Microsoft recommends that you use this feature to load-balance multiple Proxy Servers. Multihomed mapping can include up to 25 IP addresses per entry. If your network is using more than 25 Proxy Servers, you need to create a second mapping and to configure part of the clients to use the new mapping.

After the multihomed entry has been made in the WINS database, the WINS server will attempt to load-balance the requests for the Proxy Servers. It does this by first attempting to locate a Proxy Server on the same subnet as the client that is making the request. If it doesn't find a Proxy Server on the same subnet, it

Table 12.3   The configuration of the three proxy servers on Jim's network.

Computer Name	IP Address
Proxy1	10.1.199.15
Proxy2	10.1.199.16
Proxy3	10.1.199.17

Table 12.4   Jim's configurations of the A resource records on his DNS server.

Host Name	IP Address
InetServer	10.1.199.15
InetServer	10.1.199.16
InetServer	10.1.199.17

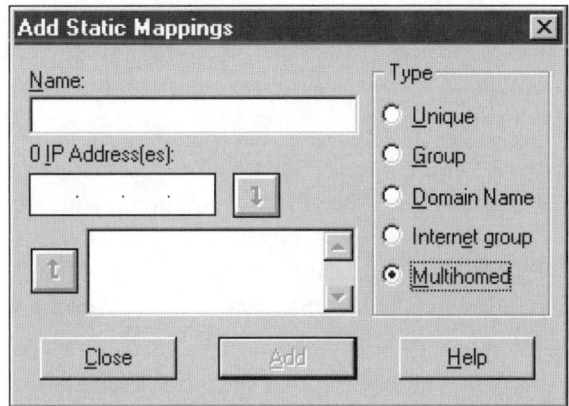

Figure 12.17   Static WINS mappings are used for load balancing in a WINS environment.

attempts to find one on the same network. If that also fails, the WINS server picks a Proxy Server at random from the list of available servers.

OTHER WINS ISSUES

There are only two other issues to consider when you use WINS and Proxy Server on the same network. First, if WINS and Proxy Server reside on the same system, it is imperative that WINS database information not be made available to external Internet users. Deny these users file access to the WINS servers and LMHOSTS file (if used), and disable all WINS services for the external network adapter.

Second, if WINS is operating on a server other than the Proxy Server, the Proxy Server may function as a WINS client. This configuration is recommended by Microsoft when a WINS server is already in place on the network.

CHAPTER SUMMARY

The Domain Name System is used to assign plain-language names to computers' IP addresses throughout the world. It is a hierarchical system that has been designed to spread the name resolution workload over many computers. This hierarchical system is known as the Domain Name Space and consists of a root level followed by seven generic domains (com, org, edu, mil, gov, int, and net) and country domains. Every computer that is part of the Internet falls into one of these top-level domains. In the Domain Name System, name servers provide host-name-to-IP-address resolution for clients (also called resolvers).

The role of the name server depends on whether it has the authority for a particular domain and whether it exchanges its DNS database with other name servers. Both DNS and WINS can run on Windows NT Server computers and are installed through the Services tab of the Network applet.

Windows Internet Name Service (WINS) provides similar services to DNS. However, it associates NetBIOS computer names to IP addresses. Without a WINS server on a network, NetBIOS name resolution takes place via broadcast. Like DNS, WINS servers are able to exchange information by using replication partners. Also like DNS, the client configuration for WINS is accomplished through the Network applet's TCP/IP Properties dialog box.

Both DNS and WINS can be used to distribute the Proxy Server workload amongst a number of servers. The DNS round robin feature automatically sends different IP addresses for each request if multiple entries with the same name exist in its database. WINS servers attempt to fulfill the client's request based on the Proxy Server's subnet and network location.

KEY TERMS

- **Advanced Research Projects Agency (ARPA)**—The Department of Defense agency that initiated the project that created TCP/IP and the Internet.

- **Advanced Research Projects Agency Network (ARPANet)**—The predecessor to today's Internet; ARPANet linked colleges and universities to allow them to share research information over a packet-switched network.

- **Berkeley Internet Name Domain (BIND)**—An implementation of DNS designed at the University of California at Berkeley. It is the basis for Microsoft's implementation of DNS.

- **BIND boot file**—The file that can be used to assist in the migration from a BIND system to a Microsoft DNS system.

- **Domain Name Space**—The name for the Domain Name System's hierarchical structure.

- **Domain Name System (DNS)**—The worldwide system for plain-language assignment of names to IP addresses. It is hierarchically organized from six generic domains.

- **Fully Qualified Domain Name (FQDN)**—The name that identifies a computer on the Internet by listing the full path through the hierarchy to the host. For example, pop3.engineering.aus-tex.inmyworld.com is an FQDN.

- **generic domain**—Any of the six top-level domains of the Domain Name Space.

- **Internet Network Information Center (InterNIC)**—The governing body of the Internet. One of its responsibilities is assigning IP addresses.

- **name server**—In the DNS environment, the computer that fulfills a name resolution request.

- **NSLOOKUP**—A Windows command-line utility that is used to query a name server.

- **replication partner**—One of two WINS servers that are configured to share information.

- **resolver**—In the DNS environment, the computer that requests name resolution.

- **resource records**—DNS records that identify specific computers on the network.

- **round robin**—A DNS feature that balances the load on servers by responding to queries with different addresses if there is more than one resource record with the same host name.

- **subdomain**—A domain that is created below a typical zone or domain. For example, in the FQDN www.hosts.lanw.com, "hosts" is the subdomain.

- **Windows Internet Name Service (WINS)**—The service that keeps track of NetBIOS names and IP addresses for computers in a Windows network.

- **WINS Proxy Agent**—A computer that is configured to assist non-WINS clients with name resolution on networks where no WINS server exists.

12

REVIEW QUESTIONS

1. Which of the following are types of queries that occur in a DNS environment?

   a. iterative

   b. recursive

   c. inverse

   d. interrogative

2. A DNS entry's ———————— specifies how long it will be kept in cache.

3. By default, a computer's DNS name is configured as its computer name in the Identification tab of the Network applet. (True or False?)

4. A _____ _____ is a server that transfers WINS data to other WINS servers.

5. Which of the following is not considered a generic domain?

a. com

b. gov

c. us

d. edu

6. When you change the TCP/IP setting on a computer, it is always a good idea to restart the computer whether you are prompted to or not. (True or False?)

7. Which of the following resource record types creates an alias to a host name that has already been defined in the DNS database?

a. A

b. CNAME

c. HINFO

d. ISDN

8. In the DNS name resolution process, the _____ requests an IP address from the name server.

9. A domain or zone can only contain resource records for the domain. (True or False?)

10. Which of the following identifies a computer with more than one network interface card?

a. network server

b. multiprotocol router

c. multinic

d. multihomed

11. To configure WINS to properly load-share Proxy Server responsibilities, a _____ must be created in the WINS database.

12. WINS and DNS can easily be configured to assist each other in the name resolution process. (True or False?)

13. The _____ utility is used to troubleshoot DNS problems.

14. Microsoft DNS is fully compatible with which of the following DNS types?

a. Stanford Research Name Domain

b. Texas Naming System

c. Berkeley Internet Name Domain

d. InterNIC

15. The _____ domain is used to locate a computer name when an IP address is used in the query.

16. Which of the following name servers provides zone lists to other name servers?

    a. master name server

    b. caching-only name server

    c. primary name server

    d. secondary name server

17. Microsoft does not recommend using WINS to load-balance Proxy Servers. (True or False?)

18. The specific host name for a computer on the network is called

    _____ .

19. Most routers can easily pass broadcast information. (True or False?)

20. Which of the following resource record types are considered experimental?

    a. MX

    b. MG

    c. MB

    d. MR

21. The DNS round robin feature is used to balance the workload of proxy servers on a DNS-enabled network. (True or False?)

HANDS-ON PROJECTS

In the hands-on projects that follow, you will install and configure DNS on a Windows NT Server, install and configure WINS on a Windows NT Server, and configure a client to use both DNS and WINS. For these projects, you will need access to both a Windows NT Server 4.0 computer and a Windows NT Workstation 4.0 or Windows 95 computer. You will need access to the installation files for each of the operating systems you use. For the client installation steps, Windows NT Workstation is used, but the Windows 95 client installation is similar.

 **PROJECT 12.1**

In this project, you will install DNS on a Windows NT 4.0 Server:

1. Log on to Windows NT 4.0 Server as Administrator or as a user with administrative access to the computer.

2. Open the Network applet by right-clicking on Network Neighborhood and selecting Properties from the shortcut menu.

3. Click on the Services tab and click on Add to bring up the Select Network Service dialog box, shown in Figure 12.18.

4. Select Microsoft DNS Server from the list of available services and click on OK.

5. As with most installations, you will be prompted to enter the path to the Windows NT setup files. This is generally the installation CD, but it may be a directory or another computer. Enter the appropriate information and click on Continue.

6. When you are returned to the Network applet, click on Close to complete the installation.

7. When prompted, click on Yes to reboot the computer.

PROJECT 12.2

In this project, you will create a zone, a subdomain, and resource records for your DNS system:

1. Once the system has restarted, log on again as Administrator or as a user with equivalent access permissions.

2. To start the DNS Manager, select Start menu/Programs/Administrative Tools (Common)|DNS Manager.

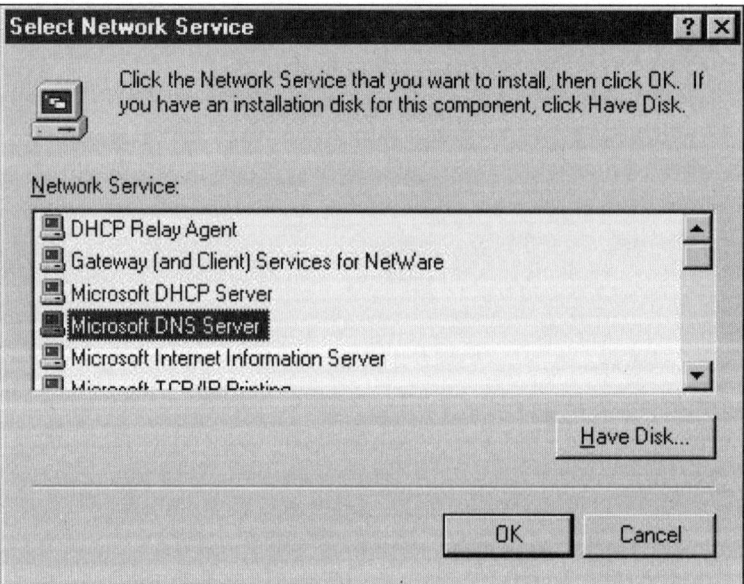

Figure 12.18   The Select Network Service dialog box.

3. Double-click on the icon for your server. The Cache object is displayed, as shown in Figure 12.19.

4. Double-click on the Cache object. Notice that the ARPA and NET folders are displayed on the left side and a list of the root name servers is displayed on the right.

5. Right-click on the icon for your server and select New Zone from the shortcut menu.

6. Select the radio button next to Primary and click on Next.

7. Enter a zone name for your domain. For the purposes of the class, you will want to create a fictitious name, such as elmerfudd.com.

8. Press the Tab key. Notice that the Zone File entry is created automatically. Click on Next.

9. To complete the new zone creation, click on Finish.

10. Notice that two records are created automatically for your new zone, an NS record and an SOA record. To begin creating a subdomain for your new zone, right-click on the zone and select New Domain from the shortcut menu.

11. Enter the name of the subdomain in the Domain Name box in the New Domain dialog box. Click on OK.

12. To begin adding resource records to your subdomain, right-click on the subdomain and select New Record from the shortcut menu.

13. Create an A record for the client computer you will be using in the next project (or for any computer on your network). Select A Record in the Record Type list.

12

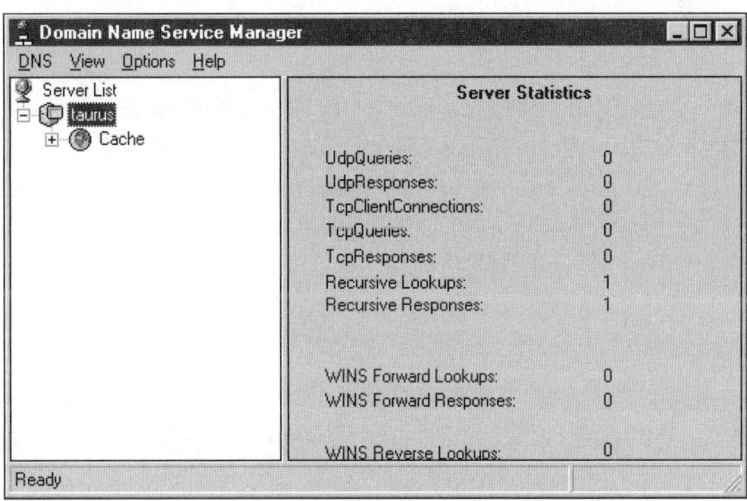

Figure 12.19   The Cache object is automatically created when a new DNS server is installed.

14. Enter the host name and IP address of the computer for which you're creating a record. Uncheck the Create Associated PTR Record option and click on OK.

15. Create another record for the same computer. Right-click on the subdomain and select New Record from the shortcut menu.

16. This time, select CNAME Record from the Record Type list. Enter another name for the computer in the Alias Name box and the name for the record created in Step 14 in the For Host DNS Name box. Click on OK.

17. Select Exit from the DNS menu to close the DNS Manager.

PROJECT 12.3

In this project, you will configure a Windows NT Workstation computer to act as a DNS client (TCP/IP must already be installed on the computer):

1. On the Windows NT Workstation computer, log on as Administrator or as a user with equivalent access permissions.

2. Open the Network applet by right-clicking on Network Neighborhood and selecting Properties from the shortcut menu.

3. Select the Protocols tab and double-click on TCP/IP.

4. Select the DNS tab, shown in Figure 12.20.

5. Enter the host name and domain for the computer in the appropriate boxes.

6. Click on Add to define a new DNS server.

7. Enter the IP address for the DNS server in the TCP/IP DNS Server dialog box and click on Add.

8. Repeat Step 7 as necessary to include all DNS servers on your network. Click on OK to close the TCP/IP Properties dialog box.

9. Click on OK to close the Network applet.

10. Although you may not be prompted to do so (TCP/IP changes are intended to take effect immediately), restart the computer to ensure that the new configuration is used.

PROJECT 12.4

In this project, you will install WINS on the Windows NT Server computer:

1. On the Windows NT Server, log on as Administrator or as a user with equivalent access permissions.

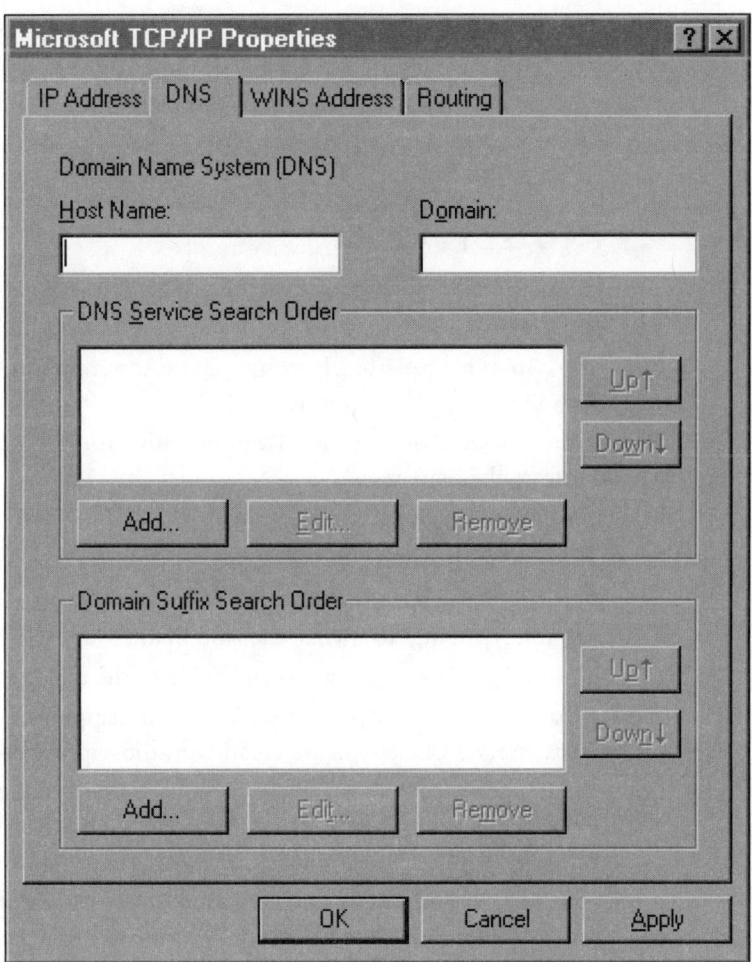

Figure 12.20   The DNS tab of the TCP/IP Properties dialog box.

2. Open the Network applet by right-clicking on Network Neighborhood and selecting Properties from the shortcut list.

3. Click on the Services tab and click on Add to bring up the Select Network Service dialog box.

4. Select Windows Internet Name Service from the list of available network services and click on OK.

5. You will be prompted to enter the path to the Windows NT setup files (as you did with the DNS installation). This is generally the installation CD, but it may be a directory or another computer. Enter the appropriate information and click on Continue.

6. When you are returned to the Network applet, click on Close to complete the installation.

7. When prompted, click on Yes to reboot the computer.

PROJECT 12.5

In this project, you will add a static mapping to the WINS database for multiple Proxy Server computers:

1. Once the system has restarted, log on again as Administrator or as a user with equivalent access permissions.

2. To start the WINS Manager, select Administrative Tools (Common) | WINS Manager from the Start menu.

3. Select your WINS server in the left pane.

4. Select Static Mappings from the Mappings menu.

5. The Static Mappings (Local) dialog box is displayed (see Figure 12.21).

6. Click on Add Mappings to invoke the Add Static Mappings dialog box.

7. Select the Multihomed type on the right side of the dialog box.

8. Notice that the options change for multihomed mappings. Enter the name of the Proxy Server object you are creating in the appropriate box.

9. Enter the IP address for the first Proxy Server computer in the 0 IP Address(es) box. Click on the down arrow to move the IP address to the list of addresses.

10. Add additional IP addresses by entering them in the X IP Address(es) box and clicking on the down arrow.

11. Click on Add to add the record to the WINS database.

12. Click on Close to close the Add Static Mappings dialog box.

13. Click on Close to close the Static Mappings (Local) dialog box and return to the WINS Manager.

14. Select Exit from the Server menu to close the WINS Manager.

PROJECT 12.6

In this project, you will configure a Windows NT Workstation computer to act as a WINS client (TCP/IP must already be installed on the computer):

1. On the Windows NT Workstation computer, log on as Administrator or as a user with equivalent access permissions.

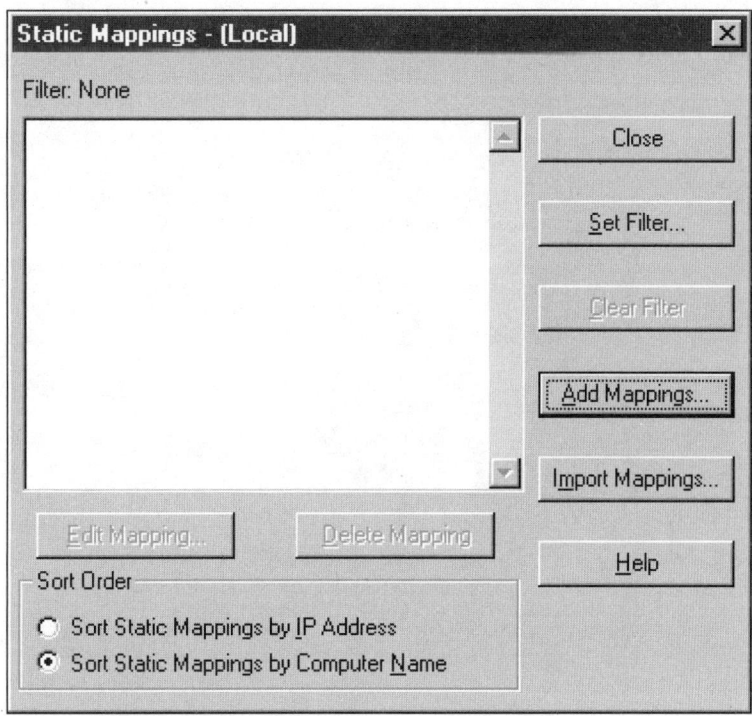

Figure 12.21 The WINS Manager's Static Mappings (Local) dialog box.

2. Open the Network applet by right-clicking on Network Neighborhood and selecting Properties from the shortcut menu.

3. Select the Protocols tab and double-click on TCP/IP.

4. In the TCP/IP Properties dialog box, select the WINS Address tab, shown in Figure 12.22.

5. Enter the IP address for the primary and secondary WINS servers on your network in the appropriate boxes.

6. Deselect the Enable LMHOSTS Lookup option and click on OK to close the TCP/IP Properties dialog box.

7. Click on OK to close the Network applet.

8. Again, although you may not be prompted to do so, restart the computer to ensure that the new configuration is used.

CASE PROJECTS

1. You are installing Proxy Server on your network, which consists of 45 Windows NT Workstation computers and three NT Servers, one of which

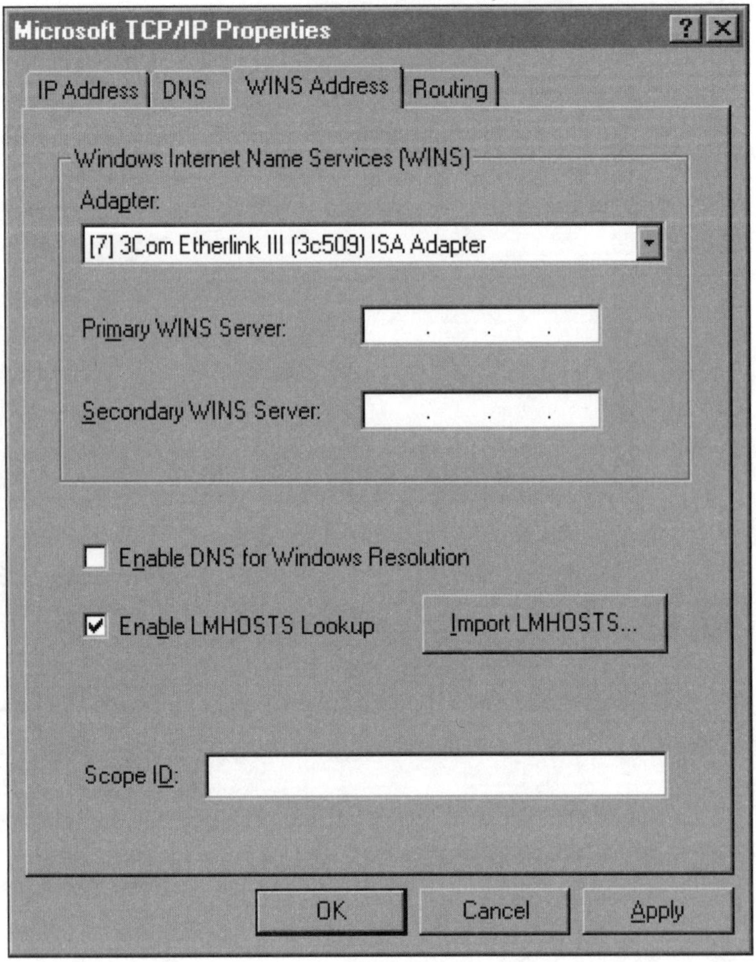

Figure 12.22   The WINS Address tab of the TCP/IP Properties dialog box.

is a DNS server. You have been using DNS successfully before the installation of Proxy Server and want to ensure that Internet communications continue unabated.

Required result: Configure the DNS to support Microsoft Proxy Server correctly.

Optional desired results: Include room for growth in the DNS scheme. The implementation should be as transparent to the users as possible.

Proposed solution: Configure the DNS server with two A records, one for the internal network interface and one for the external network interface. Which results does the proposed solution provide?

a. The proposed solution provides the required result and both optional desired results.

   b. The proposed solution provides the required result and one optional desired result.

   c. The proposed solution provides only the required result.

   d. The proposed solution does not provide the required result.

2. Traffic on your network has reached an all-time high and it's time for a change. You are currently running all 250 computers from a single 10BaseT hub. You have been using WINS for some time to provide NetBIOS name resolution on your network.

   Required result: Develop a plan to limit network traffic.

   Optional desired results: The system should support multiple subnets. The system should be easy to implement and support future expansion.

   Proposed solution: Install a router and divide the network into two subnets. To facilitate name resolution, configure two Windows NT clients as WINS Proxy Agents and install them on the network without the WINS server. Which results does the proposed solution provide?

   a. The proposed solution provides the required result and both optional desired results.

   b. The proposed solution provides the required result and one optional desired result.

   c. The proposed solution provides only the required result.

   d. The proposed solution does not provide the required result.

3. Your network is made up of 350 workstations with three Proxy Servers connecting it to the Internet. You have learned by experience that maintaining the HOSTS.TXT file is nearly impossible for a network that size, but you have been unable to convince management of the benefits of DNS. Finally, after much debating, they okay the installation of a DNS server.

   Required result: Develop a plan for implementing DNS that includes Proxy Server considerations.

   Optional desired results: The system should be easy to implement and support future expansion. The system's installation should be transparent to the users with little configuration.

   Proposed solution: Create multiple A records on the DNS server, one for the IP address of the internal network card for each proxy server. Reconfigure each client computer to point to the DNS record rather than a specific Proxy Server. Which results does the proposed solution provide?

   a. The proposed solution provides the required result and both optional desired results.

12

b. The proposed solution provides the required result and one optional desired result.

c. The proposed solution provides only the required result.

d. The proposed solution does not provide the required result.

COMPLEX DEPLOYMENT AND CONFIGURATION ISSUES

It's important to secure your internal network from possible intrusion. Sometimes, however, external clients need to access some of your internal resources. For example, clients may need to access your corporate Web server, or Internet servers may need to communicate with your internal mail servers to send and receive Internet mail. Microsoft Proxy Server 2.0 has a feature called *server proxying*, which allows you to place your mail servers (or application server) behind Proxy Server. Proxy Server then protects the mail servers from the Internet, yet the mail servers operate as if they were directly connected to the Internet.

To give administrators control over where servers are placed, and to make sure network security is not compromised, Microsoft Proxy Server 2.0 includes both *reverse proxying* and *reverse hosting*.

AFTER READING THIS CHAPTER AND COMPLETING THE EXERCISES, YOU WILL BE ABLE TO:

- Understand what needs to be done to place Microsoft Exchange Server behind a Microsoft Proxy Server.
- Understand how to implement Proxy Server's reverse proxying feature.
- Understand how to implement Proxy Server's reverse hosting feature.

Reverse proxying allows you to place your Web server behind the Proxy Server so it is protected from external attack. All Web requests are intercepted by the Proxy Server. If the request is for new information, the Proxy Server contacts the internal Web server and requests the information. However, if the information has been requested previously by another client, the Proxy Server sends the information as it is stored in its local cache.

Reverse hosting allows you to place multiple Web servers behind the Proxy Server and have them act as one. Requests to one server can be forwarded to another. You can configure this feature so it appears that clients are accessing multiple servers when they are, in fact, accessing a single Web server.

USING PROXY SERVER WITH EXCHANGE SERVER

Email is the most commonly used feature of the Internet. It has become so popular that having an email address is almost as common as having a telephone number. Most of us use email daily. It has truly made the world a smaller place.

When *Microsoft Exchange Server* was first released, it was sold as a mail system, and people still think of it as such. It is a mail server, but it is also much more. Exchange Server should be thought of as a groupware server rather than an email server.

Before integrating Microsoft Proxy Server and Exchange Server, it is important to be aware of and understand some of Exchange Server's protocols and features. In this chapter, we'll cover them in detail.

The most frequently used feature of Exchange Server is for messaging—the transfer of mail messages. It is becoming increasingly difficult to survive in today's business world without email. Today's businesses require Web page addresses, email addresses, and even chat ID numbers in addition to numbers for pagers, cellular telephones, and fax machines.

One of the drawbacks to Exchange Server version 5.0 was its 16GB limit for the Information Stores. Although this may seem like a lot of storage and information space, it wouldn't take a large organization long to fill it up. For example, if you allow your users up to 50MB of storage (in their mailbox or in public folders), you would only have 320 users on the system before you reached the Information Store limit (assuming that all users used their 50MB of space).

Exchange Server 5.5 includes:

- **Unlimited storage capacity (in the Enterprise Edition)** As stated previously, storage capacity in Exchange Server 5.5 is only limited by the physical media installed in the system.

- **Single-instance message store** Exchange Server stores messages once. If a message is sent to a distribution list (a collection of users), Exchange stores the message once and sends all the users in the distribution list a "pointer" to that one message.

- **Exchange Server clusters** With Exchange Enterprise Edition, you can cluster two Exchange Servers together so users can send or receive messages even in the event of hardware failure.

- **Exchange/NT integration** Microsoft Exchange integrates with the Windows NT user database. Therefore, information—such as usernames and password expiration—is shared between Windows NT and Exchange Server.

- **Security** Exchange Server uses several encryption standards, including Secure Sockets Layer (SSL), Enhanced Simple Mail Transport Protocol (E/SMTP), Simple Authentication and Security Layer (SASL), and digital signatures.

One of the most difficult (and important) tasks you will be responsible for is the integration of several different products, which can include new and legacy technologies. This is another area where Exchange Server excels. Exchange uses many of the most common messaging protocols, including SMTP, POP3, IMAP4, HTTP, LDAP, and NNTP:

- The *Simple Mail Transfer Protocol (SMTP)* is used to transfer mail messages between mail servers on the Internet. Because it is the standard protocol, it allows Exchange to communicate with other Exchange servers, Unix servers, Apple Macintosh servers, or any servers running SMTP.

- The *Post Office Protocol version 3 (POP3)* is used by the client (the user) to receive or pick up messages from the server. It is an Internet standard, so you can use any POP3 client to receive your messages regardless of your users' platforms.

- The *Internet Message Access Protocol version 4 (IMAP4)* is similar to POP3 in that it allows the client to receive messages from the server. The difference is that it gives the user more control as to which messages are downloaded (i.e., messages no larger than 20K), and it allows the user to connect to multiple IMAP4-compliant servers at the same time.

- The *Hypertext Transfer Protocol (HTTP)* is the protocol the client (Microsoft Internet Explorer or Netscape Navigator) uses to communicate with the Web server. This feature allows a client to access its mailbox or public folder information from anywhere on the Internet with any frame- and JavaScript-capable browser.

13

- The *Lightweight Directory Access Protocol (LDAP)* is used to search Exchange Server's directory to find users and user information such as phone numbers, email addresses, and so on.

- The *Network News Transfer Protocol (NNTP)* allows Exchange Server to act as a Usenet server. All selected newsgroups are stored as public folders that can be viewed and replied to by any Exchange user.

Microsoft Exchange Server can also connect to the following foreign mail systems:

- Lotus Notes
- cc:Mail
- MS Mail
- OfficeVision/VM (PROFs)
- Systems Network Architecture Distribution Service (SNADS), such as IBM OfficeVision/MVS or Fisher TAO
- X.500, X.400, and X.25

The *Microsoft Exchange Scripting Agent* is used to create event-driven agents, which are used to create automated collaborative applications and simple work flow. For example, you can create a form that a user can complete online. Once the user submits the form, it is sent to that user's supervisor. If the supervisor is not available or does not reply to the form within a set amount of time, Exchange Server can redirect the message to another individual who has the authority to respond to the form.

The *Microsoft Exchange Chat Service* enables realtime collaboration with any standard IRC or IRCX client. *Microsoft NetMeeting* is a conferencing tool that is integrated into the Outlook client. This tool allows users to initiate net meetings from Outlook directly. Exchange Server also includes the *Internet Locator Server (ILS)*, which allows users to use the familiar Microsoft Exchange directory to perform ILS lookups.

A new feature of Exchange Server is the *Deleted Item Recovery* feature. Deleted items or folders are hidden from the user and maintained on the server for a specified amount of time. During that time, deleted items can be recovered by the end user, which frees you to do other tasks.

Two versions of Microsoft Exchange Server 5.5 are available from Microsoft—Exchange Server 5.5 Standard Edition and Exchange Server 5.5 Enterprise Edition.

The Microsoft Exchange Server 5.5 Standard Edition contains the following:

- Exchange Server 5.5
- Outlook 97 client

- MS Mail Connector
- Internet Mail Service (IMS)
- cc:Mail Connector
- Microsoft Exchange Connector
- Lotus Notes Connector
- Collaboration Data Objects
- Internet News Service
- Microsoft Visual InterDev
- Microsoft Exchange Chat Service

The Microsoft Exchange Server 5.5 Enterprise Edition contains:

- All the components from the Standard Edition
- Unlimited Information Store storage
- X.400 Connector
- IBM OfficeVision/VM Connector
- SNADS Connector

PROXY AND EXCHANGE

Two methods can be used to allow Microsoft Exchange Server to operate with Proxy Server version 2.0:

- Colocate the Exchange services and Proxy Server on the same physical computer.
- Install Exchange Server on a different computer that is located on the protected internal network. Then configure Proxy Server's Server Proxy feature to redirect the listen( ) call of the Exchange services.

 The Server Proxy feature is only available in Microsoft Proxy Server version 2.0. It is not available in version 1.0.

EXCHANGE SERVER AND PROXY SERVER ON THE SAME COMPUTER

When you install Exchange Server and Proxy Server on the same computer, Exchange Server is able to listen for connections from any of the network interfaces (see Figure 13.1 for an example).

The server in Figure 13.1 has three network interface cards installed in it. Interface 0 connects the server to the Internet, Interface 1 connects the server to an internal

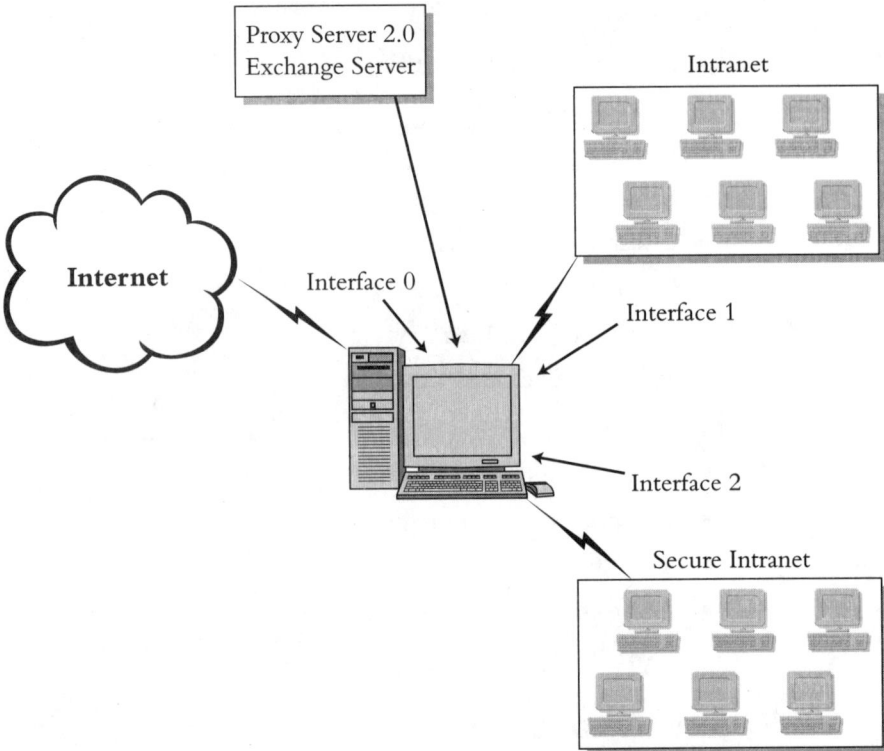

Figure 13.1   Colocating Exchange Server and Proxy Server.

intranet, and Interface 2 connects the server to an internal secure intranet (i.e., information that is not for all employees may be stored here). So any mail clients or SMTP servers on the Internet, intranet, or secure intranet are able to send and receive mail from the Exchange Server.

However, if the Proxy Server packet-filtering feature is enabled, all communication from mail clients or servers on the Internet is blocked. More specifically, all communication except ICMP requests to or from Proxy Server is blocked. Proxy Server's dynamic packet-filtering feature allows any application using the proxy services to communicate with the Internet.

Because we are installing Exchange Server and Proxy Server on the same computer, Exchange Server will not be using the Proxy services to communicate with the Internet. To prevent all communications from being blocked by Proxy Server, a static filter must be configured and enabled on the Proxy packet filter interface for each Exchange Server service.

The following steps must be taken to create a packet filter using predefined filter definitions:

1. Click on the Add button on the Packet Filters tab in the Security dialog box (see Figure 13.2). The Packet Filter Properties dialog box opens.

2. Under Allow This Microsoft Windows NT Server To Exchange Packet Of Type, click on Predefined Filter and select a protocol (for example, SMTP).

3. By default, the predefined filters allow communication to/from any host on the Internet. If necessary, change the Local Host and Remote Host settings before you click on OK.

4. Click on OK.

5. Repeat Steps 1 through 4 to add the POP and IDENTD filters.

EXCHANGE SERVER AND PROXY SERVER ON DIFFERENT COMPUTERS

Server proxying is the Proxy Server feature that allows you to locate an Exchange Server (or any mail server) on your private intranet and still have it protected by

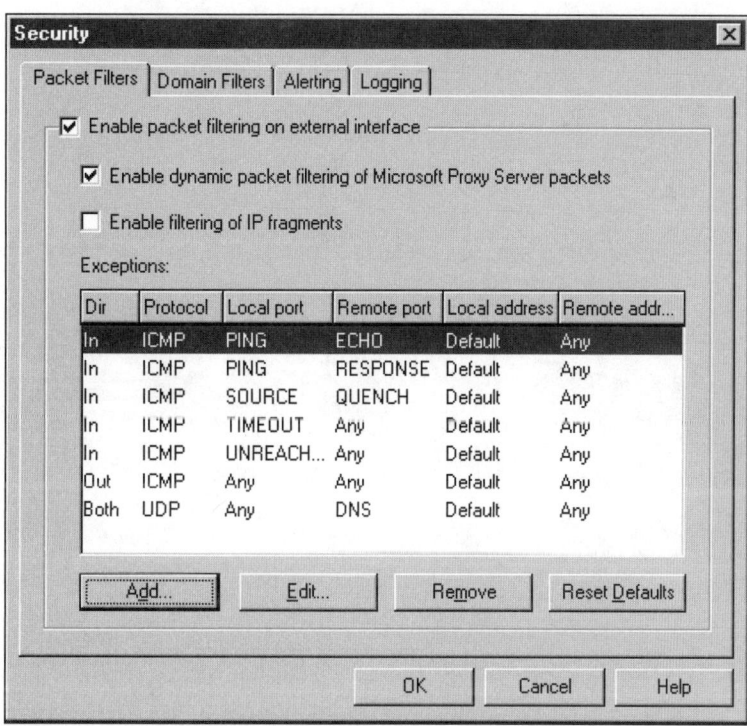

Figure 13.2   The Packet Filters tab in the Security dialog box.

Microsoft Proxy Server. Server proxying gives Proxy Server the ability to listen for inbound packets destined for a computer that is located behind the Proxy Server computer. The Proxy Server then forwards the incoming requests to the correct internal computer. The external host (the host on the Internet) sees the Proxy Server as the destination computer. For example, you can redirect incoming mail to your internal Exchange Server. The client (or server) sending the mail messages assumes that the Proxy Server is the Exchange Server. This allows you to function normally without compromising your network security. Figure 13.3 shows an example of server proxying.

The Proxy Server listens for connections on behalf of the internal service or application by binding the service or application to the external network interface card of the Proxy Server computer. See Hands-On Project 13.1 to set up the Server Proxy feature for Exchange Server version 4.0, 5.0, or 5.5. You must follow these instructions exactly or Exchange will not function properly with the Server Proxy feature.

For email to be sent successfully from anywhere on the Internet to your Exchange Server, you must configure the Domain Name System (DNS) entries for your Exchange Server computer correctly. If you are using your Internet Service Provider's (ISP's) DNS server, you must contact them and request that they add two records for your domain—an MX and an A record.

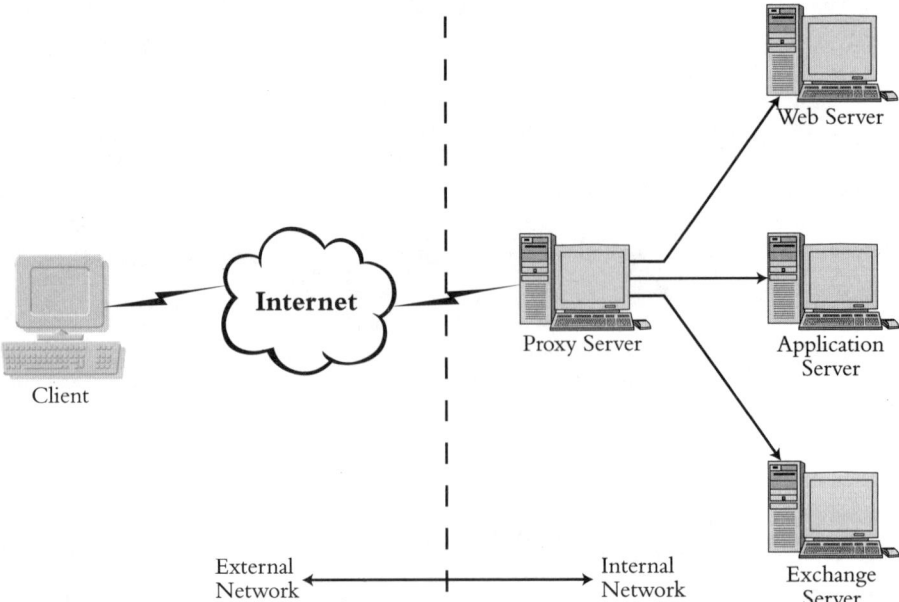

Figure 13.3   An example of server proxying.

The *MX* and *A* DNS records must refer to the IP address of your Proxy Server's external network interface card, not the internal IP address of the Exchange Server computer.

An MX Record is used to identify which server on your network is to receive mail messages from the Internet. MX stands for Mail eXchanger. The MX record is listed in the following format:

```
Company.com.            IN   MX   10      exchange.company.com.
```

In this example, the number 10 is assigned to each MX record for redundancy. For example, you can configure two different mail servers. If one server is not available, the other is used. The server with the lowest number assigned to it is contacted first. The only time a server with a higher number is contacted is if the preferred server is not available. For example, if we have two servers named Exchange and Backup-Exchange, the MX records would look like this:

```
Company.com.            IN   MX   10      exchange.company.com.
Company.com.            IN   MX   20      backup-
                                          exchange.company.com.
```

The second MX record is used only if the preferred server is not available. It will not contact both servers if the preferred server answers any mail connections.

An A record groups together an IP address to a *Fully Qualified Domain Name (FQDN)*. This combination is used to convert an FQDN to an IP address. Remember that computers do not know how to communicate by using the FQDN; they use the IP address (they actually use the Media Access Control, or MAC, address). FQDNs are used so the names are easier to remember. (When was the last time you entered in 207.68.137.53 for **www.microsoft.com**?) For example, if the previous server (exchange.company.com) has an IP address of 192.168.12.2 and your Proxy Server's external network interface card has an IP address of 10.34.122.5, the A record will look like this:

```
Exchange.company.com.   IN   A    10.34.122.5
```

Notice that the IP address of the Proxy Server's external interface card is grouped with the Exchange Server's FQDN. If you were to group the Exchange Server's IP address with its FQDN, then clients on the Internet would attempt to contact the Exchange Server directly. Their attempts would be blocked by the Proxy Server and connections would not be made.

You can also configure a *PTR* record, also known as a pointer record. A PTR record is used to convert an IP address back into an FQDN—for example:

```
5.122.34.10.in-addr.arpa.   IN   PTR   exchange.company.com.
```

This configuration is for Exchange Server specifically. Table 13.1 has some of the configuration information required for third-party SMTP servers.

The entries in Table 13.1 must be saved in a file named WSPCFG.INI.

REVERSE PROXYING

Reverse proxying is a feature that gives Microsoft Proxy Server the ability to listen to incoming requests for an Internet Web server and to respond on behalf of that server. When you configure this method, you can place a nonsecure Web server behind the Proxy Server and have it protected from the Internet. Normally, if you were to place the Web server on the external (Internet) network, it would be open to attack. Web servers usually use port 80 to communicate. Most systems, however, have several other ports that they listen to. These ports are the security holes, not port 80. Hackers can break into the Web server by using known weaknesses in protocols other than the HTTP protocol. When you place the Web server behind Microsoft Proxy Server, the Proxy Server will block all ports except port 80. Then, when hackers use known weaknesses to try to break into your Web server, it is the Proxy Server they are attempting to break into. It is less likely that a hacker will break into a Microsoft Proxy Server computer than into a Web server.

Another explanation of reverse proxying is that it causes the Proxy Server computer to impersonate a Web server to the outside world. The Proxy Server computer responds to client requests for Web content from its cache and

Table 13.1   Third-party SMTP server information.

Product	Wspcfg.ini Location	Entry
Microsoft SQL Server	Same folder as SQLSERVR.EXE	[SQLSERVR] ServerBindTCPPorts=1433 Persistent=1 KillOldSession=1
cc:Mail Server	Same folder as WINSMTP.EXE	[WINSMTP] ServerBindTcpPorts=25 Persistent=1 KillOldSession=1
cc:Mail Server (continued)	Same folder as POP3D.EXE	[POP3D] ServerBindTcpPorts=110 Persistent=1 KillOldSession=1
Lotus Notes (replicator service)	Same folder as POP3D.EXE	[NREPLICA] ServerBindTcpPorts=1352 Persistent=1 KillOldSession=1
Lotus Notes (SMTP service)	Same folder as NISESCTL.EXE	[NISESCTL] ServerBindTcpPorts=25
Lotus Notes (SMTP continued)	Same folder as NOSESHLR.EXE	[NOSESHLR] ServerBindTcpPorts=25

forwards requests to the real Web server only when the requests cannot be served directly from its cache. Figure 13.4 shows an example of reverse proxying. To configure reverse proxying, see Hands-On Project 13.2.

REVERSE HOSTING

Reverse hosting, or virtual hosting, takes reverse proxying to another level. It does this by maintaining a list of Internet server computers (not just Web servers) that have permission to publish to the Internet. Therefore, Microsoft Proxy Server listens and responds on behalf of several servers that are located behind it. It maintains a mapping table that allows multiple internal server computers to publish to the Internet using Proxy Server's external IP address. To the client, this process is transparent. There is no indication that the request is being processed through a proxy server. As far as the client is concerned, it is communicating with the Web server directly. Figure 13.5 shows an example of reverse hosting. To configure reverse hosting, see Hands-On Project 13.3.

After reverse hosting has been configured, when a client sends a request for **http://www.company.com**, the first Web server will respond. If, however, a client sends a request for **http://www.company.com/2**, the Proxy Server will redirect that request to the second Web server. To the client, the Proxy Server seems to service requests for both Web pages.

CHAPTER SUMMARY

13

Microsoft Proxy Server 2.0 has three advanced tools that allow you to configure your internal servers to operate with the Internet.

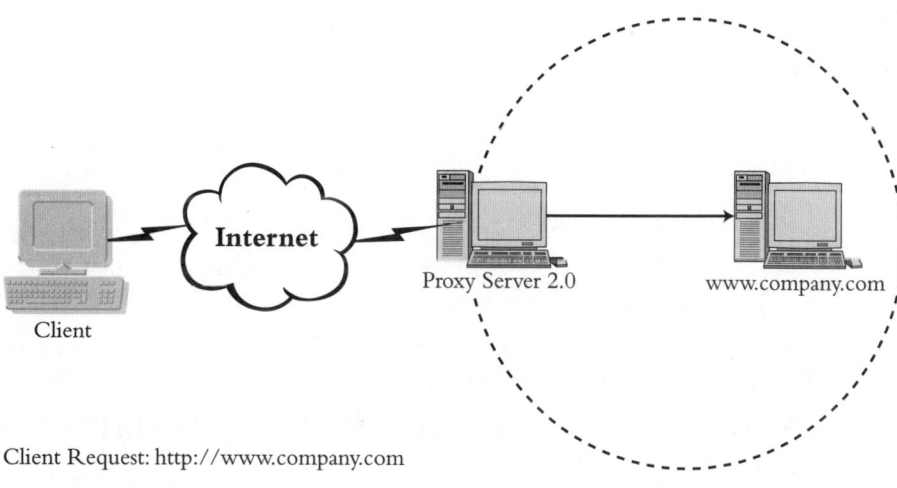

Client Request: http://www.company.com

Figure 13.4   Reverse proxying.

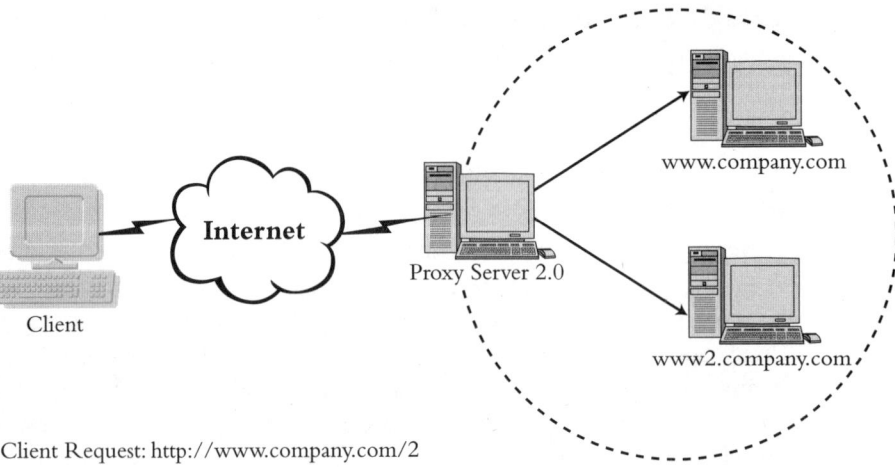

Client Request: http://www.company.com/2

Figure 13.5   Reverse hosting.

The first is called server proxying. It allows you to specify servers, such as SQL or SMTP servers, that are to be placed behind the Proxy Server. This protects them from possible attack and makes it appear to the external client that the Proxy Server and the internal server are one and the same.

The second is called reverse proxying. Reverse proxying allows you to place your Web server on the internal network and have it protected from the Internet by the Proxy Server. This saves you the trouble of having to lock down the Web server. Because the only port allowed to communicate with the Web server is the HTTP port (80), it makes it much easier to secure your Web information.

The third tool is called reverse hosting, also known as virtual hosting. This feature takes reverse proxying and extends it. Reverse hosting allows any server sitting behind Proxy Server to publish to the Internet. The Proxy Server computer simulates virtual roots on a Web server and then redirects the requests for a particular domain to a single Web server.

KEY TERMS

- **A Record**—A DNS record used to map FQDNs to IP addresses.
- **cc:Mail Connector**—A Microsoft Exchange Connector that allows Exchange to communicate with Lotus cc:Mail systems.
- **Domain Name System (DNS)**—The hierarchical database of domain name-to-IP-address relationships.
- **Fully Qualified Domain Name (FQDN)**—The full DNS path of an Internet host.

- **Hypertext Transfer Protocol (HTTP)**—The protocol used to communicate between a Web browser and a Web server (uses HTML).

- **Internet Locator Server (ILS)**—Allows users to search for other users on the Internet. ILS creates a dynamic database of users.

- **Internet Mail Service (IMS)**—A Connector that connects an Exchange site to either an SMTP mail system or a remote Exchange site.

- **Internet Messaging Access Protocol version 4 (IMAP4)**—A protocol that allows clients to send and receive messages from their mailboxes and gives them access to public folders.

- **Internet News Service**—A service that uses NNTP to connect the Microsoft Exchange Server to Usenet.

- **Internet Service Provider (ISP)**—A third party that offers Internet connectivity to individuals and businesses.

- **Lightweight Directory Access Protocol (LDAP)**—A protocol used to share Exchange Address Book information with external users.

- **Lotus Notes Connector**—A Microsoft Exchange Connector that allows Exchange to communicate with a Lotus Notes system.

- **Microsoft Exchange Chat Service**—Enables realtime collaboration using any standard IRC or IRCX client.

- **Microsoft Exchange Scripting Agent**—Allows Exchange Server to perform limited work flow and to create automated collaborative applications.

- **Microsoft Exchange Server**—The Microsoft Messaging groupware server.

- **Microsoft NetMeeting**—Allows users to initiate net meetings over the Internet or an internal network.

- **MS Mail Connector**—A Microsoft Exchange Connector that allows Exchange to communicate with MS Mail systems.

- **MX record**—A DNS record used to identify which servers are to receive messages. Known as the Mail eXchanger.

- **Network News Transfer Protocol (NNTP)**—The protocol used to send and receive Usenet messages.

- **pointer record (PTR)**—A DNS record used to map IP addresses to FQDNs.

- **Post Office Protocol version 3 (POP3)**—A standard Internet mail protocol used to read messages from a POP3 server.

- **PROFs Connector**—A Microsoft Exchange Connector that allows Exchange to communicate with a PROFs mail system (OfficeVision/VM Connector).

13

- **reverse hosting**—A method of hosting multiple Web servers internally and having Proxy Server both protect them and redirect requests to a specific Web server.

- **reverse proxying**—A method of placing an insecure Web server behind a secure Proxy Server.

- **Secure Sockets Layer (SSL) encryption**—A method used to encrypt information between hosts.

- **server proxying**—A method of placing application servers behind the Microsoft Proxy Server computer to protect them from unauthorized access.

- **Simple Mail Transfer Protocol (SMTP)**—The mail protocol used to connect two hosts running the TCP/IP protocol.

- **SNADS Connector**—A Microsoft Exchange Connector used to allow Exchange Server to communicate with a SNADS mail system.

- **SOCKS Proxy service**—A Proxy Server service that allows clients running the SOCKS protocol to access the Internet.

- **Web Proxy service**—A Proxy Server service that allows clients to use their Web browser to access information on the Internet.

- **WinSock Proxy service**—A Proxy Server service that allows clients to use WinSock applications to access the Internet.

- **X.400 Connector**—A Microsoft Exchange Connector that allows Exchange to communicate with an X.400 mail system.

REVIEW QUESTIONS

1. Which Proxy Server feature makes all your internal Web servers appear as one?
   a. server proxying
   b. reverse proxying
   c. reverse hosting

2. Which Proxy Server feature allows Internet clients to communicate with your internal application servers?
   a. server proxying
   b. reverse proxying
   c. reverse hosting

3. Which Proxy Server feature is used to forward all Web requests to one server?
   a. server proxying
   b. reverse proxying
   c. reverse hosting

4. You would like an application to work through the Proxy Server. You enable Web publishing, create a static packet filter, create a custom WSPCFG.INI file, and place the file in the application's folder. Now the other application in that folder stops working. What must you do to solve the problem?

   a. Move the nonworking application to another folder; you can only have one application per folder.

   b. Create a second WSPCFG.INI file, name it WSPCFG2.INI, and place it in the same folder as the applications.

   c. Add a unique section in the WSPCFG.INI file for the nonworking application.

   d. Create a WSPCFG.INI file for the nonworking application and place it in the MSP directory on the Proxy Server.

5. You want to allow Exchange to communicate through the Proxy Server. You have created a static packet filter for port 25. What else must you do?

   a. Create a custom WSPCFG.INI file and place it in the \WINNT\SYSTEM32 folder.

   b. Create a custom WSPCFG.INI file and place it in the \EXCHSRVR folder.

   c. Create a custom WSPCFG.INI file and place it in the same folder as STORE.EXE.

   d. Create a custom WSPCFG.INI file and place it in the same folder as MSEXCIMC.EXE.

6. You can only configure one internal application server using the server proxying feature. (True or False?)

7. When you are installing Microsoft Exchange Server behind Proxy Server, you must specify a DNS server that resides on the Internet. (True or False?)

HANDS-ON PROJECTS

 PROJECT 13.1

To allow for Microsoft Exchange Server to operate behind a Microsoft Proxy Server computer, complete the following steps:

1. Install and configure Microsoft Proxy Server version 2.0 on the computer that will act as your gateway.

2. In the WinSock Proxy Properties dialog box, select Client Configuration. The Client Installation/Configuration dialog box appears (see Figure 13.6). Set the Client Connects To Microsoft WinSock Proxy Server By option to IP Address.

13

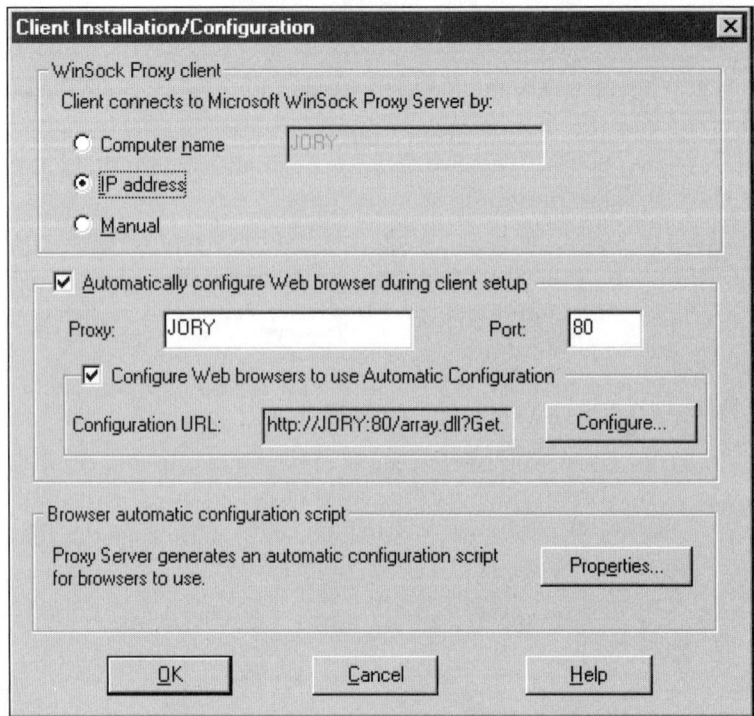

Figure 13.6 The Client Installation/Configuration dialog box.

3. Install the WinSock Proxy (WSP) client on the Exchange Server computer. If you have already installed the WSP client, reinstall it by connecting to the MSPCLNT share on the Proxy Server and running the setup program.

 A Domain Name Server (DNS) must be configured on the Microsoft Exchange computer. If you do not configure this properly, the Exchange Server computer will not be able to send Internet mail properly.

4. To configure the Domain Name Server, open the Network Control Panel, select TCP/IP Protocol from the Protocols tab, and click on the Properties button. Add your Internet Service Provider's (ISP's) DNS server address (or addresses) under Domain Name System in the DNS tab, as shown in Figure 13.7.

 If your DNS server does not work correctly, try using the Microsoft Network DNS servers to test your name resolution: 131.107.1.7 or 131.107.1.240.

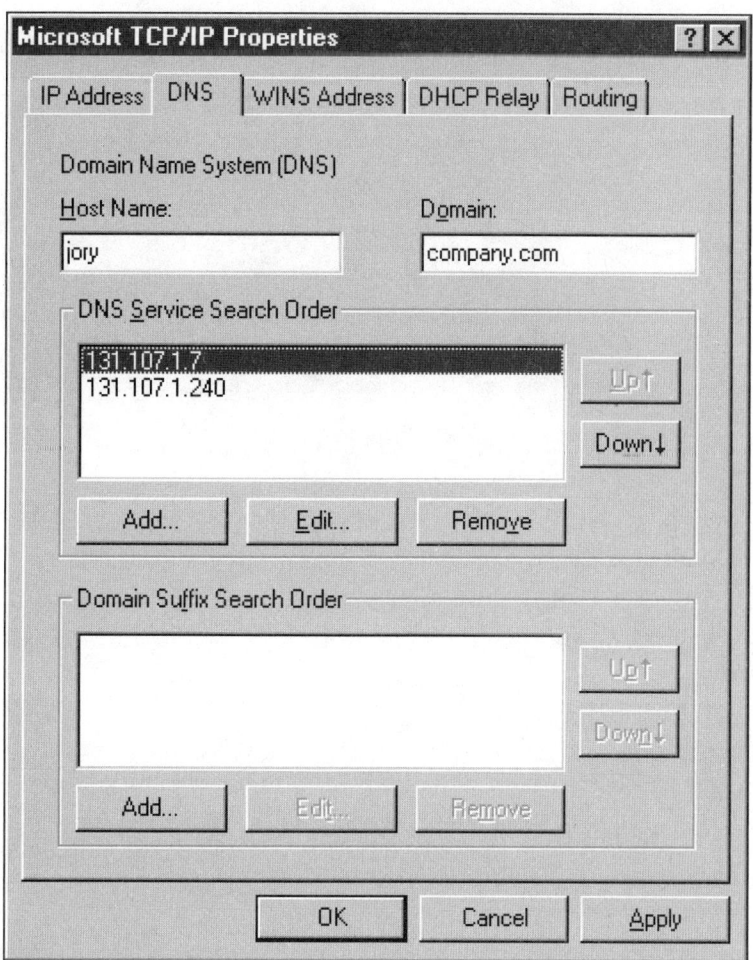

Figure 13.7   Configuring the DNS properties.

5. Test the WSP client on the Exchange Server computer by attempting to connect to a remote site. For example, open an MS-DOS prompt window and type in "FTP FTP.MICROSOFT.COM". You should see a response similar to the one in Figure 13.8.

6. You must now create two different Proxy Server Configuration files on the Exchange Server computer (the WSPCFG.INI file).

- The first WSPCFG.INI file is used by the Microsoft Exchange SMTP service. Using Notepad, create a file with the following lines. They

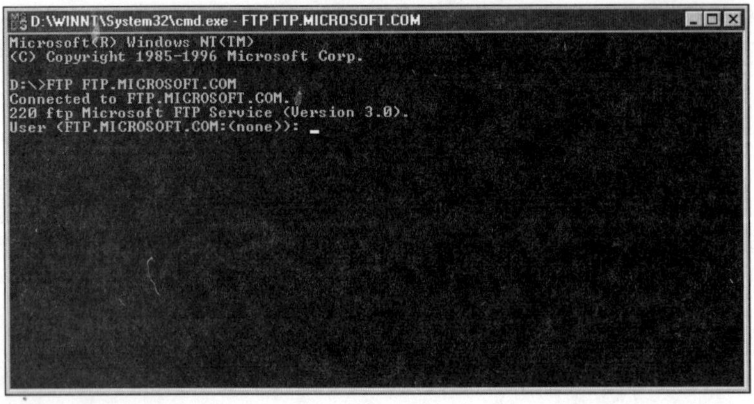

```
D:\WINNT\System32\cmd.exe - FTP FTP.MICROSOFT.COM                    _ □ ✕
Microsoft(R) Windows NT(TM)
(C) Copyright 1985-1996 Microsoft Corp.

D:\>FTP FTP.MICROSOFT.COM
Connected to FTP.MICROSOFT.COM.
220 ftp Microsoft FTP Service (Version 3.0).
User (FTP.MICROSOFT.COM:(none)): _
```

Figure 13.8   Testing the WSP client.

have to be *exactly* as shown in the following code. This is a case-sensitive operation:

```
[MSEXCIMC]

ServerBindTcpPorts=25

Persistent=1

KillOldSession=1
```

- Save this file as WSPCFG.INI in the directory where MSEXCIMC.EXE is located. By default, the MSEXCIMC.EXE file is located in the \EXCHSRVR\CONNECT\MSEXCIMC\BIN directory.

This will bind the SMTP port (25) on the Exchange Server to the Proxy Server's SMTP port.

- The second WSPCFG.INI file is used by the Microsoft Exchange Information Store (STORE.EXE). Using Notepad, create a file with the following lines. They have to be *exactly* as shown in the following code. This is a case-sensitive operation:

```
[STORE]

ServerBindTcpPorts=110,119,143

Persistent=1

KillOldSession=1
```

Save this file as WSPCFG.INI in the directory where STORE.EXE is located. By default, the STORE.EXE file is located in the \EXCHSRVR\BIN directory.

Make sure you save the two files as INI files and that they do not have a .TXT extension. The file might appear as WSPCFG.INI.TXT If it does, you need to rename it. By default, Windows NT hides all known extensions. Make sure you set Windows NT to display all extensions; otherwise, the file will appear as WSPCFG.INI, but it will actually be named WSPCFG.INI.TXT. To configure Windows NT to display all extensions, select Options from the View menu in Windows NT Explorer and clear the Hide File Extensions For Known File Types checkbox in the View tab.

7. If Access Control is not enabled on the WinSock Proxy service, skip to Step 9. If Access Control is enabled on the WinSock Proxy service, you must grant access to the Exchange service user account. This account must be a domain account rather than a local account because a local account would not be seen by the Proxy Server computer. If the Exchange service account is local, create a new domain account and grant it logon rights to all the Exchange services by using the Service Control Panel applet.

8. To give the Exchange service account access to the Proxy Server, select the Permissions tab in the WinSock Proxy Service Properties dialog box (see Figure 13.9) and assign the account the Unlimited Access right.

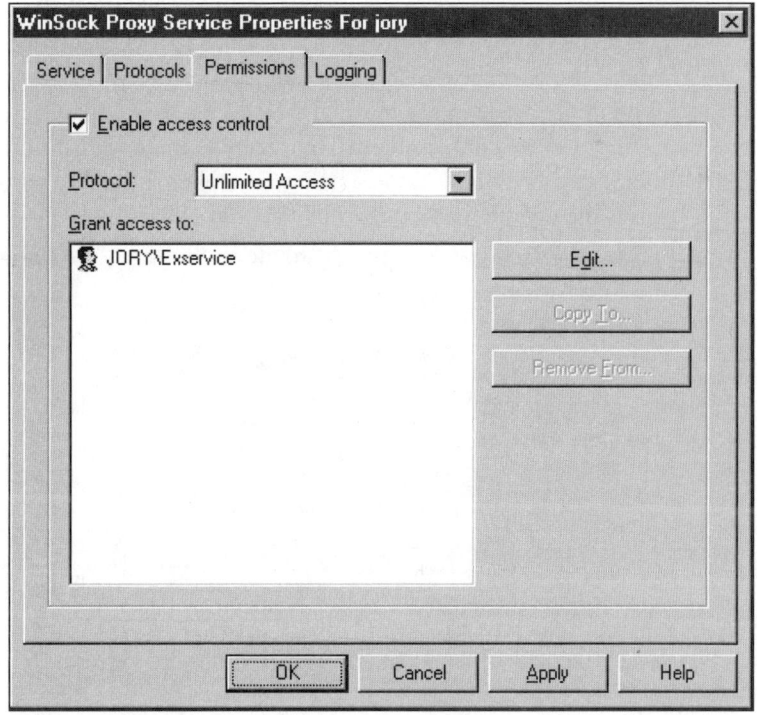

13

Figure 13.9   The Permissions tab of the WinSock Proxy Service Properties dialog box.

9. Reboot the Exchange Server computer. The Exchange Server should now be listening on the external network interface of the Proxy Server computer.

10. To test the connectivity to the Exchange Server computer, you must have access to a computer that is directly connected to the Internet (i.e., a computer that is located on the external side of the Proxy Server). From that computer, perform the following steps:

   ▪ Run TELNET.EXE from the Start/Run option.

   ▪ Select the Remote System option from the Connect menu. Enter the external IP address of the Proxy Server in the Host Name field and 25 in the Port field (see Figure 13.10) and click on OK.

   ▪ After a short time (you may have to press the Enter key), a message from the Exchange SMTP service will appear.

PROJECT 13.2

To configure reverse proxying, follow these steps:

1. From the Internet Service Manager, double-click on Web Proxy.

2. Select the Publishing tab (shown in Figure 13.11). Select the Enable Web Publishing checkbox. Select the Sent To Another Web Server radio button. Type in the name of the internal Web server in the space provided; for example, www.company.com. You can type in an FQDN (if you are using DNS) or a NetBIOS name. The port number should be set to 80 because this is the default used by the HTTP protocol.

3. Click on OK. Now any requests made to the Proxy Server are forwarded to the internal Web server.

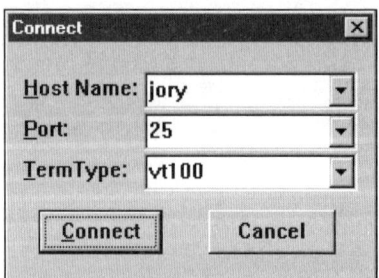

Figure 13.10   Using Telnet to connect to a remote system.

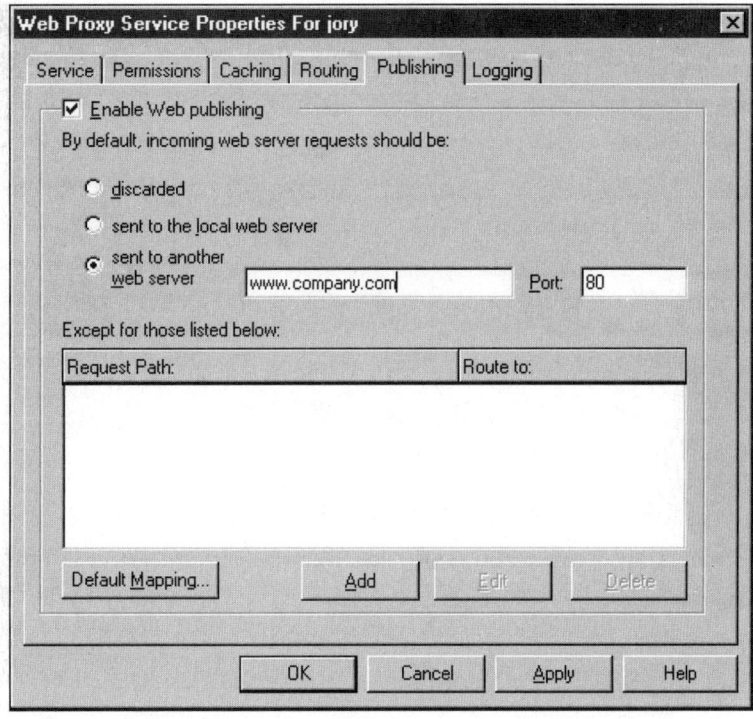

Figure 13.11   Use the Publishing tab of the Web Proxy Service
Properties dialog box to configure reverse proxying.

PROJECT 13.3

To configure reverse hosting, follow these steps:

1. From the Internet Service Manager, double-click on Web Proxy service.

2. Select the Publishing tab. Select the Enable Web Publishing checkbox and the Discarded radio button.

3. Click on Add. Enter "http://www.company.com/2" in the Path field and "http://www2.company.com" in the URL field. Click on OK. The Path and URL fields are shown in Figure 13.12.

4. Enter the default Web server name for legacy Web clients (shown in Figure 13.13). Click on OK.

5. Click on OK. Figure 13.14 shows the Publishing tab configured for reverse hosting.

Figure 13.12   The Web server Mapping dialog box.

 CASE PROJECTS

1. Your company currently uses Microsoft Proxy Server 2.0 for its Internet connectivity. You have been asked to configure Proxy Server to allow several internal Web servers to host your company's Web site.

   Required result: Make it look like there is only one Web server for your company.

   Optional desired results: Make the Web site available to your internal users. Protect the Web site from Internet attacks.

   Proposed solution: Install the Web servers and Proxy Server on the same computer. Configure Web publishing and dynamic packet filtering. Which results does the proposed solution provide?

   a. The proposed solution provides the required result and both optional desired results.

Figure 13.13   The Default Local Host Name dialog box.

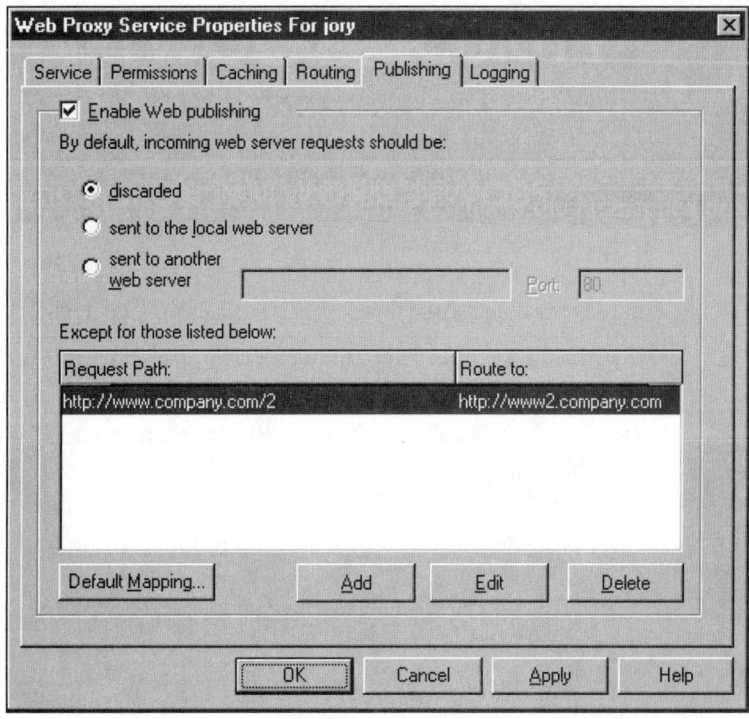

Figure 13.14   The Publishing tab of the Web Proxy Service Properties
dialog box configured for reverse hosting.

13

b. The proposed solution provides the required result and one optional
desired result.

c. The proposed solution provides only the required result.

d. The proposed solution does not provide the required result.

2. Your company currently uses Microsoft Proxy Server 2.0 for its Internet
connectivity. You have been asked to configure Proxy Server to allow several
internal Web servers to host your company's Web site.

Required result: Make it look like there is only one Web server for your
company.

Optional desired results: Make the Web site available to your internal users.
Protect the Web site from Internet attacks.

Proposed solution: Install the Web servers on a separate network. Block all
communication between this network and your internal network.
Configure Web publishing and dynamic packet filtering. Configure mapping
for your Web servers. Which results does the proposed solution provide?

a. The proposed solution provides the required result and both optional
desired results.

b. The proposed solution provides the required result and one optional desired result.

c. The proposed solution provides only the required result.

d. The proposed solution does not provide the required result.

3. Your company currently uses Microsoft Proxy Server 2.0 for its Internet connectivity. You have been asked to configure Proxy Server to allow several internal Web servers to host your company's Web site.

Required result: Make it look like there is only one Web server for your company.

Optional desired results: Make the Web site available to your internal users. Protect the Web site from Internet attacks.

Proposed solution: Install the Web servers on the internal network. Configure Web publishing and dynamic packet filtering. Configure mapping for your Web servers. Which results does the proposed solution provide?

a. The proposed solution provides the required result and both optional desired results.

b. The proposed solution provides the required result and one optional desired result.

c. The proposed solution provides only the required result.

d. The proposed solution does not provide the required result.

4. Your company uses several internal Web servers to publish information to the Internet. You have configured Web publishing on Proxy Server. What else must you specify to allow one internal Web server to receive all incoming requests?

a. Configure DNS to forward all requests to one Web server.

b. Configure DHCP to forward all requests to one Web Server.

c. Create a custom WSPCFG.INI file and place it on the Web server.

d. Enter the URL for the Web server in the Sent To Another Web Server field.

5. You can configure more than one application (such as Exchange Server and SQL Server) to work through the Proxy Server by creating multiple WSPCFG.INI files and placing them in the same folder as the server's executables. (True or False?)

6. You install Microsoft Exchange Server on a computer running the Proxy Client application. You create a custom WSPCFG.INI and place it in the Exchange folder. You configure a default mapping for the SMTP port (25). Your Exchange Server cannot communicate with the Internet. Why?

a. Microsoft Exchange Server must be on the same computer as Proxy Server.

b. You must reinstall the Proxy Client application from the server.

c. You installed Microsoft Exchange version 4.0; you must upgrade to version 5.5.

d. You must place a copy of the WSPCFG.INI file on the proxy server in the C:\MSP directory.

13

TROUBLESHOOTING PROXY SERVER

One of the toughest tasks an administrator will ever be assigned is the one of troubleshooting a system. This chapter will help you understand some of the troubleshooting tools available to you when you are attempting to solve Microsoft Proxy Server problems. The Microsoft Proxy Server Registry entries are listed, as are event messages.

AFTER READING THIS CHAPTER AND COMPLETING THE
EXERCISES, YOU WILL BE ABLE TO:

- Understand the Windows NT Registry Editor
- Use the Microsoft Performance Monitor application
- Use the Microsoft Event Viewer

THE BASICS OF TROUBLESHOOTING

Troubleshooting NT Server and Proxy Server configurations is one of the most difficult and challenging tasks you might perform as an administrator. It is a four-step process that includes identifying a problem, diagnosing the problem, implementing a solution, and verifying that the implemented solution has solved the problem.

Identifying a problem is usually a straightforward and easy process. Diagnosing the problem is much more challenging. Use the resources you have at hand. Such resources include TechNet, the online documentation, the Internet, and most importantly, other administrators. Subscribe to a mailing list such as the NTSYSADMIN-list or NTools E-News (subscribe at **www.sunbelt-software.com**). You would be amazed how far other NT administrators will go to assist an administrator they have never met (and probably never will).

When you implement a solution, document every task you perform. This will help you reverse the changes you made if necessary. Once a task is performed, verify whether or not the problem has been fixed. If it has not, reverse the change and attempt a different solution. Try not to implement change after change; if your system starts to fail in other ways, you'll have a tough time figuring out which change caused the problem. Once you have verified that a problem has been solved, document the problem and the change you made to solve the problem. Documenting the problem and storing the information (in a text file or a database) will save you and your colleagues time should the same problem occur again.

RESOURCES FOR TROUBLESHOOTING: WHERE TO LOOK FOR HELP

Because Proxy Server is part of Microsoft BackOffice, it ties in very closely with the Windows NT Event Viewer. The Windows NT Event Viewer is shown in Figure 14.1. If you are experiencing problems with Proxy Server, the system event log in the Windows NT Event Viewer is a good place to start. Proxy Server logs many messages in the format

```
Messagetext Errornumber
```

where

```
Messagetext is the explanatory message.

Errornumber is a Windows NT error code number.
```

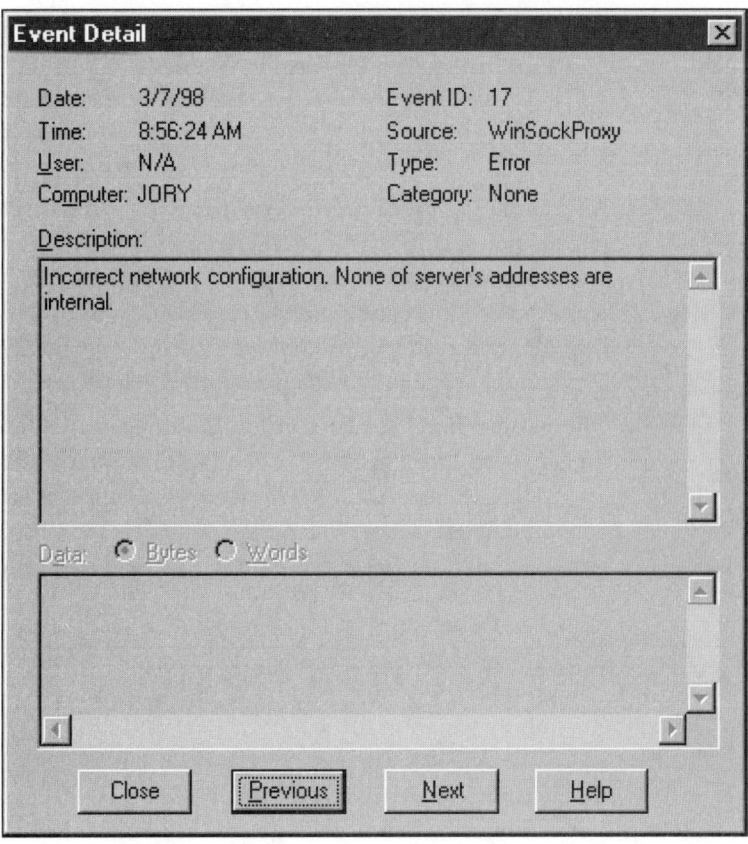

Figure 14.1   The Event Viewer error dialog box.

You can also use the Proxy Server Diagnostic Utility (MSPDIAG.EXE) to trouble-shoot common configuration problems.

Several other tools are available to help you troubleshoot Proxy Server installation and performance including:

- **Microsoft TechNet** A monthly subscription of CD-ROMs that contain an impressive amount of information of the evaluation, implementation, and support of Microsoft products. This product also contains the same Microsoft Knowledge Base that the Microsoft support engineers use to troubleshoot customer problems. Also included are the Microsoft Resource Kits, as well as service patches, hot fixes, and evaluation copies of many Microsoft products, including Proxy Server 2.0. You can find more information about TechNet on the Web at **www.microsoft.com/technet**.

14

- **Microsoft Knowledge Base** An online version of the same database used by Microsoft support engineers when they troubleshoot customer problems. Also included are troubleshooting wizards and downloadable files (such as printer and video drivers). You can access the Microsoft Knowledge Base at **support.microsoft.com**.

- **Microsoft Proxy Server home page** Includes a wealth of information specific to Microsoft Proxy Server. Most of the information available on this page is also available on TechNet. It is, however, a good idea to check this page regularly because new information is posted here before it is added to TechNet. You can access the Microsoft Proxy Server home page at **www.microsoft.com/proxy**.

- **Microsoft Proxy Server Online Documentation** An online manual for Microsoft Proxy Server 2.0; you must use Internet Explorer 4 to access all its features. You can choose to install this documentation when you install Proxy Server. The online documentation has a complete listing of the Proxy Server Registry entries and event messages.

PROXY SERVER REGISTRY ENTRIES

All configuration information for Windows NT (and Proxy Server) is stored in a database called the *Registry*. The Registry is made up of sections, called *subtrees*, such as HKEY_LOCAL_MACHINE and HKEY_CURRENT_CONFIG, at the top of the hierarchy. Below the subtrees are keys (such as HARDWARE, SOFTWARE, and SYSTEM), and below the keys are the subkeys. Each key and subkey has an entry assigned to it. These entries consist of entry names, data types, and values. One of two Registry Editors can be used to view, change, or delete these values directly: REGEDT32.EXE and REGEDIT.EXE.

 Do not edit the Registry unless it is absolutely necessary and you know what you are doing. Try to use the Windows NT Control Panel applets to make any system changes. If the Registry is edited incorrectly, you may have to reinstall some or all of your system's software.

THE WINDOWS NT REGISTRY EDITOR

When it's installed, Windows NT does not create icons for the Registry Editor by default. You must manually execute the application. To do so, select Run from the Start menu and type "regedt32" (to access REGEDT32.EXE, shown in Figure 14.2) or "regedit" (to access REGEDIT.EXE, shown in Figure 14.3).

Try to limit the number of changes you make to the Registry at one time. If you follow this advice, it will be much easier for you to troubleshoot if something goes

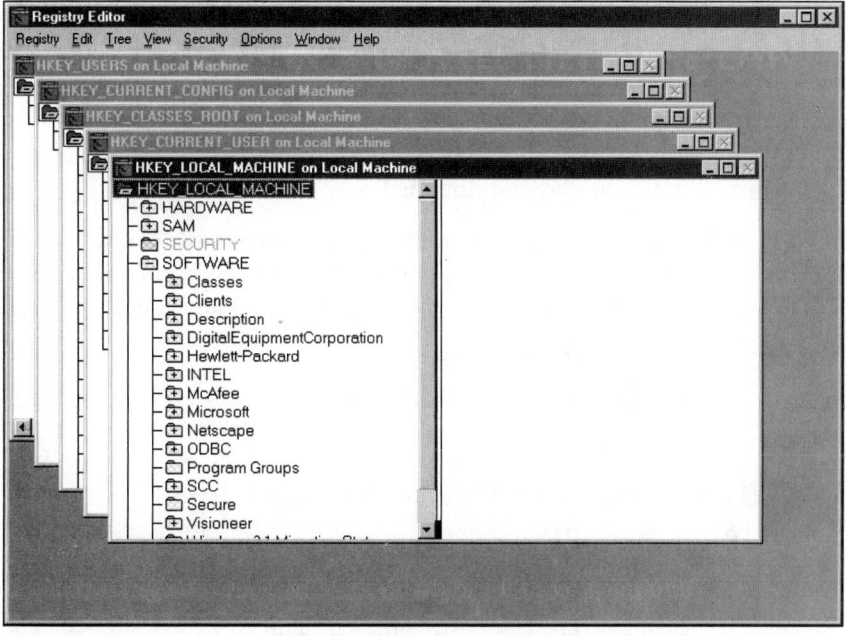

Figure 14.2   The 32-bit Registry Editor (REGEDT32.EXE).

wrong. If, for example, you change one entry in the Registry and Proxy Server (or any other application) stops working, you'll know to change the entry back to its original value. However, if you made changes to several different entries and Proxy Server stops working, you'll have to figure out which entry caused the failure.

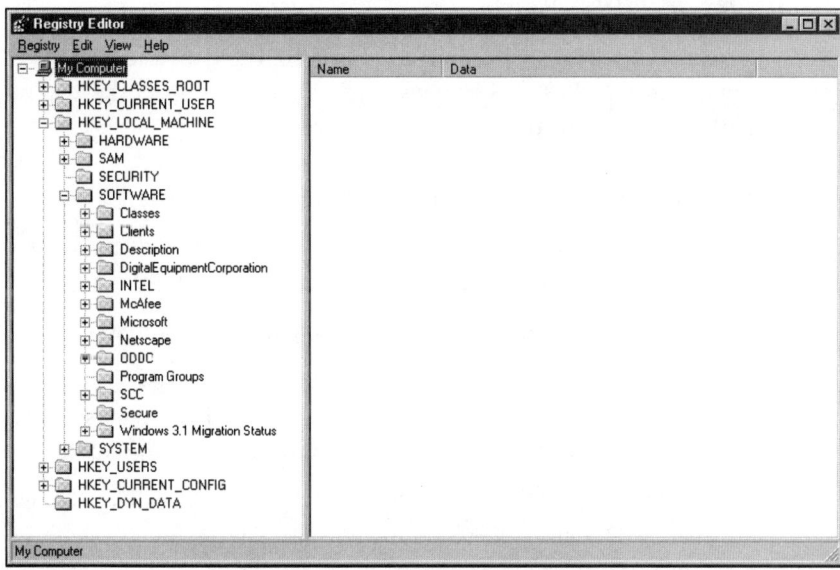

Figure 14.3   The Registry Editor (REGEDIT.EXE).

14

You should use the administrative tools in the Internet Service Manager (ISM) or the Microsoft Management Console (MMC) whenever possible. Use a Registry Editor only if the changes you require cannot be done through the ISM or the MMC. Changes made by using the ISM or the MMC take effect immediately, whereas values made by using the Registry Editor do not take effect until you start and stop the Proxy service.

In this section, we'll discuss in detail the different types of entries, where the Proxy Server Registry information is stored, and the Registry values themselves. Value entries in the Registry appear as a string, which consists of three components:

- The name of the value
- The class or type of the value entry
- The value itself

There are also five different value classes or data types:

- **REG_BINARY** Identifies a value entry as binary
- **REG_SZ** Identifies a value entry as a data string
- **REG_DWORD** Identifies a value entry as a DWORD entry
- **REG_MULTI_SZ** Identifies a value entry as a multiple string
- **REG_EXPAND_SZ** Indicates that a value entry is an expandable string

 To get more specific information about the Registry and event messages, check the online documents for Microsoft Proxy Server 2.0.

Several Registry values apply to the Web Proxy service, the WinSock Proxy service, and the SOCKS Proxy service. Their location in the Registry is covered in the following sections.

DOMAIN FILTERING KEYS

Domain filtering keys determine which Web sites the clients have permission to access. The Registry entries are located in the following subkey:

HKEY_LOCAL_MACHINE\SYSTEM\CurrentControlSet\Services\W3Proxy\Parameters\DoFilter.

Additional Registry entries exist for domains and IP addresses where access has been granted or denied. They are located in the following subkey:

HKEY_LOCAL_MACHINE\SYSTEM\CurrentControlSet\Services\W3Proxy\Parameters\DoFilter\DenySites|GrantSites. The Registry values for the domain filtering keys are listed in Table 14.1.

Table 14.1　Registry values for the domain filtering keys.

Registry Entry	Type	Setting
FilterType	REG_DWORD	0	1	2
NumDenySites	REG_DWORD	No limit to value
NumGrantSites	REG_DWORD	No limit to value
Domains	REG_MULTI_SZ	URL [URL]
IPSitex	REG_SZ	SubnetMask IPAddress

PACKET FILTERING KEYS

The packet filtering Registry keys are located in the following subkey: HKEY_LOCAL_MACHINE\SYSTEM\CurrentControlSet\Services\ mspadmin\Filters. The Registry values for the packet filtering keys are listed in Table 14.2.

PROXY SERVER ALERTING KEYS

The Registry keys used to configure mail notification for alerts are located in: HKEY_LOCAL_MACHINE\SYSTEM\CurrentControlSet\Services\mspadmin\ Parameters\Alerting.

The Registry values for the Proxy Server alerting keys are listed in Table 14.3.

PROXY SERVER ARRAY KEYS

If you change the Registry for one member of the proxy array, you must also change the Registry entries for all the other members of the array; otherwise,

14

Table 14.2　Registry values for the packet filtering keys.

Registry Entry	Type	Setting
Direction	REG_DWORD	0	4	8
FilterType	REG_DWORD	1	2	3	4	5
LocalAddress	REG_DWORD	0
LocalPort	REG_DWORD	ProtocolValue
LocalPortHigh	REG_DWORD	0x0 - 0xFFFF
PortControlFlags	REG_DWORD	
Protocol	REG_DWORD	0x0 - 0xFFFF
RemoteAddress	REG_DWORD	0x0
RemoteMask	REG_DWORD	0xFFFFFFFF
RemotePort	REG_DWORD	0x0 - 0xFFFF
RemotePortHigh	REG_DWORD	0x0 - 0xFFFF
PacketFilterEnabled	REG_DWORD	0	1	2	4	8	15
PfBindings	REG_MULTI_SZ	Text

Table 14.3   Registry values for the Proxy Server alerting keys.

Registry Entry	Type	Setting
FromAddress	REG_SZ	Text
MailServer	REG_SZ	Text
SMTPPort	REG_DWORD	0
ToAddress	REG_SZ	Text
AlertTriggerRate (per second)	REG_DWORD	0xC8
DelayBetweenAlerts (minutes)	REG_DWORD	0x5
EnableAlerting	REG_DWORD	0	1
LogEventOnAlert	REG_DWORD	0	1
SetEventOnAlert	REG_DWORD	0	1

the array members will be out of synchronization and will not perform properly. There are three important Registry keys: the array membership, the chained array, and the backup route.

The array membership keys are located in: HKEY_LOCAL_MACHINE\ SYSTEM\CurrentControlSet\Services\W3Proxy\Parameters\MemberArray\ *ComputerName.*

ComputerName is the name of the array member. The Registry values for the Proxy Server array keys are listed in Table 14.4.

Table 14.4   Registry values for the Proxy Server array keys.

Registry Entry	Type	Setting
ArrayName	REG_SZ	Text
ArrayTTL	REG_DWORD	0x00000384
ArrayUserName	REG_SZ	Text
AuthenticationType	REG_DWORD	1	2
ConfigID	REG_DWORD	0
EnableArray	REG_DWORD	0	1
EnableAuthentication	REG_DWORD	0	1
EnableSynchronization	REG_DWORD	0	1
IntraArrayAddress	REG_SZ	IPAddress
NodeCacheSize	REG_DWORD	0x00000001
NodeComputerName	REG_SZ	Text
NodeComputerPortNum	REG_DWORD	0x00000050
NodeDllUrl	REG_MULTI_SZ	Text
NodeLoadFactor	REG_DWORD	0x100
ResolveInArray	REG_DWORD	0	1

The chained array keys are located in: HKEY_LOCAL_MACHINE\ SYSTEM\CurrentControlSet\Services\W3Proxy\Parameters\ChainedArray.

The backup route keys are located in: HKEY_LOCAL_MACHINE\SYSTEM\ CurrentControlSet\Services\W3Proxy\Parameters\BackupRoute.

The Registry values for chained and backup route keys are listed in Table 14.5.

LOGGING VALUES

The logging value entries affect Proxy Server packet filtering and are located in: HKEY_LOCAL_MACHINE\SYSTEM\CurrentControlSet\Services\mspadmin\ Parameters.

The Registry values for Proxy Server logging keys are listed in Table 14.6.

STORING LOGS ON A NETWORK SHARE

You have the ability to change the log directory of Proxy Server so that it logs all of its information to another computer on the network. You are required to permit access to null sessions on the computer that contains the log files by accessing th Registry keys located in: HKEY_LOCAL_MACHINE\SYSTEM\ CurrentControlSet\Services\LanmanServer\Parameters.

The Registry value for the Proxy Server log directory keys are listed in Table 14.7.

Table 14.5 Registry values for chained and backup route keys.

Registry Entry	Type	Setting
ArrayName	REG_SZ	Text
ArrayTTL	REG_DWORD	0x1 - 0xFFFFFFFF
ArrayUserName	REG_SZ	Text
ConfigID	REG_DWORD	0
EnableArray	REG_DWORD	0 | 1
NodeCacheSize	REG_DWORD	0x00000001
NodeComputerName	REG_SZ	Text
NodeComputerPortNum	REG_DWORD	0x00000050
NodeDllUrl	REG_MULTI_SZ	Text
NodeLoadFactor	REG_DWORD	0x100
RouteType	REG_DWORD	1 | 2 | 3 | 8 | 9
UpstreamServers	REG_SZ	Text

14

Table 14.6   Registry values for Proxy Server logging keys.

Registry Entry	Type	Setting
LogFileDirectory	REG_SZ	Text
LogFileFsCompress	REG_DWORD	0x1
LogFileKeepOld	REG_DWORD	0
LogFilePeriod	REG_DWORD	0	1	2	3
LogFileStopIfFull	REG_DWORD	0x1
LogFileTruncateSize	REG_DWORD	0x1 - 0xFFFFFFFF
LogSqlDataSource	REG_SZ	Text
LogSqlPassword	REG_SZ	Text
LogSqlTableName	REG_SZ	Text
LogSqlUserName	REG_SZ	Text
Log Type	REG_DWORD	0	1	2	3	4
SmallLogFormat	REG_DWORD	0	1

Table 14.7   Registry value for the Proxy Server log directory keys.

Registry Entry	Type	Setting
NullSessionShare	REG_MULTI_SZ	COMCFG DFS$

WINSOCK PROXY SERVICE VALUES

The WinSock Proxy service Registry values are located in: HKEY_ LOCAL_MACHINE\SYSTEM\CurrentControlSet\Services\WSPSrv\ Parameters.

The Registry values for the WinSock Proxy service keys are listed in Table 14.8.

SOCKS PROXY SERVICE VALUES

The SOCKS Proxy service Registry values are located in: HKEY_ LOCAL_MACHINE\SYSTEM\CurrentControlSet\Services\W3Proxy\ Parameters\SOCKS.

The Registry values for the SOCKS Proxy service keys are listed in Table 14.9.

HANDLING WEB PROXY SERVICE PROBLEMS

This section is divided into two parts. The first covers the Web Proxy service event messages. The second lists where the Registry keys for the Web Proxy service are stored in the Registry.

Table 14.8   Registry values for the WinSock Proxy service keys.

Registry Entry	Type	Setting
Authentication	REG_DWORD	0 I 1
ConnectionQuota	REG_DWORD	0x0 - 0x100
Installation Date (2.0 Beta1)	REG_SZ	mm-dd-yyyy
InstallRoot	REG_SZ	Text
Investigation Log	REG_SZ	Text
Investigation Mode	REG_DWORD	0 I 1
LogFileDirectory	REG_SZ	Text
LogFileFsCompress	REG_DWORD	0x1
LogFileKeepOld	REG_DWORD	0
LogFilePeriod	REG_DWORD	0 - 4
LogFileStopIfFull	REG_DWORD	0x1
LogFileTruncateSize	REG_DWORD	0x0 - 0xFFFFFFFF
LogSqlDataSource	REG_SZ	Text
LogSqlPassword	REG_SZ	Text
LogSqlTableName	REG_SZ	Text
LogSqlUserName	REG_SZ	Text
LogType	REG_DWORD	0 I 1 I 2 I 3 I 4
MappingQuota	REG_DWORD	0x0 - 0x100
MaxCtrlThreads	REG_DWORD	100
MinCtrlThreads	REG_DWORD	5
RoutingTable	REG_SZ	Text
SelectiveDialOnDemand	REG_DWORD	0 I 1
ServerComment	REG_SZ	Text
SmallLogFormat	REG_DWORD	0 I 1
TcpBufferSize	REG_DWORD	0x600 or higher
UdpBufferSize	REG_DWORD	0x600 - 0xFFFF

14

WEB PROXY SERVICE EVENT MESSAGES

The Web Proxy service event messages (including arrays and chains) appear in the system event log with the WebProxyServer and WebProxyLog source names.

The Web Proxy service logs the following event messages:

- **HTTP/1.0 500 server error** An attempt has been made to operate on an impersonation token by a thread that is not currently impersonating a client.

- **HTTP/1.0 500 server error** *–number.*

Table 14.9 Registry values for the SOCKS Proxy service keys.

Registry Entry	Type	Setting
EnableBindRequests	REG_DWORD	0x1
LogFileDirectory	REG_SZ	Text
LogFileFsCompress	REG_DWORD	0x1
LogFileKeepOld	REG_DWORD	0
LogFilePeriod	REG_DWORD	0	1	2	3
LogFileStopIfFull	REG_DWORD	0x1
LogFileTruncateSize	REG_DWORD	0x1 - 0xFFFFFFFF
LogSqlDataSource	REG_SZ	Text
LogSqlPassword	REG_SZ	Text
LogSqlTableName	REG_SZ	Text
LogSqlUserName	REG_SZ	Text
LogType	REG_DWORD	0	1	2	3	4
RequestTimeoutSecs	REG_DWORD	0x10 - 0x1000
ServerComment	REG_SZ	Text
SmallLogFormat	REG_DWORD	0	1
SocketIOTimeoutSecs	REG_DWORD	0x0 - 0x78
SocksConfigFile	REG_SZ	C:\Msp\SockD.cfg
SocksServiceEnabled	REG_DWORD	0	1

- **HTTP/1.0 500 server error** The specified module could not be found.

- **115** W3Proxy failed to start because the system time is incorrect.

- **116** W3Proxy failed to start because the Microsoft Proxy Server RC program expired on *date*. Please contact Microsoft about this product.

- **118** The Web Proxy service was halted. The 60-day free evaluation period has expired.

- **125** The Web Proxy service received *number* requests from the Internet port during the past *number* seconds while Internet publishing was disabled.

- **126** The Web Proxy service configuration has been modified *number* time(s) during the past *number* seconds.

- **129** The Web Proxy service is continued.

WEB PROXY CACHE EVENT MESSAGES

The Web Proxy service cache event messages appear in the system event log with the WebProxyCache source names.

If caching does not occur, make sure sufficient disk space is available on the cache drive.

The Web Proxy service logs the following cache event messages:

- **111** Web Proxy cache initialization failed due to an incorrect configuration. Please use the administration utility or manually edit the Registry to correct the error and restart the service.

- **112** Web Proxy cache corrected a corrupted or old format URL cache by removing all or part of the cache's contents.

- **113** Web Proxy cache failed to initialize the URL cache on disk.

- **114** The hard disk used by the Web Proxy server to cache popular URLs is full. Space needs to be freed, or the Web Proxy cache needs to be reconfigured to resume normal operation.

WEB PROXY ARRAY AND CHAIN EVENT MESSAGES

The Proxy Server array and chain event messages appear in the system event log with the WebProxyServer and WebProxyLog source names.

The Web Proxy service logs the following array and chain event messages:

- **130** The Web Proxy service detected that the upstream proxy *servername* is down.

- **131** The Web Proxy service detected that the upstream proxy *servername* is back up.

- **132** The Web Proxy service detected that the array member *servername* is down.

- **133** The Web Proxy service detected that the array member *servername* is back up.

- **139** Proxy Server *servername* requires proxy-to-proxy authentication. Proxy server *servername* is not configured with this type of authentication.

WEB PROXY SERVICE REGISTRY KEYS

The Web Proxy service Registry keys are located in: HKEY_LOCAL_ MACHINE\SYSTEM\CurrentControlSet\Services\W3Proxy\Parameters.

The Registry values for the Web Proxy service keys are listed in Table 14.10.

14

Table 14.10 Registry values for the Web Proxy service keys.

Registry Entry	Type	Setting
AllowInternetHttpRequests	REG_DWORD	0 | 1
AutoDialFlags	REG_DWORD	0 | 1 | 2 | 4 | 7
BusyRetry	REG_DWORD	0-999
ClientScriptBackupRoute	REG_SZ	Text
ClientScriptBypassForLocal	REG_DWORD	0 | 1
ClientScriptReturnManualPath	REG_SZ	Text
ClientScriptReturnManual	REG_DWORD	0 | 1
ClientScriptUseBackupRoute	REG_DWORD	0 | 1
ClientScriptUseDomainList	REG_DWORD	0 | 1
ClientScriptUseIpList	REG_DWORD	0 | 1
ClusterID	REG_DWORD	Text
ConfigurationStamp	REG_DWORD	Text
ConnectCacheSize	REG_DWORD	0x1 - 0x500
ConnectCacheTimeoutInSecs	REG_DWORD	0x384 - 0xE10
DialHours	REG_BINARY	00 00 00 00 00 00 00 00 - ff ff ff ff ff ff ff ff
DiskCacheFlags	REG_DWORD	0 | 3 | 5 | 7
DnsCacheSize	REG_DWORD	0x0 - 0xFFFFFF
DnsTTLInSecs	REG_DWORD	0xE10-0x8CA0
EnableAccessControl	REG_DWORD	0 | 1
EnableSvcLoc	REG_DWORD	0 | 1
ErrorHtmlDirPath	REG_SZ	C:\msp\ErrorHtmls
FtpTTLSecs	REG_DWORD	0x15180
IntraArrayAddress	REG_SZ	IPAddress
LogFileDirectory	REG_SZ	Text
LogFileFsCompress	REG_DWORD	0x0 | 0x1
LogFileKeepOld	REG_DWORD	0x0
LogFilePeriod	REG_DWORD	0 | 1 | 2 | 3
LogFileStopIfFull	REG_DWORD	0x0 | 0x1
LogFileTruncateSize	REG_DWORD	0x1 - 0xFFFFFFFF
LogSqlDataSource	REG_SZ	Text
LogSqlPassword	REG_SZ	Text
LogSqlTableName	REG_SZ	Text
LogSqlUserName	REG_SZ	Text
LogType	REG_DWORD	0 | 1 | 2 | 3 | 4
MaxFtpThreadsFactor	REG_DWORD	0x8 - 0x24
MaxPoolThreads	REG_DWORD	0x0 - 0xFFFFFFFF

(continued)

Table 14.10 Registry values for the Web Proxy service keys *(continued)*.

Registry Entry	Type	Setting
NoAnswerRetry	REG_DWORD	0 - 999
NoHostnameInViaHeader	REG_DWORD	0 I 1
PoolThreadLimit	REG_DWORD	0x0 - 0xFFFFFF
RequestTimeoutSecs	REG_DWORD	0x10 - 0x1000
ServerComment	REG_SZ	Text
SmallLogFormat	REG_DWORD	0 I 1
SocketIOTimeoutSecs	REG_DWORD	0x0 - 0x78
SSLPortListInclusion	REG_DWORD	0 I 1
SSLPortListMembers	REG_MULTI_SZ	TwoPairsPortNumbers

WEB PROXY SERVICE MIB VALUES

The path to the dynamic link library (DLL) for the Web Proxy service Management Information Base (MIB) is located in: HKEY_LOCAL_MACHINE\SOFTWARE\Microsoft\W3Proxy\CurrentVersion.

The Management Information Base (MIB) is a set of objects that can be used by the Simple Network Management Protocol (SNMP) to manage the Proxy Server. SNMP works by sending messages, called protocol data units (PDUs), to the Proxy Server. In response, the server returns a list of its manageable objects to the SNMP requesters.

The Registry value is:

Pathname REG_EXPAND_SZ *Text*

WEB PROXY SERVICE CACHE VALUES

There are three important Registry keys: the cache parameters, the cache path, and the cache filters.

The cache parameter keys are located in: HKEY_LOCAL_MACHINE\SYSTEM\CurrentControlSet\Services\W3Pcache\Parameters.

The Registry values for the Web Proxy service cache keys are listed in Table 14.11.

14

Table 14.11　Registry values for the Web Proxy service cache keys.

Registry Entry	Type	Setting
ActiveRefreshAggressiveness	REG_DWORD	0x0 - 0x12
Age Factor(%)	REG_DWORD	0x0 - 0x64
CacheByDefault	REG_DWORD	0 | 1
CleanupFactor	REG_DWORD	0x0 - 0x64
CleanupInterval	REG_DWORD	0x0 - 0x93a40
CleanupTime	REG_DWORD	0 - 23
EnableActiveCache	REG_DWORD	0 | 1
EnableMaxObjectSize	REG_DWORD	0 | 1
EnableProtect	REG_DWORD	0 | 1
EnableTTL	REG_DWORD	0 | 1
FreshnessInterval	REG_DWORD	0x0 - 0x93a40
Max Interval Units	REG_DWORD	1 - 5
Max Interval Value	REG_DWORD	0x0 - 0x4096
Max. Protection Time (minutes)	REG_DWORD	0x0 - 0x2760
MaxObjectSize	REG_DWORD	0x0 - 0x2760
Min Interval (minutes)	REG_DWORD	0x0 - 0x5A0
Persistent	REG_DWORD	0 | 1
Protection Factor (%)	REG_DWORD	0x0 - 0x64

The cache path keys are located in: HKEY_LOCAL_MACHINE\SYSTEM\Current ControlSet\Services\W3Pcache\Parameters\Paths.

The Registry values for the Web Proxy service cache path keys are listed in Table 14.12.

The cache filters keys are located in: HKEY_LOCAL_MACHINE\SYSTEM\CurrentControlSet\Services\W3Pcache\UrlData.

The Registry value is USR REG_SZ {x,y}.

WEB PROXY SERVICE PUBLISHING VALUES

The parameters that define the reverse proxy (publishing) values of the Web Proxy service are located in: HKEY_LOCAL_MACHINE\SYSTEM\CurrentControlSet\Services\W3Proxy\Parameters\Reverse Proxy.

Table 14.12　Registry values for the Web Proxy service cache path keys.

Registry Entry	Type	Setting
CacheLimit	REG_DWORD	0x0 - 0x4096
CachePath	REG_SZ	Text

The Registry values for the Web Proxy service publishing keys are listed in Table 14.13.

Mapping routes an incoming Internet request from the system identified in the request to another system located behind the Proxy Server. The Registry keys for mapping are located in: HKEY_LOCAL_MACHINE\SYSTEM\CurrentControlSet\Services\W3Proxy\Parameters\Reverse Proxy\Mapping.

The Registry value is Requestpath REG_SZ *Routeto.*

MANAGING WINSOCK PROXY SERVER PROBLEMS

This section is divided into two parts. The first covers the WinSock Proxy Service event messages. The second lists where the Registry keys for the WinSock Proxy Service are stored in the Registry. We will not go into detail about the individual entries within those keys.

WINSOCK PROXY SERVICE EVENT MESSAGES

The WinSock Proxy service event messages appear in the system event log with the WinSockProxy and WinSockProxyLog source names.

The WinSock Proxy service logs the following event messages:

- **1** The WinSock Proxy service failed to initialize. The data is the internal error code.
- **2** The WinSock Proxy service failed to initialize the network. The data is the error.
- **3** The WinSock Proxy service started.
- **4** The WinSock Proxy service cannot initialize due to a shortage of available memory. The data is the error.
- **5** User *username* at host *hostname* has timed out after *number* seconds of inactivity.
- **6** The WinSock Proxy service cannot initialize performance counters. The data is the error.
- **7** The WinSock Proxy service has failed due to a shortage of available memory. The data is the number of connections.

Table 14.13   Registry values for the Web Proxy service publishing keys.

Registry Entry	Type	Setting
DefaultLocalHostName	REG_SZ	Servername
ReverseProxyHostName	REG_SZ	Servername:Portnumber
RouteType	REG_DWORD	5|6|7

14

- **9** The performance counters DLL for the WinSock Proxy service failed because the function *functionname* failed. The data is the error.

- **10** The WinSock Proxy service failed to initialize because of missing or corrupted Registry settings. The data is the error.

- **11** The WinSock Proxy service failed to bind its socket to *unknown* port *portnumber*.

- **12** Client from *unknown* attempts to access WinSock Proxy service by using control protocol version *versionnumber*. The server supports version *versionnumber*.

- **13, 14** The WinSock Proxy service requires Windows NT 4.0 Server.

- **15** The WinSock Proxy service failed to load security DLL.

- **16** The WinSock Proxy service failed to determine network addresses.

- **17** Incorrect network configuration. None of the server's addresses are internal.

- **18** The WinSock Proxy service failed to start because the system time is incorrect.

- **19** The WinSock Proxy service failed to start because the Microsoft Proxy Server RC program expired on *date*. Please contact Microsoft for details about this product.

- **20** Warning: The Microsoft Proxy Server RC program expired on *date*. Please contact Microsoft for details about this product.

- **36** Address *address* is missing from the configuration file.

WINSOCK PROXY SERVICE REGISTRY KEYS

The WinSock Proxy service Registry keys are located in: HKEY_LOCAL_MACHINE\SYSTEM\CurrentControlSet\Services\WSPSrv\Parameters.

The Registry values for the WinSock Proxy service keys are listed in Table 14.14.

WINSOCK PROXY SERVICE MIB VALUES

The path to the dynamic link library (DLL) for the WinSock Proxy service Management Information Base (MIB) is located in: HKEY_LOCAL_MACHINE\SYSTEM\CurrentControlSet\WSPSrv\SNMP.

The Registry value is Pathname REG_EXPAND_SZ Text.

Table 14.14   Registry values for the WinSock Proxy service keys.

Registry Entry	Type	Setting
Authentication	REG_DWORD	0	1
ConnectionQuota	REG_DWORD	0x0 - 0x100
Installation Date (2.0 Beta1)	REG_SZ	mm-dd-yyyy
InstallRoot	REG_SZ	Text
Investigation Log	REG_SZ	Text
Investigation Mode	REG_DWORD	0	1
LogFileDirectory	REG_SZ	Text
LogFileFsCompress	REG_DWORD	0x1
LogFileKeepOld	REG_DWORD	0
LogFilePeriod	RFG_DWORD	0 - 4
LogFileStopIfFull	REG_DWORD	0x1
LogFileTruncateSize	REG_DWORD	0x0 - 0xFFFFFFFF
LogSqlDataSource	REG_SZ	Text
LogSqlPassword	REG_SZ	Text
LogSqlTableName	REG_SZ	Text
LogSqlUserName	REG_SZ	Text
LogType	REG_DWORD	0	1	2	3	4
MappingQuota	REG_DWORD	0x0 - 0x100
MaxCtrlThreads	REG_DWORD	100
MinCtrlThreads	REG_DWORD	5
RoutingTable	REG_SZ	Text
SelectiveDialOnDemand	REG_DWORD	0	1
ServerComment	REG_SZ	Text
SmallLogFormat	REG_DWORD	0	1
UdpBufferSize	REG_DWORD	0x600 - 0xFFFF

14

MANAGING SOCKS PROXY SERVER PROBLEMS

This section is divided into two parts. The first covers the SOCKS Proxy Service event messages. The second lists where the Registry keys for the SOCKS Proxy Service are stored in the Registry.

EVENT MESSAGES

The SOCKS Proxy service logs entries to the event log for each successful connection—one when the connection is established and the other when the connection is closed. When the connection is closed, the number of bytes sent and received is logged. The SOCKS Proxy service event messages appear in the system event log with the SocksProxy and SocksProxyLog source names.

SOCKS PROXY SERVICE REGISTRY KEYS

The SOCKS Proxy service Registry keys are located in: HKEY_LOCAL_MACHINE\SYSTEM\CurrentControlSet\Services\W3Proxy\Parameters\SOCKS.

The Registry values for the SOCKS Proxy service keys are listed in Table 14.15.

TROUBLESHOOTING PROXY SERVER PERFORMANCE

Microsoft Windows NT has an incredibly powerful tool for monitoring system (and service) performance; it's called Performance Monitor. There are many built-in counters that allow you to monitor objects such as processor, memory, disk, network, services, and so on.

When Proxy Server is installed, several Performance Monitor counters are installed into the Performance Monitor. You use these counters to monitor the different components of Microsoft Proxy Server. The following sections list the counters for each service.

Table 14.15 Registry values for the SOCKS Proxy service keys.

Registry Entry	Type	Setting
EnableBindRequests	REG_DWORD	0x1
LogFileDirectory	REG_SZ	Text
LogFileFsCompress	REG_DWORD	0x1
LogFileKeepOld	REG_DWORD	0
LogFilePeriod	REG_DWORD	0 I 1 I 2 I 3
LogFileStopIfFull	REG_DWORD	0x1
LogFileTruncateSize	REG_DWORD	0x1 - 0xFFFFFFFF
LogSqlDataSource	REG_SZ	Text
LogSqlPassword	REG_SZ	Text
LogSqlTableName	REG_SZ	Text
LogSqlUserName	REG_SZ	Text
LogType	REG_DWORD	0 I 1 I 2 I 3 I 4
RequestTimeoutSecs	REG_DWORD	0x10 - 0x1000
ServerComment	REG_SZ	Text
SmallLogFormat	REG_DWORD	0 I 1
SocketIOTimeoutSecs	REG_DWORD	0x0 - 0x78
SocksConfigFile	REG_SZ	C:\Msp\SockD.cfg
SocksServiceEnabled	REG_DWORD	0 I 1

WEB PROXY SERVER SERVICE

The following counters are used to monitor the Web Proxy and SOCKS Proxy services:

- Array Bytes Received/sec
- Array Bytes Sent/sec
- Array Bytes Total/sec
- Cache Hit Ratio (%)
- Client Bytes Received/sec
- Client Bytes Sent/sec
- Client Bytes Total/sec
- Current Average Milliseconds/request
- Current Users
- DNS Cache Entries
- DNS Cache Flushes
- DNS Cache Hits
- DNS Cache Hits (%)
- DNS Retrievals
- Failing Requests/sec
- FTP Requests
- Gopher Requests
- HTTP Requests
- HTTPS sessions
- Maximum Users
- Requests/sec
- Reverse Bytes Received/sec
- Reverse Bytes Sent/sec
- Reverse Bytes Total/sec
- Sites Denied
- Sites Granted
- SNEWS Sessions
- SSL Client Bytes Received/sec
- SSL Client Bytes Sent/sec
- SSL Client Bytes Total/sec

14

- SSL Sessions Scavenged
- Thread Pool Active Sessions
- Thread Pool Failures
- Thread Pool Size
- Total Array Fetches
- Total Cache Fetches
- Total Failing Requests
- Total Reverse Fetches
- Total Upstream Fetches
- Total SSL Sessions
- Total Successful Requests
- Total Users
- Upstream Bytes Received/sec
- Upstream Bytes Sent/sec
- Upstream Bytes Total/sec
- Unknown SSL Sessions

WEB PROXY SERVER CACHE

The following counters are used to monitor the Web Proxy service cache:

- Active Refresh Bytes Rate
- Active URL Refresh Rate
- Bytes Committed Rate
- Bytes in Cache
- Bytes Retrieved Rate
- Max Bytes Cached
- Max URLs Cached
- Total Actively Refreshed URLs
- Total Bytes Actively Refreshed
- Total Bytes Cached
- Total Bytes Retrieved
- Total URLs Cached
- Total URLs Retrieved
- URL Commit Rate

- URL Retrieve Rate
- URLs in Cache

WinSock Proxy Server

The following counters are used to monitor the WinSock Proxy service:

- Accepting TCP Connections
- Active Sessions
- Active TCP Connections
- Active UDP Connections
- Available Worker Threads
- Back-Connecting TCP Connections
- Bytes Read/sec
- Bytes Written/sec
- Connecting TCP Connections
- DNS Cache Entries
- DNS Cache Flushes
- DNS Cache Hits
- DNS Cache Hits (%)
- DNS Retrievals
- Failed DNS Resolutions
- Listening TCP Connections
- Non-connected UDP mappings
- Pending DNS Resolutions
- Successful DNS Resolutions
- Worker Threads

SOCKS Proxy Server

The following counters are used to monitor the SOCKS Proxy service:

- SOCKS Client Bytes Received/sec
- SOCKS Client Bytes Sent/sec
- SOCKS Client Bytes Total/sec
- SOCKS sessions

14

- Total Failed SOCKS Sessions
- Total SOCKS Sessions
- Total Successful SOCKS Sessions

PACKET FILTERING

The following counters are used to monitor Proxy Server packet filtering:

- Frames dropped due to filter denial
- Frames dropped due to protocol violations
- Total dropped frames
- Total incoming connections
- Total lost logging frames

LAUNCHING PERFORMANCE MONITOR

To run the Microsoft Performance Monitor, follow these steps:

1. Select Start | Microsoft Proxy Server from the Programs menu.

2. Select Monitor Microsoft Proxy Server Performance. This starts a Performance Monitor session with some predetermined counters specific to Microsoft Proxy Server. The Windows Performance Monitor is shown in Figure 14.4.

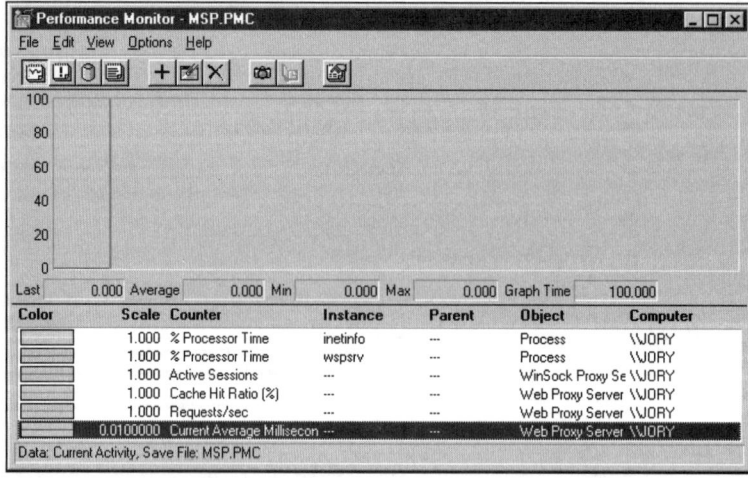

Figure 14.4   The Performance Monitor.

You can add, modify, or delete counters by following these steps:

1. Select Add To Chart from the Edit menu or click on the Add Counter icon.

2. Select a Proxy Server object from the Object drop-down menu in the Add To Chart dialog box (see Figure 14.5).

3. Select a counter from the Counter scroll box and click on the Add button.

 Some Proxy Server counters rely on monitoring disk activity. Because monitoring the hard drives in a computer can affect performance of that system, disk counters are disabled by default. You can enable the disk counters by using the **diskperf –y** command (you must reboot your system for disk monitoring to occur). You can then disable the disk counters by using the **diskperf –n** command.

CHAPTER SUMMARY

As an administrator, you have access to several tools that you can use to troubleshoot your Microsoft Proxy Server installation.

The Windows NT Registry is a database that stores all Windows NT (and its installed applications) configuration information. The information stored in the Registry includes device driver information, network information, user and group information, and so on. Windows NT comes with two graphical tools that you can use to view and edit the Registry: REGEDT32.EXE and REGEDIT.EXE.

14

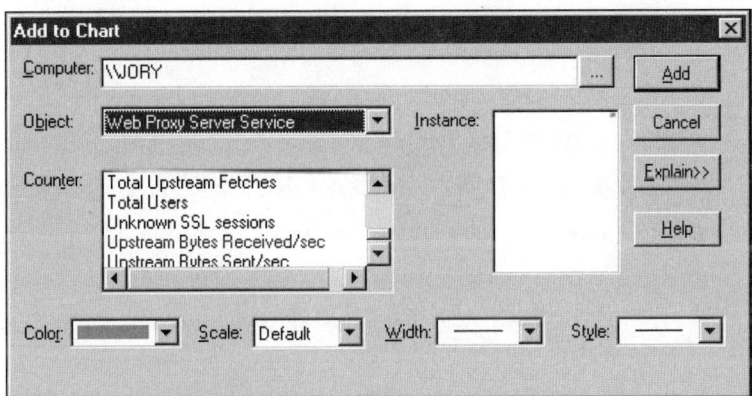

Figure 14.5   The Add To Chart dialog box.

When you install and run Microsoft Proxy Server, it automatically logs some informational and error messages to a Windows NT application called the Event Viewer. The Event Viewer is a good place to start looking for problems when Proxy Server starts to misbehave.

The Windows NT Performance Monitor is a powerful tool that you can use to monitor not only Proxy Server, but also Windows NT and many other applications and services. Because it runs in realtime, it is a useful tool for finding potential bottlenecks.

KEY TERMS

- **event messages**—The actual log messages that are logged to the Event Viewer by Microsoft Proxy Server.

- **Event Viewer**—A Windows NT application that allows the administrator to view any informational or error messages logged by Windows NT and its services.

- **Internet Service Manager (ISM)**—An interface used to manage the Internet Information Server 3.0 (and Proxy Server).

- **Microsoft Management Console (MMC)**—A new interface used to manage the Internet Information Server 4.0 (and Proxy Server).

- **Performance Monitor**—A Windows NT application that allows the administrator to monitor many different counters in realtime.

- **Performance Monitor counter**—An object that is monitored within Performance Monitor.

- **Proxy Server Diagnostic Utility (MSPDIAG.EXE)**—A utility used to diagnose the Microsoft Proxy Server installation.

- **REG_BINARY**—Identifies a value entry as binary.

- **REG_DWORD**—Identifies a value entry as a DWORD entry.

- **REG_EXPAND_SZ**—Indicates that a value entry is an expandable string.

- **REG_MULTI_SZ**—Identifies a value entry as a multiple string.

- **REG_SZ**—Identifies a value entry as a data string.

- **Registry**—A database that stores all Windows NT configuration information.

- **Registry Editor**—A tool (REGEDT32.EXE or REGEDIT.EXE) used to view and edit the Windows NT Registry.

- **SOCKS Proxy service**—A Proxy Server service that allows clients running the SOCKS protocol access to the Internet.

- **Web Proxy service**—A Proxy Server service that allows clients to use their Web browser to access information on the Internet.
- **WinSock Proxy service**—A Proxy Server service that allows clients to use WinSock applications to access the Internet.

REVIEW QUESTIONS

1. Your Web Proxy service is having some caching problems. Which source name should you look for in the Microsoft Event Viewer?
   a. WebProxyServerCache
   b. WebCache
   c. WebProxyCache
   d. CacheEvent

2. Your Web Proxy service caching has stopped working. What should be your first step for troubleshooting?
   a. Run Performance Monitor and monitor the cache objects.
   b. Reinstall Microsoft Proxy Server.
   c. Check the WPS.LOG file created in the \SYSTEMS32\LOGS directory.
   d. Check the Event Viewer for event messages.

3. What is the Registry?
   a. a database of Microsoft-specific configuration information
   b. a database of all Windows NT configuration information
   c. a database of Proxy-Server-specific configuration information
   d. a database that stores all informational and error messages logged by Windows NT

4. Which of the following Registry entries are shared by all the Proxy Server services? (Choose all correct answers.)
   a. packet filtering keys
   b. alerting keys
   c. logging values
   d. SOCKS Proxy service values

5. You run Performance Monitor and attempt to log hard disk activity. All disk activity counters read zero. Why?
   a. You have to run the **diskcount −start** command.
   b. You have to run the **diskperf −start** command.
   c. You have to run the **diskperf −y** command.
   d. You have to run the **diskcount −y** command.

14

6. You cannot use Performance Monitor to track more than one service at a time. (True or False?)

7. Your Web Proxy service is having some operational problems. Which source name should you look for in the Microsoft Event Viewer?

   a. WebProxyEvent

   b. WebProxyServer

   c. WebProxyService

   d. WebProxyServiceLog

8. You have executed the **diskperf –y** command from the DOS prompt, and Performance Monitor still tracks all disk activity at zero. Why?

   a. You must restart all Proxy Server services.

   b. You must restart the diskperf service.

   c. You must restart the Performance Monitor service.

   d. You must reboot your computer for the counters to be activated.

9. You would like to find out how many users are currently connected to the Internet through your Proxy Server. How can you find this information?

   a. Performance Monitor

   b. Event Viewer

   c. Proxy Server User Sessions dialog box

   d. Windows NT Network Monitor

10. Performance Monitor is used to monitor the performance of different components of Windows NT, including Microsoft Proxy Server. (True or False?)

HANDS-ON PROJECTS

In the following projects, you will use the Performance Monitor to track the operation of all Proxy Server services.

PROJECT 14.1

To monitor Web Proxy service performance, follow these steps:

1. Select Start | Programs | Administrative Tools (Common) | Performance Monitor.

2. Select the Add To Chart option from the Edit menu (or click on the Add Counter button on the button bar).

3. Select the Web Proxy Server Service object from the Object drop-down menu in the Add To Chart dialog box.

4. Select Upstream Bytes Total/Sec from the Counter scroll box and then click on Add.

5. Repeat Step 4 for each additional counter and then click on Done.

 PROJECT 14.2

To monitor WinSock Proxy service performance, follow these steps:

1. Select Start | Programs | Administrative Tools (Common) | Performance Monitor.

2. Select the Add To Chart option from the Edit menu (or click on the Add Counter button on the button bar).

3. Select the WinSock Proxy Server Service object from the Object drop-down menu in the Add To Chart dialog box.

4. Select Active TCP Connections from the Counter scroll box and then click on Add.

5. Repeat Step 4 for each additional counter and then click on Done.

 **PROJECT 14.3**

To monitor SOCKS Proxy service performance, follow these steps:

1. Select Start | Programs | Administrative Tools (Common) | Performance Monitor.

2. Select the Add To Chart option from the Edit menu (or click on the Add Counter button on the button bar).

3. Select the Web Proxy Server Service object from the Object drop-down menu in the Add To Chart dialog box.

4. Select SOCKS Clients Bytes Total/Sec from the Counter scroll box and then click on Add.

5. Repeat Step 4 for each additional counter and then click on Done.

14

 CASE PROJECTS

1. You have a Microsoft Proxy Server array installed on your network to allow internal users to access the Internet. The users use the Web Proxy service, the WinSock Proxy service, and the SOCKS Proxy service.

Required result: Monitor, in realtime, all the connections to the Internet.

Optional desired results: Monitor the amount of Web-related data, in realtime, received by the proxy array. Monitor the amount of Web-related data, in realtime, sent by the proxy array.

Proposed solution: Configure Windows NT Performance Monitor with the following:

- In the WinSock Proxy Server object, the Active TCP Connections counter.
- In the WinSock Proxy Server object, the Bytes Read/Sec counter.
- In the WinSock Proxy Server object, the Bytes Written/Sec counter.

Which results does the proposed solution provide?

    a. The proposed solution provides the required result and both optional desired results.

    b. The proposed solution provides the required result and one optional desired result.

    c. The proposed solution provides only the required result.

    d. The proposed solution does not provide the required result.

2. You have a Microsoft Proxy Server array installed on your network to allow internal users to access the Internet. The users use the Web Proxy service, the WinSock service, and the SOCKS service.

Required result: Monitor, in realtime, all the connections to the Internet.

Optional desired results: Monitor the amount of Web-related data, in realtime, received by the proxy array. Monitor the amount of Web-related data, in realtime, sent by the proxy array.

Proposed solution: Configure Windows NT Performance Monitor with the following:

- In the Web Proxy Server Service object, the Array Bytes Total/Sec counter.
- In the Web Proxy Server Service object, the Current Users counter.

Which results does the proposed solution provide?

    a. The proposed solution provides the required result and both optional desired results.

    b. The proposed solution provides the required result and one optional desired result.

    c. The proposed solution provides only the required result.

    d. The proposed solution does not provide the required result.

3. You have a Microsoft Proxy Server array installed on your network to allow internal users to access the Internet. The users use the Web Proxy service, the WinSock service, and the SOCKS service.

Required result: Monitor, in realtime, all the connections to the Internet.

Optional desired results: Monitor the amount of Web-related data, in realtime, received by the proxy array. Monitor the amount of Web-related data, in realtime, sent by the proxy array.

Proposed solution: Configure Windows NT Performance Monitor with the following:

- In the Web Proxy Server Service object, the Current Users counter.
- In the Web Proxy Server Service object, the Array Bytes Sent/Sec counter.
- In the Web Proxy Server Service object, the Array Bytes Received/Sec counter.

Which results does the proposed solution provide?

- **a.** The proposed solution provides the required result and both optional desired results.
- **b.** The proposed solution provides the required result and one optional desired result.
- **c.** The proposed solution provides only the required result.
- **d.** The proposed solution does not provide the required result.

14

KEY EXAM POINTS AND OBJECTIVES

To aid you in your preparation for the certification exams, Microsoft provides an Exam Preparation Guide for each test. The guides, which are located on Microsoft's Web site, give you an idea of what to expect on the exam. The Exam Preparation Guide for the Microsoft Proxy Server 2.0 exam (70-088) is located at **www.microsoft.com/mcp/exam/stat/SP70-088.htm**.

The Exam Prep Guides are divided into sections based on the organization of both the product and the test. The following sections discuss the exam objectives that appear in the Exam Prep Guide.

PLANNING

One of the most important aspects of using a Proxy Server on a network is designing and implementing a secure access strategy. The Proxy Server exam will most likely address a number of points in this area, such as outbound access for your users to the Internet and inbound access from the Internet to your Web site. The following list includes some other key considerations:

- To ensure secure access for your Proxy Server, you must understand the role of the Local Address Table (LAT) and its configuration. Remember that the LAT is used by the WinSock Proxy client software to determine whether a specific network is local or remote. The LAT should only contain IP addresses on your local network.

- Perhaps one of the most important considerations for providing a secure proxy environment is whether to grant anonymous access to your server for Internet users. Anonymous access is granted through each of the components of Internet Information Server (IIS); that is, the WWW service or the FTP service. Even if you choose to implement anonymous access, you can control what access Internet users have by managing the access rights granted to the IUSER_*servername* account.

- In addition to the option for controlling inbound access for anonymous users, there are many options for controlling both inbound and outbound access for registered users. Rather than grant anonymous access, you can specify that a user connecting to your Proxy Server from the Internet must supply a valid logon name and password, which can be sent as either a basic authentication (clear text) or a Windows Challenge/Response authentication. For outbound access, you can control which sites and protocols are granted access to the Internet according to username or group membership through the Permissions tab of the Web or WinSock Proxy Services dialog box. The Domain Filters dialog box, which is accessed through the Security dialog box, can be used to further control access by granting or denying permission to specific Internet sites based on their IP address (or IP addresses) or their domain name.

- Protocol permissions can be used to define which protocols are passed through Proxy Server to the Internet and which protocols are restricted. Once access control is enabled for a particular protocol for the Web or WinSock Proxy services, the administrator can grant access to particular users or groups for each protocol that is defined. The SOCKS Proxy service does not include user and group information; instead, it relies on the IP address of the client to control access. Also, unlike the Web and WinSock services, the SOCKS Proxy service allows the administrator to deny access to a particular protocol as well as to grant access.

Each service's protocol permissions are defined through the Permissions tab, which is accessible through its Properties dialog box. The Web Proxy service only provides four protocols to which users can be granted access: WWW, FTP Read, Gopher, and Secure (HTTP-S). As you'll see in Appendix C, the WinSock Proxy service provides a number of preconfigured protocol definitions and allows the administrator to add protocol definitions as necessary. The SOCKS Proxy service does not include any protocol definitions by default, so each protocol must be defined manually.

- Proxy service logging provides a method for auditing Proxy Server events such as protocol access. Logging is enabled through the Logging tab of each proxy service's Properties dialog box. Logging can be directed to a standard text file or to a SQL/ODBC database. If packet filtering is enabled on a Proxy Server, a separate log can be created to monitor the function of the packet filter. This option is configured through the Security dialog box's Logging tab.

- In addition to the security settings available through Proxy Server services, the Windows NT security structure lends itself to providing a secure network environment. However, many of the Windows NT security settings must be changed from the default to ensure the most secure network. You can change some of these settings to:

  - Disable IP forwarding to restrict Internet traffic from your internal network.

  - Establish a strict password policy for users on your network and enforce Challenge/Response authentication.

  - Control group and user access permissions to ensure that the users on your network are only granted access to the appropriate areas of your Proxy Server.

  - Unbind nonessential services from the external network interface.

  - Utilize NTFS for all proxy services because the NTFS file system provides extensive security control that is not available with FAT or VFAT partitions.

When you are preparing for the Proxy Server exam, it is important to understand the role of the Proxy Server in many different domain models. Key to the exam is the ability to plan Internet and intranet sites with standalone servers and single- or multiple-domain networks. Each type of Proxy Server implementation has its own advantages and disadvantages. For example, you can move a Proxy Server that is configured as a standalone server from one domain to another and still easily restrict access from the Internet to only the Proxy Server. However, establishing trusts and user access for the Proxy Server create a more administration-intensive environment. When the Proxy Server participates as a domain controller in a single-domain environment, user configuration and authentication is simplified, but it is more difficult to restrict access from the outside world. In a multiple-domain environment, Proxy Server can act as a gateway between an intranet and the rest of the network or between the internal network, an extranet, and the Internet. Determining the most efficient domain model for your Proxy Server depends on the size of your network and the administrative resources available. You must also consider the following when you are planning your Internet or intranet sites:

- Determining the right Internet connection for your network requires analyzing your current network requirements, planning for future growth, and then selecting a pipeline that will fit your current and future needs. The first step in this process is to determine the amount of bandwidth needed to service your current network. This is done by multiplying the number of users on your network who will be connecting to the Internet by the amount of bandwidth each user needs. This calculation depends on the type of Internet traffic your users are generating; for example, are your users only retrieving email from the Internet, or are they participating in full-motion video conferencing? The multiplier is generally .5Kbps to 1Kbps for email-only connections and 5Kbps to 10Kbps for more advanced connections such as Web, FTP, and video conferencing. Once this number has been calculated, it is multiplied by 1.4 to provide room for future growth. At that point, a pipeline can be chosen that provides enough bandwidth to support current and future users. The choices for a pipeline can include POTS (56Kbps maximum per line), a 56K leased line, ISDN (128Kbps maximum), a T1 or fractional T1 (56Kbps or 256Kbps chunks up to 1.544Mbps), or more advanced technologies such as ATM or SONET.

- Which Proxy Server services you choose to use on your network has a profound impact on the design and implementation of your Proxy Server and the configuration needed for the clients. The Web Proxy service supports any CERN-compliant Internet browser regardless of the operating system. This means that Unix computers running Netscape Navigator are able to utilize the Web Proxy service. Configuring these clients is a straightforward process and can be automated by using scripts. For the WinSock Proxy service, on the other hand, the clients must be running Windows operating systems and the WinSock client software must be installed on each computer that is using the Proxy Server. The SOCKS Proxy service only supports SOCKS client applications, which can be on nearly any platform— from Apple to Unix to PC—and the SOCKS applications must be configured to recognize the Proxy Server.

- Although Proxy Servers are most often used to connect networks to the Internet, there are some cases in which a Proxy Server should be used on an intranet. For example, a Proxy Server should be used on a corporate intranet in which an intranet Web server provides information from a central location at the corporate headquarters to users on a worldwide network. Rather than having the intranet server accessed directly each time a client at a remote office requests a page, a Proxy Server can be placed at the remote end of the WAN link to cache content from the intranet server, speeding up access time for the remote clients. Another use for Proxy Servers on intranets is on networks where the intranet servers must be tightly secured. A Proxy Server can be used to protect the intranet servers from unauthorized access from the local network, much the same way they are used to protect the local network from users on the Internet.

- The hardware you choose for your Proxy Server depends entirely on the size of your network and the amount of traffic it is expected to generate. For example, a low-volume network (one with fewer than 10 computers) can generally survive with a single ISDN line and a single Proxy Server configured with a Pentium 133MHz CPU, 2GB of storage for caching, and 32MB of RAM. A moderate-volume network (one with fewer than 1,000 computers) generally requires multiple ISDN lines or a fractional T1, two or more Proxy Servers in an array configured with Pentium 166MHz CPUs, 2 to 4GB of storage for caching, and 64MB of RAM. Finally, high-volume networks (enterprise corporations with thousands of computers) usually need at least a dedicated T1 connection and multiple Proxy Servers in an array configured with Pentium Pro or Pentium II CPUs, 8 to 16GB of storage for caching, and 128 to 256MB of RAM.

As a network and its Internet access requirements grow, multiple Proxy Servers are often required. Rather than configuring each client to use a specific Proxy Server, a number of different methods can be used to balance the load between multiple Proxy Servers:

A

- The most basic method is realized when the Domain Name System (DNS) is used for name resolution on a network. As you know, DNS provides IP address-to-computer-name resolution. In most situations, each computer is assigned a unique computername in the DNS database. However, you can create multiple records with the same computername and different IP addresses to allow DNS to distribute the load amongst the various servers. For example, a network may have three Proxy Servers with IP addresses of 10.1.111.111, 10.1.111.112, and 10.1.111.113. In most networks, each computer would have its own unique entry in the DNS database, but to balance the load on these Proxy Servers, you could create three records with the same computername but different IP addresses (i.e., name=Proxy, IP address=10.1.111.111; name=Proxy, IP address=10.1.111.112; and name=Proxy, IP address=10.1.111.113). When you use this configuration, the DNS server will automatically rotate through the list in order and resolve each client request with one of the three addresses. This feature is called the DNS round robin.

- In a multiple Proxy Server environment, a more intricate method can be used to balance the load between servers. Multiple Proxy Servers can be configured in an array, which enables them to share the caching load. An array is created by linking two Proxy Servers through the Internet Service Manager. Once the Proxy Servers are linked into an array, they distribute the caching load amongst all servers. The array acts as a single unit and performs Internet access functions as if it were one computer. One part of this function relies on the fact that all servers in the array are configured identically. When one server's settings are changed, the changes are propagated to all other members of the array. Because all array members function as one unit, the client is able to query any of the array members to access the Internet.

- One very important component of the array structure used with Microsoft Proxy Server 2.0 is the Cache Array Routing Protocol (CARP). CARP is used to determine which member of an array has the cached information for a particular URL that has been requested. Historically, this was done through a query process that took place between the Proxy Servers. This method, however, generated large amounts of network traffic just to decide which server had which cached Internet object. CARP removes the query process by using a hashing algorithm to determine which member has a particular object. Each member of the array has a hash number assigned to it. When a URL is accessed from the Internet, it is also assigned a hash number. When the hash number for the URL is combined with the hash numbers for all array members, the array member with the highest combined number takes ownership of the URL. Each array member keeps a list of the other array members and their hash numbers to resolve requests it receives.

One of the most crucial stages of any installation is the integration of the new with the old, especially when you are planning for a Proxy Server installation in an existing corporate environment. In addition to the information mentioned previously, the Proxy Server should be tested extensively—first in a lab environment and then with a few client computers—before being installed for use on the network at large. In addition, a system to configure the client computers must be in place before installing the Proxy Server.

One final key consideration in planning your Proxy Server implementation is determining a fault-tolerance strategy. In the event that one or more Proxy Servers are not available, how will traffic be routed to and from the Internet? This is addressed in a number of different ways, from providing backup machines that can be used in place of the nonfunctioning Proxy Server to utilizing features built in to the Proxy Server architecture, which include the following:

- As mentioned earlier, Proxy Servers can be configured as members of an array to distribute the load amongst multiple Proxy Servers. Another advantage to this system is that, in the event of a failure of an array member, the other members of the array are able to redistribute the load to compensate for the lost server.

- Another method for ensuring that Internet access is granted if an array member fails is to utilize the routing function available with Proxy Servers. A proxy chain is a hierarchical caching function in which the Proxy Servers operate independently to resolve client requests. If the first Proxy Server is not able to fulfill the request, it forwards the request to the next Proxy Server in line, and so on, until the request is fulfilled from cache or directly from the Internet. When you use a proxy chain, you are able to specify the default route to take to the Internet as well as a secondary, or backup, route. The secondary route is used to complete a client request in the event that the primary route is unavailable.

INSTALLATION AND CONFIGURATION

As mentioned earlier, the LAT is used by the Proxy Server and client software to determine whether a specific network is local or remote. The LAT is created during the Proxy Server installation process. It is automatically populated based on the contents of the routing table on the server, but it can be modified during the installation. The LAT should only contain those subnetworks and IP addresses on your local network. After the installation is complete, the LAT can be modified by clicking on Local Address Table in any service's Properties dialog box. From that point forward, the new LAT will be copied to the client when the client first accesses the Proxy Server. In addition, a LOCALLAT.TXT file that includes network addresses that should not apply to all clients can be created on the client. Any changes made to LOCALLAT.TXT remain intact because it is not overwritten during the client initialization process.

As you know, three authentication options are available for Proxy Server services: anonymous, basic authentication, and Challenge/Response. Each method is configured differently and used by a particular service. The following list describes the configuration of each authentication method:

- Anonymous authentication is the default configuration used for all services. It is, in fact, enabled for either the Web or WinSock Proxy service by deselecting the Enable Access Control option on the Permissions tab for that service. In addition, you can elect to allow anonymous logons through the Properties dialog boxes for the WWW and FTP services of IIS.

- Basic authentication is enabled by selecting the Enable Access Control option on the Permissions tab for the Web or WinSock Proxy services. If the client is a non-Windows client, or if it is outside of the Proxy Server domain or one of its trusted domains, the user will be prompted to supply a username and password. Like anonymous authentication, basic authentication can be configured for the WWW service of IIS.

- Like basic authentication, Windows NT Challenge/Response authentication is enabled when the Enable Access Control option is selected on the Permissions tab of the Web or WinSock Proxy services. The difference is that, with Windows NT Challenge/Response authentication, clients using Windows operating systems automatically respond to the username and password prompt from the server with the information the user entered to access the network. If that information does not successfully log the user on to the system, a standard username and password dialog box is presented to the user. Also like basic authentication, Windows NT Challenge/Response authentication can be configured for the WWW service of IIS.

Once the hardware requirements for your Proxy Server have been determined, you are almost ready to install Proxy Server. However, a few adjustments must be made to the standard Windows NT installation before Proxy Server can be installed. As you know, Proxy Server requires Windows NT Server 4.0, Service Pack 3 or higher, and IIS 3.0 or higher. Fortunately, IIS 3.0 is included in the Service Pack 3 update and can be installed at the same time. In addition to installing the software updates, you must have at least 100MB of available disk space on an NTFS partition to support caching. The interface cards for both the local network and the Internet must be installed and configured properly. Finally, you must have Administrator access to the NT Server to install the Proxy Server software.

A number of configuration options are available for Microsoft Proxy Server, all of which are accessed through the Internet Service Manager (ISM). To start the ISM, click on the Start menu and select Programs|Administrative Tools (Common)|Microsoft Proxy Server|Internet Service Manager. Once the ISM has been started, double-click on the Proxy Server service you wish to configure.

Eight configuration options are the same for all proxy services: Security, Array, Auto Dial, Plug-ins, Client Configuration, Local Address Table, Server Backup, and Server Restore. All of these configuration options apply to Proxy Server as a whole rather than to a particular service. Each service also has two tabs in common—Permissions and Logging—that apply only to its configuration. The Permissions tab is used to define which users and groups (in the case of the Web and WinSock Proxy services) or which computers (in the case of the SOCKS Proxy service) will be granted access to the Proxy Server and, consequently, to the Internet. The Logging tab is used to define the type of logs generated by a particular service and how those logs are managed. The SOCKS Proxy service only includes the Permissions and Logging tabs.

The Web Proxy service provides three unique tabs: Caching, Routing, and Publishing. The Caching tab is first used to define whether or not caching is enabled on the server. In addition, the type of caching and the frequency of updates are configured through this tab. The Routing tab is used to define the routing configuration for the Proxy Server, including whether a backup route will be used in the event of a failure and which server will be used as a backup. The Publishing tab defines the Web publishing configuration in use on the server. The options on the Publishing tab include what the Proxy Server will do with incoming requests (discard the request, send the request to the local Web server, or send the request to another Web server) and a list of exceptions to the rules established.

The single unique tab that is part of the WinSock Proxy service configuration is the Protocols tab. It is used to define, edit, delete, load, or save the protocol definitions that are used by the WinSock Proxy service to grant access to the Internet.

In those networks where Internet access is provided by the Proxy Server, a number of different options exist for making the connection from the Proxy Server to the Internet. Aside from direct Internet connections, dial-up connections can be used to provide access for the Proxy Server. Further, as more Proxy Servers are added to the network, the configuration becomes more intricate by degrees. The following list describes some of the other Internet access configuration tasks:

- Microsoft Proxy Server includes an auto-dialing feature that works with the Windows NT Remote Access Service (RAS) and Dial-Up Networking to automatically connect a Proxy Server to an ISP. Before Proxy Auto Dial can be configured, both RAS and Dial-Up Networking must be installed and configured to connect to your ISP. Once that has happened, you can configure the Proxy Server Auto Dial settings by opening the Properties dialog box for any proxy service and clicking on Auto Dial. The Configuration tab of the Auto Dial dialog

A

box allows you to enable dialing for WinSock and SOCKS Proxy access, Web Proxy primary route, and Web Proxy secondary route. You can also define which hours of the day Proxy Server is able to dial. The Credentials tab is used to select the phone book entry that should be used to dial your ISP. It can also be used to modify your login name and password information for your ISP.

- One of the most attractive features of Microsoft Proxy Server 2.0 is its ability to act as an IPX/IP gateway to allow IPX-only clients to communicate over the Internet. As you know, there are many instances in which clients on a network may have only NWLink (IPX/SPX) installed as their transport protocol, including those cases in which clients connect to existing NetWare servers and medium to large networks in which protocol configuration must be kept to a minimum. As long as the clients are running a Microsoft operating system such as Windows 95 or Windows NT Workstation, they are able to utilize the gateway services of Microsoft Proxy Server. Only the Windows 95 and Windows NT implementation of IPX can be utilized to support a Proxy Server gateway. In addition, because clients configured to use Proxy Server as an IPX gateway utilize the WinSock Proxy service, they are not able to take advantage of the caching functionality of the Web Proxy service.

  To configure a Windows NT server to act as an IPX/IP gateway, both protocols must be configured on the server and be communicating effectively, both internally and with your ISP. In addition, IPX must not be bound to the external network interface. To verify that this is the case, check the Bindings tab of the Network applet. Once it has been verified and Proxy Server has been installed, you must install the WSP client application on all clients that will be using the WinSock Proxy service. If both TCP/IP and IPX are installed on any client, you can force the client software to use IPX to connect to the Proxy Server by selecting Force IPX/SPX Protocol in the Microsoft WinSock Proxy Client dialog box on the client computer.

- In principle, configuring multiple Proxy Servers for Internet access is no different than configuring a single Proxy Server for Internet access. However, a number of considerations must come in to play when you are dealing with a multiple Proxy Server environment. Each consideration stems from the questions related to client configuration: How will the clients utilize the Proxy Servers? And how will they be configured to access the servers? As you know, a number of methods are available to distribute the load amongst multiple Proxy Servers. By defining which method will be used on your network, you determine how the clients will access the Proxy Servers. If you decide to use DNS to define one name for all Proxy Servers, then DNS will use its round robin feature to distribute the load evenly and all clients can be configured to access the DNS object. If Windows Internet Name Service (WINS) is used, the same principle applies, although WINS will try to direct the client to the nearest Proxy Server. If you are utilizing a caching array, the clients can be configured to access any of the Proxy Servers because the hashing algorithm will allow the Proxy Server receiving the request to direct it to the appropriate server in the array.

- In many enterprise networks, multiple Proxy Servers are used at various geographic locations to facilitate speedy local access. In this type of environment, each Proxy Server is often configured to act independently of the others. However, in some environments, particularly corporate intranets, Proxy Servers can be used across slow WAN links to cache content and ensure reasonable access times for local clients.

In addition to the ISM, a number of configuration management tools included with Windows NT can be used to start and stop proxy services and to modify the configuration and operation of the services. For example, the Service applet of the Control Panel can be used to stop and restart any proxy service without going through the ISM. Also, Registry editors, such as Regedt32, are used to tune the performance of the proxy services or to make configuration changes that are not available through the ISM.

As mentioned earlier (see "Planning"), logging provides a method for auditing Proxy Server events such as protocol access. Logging is enabled for each proxy service through the Logging tab of the Properties dialog box. The logs generated can be directed to a standard text file or to a SQL/ODBC database. If packet filtering is enabled on a Proxy Server, a separate log can be created to track the operation of the packet filter. Packet filter logging is configured through the Security dialog box's Logging tab.

One of the most important things to remember when you are working with and troubleshooting a Proxy Server installation is which application to use to configure the server. In general, most of the administrative tasks performed on the Proxy Server will be handled through the ISM. However, in the case of user access rights and permissions assignments, the User Manager For Domains is used. The Network or Services applets of the Control Panel may be used to configure the operation of the Proxy Server. Finally, a Registry editor should be used to configure the more obscure settings for the Proxy Server.

A

Knowing the licensing requirements for a particular Proxy Server installation is important to both passing the exam and remaining in compliance when you install Proxy Server. Licensing for Proxy Server 2.0 is part of the standard Microsoft licensing agreement. For Proxy Server, as with IIS and Site Server, no client access licenses are required. However, Proxy Server does require Windows NT Server 4.0 and IIS 3.0 or higher, and both must have valid licenses to comply with the licensing agreement. The Proxy Server license can be transferred between two systems as long as it is completely removed from the original system. Like all Microsoft products under this agreement, it cannot be rented or leased. It can, however, be sold with the understanding that no copies will be kept in any form. The Proxy Server software cannot be decompiled or reverse-engineered. Finally, Microsoft requires that all benchmark and testing results be submitted to Microsoft before they are released to any third party.

Although Proxy Server arrays are a function of the Web Proxy service's caching feature, they can be configured by clicking on Array from any Proxy Server service's Properties dialog box. If your Proxy Server computer is not already a member of an array, the only option available to you is Join Array. Once the Proxy Server is a member of an array, the Array dialog box displays the other members of the array and gives you the option to synchronize the configuration of array members via a check box or to remove the Proxy Server from the array. Remember, if the Synchronize The Configuration Of Array Members option is checked, configuration changes made to one array member are propagated to all array members.

A Proxy Server array can provide fault tolerance for Web Proxy client computers in a number of ways. Because array members use CARP to determine which computer has a particular cached URL, any array member can be queried to fulfill a request. If the queried array member does not have the requested information, it forwards the query to the appropriate Proxy Server and the request is fulfilled. In addition to this configuration, WINS can be configured to address the array as a whole rather than address a particular Proxy Server. In this configuration, each client can be configured to address the array and WINS will manage the address resolution. In the event that a particular array member is unavailable, the WINS server will direct the request to another member of the array.

As mentioned, packet filtering provides the tightest security on a Proxy Server. This option is configured through the Security dialog box, which is accessed from any proxy service's Properties dialog box. Items of particular interest to packet filtering include the following:

- By default, packet filtering denies all packets processed by the Proxy Server. To allow a particular protocol through the Proxy Server, click on the Add button on the Packet Filters tab of the Security dialog box. You can then select a predefined filter (such as DNS Lookup, ICMP PING Query, or SMTP), or you can configure a custom filter by providing a Protocol ID, direction (inbound or outbound), the local port, the remote port, the local host, and the remote host. Port information on many protocols is available in Appendix B and Appendix C.

- Once you have enabled packet filtering on your Proxy Server, you can configure alerting and logging for the defined packet filters. Alerting is enabled through the Alerting tab of the Security dialog box and allows you to generate alerts for rejected packets and protocol violations and when the disk is full. Each alert can be configured to record the event in the event log or to use SMTP to send an email message. Logging is enabled through the Logging tab of the Security dialog box and can be configured for either regular or verbose logging. You can record logged events to a file or to a SQL/ODBC database. If you decide to log to a file, you can have Proxy Server create a new log file daily, weekly, or monthly. In addition, you have the options to limit the number of old log files, to stop all services if the disk is full, and to define the directory to which the log files will be written. If you decide to log to a database, you are provided options for the Data Source Name, the table to which the logs will be written, and the username and password for the database.

Unlike Proxy Server arrays, hierarchical caching does not require that all servers in the chain run Microsoft Proxy Server. In this configuration, the client makes a request to the first proxy server in the chain, which attempts to resolve the request locally. If it is not able to do so, it forwards the request to its upstream proxy server, which then attempts to resolve the request. If the upsteam proxy server is unable to resolve the request, it forwards it to the next proxy server in the chain and so on until the request is resolved, either by a proxy server in the chain or by the server on the Internet. Hierarchical caching is configured through the Routing tab of the Web Proxy Service Properties dialog box. By selecting the Use Web Proxy Or Array In The Upstream Routing dialog box, you can configure the proxy server to forward unresolved requests to another server in the chain. You can also configure a backup route in case the normal upstream router is unavailable. To do so, select Enable Backup Route and specify the appropriate backup router.

SETTING UP AND MANAGING RESOURCES

As mentioned earlier, perhaps the most important feature of Microsoft Proxy Server is its ability to restrict access to the Internet for outbound users and groups. This feature can be used for either the Web Proxy or WinSock Proxy services and is configured through the Permissions tab of the service's Properties dialog box. On the service's Permissions tab, in addition to having the option to enable access control, you are presented with a list of users and groups to which access has been granted. To add a user or group to the access list, click on Edit to invoke the Permissions dialog box. Click on Add to select a user or group to which you want to grant access. Both of the proxy services control access by specifically granting access. If a particular user or group is not granted access, it is inherently denied. The Web Proxy service provides four protocols to which users or groups can be granted access: FTP Read, Gopher, Secure HTTP, and WWW. The WinSock Proxy service includes a number of predefined protocols and allows you to create protocols to which users can be granted access. In addition, unlike the Web Proxy service, the WinSock Proxy service has an option to grant unlimited access to a user or group.

Unlike specific protocol access, access to particular Internet sites cannot be granted on a user or group basis. This type of access is controlled through a domain filter, which applies to all users utilizing the services of the Proxy Server. Domain filters are established through the Domain Filters tab of the Security dialog box. After enabling domain filtering, you have the option of granting or denying access by default. Then you configure the exception list. For example, if you choose to grant access to all sites by default, the exception list you create contains those sites to which you want to deny access. When you configure the exception list, you have the option of denying access to a single computer (by IP address), to a group of computers (by IP address and subnet mask), or to a domain (by domain name). You can modify the exception list by using the Add, Edit, and Remove options on the Domain Filters tab.

As you've learned, caching of Web objects is one of the most attractive features of Microsoft Proxy Server in that it makes browsing by clients more efficient. Caching is configured via the Caching tab of the Web Proxy service's Properties dialog box. In addition to determining whether basic caching is enabled, you are given the option to enable active caching. By clicking on Cache Size, you can define the size and location of the cache on your Proxy Server. Remember that only NTFS volumes can be used for caching. Select an NTFS volume from the list of available drives, enter the size of the cache in the Maximum Size box, and click on Set to define the cache size.

Caching is configured on the Caching tab of the Web Proxy service's Properties dialog box. Select Enable Caching to enable passive caching, which caches objects as they are requested by the clients on the network. In addition to enabling passive caching, you have three options that determine how often Proxy Server will verify that a cached object is still valid. Updates Are More Important (more update checks) checks the validity of cached items more often than Fewer Network Accesses Are More Important (more cache hits). A balance between these two options is Equal Importance, which places the same value on access time and validity. Active caching allows Proxy Server to automatically update its cache for popular sites, generally when system utilization is low. This option is also available on the Caching tab, which also has three options available. The Faster User Response Is More Important (more pre-fetching) option retrieves popular items more frequently in an attempt to decrease user wait time. The Fewer Network Accesses Are More Important (less pre-fetching) option attempts to conserve bandwidth by making active requests less often than the other option. As with passive caching, an Equal Importance option provides a happy medium for active caching.

Reverse proxying is the process by which the Proxy Server listens to requests from the Internet and forwards them to a Web server on the local network. This function is part of the secure Web publishing aspect of Proxy Server and is enabled through the Publishing tab of the Web Proxy service's Properties dialog box. In this dialog box, you have the option to enable Web publishing and, once enabled, direct incoming Web server requests to the local Web server (remember that Proxy Server requires that IIS is running on the same server) or to another Web server.

The configuration of Proxy Server can be backed up and stored for later restore if necessary. To back up your Proxy Server configuration, open any proxy service's Properties dialog box and select Server Backup from the Services tab. You will be prompted to supply a path to which the system will save its configuration (the default is C:\MSP\CONFIG). To restore your Proxy Server configuration, open any proxy service's Properties dialog box and select Server Restore from the Services tab. Again, you will be prompted to supply the path to the backup file. Fill in the appropriate location information and select whether to do a partial restore or a full restore. A partial restore does not restore computer-specific configuration settings, and a Full restore restores all configuration options.

Reverse hosting is an extension of reverse proxying. In addition to listening to incoming Internet requests, Proxy Server determines which internal server to send the requests based on the domain requested. For example, you might configure Proxy Server to send requests for www.mysystem.com and ftp.mysystem.com to the internal server www.computers.com and to send requests for www.texastime.com to the internal www.testing.com server. Reverse hosting is configured through the Publishing tab of the Web Proxy Service Properties dialog box by adding listings to the Except For Those Listed Below list box.

A

INTEGRATION AND INTEROPERABILITY

After you have configured the LAT on the server, you are ready to install the WinSock Proxy Client software on client computers. The WSP Client software installation is accessed through the MSPCLNT share on the Proxy Server. From this directory (usually C:\MSP\CLIENTS\), run the setup application to install the WSP client software on the client. You will be prompted to read the end-user license agreement. Click on Continue to invoke the Microsoft Proxy Client Setup dialog box, which allows you to identify where to install the client software. Click on the icon next to Install Microsoft Proxy Client to begin the installation.

Unlike WinSock Proxy client computers, systems configured to use the Web and SOCKS Proxy services do not necessarily need to run a Windows operating system. CERN-compliant browsers, such as Microsoft Internet Explorer and Netscape Navigator, can be configured to access the Proxy Server directly. Configuring these types of browsers is the same regardless of the platform; the process for each is outlined here:

- For client computers running Microsoft Internet Explorer 4, the Proxy Server settings are accessed by choosing Internet Options from the View menu. The Connection tab of the Internet Options dialog box includes an option to access the Internet using a Proxy Server. Select this option, identify the Proxy Server by either IP address or host name, and establish the port setting (usually 80). The Advanced option allows you to define different Proxy Servers for each protocol and set an exception list of domains for which the client should not use the Proxy Server.

- The Proxy Server settings for Netscape Navigator are accessed by choosing Preferences from the Edit menu. Select Proxy in the Advanced section to define which Proxy Server the client should use. Select Manual proxy configuration and click on View to define the Proxy Server settings (IP address and port). Navigator also provides an option for defining domains with which the client should not use the Proxy Server.

As you know, the WinSock Proxy service can be used to connect IPX-only clients to the Internet by acting as a IPX-IP gateway. Once your client computers have been configured to access Proxy Server, you can install the WSP client application as described in the previous section. Once the client computer has been restarted, any Web requests will be forwarded to Proxy Server.

As you've learned, RAS and Dial-Up Networking can be used in conjunction with Auto Dial to provide dial-up access to the Internet for a small number of clients. However, you must install RAS and DUN and configure them to connect to your ISP. Once this is complete, you can configure Proxy Server's Auto Dial feature by selecting it from the Services tab of any of the proxy services' Properties dialog box.

Many browsers, including Internet Explorer and Netscape Navigator, can be configured automatically to access a Proxy Server. For both IE and Navigator, this option is enabled in the dialog box that contains the Proxy Server options. The configuration script can be used to configure not only the Proxy Server settings, but also many other browser settings. If the client is running the WSP client software, this configuration script can also be defined in the MSPCLNT.INI file and will be accessed when the client initializes.

The MSPCLNT.INI file resides on the Proxy Server and is copied to the clients each time they initialize. Therefore, any changes made to MSPCLNT.INI should be made on the server, not on the client computers themselves. Any changes made on the client will be overwritten the next time the client initializes.

MONITORING AND OPTIMIZATION

As mentioned throughout this appendix, each proxy service can be configured to log events. Event logging is configured through the Logging tab of each Proxy Server service's Properties dialog box. In addition, the alerting feature of the Security dialog box, which can be accessed from the Service tab of any proxy service's Properties dialog box, can be configured to log specific types of events to the event log. The alerting feature can log rejected packets, protocol violations, or full disks. Rejected packets are only recorded by default if there are more than 20 per second, whereas protocol violations and full disks are recorded if there is more than one per second.

The Windows NT Performance Monitor can be used to watch system performance and to determine if problems are occurring or if there is a bottleneck in the system. When Proxy Server is installed on the computer, a number of new counters that are specific to Proxy Server are added and can give greater insight into Proxy Server's performance than the default counters included with Windows NT can. Performance Monitor can be accessed through Administrative Tools (Common), which is part of the Start menu's Programs group. When you start Performance Monitor from the Start menu, a blank monitor screen appears on which you can begin to log any counter. However, to ease Proxy Server monitoring, a shortcut is added to the Proxy Server group under Start|Programs. The shortcut automatically starts Performance Monitor with a number of predefined counters: % Processor Time for inetinfo, % Processor Time for wspsrv, Active Sessions, Cache Hit Ratio (%),

A

Requests/sec, and Current Average Milliseconds/request. To start Performance Monitor this way, click on the Start menu and select Programs|Proxy Server|Monitor Proxy Server Performance.

By utilizing Performance Monitor, Task Manager, and other tools, you can easily identify problems with Proxy Server performance. For example, the Network Interface Output Queue Length should never be greater than 2. If it is, the network is not fast enough to support the requests being made to Proxy Server. If you view the Task Manager and the CPU Utilization is continuously high (above 80%), a faster CPU is necessary in your Proxy Server.

The tools available in Windows NT (mentioned in the preceding list item) can be used to identify performance issues such as the following:

- Use Performance Monitor to easily identify and correct bottlenecks in the system. For example, the Processor object's % Processor Time counter should not be consistently 80% or higher. If it remains high, a new, faster processor is required for your Proxy Server. Or, if the Memory object's Page Faults/sec counter is consistently increasing, the system is having to swap too much information to disk and more RAM should be added.

- As mentioned, the Network Interface Output Queue Length counter can be used to easily identify a network bottleneck. Another useful counter in identifying network-related performance issues is Network Interface Bytes Total/sec. If this counter is consistently close to the theoretical maximum of your network architecture (e.g., 10Mbps for 10BaseT Ethernet), a faster network is needed.

- Counters that monitor physical and logical disk performance are also included with Windows NT. However, remember that these counters can severely degrade system performance and should be used sparingly. For example, the Logical Disk Current Disk Queue Length counter should never be larger than 2. If so, the disk in use is too slow for the requests being made to the Proxy Server.

- The % Processor Time counters, both in general and for the proxy services, provide a good indication of CPU performance and can be used to identify problems in this area.

- In addition to the Memory Page Faults/sec counter, the Available Bytes counter is available to provide insight into memory-related performance. If this counter is consistently low, more memory or virtual memory should be added to the system.

After monitoring the performance of your Proxy Server and identifying possible bottlenecks, you're ready to optimize its performance. Optimization can take two forms:

- The first optimization method is geared toward increasing the throughput of your Proxy Server. This includes upgrading your network, increasing the size of the pipeline connecting your network to your ISP, increasing the CPU speed in your Proxy Server, and adding more memory to your Proxy Server.

- Another area for optimization is in the routing method used to provide cached content to clients. If you determine that access to the Internet is slowed because of the routing or caching method used, a modification is necessary. A caching array can increase performance by using CARP to quickly and easily identify which server has a cached object.

In addition to the standard logs that are available for each proxy service, you can use the Log view in Performance Monitor to track Proxy Server performance over time. One caveat to the Log view, however, is that it tracks entire objects rather than individual counters. So, to track all counters that apply to Proxy Server, you will need to log the Memory, Processor, Web Proxy Server Cache, Web Proxy Server Service, and WinSock Proxy Server objects. These logs can be saved and viewed later or on another server. In addition, you can open a log file, add counters to the Chart or Alert views, and trace the performance over time without constantly observing the server.

You can also use the Network Monitor to analyze network traffic from your Proxy Server to other computers and to the Internet. The captures generated by Network Monitor can be analyzed to determine how your Proxy Server is being utilized by clients on your network and whether it is experiencing problems from the Internet.

Through the Properties dialog box of any proxy service, you can monitor the sessions currently in use on your Proxy Server. To do so, click on Current Sessions on the Services tab of any proxy service Properties dialog box. This action invokes the Microsoft Proxy Server User Sessions dialog box, which can be used to view sessions for each service.

A

TROUBLESHOOTING

Although there are a number of specific points in the troubleshooting section of the Exam Preparation Guide from Microsoft, few of them are specific enough to warrant discussion here. Generally, the most important aspect of troubleshooting comes from your knowledge of Proxy Server, its setup and configuration, and the client configurations. The following sections outline some of the troubleshooting points to keep in mind.

For example, there are few settings to either the Proxy Server or client application installations. For a Proxy Server installation, ensure that all required components are available and that the system can support Proxy Server. From a client installation standpoint, verify that the client can communicate with the server and, if necessary, you should reinstall the WSP Client software.

Access problems most often involve a bad connection to the Internet or from the client to the server. Verify that you are able to communicate with your ISP and, if not, locate the problem at that point in the process. If the client cannot communicate with the server, verify that the client can communicate on the network in general and that other clients are not having problems communicating with the server.

When you are dealing specifically with Proxy client computers, verify that they are able to communicate on the network. If not, verify the physical connections and begin troubleshooting at the lowest level. If they are able to communicate on the network but still cannot see the proxy server, the problem may lie on the server side, which should be the next consideration.

Security problems occur more often than any other when you configure a Proxy Server. First and foremost, verify that the user has a valid logon name and password to the Proxy Server. If a user expects access to a particular protocol, verify that it has been granted, either individually or as group access. If a user is trying to access a particular site, verify that the domain filters in place are not restricting access.

Caching problems often arise when either the cache is too small or the Time-to-Live (TTL) is set too low. Track caching counters using Performance Monitor to verify that the cache is configured correctly.

TCP AND UDP PORTS ASSIGNMENTS

In Chapter 3, you were introduced to Transmission Control Protocol (TCP) and User Datagram Protocol (UDP) ports. If you will recall, TCP and UDP use port numbers to communicate over a network. Both protocols use the port number included in the packet's header information to determine which application is communicating. In many cases, both TCP and UDP use the same port number. However, there are instances where the port numbers differ; for example, port 11 is used only by UDP.

Most standard TCP/IP protocols have been assigned port numbers by the Internet Assigned Numbers Authority (IANA). The port numbers that have been assigned by the IANA range from 0 to 1023 and are called well-known ports. In addition, ports 1024 and higher have been requested by various companies and registered with the IANA. These registered ports are defined in Table B.2.

Microsoft Proxy Server is able to control the traffic that is passed through the server according to port number. This security is configured through the Permissions tab in the Proxy Service Properties dialog box. The settings can be configured to either grant or deny access on a specific port.

Table B.1 lists the decimal port number, the protocol supported, the keyword used by IANA, and IANA's description of its use. For more information on TCP and UDP ports, refer to RFC 1700 (Assigned Numbers).

Table B.1   TCP and UDP well-known ports.

Port Number	Protocol	Keyword	Description
0	TCP & UDP		Reserved
1	TCP & UDP	TCPmux	TCP Port Service Multiplexer
2	TCP & UDP	compressnet	Management Utility
3	TCP & UDP	compressnet	Compression Process
4	TCP & UDP		Unassigned
5	TCP & UDP	rje	Remote Job Entry
6	TCP & UDP		Unassigned
7	TCP & UDP	echo	Echo
8	TCP & UDP		Unassigned
9	TCP & UDP	discard	Discard
10	TCP & UDP		Unassigned
11	UDP	systat	Active Users
12	TCP & UDP		Unassigned
13	TCP & UDP	daytime	Daytime
14	TCP & UDP		Unassigned
15	TCP & UDP		Unassigned [was netstat]
16	TCP & UDP		Unassigned
17	TCP & UDP	qotd	Quote of the Day
18	TCP & UDP	msp	Message Send Protocol
19	TCP & UDP	chargen	Character Generator
20	TCP & UDP	ftp-data	File Transfer Data
21	TCP & UDP	ftp	File Transfer Control
22	TCP & UDP		Unassigned

(continued)

Table B.1 TCP and UDP well-known ports *(continued)*.

Port Number	Protocol	Keyword	Description
23	TCP & UDP	telnet	Telnet
24	TCP & UDP		Any private mail system
25	TCP & UDP	smtp	Simple Mail Transfer Protocol
26	TCP & UDP		Unassigned
27	TCP & UDP	nsw-fe	NSW User System FE
28	TCP & UDP		Unassigned
29	TCP & UDP	msg-icp	MSG ICP
30	TCP & UDP		Unassigned
31	TCP & UDP	msg-auth	MSG Authentication
32	TCP & UDP		Unassigned
33	TCP & UDP	dsp	Display Support Protocol
34	TCP & UDP		Unassigned
35	TCP & UDP		Any private printer server
36	TCP & UDP		Unassigned
37	TCP & UDP	time	Time
38	TCP & UDP		Unassigned
39	TCP & UDP	rlp	Resource Location Protocol
40	TCP & UDP		Unassigned
41	TCP & UDP	graphics	Graphics
42	TCP & UDP	nameserver	Host Name Server
43	TCP & UDP	nicname	Who Is
44	TCP & UDP	mpm-flags	MPM FLAGS Protocol
45	TCP & UDP	mpm	Message Processing Module
46	TCP & UDP	mpm-snd	MPM [default send]
47	TCP & UDP	ni-ftp	NI FTP
48	TCP & UDP		Unassigned
49	TCP & UDP	login	Login Host Protocol
50	TCP & UDP	re-mail-ck	Remote Mail Checking Protocol
51	TCP & UDP	la-maint	IMP Logical Address Maintenance
52	TCP & UDP	xns-time	XNS Time Protocol
53	TCP & UDP	domain	Domain Name Server
54	TCP & UDP	xns-ch	XNS Clearinghouse
55	TCP & UDP	isi-gl	ISI Graphics Language
56	TCP & UDP	xns-auth	XNS Authentication
57	TCP & UDP		Any private terminal access
58	TCP & UDP	xns-mail	XNS Mail
59	TCP & UDP		Any private file service

B

(continued)

Table B.1   TCP and UDP well-known ports *(continued)*.

Port Number	.Protocol	Keyword	Description
60	TCP & UDP		Unassigned
61	TCP & UDP	ni-mail	NI MAIL
62	TCP & UDP	acas	ACA Services
63	TCP & UDP	via-ftp	VIA Systems - FTP
64	TCP & UDP	covia	Communications Integrator (CI)
65	TCP & UDP	tacacs-ds	TACACS-Database Service
66	TCP & UDP	sql*net	Oracle SQL*NET
67	TCP & UDP	bootpc	BOOTP Protocol Server (DHCP is based on BOOTP)
68	TCP & UDP	bootpc	BOOTP Protocol Client (DHCP is based on BOOTP)
69	UDP	tftp	Trivial File Transfer
70	TCP & UDP	gopher	Gopher
71	TCP & UDP	netrjs-1	Remote Job Service
72	TCP & UDP	netrjs-2	Remote Job Service
73	TCP & UDP	netrjs-3	Remote Job Service
74	TCP & UDP	netrjs-4	Remote Job Service
75	UDP		Any private dial-out service
76	TCP & UDP		Unassigned
77	TCP & UDP		Any private RJE service
78	TCP & UDP	vetTCP	VetTCP
79	TCP & UDP	finger	Finger
80	TCP & UDP	www	World Wide Web HTTP
81	TCP & UDP	hosts2-ns	HOSTS2 Name Server
82	TCP & UDP	xfer	XFER Utility
83	TCP & UDP	mit-ml-dev	MIT ML Device
84	TCP & UDP	ctf	Common Trace Facility
85	TCP & UDP	mit-ml-dev	MIT ML Device
86	TCP & UDP	mfcobol	Micro Focus Cobol
87	TCP & UDP		Any private terminal link
88	TCP & UDP	kerberos	Kerberos
89	TCP & UDP	su-mit-tg	SU/MIT Telnet Gateway
90	TCP & UDP		DNSIX Security Attribute Token Map
91	TCP & UDP	mit-dov	MIT Dover Spooler
92	TCP & UDP	npp	Network Printing Protocol
93	TCP & UDP	dcp	Device Control Protocol
94	TCP & UDP	objcall	Tivoli Object Dispatcher
95	TCP & UDP	supdup	SUPDUP

(continued)

Table B.1   TCP and UDP well-known ports *(continued)*.

Port Number	Protocol	Keyword	Description
96	TCP & UDP	dixie	DIXIE Protocol Specification
97	TCP & UDP	swift-rvf	Swift Remote Virtual File Protocol
98	TCP & UDP	tacnews	TAC News
99	TCP & UDP	metagram	Metagram Relay
100	TCP	newacct	[unauthorized use]
101	TCP & UDP	hostname	NIC Host Name Server
102	TCP & UDP	iso-tsap	ISO-TSAP
103	TCP & UDP	gppitnp	Genesis Point-to-Point Trans Net
104	TCP & UDP	acr-nema	ACR-NEMA Digital !mag. & Comm. 300
105	TCP & UDP	csnet-ns	Mailbox Name Nameserver
106	TCP & UDP	3com-tsmux	3COM-TSMUX
107	TCP & UDP	rtelnet	Remote Telnet Service
108	TCP & UDP	snagas	SNA Gateway Access Server
109	TCP & UDP	pop2	Post Office Protocol—version 2
110	TCP & UDP	pop3	Post Office Protocol—version 3
111	TCP & UDP	sunrpc	SUN Remote Procedure Call
112	TCP & UDP	mcidas	McIDAS Data Transmission Protocol
113	TCP & UDP	auth	Authentication Service
114	TCP & UDP	audionews	Audio News Multicast
115	TCP & UDP	sftp	Simple File Transfer Protocol
116	TCP & UDP	ansanotify	ANSA REX Notify
117	TCP & UDP	uucp-path	UUCP Path Service
118	TCP & UDP	sqlserv	SQL Services
119	TCP & UDP	nntp	Network News Transfer Protocol
120	TCP & UDP	cfdptkt	CFDPTKT
121	TCP & UDP	erpc	Encore Expedited Remote Pro.Call
122	TCP & UDP	smakynet	SMAKYNET
123	TCP & UDP	ntp	Network Time Protocol
124	TCP & UDP	ansatrader	ANSA REX Trader
125	TCP & UDP	locus map	Locus PC Interface Net Map Server
126	TCP & UDP	unitary	Unisys Unitary Login
127	TCP & UDP	locus-con	Locus PC-Interface Conn Server
128	TCP & UDP	gss-xlicen	GSS X License Verification
129	TCP & UDP	pwdgen	Password Generator Protocol
130	TCP & UDP	cisco-fna	Cisco FNATIVE
131	TCP & UDP	cisco-tna	Cisco TNATIVE

B

(continued)

Table B.1 TCP and UDP well-known ports (continued).

Port Number	Protocol	Keyword	Description
132	TCP & UDP	cisco-sys	Cisco SYSMAINT
133	TCP & UDP	statsrv	Statistics Service
134	TCP & UDP	ingres-net	INGRES-NET Service
135	TCP & UDP	loc-srv	Location Service
136	TCP & UDP	profile	PROFILE Naming System
137	TCP & UDP	netbios-ns	NetBIOS Name Service
138	TCP & UDP	netbios-dgm	NetBIOS Datagram Service
139	TCP & UDP	netbios-ssn	NetBIOS Session Service
140	TCP & UDP	emfis-data	EMFIS Data Service
141	TCP & UDP	emfis-cntl	EMFIS Control Service
142	TCP & UDP	bl-idm	Britton-Lee IDM
143	TCP & UDP	imap2	Interim Mail Access Protocol v2
144	TCP & UDP	news	NewS
145	TCP & UDP	uaac	UAAC Protocol
146	TCP & UDP	iso-ip0	ISO-IP0
147	TCP & UDP	iso-ip	ISO-IP
148	TCP & UDP	cronus	CRONUS-SUPPORT
149	TCP & UDP	aed-512	AED 512 Emulation Service
150	TCP & UDP	sql-net	SQL-NET
151	TCP & UDP	hems	HEMS
152	TCP & UDP	bftp	Background File Transfer Program
153	TCP & UDP	sgmp	SGMP
154	TCP & UDP	netsc-prod	Netscape
155	TCP & UDP	netsc-dev	Netscape
156	TCP & UDP	sqlsrv	SQL Service
157	TCP & UDP	knet-cmp	KNET/VM Command/Message Protocol
158	TCP & UDP	pcmail-srv	PCMail Server
159	TCP & UDP	nss-routing	NSS-Routing
160	TCP & UDP	sgmp-traps	SGMP-TRAPS
161	TCP & UDP	snmp	SNMP
162	TCP & UDP	snmptrap	SNMPTRAP
163	TCP & UDP	cmip-man	CMIP/TCP Manager
164	TCP & UDP	cmip-agent	CMIP/TCP Agent
165	TCP & UDP	xns-courier	Xerox
166	TCP & UDP	s-net	Sirius Systems
167	TCP & UDP	namp	NAMP

(continued)

Table B.1 TCP and UDP well-known ports *(continued)*.

Port Number	Protocol	Keyword	Description
168	TCP & UDP	rsvd	RSVD
169	TCP & UDP	send	SEND
170	TCP & UDP	print-srv	Network PostScript
171	TCP & UDP	multiplex	Network Innovations Multiplex
172	TCP & UDP	cl/1	Network Innovations CL/1
173	TCP & UDP	xyplex-mux	Xyplex
174	TCP & UDP	mailq	MAILQ
175	TCP & UDP	vmnet	VMNET
176	TCP & UDP	genrad-mux	GENRAD-MUX
177	TCP & UDP	xdmcp	X Display Manager Control Protocol
178	TCP & UDP	nextstep	NextStep Window Server
179	TCP & UDP	bgp	Border Gateway Protocol
180	TCP & UDP	ris	Intergraph
181	TCP & UDP	unify	Unify
182	TCP & UDP	audit	Unisys Audit SITP
183	TCP & UDP	ocbinder	OCBinder
184	TCP & UDP	ocserver	OCServer
185	TCP & UDP	remote-kis	Remote-KIS
186	TCP & UDP	kis	KIS Protocol
187	TCP & UDP	aci	Application Communication Interface
188	TCP & UDP	mumps	Plus Five's MUMPS
189	TCP & UDP	qft	Queued File Transport
190	TCP & UDP	gacp	Gateway Access Control Protocol
191	TCP & UDP	prospero	Prospero
192	TCP & UDP	osu-nms	OSU Network Monitoring System
193	TCP & UDP	srmp	Spider Remote Monitoring Protocol
194	TCP & UDP	irc	Internet Relay Chat Protocol
195	TCP & UDP	dn6-nlm-aud	DNSIX Network Level Module Audit
196	TCP & UDP	dn6-smm-red	DNSIX Session Mgt Module Audit Redir
197	TCP & UDP	dls	Directory Location Service
198	TCP & UDP	dls-mon	Directory Location Service Monitor
199	TCP & UDP	smux	SMUX
200	TCP & UDP	src	IBM System Resource Controller
201	TCP & UDP	at-rtmp	AppleTalk Routing Maintenance
202	TCP & UDP	at-nbp	AppleTalk Name Binding

B

(continued)

Table B.1   TCP and UDP well-known ports *(continued)*.

Port Number	Protocol	Keyword	Description
203	TCP & UDP	at-3	AppleTalk Unused
204	TCP & UDP	at-echo	AppleTalk Echo
205	TCP & UDP	at-5	AppleTalk Unused
206	TCP & UDP	at-zis	AppleTalk Zone Information
207	TCP & UDP	at-7	AppleTalk Unused
208	TCP & UDP	at-8	AppleTalk Unused
209	TCP & UDP	tam	Trivial Authenticated Mail Protocol
210	TCP & UDP	z39.50	ANSI Z39.50
211	TCP & UDP	914c/g	Texas Instruments 914C/G Terminal
212	TCP & UDP	anet	ATEXSSTR
213	TCP & UDP	ipx	IPX
214	TCP & UDP	vmpwscs	VM PWSCS
215	TCP & UDP	softpc	Insignia Solutions
216	TCP & UDP	atls	Access Technology License Server
217	TCP & UDP	dbase	dBASE Unix
218	TCP & UDP	mpp	Netix Message Posting Protocol
219	TCP & UDP	uarps	Unisys ARPs
220	TCP & UDP	imap3	Interactive Mail Access Protocol v3
221	TCP & UDP	fln-spx	Berkeley rlogind with SPX auth
222	TCP & UDP	fsh-spx	Berkeley rshd with SPX auth
223	TCP & UDP	cdc	Certificate Distribution Center
224 to 241	TCP & UDP		Reserved
242	TCP & UDP		Unassigned
243	TCP & UDP	sur-meas	Survey Measurement
244	TCP & UDP		Unassigned
245	TCP & UDP	link	LINK
246	TCP & UDP	dsp3270	Display Systems Protocol
247 to 255			Reserved
256 to 343	TCP & UDP		Unassigned
344	TCP & UDP	pdap	Prospero Data Access Protocol
345	TCP & UDP	pawserv	Perf Analysis Workbench
346	TCP & UDP	zserv	Zebra server
347	TCP & UDP	fatserv	Fatmen server
348	TCP & UDP	csi-sgwp	Cabletron Management Protocol
349 to 370	TCP & UDP		Unassigned
371	TCP & UDP	clearcase	Clearcase
372	TCP & UDP	ulistserv	Unix Listserv

(continued)

Table B.1   TCP and UDP well-known ports *(continued)*.

Port Number	Protocol	Keyword	Description
373	TCP & UDP	legent-1	Legent Corporation
374	TCP & UDP	legent-2	Legent Corporation
375	TCP & UDP	hassle	Hassle
376	TCP & UDP	nip	Amiga Envoy Network Inquiry Protocol
377	TCP & UDP	tnETOS	NEC Corporation
378	TCP & UDP	dsETOS	NEC Corporation
379	TCP & UDP	is99c	TIA/EIA/IS-99 modem client
380	TCP & UDP	is99s	TIA/EIA/IS-99 modem server
381	TCP & UDP	hp-collector	HP performance data collector
382	TCP & UDP	hp-managed-node	HP performance data managed node
383	TCP & UDP	hp-alarm-mgr	HP performance data alarm manager
384	TCP & UDP	arns	A Remote Network Server System
385	TCP & UDP	ibm-app	IBM Application
386	TCP & UDP	asa	ASA Message Router Object Def.
387	TCP & UDP	aurp	Appletalk Update-Based Routing Pro.
388	TCP & UDP	unidata-ldm	Unidata LDM Version 4
389	TCP & UDP	ldap	Lightweight Directory Access Protocol
390	TCP & UDP	uis	UIS
391	TCP & UDP	synotics-relay	SynOptics SNMP Relay Port
392	TCP & UDP	synotics-broker	SynOptics Port Broker Port
393	TCP & UDP	dis	Data Interpretation System
394	TCP & UDP	embl-ndt	EMBL Nucleic Data Transfer
395	TCP & UDP	netcp	NETscout Control Protocol
396	TCP & UDP	netware-ip	Novell NetWare over IP
397	TCP & UDP	mptn	Multi Protocol Trans. Net.
398	TCP & UDP	kryptolan	Kryptolan
399	TCP & UDP		Unassigned
400	TCP & UDP	work-sol	Workstation Solutions
401	TCP & UDP	ups	Uninterruptible Power Supply
402	TCP & UDP	genie	Genie Protocol
403	TCP & UDP	decap	decap
404	TCP & UDP	nced	nced
405	TCP & UDP	ncld	ncld
406	TCP & UDP	imsp	Interactive Mail Support Protocol

B

(continued)

Table B.1 TCP and UDP well-known ports *(continued)*.

Port Number	Protocol	Keyword	Description
407	TCP & UDP	timbuktu	Timbuktu
408	TCP & UDP	prm-sm	Prospero Resource Manager Sys. Man.
409	TCP & UDP	prm-nm	Prospero Resource Manager Node Man
410	TCP & UDP	decladebug	DECLadebug Remote Debug Protocol
411	TCP & UDP	rmt	Remote MT Protocol
412	TCP & UDP	synoptics-trap	Trap Convention Port
413	TCP & UDP	smsp	SMSP
414	TCP & UDP	infoseek	InfoSeek
415	TCP & UDP	bnet	Bnet
416	TCP & UDP	silverplatter	Silverplatter
417	TCP & UDP	onmux	Onmux
418	TCP & UDP	hyper-g	Hyper-G
419	TCP & UDP	ariel1	Ariel
420	TCP & UDP	smpte	SMPTE
421	TCP & UDP	ariel2	Ariel
422	TCP & UDP	ariel3	Ariel
423	TCP & UDP	opc-job-start	IBM Operations Planning and Control Start
424	TCP & UDP	opc-job-track	IBM Operations Planning and Control Track
425	TCP & UDP	icad-el	ICAD
426	TCP & UDP	smartsdp	smartsdp
427	TCP & UDP	svrloc	Server Location
428	TCP & UDP	ocs_cmu	OCS_CMU
429	TCP & UDP	ocs_amu	OCS_AMU
430	TCP & UDP	utmpsd	UTMPSD
431	TCP & UDP	utmpcd	UTMPCD
432	TCP & UDP	iasd	IASD
433	TCP & UDP	nnsp	NNSP
434	TCP & UDP	mobileip-agent	MobileIP-Agent
435	TCP & UDP	mobilip-mn	MobilIP-MN
436	TCP & UDP	dna-cml	DNA-CML
437	TCP & UDP	comscm	comscm
438	TCP & UDP	dsfgw	dsfgw
439	TCP & UDP	dasp	dasp

(continued)

Table B.1   TCP and UDP well-known ports *(continued)*.

Port Number	Protocol	Keyword	Description
440	TCP & UDP	sgcp	sgcp
441	TCP & UDP	decvms-sysmgt	decvms-sysmgt
442	TCP & UDP	cvc_hostd	cvc_hostd
443	TCP & UDP	https	https Mcom
444	TCP & UDP	snpp	Simple Network Paging Protocol
445	TCP & UDP	microsoft-ds	Microsoft-DS
446	TCP & UDP	ddm-rdb	DDM-RDB
447	TCP & UDP	ddm-dfm	DDM-RFM
448	TCP & UDP	ddm-byte	DDM-BYTE
449	TCP & UDP	as-servermap	AS Server Mapper
450	TCP & UDP	tserver	Tserver
451 to 511	TCP & UDP		Unassigned
512	TCP	print	LDP Printing
512	UDP	biff	Mail notification
513	TCP	login	RLOGIN
513	UDP	who	Lists who is logged in to a computer
514	TCP	cmd	REXEC
514	UDP	syslog	
515	TCP & UDP	printer	LPD print spooler (listening port)
516	TCP & UDP		Unassigned
517	TCP & UDP	talk	Talk link across computers (listening port)
518	TCP & UDP	ntalk	
519	TCP & UDP	utime	Unixtime
520	TCP	efs	Extended file name server
520	UDP	router	Local routing process (on site)
521 to 524	TCP & UDP		Unassigned
525	TCP & UDP	timed	Timeserver
526	TCP & UDP	tempo	Newdate
527 to 529	TCP & UDP		Unassigned
530	TCP & UDP	courier	RPC
531	TCP	conference	Chat
531	UDP	rvd-control	MIT disk
532	TCP & UDP	netnews	Readnews
533	TCP & UDP	netwall	For emergency broadcasts
534 to 538	TCP & UDP		Unassigned
539	TCP & UDP	apertus-ldp	Apertus Technologies Load Determination

B

(continued)

Table B.1   TCP and UDP well-known ports *(continued)*.

Port Number	Protocol	Keyword	Description
540	TCP & UDP	uucp	Uucpd
541	TCP & UDP	uucp-rlogin	
542	TCP & UDP		Unassigned
543	TCP & UDP	klogin	
544	TCP & UDP	kshell	Krcmd
545 to 549	TCP & UDP		Unassigned
550	TCP & UDP	new-rwho	New-who
551 to 554	TCP & UDP		Unassigned
555	TCP & UDP	dsf	
556	TCP & UDP	remotefs	Rfs server
557 to 559	TCP & UDP		Unassigned
560	TCP & UDP	rmonitor	Rmonitord
561	TCP & UDP	monitor	
562	TCP & UDP	chshell	Chcmd
563	TCP & UDP		Unassigned
564	TCP & UDP	9pfs	Plan 9 file service
565	TCP & UDP	whoami	Whoami
566 to 569	TCP & UDP		Unassigned
570	TCP & UDP	meter	Demon
571	TCP & UDP	meter	Udemon
572 to 599	TCP & UDP		Unassigned
600	TCP & UDP	ipcserver	Sun IPC server
601 to 605	TCP & UDP		Unassigned
606	TCP & UDP	urm	Cray Unified Resource Manager
607	TCP & UDP	nqs	Nqs
608	TCP & UDP	sift-uft	Sender-Initiated/Unsolicited File Transfer
609	TCP & UDP	npmp-trap	
610	TCP & UDP	npmp-local	
611	TCP & UDP	npmp-gui	
612 to 633	TCP & UDP		Unassigned
634	TCP & UDP	ginad	
635 to 665	TCP & UDP		Unassigned
666	TCP & UDP	mdqs	
667 to 703	TCP & UDP		Unassigned
704	TCP & UDP	elcsd	Errlog copy/server daemon

(continued)

Table B.1   TCP and UDP well-known ports *(continued)*.

Port Number	Protocol	Keyword	Description
705 to 708	TCP & UDP		Unassigned
709	TCP & UDP	entrustmanager	EntrustManager
710 to 720	TCP & UDP		Unassigned
721 to 731	TCP	printer	NT 3.51 client LPD printing
732 to 739	TCP & UDP		Unassigned
740	TCP & UDP	neTCP	NETscout Control Protocol
741	TCP & UDP	netgw	NetGW
742	TCP & UDP	netrcs	Network-based Rev. Cont. Sys.
743	TCP & UDP		Unassigned
744	TCP & UDP	flexlm	Flexible License Manager
745 to 746	TCP & UDP		Unassigned
747	TCP & UDP	fujitsu-dev	Fujitsu Device Control
748	TCP & UDP	ris-cm	Russell Info Sci Calendar Manager
749	TCP & UDP	kerberos-adm	Kerberos administration
750	TCP	rfile	Kerberos authentication
750	UDP	loadav	
751	TCP & UDP	pump	Kerberos authentication
752	TCP & UDP	qrh	Kerberos password server
753	TCP & UDP	rrh	Kerberos userreg server
754	TCP & UDP	tell	Send; Kerberos slave propagation
755 to 757	TCP & UDP		Unassigned
758	TCP & UDP	nlogin	
759	TCP & UDP	con	
760	TCP & UDP	ns	
761	TCP & UDP	rxe	
762	TCP & UDP	quotad	
763	TCP & UDP	cycleserv	
764	TCP & UDP	omserv	
765	TCP & UDP	webster	
766	TCP & UDP		Unassigned
767	TCP & UDP	phonebook	Phone
768	TCP & UDP		Unassigned
769	TCP & UDP	vid	
770	TCP & UDP	cadlock	
771	TCP & UDP	rtip	
772	TCP & UDP	cycleserv2	
773	TCP	submit	

B

(continued)

Table B.1 TCP and UDP well-known ports *(continued)*.

Port Number	Protocol	Keyword	Description
773	UDP	notify	
774	TCP	rpasswd	
774	UDP	acmaint_dbd	
775	TCP	entomb	
775	UDP	acmaint_transd	
776	TCP & UDP	wpages	
777 to 779	TCP & UDP		Unassigned
780	TCP & UDP	wpgs	
781	TCP & UDP	hp-collector	HP performance data collector
782	TCP & UDP	hp-managed-node	HP performance data-managed node
783	TCP & UDP	hp-alarm-mgr	HP performance data alarm manager
786	TCP & UDP	concert	
787 to 799	TCP & UDP		Unassigned
800	TCP & UDP	mdbs_daemon	
801	TCP & UDP	device	
802 to 887	TCP & UDP		Unassigned
888	TCP	erlogin	Logon and environment passing
889 to 995	TCP & UDP		Unassigned
996	TCP & UDP	xtreelic	XTREE License Server
997	TCP & UDP	maitrd	
998	TCP	busboy	
998	UDP	puparp	
999	TCP	garcon	
999	UDP	applix	Applix ac
999	TCP & UDP	puprouter	
1000	TCP	cadlock	
1000	UDP	ock	
1001 to 1022	TCP & UDP		Unassigned
1023	TCP & UDP		Reserved

Although they are not controlled by the IANA, ports from 1024 to 65535 are registered for the convenience of the Internet community. Whenever possible, the same ports are used for both TCP and UDP. Ports numbered from 1024 to 5000 are sometimes referred to as *ephemeral* ports. The registered ports listed in Table B.2 are those that apply particularly to Windows NT. For a complete list of registered ports, refer to RFC 1700 or the IANA at **www.isi.edu/in-notes/iana/assignments/port-numbers**.

Table B.2 TCP and UDP registered ports.

Port Number	Protocol	Keyword	Description
1024			Reserved
1025	TCP & UDP	blackjack	Network blackjack
1109	TCP	kpop	Kerberos popup
1167	UDP	phone	
1248	TCP & UDP	hermes	
1347	TCP & UDP	bbn-mmc	Multimedia conferencing
1348	TCP & UDP	bbn-mmx	Multimedia conferencing
1349	TCP & UDP	sbook	Registration Network Protocol
1350	TCP & UDP	editbench	Registration Network Protocol
1351	TCP & UDP	equationbuilder	Digital Tool Works (MIT)
1352	TCP & UDP	lotusnote	Lotus Notes
1512	TCP & UDP	WINS	Reserved for Windows Internet Name Service
1524	TCP & UDP	ingreslock	Ingres
1525	TCP & UDP	orasrv	Oracle
1525	TCP & UDP	prospero-np	Prospero nonprivileged
1527	TCP & UDP	tlisrv	Oracle
1529	TCP & UDP	coauthor	Oracle
1600	TCP & UDP	issd	
1650	TCP & UDP	nkd	
1666	UDP	maze	
2000	TCP & UDP	callbook	
2001	TCP	dc	
2001	UDP	wizard	Curry
2002	TCP & UDP	globe	
2004	TCP	mailbox	
2004	UDP	emce	CCWS mm conf
2005	TCP	berknet	
2005	UDP	oracle	
2006	TCP	invokator	
2006	UDP	raid-cc	RAID
2007	TCP	dectalk	
2007	UDP	raid-am	
2008	TCP	conf	
2008	UDP	terminaldb	
2009	TCP	news	
2009	UDP	whosockami	

B

(continued)

Table B.2   TCP and UDP registered ports *(continued)*.

Port Number	Protocol	Keyword	Description
2010	TCP	search	
2010	UDP	pipe_server	
2011	TCP	raid-cc	RAID
2011	UDP	servserv	
2012	TCP	ttyinfo	
2012	UDP	raid-ac	
2013	TCP	raid-am	
2013	UDP	raid-cd	
2014	TCP	troff	
2014	UDP	raid-sf	
2015	TCP	cypress	
2015	UDP	raid-cs	
2016	TCP & UDP	bootserver	
2017	TCP	cypress-stat	
2017	UDP	bootclient	
2018	TCP	terminaldb	
2018	UDP	rellpack	
2019	TCP	whosockami	
2019	UDP	about	
2020	TCP & UDP	xinupageserver	
2021	TCP	servexec	
2021	UDP	xinuexpansion1	
2022	TCP	down	
2022	UDP	xinuexpansion2	
2023	TCP & UDP	xinuexpansion3	
2024	TCP & UDP	xinuexpansion4	
2025	TCP	ellpack	
2025	UDP	xribs	
2026	TCP & UDP	scrabble	
2027	TCP & UDP	shadowserver	
2028	TCP & UDP	submitserver	
2030	TCP & UDP	device2	
2032	TCP & UDP	blackboard	
2033	TCP & UDP	glogger	
2034	TCP & UDP	scoremgr	
2035	TCP & UDP	imsldoc	
2038	TCP & UDP	objectmanager	

(continued)

Table B.2   TCP and UDP registered ports *(continued)*.

Port Number	Protocol	Keyword	Description
2040	TCP & UDP	lam	
2041	TCP & UDP	interbase	
2042	TCP & UDP	isis	
2043	TCP & UDP	isis-bcast	
2044	TCP & UDP	rimsl	
2045	TCP & UDP	cdfunc	
2046	TCP & UDP	sdfunc	
2047	TCP & UDP	dls	
2048	TCP & UDP	dls-monitor	
2049	TCP & UDP	shilp	Sun NFS
2053	TCP	knetd	Kerberos de-multiplexer
2105	TCP	eklogin	Kerberos encrypted rlogon
2784	TCP & UDP	www-dev	World Wide Web—development
3049	TCP & UDP	NSWS	
4672	TCP & UDP	rfa	Remote file access server
5000	TCP & UDP	commplex-main	
5001	TCP & UDP	commplex-link	
5002	TCP & UDP	rfe	Radio Free Ethernet
5145	TCP & UDP	rmonitor_secure	
5236	TCP & UDP	padl2sim	
5555	TCP	rmt	Rmtd
5556	TCP	mtb	Mtbd (mtb backup)
6111	TCP & UDP	sub-process	HP SoftBench Sub-Process Control
6558	TCP & UDP	xdsxdm	
7000	TCP & UDP	afs3-fileserver	File server
7001	TCP & UDP	afs3-callback	Cache manager callbacks
7002	TCP & UDP	afs3-prserver	SAM database
7003	TCP & UDP	afs3-vlserver	Volume location database
7004	TCP & UDP	afs3-kaserver	AFS/Kerberos authentication service
7005	TCP & UDP	afs3-volser	Volume-management server
7006	TCP & UDP	afs3-errors	Error-interpretation service
7007	TCP & UDP	afs3-bos	Basic overseer process
7008	TCP & UDP	afs3-update	Server-to-server updates
7009	TCP & UDP	afs3-rmtsys	Remote cache manager service
9535	TCP & UDP	man	Remote man server
9536	TCP	w	

B

(continued)

Table B.2 TCP and UDP registered ports *(continued)*.

Port Number	Protocol	Keyword	Description
9537	TCP	mantst	Remote man server, testing
10000	TCP	bnews	
10000	UDP	rscs0	
10001	TCP	queue	
10001	UDP	rscs1	
10002	TCP	poker	
10002	UDP	rscs2	
10003	TCP	gateway	
10003	UDP	rscs3	
10004	TCP	remp	
10004	UDP	rscs4	
10005	UDP	rscs5	
10006	UDP	rscs6	
10007	UDP	rscs7	
10008	UDP	rscs8	
10009	UDP	rscs9	
10010	UDP	rscsa	
10011	UDP	rscsb	
10012	TCP	qmaster	
10012	UDP	qmaster	
17007	TCP & UDP	isode-dua	

PREDEFINED WINSOCK PROXY PROTOCOLS

The WinSock Proxy service includes a number of predefined protocols that can be used to easily grant or restrict access to the service. The following sections outline these protocols and their uses. The first listing for each section gives the default setting for the initial connection port, protocol type, and direction. The default port ranges for subsequent connections are also listed. These settings are found in the Protocol Definition dialog box, show in Figure C.1. The Protocol Definition dialog box is accessed through the Internet Service Manager, WinSock Proxy Properties, Protocols tab. Select a protocol and click Edit to view or modify a protocol's definition.

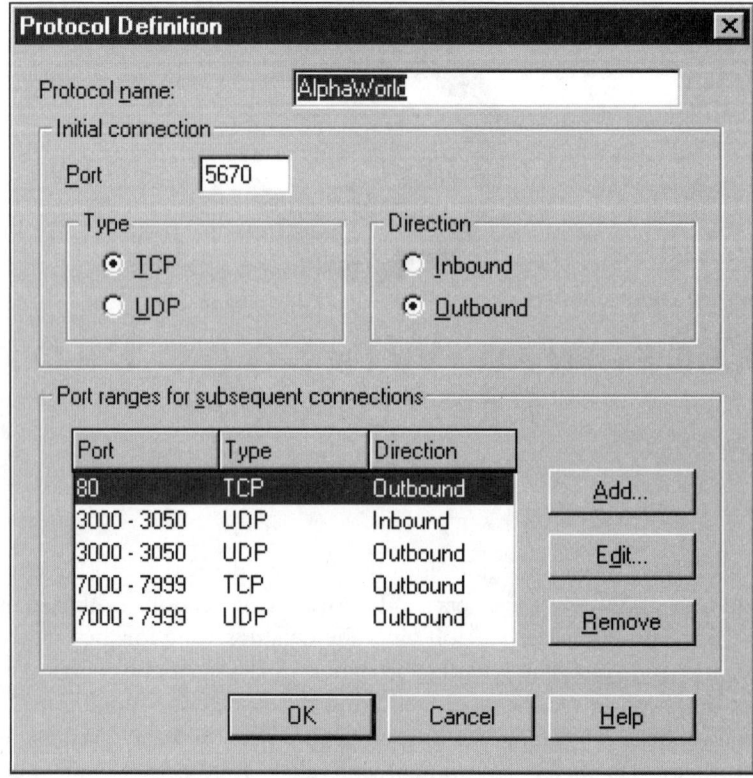

Figure C.1   Protocol settings are accessed and changed through the Protocol Definition dialog box.

 Each Request for Comments (RFC) listed in this appendix is available through a number of resources. For our search, we used the RFC editor at **www.isi.edu/rfc-editor/** and searched for each protocol or numbered RFC.

ALPHAWORLD

- **Initial connection port** 5670
- **Initial connection type** TCP
- **Initial connection direction** Outbound
- **Subsequent connection settings:**
  - 80, TCP, outbound
  - 3000–3050, UDP, inbound
  - 3000–3050, UDP, outbound

- 7000-7999, TCP, outbound
- 7000-7999, UDP, outbound

The AlphaWorld protocol is used to access one of the many interactive virtual worlds that have developed on the Internet. Specifically, AlphaWorld is the first world that was developed with the Active Worlds software, which is available from Circle of Fire Studios. Although the biggest implementation of the Active Worlds software is essentially a 3D chat room, it is also being used by many large corporations and universities to develop new and interesting ways to view Internet content. One example of this is the virtual campus recently announced by the University of Colorado.

Information on Active Worlds, Circle of Fire, and AlphaWorld is available at **www.activeworlds.com**.

AOL

- **Initial connection port** 5190
- **Initial connection type** TCP
- **Initial connection direction** Outbound
- **Subsequent connection settings** None

Perhaps the most well-known Internet Service Provider in America today, America Online (AOL) provides a simple end-user interface that has allowed many people who may otherwise have been intimidated by the Internet to get online and discover this wonderful world of information in which we live.

Unlike other ISPs, AOL does not use a standard browser to provide access; instead, it has designed its own, more intuitive interface. When you use the AOL software on a corporate network for access to the Internet, it is necessary to enable the AOL protocol. Because many of the early versions of the AOL software did not support certain features of the Web, many Webmasters designed separate versions of their pages for use with the AOL software. The newest generation of the software, however, supports standard browsers and more of the features available on the Web today.

AOL's Web site is located at **www.aol.com**.

C

ARCHIE

- **Initial connection port** 1525
- **Initial connection type** UDP

- **Initial connection direction** Outbound
- **Subsequent connection settings** 0, UDP, inbound

Archie is one of the earliest protocols used to search the Internet. It is used to search for FTP servers that contain specific information. After logging on to an Archie server, you are able to search through its list of FTP servers to find a specific file whose name contains a specified regular expression. Until recently, InterNIC maintained a list of Archie servers. The most recent update we found is from February 1997 and lists the following servers:

```
Last Update: Feb 18 1997
        archie.au                139.130.23.2      Australia
        archie.univie.ac.at      131.130.1.23      Austria
        archie.belnet.be         193.190.198.2     Belgium
        archie.bunyip.com        192.77.55.5       Canada
        archie.cs.mcgill.ca      132.206.51.250    Canada
        archie.funet.fi          128.214.248.46    Finland
        archie.cru.fr            129.20.254.2      France
        archie.th-darmstadt.de   130.83.22.1       Germany
        archie.ac.il             132.65.208.15     Israel
        archie.unipi.it          131.114.21.15     Italy
        archie.wide.ad.jp        133.4.3.6         Japan
        archie.kornet.nm.kr      168.126.63.10     Korea
        archie.sogang.ac.kr      163.239.1.11      Korea
        archie.nz                140.200.128.20    New Zealand
        archie.icm.edu.pl        148.81.209.5      Poland
        archie.rediris.es        130.206.1.5       Spain
        archie.luth.se           130.240.12.23     Sweden
        archie.switch.ch         193.5.24.1        Switzerland
        archie.ncu.edu.tw        192.83.166.12     Taiwan
        archie.doc.ic.ac.uk      193.63.255.1      UK
        archie.hensa.ac.uk       129.12.200.130    UK
        archie.unl.edu           129.93.1.14       USA (NE)
        archie.rutgers.edu       128.6.21.13       USA (NJ)
        archie.ans.net           147.225.1.10      USA (NY)
```

More information on Archie can be found at InterNIC's Web site at **www.internic.net**.

DNS

- **Initial connection port** 53
- **Initial connection type** UDP
- **Initial connection direction** Outbound
- **Subsequent connection settings** 0, UDP, inbound

As discussed in Chapters 3 and 12, the Domain Name System (DNS) is used to associate plain-language names to IP addresses. Whether your network contains a DNS server or you rely on your ISP's DNS server, if you are using the WinSock Proxy service to access the Internet, this port must be enabled to provide address resolution.

ECHO (TCP)

- **Initial connection port** 7
- **Initial connection type** TCP
- **Initial connection direction** Outbound
- **Subsequent connection settings** None

Both the Transmission Control Protocol (TCP) and User Datagram Protocol (UDP) implementations of the Echo protocol are defined by RFC 862, which was written in 1983. This troubleshooting protocol does not perform the same functions as Internet Control Message Protocol (ICMP) performs, which you might expect. Rather, the Echo server returns the information it receives from the client to ensure that transmissions are free of errors.

ECHO (UDP)

- **Initial connection port** 7
- **Initial connection type** UDP
- **Initial connection direction** Outbound
- **Subsequent connection settings** None

See Echo (TCP).

C

Enliven

- **Initial connection port** 537
- **Initial connection type** TCP
- **Initial connection direction** Outbound
- **Subsequent connection settings** None

Enliven is a series of products created by Narrative Communications. Enliven gives Webmasters the ability to place an advertisement banner on a Web page and to track information—such as number of hits, demographics, and sales—about the users who access the banner.

For more information on Enliven and Narrative, see their Web site at **www.narrative.com**.

Finger

- **Initial connection port** 79
- **Initial connection type** TCP
- **Initial connection direction** Outbound
- **Subsequent connection settings** None

Finger is a seldom-used protocol that identifies users on a Finger server. Finger can identify users on the system by their logon names, and the Finger server can supply much more detailed information, such as the user's logon time, full name, email address, and phone number. Because this private information can be revealed by the server, Finger is seldom seen on the Internet today.

The Finger protocol is defined by RFC 1288.

FTP

- **Initial connection port** 21
- **Initial connection type** TCP
- **Initial connection direction** Outbound
- **Subsequent connection settings:**
  - 0, TCP, inbound
  - 1025-5000, TCP, outbound
  - 32768-65535, TCP, outbound

As discussed throughout this book, FTP is used to manage file transfers on the Internet or an intranet. It provides easy cross-platform compatibility, which allows file transfers between dissimilar systems. Along with HTTP, FTP is one of the most often-used protocols on the Internet today.

FTP is defined in RFC 959 and is updated by RFC 2228.

GOPHER

- **Initial connection port** 70
- **Initial connection type** TCP
- **Initial connection direction** Outbound
- **Subsequent connection settings** None

Gopher provides a method for distributing text files on the Internet. It is not used often today except by colleges, universities, and government institutions.

Gopher is defined in RFC 1436.

HTTP

- **Initial connection port** 80
- **Initial connection type** TCP
- **Initial connection direction** Outbound
- **Subsequent connection settings** None

Perhaps the most widely used protocol on the Internet today, HTTP is used to transmit HTML pages from Internet servers to clients. HTML pages, the primary files that make up the World Wide Web, are the basis for all traffic on the Internet. Chances are, if you are implementing a Proxy Server, you will grant users access to the HTTP protocol. There may be some instances in which you would want to disable the protocol entirely, but a more likely scenario is one in which access is granted to a particular group of users.

HTTP 1.0 is defined in RFC 1945, but it is not a standard. The first proposed standard is HTTP 1.1, which is defined in RFC 2068.

C

HTTP-S

- **Initial connection port** 443
- **Initial connection type** TCP

- **Initial connection direction** Outbound
- **Subsequent connection settings** None

HTTP-S is the secure implementation of HTTP. It uses Secure Sockets Layer (SSL) to encrypt messages sent across the Internet. By using SSL, HTTP-S can safely send sensitive information—such as credit card or Social Security numbers—without fear of them being intercepted. If you host an e-commerce site or allow your users to make purchases over the Web, enabling HTTP-S is imperative.

The SSL protocol is defined in a number of places on the Web, including **home.netscape.com/newsref/std/SSL.html**.

I C Q

- **Initial connection port** 4000
- **Initial connection type** UDP
- **Initial connection direction** Outbound
- **Subsequent connection settings:**
    - 0, TCP, inbound
    - 0, UDP, inbound
    - 1025-5000, TCP, inbound
    - 1025-5000, TCP, outbound

ICQ (I seek you) is a new chat protocol that is used to communicate in realtime with other ICQ users on the Internet. One of the major differences between ICQ and Internet Relay Chat (IRC) is ICQ's paging feature. After installing the appropriate software, each time users connect to the Internet, they are able to receive pages telling them someone wishes to chat. In addition, ICQ goes beyond IRC in that it not only supports text transmission, it also supports voice, graphics, video, and games.

Information about ICQ abounds. A good place to start is the Lycos Community Guide to ICQ at **www.lycos.com/wguide/wire/wire_969318_53988_2_0.html** or go to **www.lycos.com** and search on ICQ.

I M A P 4

- **Initial connection port** 143
- **Initial connection type** TCP
- **Initial connection direction** Outbound
- **Subsequent connection settings** None

The Internet Messaging Access Protocol, version 4 (IMAP4) is an email transfer protocol that is used by many mail clients and servers. Whether IMAP4 is enabled on your network depends solely on which applications you and your ISP are using. IMAP4 can be used as the transport protocol for Exchange Server and Outlook clients.

IMAP is defined in a number of RFCs available through InterNIC at **www.internic.net**.

IRC

- **Initial connection port** 6667
- **Initial connection type** TCP
- **Initial connection direction** Outbound
- **Subsequent connection settings** None

The Internet Relay Chat (IRC) was one of the first chat protocols developed. It allows for text-based communication between two clients, but nothing more. It is, however, a small protocol and, consequently, fairly fast.

IRC is defined in RFC 1459.

LDAP

- **Initial connection port** 389
- **Initial connection type** TCP
- **Initial connection direction** Outbound
- **Subsequent connection settings** None

The Lightweight Directory Access Protocol (LDAP) was designed to provide users with interactive read/write access to directories. It is most often used with programs such as Microsoft's NetMeeting, which is a collaboration tool included with Internet Explorer.

Unlike some protocols used by Microsoft, LDAP is a standard and is defined in RFC 1777. LDAP version 3, which is most often used today, is defined in RFC 2251.

C

MS NETSHOW

- **Initial connection port** 1755
- **Initial connection type** TCP

- **Initial connection direction** Outbound
- **Subsequent connection settings** 1025-5000, UDP, inbound

The MS NetShow protocol definition is used by the Microsoft NetShow application. NetShow servers use push technology to distribute streaming content to users' desktops via TCP and UDP on the designated ports. NetShow is often used on intranets to disseminate information such as human resources messages to all users in the company.

For more information on NetShow and its use, go to the Microsoft site at **www.microsoft.com/ntserver/netshow**.

MSN

MSN (Microsoft Network) is a full-fledged news service from Microsoft. For more information, visit **www.msn.com**.

- **Initial connection port** 569
- **Initial connection type** TCP
- **Initial connection direction** Outbound
- **Subsequent connection settings** None

NET2PHONE

Net2Phone enables "phone" calls over the Internet. For more information, visit **www.net2phone.com**.

- **Initial connection port** 6801
- **Initial connection type** UDP
- **Initial connection direction** Outbound
- **Subsequent connection settings:**
    - 0, TCP, inbound
    - 0, UDP, inbound
    - 1025-5000, UDP, outbound

NET2PHONE REGISTRATION

Used to register your Net2Phone ID. For more information, visit **www. net2phone.com**.

- **Initial connection port** 6500
- **Initial connection type** TCP

- **Initial connection direction** Outbound
- **Subsequent connection settings** None

NNTP

- **Initial connection port** 119
- **Initial connection type** TCP
- **Initial connection direction** Outbound
- **Subsequent connection settings** None

The Network News Transfer Protocol (NNTP) is a comparatively old protocol (proposed in 1986) that is still in use today. As its name implies, it is used to transfer news messages through the Usenet news system. The choice to enable or disable this protocol is a weighty one. There are many Usenet newsgroups available that provide valuable information to users. On the other hand, there are many groups dedicated to nonbusiness activities such as cooking, antique cars, and supermodels. Although they may be interesting hobbies, transferring these types of messages in a business environment takes up valuable bandwidth and time.

NNTP is defined in RFC 977.

POP3

- **Initial connection port** 110
- **Initial connection type** TCP
- **Initial connection direction** Outbound
- **Subsequent connection settings** None

The Post Office Protocol version 3 (POP3) is another protocol used to transfer email between clients and servers. Many of the email packages available today use POP3 to receive mail messages.

POP3 is defined in RFC1725.

REALAUDIO (7070)

- **Initial connection port** 7070
- **Initial connection type** TCP
- **Initial connection direction** Outbound

- **Subsequent connection settings:**
  - 6770, UDP, outbound
  - 6970-7170, UDP, inbound

RealAudio and RealVideo are multimedia formats that are viewed through applications such as RealPlayer from RealNetworks, Inc. Both RealAudio (7070) and RealAudio (7075) support streaming audio and video from the Internet or an intranet. For example, many radio stations across the United States and around the world use streaming audio to send their broadcast in realtime. By using these applications, users can listen to their favorite music or watch video from the comfort of their desks. Enabling these protocols leaves your network open to particular clients who are using large amounts of bandwidth to entertain themselves.

For more information on RealAudio and RealVideo, visit the RealNetworks Web site at **www.real.com**.

REALAUDIO (7075)

- **Initial connection port** 7075
- **Initial connection type** TCP
- **Initial connection direction** Outbound
- **Subsequent connection settings:**
  - 6770, UDP, outbound
  - 6970-7170, UDP, inbound

See RealAudio (7070).

SMTP (CLIENT)

- **Initial connection port** 25
- **Initial connection type** TCP
- **Initial connection direction** Outbound
- **Subsequent connection settings** None

The Simple Mail Transfer Protocol is yet another email transport protocol. SMTP is often used to send email from clients to servers rather than vice versa. For example, many ISPs use separate servers to send and receive mail. A client is often configured to retrieve its mail messages from a POP3 server and send its outgoing messages to an SMTP server. Whether or not you enable this protocol on your Proxy Server depends entirely on your network configuration and the applications you and your ISP are using.

SMTP is defined in RFC 821.

TELNET

- **Initial connection port** 23
- **Initial connection type** TCP
- **Initial connection direction** Outbound
- **Subsequent connection settings** None

As mentioned in Chapter 3, Telnet is a text-based terminal emulation protocol that is used to manipulate a computer across the network as if the user were sitting at the keyboard. Although many Telnet implementations are still on the Internet, it is most often used on intranets to connect dissimilar systems, such as PCs and Unix workstations.

Telnet is one of the earliest protocols and is defined in RFC 854, but it is discussed in RFCs as early as 215, which was written in 1971.

TIME (TCP)

- **Initial connection port** 37
- **Initial connection type** TCP
- **Initial connection direction** Outbound
- **Subsequent connection settings** 0, UDP, inbound

Time is used to—you guessed it—retrieve the time setting from a server. The queried server returns the time as a 32-bit number that represents the number of seconds since midnight on January 1, 1900, Coordinated Universal Time (UTC). UTC is, at the basic level, the same as Greenwich Mean Time (GMT), which measures the different time zones against the time in Greenwich, England. UTC, however, is the recognized term to use with time-keeping applications.

The Time protocol is defined in RFC 868.

C

VDOLIVE

- **Initial connection port** 7000
- **Initial connection type** TCP

- **Initial connection direction** Outbound
- **Subsequent connection settings** 0, UDP, inbound

VDOLive is another streaming video format in use on Web sites today. It is viewed through the VDOLive Player, made by VDONet Corporation.

For more information on VDOLive and the VDOLive Player, visit the VDONet Web site at **www.vdo.net/corporate**.

VXTREME

- **Initial connection port** 12468
- **Initial connection type** TCP
- **Initial connection direction** Outbound
- **Subsequent connection settings:**
    - 0, UDP, inbound
    - 1025-5000, UDP, inbound
    - 1025-5000, UDP, outbound
    - 32768-65535, UDP, outbound

VXtreme is another streaming video format that is viewed through the Web Theater client. VXtreme Web Theater is a product of VXtreme, Inc. and is used by many sites, including CNN, to display live, streaming video.

More information is available at the VXtreme Web site at **www.vxtreme.com**.

WHOIS

- **Initial connection port** 43
- **Initial connection type** TCP
- **Initial connection direction** Outbound
- **Subsequent connection settings** None

The WhoIs protocol is used to query WhoIs servers for information on registered users. For example, the WhoIs server maintained by InterNIC at **rs.internic.net** maintains information on all registered DNS domains and the system administrators responsible for those domains. However, the information provided by a WhoIs server may be out-of-date or incomplete.

The WhoIs protocol is defined in RFC 954.

GLOSSARY

56Kbps (56K) leased line A digital communications link with a bandwidth of 56Kbps.

A

A record A DNS record used to map Fully Qualified Domain Names (FQDNs) to IP addresses.

access control A Proxy Server feature that enables user- and group-level control of service access by protocol and by extension port.

account policy A Windows NT security setting that defines restrictions on user passwords and failed logons.

Account, Global, Local, Permission (AGLP) Refers to the preferred method of assigning user permissions. User accounts are placed in global groups, which are added to local groups. Permissions are assigned to local groups.

address class A method used to delineate the network ID and host ID portions of an IP address. The address classes make this distinction along byte boundaries.

Address Resolution Protocol (ARP) The protocol that determines the physical (Media Access Control, or MAC) address for a particular IP address.

Advanced Research Projects Agency (ARPA) The Department of Defense agency that initiated the project that created TCP/IP and the Internet.

Advanced Research Projects Agency Network (ARPANet) The predecessor to today's Internet. ARPANet linked colleges and universities to allow them to share research information over a packet-switched network.

Application layer The layer of the OSI model in which network communications are interfaced with user applications.

application protocol An upper-layer protocol that provides an interface to the user and performs a specific function.

application restriction A user access control in which a specific protocol or application is restricted from use.

array-based content caching Several Proxy Server installations can be configured to operate as a single entity by using a new array-based distributed caching method. Caching arrays can be administered as a single, logical entity, and they can provide automated load balancing, add fault tolerance, and embody scalability.

Auto Dial The service that connects to the Internet automatically when an event that requires connection to the Internet occurs.

B

backbone A high-bandwidth, high-performance network link. Most ISP's networks are directly connected to a backbone; other times, the ISP is connected to someone else's network, which is connected to a backbone.

Berkeley Internet Name Domain (BIND) An implementation of DNS designed at the University of California, Berkeley; it is the basis for Microsoft's implementation of DNS.

BIND boot file The file that is used to assist the migration from a BIND system to a Microsoft DNS system.

binding Connecting a service or protocol to a network interface so the service or protocol can use or be transported over that interface.

C

cache On a server, an area used to store objects requested from the Web so that subsequent requests can be processed locally, which decreases response time and traffic over the Internet connection.

cache array A Proxy Server 2.0 configuration where two or more Proxy Servers are configured as a single entity.

Cache Array Routing Protocol (CARP) A new distributed caching protocol submitted by Microsoft to the IETF as a new industry standard. CARP uses a queryless routing method to locate and retrieve data from distributed cache whether it is in an array-based or a hierarchical-based format. This method offers significant performance improvement over traditional location methods, especially on high-volume requests with multiple Proxy Servers.

caching chain A Proxy Server 2.0 configuration in which two or more proxy servers are configured so the downline proxy servers are dependent on the upline proxy servers.

cascaded proxying In a multiple proxy server environment, a method of passing unresolved requests from one proxy server computer to an upstream proxy server computer. This is also known as hierarchical proxying or proxy chaining.

cc:Mail Connector A Microsoft Exchange Connector used to allow Exchange to communicate with Lotus cc:Mail systems.

CERN Conseil Européen pour la Recherche Nucléaire, or the European Laboratory for Particle Research, which developed much of the HTTP protocol and an HTTP proxy system.

circuit-layer restriction A user access control in which multiple protocols can be filtered or

monitored simultaneously regardless of the application or data content.

Classless Inter-Domain Routing (CIDR) The newest method for making the distinction between network ID and host ID. It counts the exact number of bits, from the left, that define the network ID.

client configuration script Allows for automatic configuration of Web Proxy clients to increase overall network performance when you are using arrays or chains. You can use predefined JavaScripts, or you can create your own scripts.

content caching The function of a proxy server; frequently accessed data on a remote server is stored locally to speed client access and to reduce network traffic.

control channel Secondary channel used by the WinSock Proxy service to provide routing and connection information and management.

counter In Performance Monitor, a single collection point of information for a system resource. DNS Cache Hits under the Web Proxy Server Cache object is an example of a counter.

D

Data Service Unit/Channel Service Unit (DSU/CSU) The device that connects a computer to a 56KB communication line.

datagram-oriented communication A connectionless communication method used by User Datagram Protocol (UDP) and the WinSock Proxy service.

dedicated service Exclusive access to a specific communications port. Dedicated service guarantees you a connection but at a higher price.

Dial-Up Networking A Windows NT and Windows 95 utility that controls the dial-out capabilities of Remote Access Service (RAS).

distributed proxying In a multiple Proxy Server environment, a method of logically connecting Proxy Servers and associated cache so Internet objects are only stored one time and all members of the array will know where the object is stored. This provides the client with a higher percentage of "hits" when it is attempting to find objects stored locally and better utilizes the cache storage space. This configuration is also known as a proxy array. Members of an array must be running Microsoft Proxy Server 2.0.

domain filter A Proxy Server security tool that limits access to external Internet resources by internal clients by restricting domains, subnets, or individual computers.

Domain Name Space The name for the Domain Name System's hierarchical structure.

Domain Name System (DNS) The worldwide system for plain-language assignment of names to IP addresses. It is hierarchically organized upon six top-level domains.

dotted–decimal format The notation used to represent IP addresses. Rather than a string of 32 ones or zeros, the address is broken into bytes and represented decimally.

Dynamic Host Configuration Protocol (DHCP) A protocol based on BOOTP and used to automatically configure a client's IP settings, such as address, subnet mask, and default gateway.

E

event messages The actual log messages that are logged to the Event Viewer by Microsoft Proxy Server.

Event Viewer A Windows NT application that allows the administrator to view any informational or error messages logged by Windows NT and its services.

F

File Transfer Protocol (FTP) The protocol used to transfer files to and from remote servers located across a TCP/IP-based network.

firewall A hardware or software product designed to restrict unauthorized or unlawful entry into an organization's network from some external point, such as the Internet.

Fully Qualified Domain Name (FQDN) The full DNS path of an Internet host.

G

gateway The next hop for a packet destined for a remote subnet.

generic domain Any of the six top-level domains of the Domain Name Space.

Gopher The protocol used to host the term-only information service of Gopher.

H

hash function The method that determines where information will be stored in a proxy array. Proxy Server computer information is hashed and combined with hashed URL information. This is done for each array member. The member with the highest combined total stores the information.

hierarchical caching When multiple LANs are connected, such as with multiple branch offices or within a large enterprise network, a hierarchical caching scheme can be implemented with multiple single proxies or arrays of proxies to distribute content based on location and use histories. Client requests are communicated upward through the proxy relation tree until the resource is located or finally retrieved from the Internet.

hierarchical proxying In a multiple proxy server environment, it is a method of passing requests not found on one proxy server computer to an upstream proxy server. This is also known as chained proxying or proxy cascading.

Hypertext Transfer Protocol (HTTP) The protocol used on the Internet to transfer Web documents.

I

Identd A simulated service of SOCKS Proxy that creates a random false username for each client and supplies it to the requesting servers in order to give Microsoft SOCKS Proxy clients access where they would be denied otherwise.

instance In Performance Monitor, it refers to multiple units of an object. For example, the PhysicalDisk object might have multiple instances if more than one hard disk is installed.

Integrated Services Digital Network (ISDN) A digital communications link with a maximum bandwidth of 128Kbps per dual-channel line.

Internet The collection of TCP/IP-based networks around the world. Information on nearly every subject is available in some form somewhere on the Internet. The Internet has become the communication medium of choice for both business and personal interaction.

Internet Assigned Numbers Authority (IANA) A governing body of the Internet that is responsible for the DNS that ensures that each organization has a unique domain name.

Internet Cache Protocol (ICP) A protocol developed in 1995 that allows proxy servers to "query" other proxy servers in an attempt to locate locally stored Internet objects.

Internet Control Message Protocol (ICMP) The protocol used by programs such as PING to return messages regarding the status of the transmission.

Internet Engineering Task Force (IETF) A governing body of the Internet made up of a number of working groups. The IETF includes the Authenticated Firewall Traversal group, which lists among its responsibilities the SOCKS protocol definition.

Internet Locator Server (ILS) Allows users to search for users on the Internet. ILS creates a dynamic database of users.

Internet Mail Service (IMS) A Connector used to connect an Exchange site to either an SMTP mail system or a remote Exchange site.

Internet Message Access Protocol version 4 (IMAP4) A protocol that allows clients to send and receive messages from their mailboxes and gives them access to public folders.

Internet News Service A service that uses Network News Transfer Protocol (NNTP) to connect the Microsoft Exchange server to Usenet.

Internetwork Packet Exchange/ Sequenced Packet Exchange (NWLink IPX/SPX compatible transport) The protocol originally developed by Novell and commonly associated with NetWare. IPX/ SPX and compatible protocols (NWLink) are supported by many Microsoft products.

Internet Protocol (IP) The primary network protocol of the TCP/IP suite, it is responsible for addressing and routing packets.

Internet Relay Chat (IRC) An Internet information service in which numerous users anywhere in the world can communicate in realtime through a text interface.

Internet Server Application Programming Interface (ISAPI) A Windows Sockets programming interface that is used to provide services for the WinSock Proxy service in the form of the ISAPI filter and ISAPI application.

Internet Service Manager (ISM) An interface used to manage the Internet Information Server 3.0 (and Proxy Server).

Internet Service Provider (ISP) A service company that sells network access to the Internet; most ISPs purchase bandwidth in bulk and resell it in smaller packages.

internetwork A network of networks; the term used to describe the early deployment of the system that became the Internet.

InterNIC A governing body of the Internet responsible for, among other things, assigning IP addresses.

IP address The unique logical address assigned to a host on an IP network.

IP forwarding A feature of Windows NT's TCP/IP protocol that can forward IP packets across multihomed computers.

IPX-to-IP gateway A gateway that enables clients on an IPX network to access Internet information services via Proxy Server 2.0. TCP/IP is no longer a requirement for a client or a network to gain access to Internet resources. The IPX-to-IP gateway currently supports Windows 95 and Windows NT Workstation 4.0 clients.

K

keep-alive A type of packet used by TCP to maintain a connection between client and server.

L

Lightweight Directory Access Protocol (LDAP) A protocol used to share Exchange Address Book information with external users.

Local Address Table (LAT) A list of IP addresses that can have valid access to the services offered by Proxy Server.

local area network (LAN) A network that is confined to a single building or geographic area and made up of servers, workstations, peripheral devices, a network operating system, and a communications link.

loopback address The IP address that is reserved for loopback testing (127.xxx.xxx.xxx).

Lotus Notes Connector A Microsoft Exchange Connector used to allow Exchange to communicate with a Lotus Notes system.

M

Management Information Base (MIB) A set of manageable objects representing various types of information about a network device that can be queried by using a Simple Network Management Protocol (SNMP) management tool.

Media Access Control (MAC) address The physical address of a network interface card. The MAC address is used at the Data Link layer to address packets.

Microsoft Exchange Chat Service Enables realtime collaboration using any standard IRC or IRCX client.

Microsoft Exchange Scripting Agent Allows Exchange Server to perform limited workflow and to create automated collaborative applications.

Microsoft Exchange Server The Microsoft Messaging groupware server.

Microsoft Management Console (MMC) A new interface used to manage the Internet Information Server 4.0 (and Proxy Server).

Microsoft NetMeeting Allows users to initiate net meetings over the Internet or an internal network.

Microsoft NetShow A streaming multimedia architecture and tool set developed by Microsoft.

MS Mail Connector A Microsoft Exchange Connector used to allow Exchange to communicate with MS Mail systems.

multihomed server A computer with two or more network interfaces connected to different networks.

MX record A DNS record used to identify which servers are to receive messages. Known as the Mail eXchanger.

N

name server In the DNS environment, the computer that fulfills a name resolution request.

National Science Foundation Network (NSFNet) A network designed for use by educational and research facilities; it was created soon after ARPANet.

network A collection of server and client computers that communicate over a wire-based media for the purpose of sharing resources.

network capacity The amount of data transmission a network is able to handle.

Network layer The OSI model layer where addressing and routing are handled.

Network Monitor A Windows NT Server utility that can inspect network packets, traffic, and protocols.

Network News Transfer Protocol (NNTP) The protocol that supports Usenet newsgroups.

network protocol Lower-level protocol responsible for addressing and routing packets.

network traffic The actual digital communications that occur over the wire media of a network.

newsgroups A messaging system on an intranet or the Internet where you can read and post information in a form called articles.

nondedicated service A type of service in which you must compete with other users to gain access to a pool of communications ports. Nondedicated service does not guarantee access at any given time and is therefore much less expensive.

NSLOOKUP A Windows command-line utility that is used to query a name server.

O

object In Performance Monitor, an object is a system resource, such as the Web Proxy Cache object that groups counters together.

OSI (Open Systems Interconnection) model An international standard that defines a seven-layer model that specifies how networking protocols operate; set by the ISO.

P

packet A single chunk of data that is transmitted across a network.

packet filter A Proxy Server security tool that filters traffic based on the protocol/application of individual packets.

packet layer Another name for the Network layer of the OSI model.

paper trail In relation to computers, a term that refers to the collection of electronic data in the form of logs, records, errors, or messages. A paper trail can be used to establish the sequence of events, process of occurrence, or evidence of failure.

password authentication An NT security feature where users are verified on one of three different security levels: anonymous logon, basic authentication, or Windows NT Challenge/Response authentication.

Performance Monitor A Windows NT utility used to monitor the activity of the system, including memory, CPU, services, applications, communication ports, networking, and more.

Performance Monitor counter An object that is monitored within Performance Monitor.

pipeline A term that refers to the communications link between your network and an ISP. The ability for a connection to support significant amounts of data protection is dependent upon the size and cost of that link.

Plain Old Telephone Service (POTS) An analog communications link with a maximum bandwidth of 56Kbps.

pointer record (PTR) A DNS record used to map IP addresses to FQDNs.

port A designation used by TCP to determine which upper-layer protocol is communicating. Ports can be used to filter traffic on a network.

Post Office Protocol version 3 (POP3) A standard Internet mail protocol used to read messages from a POP3 server.

private address IP addresses set aside by InterNIC for use on networks not connected to the Internet.

PROFs Connector A Microsoft Exchange Connector that allows Exchange to communicate with a PROFs mail system (OfficeVision/VM Connector).

Proxy Auto-Config (PAC) file An industry-standard file used to configure proxy clients. It allows clients, rather than just proxy servers, to take advantage of single-hop resolution.

proxy chaining In a multiple proxy server environment, a method of passing requests not resolved on one proxy server computer to an upstream proxy server computer. This is also known as hierarchical proxying or proxy cascading.

proxy server A software product that acts as a moderator or go-between for a client and a remote host. Most proxy servers also offer content caching and firewall capabilities.

Proxy Server Diagnostic Utility A utility (MSPDIAG.EXE) used to diagnose the Microsoft Proxy Server installation.

R

RealAudio A multimedia tool, protocol, and enhancement that streams audio (and video) over TCP/IP networks.

REG_BINARY Identifies a value entry as binary.

REG_DWORD Identifies a value entry as a DWORD entry.

REG_EXPAND_SZ Indicates that a value entry is an expandable string.

REG_MULTI_SZ Identifies a value entry as a multiple string.

REG_SZ Identifies a value entry as a data string.

Registry Editor A tool (REGEDIT.EXE or REGEDT32.EXE) used to view and edit the Windows NT Registry.

Remote Access Service (RAS) The Windows NT service that provides network communication for remote clients.

replication partner One of two WINS servers that are configured to share information.

resolver In the DNS environment, the computer that requests name resolution.

resource records DNS records that identify specific computers on the network.

reverse hosting A Proxy Server feature that is a companion to the reverse proxy feature in that it enables several distinct Web servers hosted inside of your network to be integrated by Proxy Server into what looks like a single large Web site to all external viewers. This method of Web publishing maintains tight security, isolates the Web servers from the Internet, and offers you greater flexibility in design, layout, and navigation.

reverse proxy A feature of Proxy Server that enables you to set up, within your network, a World Wide Web publishing server behind the proxy server and still be able to offer its contents to the external world of the Internet. If you use reverse proxy, you have tighter security control over your Web site. The proxy server impersonates a Web server to the outside world and only it communicates directly with the real internal Web server.

roll-back The restoration of previous configuration values for a Proxy Server.

round robin A DNS feature that balances the load on servers by responding to queries with different addresses if there is more than one resource record with the same host name.

router A device or software implementation that enables interoperability and communication across networks.

Routing and Remote Access Service Update A service update for Windows NT Server that adds routing capabilities to the Remote Access Service (RAS) server and improves the features and performance of RAS.

Routing Information Protocol (RIP) A protocol used by TCP/IP to distribute information among routers.

RPC Ports The TCP/IP service ports (1024 through 1029) used to transmit remote procedure calls (RPCs); they should be disabled on external interfaces.

S

Secure Sockets Layer (SSL) encryption A method to encrypt information between hosts.

Secure Sockets Layer (SSL) tunneling Proxy Server supports SSL tunneling via the Web proxy to maintain highly secure Web-based transactions. SSL is commonly used in electronic commerce or other state-dependent applications. SSL tunneling creates an encrypted communication path between the client and the remote server.

server proxying The ability of a server to examine inbound traffic to intercept predefined packet types so it can forward them to a specific server inside the network. Server proxying offers security without sacrificing flexibility and the capabilities of specialized information services.

Simple Mail Transfer Protocol (SMTP) The primary protocol used today for email transfer across the Internet.

Simple Network Management Protocol (SNMP) A protocol used to monitor remote hosts over a TCP/IP network.

site filtering A security feature that filters responses from specified sites or prevents requests from being processed to prevent internal users from accessing those sites. Site filtering is a form of user access control.

site restriction Another term for site filtering; the specification of an IP address, domain name, or URL that is restricted.

SNADS Connector A Microsoft Exchange Connector that allows Exchange to communicate with a SNADS mail system.

socket A unique identification number created by combining a computer's IP address and the TCP or UDP port number in use.

SOCKS A protocol used to establish a secure proxy data channel between a client and server.

SOCKS Proxy One of the components of Proxy Server. SOCKS Proxy is a cross-platform network service that creates a secured communications link between a client and a server. SOCKS Proxy supports SOCKS 4.3a and offers non-Windows or non-WinSock applications access to Internet services.

SOCKS Proxy service A Proxy Server service that allows clients running the SOCKS protocol access to the Internet.

spamming The distribution of unsolicited and unwelcome messages via email or newsgroups, often with the purpose of selling some product or service.

stream-oriented communication A connection-oriented communication method used by TCP that ensures data delivery.

subdomain A domain that is created below a typical zone or domain. For example, in the FQDN **www.hosts.lanw.com**, *hosts* is the subdomain.

subnet mask The method used by IP to determine which bits in an IP address denote the network ID and which bits denote the host ID. Bits that are masked represent the network ID.

T

T1 and fractional T1 A digital communications link with a bandwidth of 1.544Mbps (for a full T1) or 56 or 256Kbps fractional T1 chunks.

Telnet A TCP/IP utility that enables remote terminal emulation.

Time-to-Live (TTL) The length of time an object may reside in cache.

Transmission Control Protocol (TCP) The primary transport protocol of the TCP/IP suite. It is a connection-oriented protocol that ensures reliable delivery for upper-layer protocols.

Transmission Control Protocol/Internet Protocol (TCP/IP) The most commonly used network protocol and the central protocol of the Internet.

transport protocol A protocol that ensures that packets are delivered between communicating computers.

U

Uniform Resource Locator (URL) The addressing scheme used to identify resources on the Internet. URLs are most commonly associated with Web resources and are used by Web browsers. A URL consists of at least a protocol type and a domain name; it can also identify a port, a directory path, a file name, and a defined named spot.

Unlimited Access A WinSock Proxy setting that grants unlimited and unrestricted protocol access to a user or group.

Usenet The term used to refer to the collection of 20,000+ NNTP-based newsgroups supported on the Internet.

user access control A general term that refers to the security and control restrictions enforced by an administrator to specify or dictate the resources available to a user.

User Datagram Protocol (UDP) A connectionless TCP/IP protocol that provides extremely fast data transmission.

user rights Security privileges within the Windows NT network environment that gives users and groups specific abilities, such as rebooting systems, taking ownership, or logging on as a service.

V

VDOLive A streaming audio and video protocol and tool for TCP/IP networks.

virtual private network (VPN) A wide area network (WAN) that is provided by a common communications carrier. It works

like a private network, but the backbone of the network is shared with all of the customers in a public network.

W

Web Proxy One of the components of Proxy Server. Web Proxy supports those protocols and communication mechanisms typically associated with Web documents, access, and interaction.

Web Proxy service A Proxy Server service that allows clients to use their Web browsers to access information on the Internet.

well-known ports Port numbers less than 1023 that are assigned to specific functions in a TCP/IP network.

wide area network (WAN) A network that spans geographically distant segments. Often, the distance of two miles or more is used to define a WAN; however, Microsoft equates any RAS connection as establishing a WAN.

Windows Internet Name Service (WINS) A service that keeps track of NetBIOS names and IP addresses for computers in a Windows network.

Windows NT Registry A database that stores all Windows NT configuration information.

WINS Proxy Agent A computer that is configured to assist non–WINS clients with name resolution on networks where no WINS server exists.

WinSock Proxy One of the components of Proxy Server. WinSock Proxy supports client applications designed around the Windows Sockets API. This includes utilities and services such as Telnet and RealAudio.

WinSock Proxy service A Proxy Server service that allows clients to use WinSock applications to access the Internet.

X

X.400 Connector A Microsoft Exchange Connector that allows Exchange to communicate with an X.400 mail system.

INDEX

B

C

M

Q

INDEX

INDEX

X

Z